Law & Economics

THE PEARSON SERIES IN ECONOMICS

Abel/Bernanke/Croushore
Macroeconomics*

Bade/Parkin
Foundations of Economics*

Berck/Helfand
The Economics of the Environment

Bierman/Fernandez
Game Theory with Economic Applications

Blanchard
Macroeconomics*

Blau/Ferber/Winkler
The Economics of Women, Men and Work

Boardman/Greenberg/Vining/ Weimer
Cost-Benefit Analysis

Boyer
Principles of Transportation Economics

Branson
Macroeconomic Theory and Policy

Brock/Adams
The Structure of American Industry

Bruce
Public Finance and the American Economy

Carlton/Perloff
Modern Industrial Organization

Case/Fair/Oster
Principles of Economics*

Caves/Frankel/Jones
World Trade and Payments: An Introduction

Chapman
Environmental Economics: Theory, Application, and Policy

Cooter/Ulen
Law & Economics

Downs
An Economic Theory of Democracy

Ehrenberg/Smith
Modern Labor Economics

Ekelund/Ressler/Tollison
Economics*

Farnham
Economics for Managers

Folland/Goodman/Stano
The Economics of Health and Health Care

Fort
Sports Economics

Froyen
Macroeconomics

Fusfeld
The Age of the Economist

Gerber
International Economics*

Gordon
Macroeconomics*

Greene
Econometric Analysis

Gregory
Essentials of Economics

Gregory/Stuart
Russian and Soviet Economic Performance and Structure

Hartwick/Olewiler
The Economics of Natural Resource Use

Heilbroner/Milberg
The Making of the Economic Society

Heyne/Boettke/Prychitko
The Economic Way of Thinking

Hoffman/Averett
Women and the Economy: Family, Work, and Pay

Holt
Markets, Games and Strategic Behavior

Hubbard/O'Brien
Economics*

Money, Banking, and the Financial System*

Hughes/Cain
American Economic History

Husted/Melvin
International Economics

Jehle/Reny
Advanced Microeconomic Theory

Johnson-Lans
A Health Economics Primer

Keat/Young
Managerial Economics

Klein
Mathematical Methods for Economics

Krugman/Obstfeld/Melitz
International Economics: Theory & Policy*

Laidler
The Demand for Money

Leeds/von Allmen
The Economics of Sports

Leeds/von Allmen/Schiming
Economics*

Lipsey/Ragan/Storer
Economics*

Lynn
Economic Development: Theory and Practice for a Divided World

Miller
Economics Today*

Understanding Modern Economics

Miller/Benjamin
The Economics of Macro Issues

Miller/Benjamin/North
The Economics of Public Issues

Mills/Hamilton
Urban Economics

Mishkin
The Economics of Money, Banking, and Financial Markets*

The Economics of Money, Banking, and Financial Markets, Business School Edition*

Macroeconomics: Policy and Practice*

Murray
Econometrics: A Modern Introduction

Nafziger
The Economics of Developing Countries

O'Sullivan/Sheffrin/Perez
Economics: Principles, Applications, and Tools*

Parkin
Economics*

Perloff
Microeconomics*

Microeconomics: Theory and Applications with Calculus*

Perman/Common/McGilvray/Ma
Natural Resources and Environmental Economics

Phelps
Health Economics

Pindyck/Rubinfeld
Microeconomics*

Riddell/Shackelford/Stamos/ Schneider
Economics: A Tool for Critically Understanding Society

Ritter/Silber/Udell
Principles of Money, Banking & Financial Markets*

Roberts
The Choice: A Fable of Free Trade and Protection

Rohlf
Introduction to Economic Reasoning

Ruffin/Gregory
Principles of Economics

Sargent
Rational Expectations and Inflation

Sawyer/Sprinkle
International Economics

Scherer
Industry Structure, Strategy, and Public Policy

Schiller
The Economics of Poverty and Discrimination

Sherman
Market Regulation

Silberberg
Principles of Microeconomics

Stock/Watson
Introduction to Econometrics

Introduction to Econometrics, Brief Edition

Studenmund
Using Econometrics: A Practical Guide

Tietenberg/Lewis
Environmental and Natural Resource Economics

Environmental Economics and Policy

Todaro/Smith
Economic Development

Waldman
Microeconomics

Waldman/Jensen
Industrial Organization: Theory and Practice

Weil
Economic Growth

Williamson
Macroeconomics

---

* denotes ⟨X⟩ myeconlab titles

SIXTH EDITION

Law&
Economics

ROBERT COOTER
University of California, Berkeley

THOMAS ULEN
University of Illinois, Urbana-Champaign

Addison-Wesley

Boston   Columbus   Indianapolis   New York   San Francisco   Upper Saddle River
Amsterdam   Cape Town   Dubai   London   Madrid   Milan   Munich   Paris   Montréal   Toronto
Delhi   Mexico City   São Paulo   Sydney   Hong Kong   Seoul   Singapore   Taipei   Tokyo

Editorial Director: *Sally Yagan*
Editor in Chief: *Donna Battista*
Acquisitions Editor: *Noel Kamm Seibert*
Editorial Project Manager: *Melissa Pellerano*
Senior Production Project Manager: *Nancy Freihofer*
Supplements Coordinator: *Alison Eusden*
Senior Media Producer: *Angela Lee*
Director of Marketing: *Patrice Jones*
Marketing Assistant: *Ian Gold*

Senior Prepress Supervisor: *Caroline Fell*
Senior Manufacturing Buyer: *Carol Melville*
Cover Designer: *Bruce Kenselaar*
Cover Image: *Fotolia/© Serhiy Kobyakov*
Full-Service Project Management: *PreMediaGlobal*
Composition: *PreMediaGlobal*
Printer/Binder: *Courier Westford, Inc.*
Cover Printer: *Lehigh Phoenix*
Text Font: Times

Library of Congress Cataloging-in-Publication Data
Cooter, Robert.
   Law and economics / Robert Cooter, Thomas Ulen.—6th ed.
      p. cm.
   Rev. ed. of: Law & economics / Robert Cooter, Thomas Ulen.
   Includes index.
   ISBN 978-0-13-254065-0
   1. Law and economics.   I. Ulen, Thomas.   II. Cooter, Robert. Law & economics.   III. Title.
   K487.E3C665 2011
   340'.11—dc22

                                                                        2010049060

10 9 8 7 6 5 4 3 2

Addison-Wesley
is an imprint of

www.pearsonhighered.com

ISBN-10:   0-13-254065-7
ISBN-13: 978-0-13-254065-0

Contents

Preface

This sixth edition of *Law and Economics* arrives as the field celebrates its (roughly) 30th birthday. What began as a scholarly niche has grown into one of the most widely used tools of legal analysis. The subject has spread from the United States to many other countries. As scholarship deepens, the concepts in the core of law and economics become clearer and more stable, and new applications develop from the core like biological species evolving through specialization. With each new edition, we continue to refine the explanation of the analytical core and to incorporate new applications selectively as space permits. This edition expands previous discussions of empirical legal studies and behavioral law and economics. As we incorporate new material and respond to the suggestions that so many people have sent us, the book feels more like a symphony and less like a duet. We hope that you enjoy reading this book as much as we enjoyed writing it.

The book continues to cover the economic analysis of the law of property, torts, contracts, the legal process and crimes. Instructors and students who have used previous editions will notice that we have reversed the order in which we treat torts and contracts, and we have divided the material on legal process into two chapters—one on theory and one on topics—in parallel with our treatment of all the other substantive areas of the law. Below we describe what is new in this edition, followed by an account of the book's website.

New to This Edition

The Sixth Edition has been revised and updated to reflect the latest developments in law and economics. Major changes to the text are as follows:

- Tables and graphs have been updated.
- New boxes and suggested readings have been added throughout the text.
- Web Notes have been updated and added.
- Chapter 6 contains additional information on liability and customs in trade.
- Chapter 8 improves the explanation of contractual commitments through a better representation of the principal-agent problem.

- Chapter 9 now includes new material on lapses, vicarious liability, incomprehensible harms, punitive damages, mass torts, medical malpractice, and some behavioral aspects of contract remedies.
- Chapter 10 contains a new treatment of decision making by potential litigants and their lawyers, and new figures and decision trees.
- Chapter 11, a new chapter, combines new material on the legal process and an updated empirical assessment of various aspects of legal disputes.
- Chapter 12 now contains the theoretical material on crime and punishment, updated and clarified.
- Chapter 13 applies the theoretical insights of the previous chapter to wide-ranging policy issues in criminal justice and updates data and information from previous editions.

Online Resources

The Companion Website presents a wealth of supplementary materials to help in teaching and learning law and economics. "Web Notes" throughout the book indicate the points at which there is additional material on the Companion Website at www.pearsonhighered.com/cooter_ulen. These notes extend the text presentations, provide guides and links to new articles and books, and contain excerpts from cases. We also include some examples of examinations and problem sets.

An updated *Instructor's Manual,* reflective of changes to the new edition, will be available for instructors' reference. The *Instructor's Manual* is available for download on the Instructor's Resource center at www.pearsonhighered.com/irc.

Acknowledgments

We continue to be extremely grateful to our colleagues at Boalt Hall of the University of California, Berkeley, and at the University of Illinois College of Law for the superb scholarly environments in which we work. Our colleagues have been extremely generous with their time in helping us to understand the law better. And in one of the great, ongoing miracles of the academic enterprise, we continue to learn much from the students whom we have the pleasure to teach at Berkeley, Illinois, and elsewhere.

We should also thank the many colleagues and students at other universities who have used our book in their classes and sent us many helpful suggestions about how to improve the book. We particularly thank Joe Kennedy of Georgetown, who has given us remarkably thorough and singularly helpful comments on improvements in the text.

We'd like to thank the following reviewers for their thoughtful commentary on the fifth edition: Howard Bodenhorn, J. Lon Carlson, Joseph M. Jadlow, and Mark E. McBride.

We would also like to thank those who have provided research assistance for this sixth edition: Theodore Ulen, Timothy Ulen, and Brian Doxey. And, also, for their long-time support and help: Jan Crouter, Dhammika Dharmapala, Lee Ann Fennell,

Nuno Garoupa, John Lopatka, Richard McAdams, Andy Morriss, Tom Nonnenmacher, Noel Netusil, Dan Vander Ploeg, and David Wishart.

Finally, we owe particular thanks to our assistants, Ida Ng at Boalt Hall and Sally Cook at the University of Illinois College of Law. They do many big things to help us get our work done, as well as many little things without which much of our work would be impossible to do. Thanks so much.

ROBERT D. COOTER
Berkeley, CA

THOMAS S. ULEN
Champaign, IL

November, 2010

1 An Introduction to Law and Economics

For the rational study of the law the black-letter man may be the man of the present, but the man of the future is the man of statistics and the master of economics. . . . We learn that for everything we have to give up something else, and we are taught to set the advantage we gain against the other advantage we lose, and to know what we are doing when we elect.

Oliver Wendell Holmes.
THE PATH OF THE LAW, 10 HARV. L. REV. 457, 469, 474 (1897)[1]

To me the most interesting aspect of the law and economics movement has been its aspiration to place the study of law on a scientific basis, with coherent theory, precise hypotheses deduced from the theory, and empirical tests of the hypotheses. Law is a social institution of enormous antiquity and importance, and I can see no reason why it should not be amenable to scientific study. Economics is the most advanced of the social sciences, and the legal system contains many parallels to and overlaps with the systems that economists have studied successfully.

Judge Richard A. Posner, in MICHAEL FAURE &
ROGER VAN DEN BERGH, EDS., ESSAYS IN LAW AND ECONOMICS (1989)

UNTIL RECENTLY, LAW confined the use of economics to antitrust law, regulated industries, tax, and some special topics like determining monetary damages. In these areas, law needed economics to answer such questions as "What is the defendant's share of the market?"; "Will price controls on automobile insurance reduce its availability?"; "Who really bears the burden of the capital gains tax?"; and "How much future income did the children lose because of their mother's death?"

Beginning in the early 1960s, this limited interaction changed dramatically when the economic analysis of law expanded into the more traditional areas of the law, such as property, contracts, torts, criminal law and procedure, and constitutional law.[2] This

---

[1] Our citation style is a variant of the legal citation style most commonly used in the United States. Here is what the citation means: the author of the article from which the quotation was taken is Oliver Wendell Holmes; the title of the article is "The Path of the Law"; and the article may be found in volume 10 of the *Harvard Law Review*, which was published in 1897, beginning on page 457. The quoted material comes from pages 469 and 474 of that article.

[2] The modern field is said to have begun with the publication of two landmark articles—Ronald H. Coase, *The Problem of Social Cost*, 3 J. L. & ECON. 1 (1960) and Guido Calabresi, *Some Thoughts on Risk Distribution and the Law of Torts*, 70 YALE L.J. 499 (1961).

new use of economics in the law asked such questions as, "Will private ownership of the electromagnetic spectrum encourage its efficient use?"; "What remedy for breach of contract will cause efficient reliance on promises?"; "Do businesses take too much or too little precaution when the law holds them strictly liable for injuries to consumers?"; and "Will harsher punishments deter violent crime?"

Economics has changed the nature of legal scholarship, the common understanding of legal rules and institutions, and even the practice of law. As proof, consider these indicators of the impact of economics on law. By 1990 at least one economist was on the faculty of each of the top law schools in North America and some in Western Europe. Joint degree programs (a Ph.D. in economics and a J.D. in law) exist at many prominent universities. Law reviews publish many articles using the economic approach, and there are several journals devoted exclusively to the field.[3] An exhaustive study found that articles using the economic approach are cited in the major American law journals more than articles using any other approach.[4] Many law school courses in America now include at least a brief summary of the economic analysis of law in question. Many substantive law areas, such as corporation law, are often taught from a law-and-economics perspective.[5] By the late 1990s, there were professional organizations in law and economics in Asia, Europe, Canada, the United States, Latin America, Australia, and elsewhere. The field received the highest level of recognition in 1991 and 1992 when consecutive Nobel Prizes in Economics[6] were awarded to economists who helped to found the economic analysis of law—Ronald Coase and Gary Becker. Summing this up, Professor Bruce Ackerman of the Yale Law School described the economic approach to law as "the most important development in legal scholarship of the twentieth century."

The new field's impact extends beyond the universities to the practice of law and the implementation of public policy. Economics provided the intellectual foundations for the deregulation movement in the 1970s, which resulted in such dramatic changes in America as the dissolution of regulatory bodies that set prices and routes for airlines, trucks, and railroads. Economics also served as the intellectual force behind the revolution in antitrust law in the United States in the 1970s and 1980s. In another policy area, a commission created by Congress in 1984 to reform criminal sentencing in the federal courts explicitly used the findings of law and economics to reach some of its results. Furthermore, several prominent law-and-economics scholars have become federal judges and use economic analysis in their opinions—Associate Justice Stephen Breyer of the U.S. Supreme Court; Judge Richard A. Posner and Judge Frank Easterbrook of the U.S. Court of Appeals for the Seventh Circuit; Judge Guido Calabresi of the U.S.

---

[3] For example, the *Journal of Law and Economics* began in 1958; the *Journal of Legal Studies* in 1972; *Research in Law and Economics*, the *International Review of Law and Economics*, and the *Journal of Law, Economics, and Organization* in the 1980s; and the *Journal of Empirical Legal Studies* in 2004.

[4] William M. Landes & Richard A. Posner, *The Influence of Economics on Law: A Quantitative Study*, 36 J. L. & ECON. 385 (1993).

[5] See, e.g., STEPHEN M. BAINBRIDGE, CORPORATION LAW AND ECONOMICS (2002).

[6] The full name of the Nobel Prize in Economics is the Bank of Sweden Prize in the Economic Sciences in Memory of Alfred Nobel. See our book's website for a full list of those who have won the Nobel Prize and brief descriptions of their work.

Court of Appeals for the Second Circuit; Judge Douglas Ginsburg, and former Judge Robert Bork of the U.S. Court of Appeals for the D.C. Circuit; and Judge Alex Kozinski of the U.S. Court of Appeals for the Ninth Circuit.

I.   What Is the Economic Analysis of Law?

Why has the economic analysis of law succeeded so spectacularly, especially in the United States but increasingly also in other countries?[7] Like the rabbit in Australia, economics found a vacant niche in the "intellectual ecology" of the law and rapidly filled it. To explain the niche, consider this classical definition of some kinds of laws: "A law is an obligation backed by a state sanction."

Lawmakers often ask, "How will a sanction affect behavior?" For example, if punitive damages are imposed upon the maker of a defective product, what will happen to the safety and price of the product in the future? Or will the amount of crime decrease if third-time offenders are automatically imprisoned? Lawyers answered such questions in 1960 in much the same way as they had 2000 years earlier—by consulting intuition and any available facts.

Economics provided a scientific theory to predict the effects of legal sanctions on behavior. To economists, sanctions look like prices, and presumably, people respond to these sanctions much as they respond to prices. People respond to higher prices by consuming less of the more expensive good; presumably, people also respond to more severe legal sanctions by doing less of the sanctioned activity. Economics has mathematically precise theories (price theory and game theory) and empirically sound methods (statistics and econometrics) for analyzing the effects of the implicit prices that laws attach to behavior.

Consider a legal example. Suppose that a manufacturer knows that his product will sometimes injure consumers. How safe will he make the product? For a profit-maximizing firm, the answer depends upon three costs: First, the cost of making the product safer, which depends on its design and manufacture; second, the manufacturer's legal liability for injuries to consumers; and third, the extent to which injuries discourage consumers from buying the product. The profit-maximizing firm will adjust safety until the cost of additional safety equals the benefit from reduced liability and higher consumer demand for the good.

Economics generally provides a behavioral theory to predict how people respond to laws. This theory surpasses intuition just as science surpasses common sense. The response of people is always relevant to making, revising, repealing, and interpreting laws. A famous essay in law and economics describes the law as a cathedral—a large, ancient, complex, beautiful, mysterious, and sacred building.[8] Behavioral science resembles the mortar between the cathedral's stones, which support the structure everywhere.

---

[7] See Nuno Garoupa & Thomas S. Ulen, *The Market for Legal Innovation: Law and Economics in Europe and the United States*, 59 ALA. L. REV. 1555 (2008).

[8] Guido Calabresi & A. Douglas Melamed, *Property Rules, Liability Rules, and Inalienability: One View of the Cathedral*, 85 HARV. L. REV. 1089 (1972).

A prediction can be neutral or loaded with respect to social values. A study finds that higher fines for speeding on the highway will presumably cause less of it. Is this good or bad on balance? The finding does not suggest an answer. In contrast, suppose that a study proves that the additional cost of collecting higher fines exceeds the resulting benefit from fewer accidents, so a higher fine is "inefficient." This finding suggests that a higher fine would be bad. Efficiency is always relevant to policymaking, because public officials never advocate wasting money. As this example shows, besides neutral predictions, economics makes loaded predictions. Judges and other officials need a method for evaluating laws' effects on important social values. Economics provides such a method for efficiency.

Besides efficiency, economics predicts the effects of laws on another important value: the distribution of income. Among the earliest applications of economics to public policy was its use to predict who really bears the burden of alternative taxes. More than other social scientists, economists understand how laws affect the distribution of income across classes and groups. While almost all economists favor changes that increase efficiency, some economists take sides in disputes about distribution and others do not take sides.

Instead of efficiency or distribution, people in business mostly talk about profits. Much of the work of lawyers aims to increase the profits of businesses, especially by helping businesses to make deals, avoid litigation, and obey regulations. These three activities correspond to three areas of legal practice in large law firms: transactions, litigation, and regulation. Efficiency and profitability are so closely related that lawyers can use the efficiency principles in this book to help businesses make more money. Economic efficiency is a comprehensive measure of public benefits that include the profits of firms, the well-being of consumers, and the wages of workers. The logic of maximizing the comprehensive measure (efficiency) is very similar to the logic of maximizing one of its components (profits). A good legal system keeps the profitability of business and the welfare of people aligned, so that the pursuit of profits also benefits the public.

II. Some Examples

To give you a better idea of what law and economics is about, we turn to some examples based upon classics in the subject. First, we try to identify the implicit price that the legal rule attaches to behavior in each example. Second, we predict the consequences of variations in that implicit price. Finally, we evaluate the effects in terms of efficiency and, where possible, distribution.

> **Example 1:**   A commission on reforming criminal law has identified certain white-collar crimes (such as embezzling money from one's employer) that are typically committed after rational consideration of the potential gain and the risk of getting caught and punished. After taking extensive testimony, much of it from economists, the commission decides that a monetary fine is the appropriate punishment for these offenses, not imprisonment. The commission wants to know, "How high should the fine be?"

The economists who testified before the commission have a framework for answering this question. The commission focused on rational crimes that seldom occur unless the expected gain to the criminal exceeds the expected cost. The expected cost depends upon two factors: the probability of being caught and convicted and the severity of the punishment. For our purposes, <u>define the expected cost of crime to the criminal as the product of the probability of a fine times its magnitude</u>.

Suppose that the probability of punishment *decreases* by 5 percent and the magnitude of the fine *increases* by 5 percent. In that case, the expected cost of crime to the criminal roughly remains the same. Because of this, the criminal will presumably respond by committing the same amount of crime. (In Chapter 12 we shall explain the exact conditions for this conclusion to be true.) This is a prediction about how illegal behavior responds to its implicit price.

Now we evaluate this effect with respect to economic efficiency. When a decrease in the probability of a fine offsets an increase in its magnitude, the expected cost of crime remains roughly the same for criminals, but the costs of crime to the criminal justice system may change. The costs to the criminal justice system of increasing a fine's probability include expenditures on apprehending and prosecuting criminals—for example, on the number and quality of auditors, tax and bank examiners, police, prosecuting attorneys, and the like. While the cost of increasing the probability of catching and convicting white-collar criminals is relatively high, administering fines is relatively cheap. These facts imply a prescription for holding white-collar crime down to any specified level at least cost to the state: Invest little in apprehending and prosecuting offenders, and fine severely those who are apprehended. Thus, the commission might recommend very high monetary fines in its schedule of punishments for white-collar offenses.

Professor Gary Becker derived this result in a famous paper cited by the Nobel Prize Committee in its award to him. Chapters 12 and 13 discuss these findings in detail.

> **Example 2:** An oil company contracts to deliver oil from the Middle East to a European manufacturer. Before the oil is delivered, war breaks out and the oil company cannot perform as promised. The lack of oil causes the European manufacturer to lose money. The manufacturer brings an action (that is, files a lawsuit) against the oil company for breach of contract. The manufacturer asks the court to award damages equal to the money that it lost. The contract is silent about the risk of war, so that the court cannot simply read the contract and resolve the dispute on the contract's own terms. The oil company contends that it should be excused from performance because it could do nothing about the war and neither of the contracting parties foresaw it. In resolving the suit, the court must decide whether to excuse the oil company from performance on the ground that the war made the performance "impossible," or to find the oil company in breach of contract and to require the oil company to compensate the manufacturer for lost profits.[9]

War is a risk of doing business in the Middle East that one of the parties to the contract must bear, and the court must decide which one it is. What are the consequences of different court rulings? The court's decision simultaneously accomplishes two things. First, it resolves the dispute between the litigants—"dispute resolution." Second, it guides future parties who are in similar circumstances about how courts might resolve their dispute—"rule creation." Law and economics is helpful in resolving

---

[9] For a full discussion of the cases on which this example is based, see Richard A. Posner & Andrew Rosenfield, *Impossibility and Related Doctrines in Contract Law,* 6 J. LEGAL STUD. 88 (1977).

disputes, but it particularly shines in creating rules. Indeed, a central question in this book is, "How will the rule articulated by the lawmaker to resolve a particular dispute affect the behavior of similarly situated parties in the future?" And, "Is the predicted behavior desirable?"

The oil company and the manufacturer can take precautions against war in the Middle East, although neither of them can prevent it. The oil company can sign backup contracts for delivery of Venezuelan oil, and the manufacturer can store oil for emergency use. Efficiency requires the party to take precaution who can do so at least cost. Is the oil company or the manufacturer better situated to take precautions against war? Since the oil company works in the Middle East, it is probably better situated than a European manufacturer to assess the risk of war in that region and to take precautions against it. For the sake of efficiency, the court might hold the oil company liable and cite the principle that courts will allocate risks uncovered in a contract to the party who can bear them at least cost. This is the principle of the least-cost risk-bearer,[10] which is consistent with some decisions in cases that arose from the Middle Eastern war of 1967. Chapters 8 and 9 consider this principle's foundation.

> **Example 3:** *Eddie's Electric Company* emits smoke that dirties the wash hanging at *Lucille's Laundry*. *Eddie's* can completely abate the pollution by installing scrubbers on its stacks, and *Lucille's* can completely exclude the smoke by installing filters on its ventilation system. Installing filters is cheaper than installing scrubbers. No one else is affected by this pollution because *Eddie's* and *Lucille's* are near to each other and far from anyone else. *Lucille's* initiates court proceedings to have *Eddie's* declared to be a "nuisance." If the action succeeds, the court will order *Eddie's* to abate its pollution. Otherwise, the court will not intervene in the dispute. What is the appropriate resolution of this dispute?

Efficiency requires *Lucille's* to install filters, which is cheaper than *Eddie's* installing scrubbers. How can the court produce this result? The answer depends on whether or not *Eddie's* and *Lucille's* can cooperate. First, assume that *Eddie's* and *Lucille's* cannot bargain together or cooperate. If *Lucille's* wins the action and the court orders *Eddie's* to abate the pollution, *Eddie's* will have to install scrubbers, which is inefficient. However, if *Lucille's* loses the action, then *Lucille's* will have to install filters, which is efficient. Consequently, it is efficient for *Lucille's* to lose the action.

Now, consider how the analysis changes if *Eddie's* and *Lucille's* can bargain together and cooperate. Their joint profits (the sum of the profits of *Eddie's* and *Lucille's*) will be higher if they choose the cheaper means of eliminating the harm from pollution. When their joint profits are higher, they can divide the gain between them in order to make both of them better off. The cheaper means is also the efficient means. Efficiency is achieved in this example when *Lucille's* and *Eddie's* bargain together and cooperate, regardless of the rule of law. Ronald Coase derived this result in a famous paper cited by the Nobel Prize Committee when he received the award. Chapter 4 elaborates on this famous result.

---

[10] The principle assumes that the entire loss from nonperformance must be allocated by the court to one of the parties. Alternatively, the court might divide the loss between the parties.

III. The Primacy of Efficiency Over Distribution in Analyzing Private Law

We explained that economists are experts on two policy values—efficiency and distribution. The stakes in most legal disputes have monetary value. Deciding a legal dispute almost always involves allocating the stakes between the parties. The decision about how much of the stakes each party gets creates incentives for future behavior, not just for the parties to this dispute but also for everyone who is similarly situated. In this book we use these incentive effects to make predictions about the consequences of legal decisions, policies, rules, and institutions. In evaluating these consequences, we will focus on efficiency rather than distribution. Why?

By making a rule, the division of the stakes in a legal dispute affects all similarly situated people. If a plaintiff in a case is a consumer of a particular good, an investor in a particular stock, or the driver of a car, then a decision for the plaintiff may benefit everyone who consumes this good, invests in this stock, or drives a car. Most proponents of income redistribution, however, have something else in mind. Instead of contemplating distribution to consumers, investors, or drivers, advocates of income redistribution usually target social groups, such as the poor, women, or minorities. Some people passionately advocate government redistribution of income by class, gender, or race for the sake of social justice. A possible way to pursue redistribution is through private law—the law of property, contracts, and torts. According to this philosophy, courts should interpret or make private laws to redistribute income to deserving groups of people. For example, if consumers are poorer on average than investors, then courts should interpret liability rules to favor consumers and disfavor corporations.

This book rejects the redistributive approach to private law. Pursuing redistributive goals is an exceptional use of private law that special circumstances may justify but that ought not be the usual use of private law. Here is why. Like the rest of the population, economists disagree among themselves about redistributive ends. However, economists generally agree about redistributive *means*. By avoiding waste, efficient redistribution benefits everyone relative to inefficient redistribution. By avoiding waste, efficient redistribution also builds support for redistribution. For example, people are more likely to donate to a charitable organization that efficiently redistributes income than to one that spends most of its revenue on administration.

A piquant example will help you to appreciate the advantages of efficient redistribution. Assume that a desert contains two oases, one of which has ice cream and the other has none. The advocates of social justice who favor redistribution obtain control over the state and declare that the first oasis should share its ice cream with the second oasis. In response, the first oasis fills a large bowl with ice cream and sends a youth running across the desert carrying the bowl to the second oasis. The hot sun melts some of the ice cream, so the first oasis gives up more ice cream than the second oasis receives. The melted ice cream represents the cost of redistribution. People who disagree vehemently about how much ice cream the first oasis should give to the second oasis may agree that a fast runner should transport it. Also they might agree to choose an honest runner who will not eat the ice cream along the route.

Many economists believe that progressive taxation and social welfare programs—the "tax-and-transfer system," as it is usually called—can accomplish redistributive goals in modern states more efficiently than can be done through modifying or reshuffling private legal rights. There are several reasons why reshuffling private legal rights resembles giving the ice cream to a slow runner.

First, the income tax precisely targets inequality, whereas redistribution by private legal rights relies on crude averages. To illustrate, assume that courts interpret a law to favor consumers over corporations in order to redistribute income from rich to poor.[11] "Consumers" and "investors" imperfectly correspond to "poor" and "rich." Consumers of Ferrari automobiles, skiing vacations, and the opera tend to be relatively rich. Many small businesses are organized as corporations. Furthermore, the members of unions with good pension plans own the stocks of large companies. By taxing income progressively, law distinguishes more precisely between rich and poor than by taking the indirect approach of targeting "consumers" and "investors."

Second, the distributive effects of reshuffling private rights are hard to predict. To illustrate, the courts cannot be confident that holding a corporation liable to its consumers will reduce the wealth of its stockholders. Perhaps the corporation will pass on its higher costs to consumers in the form of higher prices, in which case the court's holding will redistribute costs from some consumers to other consumers.

Third, the transaction costs of redistribution through private legal rights are typically high. To illustrate, a plaintiff's attorney working on a contingency fee in the United States routinely charges one-third of the judgment. If the defendant's attorney collects a similar amount in hourly fees, then attorneys for the two sides will absorb two-thirds of the stakes in dispute. The tax-and-transfer system is more efficient.

Besides these three reasons, there is a fourth: Redistribution by private law distorts the economy more than progressive taxation does. In general, relying on broad-based taxes, rather than narrowly focused laws, reduces the distorting effects of redistributive policies. For example, assume that a law to benefit consumers of tomatoes causes a decline in the return enjoyed by investors in tomato farms. Investors will respond by withdrawing funds from tomato farms and investing in other businesses. Consequently, the supply of tomatoes will be too small and consumers will pay too high a price for them. This law distorts the market for tomatoes.

For these reasons and more, economists who favor redistribution and economists who oppose it can agree that private legal rights are usually the wrong way to pursue distributive justice. Unfortunately, lawyers without training in economics seldom appreciate these facts.

We have presented several reasons against basing private law on redistributive goals. Specifically, we discussed imprecise targeting, unpredictable consequences, high transaction costs, and distortions in incentives. For these reasons, the general principles of private law cannot rest on income redistribution. (In special circumstances, however, a private law can redistribute relatively efficiently, such as a well-designed law giving crippled people the right to sue employers for not providing wheelchair access to the workplace.)

---

[11] Courts might *always* find in favor of the individual consumer when he or she sues a corporation regarding liability for harms arising in the use of the corporation's products.

ℹ **Web Note 1.1**

Besides efficiency, what other policy values should matter to making law and applying it? In *Fairness Versus Welfare* (2002), Louis Kaplow and Steven Shavell of the Harvard Law School say "None." Others disagree. See Chris Sanchirico, *Deconstructing the New Efficiency Rationale,* 86 CORNELL L. REV. 1005 (2001), and Daniel Farber, *What (If Anything) Can Economics Say About Equity?,* 101 MICH. L. REV. 1791 (2003).

There is a more complete discussion of this literature under Chapter 1 at the website for this book and links to additional sites of interest.

IV. Why Should Lawyers Study Economics? Why Should Economists Study Law?

The economic analysis of law unites two great fields and facilitates understanding each of them. You probably think of laws as promoting justice; indeed, many people can think in no other way. Economics conceives of laws as incentives for changing behavior (implicit prices) and as instruments for policy objectives (efficiency and distribution). However, economic analysis often takes for granted such legal institutions as property and contract, which dramatically affect the economy. Thus, differences in laws cause capital markets to be organized differently in Japan, Germany, and the United States. Failures in financial laws and contracting contributed to the banking collapse of 2008 in the United States and the subsequent recession, which was less severe in Japan and Germany. Also, the absence of secure property and reliable contracts paralyzes the economies of some poor nations. Improving the effectiveness of law in poor countries is important to their economic development. Law needs economics to understand its behavioral consequences, and economics needs law to understand the underpinnings of markets.

Economists and lawyers can also learn techniques from each other. From economists, lawyers can learn quantitative reasoning for making theories and doing empirical research. From lawyers, economists can learn to persuade ordinary people—an art

Stern Warning for Students

If you are like most students who read this book—scholars of the highest moral caliber—you need not upset yourself by reading the rest of this paragraph. If you are one of those wicked students—we get a few every year—here is a stern warning for you. According to traditional Chinese beliefs, sinners are tried and punished in ten courts of hell after they die. The sixth court tries the sin of "abusing books," punishable by being sawn in half from head to toe. The eighth court tries the sin of "cheating on exams," punishable by being cut open and having your intestines ripped out. So don't you dare abuse this book or cheat on the exams!

nice

that lawyers continually practice and refine. Lawyers can describe facts and give them names with moral resonance, whereas economists are obtuse to language too often. If economists will listen to what the law has to teach them, they will find their models being drawn closer to what people really care about.

V. The Plan of This Book

To benefit from each other, lawyers must learn some economics and economists must learn some law. Readers can do so in the next two chapters. Chapter 2 briefly reviews microeconomic theory. If you are familiar with that theory, then you can read the material quickly as a review or skim the headings for unfamiliar topics. As a check, you might try the problems at the end of Chapter 2.

Chapter 3 is an introduction to the law and the legal process, which is essential reading for those without legal training. We explain how the legal system works, how the U.S. legal system differs from the rest of the world, and what counts as "law."

Chapter 4 begins the substantive treatment of the law from an economic viewpoint. The chapters on substantive legal issues are arranged in pairs. Chapters 4 and 5 focus on property law; Chapters 6 and 7, on tort law; Chapters 8 and 9, on contract law; Chapters 10 and 11, on resolving legal disputes; and 12 and 13, on criminal law. The first chapter of each pair explains the basic economic analysis of that area of law, and the second chapter applies the core economic theory to a series of topics. So, Chapter 6 develops an economic theory of tort liability, and Chapter 7 applies it to automobile accidents, medical practice, and defective products. Chapters 4 through 11 deal with laws where the typical plaintiff in a suit is a private person ("private law"), and Chapters 12 and 13 deal with criminal law where the plaintiff is the public prosecutor ("public law").

Suggested Readings

At the end of every chapter we shall list some of the most important writings on the subject. Please check the website for this book (**www.cooter-ulen.com**) for additional resources.

BOUCKAERT, BOUDEWIJN, & GERRIT DE GEEST, EDS., ENCYCLOPEDIA OF LAW AND ECONOMICS (rev. ed., 2011).

DAU-SCHMIDT, KEN, & THOMAS S. ULEN, EDS., A LAW AND ECONOMICS ANTHOLOGY (1997).

MICELI, THOMAS J, THE ECONOMIC APPROACH TO LAW (2d ed. 2008).

NEWMAN, PETER, ED., THE NEW PALGRAVE DICTIONARY OF ECONOMICS AND LAW (3 vols., 1998).

POLINSKY, A. MITCHELL, AN INTRODUCTION TO LAW AND ECONOMICS (3rd, 2003).

POLINSKY, A. MITCHELL, & STEVEN SHAVELL, EDS., HANDBOOK OF LAW AND ECONOMICS, VS. 1 AND 2 (2007).

Posner, Richard A., *The Decline of Law as an Autonomous Discipline, 1962–1987,* 100 HARV. L. REV. 761 (1987).

POSNER, RICHARD A., ECONOMIC ANALYSIS OF LAW (7th ed., 2007).

SHAVELL, STEVEN, FOUNDATIONS OF THE ECONOMIC ANALYSIS OF LAW (2003).

2 A Brief Review of Microeconomic Theory

Practical men, who believe themselves to be quite exempt from any intellectual influences, are usually the slaves of some defunct economist. . . . It is ideas, not vested interests, which are dangerous for good or evil.

JOHN MAYNARD KEYNES,
THE GENERAL THEORY OF EMPLOYMENT, INTEREST, AND MONEY (1936)

In this state of imbecility, I had, for amusement, turned my attention to political economy.

THOMAS DEQUINCEY,
CONFESSIONS OF AN ENGLISH OPIUM EATER (1821)

Economics is the science which studies human behavior as a relationship between ends and scarce means which have alternative uses.

LIONEL CHARLES ROBBINS, LORD ROBBINS,
AN ESSAY ON THE NATURE AND SIGNIFICANCE OF ECONOMIC SCIENCE (1932)

THE ECONOMIC ANALYSIS of law draws upon the principles of microeconomic theory, which we review in this chapter. For those who have not studied this branch of economics, reading this chapter will prove challenging but useful for understanding the remainder of the book. For those who have already mastered microeconomic theory, reading this chapter is unnecessary. For those readers who are somewhere in between these extremes, we suggest that you begin reading this chapter, skimming what is familiar and studying carefully what is unfamiliar. If you're not sure where you lie on this spectrum of knowledge, turn to the questions at the end of the chapter. If you have difficulty answering them, you will benefit from studying this chapter carefully.

I. Overview: The Structure of Microeconomic Theory

Microeconomics concerns decision making by individuals and small groups, such as families, clubs, firms, and governmental agencies. As the famous quote from Lord Robbins at the beginning of the chapter says, microeconomics is the study of how scarce resources are allocated among competing ends. Should you buy that digital au-diotape player you'd like, or should you buy a dapper suit for your job interview? Should you take a trip with some friends this weekend or study at home? Because you have limited income and time and cannot, therefore, buy or do everything that you might want to buy or do, you have to make choices. Microeconomic theory offers a general theory about how people make such decisions.

We divide our study of microeconomics into five sections. The first is the theory of consumer choice and demand. This theory describes how the typical consumer, con-strained by a limited income, chooses among the many goods and services offered for sale.

The second section deals with the choices made by business organizations or firms. We shall develop a model of the firm that helps us to see how the firm decides what goods and services to produce, how much to produce, and at what price to sell its out-put. In the third section, we shall consider how consumers and firms interact. By com-bining the theory of the consumer and the firm, we shall explain how the decisions of consumers and firms are coordinated through movements in market price. Eventually, the decisions of consumers and firms must be made consistent in the sense that some-how the two sides agree about the quantity and price of the good or service that will be produced and consumed. When these consumption and production decisions are con-sistent in this sense, we say that the market is in equilibrium. We shall see that power-ful forces propel markets toward equilibrium, so that attempts to divert the market from its path are frequently ineffectual or harmful.

The fourth section of microeconomic theory describes the supply and demand for inputs into the productive process. These inputs include labor, capital, land, and mana-gerial talent; more generally, inputs are all the things that firms must acquire in order to produce the goods and services that consumers or other firms wish to purchase.

The final section of microeconomics deals with the area known as welfare economics. There we shall discuss the organization of markets and how they achieve efficiency.

These topics constitute the core of our review of microeconomic theory. There are four additional topics that do not fit neatly into the sections noted above but that we think you should know about them in order to understand the economic analysis of legal rules and institutions. These are game theory, the economic theory of decision making under uncertainty, growth theory, and behavioral economics. We shall cover these four topics in the final sections of this chapter.

II.   Some Fundamental Concepts: Maximization, Equilibrium, and Efficiency

Economists usually assume that each economic actor maximizes something: Consumers maximize utility (that is, happiness or satisfaction), firms maximize profits, politicians maximize votes, bureaucracies maximize revenues, charities maximize social welfare, and so forth. Economists often say that models assuming maximizing behavior work because most people are rational, and rationality requires maximization.

One conception of rationality holds that a rational actor can rank alternatives according to the extent that they give her what she wants. In practice, the alternatives available to the actor are constrained. For example, a rational consumer can rank alternative bundles of consumer goods, and the consumer's budget constrains her choice among them. A rational consumer should choose the best alternative that the constraints allow. Another common way of understanding this conception of rational behavior is to recognize that consumers choose alternatives that are well suited to achieving their ends.

Choosing the best alternative that the constraints allow can be described mathematically as *maximizing*. To see why, consider that the real numbers can be ranked from small to large, just as the rational consumer ranks alternatives according to the extent that they give her what she wants. Consequently, better alternatives can be associated with larger numbers. Economists call this association a "utility function," about which we shall say more in the following sections. Furthermore, the constraint on choice can usually be expressed mathematically as a "feasibility constraint." Choosing the best alternative that the constraints allow corresponds to maximizing the utility function subject to the feasibility constraint. So, the consumer who goes shopping is said to maximize utility subject to her budget constraint.

Turning to the second fundamental concept, there is no habit of thought so deeply ingrained among economists as the urge to characterize each social phenomenon as an *equilibrium* in the interaction of maximizing actors. An equilibrium is a pattern of interaction that persists unless disturbed by outside forces. Economists usually assume that interactions tend toward an equilibrium, regardless of whether they occur in markets, elections, clubs, games, teams, corporations, or marriages.

There is a vital connection between maximization and equilibrium in microeconomic theory. We characterize the behavior of every individual or group as maximizing something. Maximizing behavior tends to push these individuals and groups toward a point of rest, an equilibrium. They certainly do not intend for an equilibrium to result; instead, they simply try to maximize whatever it is that interests them. Nonetheless, the interaction of maximizing agents usually results in an equilibrium.

A *stable* equilibrium is one that will not change unless outside forces intervene. To illustrate, the snowpack in a mountain valley is in stable equilibrium, whereas the snowpack on the mountain's peak may be in unstable equilibrium. An interaction headed toward a stable equilibrium actually reaches this destination unless outside forces divert it. In social life, outside forces often intervene before an interaction reaches equilibrium. Nevertheless, equilibrium analysis makes sense. Advanced microeconomic theories of growth, cycles, and disequilibria exist, but we shall not need them in this book. The comparison of equilibria, called comparative statics, will be our basic approach.

Turning to the third fundamental concept, economists have several distinct definitions of *efficiency*. A production process is said to be productively efficient if either of two conditions holds:

1. It is not possible to produce the same amount of output using a lower-cost combination of inputs, or
2. It is not possible to produce more output using the same combination of inputs.

Consider a firm that uses labor and machinery to produce a consumer good called a "widget." Suppose that the firm currently produces 100 widgets per week using 10 workers and 15 machines. The firm is productively efficient if

1. it is not possible to produce 100 widgets per week by using 10 workers and fewer than 15 machines, or by using 15 machines and fewer than 10 workers, or
2. it is not possible to produce more than 100 widgets per week from the combination of 10 workers and 15 machines.

The other kind of efficiency, called *Pareto efficiency* after its inventor[1] or sometimes referred to as *allocative efficiency,* concerns the satisfaction of individual preferences. A particular situation is said to be *Pareto* or *allocatively efficient* if it is impossible to change it so as to make at least one person better off (in his own estimation) without making another person worse off (again, in his own estimation). For simplicity's sake, assume that there are only two consumers, Smith and Jones, and two goods, umbrellas and bread. Initially, the goods are distributed between them. Is the allocation Pareto efficient? Yes, if it is impossible to reallocate the bread and umbrellas so as to make either Smith or Jones better off without making the other person worse off.[2]

These three basic concepts—maximization, equilibrium, and efficiency—are fundamental to explaining economic behavior, especially in decentralized institutions like markets that involve the coordinated interaction of many different people.

III. Mathematical Tools

You may have been anxious about the amount of mathematics that you will find in this book. There is not much. We use simple algebra and graphs.

A. Functions

Economics is rife with functions: production functions, utility functions, cost functions, social welfare functions, and others. A *function* is a relationship between two sets of numbers such that for each number in one set, there corresponds exactly one number in the other set. To illustrate, the columns below correspond to a functional relationship between the numbers in the left-hand column and those in the right-hand column. Thus, the number 4 in the *x*-column below corresponds to the number 10 in the *y*-column.

In fact, notice that each number in the *x*-column corresponds to exactly one number in the *y*-column. Thus, we can say that the variable *y* is a function of the variable *x*, or in the most common form of notation.

$$y = f(x).$$

---

[1] Vilfredo Pareto was an Italian-Swiss political scientist, lawyer, and economist who wrote around 1900.
[2] There is another efficiency concept—a potential Pareto improvement or Kaldor-Hicks efficiency—that we describe in section IX.C that follows.

This is read as "*y* is a function of *x*" or "*y* equals some *f* of *x*."

y-column	*x*-column
2	3
3	0
10	4
10	6
12	9
7	12

Note that the number 4 is not the only number in the *x*-column that corresponds to the number 10 in the *y*-column; the number 6 also corresponds to the number 10. In this table, for a given value of *x*, there corresponds one value of *y*, but for some values of *y*, there corresponds more than one value of *x*. A value of *x* determines an exact value of *y*, whereas a value of *y* does not determine an exact value of *x*. Thus, in $y = f(x)$, *y* is called the *dependent variable*, because it depends on the value of *x*, and *x* is called the *independent variable*. Because *y* depends upon *x* in this table, *y* is a function of *x*, but because *x* does not (to our knowledge) depend for its values on *y*, *x* is not a function of *y*.

Now suppose that there is another dependent variable, named *z*, that also depends upon *x*. The function relating *z* to *x* might be named *g*:

$$z = g(x).$$

When there are two functions, $g(x)$ and $f(x)$, with different dependent variables, *z* and *y*, remembering which function goes with which variable can be hard. To avoid this difficulty, the same name is often given to a function and the variable determined by it. Following this strategy, the preceding functions would be renamed as follows:

$$y = f(x) \Rightarrow y = y(x),$$
$$z = g(x) \Rightarrow z = z(x).$$

Sometimes an abstract function will be discussed without ever specifying the exact numbers that belong to it. For example, the reader might be told that *y* is a function of *x*, and never be told exactly which values of *y* correspond to which values of *x*. The point then is simply to make the general statement that *y* depends upon *x* but in an as yet unspecified way. If exact numbers are given, they may be listed in a table, as we have seen. Another way of showing the relationship between a dependent and an independent variable is to give an exact equation. For example, a function $z = z(x)$ might be given the exact form

$$z = z(x) = 5 + x/2,$$

which states that the function *z* matches values of *x* with values of *z* equal to five plus one-half of whatever value *x* takes. The table below gives the values of *z* associated with several different values of *x*:

z-column	x-column
6.5	3
12.5	15
8.0	6
6.0	2
9.5	9

A function can relate a dependent variable (there is always just one of them to a function) to more than one independent variable. If we write $y = h(x, z)$, we are saying that the function h matches one value of the dependent variable y to every pair of values of the independent variables x and z. This function might have the specific form

$$y = h(x, z) = -3x + z,$$

according to which y decreases by 3 units when x increases by 1 unit, and y increases by 1 unit when z increases by 1 unit.

B. Graphs

We can improve the intuitive understanding of a functional relationship by visualizing it in a graph. In a graph, values of the independent variable are usually read off the horizontal axis, and values of the dependent variable are usually read off the vertical axis. Each point in the grid of lines corresponds to a pair of values for the variables. For an example, see Figure 2.1. The upward-sloping line on the graph represents all of the pairs of values that satisfy the function $y = 5 + x/2$. You can check this by finding a couple of points that ought to be on the line that corresponds to that function. For example, what if $y = 0$? What value should x have? If $y = 0$, then a little arithmetic will reveal that x should equal -10. Thus, the pair $(0, -10)$ is a point on the line defined by the function. What if $x = 0$? What value will y have? In that case, the second

FIGURE 2.1

Graphs of the linear relationships
$y = 5 + x/2$ (with a positive slope) and
$y = 5 - x/2$ (with a negative slope).

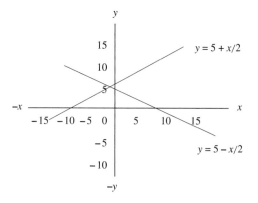

term in the right-hand side of the equation disappears, so that $y = 5$. Thus, the pair of values (5, 0) is a point on the line defined by the function.

The graph of $y = 5 + x/2$ reveals some things about the relationship between y and x that we otherwise might not so easily discover. For example, notice that the line representing the equation slopes upward, or from southwest to northeast. The *positive slope*, as it is called, reveals that the relationship between x and y is a *direct* one. Thus, as x increases, so does y. And as x decreases, y decreases. Put more generally, when the independent and dependent variables move in the same direction, the slope of the graph of their relationship will be positive.

The graph also reveals the strength of this direct relationship by showing whether small changes in x lead to small or large changes in y. Notice that if x increases by 2 units, y increases by 1 unit. Another way of putting this is to say that in order to get a 10-unit increase in y, there must be a 20-unit increase in x.[3]

The opposite of a direct relationship is an *inverse* relationship. In that sort of relationship, the dependent and independent variables move in opposite directions. Thus, if x and y are inversely related, an *increase* in x (the independent variable) will lead to a *decrease* in y. Also, a *decrease* in x will lead to an *increase* in y. An example of an inverse relationship between an independent and a dependent variable is $y = 5 - x/2$. The graph of this line is also shown in Figure 2.1. Note that the line is downward-sloping; that is, the line runs from northwest to southeast.

QUESTION 2.1: Suppose that the equation were $y = 5 + x$. Show in a graph like the one in Figure 2.1 what the graph of that equation would look like. Is the relationship between x and y direct or inverse? Is the slope of the new equation greater or less than the slope shown in Figure 2.1?

Now suppose that the equation were $y = 5 - x$. Show in a graph like the one in Figure 2.1 what the graph of that equation would look like. Is the relationship between x and y direct or inverse? Is the slope of the new equation positive or negative? Would the slope of the equation $y = 5 - x/2$ be steeper or shallower than that of the one in $y = 5 - x$?

The graph of $y = 5 + x/2$ in Figure 2.1 also reveals that the relationship between the variables is *linear*. This means that when we graph the values of the independent and dependent variables, the resulting relationship is a straight line. One of the implications of linearity is that changes in the independent variable cause a constant rate of change in the dependent variable. In terms of Figure 2.1, if we would like to know the effect on y of doubling the amount of x, it doesn't matter whether we investigate that effect when x equals 2 or 3147. The effect on y of doubling the value of x is proportionally the same, regardless of the value of x.

The alternative to a linear relationship is, of course, a nonlinear relationship. In general, nonlinear relationships are trickier to deal with than are linear relationships.

---

[3] The slope of the equation we have been dealing with in Figure 2.1 is $\frac{1}{2}$, which is the coefficient of x in the equation. In fact, in any linear relationship the coefficient of the independent variable gives the slope of the equation.

FIGURE 2.2

The graph of a nonlinear relationship, given by the equation $y = x^2$.

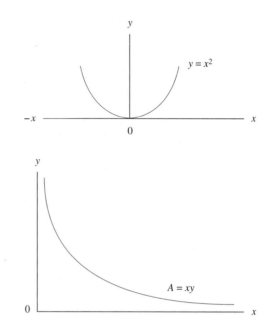

$y = x^2$

FIGURE 2.3

The graph of a nonlinear relationship, $A = xy$.

They frequently, although not always, are characterized by the independent variable being raised to a power by an exponent. Examples are $y = x^2$ and $y = 5/x^{\frac{1}{2}}$. Figure 2.2 shows a graph of $y = x^2$. Another common nonlinear relationship in economics is given by the example $A = xy$, where A is a constant. A graph of that function is given in Figure 2.3.

IV. The Theory of Consumer Choice and Demand

The economist's general theory of how people make choices is referred to as the theory of rational choice. In this section we show how that theory explains the consumer's choice of what goods and services to purchase and in what amounts.

A. Consumer Preference Orderings

The construction of the economic model of consumer choice begins with an account of the preferences of consumers. Consumers are assumed to know the things they like and dislike and to be able to rank the available alternative combinations of goods and services according to their ability to satisfy the consumer's preferences. This involves no more than ranking the alternatives as better than, worse than, or equally as good as one another. Indeed, some economists believe that the conditions they impose on the ordering or ranking of consumer preferences constitute what an economist means by the term *rational*. What are those conditions? They are that a consumer's preference ordering or ranking be *complete, transitive*, and *reflexive*. For an ordering to be *complete* simply means that the consumer be able to tell us how she ranks all the possible combinations of goods and services. Suppose that *A* represents a bundle of certain goods and services and *B* represents another bundle of the same goods and services but in different amounts. Completeness requires that the consumer be able to tell us that she prefers *A* to *B*, or that she prefers *B* to *A*, or that *A* and *B* are equally good (that is, that the consumer is indifferent between having *A* and having *B*). The consumer is *not* allowed to say, "I can't compare them."

Reflexivity is an arcane condition on consumer preferences. It means that any bundle of goods, *A*, is at least as good as itself. That condition is so trivially true that it is difficult to give a justification for its inclusion.

Transitivity means that the preference ordering obeys the following condition: If bundle *A* is preferred to bundle *B* and bundle *B* is preferred to bundle *C*, then it must be the case that *A* is preferred to *C*. This also applies to indifference: If the consumer is indifferent between *A* and *B* and between *B* and *C*, then she is also indifferent between *A* and *C*. Transitivity precludes the circularity of individual preferences. That is, transitivity means that it is impossible for *A* to be preferred to *B*, *B* to be preferred to *C*, and *C* to be preferred to *A*. Most of us would probably feel that someone who had circular preferences was extremely young or childish or crazy.

> **QUESTION 2.2:** Suppose that you have asked James whether he would like a hamburger or a hot dog for lunch, and he said that he wanted a hot dog. Five hours later you ask him what he would like for dinner, a hamburger or a hot dog. James answers, "A hamburger." Do James's preferences for hot dogs versus hamburgers obey the conditions above? Why or why not?

It is important to remember that the preferences of the consumer are *subjective*. Different people have different tastes, and these will be reflected in the fact that they may have very different preference orderings over the same goods and services. Economists leave to other disciplines, such as psychology and sociology, the study of the source of these preferences. We take consumer tastes or preferences as given, or, as economists say, as *exogenous*, which means that they are determined outside the economic system.[4]

An important consequence of the subjectivity of individual preferences is that economists have no accepted method for comparing the strength of people's preferences. Suppose that Stan tells us that he prefers bundle *A* to bundle *B*, and Jill tells us that she feels the same way: She also prefers *A* to *B*. Is there any way to tell who would prefer having *A* more? In the abstract, the answer is, "No, there is not." All we have from each consumer is the *order* of preference, not the *strength* of those preferences. Indeed, there is no metric by which to measure the strength of preferences, although economists sometimes jokingly refer to the "utils" of satisfaction that a consumer is enjoying. The inability to make *interpersonal comparisons of well-being* has some

---

[4] Many people new to the study of microeconomics will find this assumption of the exogeneity of preferences to be highly unrealistic. And there is some controversy about this assumption even within economics, some economists contending that preferences are endogenous—that is, determined within the economic system by such things as advertising. We cannot elaborate on this controversy here but are well aware of it.

important implications for the design and implementation of public policy, as we shall see in the section on welfare economics.

B. Utility Functions and Indifference Curves

Once a consumer describes what his or her preference ordering is, we may derive a *utility function* for that consumer. The utility function identifies higher preferences with larger numbers. Suppose that there are only two commodities or services, x and y, available to a given consumer. If we let u stand for the consumer's utility, then the function $u = u(x, y)$ describes the utility that the consumer gets from different combinations of x and y.

A very helpful way of visualizing the consumer's utility function is by means of a graph called an *indifference map*. An example is shown in Figure 2.4. There we have drawn several *indifference curves*. Each curve represents all the combinations of x and y that give the consumer the same amount of utility or well-being. Alternatively, we might say that the consumer's tastes are such that he is indifferent among all the combinations of x and y that lie along a given curve—hence, the name *indifference curve*. Thus, all those combinations of x and y lying along the indifference curve marked U_0 give the consumer the same utility. Those combinations lying on the higher indifference curve marked U_1 give this consumer similar utility, but this level of utility is higher than that of all those combinations of x and y lying along indifference curve U_0.

QUESTION 2.3:   Begin at point (x_0, y_0). Now decrease x from x_0 to x_1. How much must y increase to offset the decrease in x and keep the consumer indifferent?

The problem of consumer choice arises from the collision of the consumer's preferences with obstacles to his or her satisfaction. The obstacles are the constraints that force decision makers to choose among alternatives. There are many constraints, including time, energy, knowledge, and one's culture, but foremost among these is

FIGURE 2.4

The consumer's indifference map.

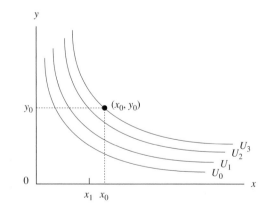

FIGURE 2.5

The consumer's income constraint or budget line.

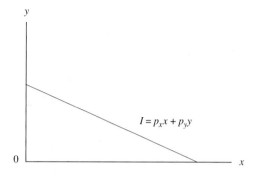

limited income. We can represent the consumer's income constraint or budget line by the line in Figure 2.5. The area below the line and the line itself represent all the combinations of x and y that are affordable, given the consumer's income, I.[5] Presumably, the consumer intends to spend all of her income on purchases of these two goods and services, so that the combinations upon which we shall focus are those that are on the budget line itself.

> **QUESTION 2.4:** In a figure like the one in Figure 2.5 and beginning with a budget line like the one in Figure 2.5, show how you would draw the new income constraint to reflect the following changes?
>
> 1. An increase in the consumer's income, prices held constant.
> 2. A decrease in the consumer's income, prices held constant.
> 3. A decrease in the price of x, income and the price of y held constant.
> 4. An increase in the price of y, income and the price of x held constant.

C. The Consumer's Optimum

We may now combine the information about the consumer's tastes given by the indifference map and the information about the income constraint given by the budget line in order to show what combination of x and y maximizes the consumer's utility, subject to the constraint imposed by her income. See Figure 2.6. There the consumer's optimum bundle is shown as point M, which contains x* and y*. Of all the feasible combinations of x and y, that combination gives this consumer the greatest utility.[6]

---

[5] The equation for the budget line is $I = p_x x + p_y y$, where p_x is the price per unit of x and p_y is the price per unit of y. As an exercise, you might try to rearrange this equation, with y as the dependent variable, in order to show that the slope of the line is negative. When you do so, you will find that the coefficient of the x-term is equal to $-p_x/p_y$. Economists refer to this ratio as *relative price*.

[6] Because we have assumed that the normal indifference curves are convex to the origin, there is a *unique* bundle of x and y that maximizes the consumer's utility. For other shapes of the indifference curves it is possible that there is more than one bundle that maximizes utility.

FIGURE 2.6

The consumer's optimum.

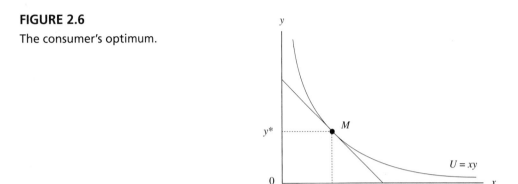

D. A Generalization: The Economic Optimum as Marginal Cost = Marginal Benefit

Because of the central importance of constrained maximization in microeconomic theory, let us take a moment to examine a more general way of characterizing such a maximum:

> A constrained maximum, or any other economic optimum, can be described as a point where marginal cost equals marginal benefit.

Let's see how this rule characterizes maximizing decisions.[7] Begin by assuming that the decision maker chooses some initial level of whatever it is he is interested in maximizing. He then attempts to determine whether that initial level is his maximum; is that level as good as he can do, given his constraints? He can answer the question by making very small, what an economist calls *marginal*, changes away from that initial level. Suppose that the decision maker proposes to *increase* slightly above his initial level whatever it is he is doing. There will be a cost associated with this small increase called *marginal cost*. But there will also be a benefit of having or doing more of whatever it is that he is attempting to maximize. The benefit of this small increase is called *marginal benefit*. The decision maker will perceive himself as doing better at this new level, by comparison to his initial level, so long as the *marginal benefit* of the small increase is greater than the *marginal cost* of the change. He will continue to make these small, or marginal, adjustments so long as the marginal benefit exceeds the marginal cost, and he will stop making changes when the marginal cost of the last change made equals (or is greater than) the marginal benefit. That level is the decision maker's maximum.

QUESTION 2.5: Suppose that, instead of increasing his level above the initial choice, the decision maker first tries decreasing the amount of whatever it is he is attempting to maximize. Explain how the comparison of marginal cost

---

[7] This rule could describe equally well an economic optimum where the goal of the decision maker is to *minimize* something. In that case, the optimum would still be the point at which $MC = MB$, but the demonstration of the stylized decision making that got one to that point would be different from that given in the text.

and marginal benefit for these decreases is made and leads the decision maker to the optimum. (Assume that the initial level is greater than what will ultimately prove to be the optimum.)

We can characterize the consumer's income-constrained maximum, M in Figure 2.6, in terms of the equality of marginal cost and benefit. Small changes in either direction along the budget line, I, represent a situation in which the consumer spends a dollar less on one good and a dollar more on the other. To illustrate, assume the consumer decides to spend a dollar less on y and a dollar more on x. Purchasing a dollar less of y causes a loss in utility that we may call the marginal cost of the budget reallocation. But the dollar previously spent on y can now be spent on x. More units of x mean greater utility, so that we may call this increase the marginal benefit of the budget reallocation.

Should the consumer spend a dollar less on good y and a dollar more on x? Only if the marginal cost (the decrease in utility from one dollar less of y) is less than the marginal benefit (the increase in utility from having one dollar more of x). The rational consumer will continue to reallocate dollars away from the purchase of y and toward the purchase of x until the marginal benefit of the last change made equals the marginal cost. This occurs at the point M in Figure 2.6.

Figure 2.7 applies constrained maximization to reduce the amount of pollution. Along the vertical axis are dollar amounts. Along the horizontal axis are units of pollution reduction. At the origin there is no effort to reduce pollution. At the vertical line labeled "100%," pollution has been completely eliminated.

The curve labeled MB shows the marginal benefit to society of reducing pollution. We assume that this has been correctly measured to take into account health, scenic, and all other benefits that accrue to members of society from reducing pollution at various levels. This line starts off high and then declines. This downward slope captures the fact that the very first efforts at pollution reduction confer large benefits on society. The next effort at reducing pollution also confers a social benefit, but not quite as great as the initial efforts. Finally, as we approach the vertical line labeled "100%" and all vestiges of pollution are being eliminated, the benefit to society of achieving those last steps is positive, but not nearly as great as the benefit of the early stages of pollution reduction.

FIGURE 2.7

The socially optimal amount of pollution-reduction effort.

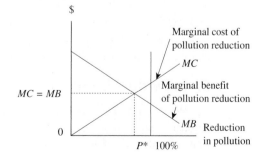

The curve labeled *MC* represents the "social" as opposed to "private" marginal cost of achieving given levels of pollution reduction. The individuals and firms that pollute must incur costs to reduce pollution: They may have to adopt cleaner and safer production processes that are also more expensive; they may have to install monitoring devices that check the levels of pollution they generate; and they may have to defend themselves in court when they are accused of violating the pollution-reduction guidelines. We have drawn the *MC* curve to be upward-sloping to indicate that the marginal costs of achieving any given level of pollution-reduction increase. This means that the cost of reducing the very worst pollution may not be very high, but that successive levels of reduction will be ever more expensive.

Given declining marginal benefit and rising marginal cost, the question then arises, "What is the optimal amount of pollution-reduction effort for society?" An examination of Figure 2.7 shows that *P** is the socially optimal amount of pollution-reduction effort. Any more effort will cost more than it is worth. Any less would cause a reduction in benefits that would be greater than the savings in costs.

Note that, according to this particular graph, it would not be optimal for society to try to eliminate pollution entirely. Here it is socially optimal to tolerate some pollution. Specifically, when pollution reduction equals *P**, the remaining pollution equals 100% − *P**, which is the "optimal amount of pollution." Few goods are free. Much of the wisdom of economics comes from the recognition of this fact and of the derivation of techniques for computing the costs and benefits.

> **QUESTION 2.6:** Suppose that we were to characterize society's decision making with regard to pollution-reduction efforts as an attempt to maximize the *net benefit* of pollution-reduction efforts. Let us define *net benefit* as the difference between marginal benefit and marginal cost. What level of pollution-reduction effort corresponds to this goal?

> **QUESTION 2.7:** Using a graph like Figure 2.7, show the effect on the determination of the socially optimal amount of pollution-reduction effort of the following:
>
> 1. Some technological change that lowers the marginal cost of achieving every level of pollution reduction.
> 2. A discovery that there are greater health risks associated with every given level of pollution than were previously thought to be the case.

If you understand that for economists, *the optimum for nearly all decisions occurs at the point at which marginal benefit equals marginal cost*, then you have gone a long way toward mastering the microeconomic tools necessary to answer most questions that we will raise in this book.

E. Individual Demand

We may use the model of consumer choice of the previous sections to derive a relationship between the price of a good and the amount of that good in a consumer's optimum bundle. The *demand curve* represents this relationship.

FIGURE 2.8

An individual's demand curve, showing
the inverse relationship between price
and quantity demanded.

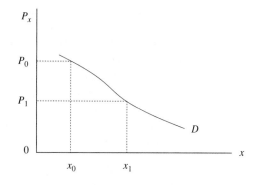

Starting from point *M* in Figure 2.6, note that when the price of *x* is that given by
the budget line, the optimal amount of *x* to consume is *x**. But what amount of *x* will
this consumer want to purchase so as to maximize utility when the price of *x* is lower
than that given by the budget line in Figure 2.6? We can answer that question by holding P_y and *I* constant, letting P_x fall, and writing down the amount of *x* in the succeed-
ing optimal bundles. Not surprisingly, the result of this exercise will be that the price of
x and the amount of *x* in the optimum bundles are inversely related. That is, when the
price of *x* goes up, P_y and *I* held constant (or *ceteris paribus*, "all other things equal,"
as economists say), the amount of *x* that the consumer will purchase goes down, and
vice versa. This result is the famous *law of demand*.

We may graph this relationship between P_x and the quantity of *x* demanded to
get the individual demand curve, *D*, shown in Figure 2.8. The demand curve we
have drawn in Figure 2.8 could have had a different slope than that shown; it might
have been either flatter or steeper. The steepness of the demand curve is related to
an important concept called the *price elasticity of demand*, or simply *elasticity of
demand*.[8]

This is an extremely useful concept: It measures how responsive consumer demand is to changes in price. And there are some standard attributes of goods that influence how responsive demand is likely to be. For instance, if two goods are similar
in their use, then an increase in the price of the first good with no change in the price
of the second good causes consumers to buy significantly less of the first good.
Generalizing, the most important determinant of the price elasticity of demand for a

[8] The measure is frequently denoted by the letter *e*, and the ranges of elasticity are called *inelastic* ($e < 1$),
elastic ($e > 1$), and *unitary elastic* ($e = 1$). By convention, *e*, the price elasticity of demand, is a positive
(or absolute) number, even though the calculation we suggested will lead to a negative number. For an inelastically demanded good, the percentage change in price exceeds the percentage change in quantity
demanded. Thus, a good that has $e = 0.5$ is one for which a 50 percent decline in price will cause a 25 percent
increase in the quantity demanded, or for which a 15 percent increase in price will cause a 7.5 percent decline in quantity demanded. For an elastically demanded good, the percentage change in price is less than
the percentage change in quantity demanded. As a result, a good that has $e = 1.5$ is one for which a 50 percent decline in price will cause a 75 percent increase in quantity demanded, or for which a 20 percent increase in price will cause a 30 percent decline in quantity demanded.

good is the availability of substitutes. The more substitutes for the good, the greater the elasticity of demand; the fewer the substitutes, the lower the elasticity. Substitution is easier for narrowly defined goods and harder for broad categories. If the price of cucumbers goes up, switching to peas or carrots is easy; if the price of vegetables goes up, switching to meat is possible; but if the price of food goes up, eating less is hard to do. So, we expect that demand is more elastic for cucumbers than vegetables and more elastic for vegetables than food. Also, demand is more elastic in the long run than the short run. To illustrate, if electricity prices rise relative to natural gas, consumers will increasingly switch to burning gas as they gradually replace furnaces and appliances. Economists often measure and remeasure the price elasticities of demand for numerous goods and services to predict responses to price changes.

V. The Theory of Supply

We now turn to a review of the other side of the market: the supply side. The key institution in supplying goods and services for sale to consumers is the business firm. In this section we shall see what goal the firm seeks and how it decides what to supply. In the following section, we merge our models of supply and demand to see how the independent maximizing activities of consumers and firms achieve a market equilibrium.

A. The Profit-Maximizing Firm

The firm is the institution in which output (products and services) is fabricated from inputs (capital, labor, land, and so on). Just as we assume that consumers rationally maximize utility subject to their income constraint, we assume that *firms maximize profits subject to the constraints imposed on them by consumer demand and the technology of production.*

In microeconomics, *profits* are defined as the difference between *total revenue* and the *total costs* of production. Total revenue for the firm equals the number of units of output sold multiplied by the price of each unit. Total costs equal the costs of each of the inputs times the number of units of input used, summed over all inputs. The profit-maximizing firm produces that amount of output that leads to the greatest positive difference between the firm's revenue and its costs. Microeconomic theory demonstrates that the firm will maximize its profits if it produces that *amount of output whose marginal cost equals its marginal revenue.* (In fact, this is simply an application of the general rule we discussed in section IV.D earlier: To achieve an optimum, equate marginal cost and marginal benefit.)

These considerations suggest that when marginal revenue exceeds marginal cost, the firm should expand production, and that when marginal cost exceeds marginal revenue, it should reduce production. It follows that profits will be maximized for that output for which marginal cost and marginal revenue are equal. Note the economy of this rule: To maximize profits, the firm need not concern itself with its total costs or total revenues; instead, it can simply experiment on production unit by unit in order to discover the output level that maximizes its profits.

FIGURE 2.9

The profit-maximizing output for a firm.

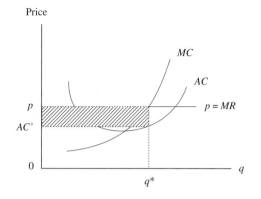

In Figure 2.9 the profit-maximizing output of the firm is shown at the point at which the marginal cost curve, labeled *MC*, and marginal revenue curve of the firm are equal. The profit-maximizing output level is denoted q^*. Total profits at this level of production, denoted by the shaded area in the figure, equal the difference between the total revenues of the firm (p times q^*) and the total costs of the firm (the average cost of producing q^* times q^*).

There are several things you should note about the curves in the graph. We have drawn the marginal revenue curve as horizontal and equal to the prevailing price. This implies that the firm can sell as much as it likes at that prevailing price. Doubling its sales will have no effect on the market price of the good or service. This sort of behavior is referred to as *price-taking* behavior. It characterizes industries in which there are so many firms, most of them small, that the actions of no single firm can affect the market price of the good or service. An example might be farming. There are so many suppliers of wheat that the decision of one farmer to double or triple output or cut it in half will have no impact on its market price. (Of course, if all farms decide to double output, there will be a substantial impact on market price.) Such an industry is said to be "perfectly competitive."

B. The Short Run and the Long Run

In microeconomics the firm is said to operate in two different time frames: the short run and the long run. These time periods do not correspond to calendar time. Instead they are defined in terms of the firm's inputs. In the short run at least one input is fixed (all others being variable), and the usual factor of production that is fixed is capital (the firm's buildings, machines, and other durable inputs). Because capital is fixed in the short run, all the costs associated with capital are called *fixed costs*. In the short run the firm can, in essence, ignore those costs: They will be incurred regardless of whether the firm produces nothing at all or 10 million units of output. (The only costs that change in the short run are "variable costs," which rise or fall depending on how much output the firm produces.) The long run is distinguished by the fact that all factors of production become variable. There are no longer any fixed costs. Established firms may expand their productive capacity or leave the industry entirely, and new firms may enter the business.

Another important distinction between the long and the short run has to do with the equilibrium level of profits for each firm. At any point in time there is an average rate of return earned by capital in the economy as a whole. When profits being earned in a particular industry exceed the average profit rate for comparable investments, firms will enter the industry, assuming there are no barriers to entry. As entry occurs, the total industry output increases, and the price of the industry output goes down, causing each firm's revenue to decrease. Also, the increased competition for the factors of production causes input prices to rise, pushing up each firm's costs. The combination of these two forces causes each firm's profits to decline. Entry ceases when profits fall to the average rate.

Economists have a special way of describing these facts. The average return on capital is treated as part of the costs that are subtracted from revenues to get "economic profits." Thus, when the rate of return on invested capital in this industry equals the average for the economy as a whole, it is said that "economic profits are zero."[9]

This leads to the conclusion that economic profits are zero in an industry that is in long-run equilibrium. Because this condition can occur only at the minimum point of the firm's average cost curve, where the average costs of production are as low as they can possibly be, inputs will be most efficiently used in long-run equilibrium. Thus, the condition of zero economic profits, far from being a nightmare, is really a desirable state.

VI.   Market Equilibrium

Having described the behavior of utility-maximizing consumers and profit-maximizing producers, our next task is to bring them together to explain how they interact. We shall first demonstrate how a unique price and quantity are determined by the interaction of supply and demand in a perfectly competitive market and then show what happens to price and quantity when the market structure changes to one of monopoly. We conclude this section with an example of equilibrium analysis of an important public policy issue.

A. Equilibrium in a Perfectly Competitive Industry

An industry in which there are so many firms that no one of them can influence the market price by its individual decisions and in which there are so many consumers that the individual utility-maximizing decisions of no one consumer can affect the market price is called a *perfectly competitive industry*. For such an industry the aggregate demand for and the aggregate supply of output can be represented by the downward-sloping demand curve, $d = d(p)$, and the upward-sloping supply curve, $s = s(p)$, shown

---

[9] When profits in a given industry are less than the average in the economy as a whole, economic profits are said to be negative. When that is the case, firms exit this industry for other industries where the profits are at least equal to the average for the economy. As an exercise, see if you can demonstrate the process by which profits go to zero when negative economic profits in an industry cause exit to take place.

FIGURE 2.10

Market equilibrium in a perfectly competitive market.

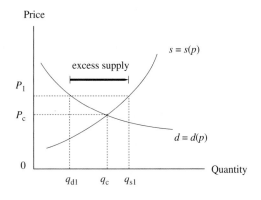

in Figure 2.10. The *market-clearing* or *equilibrium* price and quantity occur at the point of intersection of the aggregate supply and demand curves. At that combination of price and quantity, the decisions of consumers and suppliers are consistent.

One way to see why the combination P_c, q_c in Figure 2.10 is an equilibrium is to see what would happen if a different price-quantity combination were obtained. Suppose that the initial market price was P_1. At that price, producers would maximize their profits by supplying q_{s1} of output, and utility-maximizing consumers would be prepared to purchase q_{d1} units of output. These supply and demand decisions are inconsistent: At P_1, the amount that suppliers would like to sell exceeds the amount that consumers would like to buy. How will the market deal with this excess supply? Clearly, the market price must fall. As the price falls, consumers will demand more and producers will supply less, so the gap between supply and demand will diminish. Eventually the price may reach P_c. And at that price, as we have seen, the amount that suppliers wish to sell and the amount that consumers wish to purchase are equal.

B. Equilibrium in a Monopolistic Market

Monopoly is at the other extreme of market structure. In a monopoly there is only one supplier; so, that firm and the industry are identical. A monopoly can arise and persist only where there are barriers to entry that make it impossible for competing firms to appear. In general, such barriers can arise from two sources: first, from statutory and other legal restrictions on entry; and second, from technological conditions of production known as *economies of scale*. An example of a statutory restriction on entry was the Civil Aeronautics Board's refusal from the 1930s until the mid-1970s to permit entry of new airlines into the market for passenger traffic on such major routes as Los Angeles–New York and Chicago–Miami.

The second barrier to entry is technological. *Economies of scale* are a condition of production in which the greater the level of output, the lower the average cost of production. Where such conditions exist, one firm can produce any level of output at less cost than multiple firms. A monopolist that owes its existence to economies of scale is sometimes called a *natural monopoly*. Public utilities, such as local water, telecommunications, cable, and power companies, are often natural monopolies. The technological advantages of a natural monopoly would be partially lost if the single firm is allowed

Opportunity Cost and Comparative Advantage

We have been implicitly using one of the most fundamental concepts in microeconomics: *opportunity cost*. This term refers to the economic cost of an alternative that has been foregone. When you decided to attend a college, graduate school, or law school, you gave up certain other valuable alternatives, such as taking a job, training for the Olympics, or traveling around the world on a tramp steamer. In reckoning the cost of going to college, graduate school, or law school, the true economic cost was that of the next best alternative. This point is true of the decisions of all economic actors: When maximizing utility, the consumer must consider the opportunities given up by choosing one bundle of consumer goods rather than another; when maximizing profits, the firm must consider the opportunities foregone by committing its resources to the production of widgets rather than to something else.

In general, the economic notion of opportunity cost is more expansive than the more common notion of accounting cost. An example will make this point.[10] Suppose that a rich relative gives you a car whose market value is $15,000. She says that if you sell the car, you may keep the proceeds, but that if you use the car yourself, she'll pay for the gas, oil, maintenance, repairs, and insurance. In short she says, "The use of the car is FREE!" But is it? Suppose that the $15,000 for which the car could be sold would earn 12 percent interest per year in a savings account, giving $1800 per year in interest income. If you use the car for 1 year, its resale value will fall to $11,000—a cost to you of $4000. Therefore, the opportunity cost to you of using the car for 1 year is $4000 plus the foregone interest of $1800—a total of $5800. This is far from being free. The accounting cost of using the car is zero, but the opportunity cost is positive.

Comparative advantage is another useful economic concept related to the notion of opportunity cost. The law of comparative advantage asserts that people should engage in those pursuits where their opportunity costs are lower than others. For example, someone who is 7 feet tall has a comparative advantage in pursuing a career in professional basketball. But what about someone whose skills are such that she can do many things well? Suppose, for example, that a skilled attorney is also an extremely skilled typist. Should she do her own typing or hire someone else to do it while she specializes in the practice of law? The notion of comparative advantage argues for specialization: The attorney can make so much more money by specializing in the practice of law than by trying to do both jobs that she could easily afford to hire someone else who is less efficient at typing to do her typing for her.

to restrict its output and to charge a monopoly price. For that reason, natural monopolies are typically regulated by the government.

The monopolist, like the competitive firm, maximizes profit by producing that output for which marginal cost equals marginal revenue. Marginal cost of the monopolist, as for the competitive firm, is the cost of producing one more unit of output. This cost curve is represented in Figure 2.11 by the curve labeled *MC*. But marginal revenue for the monopolist is different from what it was for the competitive firm. Recall that marginal revenue describes the change in a firm's total revenues for a small, or marginal,

---

[10] The example is taken from Roy Ruffin & Paul Gregory, Principles of Microeconomics 156 (2d ed. 1986).

FIGURE 2.11

Profit-maximizing output and price for a monopolist.

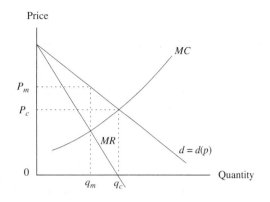

change in the number of units of output sold. For the competitive firm marginal revenue is equal to the price of output. Because the competitive firm can sell as much as it likes at the prevailing price, each additional unit of output sold adds exactly the sale price to the firm's total revenues. But for the monopolist, marginal revenue declines as the number of units sold increases. This is indicated in Figure 2.11 by the downward-sloping curve labeled *MR*. Notice that the *MR* curve lies below the demand curve. This indicates that the marginal revenue from any unit sold by a monopolist is always less than the price. *MR* is positive but declining for units of output between 0 and q_c; thus, the sale of each of those units increases the firm's total revenues but at a decreasing rate. The q_0 unit actually adds nothing to the firm's total revenues ($MR = 0$), and for each unit of output beyond q_c, *MR* is less than zero, which means that each of those units actually reduces the monopolist's total revenues.

The reason for this complex relationship between marginal revenue and units sold by the monopolist is the downward-sloping demand curve. The downward-sloping demand curve implies that the monopolist must lower the price to sell more units; but in order to sell an additional unit of output he or she must lower the price not just on the last or marginal unit but on all the units sold.[11] From this fact it can be shown, using calculus, that the addition to total revenues from an additional unit of output sold will always be less than the price charged for that unit. Thus, because *MR* is always less than the price for all units of output and because price declines along the demand curve, the *MR* curve must also be downward sloping and lie below the demand curve.

The monopolist maximizes his profit by choosing that output level for which marginal revenue and marginal cost are equal. This output level, q_m, is shown in Figure 2.11. The demand curve indicates that consumers are willing to pay P_m for that amount of output. Notice that if this industry were competitive instead of monopolized, the profit-maximizing actions of the firms would have resulted in an equilibrium price and quantity at the intersection of the aggregate supply curve, *S*, and the industry demand curve, *D*. The competitive price, P_c, is lower than the monopolistic price, and the

---

[11] This assumes that the monopolist cannot price-discriminate (that is, charge different prices to different consumers for the same product).

quantity of output produced and consumed under competition, q_c, is greater than under monopoly.

Economists distinguish additional market structures that are intermediate between the extremes of perfect competition and monopoly. The most important among these are *oligopoly* and *imperfect competition*. An oligopolistic market is one containing a few firms that recognize that their individual profit-maximizing decisions are interdependent. That means that what is optimal for firm *A* depends not only on its marginal costs and the demand for its output but also on what firms *B*, *C*, and *D* have decided to produce and the prices they are charging. The economic analysis of this interdependence requires a knowledge of game theory, which we discuss below.

An imperfectly competitive market is one that shares most of the characteristics of a perfectly competitive market—for example, free entry and exit of firms and the presence of many firms—but has one important monopolistic element: Firms produce differentiable output rather than the homogeneous output produced by perfectly competitive firms. Thus, imperfectly competitive firms distinguish their output by brand names, colors, sizes, quality, durability, and so on.

C. An Example of Equilibrium Analysis

It is useful to have an example applying this theory to a real problem. Let us imagine a market for rental housing like the one shown in Figure 2.12. The demand for rental housing is given by the curve *D*, and the supply of rental housing is given by the upward-sloping supply curve *S*. Assuming that the rental housing market is competitive, then the independent actions of consumers and of profit-maximizing housing owners will lead to a rental rate of r_1 being charged and of h_1 units of rental housing being supplied and demanded. Note that this is an equilibrium in the sense we discussed above: The decisions of those demanding the product and of those supplying it are consistent at the price r_1. Unless something causes the demand curve or the supply curve to shift, this price and output combination will remain in force.

But now suppose that the city government feels that r_1 is too high and passes an ordinance that specifies a maximum rental rate for housing of r_m, considerably below

FIGURE 2.12

The consequences of a rent-control ordinance that prescribes rents below the market-clearing rental rate.

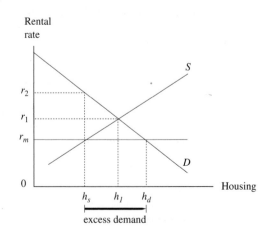

the equilibrium market rate. The hope of the government is that at least the same amount of housing will be consumed by renters but at a lower rental rate. A look at Figure 2.12, however, leads one to doubt that result. At r_m, consumers demand h_d units of rental housing, an increase over the quantity demanded at the higher rate, r_1. But at this lower rate suppliers are only prepared to supply h_s units of rental housing. Apparently it does not pay them to devote as much of their housing units to renters at that lower rate; perhaps if r_m is all one can get from renting housing units, suppliers prefer to switch some of their units to other uses, such as occupancy by the owner's family or their sale as condominiums. The result of the rate ceiling imposed by the government is a shortage of, or excess demand for, rental units equal to $(h_d - h_s)$.

If the rate ceiling is strictly enforced, the shortage will persist. Some non-price methods of determining who gets the h_s units of rental housing must be found, such as queuing. Eventually, the shortage may be eased if either the demand curve shifts inward or the supply curve shifts outward. It is also possible that landlords will let their property deteriorate by withholding routine maintenance and repairs, so that the quality of their property falls to such an extent that r_m provides a competitive rate of return to them.

If, however, the rate ceiling is *not* strictly enforced, then consumers and suppliers will find a way to erase the shortage. For example, renters could offer free services or secret payments (sometimes called *side payments*) to landlords in order to get the effective rental rate above r_m and induce the landlord to rent to them rather than to those willing to pay only r_m. Those services and side payments could amount to $(r_2 - r_m)$ per housing unit.

VII. Game Theory

The law frequently confronts situations in which there are few decision makers and in which the optimal action for one person to take depends on what another actor chooses. These situations are like games in that people must decide upon a strategy. A strategy is a plan for acting that responds to the reactions of others. *Game theory* deals with any situation in which strategy is important. Game theory will, consequently, enhance our understanding of some legal rules and institutions. For those who would like to pursue this topic in more detail, there are now several excellent introductory books on game theory.[12]

To characterize a game, we must specify three things:

1. *players,*
2. *strategies* of each player, and
3. *payoffs* to each player for each strategy.

---

[12] For those who would like to pursue game theory in more detail, there are now several excellent introductory texts: ERIC RASMUSEN, GAMES AND INFORMATION: AN INTRODUCTION TO GAME THEORY (3d ed. 2001); DAVID KREPS, GAME THEORY AND ECONOMIC MODELING (1990); and AVINASH DIXIT & BARRY NALEBUFF, THINKING STRATEGICALLY: THE COMPETITIVE EDGE IN BUSINESS, POLITICS, AND EVERYDAY LIFE (1991). More advanced treatments may be found in ROGER MYERSON, GAME THEORY (1991) and DREW FUDENBERG & JEAN TIROLE, GAME THEORY (1991). With special reference to law, see DOUGLAS BAIRD, ROBERT GERTNER, & RANDAL PICKER, GAME THEORY AND THE LAW (1995).

Let's consider a famous example—the prisoner's dilemma. Two people, *Suspect 1* and *Suspect 2*, conspire to commit a crime. They are apprehended by the police outside the place where the crime was committed, taken to the police station, and placed in separate rooms so that they cannot communicate. The authorities question them individually and try to play one suspect against the other. The evidence against them is circumstantial—they were simply in the wrong place at the wrong time. If the prosecutor must go to trial with only this evidence, then the suspects will have to be charged with a minor offense and given a relatively light punishment—say, 1 year in prison. The prosecutor would very much prefer that one or both of the suspects confesses to the more serious crime that they are thought to have committed. Specifically, if either suspect confesses (and thereby implicates the other) and the other does not, the non-confessor will receive 7 years in prison, and as a reward for assisting the state, the confessor will only receive six months in jail. If both suspects can be induced to confess, each will spend 5 years in prison. What should each suspect do—confess or keep quiet?

The strategies available to the suspects can be shown in a *payoff matrix* like that in Figure 2.13. Each suspect has two strategies: confess or keep quiet. The payoffs to each player from following a given strategy are shown by the entries in the four cells of the box, with the payoff to *Suspect 2* given in the lower left-hand corner of each cell and the payoff to *Suspect 1* given in the upper right-hand corner of the cell.

Here is how to read the entries in the payoff matrix. If *Suspect 1* confesses and *Suspect 2* also confesses, each will receive 5 years in prison. If *Suspect 1* confesses and *Suspect 2* keeps quiet, *Suspect 1* will spend six months in jail, and *Suspect 2* will spend 7 years in prison. If *Suspect 1* keeps quiet and *Suspect 2* confesses, then *Suspect 2* will spend six months in jail, and *Suspect 1* will spend 7 years in prison. Finally, if both suspects keep quiet, each will spend 1 year in prison.

There is another way to look at *Suspect 1*'s options. The payoff matrix is sometimes referred to as the *strategic form* of the game. An alternative is the *extensive form*. This puts one player's options in the form of a decision tree, which is shown in Figure 2.14.

We now wish to explore what the optimal strategy—confess or keep quiet—is for each player, given the options in the payoff matrix and given some choice made by the other player. Let's consider how *Suspect 1* will select her optimal strategy. Remember

FIGURE 2.13

The strategic form of a game, also known as a payoff matrix.

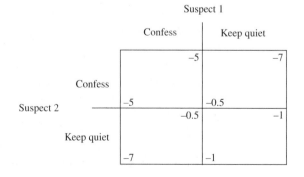

FIGURE 2.14

The extensive form of the prisoner's dilemma.

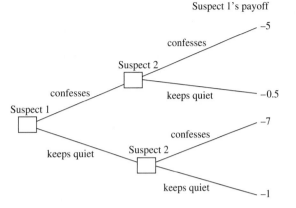

that the players are being kept in separate rooms and cannot communicate with one another. (Because the game is symmetrical, this is exactly the same way in which *Suspect 2* will select his optimal strategy.)

First, what should *Suspect 1* do if *Suspect 2* confesses? If she keeps quiet when *Suspect 2* confesses, she will spend 7 years in prison. If she confesses when *Suspect 2* confesses, she will spend 5 years. So, if *Suspect 2* confesses, clearly the best thing for *Suspect 1* to do is to confess.

But what if *Suspect 2* adopts the alternative strategy of keeping quiet? What is the best thing for *Suspect 1* to do then? If *Suspect 2* keeps quiet and *Suspect 1* confesses, she will spend only half a year in prison. If she keeps quiet when *Suspect 2* keeps quiet, she will spend 1 year in prison. Again, the best thing for *Suspect 1* to do if the other suspect keeps quiet is to confess.

Thus, *Suspect 1* will always confess. Regardless of what the other player does, confessing will always mean less time in prison for her. In the jargon of game theory this means that confessing is a *dominant strategy*—the optimal move for a player to make is the same, regardless of what the other player does.

Because the other suspect will go through precisely the same calculations, he will also confess. Confessing is the dominant strategy for each player. The result is that the suspects are *both* going to confess, and, therefore, each will spend 5 years in prison.

The solution to this game, that both suspects confess, is an equilibrium: There is no reason for either player to change his or her strategy. There is a famous concept in game theory that characterizes this equilibrium—a *Nash equilibrium*. In such an equilibrium, no individual player can do any better by changing his or her behavior so long as the other players do not change theirs. (Notice that the competitive equilibrium that we discussed in previous sections is an example of a Nash equilibrium when there are many players in the game.)

The notion of a Nash equilibrium is fundamental in game theory, but it has shortcomings. For instance, some games have no Nash equilibrium. Some games have several Nash equilibria. And finally, there is not necessarily a correspondence between the

Nash equilibrium and Pareto efficiency, the criterion that economists use to evaluate many equilibria. To see why, return to the prisoner's dilemma above. We have seen that it is a Nash equilibrium for both suspects to confess. But you should note that this is *not* a Pareto-efficient solution to the game from the viewpoint of the accused. When both suspects confess, they will each spend 5 years in prison. It is possible for *both* players to be better off. That would happen if they would both keep quiet. Thus, cell 4 (where each receives a year in prison) is a Pareto-efficient outcome. Clearly, that solution is impossible because the suspects cannot make binding commitments not to confess.[13]

We may use the prisoner's dilemma to discuss another important fundamental concept of game theory—*repeated games*. Suppose that the prisoner's dilemma were to be played not just once but a number of times by the same players. Would that change our analysis of the game? If the same players play the same game according to the same rules repeatedly, then it is possible that cooperation can arise and that players have an incentive to establish a reputation—in this case, for trustworthiness.

An important thing to know about a repeated game is whether the game will be repeated a *fixed* number of times or an *indefinite* number. To see the difference, suppose that the prisoner's dilemma above is to be repeated exactly ten times. Each player's optimal strategy must now be considered across games, not just for one game at a time. Imagine *Suspect 2* thinking through, before the first game is played, what strategy he ought to follow for each game. He might imagine that he and his partner, if caught after each crime, will learn (or agree) to keep quiet rather than to confess. But then *Suspect 2* thinks forward to the final game, the tenth. Even if the players had learned (or agreed) to keep quiet through Game 9, things will be different in Game 10. Because this is the last time the game is to be played, *Suspect 1* has a strong incentive to confess. If she confesses on the last game and *Suspect 2* sticks to the agreement not to confess, he will spend 7 years in prison to her half year. Knowing that she has this incentive to cheat on an agreement not to confess in the last game, the best strategy for *Suspect 2* is also to confess in the final game. But now Game 9 becomes, in a sense, the final game. And in deciding on the optimal strategy for that game, exactly the same logic applies as it did for Game 10—both players will confess in Game 9, too. *Suspect 1* can work all this out, too, and she will realize that the best thing to do is to confess in Game 8, and so on. In the terminology of game theory, the game *unravels* so that confession takes place by each player every time the game is played, *if it is to be played a fixed number of times*.

Things may be different if the game is to be repeated an indefinite number of times. In those circumstances there may be an inducement to cooperation. Robert Axelrod has shown that in a game like the prisoner's dilemma repeated an indefinite number of times, the optimal strategy is *tit-for-tat*—if the other player cooperated on the last play, you cooperate on this play; if she didn't cooperate on the last play, you don't on this play.[14]

---

[13] Can you think of a workable way in which the suspects might have agreed never to confess before they perpetrated the crime? Put in the language of game theory, can a participant in a game like the prisoner's dilemma make a *credible commitment* not to confess if she and her partner are caught?

[14] See ROBERT AXELROD, THE EVOLUTION OF COOPERATION (1984).

These considerations of a fixed versus an indefinite number of plays of a game may seem removed from the concerns of the law, but they really are not. Consider, for example, the relations between a creditor and a debtor. When the debtor's affairs are going well, the credit relations between the creditor and the debtor may be analogized to a game played an indefinite number of times. But if the debtor is likely to become insolvent soon, the relations between debtor and creditor become much more like a game to be played a fixed (and, perhaps, few) number of times. As a result, trust and cooperation between the parties may break down, with the debtor trying to hide his assets and the creditor trying to grab them for resale to recoup his losses.

We shall see that these concepts from game theory will play an important role in our understanding of legal rules and institutions.

VIII. The Theory of Asset Pricing

The area of microeconomic theory that deals with capital and labor markets is beyond the scope of the material in this book. There is, however, one tool from this area that we shall use: the theory of asset pricing.

Assets are resources that generate a stream of income. For instance, an apartment building can generate a stream of rental payments; a patent can generate a stream of royalty payments; an annuity can generate a fixed amount of income per year. There is a technique for converting these various streams of future income (or future expenses or, still more generally, net receipts) into a lump sum today. The general question that is being asked is, "How much would you be prepared to pay today for an asset that generated a given future flow of net receipts in the future?"

We can answer that question by computing what is called the *present discounted value* of the future flow of net receipts. Suppose that ownership of a particular asset will generate F_1 in net receipts at the end of the first year; F_2 in net receipts at the end of the second year; F_3 in net receipts at the end of the third year; and F_n at the end of the nth year. The present discounted value of that asset, supposing that the prevailing rate of interest is r, is equal to:

$$PDV = \frac{F_1}{(1 + r)} + \frac{F_2}{(1 + r)^2} + \frac{F_3}{(1 + r)^3} + \cdots + \frac{F_n}{(1 + r)^n}.$$

This result has many applications to law. For instance, suppose that a court is seeking to compensate someone whose property was destroyed. One method of valuing the loss is to compute the present discounted value of the future flow of net receipts to which the owner was entitled.

IX. General Equilibrium and Welfare Economics

The microeconomic theory we have been reviewing to this point has focused on the fundamental concepts of maximization, equilibrium, and efficiency in describing the decisions of consumers and firms. The part of microeconomic theory called *welfare economics* explores how the decisions of many individuals and firms interact to affect the well-being of individuals as a group. Welfare economics is much more philosophical than other topics in microeconomic theory. Here the great policy issues are raised. For example, is there an inherent conflict between efficiency and fairness? To what extent can unregulated markets maximize individual well-being? When and how should the government intervene in the marketplace? Can economics identify a just distribution of goods and services? In this brief introduction, we can only hint at how microeconomic theory approaches these questions. Nonetheless, this material is fundamental to the economic analysis of legal rules.

A. General Equilibrium and Efficiency Theorems

One of the great accomplishments of modern microeconomics is the specification of the conditions under which the independent decisions of utility-maximizing consumers and profit-maximizing firms will lead to the inevitable, spontaneous establishment of equilibrium in all markets simultaneously. Such a condition is known as *general equilibrium*. General equilibrium will be achieved only when competitive forces have led to the equality of marginal benefit and marginal cost in the market for every single commodity and service. As you can well imagine, this condition is unlikely to be realized in the real world. However, there are two practical reasons for knowing what conditions must hold for general equilibrium to obtain. First, while *all* real-world markets may not obey those conditions, many of them will. Second, the specification of the conditions that lead to general equilibrium provides a benchmark for evaluating various markets and making recommendations for public policy.

Modern microeconomics has demonstrated that general equilibrium has characteristics that economists describe as socially optimal—that is, the general equilibrium is both productively and allocatively efficient.

B. Market Failure

General equilibrium is, in welfare terms, such a desirable outcome that it would be helpful to know the conditions under which it will hold. Stripped of detail, the essential condition is that all markets are perfectly competitive. We can characterize the things that can go wrong to prevent this essential condition from being attained in a market. In this section we shall describe the four sources of *market failure,* as it is called, and describe the public policies that can, in theory, correct those failures.

1. Monopoly and Market Power   The first source of market failure is monopoly in its various forms: monopoly in the output market, collusion among otherwise competitive firms or suppliers of inputs, and monopsony (only one buyer) in the input market. If the industry were competitive, marginal benefit and marginal cost would be equal. But as illustrated in Figure 2.11, the monopolist's profit-maximizing output and price combination occurs at a point where the price exceeds the marginal cost of production. The price is too high, and the quantity supplied is too low from the viewpoint of efficiency.

The public policies for correcting the shortcomings of monopoly are to replace monopoly with competition where possible, or to regulate the price charged by the monopolist. The first policy is the rationale for the antitrust laws. But sometimes it is not possible or even desirable to replace a monopoly. Natural monopolies, such as public utilities, are an example; those monopolies are allowed to continue in existence, but government regulates their prices.

2. Externalities   The second source of market failure is the presence of what economists call *externalities*. Exchange inside a market is voluntary and mutually beneficial. Typically, the parties to the exchange capture all the benefits and bear all the costs, thus having the best information about the desirability of the exchange. But sometimes the benefits of an exchange may spill over onto other parties than those explicitly engaged in the exchange. Moreover, the costs of the exchange may also spill over onto other parties. The first instance is an example of an *external benefit*; the second, an *external cost*. An example of an external benefit is the pollination that a beekeeper provides to his neighbor who runs an apple orchard. An example of an external cost is air or water pollution.

   Let's explore the idea of an external cost (frequently called simply an *externality*) to see how it can lead to market failure and what public policies can correct this failing. Suppose that a factory located upstream from a populous city dumps toxic materials into the river as a by-product of its production process. This action by the factory imposes an unbargained-for cost on the townspeople downstream: They must incur some additional costs to clean up the water or to bring in safe water from elsewhere. In what way has the market failed in this example? The reason the market fails in the presence of external costs is that the generator of the externality does not have to pay for harming others, and so exercises too little self-restraint. He or she acts as if the cost of disposing of waste is zero, when, in fact, there are real costs involved, as the people downstream can testify. In a technical sense, the externality generator produces too much output and too much harm because there is a difference between *private* marginal cost and *social* marginal cost.

   Private marginal cost, in our example, is the marginal cost of production for the factory. Social marginal cost is the sum of private marginal cost and the additional marginal costs involuntarily imposed on third parties by each unit of production. The difference is shown in Figure 2.15. Social marginal cost is greater than private marginal cost at every level of output. The vertical difference between the two curves equals the

FIGURE 2.15

The difference between private and social marginal cost.

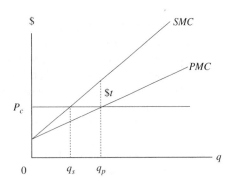

amount of the external marginal cost at any level of output. Note that if production is zero, there is no externality, but that as production increases, the amount of external cost per unit of output increases.

The profit-maximizing firm operates along its private marginal cost curve and maximizes profits by choosing that output level for which $P_c = PMC$—namely, q_p. But from society's point of view, this output is too large. Society's resources will be most efficiently used if the firm chooses its output level by equating P_c and SMC at q_s. At that level the firm has taken into account not only its own costs of production but also any costs it imposes on others involuntarily.

What public policies will induce the externality generator to take external costs into account? That is one of the central questions that this book will seek to answer. The key to achieving the social optimum where there are externalities is to induce private profit-maximizers to restrict their output to the socially optimal, not privately optimal, point. This is done by policies that cause the firm to operate along the social marginal cost curve rather than along the private marginal cost curve. When this is accomplished, the externality is said to have been *internalized* in the sense that the private firm now takes it into consideration.

QUESTION 2.8:   In Figure 2.15, if the firm is producing output, is there any external cost being generated? If so, why is this output level called a social optimum? Would it not be optimal to have *no* external cost? At what level of output would that occur? Does our earlier discussion that characterized any social optimum as the point at which (social) marginal cost equals (social) marginal benefit provide any guidance? Is the point at which social marginal cost and social marginal benefit are equal consistent with the existence of *some* external cost? Why or why not?

3. Public Goods   The third source of market failure is the presence of a commodity called a *public good*. A public good is a commodity with two very closely related characteristics:

1. *Nonrivalrous consumption:* consumption of a public good by one person does not leave less for any other consumer.
2. *Nonexcludability:* the costs of excluding nonpaying beneficiaries who consume the good are so high that no private profit-maximizing firm is willing to supply the good.

Consider national defense. Suppose, for the purposes of illustration, that national defense were provided by competing private companies. For an annual fee a company would sell protection to its customers against loss from foreign invasion by air, land, or sea. Only those customers who purchase some company's services would be protected against foreign invasion. Perhaps these customers could be identified by special garments, and their property denoted by a large white X painted on the roof of their homes.

Who will purchase the services of these private national defense companies? Some will but many will not. Many of the nonpurchasers will reason that if their neighbor will purchase a protection policy from a private national defense company, then they, too, will be protected: It will prove virtually impossible for the private company to protect the property and person of the neighbor without also providing security to the nearby nonpurchaser. Thus, the consumption of national defense is nonrivalrous: Consumption by one person does not leave less for any other consumer. For that reason, there is a strong inducement for consumers of the privately provided public good to try to be *free riders*: They hope to benefit at no cost to themselves from the payment of others.

The related problem for the private supplier of a public good is the difficulty of excluding nonpaying beneficiaries. The attempt to distinguish those who have from those who have not subscribed to the private defense companies is almost certain to fail; for example, the identifying clothes and property markings can easily be counterfeited.

As a result of the presence of free riders and the high cost of distinguishing nonpaying from paying beneficiaries, it is not likely that the private company will be able to induce many people to purchase defense services. If private profit-maximizing firms are the only providers of national defense, too little of that good will be provided.

How can public policy correct the market failure in the provision of public goods? There are two general correctives. First, the government may undertake to *subsidize* the private provision of the public good, either directly or indirectly through the tax system. An example might be research on basic science. Second, the government may undertake to provide the public good itself and to pay the costs of providing the service through the revenues raised by compulsory taxation. This is, in fact, how national defense is supplied.

Web Note 2.1

Another kind of problem that markets have is coordinating people, especially when they act collectively. See our website for a discussion of coordination and collective action applied to legal issues.

4. Severe Informational Asymmetries   The fourth source of market failure is an imbalance of information between parties to an exchange, one so severe that exchange is impeded.

To illustrate, it is often the case that sellers know more about the quality of goods than do buyers. For example, a person who offers his car for sale knows far more about its quirks than does a potential buyer. Similarly, when a bank presents a depository agreement for the signature of a person opening a checking account, the bank knows far more than the customer about the legal consequences of the agreement.

When sellers know more about a product than do buyers, or vice versa, information is said to be distributed asymmetrically in the market. Under some circumstances, these asymmetries can be corrected by the mechanism of voluntary exchange, for example, by the seller's willingness to provide a warranty to guarantee the quality of a product. But severe asymmetries can disrupt markets so much that a social optimum cannot be achieved by voluntary exchange. When that happens, government intervention in the market can ideally correct for the informational asymmetries and induce more nearly optimal exchange. For example, the purchasers of a home are often at a disadvantage vis-à-vis the current owners in learning of latent defects, such as the presence of termites or a cracked foundation. As a result, the market for the sale of homes may not function efficiently; purchasers may be paying too much for homes or may inefficiently refrain from purchases because of a fear of latent defects. Many states have responded by requiring sellers to disclose knowledge of any latent defects to prospective purchasers of houses. If the sellers do not make this disclosure, then they may be responsible for correcting those defects.

> ### Web Note 2.2
>
> One of the most important issues in welfare economics has been the derivation of a social welfare function, which aggregates individual preferences into social preferences. The Arrow Impossibility Theorem, one of the most significant intellectual achievements of modern economics, argues that a social welfare function with minimally desirable properties cannot be constructed. We describe the theorem in more detail at our website.

C. Potential Pareto Improvements or Kaldor-Hicks Efficiency

Dissatisfied with the Pareto criterion, economists developed the notion of a *potential Pareto improvement* (sometimes called *Kaldor-Hicks efficiency*). This is an attempt to surmount the restriction of the Pareto criterion that only those changes are recommended in which at least one person is made better off and no one is made worse off. That criterion requires that gainers explicitly compensate losers in any change. If there is not explicit payment, losers can veto any change. That is, every change must be by unanimous consent. This has clear disadvantages as a guide to public policy.

By contrast, a potential Pareto improvement allows changes in which there are both gainers and losers but requires that the gainers gain more than the losers lose. If this condition is satisfied, the gainers can, in principle, compensate the losers and still have a surplus left for themselves. For a potential Pareto improvement, compensation does not actually have to be made, but it must be possible in principle. In essence, this is the technique of cost-benefit analysis. In cost-benefit analysis, a project is undertaken when its benefits exceed its costs, which implies that the gainers could compensate the losers. Cost-benefit analysis tries to take into account both the private and social costs and benefits of the action being contemplated. There are both theoretical and empirical problems with this standard, but it is indispensable to applied welfare economics.

Consider how these two criteria—the Pareto criterion and the Kaldor-Hicks criterion—would help us to analyze the efficiency and distributive justice of a manufacturing plant's decision to relocate. Suppose that the plant announces that it is going to move from town *A* to town *B*. There will be gainers—those in town *B* who will be employed by the new plant, the retail merchants and home builders in *B*, the shareholders of the corporation, and so on. But there will also be losers—those in town *A* who are now unemployed, the retail merchants in *A*, the customers of the plant who are now located further away from the plant, and so on. If we were to apply the Pareto criterion to this decision, the gainers would have to pay the losers whatever it would take for them to be indifferent between the plant's staying in A and moving to B. If we were to apply the potential Pareto criterion to this decision, the gainers would have to gain more than the losers lose but no compensation would actually occur.

Web Note 2.3

See our website for much more on cost-benefit analysis as a guide to public policy, including legal change.

X. Decision Making Under Uncertainty: Risk and Insurance

In nearly all of the economic models we have examined so far, we have implicitly assumed that uncertainty did not cloud the decision. This is clearly a simplifying assumption. It is time to expand our basic economic model by explicitly allowing for the presence of uncertainty.

A. Expected Monetary Value

Suppose that an entrepreneur is considering two possible projects in which to invest. The first, D_1, involves the production of an output whose market is familiar and stable. There is no uncertainty about the outcome of project D_1; the entrepreneur can be confident of earning a profit of $200 if he takes D_1. The second course of action, D_2, involves a novel product whose reception by the consuming public is uncertain. If consumers like the new product, the entrepreneur can earn profits of $300. However, if they do not like it, he stands to lose $30.

How is the entrepreneur supposed to compare these two projects? One possibility is to compare their expected monetary values. An *expected value* is the sum of the probabilities of each possible outcome times the value of each of those outcomes. For example, suppose that there are four possible numerical outcomes, labeled O_1 through O_4, to a decision. Suppose also that there are four separate probability estimates, labeled p_1 through p_4, associated with each of the four outcomes. If these are the only possible outcomes, then these probabilities must sum to 1. The expected value (EV) of this decision is then:

$$EV = p_1 O_1 + p_2 O_2 + p_3 O_3 + p_4 O_4.$$

To return to our example, the entrepreneur can get $200 by choosing D_1. What is the expected monetary value of decision D_2? There are two possible outcomes, and in order to perform the calculation the entrepreneur needs to know the probabilities. Let p denote the probability of the new product's succeeding. Thus, $(1 - p)$ is the probability that it fails. Then, the expected monetary value of D_2 for any probability p is given by the expression:

$$EMV(D_2) = 300p + (-30)(1 - p).$$

Thus, if the probability of success for the new product equals $\frac{1}{3}$, the expected monetary value of the decision to introduce that new product equals $80.

Where does the decision maker get information about the probabilities of the various outcomes? Perhaps the seasoned entrepreneur has some intuition about p or perhaps marketing surveys have provided a scientific basis for assessing p. Still another possibility might be that he calculates the level of p that will make the expected monetary value of D_2 equal to that of the certain event, D_1. A strong reason for doing that would be that, although he might not know for sure what p is, it would be valuable to know how high p must be in order for it to give the same expected profits as the safe course of action, D_1. For example, even if there was no way to know p for sure, suppose that one could calculate that in order for the uncertain course of action to have a higher expected value than the safe course of action, the probability of success of the new product would have to be 0.95, a near certainty. That would be valuable information.

It is a simple matter to calculate the level of p that equates the expected monetary value of D_1 and D_2. That is the p that solves the following equation:

$$300p - 30(1 - p) = 200,$$

which implies that $p = .7$. The implication, of course, is that if the probability of the new product's success is .7 or greater, then D_2 has a higher expected monetary value than does D_1 and the entrepreneur will choose D_2.

B. Maximization of Expected Utility: Attitudes Toward Risk

Do people deal with uncertainty by maximizing expected monetary values? Suppose that the two decisions of the previous section, D_1 and D_2, have the same expected monetary value. Would you be indifferent between the two courses of action? Probably not. D_1 is a sure thing. D_2 is not. Upon reflection, many would hesitate to take D_2 unless the expected monetary value of D_2 was greater than that of D_1. The reason for this hesitation may lie in the fact that many of us are reluctant to gamble, and D_2 certainly is a gamble. We are generally much more comfortable with a sure thing like D_1. Can we formalize our theory of decision making under uncertainty to take account of this attitude?

The formal explanation for this phenomenon of avoiding gambles was first offered in the eighteenth century by the Swiss mathematician and cleric Daniel Bernoulli. Bernoulli often noticed that people who make decisions under uncertainty do not attempt to maximize expected monetary values. Rather, they maximize expected utility. The introduction of utility allows us to introduce the notion of decision makers' attitudes toward risk.

1. Risk Aversion   Assume that utility is a function of, among other things, money income:

$$U = U(I).$$

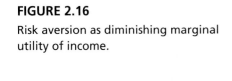

FIGURE 2.16

Risk aversion as diminishing marginal utility of income.

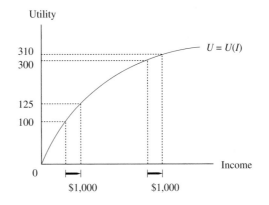

Bernoulli suggested that a common relationship between money income and utility was that as income increased, utility also increased, but at a decreasing rate. Such a utility function exhibits diminishing marginal utility of income. For example, if one's income level is $10,000, an additional $100 in income will add more to one's total utility than will $100 added to that same person's income of $40,000. A utility function like that shown in Figure 2.16 has this property. When this person's income is increased by $1000 at a low level of income, her utility increases from 100 to 125 units, an increase of 25 units. But when her income is increased by $1000 at a higher level of income, her utility increases from 300 to 310 units, an increase of only 10 units.

A person who has diminishing marginal utility from money income is said to be *risk-averse.* Here is a more formal definition of risk aversion:

> A person is said to be risk-averse if she considers the utility of a certain prospect of money income to be higher than the expected utility of an uncertain prospect of equal expected monetary value.

For example, in the preceding entrepreneur's project, a risk-averse decision maker might prefer to have $80 for certain rather than undertake a project whose *EMV* equals $80.

2. Risk Neutrality Economists presume that most people are averse toward risk, but some people are either neutral toward risk or, like gamblers, rock climbers, and race car drivers, prefer risk. Like aversion, these attitudes toward risk may also be defined in terms of the individual's utility function in money income and the marginal utility of income.

Someone who is *risk neutral* has a constant marginal utility of income and is, therefore, indifferent between a certain prospect of income and an uncertain prospect of equal expected monetary value. Figure 2.17 gives the utility function for a risk-neutral person. It is a straight line because the marginal utility of income to a risk-neutral person is constant.

The figure compares the change in utility when the risk-neutral person's income is increased by $1000 at two different levels of income. When this person's income is

FIGURE 2.17

Risk neutrality as constant marginal
utility of income.

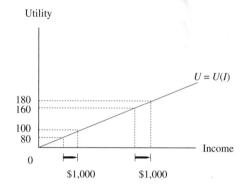

increased by $1000 at a low level of income, his utility increases from 80 to 100 units,
an increase of 20 units. And when his income is increased by $1000 at a high level of
income, his utility increases by exactly the same amount, 20 units, from 160 to 180
units. Thus, for the risk-neutral person the marginal utility of income is constant.

Economists and finance specialists very rarely attribute an attitude of risk-neutrality
to individuals. However, they quite commonly assume that business organizations are
risk-neutral.

3. Risk-Seeking or Risk-Preferring   Someone who is *risk-seeking* or *risk-
preferring* has an increasing marginal utility of income and, therefore, prefers an uncertain prospect of income to a certain prospect of equal expected monetary value.
Figure 2.18 gives the utility function of a risk-preferring individual. The figure allows
us to compare the change in utility when the risk-preferring person's income is
increased by $1000 at two different levels of income. When this person's income is in-
creased by $1000 at a low level of income, her utility increases from 80 to 85 units, an
increase of 5 units. However, when her income is increased by $1000 at a high level of
income, her utility increases from 200 to 230 units, an increase of 30 units. Thus, for
the risk-preferring person the marginal utility of income increases.

i   **Web Note 2.4**

One of the winners of the Nobel Prize in Economics in 2002 was Daniel
Kahneman, Professor Emeritus of Psychology at Princeton University.
Kahneman and his coauthor, the late Amos Tversky, did experiments to see
the extent to which people's attitudes toward risk fit those we have just studied. The experiments suggested that most people have complex feelings about
losses and gains that Kahneman and Tversky characterized as "loss aversion."
See section XII, on page 50 and our website for more on the experiments and
their implications.

FIGURE 2.18

Risk preferring as increasing marginal utility of income.

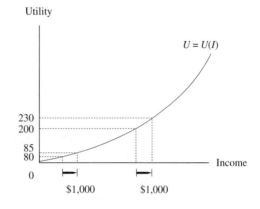

C. The Demand for Insurance

One of the most important behavioral implications of risk aversion is that people will pay money to avoid having to face uncertain outcomes. That is, a risk-averse person might prefer a lower certain income to a higher uncertain income.

There are three ways in which a risk-averse person may convert an uncertain into a certain outcome. First, he may purchase insurance from someone else. In exchange for giving up a certain amount of income (the insurance premium), the insurance company will bear the risk of the uncertain event. The risk-averse person considers himself better off with the lower certain income than facing the uncertain higher income. Second, he may self-insure. This may involve incurring expenses to minimize the probability of an uncertain event's occurring or to minimize the monetary loss in the event of a particular contingency. An example is the installation of smoke detectors in a home. Another form of self-insurance is the setting aside of a sum of money to cover possible losses. Third, a risk-averse person who is considering the purchase of some risky asset may reduce the price he is willing to pay for that asset.

D. The Supply of Insurance

The material of the previous section concerns the *demand* for insurance by risk-averse individuals. Let us now turn to a brief consideration of the supply of insurance by profit-maximizing insurance companies.

Insurance companies are presumed to be profit-maximizing firms. They offer insurance contracts not because they prefer gambles to certainties but because of a mathematical theorem known as the *law of large numbers*. This law holds that unpredictable events for individuals become predictable among large groups of individuals. For example, none of us knows whether our house will burn down next year. But the occurrence of fire in a city, state, or nation is regular enough so that an insurance company can easily determine the objective probabilities. By insuring a large number of people, an insurance company can predict the total amount of claims.

1. Moral Hazard   *Moral hazard* arises when the behavior of the insured person or entity changes after the purchase of insurance so that the probability of loss or the size of the loss increases. An extreme example is the insured's incentive to burn his home when he has been allowed to insure it for more than its market value. A more realistic example comes from loss due to theft. Suppose that you have just purchased a new sound system for your car but that you do not have insurance to cover your loss from theft. Under these circumstances you are likely to lock your car whenever you leave it, to park it in well-lighted places at night, to patronize only well-patrolled parking garages, and so on.

Now suppose that you purchase an insurance policy that will, unrealistically, compensate you for the full cost of any insured loss that you suffer. With the policy in force you now may be less assiduous about locking your car or parking in well-lighted places. In short, the very fact that your loss is insured may cause you to act so as to increase the probability of a loss.

Insurance companies attempt to set their premiums so that, roughly, the premium modestly exceeds the expected monetary value of the loss. Therefore, a premium that has been set without regard for the increased probability of loss due to moral hazard will be too low and thus threaten the continued profitability of the firm. Every insurer is aware of this problem and has developed methods to minimize it. Among the most common are *coinsurance* and *deductibles*. Under coinsurance the insuree shoulders a fixed percentage of his loss, with the insurer picking up the remaining portion of the loss; under a deductible plan, the insuree shoulders a fixed dollar amount of the loss, with the insurance company paying for all losses above that amount. In addition, some insurance companies offer reductions in premiums for certain easily established acts that reduce claims. For example, life and health insurance premiums are less for non-smokers; auto insurance premiums are less for nondrinkers; and fire insurance rates are lower for those who install smoke detectors.

2. Adverse Selection   The other major problem faced by insurance companies is called *adverse selection*. This arises because of the high cost to insurers of accurately distinguishing between high- and low-risk insurees. Although the law of large numbers helps the company in assessing probabilities, what it calculates from the large sample are average probabilities. The insurance premium must be set using this average probability of a particular loss. For example, insurance companies have determined that unmarried males between the ages of 16 and, say, 25, have a much higher likelihood of being in an automobile accident than do other identifiable groups of drivers. As a result, the insurance premium charged to members of this group is higher than that charged to other groups whose likelihood of accident is much lower.

But even though unmarried males between the ages of 16 and 25 are, on average, much more likely to be involved in an accident, there are some young men within that group who are even more reckless than average and some who are much less reckless than the group's average. If it is difficult for the insurer to distinguish these groups from the larger group of unmarried males aged 16 to 25, then the premium that is set equal to the average likelihood of harm within the group will seem like a bargain to those who know they are reckless and too high to those who know that they are safer than their peers.

Let us assume, as seems reasonable, that in many cases the individuals know better than the insurance company what their true risks are. For example, the insured alone may know that he drinks heavily and smokes in bed or that he is intending to murder his spouse, in whose insurance policy he has just been named principal beneficiary. If so, then this asymmetrical information may induce only high-risk people to purchase insurance and low-risk people to purchase none. As a result, the insurance company will find itself paying out more in claims than it had anticipated. It may, therefore, raise the premiums higher. This will drive out some more relatively safer customers, leaving an even-riskier clientele behind. The incidence and volume of claims may go up yet again, setting off a new round of premium increases, defections of less-risky customers, and so on. This process is referred to as an insurance *death spiral*.

The same devices that insurance companies employ to minimize risks of moral hazards also may serve to minimize the adverse selection problem. Coinsurance and deductible provisions are much less attractive to high-risk than to low-risk insurees so that an insuree's willingness to accept those provisions may indicate to the insurance company to which risk class the applicant belongs. Exclusion of benefits for loss arising from preexisting conditions is another method of trying to distinguish high- and low-risk people. The insurer can also attempt, over a longer time horizon, to reduce the adverse selection bias by developing better methods of discriminating among the insured, such as medical and psychological testing, so as to place insurees in more accurate risk classes. Finally, insurers frequently practice *experience rating*—the practice of adjusting the insuree's premium up or down according to his experience of insurable losses. If an insuree appears to be accident prone, then the insurer may raise his premium to reflect the greater probability or size of loss. In the limit, the insurer may refuse to cover the insuree.

XI. Profits and Growth[15]

Imagine a banker who asks to be paid by placing one penny on the first square of a chess board, two pennies on the second square, four on the third, and so on. Using only the white squares, the initial penny would double in value thirty-one times, leaving $21.5 million on the last white square. Growth compounds faster than the mind can grasp. In 1900 Argentina's income per person resembled Canada's, and today Canada's is more than three times higher. After World War II, Korea and Nigeria had similar national income per person, and today Korea's is nineteen times higher. Most people cannot imagine China with more economic influence in the world than the United States, but, if current trends continue, China will surpass the United States in national income in 2014.[16] Lifting so many people out of poverty in East Asia in the late twentieth century is one of history's remarkable accomplishments. In contrast, one of history's depressing economic failures in the late twentieth century is sub-Saharan Africa, where GDP per person declined since 1975 roughly by 25 percent.

Why do some countries grow faster than others? Sustained growth requires innovation. An innovation occurs when someone discovers a better way to make something or something better to make. Entrepreneurs make things in better ways by improving organizations

---

[15] This section draws on Chapter 1 of ROBERT COOTER & HANS-BERND SCHAEFER, LAW AND THE POVERTY OF NATIONS (2011).

[16] Because China's population is 4 to 5 times greater than the United States' population, China's income per capita in 2014 will still be one-fourth to one-fifth that of the United States. This prediction was made by Carl J. Dahlman, Luce Professor of International Affairs and Information, Georgetown University.

and markets, and scientists invent better things to make. Growth will remain mysterious until economics has an adequate theory of innovation. The only contribution to growth theory so far that merited a Nobel Prize in Economics shows the consequences of innovation for capital and labor but does not attempt to explain innovation.[17]

Law, we believe, is part of the mystery's solution. When an innovator has a new idea, it must be developed in order for the economy to grow. Combining new ideas and capital runs into a fundamental obstacle illustrated by this example: An economist who worked at a Boston investment bank received a letter that read, "I know how your bank can make $10 million. If you give me $1 million, I will tell you." The letter captures concisely the problem of financing innovation: The bank does not want to pay for information without first determining its worth, and the innovator fears disclosing information to the bank without first getting paid. Law is central to solving this problem. Later chapters in this book mention "transactional lawyers," who use law to overcome the mistrust that prevents people from cooperating in business. The most fundamental bodies of transaction law are property and contracts, which we cover in Chapters 4, 5, 8, and 9. Making these bodies of law efficient promotes economic growth by uniting innovative ideas and capital. Countries with efficient property and contract have established the legal foundation for innovation and growth.

XII. Behavioral Economics

In our review of microeconomic theory we have followed modern microeconomists in assuming that decision makers are rationally self-interested. This theory of decision making is called *rational choice theory* and has served the economics profession well over the past 60 or more years in theorizing about how people make explicitly economic decisions. But rational choice theory has been under attack over the past 30 years or so. This attack has been principally empirical. That is, it has been premised on experimental findings that people do not behave in the ways predicted by rational choice theory. (We will give examples shortly.)

Two principal names in the experimental literature that have been critical of rational choice theory are Daniel Kahneman and Amos Tversky. As we noted above, Kahneman won the Nobel Prize in Economics in 2002. The body of literature inspired by Kahneman and Tversky has as acquired the name *behavioral economics* and the legal analysis that takes account of these findings is called *behavioral law and economics.*[18]

What are some examples of behavioral economics? Let us consider two (although there are many others) that have particular relevance to the law. The first is the result of experiments involving the *ultimatum bargaining game.* In that game there are two players, neither of whom knows the identity of the other. They interact anonymously. Their task in the game is to divide a small sum of money—say, $20. One player is designated

---

[17] In 1987 Robert Solow received the Nobel Prize in Economics for his contributions to economic growth theory.

[18] For a summary of the field, see Russell B. Korobkin & Thomas S. Ulen, *Law and Behavioral Science: Removing the Rationality Assumption from Law and Economics*, 88 CAL. L. REV. 1051 (2000).

Player 1; the other, Player 2. Player 1 makes some proposal to Player 2 about how the $20 should be divided; Player 2 can then either accept that proposal, in which case the experimenter actually gives the two players the amounts proposed by Player 1, or reject the proposal, in which case neither player gets any money.

Rational choice theory predicts that Player 1 will take advantage of her position as the proposer to give herself a disproportionate share of the $20—say, $15, leaving $5 for Player 2. Player 1 might also reason that Player 2 will take $5 rather than nothing. And, in fact, Player 2 might think that Player 1 is selfish, but that, after all, $5 is better than nothing.

This game has been played in experiments in over 140 countries and among groups with vastly different incomes, ages, education levels, religions, and the like, and in countries that are wealthy and countries that are poor. The modal (most common) outcome is a 50-50 split of the stakes—each player gets $10. Equally interesting is the fact that in many countries if Player 1 tries to take more than 70 percent of the stakes (more than $14 in our $20 example), Player 2 rejects the offer and they each get nothing.[19]

We take some heart from the fact that strangers seldom take advantage of one another in the ultimatum bargaining game. Rather, the norm seems to be to treat the other party fairly; in fact, to treat him or her exactly as one treats oneself. Are there legal implications of this insight? We return to this point in Chapters 8 and 9 when we consider the concern of contract law with some forms of advantage-taking in bargaining.

A second example of a behavioral economics finding is the *hindsight bias*. This refers to the fact that things that actually happen seem, in hindsight (*ex post*), to have been far more likely than they were in foresight (*ex ante*). So, if you asked people in spring 2010 the probability that Spain would win the 2010 World Cup in South Africa, they might have said, "10 percent." But if you ask them after Spain actually won the cup, they will say it was much more likely—say, 40 percent. Is there a legal implication? Consider something that we will discuss in Chapter 6: How do we induce someone to take the right amount of precaution against harming another person? As we will see, one way to do that is to expose the possible injurer to liability for the injuries that a victim suffers if the injurer did not take a prudent amount of precaution. Here's the problem—what might seem prudent precaution *before* an accident occurs might appear, in hindsight, to have been imprudent. That is, if an accident has occurred, the hindsight bias may tell us that the accident was more inevitable than we would have thought before.

Rational choice theory cannot explain the observed behavior in the ultimatum bargaining game or hindsight bias. The central insight of behavioral economics is that human beings make predictable errors in judgment, cognition, and decision making. They are, to quote the title of a book on this topic by Dan Ariely, "predictably irrational." Economic analysis should use rational choice theory or behavioral theory, depending on which one predicts the law's effects on the behavior more accurately.

---

[19] The group that typically plays this game in line with the predictions of rational choice theory (in which Player 1 makes a proposal to take much more than half of the stakes and Player 2 accepts that) are graduate students in economics. Did they select a graduate study in economics because they already find rational choice theory attractive? Or did their graduate studies in economics convince them that rational choice was the appropriate way to behave?

Review Questions

If you are not certain whether you need to refresh your understanding of microeconomic theory, try these questions. If you find them to be too hard, read this chapter and try them again. If only some of the questions are too hard, turn to the section of the chapter that covers that material and review that section.

2.1. Define the role of the mathematical concepts of maximization and equilibrium in microeconomic theory.

2.2. Define and distinguish between *productive efficiency* and *allocative efficiency.*

2.3. What are consumers assumed to maximize? What are some constraints under which this maximization takes place? Describe the individual consumer's constrained maximum. Can you characterize this constrained maximum as a point where marginal cost and marginal benefit are equal?

2.4. A married couple with children is considering divorce. They are negotiating about two elements of the divorce: the level of child support that will be paid to the partner who keeps the children, and the amount of time that the children will spend with each partner. Whoever has the children would prefer more child support from the other partner and more time with the children. Furthermore, the partner who keeps the children believes that as the amount of child support increases, the value of more time with the children declines relative to the value of child support.

    a. Draw a typical indifference curve for the partner who keeps the children with the level of child support on the horizontal axis and the amount of time that the children spend with this partner on the vertical axis. Is this indifference curve convex to the origin? Why or why not?

    b. Suppose that the partner who keeps the children has this utility function $u = cv$, where c = the weekly level of child support and v = the number of days per week that the children spend with this partner. Suppose that initially the weekly support level is $100, and the number of days per week spent with this partner is 4. What is the utility to this partner from that arrangement? If the other partner wishes to reduce the weekly support to $80, how many more days with the children must the child-keeping partner have in order to maintain utility at the previous level?

2.5. Define *price elasticity of demand* and explain what ranges of value it may take.

2.6. Use the notion of opportunity cost to explain why "There's no such thing as a free lunch."

2.7. *True* or *False*: The cost of a week of vacation is simply the money cost of the plane, food, and so forth. (Explain your answer.)

2.8. What are firms assumed to maximize? Under what constraints do firms perform this maximization? Describe how the individual firm determines the output level that achieves that maximum. Can you characterize the firm's constrained maximum as one for which marginal cost equals marginal benefit?

2.9. Characterize these different market structures in which a firm may operate: perfect competition, monopoly, oligopoly, and imperfect competition.

Compare the industry output and price in a perfectly competitive industry with the output and price of a monopolist.

2.10. What conditions must hold for a monopoly to exist?

2.11. Suppose that the local government determines that the price of food is too high and imposes a ceiling on the market price of food that is below the equilibrium price in that locality. Predict some of the consequences of this ceiling.

2.12. The minimum wage is typically set above the market-clearing wage in the market for labor. Using a graph with an upward-sloping supply of labor, a downward-sloping demand for labor, with the quantity of labor measured on the horizontal axis and the wage rate measured on the vertical axis, show the effect on the labor market of a minimum wage set above the equilibrium wage rate.

2.13. *True* or *False:* In Japan, workers cannot be fired once they have been hired; therefore, in Japan a minimum wage law (where the minimum would be set above the wage that would cause the market for labor to clear) would not cause unemployment.

2.14. In the United States in the late twentieth century, no-fault divorce laws became the norm in the states (divorce being a matter for states, not the federal government, to regulate). Ignoring for the sake of this problem all the other factors that influence the marriage decision and that have changed during the same time period, what does the move to no-fault divorce do to the implicit (legal) price of divorce? What would be your prediction about the effect of this change in the implicit price of divorce on the quality and quantity of marriages and divorces? If, in the next decade, the states were to repudiate the experiment in no-fault divorce and return to the old regime, would you predict a change in the quality and quantity of marriages and divorces?

2.15. The Truth-in-Lending Act (15 U.S.C. §§1601–1604 (1982)) requires the uniform disclosure of the interest rate to borrowers in a readily intelligible form. Assume that before the act, there was uncertainty among borrowers about the true level of the interest rate, but that after the act, that uncertainty is reduced. What effect on the amount of borrowing would you predict from passage of the act? Would there be disproportionate effects on the poor and the rich? Why? Does the act increase the marginal cost of lenders? Does it reduce the profits of lenders?

2.16. What is general equilibrium and under what conditions will it be achieved? What are the welfare consequences of general equilibrium?

2.17. What are the four sources of market failure? Explain how each of them causes individual profit- and utility-maximizers to make decisions that may be privately optimal but are socially suboptimal. What general policies might correct each of the instances of market failure?

2.18. Which of the following are private goods and might, therefore, be provided in socially optimal amounts by private profit-maximizers? Which are public goods and should, therefore, be provided by the public sector or by the private sector with public subsidies?

    a. A swimming pool large enough to accommodate hundreds of people.

    b. A fireworks display.

    c. A heart transplant.

    d. Vaccination against a highly contagious disease.

    e. A wilderness area.

    f. Vocational education.

    g. On-the-job training.

    h. Secondary education.

2.19. What is meant by *Pareto efficiency* or *Pareto optimality*? What is the importance of the initial distribution of resources in determining what the distribution of resources will be after all Pareto improvements have been made?

2.20. A valuable resource in which we typically forbid voluntary exchange is votes. This may be inefficient in that, as we have seen, given any initial endowment of resources, voluntary exchange always makes both parties better off (absent any clear sources of market failure). Show that it would be a Pareto improvement if we were to allow a legal market for votes. Are there any clear sources of market failure in the market for votes? If so, what regulatory correctives would you apply to that market? Is it bothersome that there is a wide variance in income and wealth among the participants in this market, and if so, why is that variance more troubling in this market than in others, and what would you do about it in the market for votes?

2.21. Distinguish between the Pareto criterion for evaluating a social change in which there are gainers and losers and the Kaldor-Hicks (or potential Pareto) criterion.

2.22. What is a *dominant strategy* in a game? Where both players in a two-person game have a dominant strategy, is there an equilibrium solution for the game? What is a *Nash equilibrium*? Is a dominant-strategy equilibrium a Nash equilibrium? What are the possible shortcomings of a Nash equilibrium in a game?

Suggested Readings

ARIELY, DAN, PREDICTABLY IRRATIONAL, REVISED AND EXPANDED EDITION: THE HIDDEN FORCES THAT SHAPE OUR DECISIONS (2010).

EATWELL, JOHN, MURRAY MILGATE, & PETER NEWMAN, EDS., THE NEW PALGRAVE: A DICTIONARY OF ECONOMICS, 4 vols. (1991).

KREPS, DAVID, A COURSE IN MICROECONOMIC THEORY (1990).

LANDSBURG, STEPHEN, THE ARMCHAIR ECONOMIST (1991).

LEVITT, STEVEN D., & STEVEN J. DUBNER, FREAKONOMICS: A ROGUE ECONOMIST EXPLAINS THE HIDDEN SIDE OF EVERYTHING (2005).

LEVITT, STEVEN D., & STEVEN J. DUBNER, SUPERFREAKONOMICS: GLOBAL WARMING, PATRIOTIC PROSTITUTES, AND WHY SUICIDE BOMBERS SHOULD BUY LIFE INSURANCE (2009).

PINDYK, ROBERT, & DANIEL RUBINFELD, MICROECONOMICS (6th ed. 2004).

THALER, RICHARD H., & CASS R. SUNSTEIN, NUDGE: IMPROVING DECISIONS ABOUT HEALTH, WEALTH, AND HAPPINESS (2008).

WINTER, HAROLD, TRADE-OFFS AN INTRODUCTION TO ECONOMIC REASONING AND SOCIAL ISSUES (2005).

3 A Brief Introduction to Law and Legal Institutions

"You are old," said the youth, "and your jaws are too weak
For anything tougher than suet.
Yet you finished the goose, with the bones and the beak.
Pray, how do you manage to do it?"
"In my youth," said his father, "I took to the law,
And argued each case with my wife.
And the muscular strength, which it gave to my jaw,
Has lasted the rest of my life."

From "Father William" in LEWIS CARROLL,
ALICE'S ADVENTURES IN WONDERLAND

The life of the law has not been logic: it has been experience. The felt necessities of the time, the prevalent moral and political theories, institutions of public policy, avowed or unconscious, even the prejudices which judges share with their fellow-men, have had a good deal more to do than the syllogism in determining the rules by which men should be governed.

OLIVER WENDELL HOLMES,
THE COMMON LAW 1 (1881)

AN ECONOMIST WHO picks up a law journal will understand much more of it than a lawyer who picks up an economics journal. For this reason, it is not hard to convince a lawyer that he does not know economics. (Convincing him that he *should* learn economics is harder!) On the other hand, economists are sometimes hard to convince that any aspect of social life is not, at its root, really economics. With respect to the law, economists sometimes wonder what lawyers really study: Is the law a branch of philosophy? Is it a list of famous cases? Is it a collection of rules?

In any case, economists cannot contribute significantly to law without studying it. This chapter provides an introduction to the law for nonlawyers. We shall explain, first, differences and similarities between the two great legal traditions that spread from Europe to much of the world; second, the structure of the United States' federal and state court systems; third, how a legal dispute gets raised and resolved in systems like that of the United States; and finally, how the legal rules made by judges evolve.

I. The Civil Law and the Common Law Traditions

Legislatures make laws by enacting bills, which judges must interpret and apply. If legislation is deliberately vague or inadvertently ambiguous, judges can choose among several different interpretations. Sometimes the choice of an interpretation overshadows the enactment of the bill, in which case the judge makes the law more than the legislature. Judges make law by interpreting legislation in all legal systems with independent courts.

Judges make law in other ways as well. In medieval Europe, the king in most countries could issue pronouncements that were law, and the king's courts possessed similar powers. However, the king's courts were not free to pronounce as law any command that they wished. According to one tradition in legal theory, the courts of the English king were to examine community life and "find" law as it already existed. The courts of the English king were to select among prevailing social norms and enforce some of them. These enforceable social norms were supposedly the "laws of nature," which reason and necessity prescribed.

The finding of a rule of law by a court of the English king created a *precedent* that future courts were expected to follow.[1] A precedent in common law resembles a generally accepted interpretation in civil law. Precedent was followed flexibly, not slavishly, so the law changed gradually. Over many years, the king's courts "found" many important laws, especially in the areas of crimes, property, contracts, and accidents ("torts"). These findings are called the "common law" because they are allegedly rooted in the common practices of people. Common law is still applied in the English-language countries, except where superseded by legislation.

Legal history is different in France and the other countries of Europe: When France revolted at the end of the eighteenth century, the revolutionaries thought that the judges were as corrupt and worthless as the king, so they killed the king and extinguished his laws, thus abolishing the common law of France. A comprehensive set of statutes was required to fill the void, so people would know what counts as property, how a valid contract is formed, and who is to bear the cost of accidents. Napoleon supplied them by commissioning legal scholars to draft the rules called the *Code Napoléon*, which was promulgated in 1804. The scholars who drafted it took as their model the *Corpus Juris Civilis* ("The Body of the Civil Law"), which was compiled and edited in A.D. 528–534 at the behest of the Roman emperor Justinian. Thus, the French revolutionaries looked to ancient sources and pure reason for law, rather than to the more immediate heritage derived from medieval times.

Napoleon's armies spread the *Code Napoléon* through much of Europe, where it remained long after his troops withdrew. Similarly, Europeans spread their law throughout the world, and this influence persisted long after the colonial empires collapsed. The "civil law tradition," as it is called, predominates in most of Western

---

[1] "Precedent" refers to the practice of resolving similar cases in a similar fashion. If it is known that a court is going to resolve a dispute by applying precedent, then the disputants have a good idea what the legal resolution of their dispute might be. This can induce the disputants to settle the matter themselves against the background law that they know the court will use.

civil law tradition vs common law tradition

Europe, Central and South America, the parts of Asia colonized by European countries other than Britain, and even in pockets of the common law world, such as Louisiana, Québec, and Puerto Rico. The common law tradition, which originated in England, prevails not only in Great Britain, but also in Ireland, the United States, Canada, Australia, New Zealand, and the parts of Africa and Asia that Britain colonized, including India.

Besides these two great traditions, the unique history of each country puts its own stamp on the law. For example, Japan, which was never colonized, voluntarily adopted a code that draws heavily on the German civil code while yet remaining distinctively Japanese. In much of the Middle East, Islamic law blended with, or displaced, the law of the European colonialists. In Eastern Europe, communism bent the civil law tradition to its own purposes, and now the post-Communist regimes are trying to straighten it.

The common law and civil law traditions differ significantly with respect to how judge-made law is justified. Common law judges traditionally justify their findings of law by reference to precedent and social norms, or by broad requirements of rationality presupposed by public policy. Civil law judges traditionally justify their interpretation of a code directly by reference to its meaning, which scholars tease out in lengthy commentaries. Because common law judges rely relatively more on past court decisions and civil law judges rely relatively more on the words in statutes, the common law system is based more on precedent than the civil law system. The difference in the pattern of justification affects the training of lawyers. The common law method is taught by reading cases and arguing directly from them, whereas the civil law method is taught by reading the code and arguing from commentaries on it.

common law – precedent

All such generalizations about the difference between the two traditions, however, seem simplistic relative to the subtlety and complexity of reality. For example, although the United States is ostensibly a common law country, the American states have tried to obtain greater uniformity in commercial law by enacting the *Uniform Commercial Code*. Deciding disputes that fall under the *Uniform Commercial Code* in America has many similarities to deciding disputes that fall under the French Civil Code. Additionally, the American Law Institute, an organization founded in the 1920s, meets periodically to restate the law as it is emerging in the various states. These restatements, such as the *Restatement (Second) of Contracts* and the *Restatement (Second) of Torts,* serve a similar function to the codes that are thought to be characteristic of the civil law countries. Comparative law scholars vigorously debate whether the differences between civil and common law are more apparent than real.

Besides the difference in history between common and civil law, the laws are applied differently in the two traditions. In the common law countries, the arguments for the two sides in a dispute are made exclusively by their lawyers, and the judge is not supposed to direct a line of questioning or develop an argument. In this *adversarial process*, the judge acts more or less as a neutral referee who makes the lawyers follow the rules of procedure and evidence. The principle underlying the adversarial system is that the truth will emerge from a vigorous debate by the two sides.

In contrast, the civil law judge takes an active role in directing questions and developing arguments. In this *inquisitorial process*, the judge is supposed to ferret out the truth. The lawyers often have to respond to the judge, rather than develop the case themselves. The principle underlying the inquisitorial system is that the court has a direct interest in finding the truth regarding private disputes and crimes.

Another difference between the two systems concerns the use of juries. Juries are more commonly used in common law systems. In America, either party to a dispute usually has the right to a jury trial, although both parties sometimes waive this right and allow the judge to decide the case. In England, the jury has been abolished in almost all civil trials since 1966,[2] but it is often used in criminal trials. (Notice the different use of "civil" in the preceding sentence.[3]) In France, however, the jury has been abolished for all trials except the most serious crimes, like murder. In general, the abolition of juries is more advanced in continental Europe than in some common law countries. In a common law trial before a jury, the judge is supposed to decide questions of law, whereas the jury is supposed to decide questions of fact.

In every legal system, laws form a hierarchy. The constitution takes precedence over statutes, and statutes usually take precedence over rules issued by the executive or government agencies. In countries with common law, statutes take precedence over it. "Taking precedence" means that the higher law prevails in the event of conflict. The courts, as the main interpreters of law, must decide whether laws conflict. We have explained that judges make law indirectly by interpreting statutes or codes. Another way that judges make law is by finding a conflict between laws and setting aside the lower-level law. Finally, judges make common law directly in those countries that maintain the common law system—a process we explain later in this chapter.

Constitutions are necessarily general and vague, so their interpretation is especially problematic. The power to review legislation for its constitutionality gives courts the power, in principle, to set aside laws enacted by the legislature. This power is potentially dangerous because it brings judges into conflict with the elected representatives of the nation. The extent to which this power is exercised varies greatly from one country to another. In the United States, the federal courts have few limits on their ability to strike down laws that, in the courts' opinion, contradict the Constitution. Some of the most profound laws in America have been made by courts interpreting the Constitution, as in *Brown v. Board of Education* in 1954, which eventually ended laws mandating racial segregation of schools. In other countries, such as Great Britain, the courts do not have the power to review statutes for their constitutionality, and the courts never strike down legislation as unconstitutional. The scope of constitutional review, which is fundamental to the power and prestige of courts, has no necessary connection with whether the country's legal tradition is common or civil law.

---

[2] Except in cases involving defamation.

[3] "Civil law" has two meanings. It may refer to the system of law in most of continental Europe that rejects common law. In addition, "civil law" may refer to laws controlling disagreements between two private parties, which might arise, say, from a broken contract or an automobile accident. In this latter sense, the opposite of "civil law" is criminal or penal law, in which actions are initiated by the state's prosecutor against someone accused of violating a criminal statute, such as forgery or murder. Thus, the common law of, say, contracts can be described as "civil law," meaning "private law" or "not criminal law."

II. The Institutions of the Federal and the State Court Systems in the United States

In the United States, whether at the state or the federal level, the court systems are organized in three tiers. These tiers constitute a hierarchical pyramid, with a very broad base of many courts, an intermediate level with a smaller number of courts, and a single court at the top of the pyramid. At the lowest level are the *trial courts of general jurisdiction*. These are the "entry-level" courts that first hear a wide array of civil and criminal disputes. The trial courts of general jurisdiction are "courts of record"; that is, the proceedings are written down and saved by the government. In the state systems these courts are usually organized along county lines. For example, in the State of Illinois there are 102 counties, and each has a "Circuit Court" that serves as the trial court of general jurisdiction within the county. These trial courts have different names in different states: In California they are called "Superior Courts"; in New York State, "Supreme Courts." The nearly universal practice is for each civil and criminal case to be tried to a single judge and possibly to a jury.

In the federal system the entire country is divided into 94 judicial districts, each of which contains a federal district court, which is the trial court of general jurisdiction for the federal judiciary. Every state in the Union has at least one federal district court, and about half have *only* one. The District of Columbia has its own district court. The larger states, where larger numbers of disputes involving federal questions arise, have up to four district courts, usually organized along geographical divisions of the state. New York has four districts: the Southern, the Northern, the Eastern, and the Western. Illinois has three federal districts: the Northern, the Central, and the Southern. As the volume of federal litigation has grown, Congress has responded not by creating more districts but by appointing more judges within each district. One of the busiest districts is the Southern District of New York, which contains most of New York City. As of 2010, there were 44 district judges in that district (and 15 magistrate judges).[4] Another busy district, the Northern District of Illinois, has 32 district judges (and 14 magistrate judges).[5] The usual procedure in the federal districts is for a single judge to hear each case, but a three-judge panel sometimes hears a case.

In addition, the federal court system includes several specialized tribunals. For example, there are special tax courts, and federal administrative agencies, such as the Federal Communications Commission, have administrative law judges who hear arguments about matters before those agencies. There is also, as we shall soon see, a special appellate tribunal in the federal system for dealing with intellectual property cases.[6]

---

[4] In the last edition of this book, there were 25 district judges in that district.

[5] In the last edition there were 12 district judges in the Northern District of Illinois. Magistrate judges are appointed by district court judges in each federal district for renewable eight-year terms. Those magistrates preside over trials for federal misdemeanor crimes and hear preliminary motions in more serious federal crimes and pretrial motions for many civil cases. Magistrates may preside over federal civil trials if the parties consent.

[6] As of August 2010, there were a total of 678 federal district court judges, 179 Court of Appeals judges, 9 judges on the Court of International Trade, and 9 justices of the United States Supreme Court for a total of 875 federal judges. There are currently 98 vacancies in the federal judiciary. Because Article III of the *U.S. Constitution* provides for these judges, the 875 federal judges are called "Article III judges."

Above the trial courts in the state and federal systems are *appellate courts* or *courts of appeal*. In most state court systems, there is only one court of appeal. But about one-third of the states and the federal system have *intermediate appellate courts* that stand between the trial courts of general jurisdiction and the highest court (the *court of last resort*). For example, in Illinois there are five intermediate appellate districts with a total of just over 50 justices. Where these courts exist, parties from the trial court may appeal "as of right," which means that so long as they are willing to pay the costs involved, the parties may always seek appellate review of a lower court's judgment. Appeal is also a right in the federal system, at least from the district courts to the intermediate courts of appeal.

While there may be a right for either party to appeal the judgment of the trial courts of general jurisdiction, matters may be different if either party wishes to appeal the judgment of an intermediate appellate court. In both the state and the federal judiciary, the highest appellate court typically has a *discretionary* right of review. This means that the Supreme Court of Illinois, the Supreme Court of the United States, and all other courts of last resort may select which cases they will review, within certain limits. Some cases—for example, disputes between two states—come to the United States Supreme Court directly and without the discretion of the justices. And in many states the highest court is obligated to review death sentences. Thus, the United States Supreme Court and the highest courts in the states control most, but not all, of their docket.

An intermediate court of appeal in the federal judiciary is called the "Court of Appeals for the ___ Circuit." There are thirteen of these circuits, as Figure 3.1 indicates. Eleven of these courts of appeal are numbered; for example, the First Circuit is in New England; the Seventh Circuit covers Indiana, Illinois, and Wisconsin; and the Ninth Circuit covers the West Coast, some of the mountain states, and Alaska and Hawaii. The District of Columbia constitutes its own circuit and also has its own district court. All the other circuits include several states. An unsuccessful litigant from

FIGURE 3.1

United States Courts of Appeal and United States District Courts.

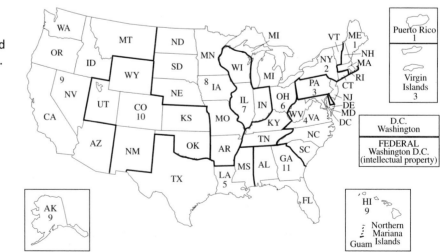

the federal district court can take an appeal, as a matter of right, to the court of appeals. Those courts often sit in a panel of three judges. Sometimes, for a particularly significant case, all of the circuit judges will sit together to decide the case. In that case the court is said to be sitting *en banc* or "in bank." Where more than one judge hears a case, the matter is decided by majority vote.

There is also a special intermediate appellate court in the federal system just for hearing matters regarding intellectual property: the United States Court of Appeals for the Federal Circuit. Congress established that court in 1982. This is the only U.S. Court of Appeals defined by its subject matter jurisdiction rather than by geography. The U.S. Court of Appeals for the Federal Circuit assumed the jurisdiction of the U.S. Court of Customs and Patent Appeals and the appellate jurisdiction of the U.S. Court of Claims. There are 15 judges on the Federal Circuit.

The Supreme Court of the United States is the highest court in the federal judiciary. That court has nine members, consisting of the Chief Justice of the United States and eight Associate Justices. All of the justices, rather than a panel, decide each case. The Court begins its work on the first Monday in October and concludes its term sometime in June of the following year. The workload of the Supreme Court increased significantly until the 1980s; since then the number of opinions that the Supreme Court issues has declined significantly. Typically, the justices decide less than 10 percent of the cases submitted to them for review. There is lively dispute about whether this figure is too large or too small. In the recent past some commentators have urged Congress to establish a national court of appeals between the courts of appeals and the Supreme Court. The argument is that this National Court would handle the more routine appeals arising from the thirteen circuits (for example, those in which there is a split among the circuits, which means that some circuits say the law is one way and other circuits say the opposite). Proponents say this would free up the Supreme Court to devote more of its energies to truly important cases.

Finally, there are rules that specify whether a dispute should be heard in the state or the federal court system.[7] This is often a matter of great strategic significance in an attorney's handling of a case. The general rules for deciding jurisdiction are relatively straightforward. State courts have jurisdiction in disputes involving state statutes or in civil actions between residents of that state or in cases arising under federal law when Congress has not given exclusive jurisdiction to the federal courts.

The jurisdiction of the federal courts is defined by Congress, through the powers assigned in the Constitution. That jurisdiction is limited to three principal areas:

1. Federal questions—that is, those matters arising under the United States Constitution or federal laws or treaties.[8]
2. Cases to which the United States is a party. Typically, these are criminal cases under federal statute law.

---

[7] The rules for resolving whether a state or federal law should apply in a particular dispute are complex and themselves constitute a special course in law school called "Conflict of Laws."

[8] There used to be a minimum dollar amount in controversy ($10,000) before a case could be a federal case, even if it was a federal question. That minimum no longer applies to matters arising under federal law.

3. Diversity cases—any civil dispute, currently involving more than $75,000, between citizens of different states. In the late eighteenth century, Congress allowed these disputes to be removed from state to federal courts because it felt that state loyalties were so strong that the citizen of another state might lose in a state court, regardless of the merits of his or her case, simply because he or she was a "foreigner."[9]

In the event that a federal district court hears a diversity dispute *not* involving a federal question, the Court will generally apply the law of the state in which it sits. Today diversity of citizenship is no longer as compelling a reason for the federal courts to assume jurisdiction as it was 200 years ago. Indeed, former Chief Justice Burger urged Congress to ease the caseload of the federal judiciary by entirely removing the diversity cases from federal jurisdiction.[10]

As to the selection and tenure of judges, there are two broad practices. For the federal bench, the rule is appointment by the president with the advice and consent of the Senate for life tenure with removal only by impeachment by the House of Representatives and conviction by the Senate. For state judges in a majority of the states, the rule is election to the bench and limited tenure. For the remainder of the states, the state judiciary is nominated by the executive branch and approved by the legislature for varying, but fixed, terms.

III. The Nature of a Legal Dispute

A legal dispute arises when someone claims to have been illegally harmed at the hands of another. It is possible that the victim and the injurer can resolve their dispute themselves, but sometimes they cannot. The person who feels injured may have a *cause of action,* that is, a valid legal claim, against another person or organization. To assert that action, he files a *complaint* and is, therefore, referred to as the *plaintiff.* The complaint must state what has happened, why the plaintiff feels that he has been injured, what area of law is involved, what statute or other law is relevant, and what relief he wishes the court to give him. The complaint and the management of the subsequent aspects of the dispute are complicated matters; typically, private citizens retain the services of a lawyer, who usually has far more experience in these matters than does the citizen, to help them in all this.[11]

The person who is alleged to have injured the victim or plaintiff is called the *defendant* and must *answer* the complaint. The answer does not go into detail about the

---

[9] In 2007 Congress raised the minimum amount in controversy in diversity cases in order to alter the caseload of the federal courts. Clearly, the greater the amount in controversy required, the fewer the number of diversity cases that will be eligible for resolution by the federal courts.

[10] But there is still an argument for maintaining federal jurisdiction in diversity cases where the benefits of a decision may accrue to the people in one state and the costs fall on the people of another state.

[11] Private citizens may, of course, represent themselves in a legal dispute. That is referred to as someone appearing *pro se*—that is, "for himself." A common joke among lawyers is that a person who represents himself has a fool for a client.

matters at hand; rather, it is a short statement of what the defendant intends to argue in detail if the matter goes to trial. Thus, the answer may say that the facts as alleged are true but that even so, the defendant is not legally responsible for the plaintiff's misfortune. Figuratively, this form of answer says, "So what?" Or the answer may say that the facts as alleged in the complaint are incorrect and that when the true facts are known, the defendant will be seen to be innocent of any wrongdoing.

The dispute may well stop at this point. For example, the parties may decide not to proceed to trial. They may drop the whole matter, or they may *settle* their dispute—that is, reach a mutually satisfactory agreement between themselves. If the case is not settled or dropped, a judge must make a determination based on the complaint and the answer whether there is sufficient reason to proceed to trial. The judge may determine that the plaintiff has failed to state a valid cause of action or that the defendant has made a complete and convincing answer to the complaint. If so, she might dismiss the complaint or enter *summary judgment* for the defendant. Usually, she will allow the parties to proceed to trial. Parties may appeal from a summary judgment or a dismissal.

If the dispute proceeds to trial, a jury may be empaneled to determine the facts, or else the case will be tried to a judge without a jury; this latter situation is called a *bench trial.* Each side will develop evidence and testimony supporting its assertions, and then the jury or judge will retire to determine who wins.[12] The standard that the jury or judge will use to make this determination is by a *preponderance of the evidence*. That means that if the plaintiff's arguments are more believable than the defendant's, then the plaintiff wins; if the defendant's are more believable, the defendant wins. Some people say that the preponderance-of-the-evidence standard means that if the plaintiff's story is 51 percent believable, she wins. Notice that this standard, which is the routine standard in cases involving private parties as litigants, is different from the one that is used in criminal proceedings. There, the prosecution must convince the jury that the defendant is guilty *beyond a reasonable doubt*, a much more exacting standard than is preponderance of the evidence.

The courts can and have established other standards for prevailing in private law disputes. For example, some jurisdictions have created a standard of *clear and convincing evidence* for some aspects of a civil case, such as the award of punitive damages. No one can be certain exactly what that standard entails, but it is certainly more demanding than the preponderance-of-the-evidence standard and less demanding than the beyond-a-reasonable-doubt standard of criminal law.

The jury returns with a *verdict*, which says, simply, which party wins. But the verdict is not the end of the matter. The judge must *enter judgment on the verdict.* It is the *judgment,* not the verdict, that is the controlling action of the court. Most of the time the judge issues a judgment that follows exactly the jury verdict. But in a few rare cases the judge decides that the jury got the matter entirely wrong and enters a *judgment non obstante verdicto* or j.n.o.v. (judgment notwithstanding the verdict), holding the exact opposite of what the jury decided.

---

[12] Even after the trial has begun but before the judge or jury returns with a verdict, the parties are free to settle the case. There are even examples—about which we have a question in Chapter 11—regarding situations in which the plaintiff has secretly settled with one of multiple defendants but allows the trial to go forward to a conclusion.

In a civil dispute, either party, winner or loser, may appeal the court's decision. The winner may appeal because he feels that he has not received everything to which he is entitled; the loser may appeal for the obvious reason that he thinks that he ought to have won. Interestingly, the ground for the appeal must be that the court below made a mistake about the relevant *law*, including the relevant general principles that the court applied and the procedures that were used in court, but not about the *facts*. For instance, the appellant (the party filing the appeal) may allege that the judge gave the jury improper instructions about what the relevant law was, or about what facts they could and could not consider, or that the judge improperly excluded some evidence or testimony from the jury's consideration.

At the appellate level there will be no new evidence or facts introduced. The appellate court takes the facts as developed in the trial court as given. The only people to appear before the appellate panel will be the attorneys for the appellant and appellee. The attorneys will submit written briefs to the appellate panel and then appear before the panel for oral argument, during which they may receive very close questioning on the matters at hand. There may be additional briefs submitted by parties who are called *amici curiae* (friends of the court); these parties are not directly involved in the legal dispute but feel that the legal issue involved touches their interests sufficiently that they would like the court to consider their arguments in addition to those of the appellant and appellee.

The appellate panel retires to consider the matter and later issues its opinion. The judges may be in unanimous agreement and issue only one opinion. However, there may be a split in the panel, and that split may result in multiple opinions: a majority and a minority or dissenting opinions. The appellate panel may *affirm* the lower court's judgment or *reverse* that judgment. In some instances, the panel *remands* the matter (that is, sends it back) to the lower court for specific corrective action, such as a recalculation of the damages owed to the plaintiff.

IV.   How Legal Rules Evolve

We now consider a sequence of cases in order to apply the preceding ideas and show how law evolves. The three cases come from England and concern *tort law*, which covers accidents.

BUTTERFIELD V. FORRESTER, 11 EAST 60 (K.B., 1809)[13]

This was an action on the case[14] for obstructing a highway, by means of which obstruction the plaintiff, who was riding along the road, was thrown down with his horse, and injured, etc. At the trial before Bayley, J.,[15] at Derby, it appeared that the defendant, for the purpose of making some repairs to his house, which was close by the roadside at

---

[13] Our selection and discussion of these cases owes a great debt to the stimulating lectures given by Professor Robert Summers to the Fifth Legal Institute for Economists.

[14] The phrase "action on the case" refers to an old legal category of dispute. Simply read it as "dispute."

[15] "J." means "Judge" or "Justice" and, by tradition, opinions are headed by the last name of the judge or justice who wrote the opinion.

one end of the town, had put up a pole across part of the road, a free passage being left by another branch or street in the same direction. That the plaintiff left a public house [a tavern] not far distant from the place in question at 8 o'clock in the evening in August, when they were just beginning to light candles, but while there was light enough left to discern the obstruction at one hundred yards distance; and the witness who proved this, said that if the plaintiff had not been riding very hard, he might have observed and avoided it; the plaintiff, however, who was riding violently, did not observe it, but rode against it, and fell with his horse and was much hurt in consequence of the accident; and there was no evidence of his being intoxicated at the time. On this evidence, Bayley, J., directed the jury, that if a person riding with reasonable and ordinary care could have seen and avoided the obstruction; and if they were satisfied that the plaintiff was riding along the street extremely hard, and without ordinary care, they should find a verdict for the defendant, which they accordingly did.

QUESTION 3.1:

a. Who is the plaintiff? What is he asking the court to do?
b. Is there a statute involved in this dispute?
c. Who won?
d. Was the jury asked to determine fact or law? How was the law stated?

When this case was tried, English law accepted the principle that a defendant whose negligence caused the plaintiff's injury would be held liable. Consequently, the judge instructed the jury that the defendant should be held liable if he could have avoided the accident by taking "reasonable" care. This case presented a novel issue: Suppose that the defendant was negligent, *but* further suppose that the *victim* was also negligent. Should the defendant still be held liable for the victim's losses? An excerpt from the opinion of the judge in this appeal follows.

LORD ELLENBOROUGH, C.J.

A party is not to cast himself upon an obstruction which had been made by the fault of another, and avail himself of it, if he does not himself use common and ordinary caution to be in the right. In case of persons riding upon what is considered to be the wrong side of the road, that would not authorize another purposely to ride up against them. One person being in fault will not dispense with another's using ordinary care for himself. Two things must concur to support this action: an obstruction in the road by the fault of the defendant, and no want of ordinary care to avoid it on the part of the plaintiff. [C]ontributory negligence is a complete bar to recovery.

QUESTION 3.2:

a. Who appealed the judgment?
b. Who won the appeal?
c. What is the judge's holding?

When precedent does not provide a clear rule for resolving a dispute, the judges must *create* such a rule. *Novel disputes* are the occasion for altering the law made by judges. Lord Ellenborough created a new precedent in this case. How broad is the new precedent? Under a narrow interpretation, the judge held that riders of horses cannot recover money damages for their injuries from a negligent defendant if they do not ride with ordinary care, and this lack of care contributes to the accident. This narrow interpretation says that the rule applies only to accidents like this one. Indeed, Lord Ellenborough's example of a horseman riding on the wrong side of the road into another horseman riding on the correct side would seem to support this narrow interpretation. But a broader interpretation of the court's holding is possible, and did, in fact, come to be the common interpretation. Under a broad interpretation of the holding, Lord Ellenborough held that no plaintiffs can recover when their own negligence contributes to their injury (even if the defendant was negligent). This was new law.

About 30 years later, another novel case arose involving similar facts.

DAVIES V. MANN, 10 M.&W. 545 (EX., 1842)[16]

At the trial, before ERSKINE, J., it appeared that the plaintiff, having fettered the fore-feet of an ass belonging to him, turned it into a public highway, and at the same time in question the ass was grazing on the off side of a road about eight yards wide, when the defendant's wagon, with a team of three horses, coming down a slight descent, at what the witness termed a smartish pace, ran against the ass, knocked it down, and the wheels passing over it, it died soon after. . . . The learned judge told the jury, that . . . if they thought that the accident might have been avoided by the exercise of ordinary

---

[16] The traditional English court system that took shape in the late twelfth century and prevailed until the late nineteenth century consisted of three common law courts and a court of equity. The first of the common law courts was the Court of Common Pleas. The members of that court were called "Justices" and were presided over by the Chief Justice. The court originally concentrated on civil disputes concerning land but came to consider a wider range of civil disputes. The Court of King's Bench, the second common law court, was originally a criminal court but over time became a court of review over the civil issues appealed from the Court of Common Pleas. The third common law court was the Court of Exchequer of Pleas or, more simply, the Court of Exchequer. The Exchequer was the King's treasury. This court originally heard disputes arising from tax liability and other matters concerning the King's revenues. By the late sixteenth century, the Court of Exchequer had extended its jurisdiction to cover nearly all civil disputes. Members of that court, in which the appeal in *Davies v. Mann* was heard, were called "Baron," abbreviated "B.," and were presided over by the Chief Baron, abbreviated "C.B."

The equity court was the Court of Chancery, so called because it was presided over by the Chancellor, the most important member of the King's Council. England established this court by the late fifteenth century as a separate court specializing in the dispensing of a more flexible kind of justice than that available in the so-called "law" courts, especially with respect to remedies. There is, therefore, a great historical and substantive difference between the courts of law and the court of equity. One of the most important of those differences has to do with the types of remedies available to a successful plaintiff. Roughly speaking, a court of law would award only compensatory money damages—an amount that would compensate the plaintiff for his injury. A court of equity would possibly do more than that if the plaintiff could demonstrate that his injuries were such that a payment of money damages would inevitably undercompensate him.

(continued)

care on the part of the driver, to find for the plaintiff. The jury found their verdict for the plaintiff. . . .

Godson now moved for a new trial, on the ground of misdirection. [That is, the defendant's lawyer appealed the judgment on the ground that the judge in the trial court had incorrectly instructed the jury on the law to be applied to the facts in this case.] The act of the plaintiff in turning the donkey into the public highway was an illegal one, and, as the injury arose principally from that act, the plaintiff was not entitled to compensation for that injury which, but for his own unlawful act would never have occurred. . . . The principle of law, as deducible from the cases is, that where an accident is the result of faults on both sides neither party can maintain an action. Thus, in *Butterfield v. Forrester*, 11 East 60, it was held that one who is injured by an obstruction on a highway, against which he fell, cannot maintain an action, if it appear that he was riding with great violence and want of ordinary care, without which he might have seen and avoided the obstruction.

LORD ABINGER, C.B. [A]s the defendant might, by proper care, have avoided injuring the animal, and did not, he is liable for the consequences of his negligence, though the animal may have been improperly there.

PARKE, B. [T]he negligence which is to preclude a plaintiff from recovering in an action of this nature, must be such as that he could, by ordinary care, have avoided the consequences of the defendant's negligence. [A]lthough the ass may have been wrongfully there, still the defendant was bound to go along the road at such a pace as would be likely to prevent mischief. Were this not so, a man might justify the driving over goods left on a public highway, or even over a man lying asleep there, or the purposely running against a carriage going on the wrong side of the road. . . .

[New trial denied.]

QUESTION 3.3:

a. Who appealed the judgment?
b. Who won the appeal?
c. What is the judge's holding? Actually, there are three opinions. Are they in accord?

A plaintiff has suffered a loss: His donkey was killed, allegedly because the defendant was driving a wagon too quickly for the conditions on the road. However, the plaintiff himself was negligent for having left his donkey unattended, although fettered, beside a public road. Strictly following the rule in *Butterfield,* the plaintiff's fault or negligence contributed to his losses and thus should bar his recovery. That is precisely what Mann's lawyer argued in appealing the judgment for the plaintiff in the lower court. But at the trial, the court believed that the facts in *Davies v. Mann* were

---

In the Judicature Act of 1873 and the Supreme Court of Judicature (Consolidation) Act of 1925, the British Parliament replaced all of these courts—and the distinction between law and equity—with a greatly simplified structure that drew no distinction between common law and equity.

As we shall see in Chapter 4, these dusty historical matters are relevant to one of the most famous examples of law and economics: the Calabresi and Melamed argument regarding the most efficient method of protecting a legal entitlement.

distinguishable from those in earlier cases in which a contributorily negligent plaintiff was not allowed to recover from a negligent defendant. There appear to be two reasons for excusing the plaintiff's negligence in Lord Abinger's and Baron Parke's opinions. First, there is the element of time. Although the plaintiff was negligent in leaving his donkey unattended on the public highway, the defendant's negligence came afterward. And if the defendant had not been driving recklessly, he would have had time to avoid the donkey by stopping or swerving—even though the donkey ought not to have been unattended where he was. Apparently, the defendant's negligence came afterward and controlled the outcome. This doctrine has come to be known as the "last clear chance" rule: If both parties to an accident are negligent, the party who had the last clear chance to avoid the accident will be held responsible for losses arising from the accident.

The second argument for excusing the plaintiff's negligence is to encourage precautions in the future by people situated like the defendant. Again, Baron Parke puts the point nicely, "[A]lthough the ass may have been wrongfully there, still the defendant was bound to go along the road at such a pace as would be likely to prevent mischief. Were this not so, a man might justify the driving over goods left on a public highway, or even over a man lying asleep there, or the purposely running against a carriage going on the wrong side of the road." This interpretation of the law suggests that rules should create incentives for avoiding accidents.

Notice that *Davies v. Mann* changes the law handed down in *Butterfield v. Forrester*. The blanket rule from the earlier case—contributory negligence is a complete bar to recovery—was amended by judges who faced a new situation. We may say that after *Davies v. Mann* the legal rule became:

> Contributory negligence is a complete bar to recovery *unless the defendant had the last clear chance to avoid the accident and did not take that chance.*

The "last clear chance" doctrine was quickly adopted throughout the common law world.[17]

---

[17] But that is not the end of the story of contributory negligence and "last clear chance." For a fascinating further episode, see *British Columbia Electric Rail Co., Ltd. v. Loach,* [1916] 1 A.C. 719. In brief, here is what was at dispute in that case: Benjamin Sands was driving a horse-drawn wagon and talking with a friend. Not paying attention to his surroundings, he pulled onto the train tracks and stopped. He looked up to see a train coming. The train's engineer applied the brakes as soon as he saw Sands and his wagon on the tracks. Unfortunately, the brakes, unknown to the engineer, were defective and failed to stop the train before it ran into and killed Mr. Sands. Loach, the executor of Sands's estate, sued the British Columbia Electric Rail Co. on a theory of negligence. The railroad claimed, following *Butterfield,* that it should not be held liable because Sands was contributorily negligent. Loach answered that the railroad had, following *Davies,* the last clear chance to avoid the injury and did not take that chance. The railroad claimed that it had not, in fact, had the last clear chance because its brakes were defective. (Everyone agreed that the train would have stopped in time had the brakes been in good working order and that the railroad should have checked the brakes before leaving the roundhouse that morning.) The holding was that the railroad should be held liable: To hold otherwise would, the court said, create an incentive not to maintain one's train (or car or wagon or other device) in good working order.

Conclusion

To summarize, we compared the two great legal traditions—the civil law and the common law. We examined the hierarchical structure of U.S. courts. We saw some of the general characteristics of a legal dispute: a plaintiff who alleges that he or she has been wronged by a defendant and seeks the courts' help in getting relief. We learned some methods that judges use to resolve novel issues. Finally, we looked at the evolution of the doctrine of contributory negligence as developed by courts. This chapter provides a brief, selective introduction to some of the basic facts about law, which we analyze using economics in the rest of the book.

Suggested Readings

BERMAN, HAROLD J., & WILLIAM R. GREINER, THE NATURE AND FUNCTIONS OF LAW (4th ed. 1980).

CARDOZO, BENJAMIN, THE NATURE OF THE JUDICIAL PROCESS (1921).

EISENBERG, MELVIN A., THE NATURE OF THE COMMON LAW (1989).

FRANKLIN, MARC A., THE BIOGRAPHY OF A LEGAL DISPUTE: AN INTRODUCTION TO AMERICAN CIVIL PROCEDURE (1968).

LEVI, EDWARD H., AN INTRODUCTION TO LEGAL REASONING (1949).

MERRYMAN, JOHN H., THE CIVIL LAW TRADITION: AN INTRODUCTION TO THE LEGAL SYSTEMS OF WESTERN EUROPE AND LATIN AMERICA (2nd ed. 1985).

4 An Economic Theory of Property

There is nothing which so generally strikes the imagination and engages the affections of mankind, as the right of property; or that sole and despotic dominion which one man claims and exercises over the external things of the world, in total exclusion of the right of any other individual in the universe.

WILLIAM BLACKSTONE,
COMMENTARIES ON THE LAWS OF ENGLAND, BK. II, CH. 1, P. 2 (1765–69)

In the African tribe called the Barotse, "property law defines not so much the rights of persons over things as the obligations owed between persons in respect of things."

MAX GLUCKMAN,
IDEAS IN BAROTSE JURISPRUDENCE 171 (1965)

[T]he theory of the Communists may be summed up in a single sentence: Abolition of private property.

KARL MARX & FRIEDRICH ENGELS,
THE COMMUNIST MANIFESTO (1848)

THE LAW OF property supplies the legal framework for allocating resources and distributing wealth. As the contrasting quotes above indicate, people and societies disagree sharply about how to allocate resources and distribute wealth. Blackstone viewed property as providing its owner with complete control over resources, and he regarded this freedom to control material things as "the guardian of every other right." Gluckman found that property in an African tribe called the Barotse conveyed to its owner responsibility, not freedom. For example, the Barotse hold rich persons responsible for contributing to the prosperity of their kin. Finally, Marx and Engels regarded property as the institution by which the few enslaved the many.

Classical philosophers try to resolve these deep disputes over social organization by explaining what property *really* is. The appendix to this chapter provides some examples of philosophical theories, such as the theory that property is an expectation (Bentham), the object of fair distribution (Aristotle), a means of self-expression (Hegel), or the foundation of liberty in community life (Burke). Instead of trying to explain what property really is, an economic theory tries to predict the effects of alternative forms of ownership, especially the effects on efficiency and distribution. We shall make such predictions about alternative property rules and institutions.

Here are some examples of problems addressed by property rules and institutions that we will analyze:

Example 1:   "This morning in a remote meadow in Wyoming, a mule was born. To whom does that mule belong?"[1] Does the mule belong to (1) the owner of the mule's mother, (2) the lumber company that has leased the land on which the mule was grazing, or (3) the federal government because the property is a national forest?

Example 2:   Orbitcom, Inc., spent $125 million designing, launching, and maintaining a satellite for the transmission of business data between Europe and the United States. The satellite is positioned in a geosynchronous orbit 25 miles above the Atlantic Ocean.[2] Recently a natural resource-monitoring satellite belonging to the Windsong Corporation has strayed so close to Orbitcom's satellite that the company's transmissions between Europe and the United States have become unreliable. As a result, Orbitcom has lost customers and has sued Windsong for trespassing on Orbitcom's right to its geosynchronous satellite orbit.

Example 3:   Foster inspects a house under construction in a new subdivision on the north side of town and decides to buy it. The day after she moves in, the wind shifts and begins to blow from the north. She smells a powerful stench. On inquiring, she learns that a large cattle feedlot is located north of the subdivision, just over the ridge, and, to make matters worse, the owner of this old business plans to expand it. Foster joins other property owners in an action to shut down the feedlot.

Example 4:   Bloggs inherits the remnant of a farm from his father, most of which has already been sold for a housing development. The remaining acreage, which his father called "The Swamp," is currently used for fishing and duck hunting, but Bloggs decides to drain and develop it as a residential area. However, scientists at the local community college have determined that Bloggs's property is part of the wetlands that nourish local streams and the fish in the town's river. The town council, hearing of Bloggs's plans, passes an ordinance forbidding the draining of wetlands. Bloggs sues for the right to develop his property, or, failing that, for an order compelling the town to buy the property from him at the price that would prevail if development were allowed.

Example 5:   A county ordinance requires houses to be set back 5 feet from the property line. Joe Potatoes buys some heavily wooded land in an undeveloped area and builds a house on it. Ten years later Fred Parsley, who owns the adjoining lot, has his land surveyed and discovers that Potatoes's house extends 2 feet over the property line onto Parsley's property. Potatoes offers to compensate Parsley for the trespass, but Parsley rejects the offer and sues to have Potatoes relocate the house in conformity with the ordinance.

---

[1] This remarkable question is how Professor John Cribbet, one of the leading scholars of property law, opened his first lecture on property to first-year law students at the University of Illinois College of Law.

[2] A geosynchronous orbit means that the satellite is traveling around the Earth at exactly the same speed at which the Earth is turning so that the satellite appears to remain stationary above a point on the Earth's surface.

These five examples capture some of the most fundamental questions that any system of property law must answer. The first and second examples ask how property rights are initially assigned. Orbitcom apparently bases its ownership claim on having placed a satellite in the orbit in dispute before anyone else. This claim appeals to a legal principle called the *rule of first possession*, according to which the first party to use an unowned resource acquires a claim to it. (How might this rule apply to the mule born on the remote Wyoming meadow?) The general issue raised here is, "How does a person acquire ownership of something?"

The second example also asks what kinds of things may be privately owned. Orbitcom asserts that a satellite orbit may be privately owned like land or a musical composition, whereas Windsong feels, perhaps, that orbits should be commonly owned by all and open to all on the same terms, like the high seas. Economics has a lot to say about the consequences of resources being privately owned, commonly owned, or unowned.

The third example concerns a problem sometimes known as "incompatible uses." May one property owner create a stench on his own property that offends his neighbors? In general, the law tries to prevent property owners from interfering with each other, but in this example, as in many other cases, there is a trade-off between competing activities. Is the cattle feedlot interfering with the homeowner by creating the stench, or is the homeowner interfering with the feedlot by moving nearby and seeking to shut it down? The legal outcome turns in part on whether the stench constitutes a "nuisance" as defined by law. Economics has a lot to say about this determination.

The fourth example, like the third, raises the question, "What may owners legitimately do with their property?" The difference is that Example 3 concerns a dispute between private owners and Example 4 concerns a dispute between a private owner and a government. The specific question in Example 4 is whether a property owner can develop his land according to his own wishes or must conform to restrictions on development imposed by a local government. The general question concerns the extent to which government may constrain a private owner's use of her property. We will show that economics has a lot to say about government's regulating and taking private property.

In the last example, one property owner has encroached on the land of another, but that encroachment has gone undetected and without apparent harm for many years. The question raised by this example concerns the remedy for trespass. Should the owner be denied a remedy because the trespass has persisted for so long? Alternatively, should the court award compensatory damages to the owner? Or should the court enjoin the trespasser and force him to move his house? As we shall see, economics predicts the effects of various remedies and thus provides a powerful tool for choosing the best one. We shall also see why courts prefer the remedy of issuing an order called an "injunction" to stop trespassing or otherwise interfering with the property owner.

The examples raise these four fundamental questions of property law:

1. How are ownership rights established?
2. What can be privately owned?
3. What may owners do with their property?
4. What are the remedies for the violation of property rights?

In the next two chapters we shall be using economics to answer these questions. Traditional legal scholarship on property law is notoriously weak in its use of theory, at least in comparison to contracts and torts.[3] This fact contributes to the feeling of many students that the common law of property is diffuse and unorganized. Through economics it is possible to give the subject more coherence and order. In this chapter we concentrate on developing fundamental tools for the economic analysis of property: bargaining theory, public goods theory, and the theory of externalities. In the next chapter we apply these tools to a large number of property laws and institutions.

I.   The Legal Concept of Property

From a legal viewpoint, property is a *bundle of rights*. These rights describe what people may and may not do with the resources they own: the extent to which they may possess, use, develop, improve, transform, consume, deplete, destroy, sell, donate, bequeath, transfer, mortgage, lease, loan, or exclude others from their property. These rights are not immutable; they may, for example, change from one generation to another. But at any point in time, they constitute the detailed answer of the law to the four fundamental questions of property law listed above.

Three facts about the bundle of legal rights constituting ownership are fundamental to our later understanding of property. First, these rights are *impersonal* in the sense that they attach to property, not persons. Any person who owns the property has the rights. In this respect, property rights are different from contract rights. Contract rights are *personal* in the sense that one person owes something to another person. Second, the owner is free to exercise the rights over his or her property, by which we mean that no law forbids or requires the owner to exercise those rights. In our example at the beginning of the chapter, Parsley can farm his land or leave it fallow, and the law is indifferent as to which he chooses to do. Third, others are forbidden to interfere with the owner's exercise of his rights. If others interfere, the court will *enjoin* them to stop—the court will issue an order that they must stop interfering on pain of punishment for contempt of court. Thus, if Parsley decides to farm his land, Potatoes cannot put stones in the way of the plow. This protection is needed against two types of interlopers—private persons and the government.

The legal conception of property is, then, that of a bundle of rights over resources that the owner is free to exercise and whose exercise is protected from interference by others. Thus, property creates a zone of privacy in which owners can exercise their will over things without being answerable to others, as stressed in the preceding quote from

---

[3] In contracts and torts there was a classical theory that dominated American law at the beginning of the twentieth century. The introductory chapters on contracts and torts describe these classical theories. There was, however, no classical theory of property of comparable coherence, detail, or stature. Instead there is a long philosophical tradition of analyzing the institution of property at a very abstract level. Some of these philosophical theories of property are described in the appendix to this chapter.

Blackstone. These facts are sometimes summarized by saying that property gives owners liberty over things.

This general definition of property is compatible with many different theories of what particular rights are to be included in the protected bundle and of how to protect those rights. It is also consistent with different accounts of the responsibilities that a person assumes by becoming an owner. The law has tended to look beyond itself to philosophy for help in deciding which rights to include in the bundle of property rights.

In the approach taken in this chapter, we focus on how alternative bundles of rights create incentives to use resources efficiently. An efficient use of resources maximizes the wealth of a nation. We begin by showing how the right to exchange property contributes to the nation's wealth.

II. Bargaining Theory[4]

To develop an economic theory of property, we must first develop the economic theory of bargaining games. At first you may not see the relevance of this theory to property law, but later you will recognize that it is the very foundation of the economic theory of property. The elements of bargaining theory can be developed through an example of a familiar exchange—selling a used car. Consider these facts:

> Adam, who lives in a small town, has a 1957 Chevy convertible in good repair. The pleasure of owning and driving the car is worth $3000 to Adam. Blair, who has been coveting the car for years, inherits $5000 and decides to try to buy the car from Adam. After inspecting the car, Blair decides that the pleasure of owning and driving it is worth $4000 to her.

According to these facts, an agreement to sell will enable the car to pass from Adam, who values it at $3000, to Blair, who values it at $4000. The potential seller values the car less than the potential buyer, so there is scope for a bargain. Assuming that exchanges are voluntary, Adam will not accept less than $3000 for the car, and Blair will not pay more than $4000, so the sale price will have to be somewhere in between. A reasonable sale price would be $3500, which splits the difference.

The logic of the situation can be clarified by restating the facts in the language of game theory. The parties to the kind of game represented by this example can *both* benefit from cooperating with each other. To be specific, they can move a resource (the car) from someone who values it less (Adam) to someone who values it more (Blair). Moving the resource in this case from Adam, who values it at $3000, to Blair,

---

[4] Bargaining theory is a form of game theory. See the section on game theory in Chapter 2 for some useful background information.

who values it at $4000, will create $1000 in value. The *cooperative surplus* is the name for the value created by moving the resource to a more valuable use. Of course, the share of this surplus that each party receives depends on the price at which the car is sold. If the price is set at $3500, each will enjoy an equal share of the value created by the exchange, or $500. If the price is set at $3800, the value will be divided unequally, with Adam enjoying 4/5 or $800, and Blair enjoying 1/5 or $200. Or if the price is set at $3200, Adam will enjoy $200 or 1/5 of the value created, whereas Blair will enjoy $800 or 4/5.

The parties typically bargain with each other over the price. In the course of negotiating, the parties may assert facts ("The motor is mechanically perfect. . . ."), appeal to norms ("$3700 is an unfair price. . . ."), threaten ("I won't take less than $3500. . . ."), and so forth. These are the tools used in the art of bargaining. The fact that the parties can negotiate is an advantage of bargaining or cooperative games relative to other games (called *noncooperative* games), such as the famous Prisoner's Dilemma, which we examined in Chapter 2. Even when negotiation is possible, however, there is no guarantee that it will succeed. If the negotiations break down and the parties fail to cooperate, their attempt to shift resources to a more valuable use will fail, and they will not create value. Thus, the obstacle to creating value in a bargaining game is that the parties must agree on how to divide it. Value will be divided between them at a rate determined by the price at which the car is sold. Agreement about the car's price marks successful negotiations, whereas disagreement marks a failure in the bargaining process.

To apply game theory to this example, let us characterize the possible outcomes as a cooperative solution and a noncooperative solution. The cooperative solution is the one in which Adam and Blair reach agreement over a price and succeed in exchanging the car for money. The noncooperative solution is the one in which they fail to agree on a price and fail to exchange the car for money. To analyze the logic of bargaining, we must first consider the consequences of noncooperation. If the parties fail to cooperate, they will each achieve some level of well-being on their own. Adam will keep the car and use it, which is worth $3000 to him. Blair will keep her money—$5000—or spend it on something other than the car. For simplicity, assume that the value she places on this use of her money is its face value, specifically, $5000. Thus, the payoffs to the parties in the noncooperative solution, called their *threat values*, are $3000 for Adam (the value to him of keeping the car) and $5000 to Blair (the amount of her cash). The total value of the noncooperative solution is $3000 + $5000 = $8000.

In contrast, the cooperative solution is for Adam to sell the car to Blair. Through cooperation, Blair will own the car, which is worth $4000 to her, and in addition, the two parties will each end up with a share of Blair's $5000. For example, Adam might accept $3500 in exchange for the convertible. Blair then has the car, worth $4000 to her, and $1500 of her $5000. Thus, the value of the cooperative solution is $4000 (the value of the car to Blair) + $1500 (the amount that Blair retains of her original $5000) + $3500 (the amount received by Adam for the car) = $9000. The surplus from cooperation is the difference in value between cooperation and noncooperation: $9000 − $8000 = $1000.

In any voluntary agreement, each player must receive at least the threat value or there is no advantage to cooperating. A reasonable solution to the bargaining problem is for each player to receive the threat value plus an equal share of the cooperative surplus: specifically, $3500 for Adam and $5500 for Blair.[5] To accomplish the division, Blair should pay Adam $3500 for the car. This leaves Adam with $3500 in cash and no car, and leaves Blair with a car worth $4000 to her and $1500 in cash.

QUESTION 4.1:   Suppose Adam receives a bid of $3200 from a third party named Clair. How does Clair's bid change the threat values, the surplus from cooperation, and the reasonable solution?

We have explained that the process of bargaining can be divided into three steps: establishing the threat values, determining the cooperative surplus, and agreeing on terms for distributing the surplus from cooperation. These steps will be used in the next section to understand the origins of the institution of property.

Before proceeding, however, we must warn you about a common problem in the economic analysis of law. In general, economic analysis sometimes uses morally or legally insensitive language to describe useful concepts. "Threat value" is an example. "Threat" connotes "coercion" and coercion often voids a contract or constitutes a tort or crime. If you are speaking to a judge or juror, do not say "threat" unless you intend to connote illegality. This is one example where you will need to substitute other terms for economic language. Refusing to cooperate with the other party and going alone is usually legal. Instead of "threat value" you might try the phrase "*fallback position*" or "*go-it-alone value.*"

III. The Origins of the Institution of Property: A Thought Experiment

The bargaining model shows how cooperation can create a surplus that benefits everyone. This type of reasoning can be used to perform a thought experiment that is helpful in understanding the origins of property.

---

[5] Economists have long struggled with the fact that self-interested rationality alone does not seem sufficient to determine the distribution of the cooperative surplus. That is why we use the term *reasonable solution,* which invokes social norms, rather than *rational solution.* To see the difference, consider this *rational* account of the division of the cooperative surplus. Suppose that somehow Adam knows that the cooperative surplus resulting from an agreement between Blair and him is $1000. Being perfectly rational, he says to Blair that he will sell the car to her for $3995. And, further, he explains to her why she should accept that price, even though it gives Adam $995 of the cooperative surplus and Blair, $5: "If you do not accept that price, I will not do business with you, in which case you will realize $0 worth of cooperative surplus. At the $3995 price, you get $5 of the cooperative surplus and that surely is better than nothing." Leaving aside all the strategic reasons that Blair might balk at this (Will Adam *really* walk away if she refuses?), this division of the cooperative surplus is perfectly rational, but it may not be reasonable. In fact, carefully controlled experiments have demonstrated that most people would *not* accept Adam's offer, rational though it be.

A Civil Dispute as a Bargaining Game

Because trials are costly, both parties can usually gain by settling out of court. That is why so few disputes ever come to trial. As we will see in Chapter 10, the best current estimate is that approximately 5 percent of all disputes that reach the stage of filing a legal complaint in the United States actually result in litigation. Here is a problem in which you must apply bargaining theory to a civil dispute:

FACTS: Arthur alleges that Betty borrowed a valuable kettle and broke it, so he sues to recover its value, which is $300. The facts are very confusing. Betty contends that she did not borrow a kettle from Arthur; even if it is proved that she borrowed a kettle from Arthur, she contends it is not broken; even if it is proved that she borrowed a kettle from Arthur and that it is broken, she contends that she did not break it.

Assume that because the facts in the case are so unclear, Arthur and Betty independently believe that the chances of either side's winning in court are an even 50 percent. Further assume that litigation in small claims court will cost each party $50 and that the costs of settling out of court are nil. So, cooperation in this case is a matter of settling out of court and saving the cost of a trial. Noncooperation in this case means trying the dispute.

QUESTIONS:
   a. What is Arthur's threat value?
   b. What is Betty's threat value?
   c. If Arthur and Betty cooperate together in settling their disagreement, what is the net cost of resolving the dispute?
   d. What is the cooperative surplus?
   e. A reasonable settlement would be for Betty to pay Arthur _____.
   f. Suppose that instead of both sides believing that there is an even chance of winning, both sides are optimistic. Specifically, Arthur thinks that he will win with probability 2/3, and Betty thinks that she will win with probability 2/3.
      1. What is Arthur's putative threat value (what he believes he can secure on his own without Betty's cooperation)?
      2. What is Betty's putative threat value (what she believes she can secure on her own without Arthur's cooperation)?
      3. The putative cooperative surplus equals _____.
      4. Describe the obstacle to settlement in a few words.

Let us imagine a simplified world in which there are people, land, farm tools, and weapons but no courts and no police. In this imaginary world, government does not vindicate and protect the rights to property asserted by the people who live on the land. Individuals, families, or alliances of families enforce property rights to the extent that they defend their land holdings. People must decide how many resources to devote to defending their property claims. Rational people allocate their limited resources so that, as we saw in Chapter 2, the marginal cost of defending land is just equal to the marginal benefit. This means that at the margin, the value of the resources used for military ends (the marginal benefit) equals their value when used for productive ends, such as raising crops and livestock (marginal [opportunity] cost). For example, the occupants are rational if allocating a little more time to patrolling the perimeter of the property preserves as much additional wealth for the defenders as they would enjoy by allocating a little more time to raising crops. The same statement could be made about allocating land between crops and fortifications, or about beating metal into swords or plowshares.

These facts describe a world in which farming and fighting are individually rational. But are they socially efficient? In Chapter 2 we offered the following definition of inefficient production: The same (or fewer) inputs could be used to produce a greater (or the same) total output. Can some mechanism be found that uses fewer resources to achieve the same level of protection for property claims? One possible mechanism is law. Suppose that the costs of operating this system of property rights are less than the sum of all individual costs of private defense. Such a mechanism would allow the transfer of resources from fighting to farming. For example, the landowners might create a government to protect their property rights at lower cost in individual taxes than each individual spends on fighting. The savings might come from economies of scale in having one large army in the society to defend everyone, rather than many small, privately financed armies.[6] In other words, there may be a natural monopoly on force.

We could imagine the parties bargaining together over the terms for establishing a government to recognize and enforce their property rights. They are motivated by the realization that there are economies of scale in protecting property. By reaching an agreement to have one government backed by one army, everyone can enjoy greater wealth and security. The bargain eventually reached by such negotiations is called the *social contract* by philosophers because it establishes the basic terms for social life.[7] It would be rational for the parties negotiating the social contract to take account of other rights of owners besides the right to exclude. Many of the rights that are currently in the bundle called property could be considered, such as the right to use, transfer, and transform. Indeed, many rights other than property rights could be a part of the social contract, such as freedom of speech and freedom of religion, but they do not concern us in this chapter.

---

[6] Recall that economies of scale occur when the cost per unit (or average cost of production) declines as the total amount of output increases. A production technology for which the unit costs are falling at every level of production, even very large levels, is called a *natural monopoly* because one producer can sell at a lower price than many smaller producers.

[7] The social contract has usually been thought of as a logical construct, but some theorists have used it to explain history. For example, it has been argued that feudalism in the Middle Ages corresponds roughly to the conditions of our imaginary world. The economic factors that caused this system to be replaced in some parts of Western Europe by a system of private property rights enforced by a central government are discussed in DOUGLASS C. NORTH & ROBERT PAUL THOMAS, THE RISE OF THE WESTERN WORLD (1973).

The same bargaining model used to explain the sale of a secondhand car can be applied to this thought experiment, in which a primitive society develops a system of property rights. First, a description is given of what people would do in the absence of civil government, when military strength alone established ownership claims. That situation—called the *state of nature*—corresponds to the threat values of the noncooperative solution, which prevails if the parties cannot agree. Second, a description is given of the advantages of creating a government to recognize and enforce property rights. Civil society, in which such a government exists, corresponds to the game's cooperative solution, which prevails if the parties can agree. The social surplus, defined as the difference between the total amount spent defending land in the state of nature and the total cost of operating a property-rights system in civil society, corresponds to the cooperative surplus in the game. Third, an agreement describes the methods for distributing the advantages from cooperation. In the car example, this agreement arises from the price that the buyer offers and the seller accepts. In the thought experiment, this agreement arises from the social contract that includes the fundamental laws of property.

To see the parallel more clearly, imagine that our world consists of only two people, *A* and *B*. In a state of nature, each one grows some corn, steals corn from the other party, and defends against theft. Each of the parties has different levels of skill at farming, stealing, and defending. Their payoffs in a state of nature are summarized in Table 4.1. Taken together, *A* and *B* produce 200 units of corn, but it gets reallocated by theft. For example, *A* steals 40 units of corn from *B* and loses 10 units of corn to *B* through theft. Notice that *A* ultimately enjoys 80 units of corn, and *B* enjoys 120 units, after taking into account the gains and losses from theft.

Instead of persisting in a state of nature, *A* and *B* may decide to enter into a cooperative agreement, recognize each other's property rights, and adopt an enforcement mechanism that puts an end to theft. Let us assume that cooperation will enable them to devote more resources to farming and fewer resources to fighting, so that total production will rise from 200 units to 300 units. One hundred units thus constitutes the social or cooperative surplus. In civil society there will be a mechanism for distributing the surplus from cooperation, such as government taxes and subsidies. The parties must decide through bargaining how this is to be done. A reasonable division of that surplus gives each party an equal share. So, in civil society, each party receives half the cooperative surplus plus the individual net consumption

TABLE 4.1

The State of Nature

Farmer	Corn Grown	Corn Gained by Theft	Corn Lost Through Theft	Net Corn Consumption
A	50	40	210	80
B	150	10	240	120
Totals	200	50	250	200

TABLE 4.2

Civil Society

Farmer	Threat Value	Share of Surplus	Net Corn Consumption
A	80	50	130
B	120	50	170
Totals	200	100	300

in the state of nature, which is each party's threat value. These facts are summarized in Table 4.2.

What is the meaning of this "thought experiment" concerning the origins of property? Read literally, you might conclude that individuals or tribes acquire government by meeting together and agreeing to create a system of law, including property rights. This literal reading is bad history and bad anthropology. Instead of a contract, a system of property law can begin with a military conquest, a rebellion against feudalism, or the disintegration of communism. Instead of history, the thought experiment is really about processes that go on all the time.

In a changing society, new forms of property arise continually. To illustrate, property law for underground gas and the electromagnetic spectrum (radio and television broadcasting) developed in the United States during the last century; and property law for computer software, music, video, and other material on the Internet, and genetically engineered forms of life developed in the last several decades. The need for a new form of property law arises in situations corresponding to our thought experiment. For example, like corn, digital music can be stolen. Without effective property law, people invest a lot of resources in stealing that music or trying to prevent its theft. These efforts redistribute music, rather than invent or manufacture it. Now the United States has property law that prevents the stealing of digital music. The imposition of these laws may have greatly stimulated the production of music. So, our thought experiment is really a parable about the incentive structure that motivates societies to continually create property.

The first question that we posed about property law is, "How are property rights established?" This is a question about how an owner acquires the legal right to property. Our thought experiment answers the question, "Why are ownership rights established?" This is a question about why a society creates property as a legal right. The two questions are closely connected. Societies create property as a legal right to encourage production, discourage theft, and reduce the costs of protecting goods. Law prescribes various ways that someone can acquire a property right, such as by finding and purchasing land with natural gas beneath it, inventing a computer program, or discovering sunken treasure.

We now turn to the elaboration of how bargaining theory can help the law prescribe ways for the acquisition of property that also encourage production, or discourage theft, and reduce the costs of protecting goods.

QUESTION 4.2:

a. Is the cooperative solution *fair*? Can the resulting inequality in civil society be justified? To answer these questions, draw on your intuitive ideas of fairness or, better still, a concept of fairness developed by a major philosopher such as Hobbes, Locke, Rawls, or Aristotle.

b. Suppose that the bargaining process did not allow destructive threats, such as the threat to steal. How might this restriction affect the distribution of the surplus?

c. What is the difference between the principle, "To each according to his threat value," and this principle, "To each according to his productivity"?

IV. An Economic Theory of Property

The fact that the same theory of bargaining can be applied to selling a used car or creating a civil society is proof of that theory's generality and power. Indeed, bargaining theory is so powerful that, as this section will show, it serves as the basis for an economic theory of property and of property law. Let us briefly summarize where we are going.

By bargaining together, people frequently agree on the terms for interacting and cooperating. But sometimes the terms for interacting and cooperating are imposed on people from the outside—for example, by law. The terms are often more efficient when people agree on them than when a lawmaker or conqueror imposes them. It follows that law is unnecessary and undesirable where bargaining succeeds, and that law is necessary and desirable where bargaining fails.

These propositions apply to the four questions about property that we asked above. In certain circumstances we do not need property law to answer the four questions that we posed at the beginning of this chapter. Rather, in those special circumstances, private bargaining will establish what things are property, who has claims to that property, what things an owner may and may not do with the property, and who may interfere with an owner's property. The special circumstances that define the limits of law are specified in a remarkable proposition called the *Coase Theorem*. This theorem, to which we now turn, helped to found the economic analysis of law and won its inventor the Nobel Prize in economics.

A. The Coase Theorem[8]

Different commentators formulate the Coase Theorem differently. We will expound a simple version of the theorem and then acquaint you with some of the commentary.

---

[8] The theorem is discussed in Professor Ronald H. Coase's *The Problem of Social Cost*, 3 J. LAW & ECON. 1 (1960). The article has been reprinted in numerous legal and economic anthologies, notably R. BERRING ED., GREAT AMERICAN LAW REVIEWS (1984) (a compendium of the 22 "greatest" articles published in the United States' law reviews before 1965).

FIGURE 4.1

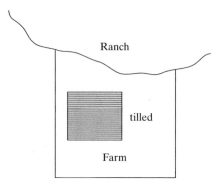

Consider the example of the rancher and the farmer as depicted in Figure 4.1. A cattle rancher lives beside a farmer. The farmer grows corn on some of his land and leaves some of it uncultivated. The rancher runs cattle over all of her land. The boundary between the ranch and the farm is clear, but there is no fence. Thus, from time to time the cattle wander onto the farmer's property and damage the corn. The damage could be reduced by building a fence, continually supervising the cattle, keeping fewer cattle, or growing less corn—each of which is costly. The rancher and the farmer could bargain with each other to decide who should bear the cost of the damage. Alternatively, the law could intervene and assign liability for the damages.

There are two specific rules the law could adopt:

1. The farmer is responsible for keeping the cattle off his property, and he must pay for the damages when they get in (a regime we could call "ranchers' rights" or "open range"), or
2. The rancher is responsible for keeping the cattle on her property, and she must pay for the damage when they get out ("farmers' rights" or "closed range").

Under the first rule, the farmer would have no legal recourse against the damage done by his neighbor's cattle. To reduce the damage, the farmer would have to grow less corn or fence his cornfields. Under the second rule, the rancher must build a fence to keep the cattle on her property. If the cattle escape, the law could ascertain the facts, determine the monetary value of the damage, and make the rancher pay the farmer.

Which law is better? Perhaps you think that fairness requires injurers to pay for the damage they cause. If so, you will approach the question as traditional lawyers do, by thinking about causes and fairness. The rancher's cows harm the farmer's crops, but the farmer's crops do not harm the rancher's cows. The cause of the harm runs from rancher to farmer, and many people believe that fairness requires the party who causes harm to pay for it.

Professor Coase, however, answered in terms of *efficiency*. All other things equal, we would like the legal rule to encourage efficiency in both ranching and farming.

This approach yielded a counterintuitive conclusion, which can be explained using some numbers. Suppose that, without any fence, the invasion by the cattle costs the farmer $100 per year in lost profits from growing corn. The cost of installing and maintaining a fence around the farmer's cornfields is $50 per year, and the cost of installing a fence around the ranch is $75 per year. Thus, we are assuming that damage of $100 can be avoided at an annual cost of $50 by the farmer or $75 by the rancher. Obviously, efficiency requires the farmer to build a fence around his cornfields, rather than the rancher to build a fence around her ranch.

Now, consider what will happen under either legal rule. Under the first legal rule (ranchers' rights), the farmer will bear damage of $100 each year from the wandering cattle. He can eliminate this damage at a cost of $50 per year, for a net savings of $50 per year. Therefore, the first rule will cause the farmer to build a fence around his cornfields. Under the second rule (farmers' rights), the rancher can escape liability for $100 at a cost of $75. Consequently, the second rule will cause the rancher to build a fence around her ranch, thus saving $25. Apparently, the first rule, which saves $50, is more efficient than the second rule, which saves $25. But this efficiency is only apparent; it is not real.

We may begin our understanding of this apparent puzzle by first imagining how the rancher and the farmer could have resolved their problem by cooperative bargaining and then comparing that outcome with the apparent outcomes under the different legal rules. Suppose that the farmer and the rancher had fallen in love, married, and combined their business interests. They would then maximize the combined profits from farming and ranching, and these joint profits will be highest when they build a fence around the cornfields, not around the ranch. Consequently, the married couple will build a fence around the cornfields, regardless of whether the law is the first rule or the second rule. In other words, they will cooperate to maximize their joint profits, regardless of the rule of law.

We have seen that the first rule is more efficient than the second if the farmer and the rancher follow the law without cooperating, but that the law makes no difference to efficiency when they cooperate. The farmer and the rancher do not need to get married in order to cooperate. Rational businesspeople can often bargain together and agree on terms of cooperation. By bargaining to an agreement, rather than following the law noncooperatively, the rancher and the farmer can save $25. That is, if the parties can bargain successfully with each other, the efficient outcome will be achieved, regardless of the rule of law.

Recall that the most efficient outcome is for the farmer to build a fence around his cornfields, and that when the parties simply follow the law without cooperating, the second rule (farmers' rights) leads to the apparent inefficiency of the *rancher's* building a fence around her ranch. But consider how bargaining might proceed under the second rule:

> **RANCHER:** *"The law makes me responsible for any damage that my cattle do to your crops. There would be no damage if there was a fence. I can fence my ranch for $75 per year, whereas you can fence your cornfields for $50 per year. Let's make a deal. I'll pay you $50 per year to fence your cornfield."*

> **FARMER:**   *"If I agree, and you pay me $50 per year to fence my cornfields, I won't be any better off than if I did nothing and you had to fence your ranch. However, you'll save $25. You shouldn't receive all of the gains from cooperation. You should give me a share of the gains by paying me more than $50 per year for fencing my cornfields."*

> **RANCHER:**   *"OK. Let's split the savings from cooperation. I'll pay you $62.50 per year, and you build the fence. That way we'll each receive half of the $25 gained by cooperating."*

> **FARMER:**   *"Agreed."*

Note the important implication: Cooperation leads to the fence's being built around the *farmer's* cornfields, despite the fact that the second legal rule (farmers' rights) was controlling. The greater efficiency of the first legal rule is apparent, not real. Note, also, the parallel between bargaining over the right of ownership of a used car from earlier in the chapter and the rights of ownership of land. Adam owns the car, and Blair values it more than Adam. By bargaining to an agreement, they can create a surplus and divide it between them. Similarly, the second legal rule imposes an obligation on the rancher to constrain her cattle, but the farmer can constrain them at less cost than the rancher. By bargaining to an agreement, both parties can save costs and divide the savings between them.[9]

Let's generalize what we have learned from this exercise. When one activity interferes with another, the law must decide whether one party has the right to interfere or whether the other party has the right to be free from interference. Fairness apparently requires the party who causes harm to pay for it. In contrast, efficiency requires allocating the right to the party who values it the most. When the parties follow the law noncooperatively, the legal allocation of rights matters to efficiency. When the parties bargain successfully, the legal allocation of rights does not matter to efficiency. Given successful bargaining, the use of resources (the placement of a fence, the number of cattle run, the extent of land planted in cornfields, and so forth) is efficient, regardless of the legal rule.

We have discussed "successful bargaining," but we have not discussed why bargains sometimes succeed and sometimes fail. Bargaining occurs through communication between the parties. Communication has various costs, such as renting a conference room, hiring a stenographer, and spending time in discussion. Coase used the term "transaction costs" to refer to the costs of communicating, as well as to a variety of

---

[9] The bargaining situation is quite different if the law adopts the first rule (ranchers' rights), rather than the second rule (farmers' rights). Under the first rule, the farmer is responsible for building a fence to keep the cattle out of his cornfields. In these circumstances, cooperation between the farmer and the rancher does not save costs relative to following the law noncooperatively. Consequently, under the first rule, the farmer will go ahead and build the fence, without any bargaining. The first rule has an analogy in the used-car example. Recall that Blair values the car more than Adam does, which is why a surplus can be created by Adam's selling the car to Blair. If Blair initially owns the car, there is nothing to be gained by bargaining with Adam or cooperating with him. Thus, Blair's owning the car is analogous to ranchers' rights. In the car example, there is no scope for a bargain because the party who values the car the most already owns it; in the cattle-corn example, there is no scope for a bargain because the party who can fence the cattle at least cost already has the duty to build the fence.

other costs that we will discuss later. In fact, he used "transaction costs" to encompass *all* of the impediments to bargaining. Given this definition, bargaining *necessarily* succeeds when transaction costs are zero. We can summarize this result by stating this version of the Coase Theorem:

> When transaction costs are zero, an efficient use of resources results from private bargaining, regardless of the legal assignment of property rights.

Now we must relate the Coase Theorem to our larger project of developing an economic theory of property. The theorem states abstractly what our example showed concretely: If transaction costs are zero, then we do not need to worry about specifying legal rules regarding property in order to achieve efficiency. Private bargaining will take care of such issues as which things may be owned, what owners may and may not do with their property, and so on.

By specifying the circumstances under which property law is unimportant to efficient resource use, the Coase Theorem specifies implicitly when property law *is* important. The assignment of property rights might be crucial to the efficient use of resources when transaction costs are *not* zero.

To make the point more explicit, we posit this corollary to the Coase Theorem:

> When transaction costs are high enough to prevent bargaining, the efficient use of resources will depend on how property rights are assigned.

Figure 4.2 represents the corollary graphically. Transaction costs lie on a spectrum from zero to infinity. In any particular situation, a threshold level of transaction costs divides the spectrum into a region in which bargaining succeeds and one in which it fails.

To appreciate the corollary, let us return to the rancher and the farmer. Bargaining to an agreement requires communication. Assume that communication is costly. Specifically, assume that the transaction costs of bargaining are $35. Transaction costs must be subtracted from the surplus in order to compute the net value of cooperating. Suppose that the second legal rule (farmers' rights) prevails, so that a surplus of $25 can be achieved by an agreement that the rancher will pay the farmer to fence the cornfields. The net value of the bargain is the cooperative surplus minus the transaction costs— $25 − $35 = −$10. Recognizing that the net value of the bargain is negative, the parties will not bargain. If the parties do not bargain, they will follow the law noncooperatively. Specifically, the farmer will assert his right to be free from invasions of cattle, and the rancher will fence the ranch, which is inefficient. In order to avoid this inefficiency, the law would have to adopt the first rule (ranchers' rights), in which case the parties will not bargain, and they will achieve efficiency by following the law noncooperatively.

FIGURE 4.2

A threshold level of transaction costs that distinguishes the areas in which the Coase Theorem applies and does not apply.

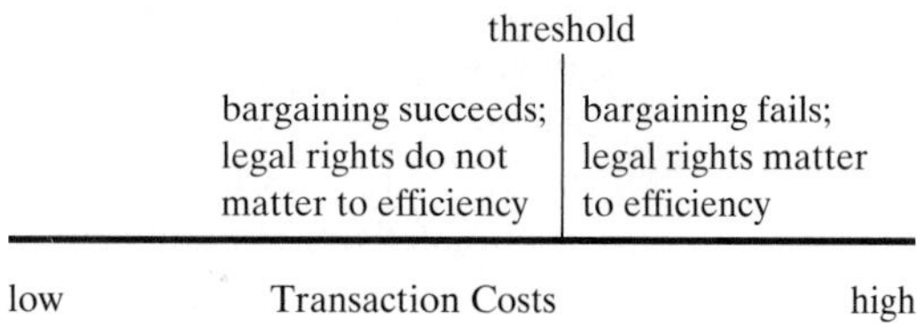

	threshold	
bargaining succeeds; legal rights do not matter to efficiency		bargaining fails; legal rights matter to efficiency
low	Transaction Costs	high

Sometimes the threshold's location is obvious to everyone. For example, when a minor road crosses a main road, the law should prescribe that drivers in the minor road must yield to drivers on the main road. Motorists do not have time to bargain with each other and arrive at this result on their own. Sometimes the threshold's location is not obvious and people sharply disagree over policy. Motorists cannot buy insurance against their own pain and suffering from an accident. Legal scholars disagree sharply over whether such insurance is unavailable because transaction costs are prohibitively high or because motorists do not value compensation for pain and suffering enough to pay for it.

QUESTION 4.3: Suppose that a railroad runs beside a field in which commercial crops are grown. The railroad is powered by a steam locomotive that spews hot cinders out of its smokestack. From time to time those cinders land on the crops nearest to the track and burn them to the ground. Assume that each year, the farmer whose crops are burned loses $3000 in profits, and that the annual cost to the railroad of installing and maintaining a spark-arrester that would prevent any damage to the crops is $1750. Does it matter to the efficient use of the farmer's land or to the efficient operation of the railroad whether the law protects the farmer from invasion by sparks or allows the railroad to emit sparks without liability? Why or why not?

The Coase Theorem is so remarkable that many people have questioned it. Although we cannot discuss this rich literature here, we have embodied some of the most important points in the following questions:

QUESTION 4.4: **The long run.** Some commentators thought that the Coase Theorem might be true in the short run but not in the long run. In the example of the farmer and the rancher, changing the use of fields takes time. For example, to convert a field from grazing land to farmland, the farmer must fence and plough the land. The efficiency of the Coase Theorem in the long run depends on the ability of private bargaining to accommodate any additional costs of altering resource use over long time periods as relative prices and opportunity costs change. Discuss some ways that a contract for long-run cooperation between the rancher and the farmer would differ from a contract for short-run cooperation.

QUESTION 4.5: **Invariance.** With zero transaction costs, the farmer fences the cornfield rather than the rancher fencing the ranch—regardless of the rule of law. Notice that in this example, the use of the fields for cattle-ranching and corn-growing is the same, regardless of the initial assignment of property rights. This version of the Coase Theorem is called the *invariance* version (because the use of resources is *invariant* to the assignment of property rights). This version turns out to be a special case. The more general case is one in which the resource allocation will be *efficient* (but not necessarily identical), regardless of the assignment of property rights. There will be a Pareto-efficient allocation of goods and services, but it may be different from the Pareto-efficient allocation that would have resulted from assigning that same entitlement to someone else.

To illustrate, assume that farmers like to eat more corn and less beef, whereas ranchers like to eat more beef and less corn. Assume that farmers and ranchers own their own land, that transaction costs are zero, and that fence is costly relative to their incomes. The change from "ranchers' rights" to "farmers' rights" will increase the income of farmers and decrease the income of ranchers. Consequently, the demand for corn will increase, and the demand for beef will decrease. Greater demand for corn requires the planting and fencing of more cornfields. Thus, the change in law causes the building of more fences. Remember the distinction between "price effects" and "income effects" in demand theory? Can you use these concepts to explain this example?[10]

QUESTION 4.6: Endowment effects. Surveys and experiments reveal that people sometimes demand much more to give up something that they have than they would be willing to pay to acquire it. To illustrate, contrast a situation in which people have an opportunity to "sell" the clean air that they currently enjoy to a polluter to the situation in which people currently not enjoying clean air have an opportunity to "buy" clean air from a polluter. Evidence suggests that people may demand a higher price to "sell" a right to clean air than they would pay to "buy" the same right. An *endowment* is an initial assignment of ownership rights. The divergence between buying and selling price is called an *endowment effect* because the price varies depending on the initial assignment of ownership.

Why might farmers place a different value on the right to be free from straying cattle depending on whether they were selling or buying that right? Is it rational to place different values on those rights? How do these flip-flops in the relative valuation complicate an efficiency analysis of the assignment of property rights?

QUESTION 4.7: Social norms. Social norms often evolve to cope with external costs, without bargaining or law. For example, a social norm in a county in northern California requires that ranchers assume responsibility for controlling their cattle, even though parts of the county are "open range" (that is, areas in which legal responsibility rests with farmers). Furthermore, the ranchers and farmers in this county apparently do not engage in the kind of bargaining envisioned by the Coase Theorem. How damaging are these facts to Coase's analysis? Why would you expect neighbors in long-run relationships to adopt efficient norms to control externalities?[11]

---

[10] In the long run, ranchland will be more valuable if the rancher does not have to install fences, and farmland will be more valuable if the farmer does not have to install fences. If ranchers and farmers rent their land, the rule that determines the cost of fencing may affect the rental value of the land, not the profitability of the activity that occurs on it. On the various versions of the Coase Theorem, see ROBERT D. COOTER, *The Coase Theorem*, in THE NEW PALGRAVE: A DICTIONARY OF ECONOMICS (1987). On the special assumptions underlying the invariance version of the Coase Theorem, see the graphical treatment in THOMAS S. ULEN, *Flogging a Dead Pig: Professor Posin on the Coase Theorem*, 38 WAYNE L. REV. 91 (1991).

[11] See Robert Ellickson, *Of Coase and Cattle: Dispute Resolution Among Neighbors in Shasta County*, 38 STAN. L. REV. 623 (1986).

ⓘ **Web Note 4.1**

There is more on the Coase Theorem at our website, where we pose additional questions and describe some experimental studies designed to test the Coase Theorem.

B. The Elements of Transaction Costs

What are transaction costs? Are they ever really negligible? We cannot use the Coase Theorem to understand law without answering these questions. Transaction costs are the costs of exchange. An exchange has three steps. First, an exchange partner has to be located. This involves finding someone who wants to buy what you are selling or sell what you are buying. Second, a bargain must be struck between the exchange partners. A bargain is reached by successful negotiation, which may include the drafting of an agreement. Third, after a bargain has been reached, it must be enforced. Enforcement involves monitoring performance of the parties and punishing violations of the agreement. We may call the three forms of transaction costs corresponding to these three steps of an exchange: (1) search costs, (2) bargaining costs, and (3) enforcement costs.

QUESTION **4.8:**   Classify each of the following examples as a cost of searching, bargaining, or enforcing an agreement to purchase a 1957 Chevrolet:

a. Haggling over the price.
b. Collecting the monthly payments for the purchase of the car.
c. Taking time off from work for the buyer and seller to meet.
d. Purchasing an advertisement in the "classified" section of the newspaper.
e. Purchasing a newspaper to obtain the "classified" section.
f. The buyer asking the seller questions about the car's ignition system.

When are transaction costs high, and when are they low? Consider this question by looking at the three elements of the costs of exchange. Search costs tend to be high for unique goods or services, and low for standardized goods or services. To illustrate, finding someone who is selling a 1957 Chevrolet is harder than finding someone who is selling a soft drink.

Turning from search costs to bargaining costs, note that our examples of bargaining assumed that both parties *know* each other's threat values and the cooperative solution. Game theorists say that information is "public" in negotiations when each party knows these values. (Game theorists refer to these negotiations as "common knowledge" situations.) Conversely, information is "private" when one party knows some of these values and the other does not. If the parties know the threat values and the cooperative solution, they can compute reasonable terms for cooperation. In general, public information facilitates agreement by enabling the parties to compute reasonable terms for cooperation. Consequently, negotiations tend to be simple and easy when information about the threat values and the cooperative solution is public. To illustrate, negotiations for the sale of a watermelon are simple because there is not much to know about it.

Negotiations tend to be complicated and difficult when information about threat values and the cooperative solution is private. Private information impedes bargaining because much of it must be converted into public information before computing reasonable terms for cooperation. In general, bargaining is costly when it requires converting a lot of private information into public information. To illustrate, negotiations for the sale of a house involve many issues of finance, timing, quality, and price. The seller of a house knows a lot more about its hidden defects than the buyer knows, and the buyer knows a lot more about his or her ability to obtain financing than the seller knows. Each attempts to extract these facts from the other over the course of negotiations. To a degree, the parties may want to divulge some information. But they may be reluctant to divulge all. Each party's share of the cooperative surplus depends, in part, on keeping some information private. But concluding the bargain requires making some information public. Balancing these conflicting pulls is difficult and potentially costly.

There is an extensive literature on bargaining games, including a large number of carefully constructed experiments testing the Coase Theorem.[12] One of the most robust conclusions of these experiments is that bargainers are more likely to cooperate when their rights are clear and less likely to agree when their rights are ambiguous. Put in more formal terms, bargaining games are easier to solve when the threat values are public knowledge. The rights of the parties define their threat values in legal disputes. One implication of this finding is that property law ought to favor criteria for determining ownership that are clear and simple. The most immediate prescription for efficient property law is to make rights clear and simple. For example, a system for the public registration of ownership claims to land avoids many disputes and makes settlement easier for those that arise. Similarly, the fact that someone possesses or uses an item of property is easy to confirm. In view of this fact, the law gives weight to possession and use when determining ownership. Conversely, unclear ownership rights are a major obstacle to cooperation and a major cause of wasted resources. Thus, squatters who occupy land owned by others in developing countries fail to improve their dwellings because it is not clear that they would own the improvements.

Most of our bargaining examples concern two parties. Communication between two parties is usually cheap, especially when they are near each other. However, many bargains involve three or more parties. Bargaining becomes more costly and difficult as it involves more parties, especially if they are dispersed from one another. This fact may explain why treaties involving many nations are so difficult to conclude.

Finally, the parties may want to draft an agreement, and this may be costly because it must anticipate many contingencies that can arise to change the value of the bargain.

---

[12] See J. KEITH MURNIGHAN, BARGAINING GAMES (1992) for a highly readable summary of this literature. For specific experiments on the Coase Theorem, see Elizabeth Hoffman & Matthew Spitzer, *The Coase Theorem: Some Experimental Tests*, 25 J. LAW & ECON. 73 (1982), and Hoffman & Spitzer, *Experimental Tests of the Coase Theorem with Large Bargaining Groups*, 15 J. LEGAL STUD. 149 (1986). Ian Ayres has recently argued that, contrary to these findings, ambiguous rights induce bargaining. See our website for more.

Another obstacle to bargaining is hostility. The parties to the dispute may have emotional concerns that interfere with rational agreement, as when a divorce is bitterly contested. People who hate each other often disagree about the division of the cooperative surplus, even though all the relevant facts are public knowledge. To illustrate, many jurisdictions have rules for dividing property on divorce that are simple and predictable for most childless marriages. However, a significant proportion of these divorces are litigated in court rather than settled by negotiation. In these circumstances, lawyers can facilitate negotiations by interposing themselves between hostile parties.

Even without hostility, however, bargaining can be costly because negotiators may behave unreasonably—for example, by pressing their own advantage too hard (what lawyers refer to as "overreaching"). An essential aspect of bargaining is forming a strategy. In forming a bargaining strategy, each party tries to anticipate how much the opponent will concede. If the parties miscalculate the other party's resolve, each will be surprised to find that the other does not concede, and as a result, negotiations may fail. Miscalculations are likely when the parties do not know each other, when cultural differences obscure communication, or when the parties are committed to conflicting moral positions about fairness.

Enforcement costs, the third and final element of transaction costs, arise when an agreement takes time to fulfill. An agreement that takes no time to fulfill has no enforcement costs. An example is simultaneous exchange, in which I give you a dollar and you give me a watermelon. For complex transactions, monitoring behavior and punishing violations of the agreement can be costly. To illustrate, consider the example from the beginning of this chapter of Bloggs's desire to drain a wetlands on his property in order to develop it as a residential area. Suppose that the city permits him to build on a small part of the wetlands, provided that he does not harm the rest. Officials must watch him to be sure that he keeps his promise. Furthermore, officials may require Bloggs to post bond, which will be confiscated if he harms the rest of the wetlands and returned to him if he completes construction without doing harm. In general, enforcement costs are low when violations of the agreement are easy to observe and punishment is cheap to administer.

Let us summarize what we have learned about transaction costs. Transactions have three stages, each of which has a special type of cost—search costs, bargaining costs, and enforcement costs. These costs vary along a spectrum from zero to indefinitely large, depending on the transaction. Characteristics of transactions that affect their costs are summarized in Table 4.3.

QUESTION 4.9:   Rank the following six transactions from lowest to highest transaction costs. Explain your ranking by reference to the costs of search, bargaining, and enforcement. (There is no uniquely correct answer.)

a. Getting married.
b. Buying an artichoke.
c. Acquiring an easement to run a gas line across your neighbor's property.
d. Selling a Burger King franchise.
e. Going to college.
f. Purchasing a warranty for a new car.

TABLE 4.3

Factors Affecting Transaction Costs

Lower Transaction Costs	Higher Transaction Costs
1. Standardized good or service	1. Unique good or service
2. Clear, simple rights	2. Uncertain, complex rights
3. Few parties	3. Many parties
4. Friendly parties	4. Hostile parties
5. Familiar parties	5. Unfamiliar parties
6. Reasonable behavior	6. Unreasonable behavior
7. Instantaneous exchange	7. Delayed exchange
8. No contingencies	8. Numerous contingencies
9. Low costs of monitoring	9. High costs of monitoring
10. Cheap punishments	10. Costly punishments

QUESTION 4.10: Consider the right to smoke or to be free from smoke in the following situations. In which situations do you think that transaction costs are so high that they preclude private bargains, and in which cases do you think that transaction costs are low enough for private bargains to occur? Explain your answer.

a. Smoking in a private residence.
b. Smoking in a public area, such as a shopping mall, an indoor arena or concert hall, or an outdoor stadium.
c. Smoking in hotel rooms.
d. Smoking on commercial airline flights.

What sorts of arguments might be made for and against a bargaining or more interventionist means of dealing with each issue? To what extent are social norms, not law, determinative of the outcome?

C. The Normative Coase and Hobbes Theorems

We have been speaking thus far as if the Coase Theorem's only lesson for property law is that the law should determine the level of transaction costs and react accordingly. But we can go further.

Thus far, we have spoken of transaction costs as if they are exogenous to the legal system—that is, as if they are determined solely by objective characteristics of bargaining situations outside the domain of the law. This is not always the case. Some transaction costs are *endogenous* to the legal system in the sense that legal rules can lower obstacles to private bargaining. The Coase Theorem suggests that the law can encourage bargaining by lowering transaction costs.

To illustrate numerically, if the surplus from exchange is $25 and transaction costs are $30, then the parties can obtain a net benefit of $25 − $30 = −$5 from a private agreement. In other words, at least one of the parties will lose from private exchange. A rational person will not voluntarily trade at a loss. So, private exchange will not occur among rational people when the net benefit is negative. If, however, law lowers transaction costs to $10, then the net benefit of exchange is $25 − $10 = $15. When the surplus exceeds transaction costs, the net benefit from private exchange is positive, so both parties can gain from private exchange. Private exchange will ordinarily occur among rational people when the net benefit is positive.

Lowering transaction costs "lubricates" bargaining. An important legal objective is to lubricate private bargains by lowering transaction costs. One important way for the law to do this is by defining simple and clear property rights. It is easier to bargain when legal rights are simple and clear than when they are complicated and uncertain. To illustrate, the rule "first in time, first in right" is a simple and clear way to determine ownership claims. Similarly, requiring public recording of property claims makes determining ownership easier. Further, making those records searchable on the Internet may lower transaction costs even more. You will encounter many examples throughout this book of other ways that law lubricates bargaining. By lubricating bargaining, the law enables the private parties to exchange legal rights, thus relieving lawmakers of the difficult task of allocating legal rights efficiently.[13]

We can formalize this principle as the *Normative Coase Theorem*:

> Structure the law so as to remove the impediments to private agreements.

The principle is *normative* because it offers prescriptive guidance to lawmakers. The principle is inspired by the Coase Theorem because it assumes that private exchange, in the appropriate circumstances, can allocate legal rights efficiently. To illustrate the principle's application, the dramatic worldwide trend toward privatization in the 1990s removed many regulatory impediments to private agreements.

Besides encouraging bargaining, a legal system tries to minimize disagreements and failures to cooperate, which are costly to society. The importance of minimizing the losses from disagreements was especially appreciated by the seventeenth-century English philosopher Thomas Hobbes. Hobbes thought that people would seldom be rational enough to agree on a division of the cooperative surplus, even when there were no serious impediments to bargaining.[14] Their natural cupidity would lead them to quarrel unless a third, stronger party forced them to agree. These considerations suggest the following principle of property law, which we may call the *Normative Hobbes Theorem*:

> Structure the law so as to minimize the harm caused by failures in private agreements.[15]

---

[13] As we shall see in Chapter 8, contract law may be seen as an application of the Normative Coase Theorem in that much of that area of the law may be seen as an attempt to lower the transaction costs of concluding consensual agreements.

[14] Because Hobbes wrote in the seventeenth century, he did not express himself in quite these terms, but this kind of argument is pervasive in his classic work, LEVIATHAN (1651). The modern idea underlying the pessimism of Hobbes concerning distribution is the fact that game theory has no generally accepted way to choose among core allocations.

[15] This idea is developed at length in Cooter, *The Cost of Coase*, 11 J. LEGAL STUD. 1 (1982).

According to this principle, the law should be designed to prevent coercive threats and to eliminate the destructiveness of disagreement.

When the parties fail to reach a private agreement where one is, in fact, possible, they lose the surplus from exchange. To minimize the resulting harm, the law should *allocate property rights to the party who values them the most.* By allocating property rights to the party who values them the most, the law makes exchange of rights unnecessary and thus saves the cost of a transaction. To illustrate, the Normative Hobbes Theorem requires the law to create "open range" (ranchers' rights), rather than "closed range" (farmers' rights) in situations corresponding to our previous example.

These two normative principles of property law—minimize the harm caused by private disagreements over resource allocation (the Normative Hobbes Theorem), and minimize the obstacles to private agreements over resource allocation (the Normative Coase Theorem)—have wide application in law. In combination with the Coase Theorem discussed earlier and its corollary, these principles will form the heart of our economic analysis of property law in the remainder of this and the following chapter.

D. Lubricate or Allocate? Coase versus Hobbes

The Coase and Hobbes Theorems characterize two ways that law can increase efficiency when transaction costs are positive. First, law can *lubricate* private exchange by lowering transaction costs. Second, law can *allocate* rights to the party who values them the most.

Now we consider how a lawmaker might choose between lubricating and allocating. Return to our example of the farmer and the rancher, where fencing costs the rancher $75 and the farmer $50. Assume that law assigns the obligation to fence to the rancher (farmers' rights). Given these facts, a surplus of $25 could be achieved by transferring the obligation to fence from the rancher to the farmer (ranchers' rights). Assume, however, that transaction costs of private exchange equal $35, so the transfer is blocked. What is to be done? If law can lower the transaction costs of exchange from $35 to $10, transaction costs will no longer block private exchange. When private exchange is not blocked, the obligation of the rancher to build the fence can be transferred to the farmer, thus creating a net benefit of $15.

Alternatively, assume that the law cannot lower the transaction costs of exchange. The other possible remedy is to change the law and assign the obligation to fence to the farmer (ranchers' rights), not the rancher (farmers' rights). If the farmer has the obligation to fence, the legal rights are allocated efficiently. When the right is already allocated efficiently, exchange of the right would produce a negative surplus. Exchange is unnecessary and will not occur.

Unfortunately, however, lawmakers often do not know who values rights the most, and finding out can be difficult. To illustrate, consider the problem of finding out the cost of fencing the farmer's crops. When testifying in court, the farmer has an incentive to exaggerate these costs. Knowing this fact, the judge and the jury are not sure whether to believe the farmer.

Lawmakers with limited information face a trade-off between transaction costs and information costs. On one hand, by strictly following precedent, courts avoid the information costs of determining who values a right the most. With strict adherence to precedent by courts, the parties must bear the transaction costs of correcting inefficient legal allocations of rights. On the other hand, the courts can attempt to determine who values a legal right the most and adjust the law accordingly. With legal reallocation of rights, the courts or other lawmakers must bear the information costs of determining who values a right the most. Efficiency requires the courts to do whichever is cheaper.

To formalize this claim, let *IC* denote the information costs to a court of determining who values a legal right the most. Let *TC* indicate the transaction costs of trading legal rights. Efficient courts would follow this rule:

$IC < TC \Rightarrow$ allocate the legal right initially to the person who values it the most;
$TC < IC \Rightarrow$ strictly follow precedent.

To illustrate the application of this principle, as population increases and land use intensifies, areas in the western United States convert from open to closed range. Assume that a judge or panel of legal experts must consider whether to leave some range in the country open or to close it. In approaching the question, the judge or commission should balance the transaction costs of private bargains between ranchers and farmers, and the cost to lawmakers of trying to determine the fencing costs of ranchers and farmers.

QUESTION 4.11:

a. When transaction costs are low enough, efficient resource allocation will follow regardless of the particular assignment of property rights. When transaction costs are high enough, efficient resource allocation requires assigning property rights to the party who values them the most. Give an example of each case.

b. Can you use the Normative Hobbes Theorem to justify legislation regulating the collective bargaining process between employers and employee unions?

c. When people strongly disagree, they may try to harm each other, or they may walk away from a potentially profitable exchange. What does the Normative Hobbes Theorem suggest the response of the law should be to these two possibilities?

V. How Are Property Rights Protected?

Now we have the tools to answer another of the four fundamental questions of property law that we posed at the beginning of this chapter: "What are the remedies for the violation of property rights?" This question concerns how a court should respond when a private person or the government interferes with someone's property rights. Our discussion in this chapter will focus on interference by a private person. We consider government interference in the next chapter.

A. Damages and Injunctions

First, we need some background. The remedies available to a common law court are either *legal* or *equitable*. The principal *legal* remedy is the payment of *compensatory money damages* by the defendant to the plaintiff. These damages are a sum of money that compensates the plaintiff for the wrongs inflicted on her by the defendant. The court determines the appropriate amount of money that will, as the saying goes, "make the plaintiff whole." The measurement of this sum is a complex subject itself, which we discuss later.[16] *Equitable* relief consists of an order by the court directing the defendant to perform an act or to refrain from acting in a particular manner. This order is frequently in the form of an *injunction*, which is said to "enjoin" the defendant to do or to refrain from doing a specific act.[17]

Notice that legal relief is "backward-looking" in the sense that it compensates a plaintiff for a harm already suffered, whereas equitable relief is "forward-looking" in the sense that it prevents a defendant from inflicting a harm on the plaintiff in the future. Thus, a court may combine the two forms of relief, awarding money damages for past harms and enjoining acts that could cause future harm.

Damages are the usual remedy for broken promises and accidents, whereas injunction is the usual remedy for appropriating, trespassing, or interfering with another's property. In other words, damages are the usual remedy in the law of contracts and torts, whereas injunction is the usual remedy in the law of property. For these reasons, damages are often referred to in the legal literature as a "liability rule," while equitable relief is typically called a "property rule." To illustrate, the farmer will have to pay damages to the rancher for breach of a contract to deliver hay or for accidentally shooting the rancher's cow while hunting. But if the cattle trespass on the farmer's crops (and if farmers have a right to be free from the depredations of stray cattle), then the court will probably award damages for past harm and enjoin the rancher to constrain her cattle in the future.

B. Laundry and Electric Company: An Example

An injunction may appear to be an absolute proscription on an act. For example, if the court were to enjoin the future invasion of the farmer's cornfields by the rancher's cattle, one might interpret that as meaning that the rancher will have to erect a fence. This is a mistake. The injunctive remedy does not prevent the invasion of the farmer's property by the rancher's cattle from ever occurring, only from its occurring without the consent of the farmer. The farmer is free to make a contract promising *not* to enforce the

---

[16] There are two more things you should be aware of. First, if a defendant fails to pay a judgment that a court has awarded against him or her, the defendant's property may be seized and sold in order to raise the judgment amount. Second, compensatory damages are to be distinguished from punitive damages, which are money damages over and above compensatory damages assessed against the defendant. The purpose of punitive damages is to punish the defendant, not to compensate the plaintiff. We discuss punitive damages in Chapter 7.

[17] The consequences to a defendant of violating an equitable decree are far more serious than the consequences of failing to pay a monetary judgment. A defendant's failure to abide by an injunction not only leaves the plaintiff at a loss, but it also constitutes an insult to the authority of the court. A defendant who ignores an equitable order may be held in contempt of court and imprisoned until she agrees to abide by the order.

injunction. To illustrate, the farmer might agree not to enforce the injunction in exchange for payment of a sum of money by the rancher.[18]

Given these facts, the right to an injunction should be regarded as a clear assignment of a property right. Once the property right is clearly assigned, its owner may strike a bargain to sell it. Thus, if the court enjoined the rancher from allowing future invasion by her cattle, this could be viewed as a declaration that the farmer has the legally enforceable right to be free from invasion by cattle. If the rancher's value on being allowed to invade the farmer's property is greater than the farmer's value on being free from invasion, there is scope for a bargain in which the rancher buys the right from the farmer.

Most legal disputes are settled by bargaining between the parties without going to trial, but the terms of the bargain are affected by the remedy that would be available at trial.[19] Specifically, the terms of the bargain are different depending on whether the remedy is damages or injunction. An example from Chapter 1 will help you to understand the relationship between remedies and bargains.

> FACTS: The *E* Electric Company emits smoke, which dirties the wash at the *L* Laundry. No one else is affected because *E* and *L* are near each other and far from anyone else. *E* can abate this external cost by installing scrubbers on its stacks, and *L* can reduce the damage by installing filters on its ventilation system. The installation of scrubbers by *E* or filters by *L* completely eliminates the damage from pollution. Table 4.4 shows the profits of each company, depending on what action is taken to reduce the pollution. (The profits that are shown in the matrix exclude any compensation that might be paid or received as a consequence of a legal dispute.)

The numbers in Table 4.4 can be explained as follows. When *E* does not install scrubbers, its profits are $1000 (regardless of what the laundry does). When *L* does not install filters and does not suffer pollution damages (because *E* has installed scrubbers), *L*'s profits are $300. Pollution destroys $200 of *L*'s profits. *L* can avoid this by installing filters at a cost of $100, or *E* can avoid it by installing scrubbers at a cost of $500. Check to see that you can use these facts to explain the numbers in the table.

The most efficient outcome is, by definition, a situation in which the total profits for the two parties, called the "joint profits," are greatest. The joint profits are found by adding the two numbers in each cell of the table. Joint profits are maximized in the northeast cell, where $1200 is attained when *E* does not install scrubbers and *L* installs filters.

The harm caused by pollution represents a source of contention between *E* and *L*. They may be able to settle their disagreement and cooperate with each other, or they may fail to cooperate and litigate their dispute. What we are interested in determining here is how the remedy available from a court may induce the parties to achieve the efficient solution and thus to minimize the harm of pollution.

---

[18] This inducement to bargain may be more theoretical than real. For a discussion of research by Ward Farnsworth about post-injunction bargains, see the material at Web Note 4.2 on our website.

[19] This is referred to as "bargaining in the shadow of the law."

TABLE 4.4
Profits Before Legal Action[‡]

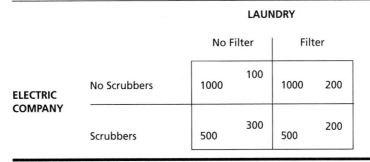

		LAUNDRY	
		No Filter	Filter
ELECTRIC COMPANY	No Scrubbers	1000 100	1000 200
	Scrubbers	500 300	500 200

[‡]The electric company's profits are given first in the lower-left corner of each cell; the laundry's profits are given in the upper-right corner of each cell.

Suppose that E and L litigate their disagreement. Three alternative rules of law could be applied in the event of a trial:

1. *Polluter's Right:* E is free to pollute.
2. *Pollutee's Right to Damages:* L is entitled to compensatory damages from E. (Compensatory damages are a sum of money that E pays to L to make up for L's reduced profits due to E's pollution.)
3. *Pollutee's Right to Injunction:* L is entitled to an injunction forbidding E to pollute. (An injunction is a court order requiring E to stop polluting.)

Let us determine the value of the noncooperative solution under each of these rules as depicted in Table 4.5.

Beginning with rule 1, if E is free to pollute, the most profitable action for E is not to install scrubbers and to enjoy profits of $1000. The most profitable response for L is to install filters and enjoy profits of $200. Thus, the noncooperative value of the rule of free pollution is $1200. This is the efficient solution, which is in the northeast cell of the table.

TABLE 4.5
Profits from Bargaining Under Three Legal Rules

	Noncooperation		Surplus	Cooperation	
	E	L		E	L
Rule 1 *Polluter's Right*	1000	200	0	1000	200
Rule 2 *Damages*	800	300	100	850	350
Rule 3 *Injunction*	500	300	400	700	500

Turning to rule 2, assume that E must pay damages to L and also assume that L has no legal duty to install filters (no duty to "mitigate"). If E must pay damages to L for polluting, then L will not bother to install filters. E will have to pay damages to L equal to the difference between the profits L enjoys when there is no pollution, $300, and the profits L enjoys with pollution, $100. E has a choice between installing the scrubbers and paying damages of $200 to L. The more profitable alternative is for E *not* to install the scrubbers: It initially realizes $1000 in profits, from which $200 must be subtracted to pay damages, leaving E with net profits of $800. L enjoys net profits of $300 ($100 from its operations plus $200 from E). The noncooperative value under rule 2 (a rule of liability for compensatory damages) is then $1100 = $300 + $800. This is the value in the northwest cell in the table.

Turning to rule 3, if E is enjoined from polluting and responds by installing scrubbers, E's profits equal $500. When E installs scrubbers, L will not bother to install filters, so L's profits will be $300. Thus, the noncooperative value under the rule of enjoining pollution is $800 = $500 + $300, which corresponds to the southwest cell of the table.

Under the pessimistic assumption that E and L cannot cooperate, only one of the legal rules produces an efficient outcome—namely, rule 1. Instead of making the pessimistic assumption that the parties will be unable to cooperate, suppose we make the optimistic assumption that the parties can settle their disagreement cooperatively. (We are assuming that transaction costs are very low.) When E and L cooperate, their best strategy is to maximize the joint profits of the two enterprises. The profits are maximized when they take the efficient course of action, which, in this case, is for L to install filters and E not to install scrubbers, yielding joint profits of $1200. This is the efficient solution in the northeast cell.

There are, thus, two ways to achieve the efficient solution. One way is for the law to adopt the rule for which the noncooperative solution is efficient. This solution is commended by the Normative Hobbes Theorem. In our example (but not necessarily other pollution examples), the noncooperative solution is efficient under rule 1, which gives E the freedom to pollute. The other way to achieve efficiency is for the parties to cooperate. The cooperative solution is efficient under all three of the possible laws. According to the Coase Theorem, inefficient allocations of legal rights by laws such as rules 2 and 3 will be cured by private agreements, provided that bargaining is successful.

If transaction costs equal zero and successful bargaining can cure inefficient laws, what difference does the law make? One answer is that the law affects the distribution of the cooperative product, which affects bargaining. To illustrate this point about distribution, recall how the structure of the law—such as rules 1, 2, and 3—affects the threat values of the parties. A reasonable bargaining solution is for each party to receive his or her threat value plus an equal share of the cooperative surplus. Each party to a bargain would prefer the rule of law that provides him or her with the largest threat value. Specifically, the threat value of the plaintiff in a property dispute is at least as great when the remedy for future harm is injunctive relief as when the remedy is damages. The plaintiff, consequently, prefers the remedy of injunctive relief for future harm, or, better yet, injunctive relief for future harm and damages for past harm.

In contrast, the defendant prefers the damage remedy for future harm or, better yet, no remedy.

The effect of the rule of law on the distribution of the cooperative product can be computed precisely for E and L. Imagine that E and L enter into negotiations, and, to keep the arithmetic simple, assume that negotiating a settlement or going to trial is costless for the parties (swallow hard!). The noncooperative payoffs—that is, the profits the parties can get on their own if negotiations fail—are shown in Table 4.5 under each of the three rules. The cooperative surplus, which equals the difference between the joint profits from cooperation and the threat values, is shown in the middle column. A reasonable bargaining solution is for each party to receive his or her threat value plus half the surplus from cooperation. The payoffs to the two parties from cooperation are given in the two columns on the right side of the table. Notice that in each case the cooperative payoffs sum $1200, but that L receives the largest share under the injunctive rule (rule 3), an intermediate share under damages (rule 2), and the smallest share when E is free to pollute (rule 1).

> **QUESTION 4.12:** In the preceding example, implementing an injunction to end future interference costs the defendant more than damages for future interference. Is this fact generally true or just a special feature of this example?

C. Efficient Remedies

We mentioned that injunction is the usual remedy for breach of a property right. We would like to explain this generalization, as well as exceptions to it, in terms of efficiency. The preceding example showed that damages and injunctions are equally efficient remedies when transaction costs equal zero. Consequently, differences in efficiency must depend on transaction costs. If transaction costs are so high as to preclude bargaining, then the more efficient remedy is damages, not injunctions.

The reason that damages are more efficient than injunctions when transaction costs preclude bargaining is easy to see from the example of the laundry and electric company. If damages perfectly compensate the laundry, its profits remain the same (specifically, $300) regardless of whether the electric company pollutes. So, the laundry is indifferent between the damage and injunction remedies (assuming no bargaining). Under the damage remedy, the electric company can pollute and pay damages, or it can abate and not pay damages. Its profits increase from $500 to $800 when it pollutes and pays damages, rather than abating. In contrast, an injunction (with no bargaining) removes this choice. Specifically, the injunction forces the electric company to abate, in which case its profits are $500. In general, when transaction costs preclude bargaining, a switch in remedy from injunction to compensatory damages makes the victim no worse off, whereas the injurer may be better off and cannot be worse off. In the example of the laundry and electric company, a switch makes the electric company strictly better off. According to Table 4.5, the noncooperative solution yields $800 to the electric company under a damage remedy and $500 under an injunction, whereas the laundry enjoys $300 in either case.

We have explained the superiority of the damages remedy when transaction costs are high. What about the converse proposition? Are injunctions the superior remedy when transaction costs are low? The traditional answer, which we will explain, is "Yes." Earlier we noted that bargaining tends to succeed when the legal rights of the parties are clear and simple. Injunction is traditionally regarded as clearer and simpler than damages, because the determination of damages by courts can be unpredictable. To illustrate, it is difficult for a court to assign monetary value to the damage caused by the Windsong satellite's straying into the orbit of Orbitcom's satellite in Example 2. Similarly, it is difficult for a court to assign monetary value to the damage caused by the intrusion of Potatoes's house onto 2 feet of Parsley's land in Example 5. In contrast, the right to an injunction gives the parties a clear position from which to bargain. In the course of bargaining, they may establish the value of the damage themselves. Thus, the traditional argument concludes that the injunctive remedy is more efficient than damages when the parties can bargain with each other.

We have reached the conclusion of a famous article by Judge (then Professor) Guido Calabresi and A. Douglas Melamed,[20] who proposed the following rules for determining the best remedy for violating a legal right:

> Where there are few obstacles to cooperation (that is, low transaction costs), the more efficient remedy is to enjoin the defendant's interference with the plaintiff's property.

> Where there are obstacles to cooperation (that is, high transaction costs), the more efficient remedy is to award compensatory money damages.

Most property disputes involve small numbers of contiguous landowners. Communication costs are low; the parties can monitor conformity to their agreements; and neighbors take a long-run view towards each other, which limits opportunism and strategic behavior. Bargaining is likely to be successful in these circumstances. According to the preceding prescription, the usual remedy in property disputes ought to be injunctive relief, and that is the law in fact.

Some property disputes, however, involve large numbers of people. As the numbers increase, communication costs rise, monitoring becomes difficult, and short-sighted behavior increases. Private bargaining is unlikely to succeed in disputes involving a large number of geographically dispersed strangers, such as disputes over nuisances like air pollution and the stench from the feedlot in Example 3. According to the preceding prescription, the usual remedy in nuisance suits with large numbers of people should be damages. Chapter 5 explains that some courts have followed this principle and others have not.

The two preceding rules constitute the "traditional prescription" in law and economics to choose between damages and injunctive remedies. In most circumstances, the traditional prescription suffices, but more careful thinking about information has refined it. When a person's activity spills over and affects other property owners, the

---

[20] Calabresi & Melamed, *Property Rules, Liability Rules, and Inalienability: One View of the Cathedral*, 85 HARV. L. REV. 1089 (1972). As the title indicates, the authors consider a third method of encouraging the efficient use of property—inalienability, the forbidding of a bargaining solution to the use of a property right. We discuss the efficiency of that method briefly in the next chapter.

court needs different information depending on whether its remedy is damages or injunction. When transaction costs obstruct bargaining, creating efficient incentives by awarding damages requires the court to measure the harm correctly. If the court mismeasures the harm, damages will be set too high or too low, which will distort the injurer's incentives. Chapter 6 explains this point in detail.

Alternatively, when transaction costs obstruct bargaining, creating efficient incentives requires the court to know which party values the right the most in order to decide between an injunction and no injunction.[21] If the electric company values the right to pollute more than the laundry values the right to be free from pollution, then the court should allow the electric company to pollute and refuse the laundry's request for an injunction. Conversely, if the laundry values the right to be free from pollution more than the electric company values the right to pollute, then the court should grant the laundry's request for an injunction against the electric company's pollution.

In sum, when transaction costs obstruct bargaining, what the court should do depends on what it knows. The court must know the absolute value of the harm caused by a spillover in order to provide efficient incentives by a damage remedy. The court needs to know the relative value of the spillover in order to achieve efficiency by the injunctive remedy. Now we can restate the first prescription's refinement:

> When transaction costs preclude bargaining, the court should protect a right by an injunctive remedy if it knows which party values the right relatively more (even if it does not know how much either party values the right absolutely). Conversely, the court should protect a right by a damage remedy if it knows how much one of the parties values the right absolutely (even if it does not know which party values the right relatively more).

The second prescription—award an injunction when low transaction costs permit bargaining—also requires qualification in light of problems of information. This prescription assumes that voluntary exchange of a right occurs more easily when it is protected by an injunction, because the injunctions are simpler and clearer than damages. While this is usually true, it is not always so. In bargaining, what matters is costs, not physics. No matter how clear the injunction, the cost of complying with it may be unclear. To lubricate bargaining, each party needs to know the other's threat value or go-it-alone value. Injunctions do not solve the problem that private information about costs and values inhibits bargaining. To illustrate, the injunction for the electric company to stop polluting is clear, but the cost to the electric company of complying, which may or may not be clear to the electric company, is unclear to the laundry.

The truth is more equivocal than the traditional analysis suggests. With the injunctive remedy, the obstacle to private agreement includes the plaintiff's uncertainty about

---

[21] The court knows the relative values of the entitlement if the unobservable elements of individual valuations correlates positively with the observable elements. See Louis Kaplow & Steven Shavell, *Property Rules Versus Liability Rules: An Economic Analysis*, 109 HARV. L. REV. 715 (1996). But see Ian Ayres & Paul Goldbart, *Correlated Values in the Theory of Property and Liability Rules*, 32 J. LEGAL STUD. 121 (2003) (rejecting the correlated values claim—that "liability rules cannot harness private information when the disputants' values are correlated").

the defendant's costs of complying with a court order. Conversely, with the damage remedy, the obstacle to private agreement includes the defendant's uncertainty about the money value of the plaintiff's harm.[22]

QUESTION 4.13: Use the theory of transaction costs to justify protecting the following rights by injunction or damages:

a. A landowner's right to exclude from his property a neighbor's gas line.
b. A new car owner's right to have her car's defective transmission replaced by the seller.
c. A homeowner's right to be free from air pollution by a nearby factory.
d. A spouse's right to half the house on divorce.

QUESTION 4.14: Suppose that two people choose to litigate a dispute. Should the law presume that if two parties are prepared to litigate, transaction costs must be high, and therefore the court should choose damages as the remedy, not an injunction?

ⓘ Web Note 4.2

There has been a surprising amount of recent scholarship on the Calabresi-Melamed contention about the efficiency of remedies. We discuss much of that literature on our website, including looking at the empirical literature on whether the issuing of injunctions is typically followed by bargaining.

VI.   What Can Be Privately Owned?—Public and Private Goods[23]

In this section we turn to another fundamental question of property law: should property rights be privately or collectively held? First, we use the economic distinction between public and private goods (developed in Chapter 2) to differentiate those resources that will be most efficiently used if privately owned from those that will be most efficiently used if publicly owned.

Most examples of property that we have discussed thus far in this book are what economists call "private goods." Goods that economists describe as purely private have the characteristic that one person's use precludes another's: For example, when one person eats an apple, others cannot eat it; a pair of pants can be worn only by one person at

---

[22] Taking these arguments into account leads to a more convincing version of the second rule:
Where there are few obstacles to cooperation (i.e., low transaction costs), the more efficient remedy is the award of an injunction when the plaintiff can estimate the defendant's compliance costs more readily than the defendant can estimate the plaintiff's damages.

[23] Before reading this section, you may find it helpful to review the material on public goods in Chapter 2.

a time; a car cannot go two different directions simultaneously; and so forth. These facts are sometimes summarized by saying that there is rivalry in the consumption of private goods.

The polar opposite is a purely public good, for which there is no rivalry in consumption. A conventional example of a public good is military security in the nuclear age. Supplying one citizen with protection from nuclear attack does not diminish the amount of protection supplied to other citizens.

There is also another attribute that distinguishes private and public goods. Once property rights are defined over private goods, they are (relatively) cheap to enforce. Specifically, the owner can exclude others from using them at low cost. For example, a farm can be fenced at relatively low cost to exclude trespassing cattle. With public goods, however, it is costly to exclude anyone from enjoying them. To illustrate, it is virtually impossible to supply different amounts of protection against nuclear attack to different citizens.

Having explained the private-public distinction in economics and law, we can now relate them to each other. The relationship is very simple: Efficiency requires that private goods should be privately owned and that public goods should be publicly owned. In other words, efficiency requires that rivalrous and excludable goods should be controlled by individuals or small groups of people, whereas nonrivalrous and nonexcludable goods should be controlled by a large group of people such as the state. Thus, the distinction between private and public goods should guide the development of property rules to answer the question, "What can be privately owned?"

We can explain the central idea, not the details, for this prescription. Being rivalrous, private goods must be used and consumed by individuals, not enjoyed equally by everyone. Efficiency requires the use and consumption of each private good by the party who values it the most. In a free market, exchanges occur until each good is held by the party who values it the most. Thus, the law can achieve the efficient allocation of private goods by, for example, lowering bargaining costs by assigning clear and simple ownership rights. Once the state recognizes private property rights, the owner of a private good can exclude others from using or consuming that right, except by the owner's consent. The owner's power to exclude channels the use or consumption of private goods into voluntary exchange, which fosters the efficient use of those goods. This is an example of "lubricating bargaining."

In contrast, the technical character of public goods obstructs the use of bargaining to achieve efficiency. To illustrate, suppose that a particular city block is plagued by crime and some residents propose hiring a private guard. Many residents will voluntarily contribute to the guard's salary, but suppose that some refuse. The paying residents may instruct the guard not to aid nonpayers in the event of a mugging. Even so, the presence of the guard on the street will make it safer for everyone, because muggers are unlikely to know who has and who has not paid for the guard's services. Given these facts, there is not much that the payers can do to compel nonpayers to contribute.

Those people who do not pay for their consumption of a public good are called "free riders." To appreciate this concept, imagine that a street car has an electric meter in it and, in order to make the street car move, the riders must put money into the meter.

The riders will realize that anyone who pays provides a free ride for everyone else. Perhaps some riders will, nonetheless, put their full fare into the meter; some will put some money in but not their full fare; and some will not put anything in at all. Because of "free riders," not enough money will be put in the meter, so the street car company will provide fewer street cars than efficiency requires. In general, markets supply too little of a public good because the private supplier cannot exclude users of it who do not pay their share of the costs.

We have explained that private goods, which exhibit rivalry and exclusion, ought to be privately owned, and that public goods, which exhibit nonrivalry and nonexclusion, ought to be publicly owned. We illustrate this proposition as applied to land. Some efficient uses of land involve a small area and affect a small group of people, such as building a house or growing corn. "Housing" and "corn" are rivalrous goods with low exclusion costs, so markets easily form for housing and corn. Other efficient uses of land involve a large area and affect a large group of people. For example, the use of an uncongested airspace by airplanes or the use of the high seas for shipping are not rivalrous and exclusion is costly. Thus, airspace and the high seas are public goods. As congestion increases from more planes and ships, governments impose rules on the use of the air and seas.

These are examples in which private goods are privately owned and public goods are publicly owned, as required for efficiency. There are, however, many examples of private goods that are publicly owned. Public ownership of a private good typically results in its misallocation, by which we mean that it is used or consumed by someone other than the person who values it the most. For example, leases for grazing cattle on public lands may be granted to the friends of politicians. Similarly, the officials who administer the leases may not monitor compliance to prevent overgrazing, and the ranchers who overgraze the land may cause it to erode. Much of the impetus for "deregulation," which was a worldwide movement in the 1990s, came from the realization that much government activity concerns private goods where markets should be lubricated, rather than government intruding directly in the process of allocation. For example, the realization that transportation by railroad, airplane, and barge are private services that should be supplied by free markets has led to the dismantling of the Interstate Commerce Commission, the Civil Aeronautics Board, and other regulatory agencies in the United States.

One way to contrast private and public ownership is in terms of transaction costs. Private ownership imposes various transaction costs of private enforcement and exchange. Public ownership imposes transaction costs in terms of public administration and collective decision making. To illustrate the difference, consider two possible ways to control air pollution from a factory. The private property approach is to grant each property owner the right to clean air, protected by the remedy of compensatory damages. This method will result in many landowners suing for damages or bargaining to settle out of court. Alternatively, the public property approach would declare that clean air is a public good, and assign the task of air quality control to a government agency. This method will result in political bargaining and regulations. From this perspective, the choice between private and public ownership should depend on whether the costs of private enforcement and exchange are more or less than the costs of public administration and political bargaining.

In the next chapter we will continue developing these themes by discussing two important questions: For what specific resources is private ownership more efficient than public or communal ownership and vice versa? And under what circumstances should government be allowed to take private property from citizens?[24]

QUESTION 4.15: If everyone has free access to a public beach, who, if anyone, has the power to control the use of this resource?

QUESTION 4.16: Discuss how to adjust private and public property rights to promote ecotourism in Africa.

VII. What May Owners Do with Their Property?

We used the theory of private and public goods to answer the question, "What can be privately owned?" Closely related to the theory of public goods is the theory of externalities, which we discussed in Chapter 2. Now we return to that theory in order to answer the question, "What may owners do with their property?"

Legislation imposes many restrictions on what a person may do with his or her property. But at common law there are relatively few restrictions, with the general rule being that any use is allowed that does not interfere with other peoples' property or other rights. Indeed, we could say that common law approximates a legal system of *maximum liberty*, which allows owners to do anything with their property that does not interfere with other people's property or other rights. The restriction of noninterference finds justification in the economic concept of *external cost*. Recall that external costs are those costs involuntarily imposed on one person by another. Because market transactions are voluntary, externalities are outside the market system of exchange—hence their name. For example, a factory that emits thick, cloying smoke into a residential neighborhood is generating an externality. In Example 3 at the beginning of this chapter, the stench from the cattle feedlot is an externality that interferes with Foster's enjoyment of her house. In Example 4, the development of Bloggs's wetlands will interfere with the town's enjoyment of its rivers and streams. Notice that these types of interference are like a public good in that they affect many property owners. There is, as it were, no rivalry or exclusion from smelling the feedlot's stench among Foster and her neighbors. These forms of interference are thus like a public good, except they are bad rather than good.

---

[24] We are not, of course, suggesting that the current division of responsibility between public and private providers of goods and services necessarily follows the rules we have just set down. That is, there are current instances of the government provision or subsidization of private goods and of the private (under-) provision of public goods. The extent to which these anomalies exist and why they persist are two of the central concerns of the branch of microeconomic theory called "public choice theory."

We have already explained why markets cannot arise to supply public goods efficiently. The same set of considerations explains why private bargaining cannot solve the problem of externalities, or, as we called them in a previous section, public bads. To illustrate, suppose that Foster had enough money to pay the feedlot to stop emitting its stench. If she made this private deal with the feedlot, all of her neighbors would also benefit but without having to pay for that benefit. This fact suggests that Foster will not pay the feedlot to stop its malodorous activities. More generally, the free-rider problem prevents private bargaining solutions to the problem of externalities or public bads. Some form of legal intervention is called for. One possibility is a rule forbidding involuntary invasion, supported by provisions for remedies if that invasion takes place. We have already noted how bargaining theory can help to design the form that remedy should take, namely, the payment of compensatory money damages. An alternative remedy that we will consider in the following chapter is regulation of the public bad or external-cost-generating activity by an administrative agency.

By contrast, *private* bads may be self-correcting through private agreements (recall the rancher-farmer example), so that there may be no need for an intrusive legal solution. Instead, the courts can stand prepared to issue an injunction in the confident expectation that they will seldom be required to do so.

VIII. On Distribution

We have developed an economic theory of property based on efficient ownership. However, some critics of economics believe that property law should be based on distribution, not efficiency.

Some people think that government should redistribute wealth from rich to poor for the sake of social justice, whereas other people think that government should avoid redistributing wealth, allowing individuals to receive all the rewards of their hard work, inventiveness, risk-taking, and astute choice of parents. Like the rest of the population, economists disagree among themselves about redistributive *ends*. However, economists often agree about redistributive *means*.

Given the end of redistribution, economists generally prefer to pursue it by the most efficient means. For each dollar of value transferred from one group to another, a fraction of a dollar is typically used up, as, for example, in administrative costs. The most efficient means of redistribution uses up the least value to accomplish the transfer. Chapter 1 illustrated this fact by the example of ice cream melting during its transfer across the desert from one oasis to another. Another example is the percentage of donations that a charity spends on administrative costs. Many economists believe that redistributive goals can be accomplished more efficiently in modern states by progressive taxation than by reshuffling property rights. Besides avoiding waste, more efficient redistribution generates more support from the people who must pay for it. If the economists are right, redistribution for social justice should focus mostly on taxation and expenditure, not property rights.

Progressive taxation and expenditure is usually more efficient than reshuffling property rights to achieve redistribution for a variety of reasons. The most wasteful way to redistribute wealth is for courts to tilt trials in favor of the plaintiff or defendant depending on who is poorer. If courts favor the poorer party in legal disputes, each person prefers to avoid interacting with relatively poorer people whenever a lawsuit could arise. Thus, a person would want to avoid owning real estate in a neighborhood occupied by people who are poorer than he is. Similarly, favoring the poorer party in a contract dispute makes a person reluctant to do business with anyone who is poorer than he is.

Several other reasons also make taxation superior to property law as a means of redistribution. First, the income tax precisely targets inequality, whereas property law relies on crude averages. To illustrate, suppose that the rule of law in a particular county in Montana is "ranchers' rights." If ranchers are richer than farmers on average in this county, then changing the rule to "farmers' rights" would redistribute wealth toward greater equality. However, although ranchers are richer than farmers *on average*, some farmers are undoubtedly richer than some ranchers. Changing the property rights to favor farmers over ranchers will aggravate the inequality between the rich farmers and poor ranchers. In contrast, progressive taxation will ameliorate unequal incomes.

A second objection is that reshuffling property rights may not really have the distributive effects anticipated. To illustrate, suppose that both farmers and ranchers rent their land from absentee owners. If property law shifts the cost of fencing from farmers to ranchers, competition among landlords may cause them to adjust rents to offset the change in costs. Specifically, the landlords who own farm land may increase the rent charged to farmers, and the landlords who own ranch land may decrease the rent charged to ranchers. Consequently, the reshuffling of property rights may not affect the distribution of wealth between farmers and ranchers. Instead, the landlords who own farms may gain and the landlords who own ranches may lose. In general, any change in the value of land gets "capitalized" into rent. Consequently, the wealth effects of reshuffling property rights in a world with zero transaction costs tend to fall on the owners of land, not its users.[25]

In addition, there is another reason for the relative inefficiency of redistribution by property law. Redistribution by property law distorts the economy more in the long run than does progressive taxation. For example, if property law favors farmers over ranchers, some rich ranchers may switch to farming to gain valuable legal rights. In contrast, a comprehensive income tax precludes people from reducing their tax liability by changing the source of their income.[26] For these reasons and more, economists who favor redistribution and economists who oppose it can agree that property law is usually

---

[25] Professor Coase made this argument in "Notes on the Problem of Social Cost" in THE FIRM, THE MARKET, AND THE LAW (1988). In general, taxes and other government impositions finally fall on factors in relatively fixed supply, such as land.

[26] A fundamental principle in public finance is that taxes distort less when applied to a broad base rather than to a narrow base. Distortion decreases with the breadth of the base because demand becomes less elastic. To illustrate, the demand for food is less elastic than the demand for vegetables, and the demand for vegetables is less elastic than the demand for carrots. Income is a very broad base.

the wrong way to pursue distributive justice. Unfortunately, these facts are not appreciated by many lawyers who have not studied economics.[27]

We have presented several reasons against basing property law on redistributive goals. Specifically, we discussed imprecise targeting, unpredictable consequences, high transaction costs, and large distortions in incentives. While the general principles of property law cannot rest on wealth redistribution, special kinds of redistributive laws can ameliorate these objections and blunt this criticism. An example is laws requiring employers to construct buildings that provide access to people in wheelchairs. If properly designed, these laws can precisely target handicapped people in a predictable way, enforcement by private legal action can be inexpensive, and the distortion in incentives can be modest. Designing such laws to produce these desirable outcomes, however, requires more careful attention to the underlying economics than regulators typically show.

Conclusion

Property is a bundle of rights with incentive effects. Efficient property rights create incentives to maximize a nation's wealth in two different ways. First, property rights are the legal basis of voluntary exchange, which achieves *allocative efficiency* by moving goods from people who value them less to people who value them more. Second, property rights are part of the law that makes owners internalize the social costs and benefits of alternative uses of the goods that they own. Owners achieve *productive efficiency* by balancing the social costs and benefits of what they do with what they own.

Suggested Readings

Bell, Abraham, & Gideon Parchomovsky, *A Theory of Property*, 90 CORNELL L. REV. 531 (2005).

Calabresi, Guido, *The Pointlessness of Pareto: Carrying Coase Further*, 100 YALE L. J. 1043 (1991).

Cooter, Robert, *The Cost of Coase*, 11 J. LEGAL STUD. 1 (1982).

Ellickson, Robert D., *Property in Land*, 102 YALE L.J. 1315 (1993).

ELLICKSON, ROBERT, ORDER WITHOUT LAW: HOW NEIGHBORS SETTLE DISPUTES (1991).

Lueck, Dean, & Thomas Miceli, *Property*, in A. MITCHELL POLINSKY & STEVEN SHAVELL, EDS., HANDBOOK OF LAW AND ECONOMICS, vol. 1 (2007).

Merrill, Thomas W., & Henry E. Smith, *Optimal Standardization in the Law of Property: The Numerus Clausus Principle*, 110 YALE L.J. 1 (2000).

Merrill, Thomas W., & Henry E. Smith, *What Happened to Property in Law and Economics?*, 111 YALE L.J. 357 (2001).

Polinsky, A. Mitchell, *Resolving Nuisance Disputes: The Simple Economics of Injunctive and Damage Remedies*, 32 STAN. L. REV. 1075 (1980).

---

[27] An important technical conclusion in formal welfare economics (the Second Fundamental Theorem of Welfare Economics) reinforces the general point made in the text—namely, that efficiency and equity are separable. With specific reference to property law, that conclusion can be read to say that property law should seek to allocate and enforce entitlements so that a society uses resources efficiently and should then use the tax-and-transfer system to achieve distributive equity. See, for example, Steven Shavell, *A Note on Efficiency v. Distributional Equity in Legal Rulemaking: Should Distributional Equity Matter Given Optimal Income Taxation?*, 71 AM. ECON. REV. 414 (1981), and Louis Kaplow & Steven Shavell, *Why the Legal System Is Less Efficient Than the Income Tax in Redistributing Income,* 23 J. LEGAL STUD. 667 (1994).

The Philosophical Concept of Property

PHILOSOPHERS GENERALLY PERCEIVE property to be an instrument for pursuing fundamental values. Some philosophers of property have concentrated on its ability to advance values such as utility, justice, self-expression, and social evolution. These traditions of thought have influenced the law. This appendix introduces the reader to four of these traditions and relates them to the economic analysis of property.

1. Utilitarianism

Utilitarians measure the value of a good or an act by the net pleasure or satisfaction that it creates. For utilitarians, the purpose of the institution of property is to maximize the total pleasure or satisfaction obtained from material and other resources. Bentham thus defines property as an expectation of utility: "Property is nothing but a basis of expectation; the expectation of deriving advantages from a thing, which we are said to possess, in consequence of the relation in which we stand toward it."[28] The objective of maximizing total utility constitutes a standard against which property rules can be evaluated. In our examples at the beginning of the chapter, each of the disputes could be resolved on utilitarian grounds by establishing a legal rule that seeks to maximize the sum of utilities or pleasure of society as a whole.

The utilitarian approach makes a person's claim to property tentative. It can be taken from him in principle if the beneficiaries of the expropriation gain more in utility than the owner loses. Suppose, for example, that a young son is living with his aged parents in their home. On utilitarian grounds, the young son may be excused for throwing the parents out of the home if their loss in utility from being dispossessed is less than his gain in utility from having them out of the house. Critics of utilitarianism have often wondered whether the theory makes ownership too tentative. Isn't ownership more than an expectation? Do we really think that a person could be rightfully deprived of his property just because the loss is more than offset by the gain to others?

This objection to the utilitarian theory of property applies with equal force to the conventional economic theory that holds that the purpose of property is to maximize wealth. Isn't ownership more than a right to a stream of income? Do we really think

---

[28] JEREMY BENTHAM, THEORY OF LEGISLATION: PRINCIPLES OF THE CODE 111–113 (Hildreth ed. 1931).

that a person could be rightfully deprived of her property just because the loss of wealth is more than offset by the gain in wealth to others?

2. Distributive Justice

Another philosophical approach to property law emphasizes property law's ability to achieve distributive justice, rather than pleasure or satisfaction. Aristotle, for example, held that a conception of distributive justice is implicit in various forms of social organization. For Aristotle, the principle of justice is different for different societies, but it is appropriate for each type of society to promote its own conception of distributive justice through its constitution and laws, including its notion of property rights. He argued that a democracy will favor an equal distribution of wealth, whereas an aristocracy (the form preferred by Aristotle) will favor the distribution of wealth according to the virtues of various classes. In Aristotle's conception, it is just that aristocrats receive an unequal share of wealth because they use it for more worthy ends than do others.

From the Aristotelian conception of democratic equality we might infer a policy of redistributive justice whereby the valuable assets of society are periodically redistributed so as to achieve a roughly equal distribution of that property. In general, this sort of redistribution would favor the poor and penalize the wealthy. On the other hand, from the Aristotelian justification of aristocratic inequality we might infer the polar-opposite policy of redistributive justice whereby the assets of society would be periodically redistributed to the aristocrats. To the extent that the aristocracy and the wealthy are the same group, this redistribution of property would favor the rich and penalize the poor. In either case, these notions of distributive justice make property claims as tentative as they were under utilitarianism and, therefore, open to the same criticisms.

There is another school of philosophical thought relating to distributive justice and property that emphasizes a just *process* for defining and enforcing property rights rather than a just *outcome* or end result in the distribution of wealth from property.[29] According to one version of this theory, any distribution of wealth is just provided that it starts from a just initial distribution of resources and achieves the final distribution by voluntary exchange. In practice, this means that the process of voluntary market exchange is just and that ownership claims are most justly established and enforced in an unfettered market in which there is free and perfect competition. In Nozick's memorable rephrasing of Marx, "From each as he chooses; to each as he is chosen." Whatever distribution of wealth results from this just process is also just. Thus, according to this theory, redistributing property to dilute the effects of competition is unjust.

Several criticisms have been made of this notion of distributive justice. The most telling criticism is that the competitive process can lead to a multitude of distributive outcomes, from one in which each individual has an equal share to one in which one individual has 99 percent of the property and everyone else divides up the remaining 1 percent. All of the outcomes are efficient. But clearly not all of them are equitable or just. The notion of the competitive process as distributive justice is not a sufficient

---

[29] The most forceful modern statement of this view is in R. Nozick, Anarchy, State, and Utopia (1974).

guide to designing rules of property law. At a minimum, there must be an additional, independent standard by which to appraise various initial endowments of property.

3. Liberty and Self-Expression

Besides utility and distributive justice, another value that may underlie property law is liberty. Private property is a precondition for markets, and markets are a decentralized mechanism for allocating resources. Most markets can, and do, operate without extensive government interference or supervision. The practical alternative to markets in the modern economy is some form of government planning. Government planning involves centralizing power over economic matters in the hands of state officials. Control over economic life provides officials with leverage that can be used to control other aspects of life, whereas private property creates a zone of discretion within which individuals are not accountable to government officials. Private property has thus been viewed by some philosophers as a bulwark against the dictatorial authority of governments.[30] It has been argued, for example, that capitalism was deliberately invented to thwart absolutism by depriving the king of economic power. The U.S. Constitution was probably drafted with this idea in mind.

Another connection between property and liberty focuses on individual self-expression. Hegel stressed the idea that people, through their works, transform nature into an expression of personality, and, by doing so, perfect the natural world. A painter takes materials in no particular order and rearranges them into a work of art. By investing personality in work, the artist transforms natural objects and makes them the artist's own. It is difficult to imagine a system of property law that did not recognize this fact. Thus, to encourage self-expression, the state needs to recognize the creators' rights of ownership over their creations. Notice that this proposition extends beyond art to most of the works of humans.

4. Conservatism and the Origins of Property

The philosophical theories discussed so far tend to regard the institution of property as serving ultimate values, such as utility, distributive justice, or liberty. Another philosophical tradition focuses not on the purposes of property but on its origins. To illustrate, in medieval times there were many encumbrances and restrictions on the use and sale of real estate. The common law of private property emerged from feudalism and acquired its modern character by chipping away at these encumbrances on the marketability of real property. Political conservatives like Burke and Hayek idealize forms of social order that, like the common law of property, evolve over time in much the same manner as the myriad species of life. Like organisms, social forms are, in this view, subject to the rules of natural selection. The conservative philosophers condemn institutions imposed on us by planners, engineers, politicians, and other societal decision makers for much the same reasons that environmentalists condemn actions that interfere with an area's environment.

---

[30] This is a theme in THE FEDERALIST PAPERS (1786) and in the work of Friedrich Hayek (see, for example, The CONSTITUTION OF LIBERTY (1972)).

5

Topics in the Economics of Property Law

I N THE PRECEDING chapter, we developed an economic theory of property rights and remedies. We saw that property law creates a bundle of rights that the owners of property are free to exercise as they see fit, without interference by the state or private persons. Consistent with this freedom is a system of allocation by voluntary exchange. Property law fosters voluntary exchange by removing the obstacles to bargaining. When the obstacles to bargaining are low, resources will be allocated efficiently. We used this framework and economic theory to answer the following four questions that must be addressed by a theory of property law:

1. What can be privately owned?
2. How are ownership rights established?
3. What may owners do with their property?
4. What are the remedies for the violation of property rights?

To answer the first question, we distinguished between private and public goods, and we claimed that the former should be privately owned. Private ownership is appropriate when there is rivalry and exclusion in the use of goods. To answer the second question, we presented a thought experiment to illustrate how property law encourages production, discourages theft, and reduces the cost of protecting goods. According to this thought experiment, people agree to establish property rights to share the benefits from increased productivity. We answered the third question by developing the theory of externalities, especially the connection between public bads in economics and nuisances in law. We noted that common law approximates a system of maximum liberty, which allows any use of property by its owner that does not interfere with other people's property or protected rights. In answering the fourth question, we used bargaining theory to conclude that the injunctive remedy is preferred for private bads with low transaction costs for private bargaining. Conversely, the damage remedy is preferred for public bads with high transaction costs that preclude private bargaining.

These answers given in the previous chapter are very general. In this chapter, we reexamine these questions in detail, with concrete applications. The topics are organized roughly according to the four fundamental questions of property law.

I. What Can Be Privately Owned?

The economic distinction between public and private goods characterizes two ideal types. Although reality is never ideal, understanding these ideal types increases your understanding of laws governing real goods. In this section we discuss the application of property law to information, which has some features of a public good. Four principal areas of law create property in information and are called "intellectual property law." The *patent system* establishes ownership rights to inventions, processes, and other technical improvements. The *copyright system* grants ownership rights to authors, artists, and composers. The *trademark system* establishes ownership for distinctive commercial marks or symbols that uniquely identify an individual's or organization's output. The area of law known as *trade secrets* deals with business practices in which commercial enterprises have a property interest. (We discuss trade secrets briefly below and more extensively on our website.) After discussing the economics of information, we will turn to its application to the law of patents, copyright, and trademark. Then we will turn to a new section on the ownership of organizations, specifically corporations.

A. Information Economics

Five thousand years ago people slept under grass roofs, covered themselves with skins, and fastened sharp stones on sticks to throw at animals. An American Indian friend of Professor Cooter said, "My father lived in the stone age, I grew up in the iron age, and I'm dying in the computer age." The technical innovations that drove these changes have accelerated. Since the industrial revolution, innovation has caused wealth to grow at compound rates. Compounded over a century, a 2 percent annual growth rate increases wealth more than six times; a 5 percent annual growth rate increases wealth more than 130 times; and a 10 percent annual growth rate increases wealth almost 14,000 times.

This section concerns some laws that promote innovation and cause compound growth. To understand how these laws affect growth, we must first explain the basic economics of innovations, beginning with the effects of innovation on welfare. An economic innovation provides a better way to make something or something better to make. A better way to make something lowers its cost, so the supply curve shifts down and to the right. This shift causes the price of the good to fall for consumers. The amount of their gain is measured by the increase in consumers' surplus in the market for the cheaper good. Similarly, finding something better to make creates a new good that some consumers buy.

Consumers benefit from the fall in the price of a good that they buy or from the introduction of a new good. In addition, innovations can make whole industries appear, disappear, or restructure. Only historians remember the American Ice Trust, which was one of America's largest corporations in 1900. By changing wages and employment, innovation disrupts communities, causing some to grow and others to wither. The mechanization of agriculture in the U.S. emptied the countryside in the early twentieth century and left vacant buildings boarded shut in small towns. Although many agricultural workers moved to the city for higher wages, a ploughman with a team of horses who remained in the countryside found few employers who valued his skill. In Europe, the industrial revolution shoved the nobles with large estates out of the centers of political power. Joseph Schumpeter appropriately called innovation "creative destruction."

Most societies value the gains from faster growth more than they fear its destructive effects. Property law can help to secure rapid economic growth. To understand why, we must shift from consumers and workers to companies. A company that innovates gains a competitive advantage, which immediately creates extraordinary profits. Extraordinary profits reward the innovator for the resources and effort devoted to a very risky activity. In the long run, however, competition causes the innovation to diffuse, and many companies make use of it. When the innovation diffuses fully, the innovator loses its competitive advantage, and its profits fall to the ordinary level. When diffusion is complete, the economy reaches a new equilibrium whose benefits diffuse even more broadly than the innovation.

In this life cycle of an innovation, the innovation causes a disequilibrium, and the innovator earns extraordinary profits as long as it persists. The reward for innovation thus depends on how long the disequilibrium persists. A quick move to equilibrium gives little reward to the innovator for the resources that it invested and the risk that it assumed. Without legal intervention, competition can quickly destroy the profits from innovation, which results in too little innovation.

To see why, we must understand some elements of the economics of information. Everyone with a television or computer buys information, but information differs from other commodities like oranges or razor blades. What special problems exist in defining property rights and establishing markets in information? Information has two characteristics that make transactions in information different from transactions in ordinary private goods. The first characteristic is *credibility,* which we discuss in Chapter 9. The second characteristic, which we discuss now, is *nonappropriability.* Information is generally costly to produce and cheap to transmit.

To illustrate, popular music is costly to make and recordings are cheap to copy. The instant the producer sells information to the buyer, that buyer becomes a potential competitor with the original producer. For example, when someone buys a compact disk recording at a music store, the buyer can copy the disk immediately and resell it to others. Furthermore, the reseller bears only the cost of transmission, not the cost of production. Thus, resellers who pay for transmission undercut producers who pay for production. Consumers try to "free ride" by paying no more than the cost of transmission.

The fact that producers have difficulty selling information for more than a fraction of its value is called the problem of *nonappropriability.* To illustrate, Hong Kong shops traditionally resell American software at the cost of a diskette. Producers use various devices to try to protect their products against appropriation, such as writing computer programs that are hard to copy. (The industry calls this "digital rights management.") But for every program obstructing copying, there is a hack.

Consider the connection between nonappropriability and public goods. Information contains ideas. One person's use of an idea does not diminish its availability for others to use. Thus, information use is *nonrivalrous.* Excluding some people from learning about a new idea can be expensive, because the transmission of ideas is so cheap. Thus, information is *nonexcludable.* These are the two characteristics of public goods identified in Chapter 2. Nonappropriability of information is essentially the same problem as non-excludability for public goods.

Because of these problems, private markets often undersupply public goods. Similarly, economists who developed the original economics of information concluded that a private market would provide less than the efficient amount of information. These theoretical considerations suggest that an unregulated market will undersupply creative works that embody ideas, such as science, inventions, books, and paintings. The problem has four different remedies that we will describe.

The first remedy is for the state to *supply or subsidize art and science,* especially basic research. Thus, the state owns or subsidizes many universities. More relevant to this book are subsidies for trials. In many civil law countries such as Mexico and Chile, the citizens have a right to use the courts for free. In the United States litigants are assessed court fees, but fees fall far short of court costs, so trials are subsidized. In Chapter 10 we will argue that common law precedents are a valuable stock of ideas. From this fact we will conclude that U.S. courts should stop subsidizing the resolution of private disputes and continue subsidizing the creation of legal precedents.

The second remedy is *charitable contributions.* A great tradition in the United States and some other countries (but not all) is the expectation that wealthy people will make substantial voluntary contributions to the arts and sciences. Besides social norms requiring such gifts, the tax system in the United States allows for the deduction of charitable donations from the donor's taxable income. In practice, the charitable deduction means that donors contribute roughly two-thirds of the donation's value and the U.S. Treasury contributes the other one-third. Other countries such as Switzerland do not allow such deductions, apparently because of sentiment that the state, not the rich, should control the arts and sciences. Charity, however, enjoys this significant advantage over government: donors monitor the use of their money by their favorite charities more carefully than taxpayers monitor the government's use of taxes, and monitoring reduces waste.

The third remedy, broadly described as *trade secrets protection,* comes from contract and tort law. An employee or contractor with a Silicon Valley company is routinely required to sign a non-disclosure agreement (NDA). In an NDA, the employee or contractor promises not to disclose any of the company's secrets. For example, the employee or contractor promises not to speak or write about the company's machinery, equipment, research, or business practices. Trade secrets protection ideally prevents the transmission of information and allows its producer to appropriate its value.

Trade secrets laws, however, have weaknesses that impair their effectiveness. Assume that inventor A employs person B who signs an NDA, and then person B leaks A's secrets to company C:

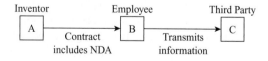

A has a contract with B and no contract with C. Because C has no contractual obligations to A (in legalese, A and C do not have "privity" of contract), A has limited legal powers to prevent C from using A's trade secrets or transmitting them to others. If C knew or had reason to know that B violated the NDA, then A could sue C. If C induced B to violate the NDA, then A could sue C. But if C did not know, or have reason to know, or induce B's breach of contract with A, then C did nothing wrong in receiving the information. Furthermore, if the information has thoroughly leaked and become common knowledge in the industry, anyone can use it for free, even if they know that the information originally escaped into the public sphere by breach of contract.

Recent survey research concludes that trade secrets protection is not very effective in Silicon Valley. In reality, employees change jobs frequently in Silicon Valley, and they carry many of the old firm's secrets to the new firm. In fact, many Silicon Valley employees do not understand when they breach trade secrets laws, partly because these laws depart so far from business practices in Silicon Valley.

The fourth remedy, which usually supplements trade secrets protection, is *intellectual property law*. In addition to non-disclosure agreements with his employees, associates, and business customers, inventor A may try to obtain a patent, copyright, or trademark. If his application succeeds, A will have property rights in the information that he produced. For this reason, these three bodies of law belong to the study of *intellectual property*, which is our next topic.

Web Note 5.1

We discuss the burgeoning law-and-economics literature on trade secrets on our website.

B. Intellectual Property

As with real estate, ownership of the mind's products implies the right to exclude others from using them. When intellectual property rights are effectively enforced, the owner of a new computer chip or novel can use the power of exclusion to extract a price from other users. The price rewards the creator, which results in more innovations and faster growth—a form of "dynamic efficiency."

After making an innovation, disseminating it allows more people to enjoy its advantages. Intellectual property rights can also increase dissemination. Without property rights, the innovator may try to keep the innovation secret in order to profit from it. Thus, Renaissance Venetians carefully guarded the secrets of glassmaking, and Shakespeare carefully guarded the texts of his plays so that only his company could perform them. With effective intellectual property rights, however, the innovator need not fear that others will steal the innovation. Instead of keeping it secret, the owner can disseminate it and charge fees for its use, such as licensing fees for patents or performance fees for plays. Replacing secrecy with property increases dissemination, which results in wider use—an increase in "static efficiency."

Although secure intellectual property rights cause the owner to disseminate an innovation, dissemination usually stops short of the point required for static efficiency. Monopoly theory explains why. A valuable invention creates a better product or a better way to make an old product. If the invention has no close substitutes, granting a patent or copyright creates "monopoly power," which means that the seller can raise the price. To maximize profits, the owner-monopolist sets the user fee too high for social efficiency, so use is too low. Thus, intellectual property law may result in less dissemination of an innovation than required for static efficiency.

Patents and copyright may be temporary monopolies that can vary in breadth and duration. Narrowing the breadth or shortening the duration of intellectual property rights often decreases monopoly profits and increases dissemination. To illustrate, assume that one person writes a novel and another adapts it for a movie. Narrow copyright law gives the novelist ownership of the novel and the adapter ownership of the movie rights. In contrast, broad copyright law gives the novelist ownership of the novel and the movie rights, which are an example of what are called "derivative works." Similarly, a patent on a computer chip can last different lengths of time in different countries. Starting from narrow, short intellectual property rights, broadening and lengthening them rewards the creator and encourages more innovation. If the innovation can be kept secret, then broadening and lengthening the intellectual property rights rewards dissemination by increasing user fees. Thus, increasing incentives for creation also increases incentives for dissemination, at least up to a point. Beyond this point, however, broadening the scope or duration of the creator's property rights increases monopoly power, which rewards creation and reduces dissemination. Thus, incentives for creation and dissemination trade off. (Later we explain that increasing the scope or duration of the creator's property rights still further may eventually reduce creation and dissemination.)

To appreciate the problem of dissemination, consider bridge tolls. Efficiency requires the toll to equal the marginal cost of crossing the bridge. The cost of allowing another motorist to cross an *uncongested* bridge is approximately zero, so the optimal toll is approximately zero. If the optimal toll is not zero, someone who values crossing the bridge will fail to do so, which is a waste. Suppose the toll is $1. A person who is willing to pay $.75 will not cross, so the toll destroys $.75 in benefits that could have been created at no cost. (The conclusion is different for a congested bridge, where increased congestion is the cost of allowing another motorist to cross.) Similarly, the cost of allowing another person to use a patented computer program or music recording is approximately zero, so the optimal user fee is approximately zero. However, the fee that maximizes profits for the owner is much larger than zero. Thus, intellectual property may result in too-high user fees and too-low dissemination.

The innovation-diffusion tradeoff causes major trade tensions in the contemporary world. The world's developed countries create far more innovations that result in patents or copyrights than developing countries do. The developed countries, consequently, focus on the benefits of strong intellectual property rights that protect their creators. In contrast, the developing countries benefit from wide diffusion of technology at low cost. The developing countries, consequently, lack enthusiasm for enforcing intellectual property rights that raise prices to their consumers. Thus, Microsoft wants China to suppress illegal copying of its software, and China apparently lacks enthusiasm for this effort. The net result is that the latest Microsoft software sells in Hong Kong street markets for the cost of a diskette, and the U.S. threatens to sue

China in the World Trade Organization.[1] These tensions should ameliorate as China finds that weak intellectual property law retards its own development of software and other creative industries.

Intellectual property law confronts the innovation-dissemination tradeoff and resolves it somewhat differently in each of its three principal areas—patents, copyrights, and trademarks. Intellectual property law, however, is a historical accretion that developed without a scientific basis. Only recently has property law come under economic analysis. Even today, however, available economic analysis is insufficient to the task. The usual technique of economic analysis involves comparing equilibria with fixed technology ("static equilibrium analysis"), whereas intellectual property law requires an analysis of innovation and changing technology ("growth theory"). Improvements in the economics of information will no doubt produce new, better critiques of intellectual property law. In the meantime, the economic analysis of intellectual property law must proceed with the tools at hand. Besides inadequate scientific tools, intellectual property law aligns poorly with economic efficiency because the legislators respond to politically powerful special interest groups who care about their own profits more than the nation's wealth. The development of high technology industries challenges both economic theory and the law. Almost all questions regarding intellectual property law are open. This fact makes the subject both exciting and confusing.

1. Patents: Broad or Narrow?   To appreciate the history of patent law, consider its evolution. European patents for inventions began in the Republic of Venice in 1474 and were formalized in England in the Statute of Monopolies in 1623. Article I, Section 8 of the U.S. Constitution gives Congress the power "to promote the progress of science and useful arts, by securing for limited time to authors and inventors the exclusive right to their respective writings and discoveries." To put this power into action with respect to patents, the U.S. Congress passed America's first patent law in 1790, which was revised in 1793, 1836, 1952, and 1995. To secure an exclusive right to an invention, the inventor must submit an application to the U.S. Patent Office establishing that the invention is for a "new and useful process, machine, manufacture, or composition of matter, or [a] new and useful improvement thereof." (35 U.S. Code 101.) The invention must be "non-obvious," must have "practical utility" (a characteristic that is more or less presumed for all applicants), and must not have been commercialized or known to the public for more than a year before the date of application. A patent examiner—a government official who is, ideally, a lawyer with a strong scientific background—must decide whether to grant the patent. Approximately three-fourths of all applications are granted by the Patent Office. Throughout the 1970s, between 70,000 and 80,000 patents were granted per

---

[1] The Agreement on Trade Related Aspects of Intellectual Property, or TRIPS, applies to all members of the World Trade Organization. Intellectual property rights are also enforced internationally through the World Intellectual Property Organization, or WIPO.

year.[2] But in the 1990s patent applications and the number of patents granted in the United States exploded to nearly 150,000 per year. The successful applicant now receives a 20-year monopoly on the use of the invention.[3] No one can use the invention except by its owner's consent. Others who wish to use the invention must purchase the right to do so from the patent-holder. The holder may, at his or her discretion, *license* the use of the patent in exchange for the licensee's payment of a fee known as a *royalty*.

If a patent-holder believes that another is using his patent without permission, he or she may bring an action for infringement and seek both injunctive and legal relief.

Web Note 5.2

See our website for more on recent developments in patent laws in the United States and other nations, including speculation on the causes of the tremendous upsurge in the number of patents in the 1990s and early 2000s.

An inventor who applies for a patent risks more than lawyers' fees. The information in the application is accessible to the public. If the application fails, competitors will be able to freely use the invention described in the application. If the application succeeds, competitors will have a precise description of the invention, so they can try to emulate it without trespassing on the patent ("engineer around the patent"). For these reasons, some inventors prefer to rely on trade secrets protection and not apply for a patent. More typically, however, an inventor relies on both trade secrets laws and patents to protect his intellectual property.

Patents create an exclusive property right in an invention with two dimensions: *duration* and *breadth*. "Duration" refers to the number of years between a patent's registration and its expiration. For example, most U.S. patents last for 20 years from the date of application. "Breadth" refers to how similar another invention can be without infringing on the patent for the original invention. To illustrate, the Rubik's Cube is a popular puzzle in which each of the six sides of the cube are divided into a 3 × 3 grid, and each of the cells in the grid is colored. The object of the game is to manipulate the cube in order to align rows of same-colored cells. An American court ruled that the Rubik's Cube did not infringe an earlier patent by Moleculon for a similar game using a 2 × 2 grid.[4]

---

[2] Of those issued between 1971 and 1975, 51 percent were granted to domestic corporations, 23 percent to foreign corporations and governments, 2 percent to the U.S. federal government, and 23 percent to individual inventors. This distribution represents a trend in the century toward corporate ownership and away from individual ownership of new patents. FREDERICK SCHERER, INDUSTRIAL MARKET STRUCTURE AND ECONOMIC PERFORMANCE (2d ed. 1980).

[3] In 1995, as part of the agreement establishing the World Trade Organization, the U.S. Congress changed the patent life from 17 years from the date of approval to 20 years from the date of application. The change, which brings the U.S. system into conformity with other national patent systems, arose from the approval of the latest international trade agreement.

[4] *Moleculon Research Corp. v. CBS, Inc.,* 872 F.2d 407, 409 (Fed. Cir. 1989).

1a. Breadth An important policy question concerns the efficient breadth of a patent. To understand the difference in incentive effects between narrow and broad patents, contrast two inventors, two inventions, and two rules. Assume that two inventors are contemplating investing in research on two inventions. The first invention would improve oil-cracking processes, and the second invention would provide a substitute for lead in gasoline. The inventors expect the two inventions to be similar but not identical. Under a broad rule, a single patent would encompass both inventions. Because the party who makes the first invention receives exclusive rights to both inventions, the party who makes the first discovery gets all of the profits, and the other party gets nothing. Thus, the broad rule encourages fast, duplicative research. In contrast, under a narrow rule, a separate patent would be required for each invention. The party who makes the first invention would receive exclusive rights to it, and the party who makes the second invention would have exclusive property rights to it. Thus, the narrow rule encourages slower, complementary research.

To appreciate this contrast between broad and narrow patents, consider a typical relationship between research and development (R&D). Research sometimes yields a pioneering discovery with no immediate commercial value, but with large commercial potential. To realize its potential, a pioneering discovery must be developed and "brought to market." Development involves a series of small improvements. A patented pioneering invention can be followed by a valuable application patented by another inventor. In such cases, U.S. law has an interesting feature: Neither party can use the application without the other's permission. As long as both patents endure, the owner of the application cannot use his patent without a license from the owner of the pioneering invention, and the owner of the pioneering invention cannot use the application without a license from its owner. The result is that they have to negotiate with each other and reach an agreement before anyone can use the application and make money from it. U.S. patent law for pioneering inventions and applications creates an incentive for each to bargain with the other.

These mutual rights get triggered when the subsequent invention is an application of the prior invention. The legal question is how broadly the pioneering discovery extends over the follow-on inventions. Broad patents encourage fundamental research, and narrow patents encourage development. Thus, suppose that an investment of $100,000 in research yields a pioneering invention that has no commercial value. Subsequently, an investment of $50,000 in development yields an improvement to the pioneering invention that has commercial value of $1 million. If the law grants broad patents, a patent for the pioneering invention would also cover the improvement, but if the law grants narrow patents, separate patents would be required for the pioneering invention and the improvement.

What breadth of patents is most efficient? If the social value of investment on fundamental research exceeds the social value of investment on developing applications, then patents should be broadened. Conversely, if the social value of investment on developing applications exceeds the social value of investment on fundamental research, then patents should be narrowed.

In reality, questions of breadth are decided in law according to the "doctrine of equivalents," which refers to a series of court findings about how nearly equivalent two inventions must be before finding patent infringement. This doctrine is obscure and unpredictable. Courts have sometimes reasoned that an improvement with great commercial value should not be interpreted as infringing on a pioneering invention with little stand-alone value.[5] After all, the improvement, not the pioneering invention, is what people really value.

Howard Chang, an economist-lawyer, has recently shown that this argument is flawed for purposes of maximizing the social value of inventive activity.[6] If the people who do fundamental research receive the sale value of the pioneering invention, but they do not receive any of the sale value of the commercial applications, there will not be enough fundamental research. To see why, consider an analogy between pioneering inventions and raising sheep. Sheep are sold for mutton and wool. Assume that the mutton from a sheep is worth much more than the wool. If shepherds are paid the value of the wool, but not the value of the mutton, then shepherds will not be paid enough, and they will raise too few sheep. Mutton and wool are *joint products* of rearing sheep. Efficient incentives require that shepherds receive the sale value of their product (sheep), which is the sum of the sale value of mutton and wool.

Similarly, commercial applications and pioneering inventions are joint products of fundamental research. Commercial applications require pioneering inventions, and pioneering inventions require fundamental research. A joint product will be undersupplied if the supplier's compensation equals the commercial value of only one of the joint products. Ideally, the fundamental research and commercial development would be joined together in a single firm. If the activities are joined under a single producer, then the producer will receive the sum of the value of the fundamental research and commercial application, just like paying the shepherd the sum of the value of the mutton and wool.

Even if one firm conducted fundamental research and another firm developed commercial applications, the incentive problem could be solved if transaction costs were zero. If transaction costs were zero, then the Coase Theorem would apply: breadth of patent does not matter to economic efficiency so long as inventors can bargain with each other costlessly and make efficient contracts.

Problems arise under the realistic assumption that transaction costs impede bargaining between suppliers of fundamental research and commercial development. Two legal remedies are available: lubricate bargaining (Normative Coase Theorem) or allocate rights to the party who values them the most (Normative Hobbes Theorem). Instead of pursuing these two remedies, U.S. law has been perverse in both respects.

Bargaining among inventors sometimes leads to joint research ventures, in which competing manufacturers share an R&D facility and compete with each other in production and sales. In America, antitrust laws have inhibited joint ventures for research and development. Thus, the application of antitrust law to R&D obstructed a solution to the problem of the joint production of inventions. Fortunately, American officials have recognized this failure in policy and taken steps to correct it.

---

[5] See *Westinghouse v. Boyden Power Brake Co.*, 170 U.S. 537, 572 (1898).

[6] See Howard F. Chang, *Patent Scope, Antitrust Policy, and Cumulative Innovation,* 26 RAND J. ECON. 34 (1995). See also Robert P. Merges & Richard R. Nelson, *On the Complex Economics of Patent Scope,* 90 COLUM. L. REV. 839 (1990).

When separate producers make joint inventions, officials face a difficult problem in determining the breadth of the patents. If the pioneering invention has little stand-alone value, then some of the improvement's value must be paid to the pioneer in order to provide an adequate incentive for pioneering inventions. On the other hand, if the pioneering invention has large stand-alone value, then its inventor often will be rewarded adequately already, even if he or she receives no share of the value of the improvement. Thus, patent protection for pioneering inventions should be *broader* for those with *little* stand-alone value, and the patent protection for pioneering inventions should be *narrower* for those with *large* stand-alone value. This is just the opposite of the result sometimes reached by U.S. courts.[7]

QUESTION 5.1:   When the patent expired on a drug named "Librium" (a sedative that was the forerunner of Valium), its price dropped from $15 to $1.10.[8] Explain why this drop in price occurred. Relate your explanation to the problem of efficient incentives for creating and transmitting an idea.

QUESTION 5.2:   Recall our example of an investment of $100,000 in research that yields a pioneering invention that has no commercial value, and a subsequent investment of $50,000 in development that yields an improvement that has commercial value of $1 million. Assume that Firm A is uniquely situated to do the pioneering research, and Firm B is uniquely situated to develop the application. Predict the difference in investment resulting from a broad patent law and a narrow patent law. In making your prediction, distinguish between a situation in which transaction costs prevent Firm A and Firm B from bargaining with each other and a situation in which transaction costs of bargaining are zero.

QUESTION 5.3:   When inventions take the form of discovery and application, the authorities may issue a "dominant patent" to the pioneering discovery and a "subservient patent" to the improvement. The subservient invention cannot be manufactured legally without the agreement of the holders of the dominant patent and the subservient patent. Thus, the two parties are compelled to bargain, each having veto power, and agree on the division of future profits before manufacturing the improvement. Absent such an agreement, only the pioneering invention can be manufactured. Answer Question 5.2 under the assumption that, instead of prescribing broad or narrow patents, the law grants a dominant patent and a subservient patent.

---

[7] The technical name for the legal doctrine giving perverse results is the "doctrine of equivalents." Applying this doctrine, courts may find that a pioneering invention with little stand-alone value *is not equivalent* to an application of it, so the patent for the former does not extend to the latter. In contrast, the courts may find that a pioneering invention with stand-alone value *is equivalent* to an application of it, so the patent for the former extends to the latter.

[8] "'When Librium, Hoffmann-LaRoche's forerunner to Valium, came off patent, prices dropped from $15 to $1,' said William Haddad, president of the Generic Pharmaceutical Industry Association." See "The Shift to Generic Drugs," *New York Times*, July 23, 1984, p. 19.

1b. Duration   As noted, the rights to a patent last for a fixed time period. What is the optimal patent life? We provide an economic framework for answering this question. Because patents may create a temporary monopoly that rewards the inventor and over-charges buyers, the optimal life of a patent strikes the best balance between encouraging creativity and discouraging dissemination. As the duration of patents increases, society enjoys more benefits from more innovation. However, the rate at which these benefits increase presumably decreases. Consequently, the marginal benefit from more innovation decreases as the duration of patents increases. As the duration of patents increases, society suffers more costs from less dissemination. Society responds to long patents by searching for substitutes for patented goods. The longer a society searches, the more substitutes it finds. As with benefits, the rate at which the social costs of patents increases presumably decreases with duration. Consequently, the marginal cost from less dissemination presumably decreases as the duration of patents increases.

Marginalist reasoning describes the optimal patent life in abstract terms. But what particular life is optimal? Ideally, there would be a different patent life for each invention, depending on its individual characteristics.

Such a scheme of individualized patent terms is impractical, but practical alternatives exist to granting a 20-year patent for every invention (the current international default patent term). Germany, for example, has established a two-tiered patent system. Major inventions in Germany receive full-term patents, while minor inventions and improvements receive *petty patents* for a term of 3 years. In addition, Germany requires patent-holders to pay an annual fee to continue the patent. The annual fee is relatively modest for the first several years of a patent's life, but thereafter escalates at regular intervals until the patent period is exhausted. Consequently, fewer than 5 percent of German patents remain in force for their entire term, the average patent life being a little less than 8 years. This fact is not surprising when you consider that, given an interest rate of 10 percent, a promise to pay $1 in 8 years is worth less than $.50 today, and a promise to pay $1 in 20 years is worth less than $.20 today.

Would economic efficiency increase by changing the U.S. system to resemble the German system? Perhaps. A convincing answer, however, requires much statistical research to provide evidence about broad averages, and that research remains to be done.

1c. Too Much Patent   Despite absence of statistical research, evidence exists that patent law has extended too far and threatens to choke creativity in some areas. Pharmaceutical research provides an example of such a problem that legislation cured. To develop a new drug, companies often have to use an existing drug. Fearing competition, the owners of patents on drugs are reluctant to license their use in research to competitors. This is a case where patent law suppresses the innovation that is the purpose of it. The Drug Price Competition and Patent Term Restoration Act (1984) (amending the Food, Drug, and Cosmetic Act, and known as the Hatch-Waxman Act) addressed part of the problem by allowing the free use of patented compounds in research to develop a generic alternative. In *Merck KGaA v. Integra Lifesciences I, Ltd.*, 545 U.S. 193 (2005), the Supreme Court extended this law to research aimed at developing entirely new drugs.

Another example of overextended patent law concerns business methods. In the past, no one thought that a business method could be patented. However, creative

Optimal Patent Life: Orphan Drugs

We have already remarked on the fact that there is one patent term—20 years. The analysis of this section has implied that this is not optimal; clearly the social costs and benefits of inventions and innovations differ, sometimes markedly. Ideally, the patent system would recognize these variations by granting different patent terms depending on the net social benefit of each invention. But the administrative costs of making an invention-by-invention determination of optimal patent life—or even of putting inventions into classes with different patent terms—are probably prohibitively high. There are, no doubt, social costs—perhaps, *significant* social costs—that follow. For instance, there may be a valuable invention that is extremely costly to develop but that simply could not generate enough revenues if sold at a reasonable cost within the 20-year patent term to justify development.

The United States Congress has recognized several important examples of such inventions. One is the Hatch-Waxman Act (Drug Price Competition and Patent Restoration Act) of 1984. That Act added up to five years of patent life for pharmaceuticals to make up for time lost in the pre-approval testing of new drugs required by the Food and Drug Administration (FDA). The Act also eliminated duplicative safety and effectiveness testing for generic drugs (those that share the chemical composition of drugs that are coming off patent).

Congress went even further in the Orphan Drug Act of 1983 and its later amendments. Congress addressed that Act at an instance of the problem we mentioned above—a valuable invention that might not be developed because the standard patent life was not long enough to justify the development costs. An "orphan drug" is one for treatment of "any disease or condition which occurs so infrequently in the United States that there is no reasonable expectation that the cost of developing or marketing the drug will be recovered by sales." A later amendment further defined such diseases or conditions as those affecting fewer than 200,000 people in the United States. The Act gives developers of orphan drugs tax credits for the costs of clinical studies and other subsidies for development costs. In addition, developers of orphan drugs are given a period of seven-year exclusivity, which may be revoked if the developer fails to provide the patient population with the drug or abandons the drug.[9] Finally, the FDA greatly accelerates the approval process for orphan drugs, sometimes taking only eight months for approval.

---

[9] This term of exclusivity may strike some readers as odd. Aren't *all* patents grants of exclusivity? Yes, but there is a very important qualification. A normal patent gives the holder exclusive rights to *that* invention or innovation. But others are free to develop distinct but different inventions that substitute for (but do not infringe upon) existing patents. (See our brief discussion of the "doctrine of equivalents" in this section.) So, you may have developed and patented a pharmaceutical that lowers bad blood cholesterol. But others can develop other chemicals directed at the same end, so long as they are not close copies of your drug. (Consider that your ownership of a piece of real property gives you exclusive rights to *that* property but not to similarly situated pieces of property.) The distinction in the Orphan Drug Act is that once one has developed a pharmaceutical that meets the criteria for being designated an orphan drug, no one else can develop even a different drug addressed to the same condition or disease for seven years (at least under the original formulation of the Act).

The Act apparently had the desired effect. In the 20 years before 1983, the FDA had approved only 10 orphan drugs. But in 1984 alone it approved 24. During the Act's first 15 years, the number of orphan drugs increased fivefold, while the number of non-orphan drugs increased by twofold.[10]

This record of success notwithstanding, there are some concerns with the Orphan Drug Act. One has to do with the exclusivity period. That seven-year period, for example, encourages initial development but discourages development of competing but chemically different drugs. Congress found this to be undesirable, so in 1993 they passed amendments to the Act that allowed patenting of second and third orphan drugs directed at the same disease or condition as the original orphan drug so long as those second and third drugs were clinically superior in defined ways. There also have been some additional concerns with the status of orphan drugs. Suppose, for example, that the patient population turns out to expand beyond the 200,000 threshold or that the orphan drug turns out to be effective in treating other, non-orphaned conditions or diseases or that the orphan drug turns out to be extremely profitable. Should the orphan status be revoked in these instances? Congress has addressed these issues but has not yet reached agreement on what to do about them.

lawyers induced the U.S. Patent Office to issue patents on some business methods. The most famous example is Amazon's patent on "one-click" Internet orders. Most scholars believe that innovators who create new business methods should not be able to patent them.

QUESTION 5.4: One possible pitfall of the renewal-fee system for determination of optimal patent life is that, ideally, we want the patent-holder to compare the renewal fee with the *social* benefit of continuing the patent for another year, not just the *private* benefit. Can you suggest how, in setting the annual renewal fee, we might induce patent-holders to make the appropriate social calculation?

QUESTION 5.5: A third means of reducing the social costs of granting a patent life that is too long is a policy of *compulsory licensing*. This policy, which forms part of the patent systems of most Western European countries, allows frustrated licensees to ask courts to compel patentees to license to them if they can show that patent-holders have failed to use their patents in the domestic market within a specified time period, have failed to license when that is essential to bringing a complementary invention into use, or have abused their positions by, for example, excessively restricting the supply of their inventions. If the court is persuaded by the prospective licensee to compel licensing, then it also determines a *reasonable* royalty. Give an economic evaluation of the policy of compulsory licensing.

---

[10] See Frank Lichtenberg & Joel Waldfogel, "Does Misery Love Company? Evidence from Pharmaceutical Markets Before and After the Orphan Drug Act," NBER Working Paper No. 9750 (2007).

1d. Conclusion on Patents   As explained, the original economics of information concluded that an unregulated private market will undersupply information. Remedies to the problem include public supply or subsidies for scientific research, charitable donations, and intellectual property rights. This view still dominates most policy discussions. However, special situations can occur in which no regulation or subsidies results in too much information or just the right amount.[11]

To see why, consider the invention of a superior means of forecasting the weather. The original theory argued that the inventor cannot appropriate the value of the invention because people who buy her forecasts can resell them to others. However, there are alternative means for inventors to earn profits. The inventor of the weather forecast, for example, can profit by speculating on agricultural prices. To see how, let's suppose that the inventor forecasts a rainy autumn that will reduce harvests and cause the price of corn to rise. She can keep this information secret and buy corn in the summer for delivery in the autumn. Presumably, if everyone else anticipates normal fall weather, the price of corn in the summer for autumn delivery will be low—too low, the inventor of the weather forecasting method knows. When the harvest arrives in the fall, farmers will fulfill their contracts by delivering corn to the inventor at the low, summer price. Subsequently, the inventor can resell the corn on the spot at the high price caused by a rainy autumn. Thus, Aristotle asserts that Thales of Miletus used philosophy to predict the weather and made a fortune on what amounted to olive press call options.[12]

In general, the producers of information can obtain profits from speculative investments. In Silicon Valley, an inventor often participates in founding a firm and owns a lot of its stock. The inventor presumably knows more than the public about the firm's future performance. The invention may give the firm a competitive advantage in several respects beyond its immediate application. For example, the firm may learn many things about applying and marketing the invention in various fields ahead of its competitors. Also, the firm may establish its brand name over products associated with the invention. Once the market learns the firm's true value, the inventor's stock will appreciate.

Following this line of thought, some scholars have argued that some markets produce too much investment in information. For example, consider the stock market as a whole. An investor who finds out sooner than others that one corporation is buying another can make large profits by purchasing the target company's stock. The gains to society from faster price movements in the target company's stocks are modest compared to the vast wealth redistributed from uninformed stockholders to informed investors. This fact is one reason why securities laws in the United States and elsewhere forbid members of a firm from trading its stock based on information that they have not yet made public—the prohibition against *insider trading*.

Investors race to buy a stock whose price will rise before someone else does, which creates the possibility of excessive trading. Similarly, fishermen race to catch the fish

---

[11] J. Hirshleifer *The Private and Social Value of Information and the Reward to Innovative Activity*, 61 Am. Econ. Rev. 561 (1971). See also R. Posner, *The Social Costs of Monopoly and Regulations*, 83 J. Pol. Econ. 807 (1975), and E. Rice & T. Ulen, *Rent-Seeking and Welfare Loss*, 3 Res. in Law & Econ. 53 (1981).

[12] Aristotle's *Politics*, Book 1, Chapter 11. Thanks to Eric Rasmusen for this example.

in the sea before someone else does, which causes tragic over-fishing. Inventors race to secure patents. Unlike the Olympics, patent law typically (but not always) has no silver medals—the second-place finisher often gets nothing. Are inventions like fish in the sea? No. The advantages of growth are so vast that society benefits from the innovation race, even when it is frenetic. Beating the competition in a patent race has negative externalities, but inventions cause much larger positive externalities that the public enjoys as the innovations disseminate.

Before concluding this section, we want to mention a reason why patent protection for some inventions is higher than commended by economic efficiency. In addition to the legal monopoly sometimes given by a patent, some inventions create natural monopolies. A natural monopoly exists when average costs fall as the scale of production rises. Given a natural monopoly, the largest firm with the lowest costs can drive out the competition. For example, spreading research and development costs over larger production volumes reduces the average cost of innovation. Thus, the average cost of developing an operating system for users of personal computers falls as the number of users increases. In information technologies, industry standards provide an additional element of natural monopoly. To illustrate, standardizing the key strokes required to move the cursor in a word processing program lowers the learning cost of word processing to everyone. As the standard becomes more dominant, users value it more. Consequently, any company that can establish exclusive rights over an industry standard can enjoy an element of natural monopoly and exploit this power in licensing the right to use the standard.

If an invention is the basis of a natural monopoly, then the inventor can obtain monopoly profits even without a patent. To do so, the inventor must use his lead-in time to expand his business and innovate faster than the competition. By growing and innovating faster than the competition, the leader enjoys increasing returns to scale, which convey monopoly profits. To illustrate, assume that a computer software product begins with a fundamental discovery and then undergoes constant improvement through innovation. To finance constant improvement, a company needs a significant level of sales. The original inventor may achieve the critical sales level before anyone else and then price the product low enough to preclude entry by other firms. The price that precludes entry into the market by competitors (the so-called "entry-limiting price") can still yield supra-competitive profits to the producer.

Natural monopoly is such a common feature of networks that its occurrence in networks has a special name—*network effects*. The economic analysis of network effects began with railways in the nineteenth century. The most efficient organization of a railway usually requires lines to radiate from a central terminal. The central terminal is the "hub" and the radiating lines are the "spokes." (This same language is now applied to airlines.) The owner of the central terminal can favor connections to its own railway lines and disfavor connections to competing railway lines. This network effect in railways confers a large advantage on the owner of the central terminal for a region. Similarly, information-based industries often rely on connections analogous to the central railway terminal. For example, all the software on a personal computer must use its operating system. An exclusive owner of the operating system for personal computers can favor the use of its own software and disfavor the use of rival software.

Such a pattern of abuse was the central allegation of the U.S. Justice Department in its recent antitrust suit against Microsoft. Owning a computer operating system has been analogized to having a patent on use of the English language.

> **QUESTION 5.6:** Suppose that the inventor of a weather-forecasting technique determines that the weather during the growing season will be perfect, causing a bumper harvest. Explain how the inventor could use this information to make profitable investments.

> **QUESTION 5.7:** The directors of a corporation are often the first people to know about facts that affect its stock price. American law forbids directors and other "insiders" from using "inside information" to speculate on the value of the company's stocks. Use the theory of first appropriation and the economics of information to make arguments for and against the efficiency of this prohibition.

Web Note 5.3

See our website for additional law-and-economics literature on patent issues.

Patent (and Other) Prizes

The economic argument for patents asserts that giving the developer of a new, useful, and nonobvious invention or innovation an exclusive right encourages investment in and dissemination of new methods, machines, and practices. But there has always been skepticism about the necessity of the patent system. Critics have long argued that the shortcomings of that system—particularly the high prices and restricted output of monopoly—are not worth the alleged benefits.[13] Indeed, because of their deep concerns about the ill effects of the IP system, several European countries, including Sweden and the Netherlands, suspended their intellectual property systems for several decades in the mid- and late nineteenth century.

But if there is no patent system, how can society encourage investment in invention and dissemination? One possible method is through the award of prizes. These can be monetary rewards for designated accomplishments or for general innovations, and they can be offered by either public or private parties or both simultaneously. Perhaps the best example of a public reward designed to induce a particular invention is the English government's search for an accurate method of measuring longitude.[14] Using sightings of the sun, ships could relatively easily measure latitude, their distance north or south of the equator. But with regard to longitude they were—well, at sea. The results of not knowing where one was could be, and sometimes were, disastrous. In response to a famous ship disaster, the English Parliament decided to do something. In 1714 they offered a reward of £20,000 to the first person who could

---

[13] See for example, Michelle Boldrin & David Levine, *The Case Against Intellectual Property*, 92 AM. ECON. REV. 209 (2002). See also the authors' *Against Intellectual Property* (2008).

[14] See DAVA SOBEL, LONGITUDE (1997).

accurately measure longitude at sea. To evaluate the submissions, Parliament appointed a Board of Longitude, with Sir Isaac Newton as its Prime Commissioner, and they required a testing voyage to the West Indies with criteria for success.

A carpenter and clockmaker in Yorkshire, John Harrison, thought that the key to measuring longitude was an extremely accurate clock. (Most of the other inventors who pursued the prize thought the key lay in accurate sightings of celestial objects.) Harrison's insight was that the Earth turned through 360 degrees, a complete rotation, in the course of 24 hours. As a result, the Earth turns through 15 degrees each hour of each day. A traveler who departed from London to Moscow could set his watch for London time and compare it to the time when he reached Moscow. He would find that his watch said 9:00 am when it was noon in Moscow, which would enable him to deduce that Moscow is east of London by 45 degrees of longitude. If it were possible to measure the time difference between a ship at sea and at a fixed point on the Earth's surface (such as at London), then one could tell how far around the Earth one had gone. For this method of measurement to work would require having an extremely accurate clock. And that was the task that Harrison set himself.

In the eighteenth century, ships' clocks were inaccurate because the motion of the ship disrupted the clock's mechanism. In 1759, Harrison finally developed an extremely accurate ship's clock, which he called H-4. In 1764 the Board of Longitude ordered H-4 to be tested on a ship traveling from Portsmouth to Barbados, and Harrison's son, William, went to Barbados to oversee the test. The clock performed marvelously, but rivals blocked Harrison from receiving the prize until his son made a dramatic and successful appeal to King George III. Harrison finally received his reward 43 years after he had begun his quest.

England was not put off by this experience. Parliament later offered a reward for the first successful vaccine against smallpox.

There are many—indeed, an increasing number of—private prizes designed to elicit particular inventive activity. The Ansari X Prize, created in 1996, famously offered $10 million to the first private team that could finance, build, and launch a spaceship capable of carrying three people to a height of 100 km (62.5 miles) above the Earth, return safely to Earth, and then repeat the trip with the same ship within 2 weeks. A group headed by Burt Rutan and Paul Allen, the cofounder of Microsoft, won the prize in October, 2005. Recently, the Progressive Insurance Company announced a $5 million prize for the first team or individual to develop a car with an internal combustion engine capable of getting 100 miles per gallon of gasoline.

Some have suggested that the successes of rewards for particular achievements can be extended to general inventions. Steve Shavell and Tanguy van Ypersele have argued that a system of general governmental rewards for the developing of new, useful, and nonobvious inventions is superior to the current system of awarding patent rights.[15] Are the social costs and benefits of a reward system clearly superior to those of the current patent system? Could one argue that public and private rewards for inventive activity complement the patent system so that the two systems should operate together?

---

[15] See Steven Shavell & Tanguy van Ypersele, *Reward Versus Intellectual Property Rights*, 44 J. LAW & ECON. 525 (2001). See also Michael Abramowicz, *Perfecting Patent Prizes*, 56 VAND. L. REV. 115 (2003).

2. Copyright   In our analysis of patents, we applied the economics of information to answer the two fundamental questions about breadth and duration. This same framework applies to other topics in intellectual property, notably copyright and trademark, which we discuss briefly. Copyright grants writers, composers, and other artists property rights in their creations on demonstration that their works are *original expressions*.[16] Unlike the patent system, the U.S. copyright system does not require creators to register their works in order to receive the protection of copyright. But very much like the patent law, copyright protection is limited in breadth and duration.

The breadth of a copyright concerns the uses to which copyrighted material can be put without authorization. A broad copyright forbids any unauthorized use, whereas a narrow copyright permits some unauthorized uses. For example, books are quoted in reviews and satires, or photocopied or distributed electronically for educational purposes. The law handles these uses through so-called *fair-use* exceptions. For example, in *Sony Corporation of America v. Universal City Studios, Inc.*, 464 U.S. 417 (1984), the *Betamax* case, the U.S. Supreme Court held that recording over-the-air copyrighted television programs on a videocassette recorder is fair use when done for "time-shifting" purposes, but not necessarily for purposes of "archiving." A vague line, frequently litigated, divides fair and unfair unauthorized copying.

Since its eighteenth century beginning, the United States has lengthened the duration of a copyright until it now stands as the creator's life plus 70 years.[17] The optimal duration of a copyright involves a different problem from patents—specifically, *tracing costs*.[18] Before producing her own copyrightable material, a creator may want to check to see if her ideas for a novel, say, are original. The costs of searching among all novels to make sure her idea does not, unintentionally, infringe on someone else's copyright can be extensive. To limit these costs, creators are given limited duration and relatively narrow breadth for their creations. However, the increasing ease of copying and the spread of literacy increase the ability of others to avoid paying the copyright-holder a royalty. So, the lengthening of copyright protection allows creators a longer time to recoup their just royalties.

In some areas, copyright and patent law have extended too far and threaten to choke creativity. To appreciate the problem, imagine that someone obtains copyright to the English language. No one would be able to say anything without paying a license fee. This copyright would suppress language creativity. Similarly, many computer experts believe that fundamental computer languages should remain in the public domain where people can freely modify, adapt, improve, and use them. In this way the Linux operating system has developed into a powerful programming tool. As we move

---

[16] As Lord Macaulay put it, copyright is "a tax on readers for the purpose of giving a bounty to writers." THOMAS B. MACAULAY, SPEECHES ON COPYRIGHT 25 (C. Gaston ed. 1914).

[17] In October, 1998, Congress passed the Sonny Bono Copyright Term Extension Act, which lengthens copyright protection for works created on or after January 1, 1978, to the life of the author plus 70 years, and extends existing copyrights "created for hire and owned by corporations" to 95 years. Before the change, the 1976 Copyright Act had given protection for the author's life plus 50 years. Whatever other reasons there may be for the Copyright Term Extension Act, one justification is that it brings U.S. practice into conformity with Western European practice.

[18] William Landes & Richard A. Posner, *An Economic Analysis of Copyright Law*, 18 J. LEGAL STUD. 325 (1989). See also Wendy Gordon, *On Owning Information: Intellectual Property and the Restitutionary Impulse*, 78 VA. L. REV. 149 (1992).

away from operating systems to more applied programs, however, private owners control the most successful programs. Examples are Microsoft *Word* and *Google*. We could analogize operating systems to the English language and applied programs to novels. These facts suggest a natural boundary between open source and proprietary software. Computer programs hotly contest the proper location of this boundary. Their rhetoric can sometimes sound like a religious war of the seventeenth century or the bitter dispute between socialists and capitalists in the twentieth century.

The historical legacy of copyright law often hinders and obstructs communications among scholars and slows scientific development. Before the Internet, scholars communicated mostly on paper when they did not talk to each other. Publishing an academic journal on paper is costly, so the publisher has to restrict access by charging high subscription fees. With the Internet, the cost of disseminating journal articles plummeted; yet, the same academic journals with their high subscription fees dominate many academic fields. To change the situation, some scholars now refuse to transfer copyright over their articles to the publishers of journals with high subscription fees, or they reserve Internet dissemination rights for themselves. An initiative called the "Creative Commons" attempts to create a new, private copyright standard that guarantees for authors the right of cheap dissemination of their scholarship on the Internet.[19]

What is the future of copyright in the digital age? According to one vision of the future, most users of digital information will download it from a few large sellers who impose uniform charges. In this system, obtaining information resembles putting money in a jukebox to hear a song. According to the "celestial jukebox" model (see Paul Goldstein's book, cited at the end of this chapter), every user of digital information will resemble contemporary U.S. radio stations that must pay standardized royalties to a central clearinghouse whenever they broadcast a song. If the celestial jukebox succeeds, copyright will become the dominant law of the digital age. According to an alternative vision, however, copyright law will die because technology will make law unnecessary. In the model of "digital libertarianism," technical protection through cheap encrypting will be more efficient than legal protection of intellectual property. Cheap encrypting will allegedly enable producers of digital information to control who uses it without much need for law. Are new laws the answer to new machines, or are new machines the answer to new machines? If you think you know whether the future will bring the celestial jukebox or digital libertarianism, then you should immediately go buy technology stocks.

Web Note 5.4

Our website considers much more on the economics of copyrights, such as the recent legal controversy regarding downloading copyrightable material from the Internet, constitutional objections to the copyright extensions of the late 1990s, further proposals for copyright reform, and a recent proposal by Judge Richard Posner and Professor William Landes for an indefinitely renewable copyright.

---

[19] The Creative Commons, a project of Professor Lawrence Lessig of the Stanford Law School, allows authors, composers, and other creators to choose among a variety of protections for their expressions. See www.creativecommons.org.

3. Trademark   Many modern businesses and service organizations invest vast sums of money to establish easily recognizable symbols for their products. For example, children in many countries recognize the golden arches signaling the location of a McDonald's franchise. Such symbols are trademarks or servicemarks. The common law and statutes protected trademarks from as early as the 13th century in England. Proprietary rights in a trademark can be established through actual use in the marketplace, or through registration with the trademarks office. Modern trademark law in the United States stems from the Federal Trademark Act of 1946, commonly called the Lanham Act. The act provides a method for obtaining federal registration for trademarks or servicemarks.[20] As in the case of patents, the successful applicant must establish that the mark passes certain criteria, the most important of which is distinctiveness. Registration with the U.S. Trademark Office entitles the holder to certain protections and rights, among which is the privilege of placing beside one's trademark a sign, ®, that indicates a registered trademark.[21] The owner of a trademark can sue for infringement to prevent unauthorized use .

Trademarks help to solve the problem of consumer ignorance about the quality of a product. When quality is opaque, the consumer can use the trademark as a signal of quality. Furthermore, trademarks reduce the cost to consumers of searching for a product with specific qualities. The principal economic justifications for granting property rights to trademarks are that they lower consumer search costs and create an incentive for producers to supply goods of high quality.

Marketing in Eastern Europe before the fall of communism in 1989 shows what can happen without trademarks. State stores sold unbranded goods with generic labels—"bread," "shirt," "oil," or "pen." A consumer would find one or two unbranded pens on a store's shelf, so he or she could not tell who designed or manufactured them. A purchase was a random draw from the universe of state factories. Because factories could not acquire reputations with consumers, they could not compete to improve quality. In contrast, trademark law enables a company to build up a reputation for high quality and credible advertising, so it can compete with other companies on these dimensions.

The general problem of credibility is central to information economics. Buyers of information generally cannot determine its value until they have it. To illustrate, a banker recently received a letter that read, "If you pay me $1 million, I'll tell you how your bank can make $2 million." The only way to make this claim credible is by providing the information to the bank. After the bank has the information, however, it has no reason to pay for it. Similarly, to assess the value of innovative software, a large buyer like Microsoft must understand how it works. After learning how the product works, however, Microsoft may produce its own version of the product rather than paying royalties to the small company.

Notice that the economic justification for trademarks is different from those for patents and copyrights. Unlike patents and copyrights, the economics of trademarks

---

[20] Note, however, that one does not have to register a mark in order to receive a property right in that mark.

[21] Some producers place the symbol TM or SM (for servicemark) on their products, but those symbols have no legal status.

does not concern innovation, temporary monopoly, or constrained dissemination. Consequently, we cannot make the same economic argument for limiting the duration of the property rights in trademarks as we did in the case of patents and copyrights. Limits on the duration of patents and copyrights were justified as attempts to minimize the social costs of monopoly and tracing. However, trademarks encourage competition and do not impose tracing costs.[22] Perhaps this is why trademarks can last forever, until abandoned. In this respect, trademarks are like property rights in land and unlike other forms of intellectual property.

The question of breadth in trademarks has an interesting twist. Nothing is more settled in the law of trademarks than the proposition that generic product names cannot be trademarks. For example, no producer of cameras may register the word "camera" as a trademark. To allow such a trademark would enable its owner to sue every camera manufacturer that advertised its product by use of the word "camera." If generic product names could be trademarks, then the law of trademarks would create monopoly power, rather than facilitating competition. Sometimes, however, a competitive product succeeds so far that its trademark becomes a generic name. For instance, people today speak of "xeroxing" when they mean "photocopying," or they speak of "Scotch tape" when they mean cellophane tape, or they speak of a "Hoover" when they mean a vacuum cleaner. When this situation arises, the trademark owner must protect the trademark by suing rivals who use the generic name to describe their products. Otherwise, the producer loses its property right in the generic name.

This sort of thing happened to the Sterling Drug Company in 1921. In that year a U.S. federal district court determined that Sterling's trademarked name for acetylsalicylic acid, "Aspirin," had become the common word for any brand of that drug, not just Sterling's. After this ruling, all producers of acetylsalicylic acid could use the term "aspirin" to describe their product. Bayer has managed to prevent this erosion of its trade name Aspirin in Mexico and Canada, where no company but Bayer may describe its acetylsalicylic acid as "aspirin."[23] To learn how manufacturers of very successful products protect their trademarks, read the box on "Coke" on page 134.

Besides quality, trademarks also signal prestige. In some east Asian markets a consumer can choose an unbranded watch and then choose the brand name to put on it. Thus, a consumer can get the prestige of a watch that proclaims itself to be a "Rolex" without paying the cost. These "knockoffs," which violate trademark laws, reward the consumer and cheat the manufacturer of the authentic good. Unfortunately, standard economic tools were not designed for prestige, and they do not do a good job of measuring the costs and benefits of knockoffs.

---

[22] See, for general information, William Landes & Richard A. Posner, *Trademark Law: An Economic Perspective*, 30 J. LAW & ECON. 265 (1987).

[23] The Bayer Company of Germany had discovered acetylsalicylic acid in the late 1890s. The U.S. government seized the trademark "Aspirin" during World War I and sold the right to use that tradename to the Sterling Drug Company in 1918. Interestingly, Bayer purchased Sterling in 1994.

QUESTION 5.8: The duration of copyright increased under U.S. law in several steps since the eighteenth century until it reached the life of the author plus 70 years. Suppose that a writer completes a novel at age 40. If the writer lives to be 75, then the copyright will last for 105 years. At an interest rate of 10 percent, the present value of $1 paid after 105 years equals much less than 5 cents. What does this fact suggest about whether the efficient duration of copyright is longer or shorter than currently provided by law?

QUESTION 5.9: In 1939 the composer Igor Stravinsky received $6000 from Walt Disney for the right to use "The Rite of Spring" in the animated film "Fantasia," featuring Mickey Mouse. Should Disney own the exclusive right to release the film in videocassette, which generated $360 million in revenues in the first two years after its release in 1996, or are Stravinsky's assignees entitled to some of the money?[24]

"Coke" Is It!

One of the best-known trademarks in the world is the word "Coke" to describe the Coca-Cola Company's cola soft drink. Precisely because it is so well known, there is the danger to the Coca-Cola Company that consumers might use the designation "Coke" to refer to any cola soft drink and not just the one the Coca-Cola Company produces. If that should happen, then "Coke" will have become a generic product name that any producer may use. The Coca-Cola trade research department, which has an annual budget of redundant millions of dollars and employs a team of investigators whose job it is to roam the United States asking at restaurants and soda fountains for "Coke" and "Coca-Cola." The investigators then send samples of what they are served to the corporate headquarters in Atlanta for chemical analysis. If the company determines that a restaurateur has served them something other than Coca-Cola, then that business is advised of its wrongdoing.

Since 1945, Coca-Cola has sued approximately 40–60 retailers per year. Retailers claim that what lies behind the company's vigorous campaign is not a fear of trademark infringement but an insidious and anticompetitive attempt to browbeat retailers into dealing only with the Coca-Cola Company. They note that it is frequently too costly for them—as on a busy night—to tell each customer who asks for a rum and Coke that they are really going to get a rum and Pepsi. Rather than face a lawsuit for trademark infringement, many of the retailers simply signed up with Coca-Cola as their exclusive supplier, saying that to do so was less costly to them. The retailers point to the fact that Coke has an 80 percent market share in the fountain-soda market but a much smaller share of the supermarket sales as evidence that the trade research department's work is part of an anticompetitive marketing operation.

(See "Mixing with Coke Over Trademarks Is Always a Fizzle: Coca-Cola Adds a Little Life in Court to Those Failing to Serve the Real Thing," *Wall Street Journal*, March 9, 1978, p. 1, col. 4.)

---

[24] James Zinea, "A Discordant Ruling," *Forbes*, October 5, 1998, p. 66.

QUESTION 5.10: No one may use a patent without the patent-holder's permission. But in a limited set of circumstances, others may use copyrighted material without the copyright-holder's permission. These circumstances—called the "fair use" exception—allow, for example, reviewers to quote from copyrighted material without permission, teachers to photocopy or distribute electronically and assign limited portions of copyrighted material to their classes, and musical groups to include or "sample" copyrighted music in their own compositions.

Use economic theory to explain why it may be efficient to allow the fair use exception.

QUESTION 5.11: Why is it efficient to limit the duration of patents and copyrights, whereas real property rights endure almost forever (with an important exception to be noted later in this chapter)?

QUESTION 5.12: Trademark law does not allow a holder to sell a trademark independent of the good to which it is attached. Thus, Coca-Cola cannot sell its use of the trademark "Coke" to another producer of cola syrup; that mark may be sold only with the syrup produced by or under the supervision of the Coca-Cola Company. Can you provide an economic rationale for this restriction?

Web Note 5.5

What are the appropriate remedies for unlawful use of a patent, copyright, or a trademark? See our website for a discussion of the economics of those issues.

Web Note 5.6

This section has only skimmed the surface of the remarkable developments in intellectual property of the last 10 years. See our website for more on the issues of the law, such as private ownership versus "open source" software, how the fashion industry uses IP, and how magicians, cooks, and comedians protect their intellectual property.

C. Organizations as Property

Families, clubs, churches, cooperatives, trusts, charities, and the state are organizations that own property, such as land, buildings, and machinery. An organization, however, is not the same as the property that it owns. For some kinds of organizations, the members can buy and sell assets, but no one can buy or sell the organization. To illustrate, no one owns a family, club, church, cooperative, trust, charity, or state. In contrast, corporations have owners who buy and sell, not just the corporation's assets, but also the corporation itself. In brief, many organizations own property and some organizations *are* property.

Owned and unowned organizations perform different roles in society. Unowned organizations play the central role in social life, religion, and government, whereas corporations play the central role in production and economic growth. We will explain the connection between the difference in ownership and the difference in function.

To begin, consider what an organization is. Organizations generally have a structure of offices created by laws and contracts, such as Chairman, Treasurer, or Ombudsman. While some members of organizations have offices, all members have roles to play. Standardization in the division of labor creates roles like bookkeeper, mechanic, or purchasing agent. By supplying a structure of offices and roles, an organization coordinates the behavior of its members so that it can pursue goals. When coordination is tight enough, observers of the organization ascribe goals to it, not just to its individual members. Thus, we can define an organization as *a structure of offices and roles capable of corporate action.*

Organizations adjust their structure to improve performance or change goals. Owned organizations adjust in response to pressure from markets for organizations. For example, corporate officers who fail to perform may find their company bought by a new owner who fires the old managers and replaces them with new managers. In contrast, an unowned organization avoids pressure from the market for organizations because no one can buy or sell it.

We must consider how a market for organizations changes their behavior. According to the bargain theory of property developed in this book, markets tend to move property from people who value it less to people who value it more. Thus, the market for organizations tends to move organizations from owners who value them less to owners who value them more. Corporations are primarily instruments to make money, so the owners of corporations tend to value them according to their profitability. Consequently, the market for corporations tends to bring the ownership of each corporation to the people who can make the most profit from them. Under ideal conditions described in the model of perfect competition, profitability measures the social value created by a corporation. When reality approximates these conditions, the market for corporations maximizes the nation's wealth by transferring ownership to the people who can run corporations most profitably.

Because no one owns a family, club, church, cooperative, trust, charity, or state, there are no markets to move control of these organizations to the people who can make the most profit from them. Consequently, the primary purpose of these organizations is not profits. Instead of being an instrument for wealth, most members regard these organizations as primarily serving other purposes. If these organizations were owned, pressure from the market for organizations would divert their purpose to profitability. Consequently, no one should own an organization whose purpose is not profit, which is what we observe in fact.

The owner of property enjoys discretionary power over it, including the right to transform it. When an organization is owned, the owner usually has the power to restructure its offices and roles, and change the people who fill them. This owner's legal power over an organization often suffices to control it. When an organization is unowned, however, no one may control its offices and roles. *The alternative to ownership is often governance.* A system of governance involves politics and collective control. To illustrate the difference, the owner of a small corporation controls it and does with it as he wishes, whereas the members of a club, church, cooperative, or democratic state make collective decisions and engage in politics. Ownership is usually best for pursuing wealth, and governance is usually best for pursuing more diffuse goals.

We have explained that different organizations have different functions, and the primary function of corporations is to create wealth by pursuing profits. The market for corporations helps to keep management focused on this task. Markets for corporations, however, are often "thin," by which we mean that there are few buyers or sellers. To illustrate, economic recession at the turn of the 21st century and destruction of the World Trade Center by terrorists caused a significant decline in the number of air travelers. In this environment, many (but not all) airlines are unprofitable. This situation creates pressure for the owners of unprofitable airlines to sell them. The potential buyers are few in number, because airlines are very expensive to buy and running them requires expert knowledge. The market for airlines is "thin" in the sense of having few buyers and sellers. The problem of thin markets is aggravated by antitrust authorities who may prevent one airline from merging with another. In general, blocking mergers to thicken product markets thins the market for corporations.

As a market thins, competitive pressures diminish. Specifically, thin markets for corporations allow their members to pursue goals other than maximizing the company's profits. Understanding this fact requires appreciation of the history of corporate law. Corporations are very old forms of organization. For example, the British government financed itself in the past partly by selling exclusive licenses to large corporations to develop trade in the colonies. As a specific example, the Hudson's Bay Company was formed in 1670 and was soon thereafter given control over fur trading and other businesses in the area amounting to one-third of present-day Canada.

Two important legal innovations distinguish these historic corporations from modern corporations. First, like the Hudson's Bay Company, the charters of the historic companies restricted them by activity and geography. In contrast, modern corporations can enter almost any form of business in any place. To illustrate, a corporation chartered in Indiana can enter almost any kind of business in any other U.S. state. (Corporations are restricted from entering a few lines of business in the United States that are reserved for partnerships, notably law and accounting, or require separate incorporation, notably commercial banks.) Removing restrictions on activities and geography vastly increases competition among corporations.

Second, the owners of the historic corporations were liable for the corporation's debt. To illustrate, if the Hudson's Bay Company had gone bankrupt in the eighteenth century, then its creditors could obtain repayment by seizing the wealth of its stockholders. Given unlimited liability of investors in a company for its debts, people who invest must carefully monitor and control the company's policies. In contrast, the owners of modern corporations are not liable for the corporation's debts. To illustrate, if an airline goes bankrupt, its creditors can liquidate its assets, but its creditors cannot seize the homes, cars, or bank accounts of its stockholders. As a result of *limited liability,* people who invest in stock run the risk of losing their investment and nothing more. Limited liability allows people to invest in a company without monitoring or controlling the company's policies so thoroughly.

Limited liability is an aspect of the more general problem of separating the assets of a company from the assets of its owners and managers. Limited liability prevents the creditors of the company from reaching the personal assets of the company's owners. An equally important body of law prevents the creditors of the owners from reaching the assets of the company. Separating the assets is called "partitioning," and not separating the assets is called "co-mingling." Modern corporate law partitions the assets of corporations and their owners, whereas the law historically co-mingled them.

Limited liability has created a situation commonly described as the *separation of ownership from control*. This phrase refers to the fact that many stockholders in large companies sold on public stock exchanges do little monitoring of it and have no control over it. Sometimes a small number of large investors monitor and control the corporation. Often, however, none of the owners exercises control over the corporation. Instead, control over the corporation rests with its management. Most investors want to make money, so they want the managers to maximize profits. The managers, however, have their own goals to pursue.

A vigorous market for corporations can prevent managers from pursuing goals other than maximizing the company's profits. In general, the stock market bids up the price of a company's stock until it equals the sum of the company's expected future earnings discounted to present value. If managers fail to maximize the company's profits, then the expected future earnings of the company fall and its stock price declines. Under these circumstances, an outsider may attempt to buy the company and replace its management. As this theory predicts, econometric evidence demonstrates that the stock price of firms rises and remains higher as a consequence of a successful hostile takeover. So, the new managers must make the acquired firm more profitable. Foreseeing the possibility of a hostile takeover helps to prevent managers from departing very far from the goal of maximizing the company's profits. Conversely, a thin market for corporations makes hostile takeovers unlikely, so managers can pursue other goals than profits.

In recent years, much scholarship and research on corporations concerns how the law ameliorates or exacerbates problems created by the separation of ownership from control. For example, managers employ various contractual devices to reduce the possibility that someone will buy the company and bring in new managers (for example, "poison pill," "golden parachute," "lock-ups," and non-voting shares of stock). Also, managers have succeeded in persuading legislators to enact statutes to reduce the effectiveness of the market for corporate control (notably the Williams Act).

Before beginning a new topic, we want to connect this discussion of organizations as property to the discussion of contracts in Chapter 8. The problem of the separation of ownership from control in the modern corporation has a general analytical form. Owners often placed their assets under the control of someone else. In these circumstances, economists describe the owner as the "principal" and the controller as the "agent." The principal-agent problem is to write a contract that gives the agent incentives to manage the asset in the best way for the principal. A later chapter uses the principal-agent model to develop the theory of contracts.

QUESTION 5.13:

a. Give a concrete example of the difference between ownership and governance in organizations. In your example, which form of organization has a higher transaction cost of making decisions?

b. Find a concrete example of a corporation whose managers faced a hostile take-over bid that succeeded. After the take-over, what happened to the managers of the acquired firm?

D. Public and Private Property

Having discussed the ownership of organizations, we return to a discussion of the ownership of assets like land, buildings, and machinery by organizations. We will use our theory of property to explain the difference between private and public ownership of a resource. Private and public externalities differ according to the number of affected people. Similarly, private and public ownership can be distinguished by the number of owners. A resource owned by a single individual is private. A corporation owned by a small group of stockholders ("closely held corporation" or "close corporation") is a "private company." Corporations owned by many shareholders are "public companies." Similarly, the state is called the "public sector." When the state owns a resource, such as a public park, we sometimes say that the resource belongs to all of the citizens or that it belongs to no one other than the state.

What difference does the number of owners make? In discussing the Coase Theorem, we described bargaining among the owners of separate properties, such as the rancher and the farmer. Bargaining also occurs when several people own the same property. For example, the partners in a business bargain over the allocation of tasks. The difference between private and public ownership can be described as a difference in the structure of bargaining.

Private ownership divides people into small groups. So long as externalities are private, private owners can advance their interests by cooperating with a small number of people. Bargaining among small groups of people tends to result in cooperation and to achieve efficiency. Consequently, the case for private ownership is easy to make when production and utility functions are separable, or when externalities affect few people. In these circumstances, public ownership is a costly mistake.

An illustration comes from a study of oyster beds along the Atlantic and Gulf coasts of the United States.[25] At an early stage in their lives, oysters attach themselves permanently to some subaqueous material, such as rock. This attachment makes it possible to imagine defining private property rights in oysters for commercial fishing operators. However, the states along the Atlantic and Gulf coasts that have commercial oyster industries have not settled on a single system of property rights for oysters. Some states have determined that the subaqueous areas where oysters tend to congregate are to be *common* property for oyster harvesters; any of them may take oysters from those areas, and none may exclude another. Other states have held that these areas are to be available for private leasing from the state and that the lessee will have the usual rights to exclude and transfer (with some limitations). This difference allowed Professors Agnello and Donnelly to compare the relative efficiency of the private and communal property-rights systems. The measure of efficiency they used was labor productivity (output per person-hour in oyster fishing). Their finding was that labor was much more productively employed in the privately leased oyster beds than in the communal oyster beds. Put dramatically, the authors of this study concluded that if all oyster beds had been privately leased in 1969, the average oyster harvester's

---

[25] See R.J. Agnello & L.P. Donnelly, *Property Rights and Efficiency in the Oyster Industry*, 18 J. Law & Econ. 521 (1975). See also G. Power, *More About Oysters Than You Wanted to Know*, 30 Md. L. Rev. 199 (1970).

income would have been 50 percent higher than it was. That implies a sizable welfare loss due to public ownership.

The public oyster beds are an example of the depletion of an open-access resource by overuse, which is called "the tragedy of the commons."[26] Open access to a congested natural resource has a remorseless logic with a terrible ending, like a Greek tragedy. There were two clear correctives to the problem: Turn ownership of the resource over to an individual (who would then have the appropriate incentive to invest in its preservation or use and to exclude others from using it) or devise an enforceable and effective method of restricting access to the common resource.[27]

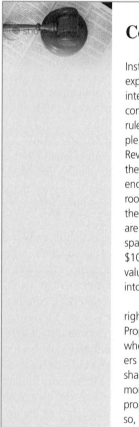

Commons and Anticommons

Instead of a tragedy of the commons, the breakup of the Soviet Union in the early 1990s exposed the symmetrically opposite problem of property rights.[28] Rather than too few property interests—the problem of the commons—there were too many property interests. How did this come to be? Private property interests were largely unknown during the 70 years of communist rule, and people came to have ownership claims to resources in idiosyncratic ways. So, for example, a large apartment with many rooms, which had been privately owned before the 1917 Revolution, had come to be home to several different families. Each family might occupy one of the rooms of the apartment and share the use of the kitchen and bathroom. When communism ended, these families thought that they had continuing ownership claims to their individual rooms and the common spaces. Suppose that if integrated into an apartment for a single owner, the apartment—or *komunalka,* as it was called—would be worth $500,000. Assume that there are currently four tenant families, each occupying one room and sharing use of the common spaces. If sold separately, the interests of the tenants would fetch, we assume, $25,000—or $100,000 in total. Converting the *komunalka* into a single apartment would create $400,000 in value. But it was frequently the case that the costs of assembling the individual tenant interests into the more valuable whole were so great as to preclude the more valuable use of the resource.

The tragedy of the anticommons occurs when multiple owners are each endowed with the right to exclude others from a scarce resource, and no one has an effective privilege of use. Property interests can be so finely divided as to impose significant assembly costs on later users who would like to consolidate the property interests into a more valuable whole. Heller and others have argued that precisely this anticommons problem arises in biomedical research.[29] We shall see an additional example in the box on the public domain later in this chapter. The commons and the anticommons suggest symmetric problems of "under-propertization" and "over-propertization." Just as the porridge of the three bears could be too hot or too cold or just right, so, too, the law can define property interests too finely or not at all or in just the right measure.

---

[26] G. Hardin, *The Tragedy of the Commons,* 162 SCIENCE 1243 (1968).

[27] See ELINOR OSTROM, GOVERNING THE COMMONS: THE EVOLUTION OF INSTITUTIONS FOR ACTION (1990).

[28] See Michael Heller, *The Tragedy of the Anticommons: Property in the Transition from Marx to Market,* 111 HARV. L. REV. 621 (1998).

[29] Michael A. Heller & Rebecca Eisenberg, *Can Patents Deter Innovation?: The Anticommons in Biomedical Research,* 280 SCIENCE 698 (1998).

We have discussed the easy case in which private ownership can separate utility and production functions and in which externalities are private. A more difficult case for choosing between public and private ownership arises when production and utility functions of many owners are interdependent and externalities are public. To address this problem through private ownership, the affected parties must bargain with each other, and the transaction costs are prohibitive. Public ownership is a possible solution. Instead of unstructured bargaining and a requirement that everyone agree, the switch from private to public ownership substitutes structured bargaining and a collective-choice principle, such as majority rule.

To illustrate, consider pasture land in the mountains of Iceland.[30] Dividing the mountain pasture among individual owners would require fencing it, which is prohibitively expensive. Instead, the highland pasture is held in common, with each village owning different pastures that are separated by natural features, such as lakes and mountain peaks. If each person in the village could place as many sheep as he or she wanted in the common pasture, the meadows might be destroyed and eroded by overuse. In fact, the common pastures in the mountains of Iceland have not been overused and destroyed because the villages have effective systems of governance. They have adopted rules to protect and preserve the common pasture. The sheep are grazed in common pasture in the mountains during the summer and then returned to individual farms in the valleys during the winter. The total number of sheep allowed in the mountain pasture during the summer is adjusted to its carrying capacity. Each member of the village receives a share of the total in proportion to the amount of farmland where he or she raises hay to feed the sheep in the winter.[31]

Some discussions of the superiority of private ownership over public ownership equate public ownership with open access to resources. This equation is too simple. In fact, the general public does not have free access to most public property. To illustrate, the national parks in the United States are publicly owned, but a fee is charged to enter; many activities require reservations in advance (a form of rationing by time), and no one can graze animals or cut wood. The tragedy of the commons, in its fully disastrous form, requires a political paralysis that prevents government from stopping the destruction of a resource. This paralysis seems to have reached an advanced stage for some resources, such as fisheries. For other resources, there are symptoms of paralysis, but not the full disaster. For example, the federal government owns vast lands in the American West and sells permits for grazing, forestry, and mining on these lands. The federal domain is inefficiently managed. As a result, the environment has deteriorated.[32]

Communism's collapse in Eastern Europe identified a kind of property problem that had gone unnoticed. Many shops in Moscow remained closed for several years while busy street kiosks appeared on the street in front of them. Potentially profitable shops remained closed because too many people had the legal or effective power to prevent

---

[30] See the discussion of common mountain pastures in Iceland in THRAINN EGGERTSSON, ECONOMIC BEHAVIOR AND INSTITUTIONS (1990).

[31] Professor Elinor Ostrom won the 2009 Nobel Prize in Economics for her studies of governance systems of public and common resources.

[32] For an introduction to federal ownership of American land, see MARION CLAWSON, THE FEDERAL LANDS REVISITED (1983).

anyone from using them. Multiple vetoes resulted from the overhang of socialist laws enacted under the communist regime. The situation where everyone could prevent anyone from using a Moscow shop is the mirror image of the sea where no one could prevent anyone from fishing. The problem of the sea was already called the "tragedy of the commons," so the problem of the Moscow shops was named the "tragedy of the anticommons." Once an anticommons emerges, collecting rights into usable private property bundles can be brutal and slow.

Private ownership assigns each resource to a person who owns it, and the owner can control access by excluding users. Private owners must bear the cost of boundary maintenance. Private ownership works well when production and utility functions are separable or externalities affect few people who can bargain with each other. *Public ownership* comes in three forms. First, *open access* allows everyone to use a resource, and no one can exclude anyone from using it. Nothing is spent on boundary maintenance. Open access works well when the resource is uncongested, but congestion causes tragic overuse. Second, *political control* allows lawmakers or regulators to impose rules concerning access. Limited access is the most common rule for the state's property, including public lands. Third, the opposite of open access is *unanimous consent,* which allows no one access unless everyone agrees. The need for unanimous consent among multiple owners causes tragic underuse. In special circumstances where the aim is to preserve a resource in its unused condition, underuse is serendipitous rather than tragic.

It would be surprising if a small, homogeneous village in Iceland were paralyzed politically to the point of being unable to manage public resources. However, a large, heterogeneous country such as the United States faces far more difficult problems in managing public resources. One solution is to reduce public ownership by selling federally owned land. The market value of the products yielded by lands in the American West would surely be higher if the land currently under public control were transferred to private control.

This argument, however, is unlikely to persuade those who *want* to see the wilderness underutilized. Most ecologists believe that public land should *not* be managed with the aim of maximizing the market value that it yields. Everyone tends to think that some things are more valuable than wealth (at least at the margin), such as liberty or truth; for some people, wilderness is such a value. People who love liberty would never decide whether persons have the right to speak by asking whether people would pay more to hear them or to shut them up. Similarly, those who love the wilderness would never decide whether to build condominiums on the nesting site of the California condors by asking whether developers would pay more for the land than would the ecologists. Ecologists usually oppose the sale of public lands to private interests because their aim is to limit development rather than to increase yield. Given the scope of disagreement between ecologists and developers, it seems certain that vast resources will be used up in political disputes over the governance of public lands in the western United States.

Question 5.14: Cooperative enterprises are collectively owned, and their affairs are directed through shared governance. Use the preceding theory to discuss the management of some cooperative enterprises with which you are familiar, such as a cooperative dairy, a cooperative apartment building, an Israeli kibbutz, a Hutterite farm, a commune, and so on.

II. How are Property Rights Established and Verified?

As explained in the preceding chapter, the clear delineation of property rights typically facilitates bargaining and voluntary exchange. If property rights are unclear, the parties have an incentive to bargain and clarify them. However, delineation and enforcement of property rights is costly. It is necessary, consequently, to balance the benefit from delineating property rights against the costs. In this section we consider how law strikes the balance.

A. Establishing Property Rights Over Fugitive Property: First Possession versus Tied Ownership

The problem of defining property rights seems straightforward for objects like land and houses, which have definite boundaries and stay put. But what about objects that move around or have indefinite boundaries, like natural gas or wild animals? "Fugitive property," as such things are called, creates a legal problem as illustrated by the case of *Hammonds v. Central Kentucky Natural Gas Co.,* 255 Ky. 685, 75 S.W.2d 204 (Court of Appeal of Kentucky, 1934). The Central Kentucky Natural Gas Company leased tracts of land above large deposits of natural gas. Some of the leased tracts were separated from one another by land that the company did not own or lease. The geological dome of natural gas from which the company drew its supply lay partially under the leased land and partially under unleased land. Hammonds owned 54 acres of land that lay above the geological dome tapped by the Central Kentucky Natural Gas Company, but she had not let the subsurface rights in her land to the company. When the Central Kentucky Natural Gas Company extracted natural gas and oil from the dome, she sued the company on the theory that some of the natural gas that was under her land had been wrongfully appropriated by the defendant.

It is difficult in this case, if not impossible, to identify which natural gas came from under unleased land and which came from under leased land. Two general principles can solve the problem of establishing ownership:

1. *First possession:* oil and gas are not the property of anyone until reduced to actual possession by extraction, or
2. *Tied ownership:* the owner of the surface has the exclusive right to subsurface deposits.

Under the first rule, the Central Kentucky Natural Gas Company was entitled to extract all the natural gas from the dome, regardless of whether it held the surface rights. But under the second rule, the Central Kentucky Natural Gas Company was only entitled to extract the natural gas under the ground that it owned or leased.

The consequences of these two rules for the efficient exploration and extraction of natural gas are very different. According to the first rule, fugitive oil or gas is not owned by anyone until someone possesses it, and the first person to possess it thereby becomes the owner. This rule can, consequently, be called the *rule of first possession.* The rule of first possession applies the legal maxim "first in time, first in right." This rule has been used to establish ownership rights for centuries. To illustrate, in the arid

American Southwest, state law allowed a person to obtain a right to water in a stream by being the first to tap it for use in mining or irrigation. (See the box entitled "Owning the Ocean" on page 156.) By now, there are few opportunities to claim unpossessed land or water, but the rule of first possession applies to important forms of intangible property, such as inventions.

A great advantage of the rule of first possession is that it focuses on a few simple facts, so it is relatively easy and cheap to apply. In the event of a dispute about ownership, determination of who first possessed the property in question is usually straightforward. For example, material evidence usually proves who tapped a water supply first. There is, however, an economic disadvantage of the rule of first possession: it creates an incentive for some people to preempt others by making uneconomic investments to obtain ownership of property. The reason why the rule of first possession creates an incentive to invest too much too early is easily explained. According to the rule of first possession, an appropriate investment transfers the ownership of a resource to the investor. The owner of a scarce resource can rent it to others. Rent increases as a resource becomes more scarce. Indeed, rent is the scarcity value of the resource. Under the rule of first possession, an investment thus yields two types of benefits to the investor: (1) production (more is produced from existing resources), and (2) future rent (scarcity value of the resource in the future).

To illustrate, assume that the law allows a person to acquire ownership of "waste" land by fencing it. Fencing land increases its productivity from, say, grazing cattle on it. By assumption, fencing the land also transfers ownership to the person who built the fence. Assume that fencing waste land costs more than the profit from grazing cattle on it at current prices, but everyone expects the use value of the land to increase as population grows in the future. Investors may build useless fences to "preempt" others and secure title to the land.

Preemptive investment illustrates a general economic principle applicable to the rule of first possession. When the state awards property rights, people contest vigorously to obtain title. In a contest for title, persons try to get ownership rights transferred to themselves. Economic efficiency, however, concerns the *production* of wealth, not the *transfer* of it. Investments for the sake of transferring wealth, not producing it, are socially inefficient.

In technical terms, social efficiency requires investors to invest in a resource until the marginal cost equals the marginal increase in productive value. The rule of first possession causes people to invest in a resource until the marginal cost equals the marginal value of the sum of increased production *plus* transferred ownership. The transfer effect under the rule of first possession thus causes over-investment in the activities that the law defines as necessary to obtain legal possession. It is in the self-interest of investors, but not in the interests of social efficiency, to improve property in order to transfer ownership.

To illustrate, consider the Homestead Act of 1862 in the United States, which established rules allowing private citizens to acquire up to 160 acres of public lands in the West. The act required claimants to fulfill certain requirements before they acquired title. For example, the claimant had to file an affidavit swearing that he or she was either the head of a family or 21 years old, and that the claim was "for the purpose of actual settlement and cultivation, and not, either directly or indirectly, for the use or benefit of any other person or persons whomsoever." Moreover, before full title was acquired for $1.25 per acre, the claimant had to reside on the claim for 6 months and make "suitable" improvements on the land. These requirements were meant to minimize transfer effects and to encourage production. In practice, however, the requirements were fleetingly enforced (as was usually the case with the residence requirement) and easily evaded (as when "suitable" improvements consisted of placing miniature houses—really large doll houses—on the claim). The occupation and development of the American frontier occurred at a faster pace than competitive markets or a strictly enforced Homestead Act would have produced.

In contrast to the rule of first possession, there is no gap in ownership under the second rule for fugitive gas, according to which all the gas under the ground already belongs to the people who own the surface. By extension, the second rule suggests that wild animals belong to the owners of some piece of land, such as the land where the wild animal was born. Ownership of fish and other marine resources should perhaps be tied to ownership of the ocean floor. In general, the second rule, called the *rule of tied ownership,* ties ownership of fugitive property to settled property.

The common and civil law often tie ownership by applying the principle of *accession.* According to this principle, a new thing is owned by the owner of the proximate or prominent property. Thus, a newborn calf belongs to the owner of the mother cow, new land created by a shift in a river belongs to the owner of the river's bank; the owner of a brand name has an exclusive right to use it in an Internet domain name; the owner of copyright has an exclusive right to adapt the work to another medium; an owner of an apartment also owns any fixtures that a tenant attaches to the walls; a new business opportunity discovered by a corporate employee in the course of work belongs to the corporation; and a carpenter who unknowingly uses someone else's wood to make a barrel owns it (but he must pay restitution to the wood's owner).[33]

Tying ownership of fugitive property to settled property avoids preemptive investment *so long as the ownership claims in the resource to which the fugitive property is tied are already established.* To illustrate, all the gas is already owned under the second rule because all the surface rights are already owned, so the rule does not provide an incentive to acquire ownership by extracting too much gas too soon. Similarly, if salmon were the property of the people who own the streams where they spawn, the owners would not deplete the salmon by catching too many of them.

The problem with the second rule, as illustrated by the facts in *Hammonds,* is the difficulty of establishing and verifying ownership rights. The homogeneity of natural gas and its dispersion in caverns makes proving its original underground location difficult and costly.

Our analysis of fugitive resources reveals a common trade-off in property law:

> Rules that tie ownership to possession have the advantage of being easy to administer and the disadvantage of providing incentives for uneconomic investment in possessory acts, whereas rules that allow ownership without possession have the advantage of avoiding preemptive investment and the disadvantage of being costly to administer.

---

[33] Thomas A. Merrill, "Establishing Ownership: First Possession versus Accession." BERKELEY LAW AND ECONOMICS WORKSHOP (26 February 2007).

Choosing the more efficient rule in a case such as *Hammonds* requires balancing the incentive to overinvest under the rule of first possession against the cost of administering and enforcing ownership without possession. (Besides first possession and tied possession, other ways of allocating initial rights include auctions, lotteries, and preferences based on attributes such as needs, accomplishments, ethnicity, and gender.)

QUESTION 5.15:   Here is the critical part of the case of *Pierson v. Post*,[34]

" . . . Post, being in possession of certain dogs and hounds under his command, did, 'on a certain wild and uninhabited, unpossessed and waste land, called the beach, find and start one of those noxious beasts called a fox,' and whilst there hunting, chasing and pursuing the same with his dogs and hounds, and when in view thereof, Pierson, well knowing the fox was so hunted and pursued, did, in the sight of Post, to prevent his catching the same, kill and carry it off. A verdict having been rendered for [Post, who was] the plaintiff below, [Pierson appealed] . . . However uncourteous or unkind the conduct of Pierson towards Post, in this instance, may have been, yet his act was productive of no injury or damage for which a legal remedy can be applied. We are of opinion the judgment below was erroneous, and ought to be reversed."

Does this decision implement a principle of tied ownership or a principle of first possession? Note that the case, which is a staple in introductory courses on property law in American universities, seems irrelevant to modern conditions because first possession of foxes apparently does not lead to capturing too many of them too soon.

Economic analysis suggests that it should not be because of concerns about which hunter owns a fox. Explain the costs and benefits to weigh in an efficiency analysis of this case.

QUESTION 5.16:   Can you make any sense of the proposition that the rule of first possession is a principle of "natural justice"?

B. When to Privatize Open-Access Resources: Congestion versus Boundary Maintenance

We have discussed various examples from history of unowned resources that become private property. *When* do unowned resources become owned? Economics suggests an answer.

The rule of first possession often applies when property is owned in common and accessible to the public. Property that is accessible for use by a broad public is called an *open access resource*. To illustrate, the seas are common property to which the public has access. In many cases, the fish and mammals in the sea can be owned by whoever catches them. Consequently, fish and marine mammals have been hunted far

---

[34] Cal. R. 175, 2 Am. Dec. 264 (Supreme Court of New York, 1805).

beyond the economic level, some to the brink of extinction. Similarly, in much of the world, common hunting land is over-hunted, common pasture land is over-grazed, and public forests are over-harvested. Much of the world's soil erosion and forest depletion is caused by the open-access rule.

Some technical terms follow to help explain the economic irrationality of the situation. The "maximum sustainable yield" is the largest yield sustainable in the long run. To maximize the yield, the application of labor and capital must expand until the marginal products of labor and capital are zero. All of the world's major fisheries are currently fished beyond the maximum sustainable yield, which means that the marginal product of labor and capital is negative. In these circumstances, the catch on the fisheries would increase simply by making less effort and reducing expenditures on labor and capital. Similarly, the yield on many open-access forests would increase by investing less effort and cutting fewer trees, and the yield on many open-access pastures would increase by investing less effort and keeping fewer animals. Overused fisheries, forests, and pastures are analogous to a factory with so many workers that they get in each others' way and slow each other down, so the factory's total product would increase merely by reducing its total employment. Nothing could be more irrational than assigning people to work at jobs with negative productivity.

Preventing overuse of common resources involves controlling use by means other than the open-access rule. Tied ownership is one method. For example, to prevent over-grazing of common pastures, small communities in Iceland traditionally tied access to common pastures to production on private pastures. Specifically, farmers were allowed to graze animals in the common, high lands in the summer according to a formula based on the number of animals each farmer sustained in the winter from hay grown on private pastures in low lands.[35]

Another method to prevent overuse is *privatization,* which means in this context converting from public to private ownership. To illustrate, many people could homestead land, fish in the sea, or gather coral from reefs. In contrast, a private owner can exclude others from using his or her resource. Granting private property rights over land, whales, or elephants would close access by limiting it to the owner. Thus, homesteading land converts it from public to private ownership; some salmon streams have been converted to private ownership; and some villages have been given ownership of coral reefs.

The conversion from common ownership to private ownership involves this trade-off: A rule of open access causes over-use of a resource, whereas private property rights require costly exclusion of non-owners. This formulation suggests when an economically rational society will change the rule of law for a resource from open access to private ownership. When the resource is uncongested and boundary maintenance is expensive, open access is cheaper than private ownership. As time passes, however, congestion may increase, and the technology of boundary maintenance may improve. Eventually, a point may be reached where private ownership is cheaper than open

---

[35] See T. Eggertsson, *Analyzing Institutional Successes and Failures: A Millennium of Common Mountain Pastures in Iceland,* 12 INTN'L. REV. LAW & ECON. 423 (1992).

access. An economically rational society will privatize a resource at the point in time where boundary maintenance costs less than the waste from overuse of the resource.[36]

This theory makes definite predictions about privatization. For example, it predicts that the invention of barbed wire, which lowered the cost of boundary maintenance in areas where there were few fencing materials, would promote the privatization of public lands in the American West. As another example, it predicts that property rights will be created in the electromagnetic spectrum when broadcasters begin to interfere with each other. The predictions of this theory are confirmed by some facts and disconfirmed by others. Apparently, societies are often rational, as the theory assumes, but not perfectly rational. Politics leads to bargains and compromises that violate the requirements of economic efficiency. For examples of these compromises, read the box entitled "Owning the Ocean."

Owning the Ocean

Water covers 70 percent of the Earth's surface in the form of oceans; yet, almost all of that vast amount of water is unaffected by well-defined property rights. In the late sixteenth and early seventeenth centuries, the great voyages of discovery and the resulting sea-borne empires in Europe necessitated internationally accepted rules on rights to use the ocean. These rights were first catalogued in the famous *Mare Liberum* of Hugo Grotius of Holland. He noted that the "sea, since it is as incapable of being seized as the air, cannot have been attached to the possessions of any particular nation." In the system that Grotius suggested and that prevailed in international law for nearly 300 years, each nation was to have exclusive rights to the use of the ocean within three miles of its shoreline, with that area to be called the "territorial seas." (The three-mile distance was not picked at random; it was the distance that an early seventeenth-century cannonball could carry.) Beyond the three-mile limit, Grotius urged that the "high seas" should be a common resource from which none, save pirates, could legitimately be excluded.

Increasing use of the high seas in the early and mid-nineteenth century led to the replacement of the doctrine of "free use" with that of "reasonable use." After World War II, the increasing importance of shipping, fishing, offshore oil and gas deposits, and seabed mining caused the legal system of ocean rights to crumble. In 1945 President Truman announced that the United States' exclusive rights to subaqueous organic resources—such as oil and natural gas—extended to the edge of the continental shelf or margin, an area that stretched 200 miles from the Atlantic Coast of the United States. Other nations quickly made similar claims. Unlike these unilateral actions, attempts at international cooperation have achieved mixed results.

---

[36] This is the central point made by Harold Demsetz in *Toward a Theory of Property Rights,* 57 AM. ECON. REV. 347 (1967). He argues, for example, that American Indians did not establish property rights in land when the costs of administering the rules exceeded the benefits from private ownership. Proceeding along these lines, he tries to explain why certain North American Indian tribes, such as those in the Northeast, whose principal economic activity was trapping animals for their fur, developed a notion of property rights and others, such as the Plains Indians, whose principal resource was the migratory buffalo, did not. The extent to which his arguments can be squared with history or anthropology is still open to question.

To illustrate, when the third United Nations Convention on the Law of the Sea (UNCLOS) convened in 1973, there was widespread agreement that the territorial sea would be established at the 12-mile limit and that there should be an "exclusive economic zone," largely but not completely controlled by the coastal state, stretching to 200 miles beyond the shoreline, the general extent of the continental shelf.

There was not general agreement on what to do with property rights to the areas beyond this 200-mile limit, and it was the disposition of these areas that raised the really hard issues. The developed countries urged a private-property-rights-based system of development, whereas the developing countries offered a common-property-rights system. In the end a compromise, called the *parallel system,* was agreed on. There would be both private development and a UN-funded and UN-operated company, called the "Enterprise." In order to give the Enterprise the ability to compete with the more advanced countries of the developed world, an International Seabed Authority (ISA) would be created to allocate rights to mine the oceans. The conference specified an ingenious variant of the "I cut, you choose" method of cake-cutting in order to allocate mining rights. Before it could begin operation, a private or state organization had to submit to the ISA two prospective sites of operations. The Authority would then choose one of those sites for later development by the Enterprise and allow the applicant to proceed with the mining of the other.

The United States refused to sign the final treaty, although 117 countries eventually signed it in December, 1982. Over time, the U.S. objections to the missing provisions of UNCLOS III have faded or been proven unfounded. The treaty went into effect in 1994. The U.S. has signed the treaty, but Congress has not ratified it.

QUESTION 5.17: In what ways do these historical developments respond to efficiency, and to what extent do they respond to political power and distribution?

QUESTION 5.18: Read the following account of the history of water law and discuss whether the law appears to have evolved toward economic efficiency.

Water has always been one of the most valuable natural resources, but because it tends to run away, there have always been problems in defining and assigning property rights in water. Centuries ago in England, the general rule was that rights were vested in the "riparian owner," that is, in the person who owned the land on the bank of the river. The riparian owner's principal right was to a flow of water past his land. It would be a violation of someone else's rights for an upstream user to use the water that passed by his property in such a way as to reduce the flow to downstream users. The upstream user could not, therefore, divert so much of the water to his own use that the flow was significantly diminished for those downstream. A riparian was restricted in his ability to sell water to nonriparians (that is, people who do not own land along the water).

However, in the nineteenth century, this legal arrangement had to be altered because industrial demand on the natural flow of a river frequently exceeded the supply. In the eastern United States, these issues were resolved by elaborating the natural-flow theory of water rights that had been adopted from the English common law. An alternative theory of water rights appeared in the western United States. Under the *reasonable-use theory*, the riparian owner is entitled to use the water flow in any reasonable way. It was deemed reasonable for one owner to use all of the water in a stream or lake when others are making no use of it. Under the reasonable-use theory, a riparian owner does not have a right to the natural water flow. Furthermore, a riparian owner may transfer rights to nonriparians.

C. Recording and Transferring Title: Verification Costs versus Registration Costs

Branding cattle, stamping a serial number on an automobile engine, stenciling a Social Security number on a TV—these are some ways that private persons try to prove their ownership of valuable goods. In addition to these private remedies, the state sometimes provides registries of ownership. Thus, trademarks are registered to avoid duplication or overlap. Brand inspectors employed by the state or private companies may police violations. Despite these devices, people sometimes "buy" goods that were not the seller's to sell. This section concerns verifying ownership and remedies when a good is "sold" without the owner's permission.

Suppose you decide to fulfill a lifelong dream and buy a farm. You find a parcel in the country that you like and approach the farmer who is living there. After discussing the parcel's boundaries, fertility, and drainage, the farmer offers to sell the land at an attractive price. You shake hands to seal the agreement. The next week you return with a check, hand it over to the farmer, and shortly thereafter move onto the property. Two weeks later, a man knocks at the cottage door, announces that he is the owner of the property, and explains that he has come to evict the nefarious tenant who rented the cottage in which you are living. At this point you recall the joke that begins: "Hey buddy, how would you like to buy the Brooklyn Bridge?"

When you buy property, you should ascertain the rightful owner and deal with him or her. A reliable and inexpensive method for determining ownership prevents fraudulent conveyances, such as tenants representing themselves as owners. There are various ways to create a record of ownership. Consider the story—presumably apocryphal—of "recording" title in England in the Middle Ages, when few people could read. It is said that the seller handed the buyer a clod of turf and a twig from the property in a ceremony before witnesses known as *livery of seisin*. Then, the adults thrashed a child who had witnessed the passing of turf and twig severely enough so that the child would remember that day as long as he or she lived, thus creating a living record of the transfer.

Fortunately, we now have better methods of recording title in land. In the United States, there is no uniform method of land registration,[37] but each of the fifty states has some system for the public recording of title to land. A change in ownership of real

---

[37] There is an alternative land registration system, known as the *Torrens system,* after Sir Richard Torrens, who introduced this simplified mechanism into South Australia in 1858, and that system or something like it is in use in many parts of the world. In the Torrens system, the state operates a registry and a title insurance fund. Defects in title caused by the state record-keeper are compensated from the insurance fund. Several of the United States tried the Torrens system, but every one of them has abandoned the system, because incompetent bookkeeping caused such a drain on the state-operated title insurance funds that the funds went bankrupt. (See SHELDON KURTZ & HERBERT HOVENKAMP, AMERICAN PROPERTY LAW 1151–1244 [1987].)

property must be recorded in an official registry of deeds, such as the county recorder's office. Recording is a formal process, and the records are open to the public. The record of ownership on file usually contains a formal description of the property's location, a list of restrictions that apply to the property, and an account of who has owned the property at each point in time.

While a system of recording title is maintained for land and a few other valuable items, like automobiles, there is no such system for most goods. In most exchanges the buyer does not devote resources to determining whether the seller truly owns what he or she is selling. For example, you rarely question whether the books you purchase at the bookstore were rightly the bookstore's to sell. Your presumption is that whoever possesses a book rightfully owns it. Further proof of ownership is in the memory of witnesses to the sale, like the child in the medieval example, or perhaps in a written sales contract. A system of recording the ownership of books would burden commerce and impede the efficient movement of goods.

The security of major contracts is strengthened by a system of official witnesses to the event. Official witnesses, called "notaries," record the event in an official document and fix their seal to it. Some U.S. states license many notaries, so their fees are low. At the other extreme, some countries like Italy restrict notaries to specialized lawyers who pass difficult exams, perform complicated services far beyond witnessing a document, and enjoy high monopoly profits, especially in real estate transactions.

We have encountered another trade-off in property law. On the one hand, verifying title by formal means, such as recording the transfer of a deed, reduces the uncertainties that burden commerce. On the other hand, the verification of title through formal means is costly. Property law thus has to develop rules that *balance the impediments to commerce created by uncertain ownership against the cost of maintaining a system of verification*. For costly items like houses and cars, the law reduces the uncertainties that burden commerce by providing a system for recording title, and the law typically forces all sales through the recording process by refusing to protect unrecorded transactions in these items. For small transactions, however, the cost of maintaining a system of verification would exceed the benefit from reduced risk.[38]

D. Can a Thief Give Good Title?

Let us consider how people respond to laws allocating the responsibility to verify ownership. Imagine that you have made a shrewd deal for the purchase of a television from a person whom you met in the parking lot outside a local bar. The seller told you a tale about his urgent need to raise cash by selling his TV and handed it over from the trunk of his car. One evening while you are enjoying your new television, the police arrive at your apartment with the person from whom the TV was stolen. Should the law allow you to keep the TV or require you to return it? This example poses the general question: if a good is stolen from owner A by thief B, and B disappears with the money after selling the good to innocent buyer C, does the good belong to A or C?

---

[38] You should recognize that this argument in favor of a system of recordation of ownership claims is a general instance of the Normative Coase Theorem of the last chapter.

This figure depicts the facts:

This question is answered differently in different jurisdictions. According to the rule in America, transferors can usually convey only those property rights that they legitimately have. Thus, a person without title cannot convey title to a purchaser.[39] In this example, the thief did not have good title to the television, so he could not give you good title to it. Instead, title rests with the person from whom the TV was stolen. According to the American rule, you must return the television set to its owner. You are entitled to recover your money from the thief (technically, the thief breached his warranty of title), if the thief is caught and has money.

A different rule prevails in much of Europe, where the buyer acquires title by purchasing the good "in good faith."[40] The good-faith requirement means that the buyer must genuinely believe that the seller owns the good. The good-faith requirement prevents a "fence" of stolen goods from hiding behind the law. The law may also require the buyer to make reasonable efforts to verify ownership, such as checking that the serial number was not filed off the television. Applied to this example, the European law presumably permits you to keep the television. The original owner may recover your money from the thief, if possible.

In general, law must allocate the risk that stolen goods will be bought in good faith. The American rule places the entire risk on the buyer, whereas the European rule places that risk on the original owner. The American rule gives buyers an extra incentive to verify that the seller is truly the owner. The European rule gives owners an extra incentive to protect their property against theft. One of these rules is more efficient in the sense of imposing a lower burden on commerce and promoting the voluntary exchange of property.

Which rule is it? Here is a method for finding out. Let C_o indicate the lowest cost to the original owner of protecting against theft by, say, engraving his or her Social Security number on the object. Let C_B indicate the lowest cost to the purchaser of verifying that the seller is the owner by, say, confirming this fact with the party from whom the seller originally obtained the good. For the sake of efficient incentives, liability

---

[39] This is true as a generalization, but there are important exceptions. For example, if a thief steals money and uses it to buy goods from a merchant, the original owner of the money cannot recover the money from the merchant. A thief can convey good title to money. Moreover, the *Uniform Commercial Code* allows regular dealers in goods sometimes to give *better* title than they got. Thus, if a television store happens to have taken possession of and sold a stolen television, the buyer is entitled to presume that the dealer had good title to the television. Any liability to the true owner of the television lies with the dealer. Can you suggest an economic reason why this is a sensible rule?

[40] Our simplification of the European rule omits nuances in civil law. Thus, rule §935 of the *German Code of Civil Law* distinguishes an owner who lost possession of a movable good voluntarily as opposed to involuntarily. An owner who lost possession involuntarily has a relatively strong claim against a good faith purchaser of it.

should fall on the party who can verify ownership at least cost. Thus, the efficiency of the competing rules may be determined as follows:

1. If it is generally true that $C_o < C_B$, then it is more efficient for the good-faith buyer to acquire good title against the original owner.
2. If it is generally true that $C_o > C_B$, then it is more efficient for the original owner to retain title against the good-faith buyer.

Unfortunately, the absence of empirical evidence about the values of C_o and C_B prevents us from answering decisively whether one rule is better than the other. Indeed, the lack of evidence also prevents different countries from identifying the more efficient rule and adopting it. However, the example of Spain suggests what is probably the best approach. In Spain, the "American Rule" typically applies when the thief steals the good from a household and sells to a merchant. In other words, a Spanish merchant cannot get good title from a thief. Merchants who buy from a thief encourage thievery by making it more profitable. The Spanish practice of applying the American Rule to merchants who buy from thieves discourages merchants from "fencing" stolen goods, thus reducing the profitability of theft. In Spain, however, the "European Rule" that a buyer can acquire good title from a thief typically applies when the thief steals the good from a merchant and sells it to another merchant or a household. Thus, the Spanish practice increases the ease with which goods circulate among merchants in commerce and passes to the final consumer.[41]

E. Breaks in the Chain of Title

Uncertain ownership burdens commerce and causes deep discounting of the value of an asset by prospective purchasers. Consequently, economic efficiency requires clearing away uncertainties, or "clouds," from the title to property. This section briefly examines how property law removes the clouds that accumulate over titles.

1. Adverse Possession   In the preceding chapter we discussed an example in which Joe Potatoes unwillingly built his house so that two feet of it extended over the property line onto Fred Parsley's lot. Recall that Parsley did not discover the trespass and sue until 10 years had passed. Has Potatoes acquired any right to the part of Parsley's property that he has occupied? According to Anglo-American law, he may have. If the owner "sleeps on his rights," allowing trespass to age, the trespasser may acquire ownership of the property.

The relevant legal doctrine is *adverse possession*. The phrase refers to the fact that a trespasser's possession of the land is adverse to the owner's interest.[42] Someone can

---

[41] C. Paz-Ares, *Seguridad Jurica y Seguridad del Trafico,* Rev. de Derecho Mercantil 7–40 (1985).

[42] It is also possible to acquire an easement by adverse use of another's property. For example, someone who habitually cuts across someone's property without protest by the owner may acquire the right to continue cutting across the property.

acquire ownership of another's property by occupying it for a period of time specified in a statute, provided the occupation is adverse to the owner's interests, and the original owner does not protest or take legal action.[43]

The economic advantage of adverse possession is that it clears the clouds from title and allows property to move to higher-valuing users. To illustrate, assume that you want to buy a house that was built in 1910 and sold in the years 1925, 1937, and 1963. Your search of title reveals a confusion in the legal records about whether the sale in 1937 was legal. However, the current owner has resided on the property since 1963 without a legal challenge. The law for this jurisdiction stipulates that adverse possession for 25 years transfers ownership to the trespasser. The adverse-possession statute and the current owner's unchallenged occupancy since 1963 have thus removed the cloud from the title dating to 1937. In general, a rule for acquiring title by adverse possession lowers the cost of establishing rightful ownership claims by removing the risk that ownership will be disputed on the basis of the distant past.

Another efficiency justification for adverse possession was emphasized in the past: adverse possession prevents valuable resources from being left idle for long periods of time by specifying procedures for a productive user to take title from an unproductive user. Under such a rule, persons who neglect to monitor their property boundaries run the risk of losing idle parts of them to someone who makes use of them. In this respect the rule tends to move property from idleness to productive use. Sometimes squatters have acquired land from absentee owners through adverse possession. In the American West, settlers historically acquired much Indian land through adverse possession. The settlers viewed themselves as putting the land to a higher use, whereas the Indians viewed the settlers as thieves.

Besides the two types of economic benefit, adverse possession has a cost. The cost is that owners must actively monitor their land to eject trespassers who might otherwise become owners through adverse possession. Without adverse-possession statutes, owners might reduce monitoring costs and more trespassers would enjoy using other people's land.

QUESTION 5.19:   Apply the concept of adverse possession to the electromagnetic spectrum.

---

[43] To be precise, traditional scholarship distinguishes four conditions that adverse possession must satisfy:

1. The adverse possessor must have actually entered the contested property and have assumed exclusive possession.
2. That possession must be "open and notorious." This phrase means that the trespass must not be done in secret; an alert owner should be able to detect it.
3. The trespasser's possession must be adverse or hostile and under a "claim of right." This condition requires the trespass to be inconsistent with the owner's use rights and against the owner's interests.
4. Finally, the trespass must be continuous for a statutorily specified period. Some states in the American West also require the adverse possessor to pay property taxes for a statutorily specified period before acquiring title. See LAWRENCE FRIEDMAN, A HISTORY OF AMERICAN LAW 360–361 (2d ed. 1985). Note that these conditions do not inquire into the intentions of the adverse possessor. Despite this, there is evidence that courts are more likely to apply the adverse-possession rule when the trespass is accidental. See Richard Helmholz, *Adverse Possession and Subjective Intent*, 61 WASH. U. L. Q. 331 (1983).

QUESTION 5.20: Why do you think that the statutory time period for adverse possession tends to be short in states like Oklahoma where Indians owned a lot of land?

QUESTION 5.21: Suppose the statute of limitations for adverse possession is 10 years. After 9.9 years of trespass owners retain full rights, but after 10 years of trespass owners lose all of their rights. Instead of owners losing their rights abruptly at the end of 10 years, the statute could be written so that the rights depreciate gradually over time. For example, the trespasser could be granted a 10 percent interest in the property for each year of adverse possession, so that after one year the trespasser would own 10 per cent of it and after 10 years the trespasser would own all of it. Compare the efficiency of the "discontinuous rule" and the "continuous rule."

2. Estray Statutes

Suppose that while strolling down an alley in Manhattan you stumble over a brown paper bag. Opening the bag, you find that it contains a diamond brooch. Naturally, you would like to claim it for your own. But clearly someone has lost it. Are you entitled to keep it if the owner does not demand it back after a reasonable period of time? Are you obligated to make efforts to locate the owner, say, by advertising in the paper? Who owns property that has been abandoned, lost, or mislaid? *Estray statutes* answer these questions.

A typical estray statute in the United States stipulates a procedure for the finder to acquire ownership of lost or abandoned property. If the property exceeds a stipulated value, the finder may have to appear before a court official and sign a document concerning the facts about the property found. The court official then places an advertisement concerning the found item. If the owner does not appear to claim it within a stipulated time period (for example, one year), the finder becomes the owner. A finder who keeps the item without complying with the statute is subject to a fine.

Like registering title, estray statutes discourage the theft of property. Given an estray statute, a thief who is caught with another's property cannot avoid liability by claiming that he or she found it. ("Where did you get that watch?" Sherlock asked the suspect. "It fell off the back of a truck," he replied.) Thus, an estray statute helps to distinguish a good-faith finder from a thief. Like adverse-possession rules, estray statutes tend to clear the clouds from title and transfer property to productive users. Like adverse-possession rules, estray statutes also provide an incentive for owners to monitor their property. Finally, estray statutes induce the dissemination of information by finders and thus reduce the search costs of owners who lose or mislay their property.

QUESTION 5.22: If the value of a lost object is low enough, the estray statutes do not apply. Consequently, the finder has no legal obligation to advertise. Discuss the costs that need to be balanced to the most efficient lower bound in the value of a lost object for purposes of the estray statutes.

QUESTION 5.23: In admiralty law, there have to be rules for allocating ownership rights to property lost at sea. In the United States, the finder of an abandoned ship is generally awarded ownership, but in some cases the government takes possession of abandoned ships in its waters. Where that latter condition holds, a salvor (that is, one who salvages an abandoned ship) is usually entitled to a salvage award determined by the court.

Does this practice of making awards to salvors encourage dishonesty, or does it attract an efficient number of resources into the business of searching for lost ships? Is the system of awarding complete ownership rights to the finder more or less efficient than the award-to-salvors system?

III. What May Owners Do with Their Property?

What may owners do with their property? In this section we analyze some traditional restrictions on property rights. We postpone discussing modern government regulations such as zoning ordinances till the final section of the chapter.

A. Bequests and Inheritances: Circumvention Costs and Depletion Costs

In a feudal or tribal world, law typically stipulates the heirs to land, rather than the owner choosing heirs. To illustrate, the eldest son inherited all of his father's land in medieval England,[44] and in matrilineal tribes the land is often inherited by the niece from her aunt. Furthermore, feudal and tribal societies typically restrict the sale of land. As law modernizes, owners increase their power to stipulate the terms of inheritance and sales. The law in Western countries has evolved over centuries toward more freedom for the owner to specify who may have the property after his or her death and what they may do with it. We discuss briefly the economic analysis of this trend.

Any restriction on the owner's choices creates an incentive to circumvent it. To illustrate, imagine an owner who wants to bequeath her land to a particular friend, and imagine that the law will award the property to someone else. The owner can circumvent the law, say, by transferring title to the friend today and leasing it back for $1 per year until her death. Circumventing the law usually requires the assistance of a good lawyer. In general, owners use costly legal resources to circumvent restrictions on the use of property.

Now change the example and imagine that tight laws and costly lawyers prevent the owner from circumventing restrictions on bequests. Because her desire to designate her heir was frustrated, the owner may deplete her property before she dies. For example, she might cut timber prematurely, or exhaust the soil's fertility by intensive farming, or postpone needed improvements to buildings. In general, rules that restrict transfer undermine the owner's incentive to maximize the value of the property.

Circumvention costs and depletion costs provide two reasons for allowing an owner freedom in transferring property at death. However, these same reasons justify restricting

---

[44] In most of England from 1066 (the date of the Norman conquest) until 1925, the general rule for disposing of real estate on one's death was that it passed intact to the decedent's eldest son, a system called *primogeniture*. Testators were not free to alter this rule except under very narrow circumstances.

the freedom of an owner in special circumstances. Most property rights live forever, but all owners die. Sometimes one generation of owners wants to limit the discretionary power of subsequent owners. To illustrate, suppose that I own my family's ancestral home, Blackacre, and I stipulate in my will that no one will ever use Blackacre for purposes other than as a residence. Subsequently, I die and my heir wants to develop Blackacre into a golf course. Should the law enforce the restrictions in my will or set it aside and allow my heir to build a golf course? If the law routinely sets aside such restrictions, then I have an incentive to deplete the resource or circumvent the law prior to my death. If the law enforces such restrictions, then my wishes may be fulfilled but at the social cost of making it difficult, if not impossible, to move Blackacre to a higher-valued use than its use as a residence.

In the preceding example, the owner apparently wants to restrict future uses of Blackacre for his own, perfectly legitimate reasons. In other examples, an owner creates a trust (called a "spendthrift" trust) to protect someone from his or her own bad judgment,[45] or a bequest attempts to keep property in the family forever,[46] or a restrictive covenant attempts to channel future sales to certain classes of buyers.[47] In general, the principle that the current owner should be free to structure transactions as he or she wishes runs up against a difficulty when the owner wants to restrict future owners. In these cases, a conflict exists between the freedom of sequential owners of the same property. Any reduction in the freedom of any owner in the sequence may cause economic waste, regardless of whether the reduction in freedom comes from law or a private transaction.

English common law responded to these facts generally by being skeptical of "restraints on alienation," as they are called, and specifically in the case of bequest by a complicated law called the *rule against perpetuities*. The rule imposes a time limit on property restrictions imposed by the terms of a gift, sale, bequest, or other transaction. Instead of lasting in perpetuity, restrictions automatically lapse when a legal time limit expires. The legal time limit has the curious formulation "lives-in-being plus 21 years." To illustrate its meaning, assume that my only child is an unmarried daughter, and I stipulate in my will that she will inherit my ancestral home, Blackacre, on the condition that it never be used except as a residence. According to the rule, the restriction must ordinarily lapse 21 years after my daughter's death.[48]

Notice that the rule against perpetuities is a "generation-skipping rule." By this phrase we mean that it allows an owner to skip over the living generation by restricting their use of the property, but the property passes unrestricted to the unborn when they reach the age of 21 and become legal adults. A generation-skipping rule has an economic rationale. Assume that you must choose a principle concerning the power

---

[45] For example, a trust is created in which the beneficiary receives the interest income from the trust property but cannot touch the capital until she is middle-aged.

[46] For example, the owner leaves instructions that, at his death, his land is to be given to his oldest son, at whose death the land is to be given to *his* oldest son, and so on.

[47] In the past in America, covenants sometimes blocked future sales to buyers belonging to certain races.

[48] This account of the rule against perpetuities is roughly, but not exactly correct. The "life in being" designated as the "measuring life" does not have to be that of the daughter. It could, for example, be the first child born in Kinshasa the month before the testator's death. The rule, to be brief, is extremely complicated—so complicated that it invites creativity to avoid it.

of one generation to impose restrictions on the use of property by subsequent genera-tions. The principle that you choose will apply to every generation. You know that the world changes in unpredictable ways, so no restriction is good forever. You also know that most owners are prudent and benevolent toward their heirs, and a few are foolish and venal. In effect, you want a principle to protect against an occasional fool in an unending sequence of owners, given a constantly changing world.

A prudent owner will not restrict a prudent heir, and a prudent owner will restrict a foolish heir. Given these facts, an attractive principle for you to choose allows each generation to restrict the next generation, but not subsequent generations. When pru-dent owners apply this principle, only foolish heirs will be restricted. Furthermore, the restrictions that prudent owners impose on foolish heirs may prevent the foolish heirs from imposing restrictions on the next generation. So, the rule against perpetuities ap-pears to maximize the value of property across generations.

A trust is an organization where one person owns and manages money for the ben-efit of another. Trusts have different purposes, such as transferring wealth to one's heirs while avoiding inheritance taxes. When a person creates and endows a trust, it pays money to the beneficiary, which is not an inheritance, so no inheritance tax is owed. Eventually, however, the trust is dissolved, and the tax authorities may recapture part of the taxes that the trust avoided. To further reduce tax liability, some U.S. states have enacted laws allowing citizens to create "perpetual trusts" or "dynasty trusts." Because they never dissolve, they avoid the tax liabilities triggered by dissolution, but they are also inconsistent with the rule against perpetuities.

U.S. citizens in one state can establish a trust in another state. States compete to attract trust business by making favorable laws, especially for avoiding taxes owed to the federal gov-ernment or other states. Perpetual trusts are an example. Besides avoiding taxes, competition for trust business can also improve the efficiency of trusts. The management of stock portfo-lios, which trusts often have, illustrates such an improvement. In the nineteenth century, most U.S. states adopted a rule making the trustee liable if the portfolio included speculative stocks that lost their value. This rule caused trustees to buy bonds and very conservative, "blue-chip" stocks. Low risk, however, characterizes the portfolio as a whole, not each stock in it. In a bal-anced portfolio, the risk from one stock offsets the risk from another. In technical terms, hold-ing stock with negatively correlated risk results in low risk for the portfolio as a whole, even though individual stocks are high risk. Some innovative states responded to these facts by changing the rules of trust management. Under the revised rules, the trustee who holds a bal-anced portfolio is not liable for losses caused by a fall in value of individual stocks. This change in the rule caused trust portfolios to shift away from conservative bonds and toward more individually risky stocks. States making the change attracted more trust business, which puts pressure on other states to modernize their rules of trust management.[49]

---

[49] See Max M. Schanzenbach & Robert H. Sitkoff, *Did Reform of Prudent Trust Investment Laws Change Trust Portfolio Allocation?*, 50 J. Law & Econ 681 (2007). See also those authors' *Lawyers, Banks, and Money: The Revolution in American Trust Law* (2011). As another example of competition among juris-dictions, the trust was developed in the common law, not in civil law. The success of London banks in the trust business has put pressure on Paris banks to modify French civil law to gain all the advantages of the trust in English common law.

QUESTION **5.24:**   Instead of "lives-in-being plus 21 years," the rule might be "lives-in-being plus 10 years," or "lives-in-being plus 35 years." Compare these rules as means for "generation-skipping."

QUESTION **5.25:**   Suppose that a testator imposes a condition that cannot be met. For example, the decedent gives her property to be used for a medical school in Lebanon, Indiana, but after the testator's death, the State of Indiana abandons its plans to build a medical school there. In this situation, American courts apply the doctrine of *cy pres* (pronounced "see pray" and meaning, in law French, "so nearly" or "as near as possible"). Under that doctrine the court will find an alternative condition that is as close as possible to the decedent's intentions. For example, the proceeds from the sale of the decedent's property in Lebanon, Indiana, might be given to a medical school located somewhere else. Use the concepts of circumvention costs and depletion costs to provide an economic rationale for this rule.

QUESTION **5.26:**   We suggested above that an annually increasing renewal fee would be an efficient means of setting optimal patent life. Similarly, suppose that owners who wanted to restrict future use of their property had to pay a fee for each year that the restriction runs. For example, if my will stipulates that Blackacre should be used exclusively as a residence for 100 years, then I would have to make provision in my will to pay the state for each year that the restriction runs. In effect, the state deducts an annual fee from a bequest for a testator who desires to impose posthumous restrictions on property for a specified number of years. At what level would you set such a fee? Would it be the same for all types of conditions and all types of property? Is such a fee more efficient than the rule against perpetuities?

B. Rights to Use Someone Else's Property

In general, no one may use another's property without the permission of the owner. Use of another's property without the owner's permission is an illegal trespass. As we saw in Chapter 4, this rule and moderate transaction costs induce those who want to use another's property to bargain with the owner. Bargaining leads to the use of property by the party who values it the most, as required for allocative efficiency.

Can someone ever use another's property lawfully without the owner's permission? We have already seen that the "fair use" exception allows one to use copyrighted material without the owner's permission—in limited circumstances. (See question 5.11 on page 135). This issue arose in the famous case of *Ploof v. Putnam*.[50] Putnam was the owner of a small island in Lake Champlain, a large body of water in northern Vermont. In November, 1904, Ploof was sailing on that lake in a sloop with his wife and two children when a violent storm arose very suddenly. Ploof needed a safe harbor quickly, and the nearest one was Putnam's island. Ploof moored his sloop to a pier on that island, hoping that his ship and family would be able to ride out the storm in safety.

---

[50] 81 Vt. 471, 71 A 188 (Supreme Court of Vermont, 1908).

However, an employee of Putnam's, fearing that the sloop would damage his employer's property by being cast repeatedly against it during the storm, untied the ship from the pier and pushed it away. The sloop and its passengers were then at the mercy of the storm. The ship was ultimately driven by the storm onto the shore and wrecked.

Ploof sued Putnam, alleging that the losses to his ship and the injuries to himself and his family were the result of wrongful action by the defendant, through his employee. Ploof argued that the storm caused an emergency that justified his trespassing on the defendant's property, even without permission. He asked for compensatory damages for his losses. Putnam replied that every property owner has a right to exclude trespassers. This principle is so firmly settled, he asserted, that the court should award him summary judgment without proceeding to trial. The trial judge denied the defendant's motion for summary judgment, and the defendant appealed. The Supreme Court of Vermont affirmed the decision and held that *private necessity* like that of Ploof was an exception to the general rule against trespass.

In an emergency, one person can use another's property without permission. However, the user must compensate the owner for the costs of use. To illustrate, a hiker who gets lost in a remote wilderness may break into an uninhabited cabin in order to obtain food and shelter, but the hiker must compensate the owner for damage to the cabin and food consumed. As another example, X becomes deathly ill during the night, the only pharmacy in town is closed, and its owner Z is unreachable, so X breaks into Z's pharmacy and takes the required medicine. The law will excuse the trespass, but X must pay damages to Z. As a final example, X, who is about to be murdered by Y, picks up the nearest heavy object, Z's valuable china vase, and crashes it over Y's head, thereby saving X's life. X must pay damages to Z for the vase. In brief, the private-necessity doctrine allows compensated trespass in an emergency.

Bargaining theory rationalizes the *private necessity* exception to the general rule against trespass. In an emergency, transaction costs may preclude bargaining. For example, the suddenness with which the storm arose precluded Ploof from finding Putnam and bargaining with him. When bargaining is precluded, voluntary transactions do not necessarily cause goods to be used by the party who values them the most. A rule allowing compensated trespass assures that trespass occurs only when its value to the trespasser exceeds the cost to the owner.[51]

QUESTION 5.27: An interesting variation on the facts in *Ploof* occurred in *Vincent v. Lake Erie Transport Co.,* 109 Minn. 456, 124 N.W. 221 (Supreme Court of Minnesota, 1910). In late November, 1905, the steamship *Reynolds,* owned by the defendant, was moored to the plaintiff's pier in Duluth and discharging cargo. A storm suddenly arose on Lake Superior. The *Reynolds* signaled for a tug to take her away from the pier,

---

[51] Suppose that Ploof had found Putnam on the pier and bargained with him. The emergency has conveyed monopoly power on Putnam, who has the *only* nearby pier. Given Putnam's monopoly and Ploof's desperation, Putnam might demand an exorbitant amount of money for use of the pier. Ploof might promise to pay it, and then refuse to do so after the emergency passes. Litigation of such "bad-Samaritan contracts" is discussed later, when we come to the "necessity doctrine" in contract law.

but because of the storm, none could be found. The ship remained moored to the pier during the storm. The violence of the storm threw the steamship repeatedly against the plaintiff's pier, causing damage in the amount of $300. The plaintiff asked for that amount. The Lake Erie Transport Co. contended that its steamship was an involuntary trespasser. The *Reynolds* had tried to leave the plaintiff's property but had not been able to do so *through no fault of its own*. The court held that the plaintiff was entitled to damages. Argue that this holding is efficient.

C. Inalienability

The law forbids the sale of some valuable things, such as body organs, sex, heroin, children, votes, atomic weapons, or human rights. You cannot even *give away* some of these things, such as heroin or your vote in a national election. You cannot lose some of these things by *any* legal means, such as your human rights. One meaning of *alienation* is losing something, especially an intimate part of yourself. In law, the term *inalienable* refers to something of yours that you cannot lose by specified means. Thus, body organs, sex, and children are inalienable by sale, your vote is inalienable by sale or gift, and your human rights are inalienable by any means.

The sale of sex or children is prohibited by conventional morality, as well as law. Many forms of inalienability express conventional morality. Other forms of inalienability, such as the enactment of human rights, express the aspirations of eminent political theorists. What about economic theorists? What have they had to say about the efficiency of inalienability? Occasionally, a regulation increases the efficiency of a transfer. This fact provides an economic rationale for regulation. However, inalienability goes far beyond regulation. Whereas regulations restrict transfers, inalienability prohibits them. The efficiency of a transfer cannot increase by prohibiting it. In general, prohibitions on transfers are inefficient because they prevent people from getting what they want. Following this line of thought, some economic writers have attacked laws that make certain goods inalienable.[52] Is there *any* economic rationale for inalienability?[53]

Some theorists argue that the sale of certain commodities undermines their transfer by superior means. For example, consider the supply of blood to hospitals. Two complementary means are used to ensure that blood is free from infection: A medical history is taken from the individuals who supply blood, and the blood is tested in laboratories. The individual suppliers are more likely to provide an accurate medical history when they give their blood away than when they sell it.

---

[52] For example, see Elizabeth Landes & Richard A. Posner, *The Economics of the Baby Shortage*, 7 J. LEGAL STUD. 323 (1978) and J. Robert Pritchard, *A Market for Babies?*, 34 U. TORONTO L. J. 341 (1984). See also the 1987 symposium on the economics of selling babies in the *Boston University Law Review*.

[53] See Susan Rose-Ackerman, *Inalienability and the Theory of Property Rights*, 85 COLUM. L. REV. 931 (1985), Margaret Jane Radin, *Market-Inalienability*, 100 HARV. L. REV. 1849 (1987), and Richard Epstein, *Why Restrain Alienation?*, 85 COLUM. L. REV. 970 (1985).

Consequently, donated blood is freer from infection. This fact provides an economic rationale for obtaining blood by donations rather than purchases, but not a reason for prohibiting the sale of blood.[54] For example, in the United States most blood is obtained by donations, but some blood is purchased.[55]

However, assume that the sale of blood undermines voluntary donations. For example, people might feel that giving blood away for free is stupid so long as it can be sold. If these facts were true, then prohibiting the sale of blood might be necessary in order to divert transfers into the superior channel of gifts. Similarly, anthropologists have argued that markets destroy gift economies among tribal people. Although plausible, the factual support for this theory is not strong enough to provide a convincing defense of inalienability. It seems, then, that inalienability rests on conventional morality and political philosophies that stress values other than Pareto efficiency.

QUESTION 5.28: Assume that every adult in a particular jurisdiction is eligible to serve as a juror. Panels of potential jurors are drawn by rotation from the qualified population. Currently, no jurisdiction allows someone called for jury service to hire a qualified replacement. Would society be better off if people were allowed to engage in a market for jurors?

Web Note 5.7

As the technology for making use of transplantable human organs improves, the demand for those organs has far outstripped the supply available under the inalienability rules. See our website (and the box on "Inalienable Bodily Organs") for a discussion of how a regulated market in human organs might significantly increase the supply.

D. Unbundling Property Rights

In England, the boundaries of property are often based on enduring natural objects and countours of the land such as rocks, trees, or hills. In the United States, much of the land was surveyed and divided into uniform parcels in the countryside and in towns.[56] Standardizing property simplifies comparing one property to another. Easy

---

[54] See RICHARD TITMUSS, THE GIFT RELATIONSHIP: FROM HUMAN BLOOD TO SOCIAL POLICY (1971), in which the author argues that inalienability is an efficient method of assuring quality control. See also Kenneth Arrow, *Gifts and Exchanges,* 1 PHILOSOPHY & PUBLIC AFFAIRS 343 (1972), and Reuben Kessel, *Transfused Blood, Serum Hepatitis, and the Coase Theorem,* 17 J. LAW & ECON. 265 (1974).

[55] Blood can be purchased in the United States, but the federal Food and Drug Administration requires labels to distinguish whether the source is a "paid donor" or "volunteer donor." Note that nonprofit institutions that collect blood from "volunteer donors" usually sell it to hospitals.

[56] A grid for land boundaries ("rectangular survey") was an innovation that spread in the British Empire during the nineteenth century, replacing the demarcation of land boundaries by natural objects such as trees and rocks ("metes and bounds").

Inalienable Bodily Organs

Advances in medical technology have sharply increased demand for transplantable bodily organs.[57] Each year in the United States there are almost 80,000 people waiting for organ transplants. But the supply of suitable organs, is much smaller—approximately 10,000 organs per year. Excess demand in a market causes the price to rise, which brings supply and demand into equilibrium. This cannot happen to transplantable organs because all states adopted the Uniform Anatomical Gift Act of 1968, which forbids the sale of organs. Consequently, gifts or donations are the only means by which to supply transplantable bodily organs. The donor may consent to give up transplantable organs in the event of his or her death. People often have the opportunity to consent when renewing a driver's license. However, less than 20 percent of the United States' driving-age population has filled out the donor cards. Absent consent, the current system typically requires physicians to ask next of kin whether they may "harvest" the organs of the decedent. This is not the best time to make such a request.

To cope with excess demand, the United States has a non-market method of allocating organs. The rules are very complicated, but most organs are awarded in the order in which patients have been on an official waiting list. In 2006 the organization overseeing organ transplantation (UNOS) suggested an alternative rule—organs may be given first to those likely to live the longest after a transplant. That controversial proposal is still under discussion.

How to increase the supply of organs for transplant? Technology may develop more artificial organs, or technology may make it increasingly possible to transplant organs from other animals into humans. Alternatively, a regulated market in human organs might be allowed somewhere in the world. (The virtues and pitfalls of such a market are explored in the sources that follow.)

However, some nations have already implemented a rule that dramatically increases the supply of organs. We called the current donation rule "required consent." While less than 20 percent of the United States' driving-age population has filled out the donor cards, 85 percent of that same population say that they are willing to make a donation of their organs. An alternative to required consent is a rule of "presumed consent": Everyone is presumed to have consented to his or her organs being harvested upon death unless they have affirmatively declared otherwise. Data suggests that switching from required consent to presumed consent dramatically increases the supply of organs. The four European countries with a rule of required consent (Denmark, Germany, the Netherlands, and the United Kingdom) have much lower rates of donation (ranging from 4.25 percent in Denmark to 27.5 percent in the Netherlands) than do the six countries (Austria, Belgium, France, Hungary, Poland, Portugal, and Sweden) that use a rule of presumed consent (ranging from a low of 85.9 percent to a high of 99 percent).

SOURCES:

See Lloyd R. Cohen, *Increasing the Supply of Transplantable Organs: The Virtues of a Futures Market,* 58 Geo. Wash. L. Rev. 1 (1989).

Gregory Crespi, *Overcoming the Legal Obstacles to the Creation of a Futures Market in Bodily Organs,* 55 Ohio St. L. J. 1 (1994).

Richard Epstein, Mortal Peril: Our Inalienable Right to Health Care? (1997).

Eric J. Johnson & Daniel Goldstein, "Do Defaults Save Lives?," 302 Science 1338 (2003).

---

[57] An economist joke about this situation goes like this: A patient waiting for a heart transplant learns from his doctor that there are suddenly two hearts available—one from a 24-year-old marathon runner and one from an elderly economist. Without hesitation the patient chooses to receive the heart of the economist. It explains to his astonished doctor, "It is unused."

comparison of property opens the real estate market to broader competition because potential buyers need less information to compare the value of one property relative to another. Besides real estate, uniformity lubricates sales for stocks, bonds, wheat, oil, and many other goods.

Conversely, inconsistent bundles of rights make properties incomparable to each other, so prices must be negotiated individually. Thus, one share of stock issued by Honda is the same as another share of the same class of stock. Honda shares have a public price in the stock market at which they can be bought or sold. In contrast, investment banks have created bundles of unstandardized real estate mortgages ("derivatives") whose prices are individually negotiated. Unlike stock market prices, individually negotiated prices for securities are not public information. Most people do not know the price at which such a security last sold. When securities prices plummeted in the financial meltdown of 2008, Harvard University held many unstardardized securities without a public price, so it did not know how much value its portfolio had lost.

In general, the owners of property possess a bundle of rights. To standardize property, the law must restrict the owner's ability to repackage these rights. The owner of a good may have rights w, x, y, and z over it. The owner may want to unbundle these rights and sell w and x to one person, while retaining y and z for himself. Sometimes, however, law only allows sales of the complete bundle. For example, the owner of a city lot can sell it as a whole, but city regulations may prevent him from cutting it in half and selling half of it.

Zoning illustrates specific regulations that prevent unbundling some property rights. A deeper question is whether something in the nature of property generally limits or restricts unbundling. To illustrate what is at stake, assume that A inherits his family's heirloom pocket watch. B, who is A's brother, would like to wear the watch to a Christmas party each year. B pays some money to A in exchange for A's promise to let B wear the watch every Christmas. A's refusal to let B wear the watch on Christmas in a future year would breach their contract, so B could sue A for money damages.

Continuing the example, assume that A sells the watch to C. In making the sale, A tells C nothing about B. C remains ignorant about A's contract with B until Christmas approaches and B asks C for the watch to wear. C refuses. What can B do? Nothing to C. C does not have to let B wear the watch on Christmas. B's only available remedy is to sue A for compensatory damages for breach of contract.

As this example illustrates, the contract between A and B does not give B security that he will always get to wear the watch on Christmas. What B wants is a right to use the watch on Christmas that he can assert against anyone who owns the watch. B might take a novel legal approach in an attempt to get security: Let A sell B the use rights over the watch on Christmas, and let A retain all other rights over the watch. If A did not own use rights to the watch on Christmas, then presumably A could not sell those rights to anyone else. Further, anyone who tried to prevent B from using the watch on Christmas would presumably interfere with his property rights. Specifically, if C refused to let B use the watch on Christmas then B could sue C for "trespass" and obtain specific performance. (We will explain these terms in more detail in Chapters 8 and 9.)

Notice what happens when A and B replace A's contractual promise to B with A's sale of use rights to B. Damages are the usual remedy for breach of contract. Hence B's contractual right to wear the watch on Christmas is protected by A's liability to pay damages for breach. In contrast, injunctions are the usual remedy for trespass on property rights. Hence B's ownership of the right to wear the watch on Christmas is protected by his ability to obtain an order from the court requiring C to allow B to wear the watch on Christmas.

The example of the watch illustrates how unbundling can hinder commerce. Specifically, if unbundling is allowed, C would be uncertain exactly what rights he acquired by buying the watch from A, which would dampen C's interest in buying the watch. A vigorous market requires certainty of buyers concerning the rights that they acquire.

This example raises the general question, "Can the owner of property, who has a bundle of rights, rearrange the bundle of rights freely, transfer them as he wishes, and force courts to protect the transfer of rights by injunctions?" While this problem seldom arises with watches or similar objects, it often arises with real estate. To illustrate, assume that I own my family's ancestral home, Blackacre, and I want to assure that no one will ever use it for purposes other than a residence. To secure this end, I would like to remove the development rights from the bundle of ownership rights. Can I do it? According to the common law of property, I can only restrict the use by the future owners of Blackacre for a limited period of time. (See the preceding discussion of the rule against perpetuities.) In general, an owner cannot freely unbundle and repackage real property rights in common law. Similarly, civil law systems in countries like France go beyond these common law restrictions by enumerating rights of real property that the owners cannot change. According to the civil law tradition, the enumerated rights attach to the property itself, not to the person who happens to own the property.[58]

Another important kind of property that provokes disputes about bundling and unbundling is the corporation. The stockholders of a corporation are its legal owners. Each share of stock traditionally conveys to its owner the right to one vote at stockholders' meetings. In recent years, however, some corporations have created new kinds of stock that do not give voting rights to their owners. There are many other examples where corporations have unbundled and rearranged the traditional rights enjoyed by their owners.

Instead of entangling ourselves in the details of real estate or corporate law, we must focus on the general point underlying these controversies. In the example of the heirloom watch, the fundamental issue is whether the owner of property can give several different people rights over it that they can enforce by specific performance against anyone who interferes.

Economic efficiency generally favors allowing unbundling whenever it increases the market value of the property, and prohibiting unbundling when it decreases the market value of the property. Property owners generally want to maximize its market value, and they are better situated than the state to know how to do this. Consequently, the state seldom has reason to prevent owners who want to unbundle from doing so. Recall,

---

[58] In legal language, *numerus clausus* refers to a restricted list of rights, including property rights. In property, these rights are *in rem,* meaning that they attach to the property regardless of its owner, whereas contract rights are *in personam,* meaning that they attach to the particular people who made the contract. See the article by Thomas Merrill and Henry Smith noted at the end of Chapter 4.

however, our previous discussion about the "anticommons." Unbundling may impose future costs on those who would like to repackage the rights into a new configuration. Insofar as there is an economic argument against unbundling, it is based on this desire to minimize future costs of assembling those rights into a more valuable whole.

Some theorists have argued that individuals can sometimes increase the value of their own property by unbundling in ways that increase transaction costs for the sale of other properties. To illustrate, a standard form contract lowers the bargaining costs of everyone in an industry. One seller who departs from the standard form reduces standardization, which imposes costs on other sellers. In general, a common pool of knowledge about contracts lowers transaction costs of exchange, and unbundling drains the common pool. This view implies that property law requires constraints against fragmentation by particularization.

This argument, however, is unconvincing. Much of contract law imposes rules that apply unless the parties stipulate otherwise in the contract. (See our discussion of "default rules" in Chapter 8.) The state does not have to police contracts to make sure that they remain sufficiently standardized. State requirements of standardized contracts are typically misguided for the same reason that state restrictions on unbundling property are misguided. The law should obligate sellers to disclose improbable restrictions on ownership due to past transactions, but as long as the parties understand what they are purchasing, the law should generally enforce agreements to unbundled property rights.

IV. What are the Remedies for the Violation of Property Rights?

As noted in Chapter 4, common law approximates a legal system of *maximum liberty,* which allows owners to do anything with their property that does not interfere with other people's property. When applying this principle, the amount of liberty afforded to owners depends on disentangling one owner's use of property from another's. When uses are separate, the effect of one owner on another occurs through voluntary agreements, such as market exchange. When uses join, one owner affects another involuntarily, as when my smoke blows over your property. In this section we discuss the special legal and economic problems caused by entangled uses.

A. Externalities and Public Bads

When people agree to impose costs and benefits on each other, they often make a contract. In contrast, when the utility or production functions of different people are interdependent, they impose benefits or costs on each other, regardless of whether they have agreed. Such interdependence is called an *externality,* because the costs or benefits are conveyed outside of a market. To illustrate the difference, if I buy so many watermelons at my local fruit store that the seller raises the price, my action affects other buyers, but bidding up a price exemplifies the ordinary working of markets, not an externality. In contrast, if my rooster's crowing annoys my neighbors, my action affects them independent from market transactions; so, the noise is an externality.

Costs or benefits conveyed outside of the market are not priced. Whenever costs or benefits are not priced, the supplier lacks incentives to supply the efficient quantity. Overcoming this incentive problem requires pricing the externality. When an externality gets priced, its supply is channeled through a market, which is called *internalizing the externality*. Thus, the solution to interdependent uses of property is to channel them through the market, or to internalize the externality.

The efficient solution to the problem of internalization depends on the number of affected people. If interdependence affects a small number of people, the externality is "private." For example, the crowing of my rooster affects a few neighbors, so the noise is a private externality. If the interdependence affects a large number of people, the externality is "public." For example, the smoke from a factory affects many households, so it is a public externality. Similarly, when one additional car enters a congested freeway, all the other drivers slow down a little, so congestion is a public externality. The private-public distinction in economics rests on a continuum describing the number of people who are affected by someone's actions. As the number of people affected by someone's action increases, a vague boundary is crossed separating "private" from "public."

In Chapter 4 we explained that one person's consumption of a public good does not diminish the amount available to others, and that excluding some people from enjoying a public good is difficult. Public externalities typically have these characteristics of nonrivalry and nonexcludability. For example, when one person breathes dirty air, just as much dirty air remains for others to breathe, and preventing some people in a given air-quality region from breathing the air is difficult. Consequently, harmful public externalities are also called "public bads."

We summarize these points by using some notation. Imagine a small economy with two people, denoted a and b, and three private goods, denoted x_1, x_2, x_3. Consumption of the first two goods involves no externalities, but consumption of the third good imposes external costs. For example, the first two goods might be apples and pears, and the third good might be cigarettes. We attach a superscript on a good to indicate who consumes. Thus, the utility of person a can be written as a function of the three goods that she consumes: $u^a = u^a(x_1^a, x_2^a, x_3^a)$. Assume that person b consumes the first two goods, but not the third good; that is, person b does not smoke cigarettes. Furthermore, assume that person b dislikes breathing the smoke from person a's cigarettes. Thus, the utility of person b can be written $u^b = u^b(x_1^b, x_2^b, x_3^a)$. (Note that b's utility will typically increase if she consumes more of x_1 and x_2 but that her utility will *decrease* if a consumes more x_3.) The utility functions of a and b are interdependent because a's consumption of the third good is an argument in b's utility function. In other words, the presence of a variable in b's utility function bearing the superscript a indicates an externality.

Let us add additional notation to indicate incomplete markets. Suppose that the three goods $(x_1, x_2 \, x_3)$ are purchased in a store at prices (p_1, p_2, p_3). The price that person a must pay for x_3 presumably reflects the cost at which the store purchases the good. This price does not include the cost of the harm that a's consumption of x_3 imposes on b.

Consequently, there is no price associated with the variable x_3^a in b's utility function. In order to attach such a price, persons a and b would have to bargain with each other.

Through such bargaining, the externality might be internalized. Our two-person example is a private externality. Alternatively, assume that there are 1, 2, 3, . . . , n people just like person b. Choose any one of these n people and call this person j. Person j's utility function has the form $u^j = u^j(x_1^j, x_2^j, x_3^q)$, for $j = 1, 2, 3, . . . , n$. Now the harmful externality from a's consumption of x_3 affects so many people that it is a public bad. The transaction cost of bargaining with n people is presumably prohibitive, so the externality cannot be internalized by a private bargain. Instead, an alternative means of pricing the externality must be found.

> **QUESTION 5.29:**   Classify the items in the following list as markets, private externalities, or public externalities.
> a. A lighthouse warns ships about rocks.
> b. My building blocks your sunlight.
> c. You outbid me at the auction.
> d. Bees pollinate your apple trees.
> e. Noise lowers the sale value of my house.

> **QUESTION 5.30:**   Assume that the third good, x_3, represents miles driven in cars by persons 1, 2, 3, . . . , n, and assume that cars are polluting. Rewrite the utility function of person j in the preceding formulation to represent these facts.

B. Remedies for Externalities

In property law, a harmful externality is called a *nuisance*. Remember that our discussion of remedies for nuisance in Chapter 4 distinguished between injunctions and damages, and that the relative efficiency of these remedies has a lot to do with the public-private distinction. If the nuisance is private, few parties are affected by it, and, as a result, the costs of bargaining together are low. When bargaining costs are low, the parties will ordinarily reach a cooperative agreement and do what is efficient. Consequently, in those circumstances the choice of remedies makes little difference to the efficiency of the bargaining outcome. The traditional property law remedy—injunctive relief—is attractive under these circumstances, because the court need not undertake the difficult job of computing damages. If one views an injunction as always and forever prohibiting the offensive activity, then its inflexibility is costly. However, if one views an injunction as an instruction to the parties to resolve their dispute through voluntary exchange, then it is an attractive remedy for private nuisances.

In contrast, trying to correct a harmful externality of the public-bad type by bargaining would involve the cooperation of all the affected parties. Bargaining fails in these circumstances because it requires the cooperation of too many people. The law refers to a harmful externality of the public type as a *public nuisance*. Our analysis suggests that damages will be a more efficient remedy for a public nuisance than an injunction would be.

To apply this prescription for choosing between injunctions and damages, the court has to examine the number of people affected by the externality. However, the court does not have to perform a cost-benefit analysis comparing injunctions and damages.

Cost-benefit analysis requires more information than courts typically possess, so legal rules whose application requires a cost-benefit analysis should be avoided.

When compensatory damages are perfect, they restore the victim to the same utility curve as he or she would have enjoyed without the harm. Compensatory damages can be *temporary* or *permanent*. With temporary damages, the plaintiff receives compensation for the harms the defendant has inflicted on him or her in the past. If harms continue in the future, the plaintiff must return to court in order to receive additional damages. Thus, temporary damages impose high transaction costs for dispute resolution. With temporary damages, reductions in future harms translate directly into reductions in liability. Consequently, temporary damages create incentives for injurers to continually adopt technical improvements that reduce external costs.

With permanent damages, the plaintiff receives compensation for past harms plus the present discounted value of all reasonably anticipated future harms.[59] One lump-sum payment extinguishes claims for past and future harms at the level specified in the judgment. Unfortunately, future changes in technology and prices are difficult to predict, so the estimation of future harms suffers from error. Thus, permanent damages impose high error costs. Furthermore, by paying permanent damages the injurer "purchases" the right to external harm up to the amount stipulated in the judgment. Consequently, permanent damages create no incentive for injurers to adopt technical improvements that reduce external costs below the level stipulated in the judgment.[60]

As explained, temporary damages impose high transaction costs, whereas permanent damages impose high error costs and undermine incentives for reducing future harms. Transaction costs of resolving disputes, whether by trial or settlement, are low when liability is certain and damages are easily measured. Error costs are high when innovation improves abatement technology and changes the understanding of the harms caused by externalities. Thus, temporary damages tend to be more efficient given easily measured damages and rapid innovation. Conversely, permanent damages tend to be more efficient given costly measurement of damages and slow innovation.

We commend damages as the remedy for a public nuisance. However, common law has not traditionally followed this prescription. When the public is harmed by a nuisance, courts traditionally allow the affected parties to enjoin it. The following case suggests that the common law has become more receptive to damage remedies for public nuisances. Read the case, bearing in mind the difference between the traditional remedy for a nuisance (damages for past harm and an injunction against future harm), recurring damages, and permanent damages. After reading the case, test your knowledge of externality theory by answering the questions.

---

[59] See the section on asset-pricing in Chapter 2 for more on discounting.

[60] In his dissent in *Boomer v. Atlantic Cement Co.,* which we discuss next, Justice Jasen recognized this point in his criticism of the majority's award of permanent damages. He wrote, "Furthermore, once permanent damages are assessed and paid, the incentive to alleviate the wrong would be eliminated, thereby continuing air pollution in an area without abatement."

BOOMER v. ATLANTIC CEMENT CO., INC. 309 N.Y.S.2d 312, 257 N.E.2d 87 (Court of Appeals of New York, 1970)

BERGAN, J. Defendant operates a large cement plant near Albany. These are actions for injunction and damages by neighboring land owners alleging injury to property from dirt, smoke and vibration emanating from the plant.

[At the trial court and on appeal, the defendant's cement-making operations were found to be a nuisance to the plaintiff-neighbors. Temporary damages were awarded, but an injunction against future dirt, smoke, and vibration from the plant causing the same or greater harms was denied. Plaintiffs have brought this appeal in order to receive the traditional remedy against a nuisance—an injunction.]

The ground for denial of injunction . . . is the large disparity in economic consequences of the nuisance and of the injunction. This theory cannot, however, be sustained without overruling a doctrine which has been consistently reaffirmed in several leading cases in this court and which has never been disavowed here, namely, that where a nuisance has been found and where there has been any substantial damage shown by the party complaining, an injunction will be granted.

The rule in New York has been that such a nuisance will be enjoined although marked disparity be shown in economic consequences between the effect of the injunction and the effect of the nuisance . . . .

The court at Special Term [the trial court] also found the amount of permanent damage attributable to each plaintiff, for the guidance of the parties in the event both sides stipulated to the payment and acceptance of such permanent damage as a settlement of all the controversies among the parties. The total of permanent damages to all plaintiffs thus found was $185,000 . . . .

This result . . . is a departure from a rule that has become settled; but to follow the rule literally in these cases would be to close down the plant at once. This court is fully agreed to avoid that immediately drastic remedy; the difference in view is how best to avoid it. [Footnote by Court: Atlantic Cement Co.'s investment in the plant is in excess of $45,000,000. There are over 300 people employed there.]

If the injunction were to be granted unless within a short period—e.g., 18 months—the nuisance be abated by improved techniques found, there would inevitably be applications to the court at Special Term for extensions of time to perform on showing of good faith efforts to find such techniques. The parties could settle this private litigation at any time if defendant paid enough money and the imminent threat of closing the plant would build up the pressure on defendant . . . .

Moreover, techniques to eliminate dust and other annoying by-products of cement making are unlikely to be developed by any research the defendant can undertake within any short period, but will depend on the total resources of the cement industry nationwide and throughout the world. The problem is universal wherever cement is made.

For obvious reasons the rate of the research is beyond control of defendant. If at the end of 18 months the whole industry has not found a technical solution, a court would be hard put to close down this one cement plant if due regard be given to equitable principles.

On the other hand, to grant the injunction unless defendant pays plaintiffs such permanent damages as may be fixed by the court seems to do justice between the contending parties. All of the attributions of economic loss to the properties on which plaintiffs' complaints are based will have been redressed. . . .

It seems reasonable to think that the risk of being required to pay permanent damages to injured property owners by cement plant owners would itself be a reasonably effective spur to research for improved techniques to minimize nuisance . . . Thus, it seems fair to both sides to grant permanent damages to plaintiffs which will terminate this private litigation. . . . The judgment, by allowance of permanent damages imposing a servitude on land, which is the basis of the actions, would preclude future recovery by plaintiffs or their grantees.

This should be placed beyond debate by a provision of the judgment that the payment by defendant and the acceptance by plaintiffs of permanent damages found by the court shall be in compensation for a servitude on the land.[61]

The orders should be reversed, without costs, and the cases remitted to Supreme Court, Albany County, to grant an injunction which shall be vacated on payment by defendant of such amounts of permanent damage to the respective plaintiffs as shall for this purpose be determined by the court.

JASEN, J., dissenting. I agree with the majority that a reversal is required here, but I do not subscribe to the newly enunciated doctrine of assessment of permanent damages, in lieu of an injunction, where substantial property rights have been impaired by the creation of a nuisance. . . .

I see grave dangers in overruling our long-established rule of granting an injunction where a nuisance results in substantial continuing damage. *In permitting the injunction to become inoperative on the payment of permanent damages, the majority is, in effect, licensing a continuing wrong. It is the same as saying to the cement company, you may continue to do harm to your neighbors so long as you pay a fee for it.* [Our emphasis.] Furthermore, once such permanent damages are assessed and paid, the incentive to alleviate the wrong would be eliminated, thereby continuing air pollution of an area without abatement.

It is true that some courts have sanctioned the remedy here proposed by the majority in a number of cases, but none of the authorities relied on by the majority are analogous to the situation before us. In those cases, the courts, in denying an injunction and awarding money damages, grounded their decision on a showing that the use to which the property was intended to be put was primarily for the public benefit. Here, on the other hand, it is clearly established that the cement company is creating a continuing air pollution nuisance primarily for its own private interest with no public benefit. . . . The promotion of the interests of the polluting cement company, has, in my opinion, no public use or benefit. . . . .

I would enjoin the defendant cement company from continuing the discharge of dust particles on its neighbors' properties unless, within 18 months, the cement company abated this nuisance. . . .

---

[61] A *servitude on the land* is a restriction or burden on a piece of real property. The servitude typically "runs with the land," which means that it becomes permanently attached to the particular piece of land and is not, therefore, dependent on the identity of the owner. In your discussion of the case, see if you can explain why the court wishes to make the obligation to pay permanent damages for the nuisance a servitude on the land rather than being a mere obligation to pay particular individuals.

QUESTION 5.31:   Is the externality in *Boomer* private or public?

QUESTION 5.32:   Are the transaction costs of bargaining among the parties low or high?

QUESTION 5.33:   Suppose the households had a right to enjoin the cement company to stop polluting. What obstacles would the cem ent company face if it tried to purchase the right to pollute from the households?

QUESTION 5.34:   Explain the remedy given by the court. Suppose that at some time in the future the cement company doubles its rate of output, thus increasing the noise, smoke, dust, and vibration inflicted on the neighbors. Do the homeowners have a remedy?

QUESTION 5.35:   Contrast the difference between temporary and permanent damages on the incentives of people to build new houses near the cement factory.

QUESTION 5.36:   To what extent can the private law of property solve the problem of pollution?

Web Note 5.8

See our website for an additional case and some additional questions on using nuisance law to correct externalities. We also summarize there some new literature on the choice between property and liability rules as remedies.

C. Graphing Externalities

Let us graph how the award of damages can internalize an externality and restore efficiency. We assume that a firm like Atlantic Cement is held liable for the external costs it inflicts on others. The situation facing the firm is shown in Figure 5.1. The company's marginal private-cost curve, *MPC*, indicates the private cost to the firm of producing different quantities of cement. Private costs include the capital, labor, land, and materials but not the external harm caused by pollution. The external costs of pollution are added to the private costs to yield the social costs of producing cement. Figure 5.1 depicts two marginal social-cost curves representing two different technologies. Under the old technology, the addition of external costs of pollution to the private costs of production yields the marginal social-cost curve *MSC*. This curve depicts the true cost to society of each level of production under the old technology. There is, however, a new technology that pollutes less. Its marginal social costs are shown along line *MSC'*. The superiority of the new technology lies in the fact that it causes half as much pollution at any given level of output as the old technology. For example, the old technology might use filters in the smoke stack, and the new technology might use scrubbers in the smoke stack.

Figure 5.1

The incentives to adopt a new, superior technology under a rule of temporary damages.

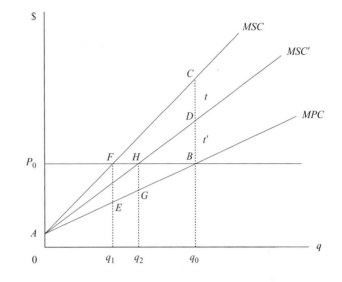

Under either technology and in the absence of any court or regulatory action, the company's profit-maximizing rate of output, q_0, is determined at the intersection of the private marginal-cost curve and the prevailing output price, P_0. Under the old technology, the total amount of external cost inflicted by the output rate q_0 is the area ABC. Under the new technology, the total amount of external cost inflicted by the output rate q_0 is the area ABD. The net social cost inflicted by the last unit of output is $t' + t$ under the old technology and t' under the new technology. Note that it is easy to see here that, even if there is no legal compulsion for the firm to take external costs into account, society is better off if the firm is producing under the new technology rather than under the old technology. However, if the firm is not required to internalize these external costs, it has no incentive to adopt the new technology.

However, matters change if the firm can be made to internalize the social cost of its production of cement. Under the old technology and with the firm held responsible for its external costs, the profit-maximizing rate of output is determined by the intersection of P_0 and MSC at q_1. At this point the cost of pollution is area AEF. But under the new technology and with the firm held responsible for its external costs, the profit-maximizing rate of output is determined by the intersection of P_0 and MSC' at q_2. Social efficiency requires the firm to adopt the new technology and produce at q_2. (Can you identify the cost of pollution at production level q_1 under the old tenchology, and at q_2 under the new technology?[62]

---

[62] At q_1 under the old technology, the cost of pollution is AEF. At q_2 under the new technology, the cost of pollution is AGH.

But what about the firm? Is it indifferent between the two technologies? No. Assuming that the firm pays pollution costs, its maximum profits under the old technology are the area AP_0F, whereas maximum profits under the new technology are $AP_0 H$. It is obvious that $AP_0 H > AP_0 F$.

How do these considerations relate to the question we asked above about the incentives for adopting superior technologies of production under the alternative damage measures? The intuitively plausible answer is that the cement company will adopt the cleaner technology more quickly under temporary damages than under permanent damages, and that intuition is borne out by our formal analysis. However, these economic advantages to temporary damages over permanent damages must be balanced against the potentially higher administrative costs of temporary awards.

QUESTION 5.37: The price line P_0 is horizontal in Figure 5.2. What does this fact indicate about competition?

QUESTION 5.38: Assume that science reveals a new health hazard caused by breathing pollution from cement factories. How would such a discovery modify the graph and change the efficient level of production of cement?

D. Takings

The theory of property developed in Chapter 4 stresses that clear and certain property rights may facilitate bargaining, which creates a surplus from cooperation and exchange. Conversely, unclear and uncertain property rights may impede bargaining, which destroys the social surplus. The power of the state to take property (that is, to compel its sale to the state) and regulate its use reduces the clarity and certainty of

Figure 5.2

The incentive effects on private investors of a difference between compensable takings and noncompensable regulations.

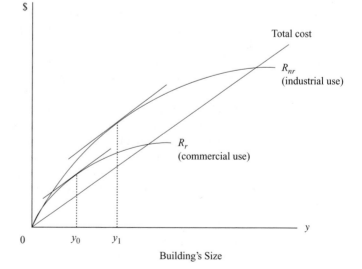

property rights. The resulting destruction in social surplus represents the economic cost of the state's power to take property and regulate its use. Offsetting the economic cost is the benefit of providing public goods at lower cost. In this section we develop these ideas into an economic theory of the taking and regulatory powers.

In many countries, the constitution circumscribes the state's power to take private property. For example, the takings clause of the Fifth Amendment to the U.S. Constitution reads, "nor shall private property be taken for public use, without just compensation." Thus, the Fifth Amendment prohibits the state from taking private property except under two conditions: (1) the private property is taken for a public use, and (2) the owner is compensated. We will explain the economic rationale for these two conditions.

1. Compensation

To understand the compensation requirement, we proceed in two stages. First, assume that there were no requirement to compensate (as was the case in England centuries ago) so that expropriating private property might be a means of financing the government. Second, assume that there is a requirement to compensate and examine its incentive effects for the government to use private property. (We will examine compensation's effect on the private property owner's use of the property in a subsequent section.)

First, contrast takings and taxes as means of financing government. Taxes are assessed on a broad base, such as income, property, sales, or bequests. Everyone subject to the tax faces the same schedule of rates. In contrast, a taking involves a particular piece of property owned by a particular person. Tyrannies sometimes finance government and enrich officials by taking property from individuals. To finance the state by takings, the private owner whose property is appropriated must not receive compensation. If the private property owner received compensation equal to the market value for his or her property, the state could not profit from taking it. So the requirement of compensation can be viewed as a device to channel government finance into taxes and away from takings.

Economics provides strong reasons for financing the state by taxes rather than takings. Any kind of expropriation distorts people's incentives and causes economic inefficiency, but taxes distort far less than uncompensated takings. To see why, consider the basic principle in public finance that focused taxes distort more than broad taxes. Applying this principle, a given amount of revenues can be raised with less distortion by a tax on food rather than vegetables, or a tax on vegetables rather than carrots. This principle follows from the fact that avoiding broad taxes is harder than avoiding narrow taxes. For example, avoiding a tax on food requires eating less, whereas avoiding a tax on carrots requires eating another vegetable, such as cucumbers. Broad taxes distort behavior less because many people cannot change their behavior to avoid broad taxes. Thus, efficiency requires the state to collect revenues from broad taxes such as income or consumption.[63] In contrast, takings have a very narrow base. Individual owners will go to

---

[63] The precise proposition is that goods should be taxed at a rate inversely proportional to their elasticity of demand and supply. Broad taxes fall on aggregates that are inelastically demanded and supplied.

great expense to prevent the state from taking their property without compensation. Indeed, the possibility of uncompensated takings would divert effort and resources away from production and toward the politics of redistribution.

Now let us examine the effect of the compensation requirement on government's actions. Courts have held that the compensation requirement necessitates the government's paying roughly the fair market value to a property owner if her property is taken. For reasons that we will soon explain, that value may not be exactly what the owner would like or that would be reached in an arm's-length transaction between the owner and another buyer. Nonetheless, the government cannot make money by paying the market value for property that it takes. This fact discourages the government from excessive takings of private property.

2. Public Use   The requirement of compensation does not preclude another political abuse, in which the state takes one person's property and sells it to someone else. To appreciate the problem, consider the difference between a taking and a sale. Sales are motivated by mutual gain, which is created by moving property from lower-valued to higher-valued uses. To illustrate, Blair's purchase of Adam's 1957 Chevrolet creates a surplus because Blair values it more than Adam does. The fact that both parties must consent to the sale guarantees mutual gain. In contrast, a taking does not require the consent of the property owner, so unilateral gain can motivate a taking. A property owner may value his or her property more than whoever takes it.

For example, assume that Samson owns his family's estate, the market value of which equals $30,000, but Samson does not want to sell it because he values the estate at $100,000 for sentimental reasons. Delilah covets Samson's estate and would be willing to pay up to $40,000 for it. Assume that the state can compel Samson to sell his property at its "fair market value." So, Delilah contributes $5000 to the campaign fund of a prominent government official, who takes Samson's estate, pays him $30,000, and resells the estate to Delilah for $30,000. Thus, Delilah and the government official each gain $5000, although Samson loses $70,000.

By taking Samson's property and giving it to Delilah, the state transfers property from one private person to another, so that Delilah does not have to pay Samson's subjective price for the estate. The requirement of compensation at market prices does not prevent this abuse, which occurs because the owner's subjective value exceeds the market price paid as compensation. To eliminate the abuse, the state could compensate the owner's subjective price rather than the market price. However, no one but the owner knows the subjective price. In a voluntary sale, the owner receives at least the subjective price or does not sell. If the state wanted to compensate at least the owner's subjective price, the state would have to buy the property, not take it.

The "public-use" requirement avoids the abuse in this example. Delilah's use of Samson's estate is private, not public. Consequently, the taking in this example violates the public-use requirement. The public-use requirement forbids the use of takings to bypass markets and transfer private property from one private person to another. Instead, property must be taken for a public use. For example, Samson's estate could be taken for a park, school, or highway.

The public-use requirement does not solve the problem of inefficiency in involuntary transfers. To illustrate, suppose that motorists would be willing to pay $40,000 to use a highway through Samson's estate, the market value of which is $30,000. By taking the land, paying Samson $30,000, and building a highway, the government anticipates a surplus of $10,000. In reality, Samson values his estate at $100,000, so the net social loss will equal $60,000, and Samson will lose $70,000.

This example suggests that the state should not take property with compensation merely to produce a public good. In reality, the state buys most of the resources that it uses to supply public goods. For example, the state buys cement, pencils, trucks, light bulbs, and labor. In fact, takings are circumscribed more than the requirements of compensation and public use suggest.

3. Holdouts   The government must purchase large tracts of land from many owners in order to provide some public goods, such as military bases, airports, highways, and wilderness areas. These projects often demand "contiguity," which means that the parcels of land must touch each other. To illustrate, the segments of a highway do not connect unless they are on contiguous parcels of land. Contiguity disrupts bargaining by creating opportunities for owners to hold out.

To illustrate, assume that the state proposes to construct a road across three parcels of land owned by three different people. The state determines that motorists would pay $200,000 more than the construction costs for such a road. Consequently, efficiency requires undertaking the project provided that the land's value is less than $200,000. The three owners value the land at $30,000 per parcel, so construction of the road would create a social surplus of $110,000. Assume that the state acquires an option to buy one of the parcels for $30,000. The state could pay up to $170,000 for the other two parcels and still come out ahead. Knowing this, each of the owners demands $100,000 for her parcel of land. If the state must buy the land, not take it, the project fails.

The last owner frequently "holds out" when the state acquires contiguous parcels of land needed for a public project. In a real-life example, the developers of a new baseball stadium in Denver purchased all the land except for the property of one "holdout," whom the newspaper called "the guy who owns first base." Even when owners do not hold out, the possibility of doing so can dramatically increase the transaction costs of purchasing contiguous property. The taking power eliminates this problem. The government should resort to compulsory sale principally when there are many sellers, each of whom controls resources that are necessary to the project. Thus, takings should be guided by this principle: *in general, the government should only take private property with compensation to provide a public good when transaction costs preclude purchasing the necessary property.*

> **QUESTION 5.39:**   What if the government needs to purchase a single, large piece of property in order to provide a public good, say, a satellite-tracking station? There is only one private owner with whom to deal. And his property is the only one that is suitable for the station. Should the government be allowed to compel this individual, a monopolist for the contemplated public use, to sell at fair market value?

QUESTION 5.40:   In *Kelo v. City of New London*, 545 U.S. 469 (2005), the U.S. Supreme court decided a case in which landowners challenged the power of a city in Connecticut to take their property for redevelopment. The redevelopment plan did not contemplate that all of the land would be open to the public. Parts would be privately developed. The plaintiffs alleged that the taking was unconstitutional because it was not for a public purpose. The Supreme Court rejected this claim. Use economic analysis to argue for or against the view that such a mixed development plan should be regarded as serving a public purpose. (For some recent cases like this one, see Web Note 5.9.)

QUESTION 5.41:   Compare the efficiency of the following two methods of amending the just-compensation constraint:

a. Define just compensation to be fair market value (including relocation costs) plus, say, 20 percent.
b. Allow private property owners to make their own assessments of the value of their property. Property owners agree to pay property taxes on that self-assessed value. If the government ever takes the property, it agrees to pay the self-assessed property value as just compensation.

4. Insurance   People typically purchase insurance on assets whose value constitutes a significant proportion of their wealth, such as a house. Most homeowners purchase fire insurance. Similarly, people want insurance against takings. Private companies provide fire insurance, whereas the state provides insurance against takings by compensating property owners. Why does the private sector provide insurance against fires, and the state sector provide insurance against takings?

This question challenges you to relate takings to the economics of insurance. Insurance spreads risk among policy holders. In general, spreading risk more broadly reduces the amount that anyone must bear. The state can spread the risk of takings through the base of all taxpayers, which is broader than the base of all policy holders in any insurance company. So, risk-spreading argues for public insurance.

Administrative efficiency argues for private insurance. The discipline of competition causes a higher level of administrative efficiency in private insurance funds than in state insurance funds. Many state insurance funds, such as depository insurance in American savings banks, have a dismal history.

Risk-spreading and administrative costs are not decisive. The decisive case for public insurance against takings rests on incentive effects for the state. Decisions about takings are made by the state. If the state did not have to pay compensation, it might take property to finance itself, or it might take property for redistribution to the friends of politicians, or it might purchase too many public goods.[64]

5. Regulations   Earlier in this chapter we discussed how interdependent utility or production functions can cause the externalization of social costs. Nuisance suits provide

---

[64] For more on takings as insurance, see Lawrence Blume & Dan Rubinfeld, *Compensation for Takings: An Economic Analysis,* 72 CAL. L. REV. 569 (1984).

a remedy. State regulations provide another remedy. Regulations restrict the use of the property without taking title from the owner. Enacting regulations involves a political fight between the beneficiaries and victims. Since the outcome depends on politics, not cost-benefit analysis, the total costs of regulations often exceed the total benefits. However, a chapter on property is not the place to develop a full critique of regulations. In this section, we focus on a narrower issue related to takings.

Regulations typically cause a fall in the value of some target property, which may prompt a suit for compensation. To illustrate, an industrialist who acquires land to build a factory may be blocked when the local government "downzones" and forbids industrial uses. The industrialist may sue, alleging that the state took a substantial portion of the value of the property but not the title. When courts find for the plaintiff in such cases, they say there was a "taking." When courts find for the defendant in such cases, they say there was a "regulation." The difference is that a taking requires compensation and a regulation requires no compensation.

We want to discuss the incentive effects of this classification into compensated restrictions (takings) and uncompensated restrictions (regulations). If the state need not compensate for restrictions, then it will impose too many of them. If there are too many restrictions, then resources will not be put to their highest-valued use. Thus, uncompensated restrictions result in inefficient uses. Conversely, if the state must compensate fully for restrictions, then property owners will be indifferent about whether the state restricts them. If property owners are indifferent about whether the state restricts them, they will improve their property as if there were no risk that restrictions will prevent the use of the improvements. If restrictions subsequently prevent the use of the improvements, the investment will be wasted. Thus, compensated restrictions result in wasteful improvements.

We illustrate this argument by an example.[65]

> **FACTS:** Xavier is a government official whose wall contains a map with a thick blue line across it. Currently, the land-use planning laws allow the area to the south of the blue line to be used for any commercial, industrial, or residential purpose. The government proposes to change the law and forbid industrial uses, although commercial uses would still be allowed.
>
> Yvonne owns a building that is located on the blue line. She currently uses the building as a retail outlet, but she is contemplating expanding and improving the building for use as a factory. Yvonne must decide how much to invest in improving her building. If she abandons the idea of using her building as a factory, she will make a smaller investment in improving it for use as retail space, and the government's land-use regulation decision will not affect her. But if she proceeds with the idea of using her building as a factory, she will make a large investment, and the government's decision *will* affect her. Should the government carry out its proposed change, she will lose money on the large investment, and a court will then have to decide whether she is entitled to compensation for the loss. The decision will turn on whether the court declares the change in the governmental land-use plan to be a regulation, in which case no compensation is due, or a taking, in which case compensation is due.

---

[65] See Cooter, *Unity in Tort, Contract, and Property: The Model of Precaution,* 73 CAL. L. REV. 1 (1985).

Consider the incentive effects of the court's decision on Yvonne. If she is confident that downzoning is a taking and that she will receive compensation, she bears no risk from making a large investment; so, she will invest as if there were no risk of loss from governmental action. On the other hand, if she is confident that downzoning is a regulation and that she will not receive compensation, she bears the risk that the value of her investment would be destroyed by the governmental action, and she will restrain her investment.

Figure 5.2 on page 174 illustrates these facts. The vertical axis indicates dollars, and the horizontal axis measures the size of Yvonne's renovated building. The straight line labeled "Total Cost" indicates the amount that she spends on enlarging the building. Two curves, labeled and R_{nr} and R_r, indicate possible revenues yielded by the building as a function of its size. The higher revenue curve, labeled R_{nr}, indicates the revenues obtainable when there is no regulation, so that the building can be used as a factory. The lower revenue curve, labeled R_r, indicates the revenues obtainable when there is regulation, so that the building cannot be used as a factory.

Applying the usual economic logic, Yvonne will maximize profits by choosing the size of building for which the marginal cost equals the marginal revenues. Marginal values are given by the slopes of total value curves in the graph. y_0 is the point at which the slope of the lower revenue curve equals the slope of the total cost curve, so y_0 is the profit-maximizing investment level when industrial use is forbidden. If Yvonne were certain that the courts would hold that downzoning is a regulation, then she would maximize profits by investing at the low level y_0.

y_1 is the point at which the slope of the higher revenue curve equals the slope of the total cost curve; so, y_1 is the profit-maximizing investment level when industrial use is allowed. If Yvonne were certain that downzoning would be deemed a taking by the courts, then she would maximize profits (including compensation) by investing at the high level.

Now consider the efficient level of investment. Social efficiency requires Yvonne to take account of real risks, including the risk that the value of her contemplated investment will be destroyed by governmental action. If it were certain that government would *not* alter the land-use regulations in this area, then efficiency would require Yvonne to invest at the high level y_1. On the other hand, if it were certain that government would alter the rules, then efficiency would require Yvonne to invest at the low level y_0. In reality, it is uncertain whether government will make the alteration, so efficiency requires Yvonne to invest at a level in between y_1 and y_0.[66]

No compensation causes Yvonne to internalize the risk. When she internalizes the risk, she invests efficiently, at a level above y_0 and below y_1. We conclude that *no compensation for the loss of value in investments caused by uncertain governmental action provides incentives for efficient private investment.* However, compensation causes her to invest at y_1, as if the risk were zero. We conclude that *full compensation for the loss of value in investments caused by uncertain governmental action provides incentives for excessive private investment.*

---

[66] To be precise, efficiency requires her to make additional improvements until the resulting increase in her profits when there is no government action, multiplied by the probability of no governmental action, equals the loss in profits when there is government action, multiplied by the probability of governmental action.

This argument concerns incentives for private persons, not the state. The effect of the two legal institutions—regulations and takings—is quite different when we turn from private persons to government officials. If the court decides that the alteration in the allowable uses of land in the relevant area is a mere regulation, so that compensation need not be paid, then the alteration costs the government nothing. On the other hand, if the court decides that this particular action is a taking so that compensation must be paid, then this type of action is very costly to the government. Obviously, *the noncompensability of regulations gives government officials an incentive to overregulate, whereas the compensability of takings makes government officials internalize the full cost of expropriating private property.* When government action is likely to be judged a taking, the government internalizes the cost of its actions and thus restrains its taking of private property. On the other hand, when government action is likely to be judged a mere regulation, the government lacks material incentives to conserve its use of valuable private property rights.

If the state compensates property owners for governmental takings, property owners have an incentive toward excessive improvements, whereas if the state does not compensate, the government has an incentive to overregulate private property. This is the *paradox of compensation,* which we shall meet again in our study of contracts and torts. Officials should consider this paradox when they must decide whether a state action that reduces private property values is a taking or a regulation. If private owners will respond to compensation by making excessive improvements, then their behavior will improve by declaring the state action to be a regulation. Conversely, if the government will respond to non-compensation by excessive action that harms property owners, then its behavior will improve by declaring the state action to be a taking. In technical terms, *elasticity in the supply of private investment with respect to compensation favors regulation instead of takings, and elasticity in the supply of state action with respect to compensation favors takings instead of regulations.*

Web Note 5.9

There have been some fascinating recent U.S. cases regarding noncompensable regulations and compensable takings. We review some of those cases and some of the recent literature on these issues on our website.

E. Bargaining With the State

Now we turn to a famous case where a landowner successfully sued the state for taking a property right by the way it regulated development. North of Los Angeles, the magnificent coastline of California remains largely unspoiled by development, and the California Coastal Commission is responsible for keeping it that way. A property owner named Nollan sought a permit from the Commission to enlarge a small coastal dwelling into a house. The property was located between the beach and a public road, as depicted in Figure 5.3. The house would have diminished and degraded the view of the coast from the road. The Commission wanted to protect the view from the road. To protect the view, the Commission could have refused permission to build the house. The Commission,

Figure 5.3

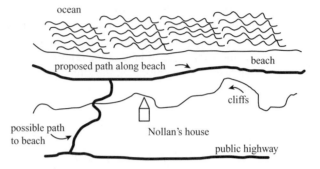

however, took another approach because it had another goal: to create a public walking path along the beach, as indicated in the figure. The Commission asked the owner to donate a public path along the beach in exchange for permission to build the house. Private developers often donate land in exchange for permits, as when a housing developer donates land for a school and a road in exchange for a permit to build houses on farmland. Instead of donating the path, however, the owner sued the Commission.

The law clearly allows the state to regulate property to protect the public against harm, and the law clearly forbids the state from expropriating selected property owners without compensation in order to finance public goods. Was the Coastal Commission protecting the public or forcing a private person to pay for a public easement? The U.S. Supreme Court reached the latter conclusion in a complex opinion written by Justice Scalia. The Court looked for a "nexus" between the harm caused by the owner (obstructing the public view from the road) and the remedy demanded by the Commission (donating a public path along the beach). The Court reasoned that without such a nexus, the regulation was an illegal taking. Because the Court could not find a nexus, the owner won the dispute.

A legal principle can be abstracted from these facts. In order for a regulation to count as protecting the public from harm, the regulation must *mitigate* the harm. The state may condition a permit on mitigating the harm caused by its exercise. A donation of land to mitigate harm is allowed. For example, the Commission might have asked Nollan to donate a path to get around the house and reach the beach. (See "possible path to beach" in the picture.) A donation of land for a purpose *un*related to the harm does not mitigate it. Instead, a donation for another purpose *offsets* the harm by supplying something else of value. *Nollan* can be interpreted as standing for the principle that the state may not condition a permit on offsetting the harm caused by the permit's exercise.

Some hypothetical numbers inspired by *Nollan* show a problem with this policy of forbidding permits conditional on offsets. According to Figure 5.4, the property owner values building the house at 1000, and the Commission values the public's loss of view at 300. Figure 5.4 shows the valuations for "build" and "don't build" in the two columns of the figure.

Figure 5.5 shows the valuations for "mitigate" and "offset." Mitigating requires redesigning the house to improve the view, which costs the owner 300 and benefits the public by 250 as estimated by the Commission. Alternatively, donating a path along the beach costs the owner 250 and benefits the public by 400.

Figure 5.4

Value of building and not building.

	Act (build house)	Don't act (don't build house)
Property owner	+1000	0
Public commission	− 300	0

Figure 5.5

Value of mitigation and offset.

	Redesign house (mitigate)	Path along beach (offset)
Property owner	−300	−250
Public commission	+250	+400

Figure 5.6

Net values.

	Don't act	Act and mitigate	Act and offset
Property owner	0	700	750
Public commission	0	−50	100
Total	0	650	850

Figure 5.6 combines the numbers from the two previous figures to give the net benefits of alternative acts. "Don't act" yields 0 to both parties. "Act and mitigate" yields 700 to the property owner (1000 − 300 = 700) and −50 to the public (−300 + 250 = −50), for a net benefit of 650. These two choices ("Don't act" and "Act and mitigate") are apparently the only ones allowed by the Court in *Nollan*. Given these two choices, the Commission will presumably refuse to issue a permit, and the result will be 0 benefits to both parties.

The Court apparently will not allow the parties to act and offset, which would benefit both of them. "Act and offset" yields 750 to the property owner (1000 − 250 = 750) and 100 to the public commission (−300 + 400 = 100) for a total benefit of 850.

With these hypothetical numbers, the holding in *Nollan* results in a payoff of 0 to both parties (the Commission denies the building permit), whereas allowing the Commission to demand an offset results in a payoff of 850 (Commission gives permit, and owner donates the path). These hypothetical numbers show that the principle in *Nollan* can easily cause inefficient blocking of building permits. The Supreme Court apparently arrived at this principle because it feared that the state will abuse offsets. The state might demand offsets from politically vulnerable property owners instead of collecting taxes. For example, a mayor elected by tenants might demand offsets whenever landlords need building permits. The mayor could use the offsets to finance public goods instead of imposing taxes that fall partly on tenants.

The potential scope for such abusive offsets is large for two reasons. First, the state has extensive powers of regulation, many of which go unused. The state might start to introduce unnecessary restriction on those seeking building (and other) permits just to obtain offsets. Second, the state can demand an offset whose value exceeds the harm caused by exercising the permit. In Figure 5.4, building benefits the owner by 1000. Thus, the state can demand up to 1000 in offsets as a condition for allowing the owner to build, and the owner gains from accepting the offer, even though building harms the public by only 300.

Fear of abuse is reasonable, but the Court should have solved the problem in a different way that avoids inefficiency. A better solution prohibits offsets unless the state also gives the property owner the opportunity to mitigate. This approach implies that the Commission should give the property owner the permit to build the house conditional on the owner *either* mitigating *or* offsetting. The relationship "either . . . or . . ." is disjunctive. We are proposing a disjunctive conditional permit.

The additional choice can benefit both parties. In Figure 5.6, the disjunctive conditional permit allows the owner to redesign the house at a cost of 300 (mitigate) or donate a path along the beach at a cost of 250 (offset). The owner will choose the latter, which will benefit the public much more than the former. In general, allowing the state an additional choice—to issue a permit conditional on mitigating or offsetting—cannot make the state worse off. By issuing a disjunctive conditional permit, the state gives the property owner an additional choice. The property owner in Figure 5.6 will choose to offset. In general, allowing the property owner an additional choice—to mitigate or offset—cannot make the property owner worse off. So, allowing the state to choose or reject issuing a disjunctive conditional permit is more (Pareto) efficient than not allowing it to do so.

> **QUESTION 5.42:** Assume that Figures 5.4 and 5.5 describe the facts in *Nollan*. Why might the property owner challenge the Commission and litigate instead of accepting the Commission's offer to give a permit in exchange for donating a pathway along the beach?

> **QUESTION 5.43:** The picture of the *Nollan* case indicates the "proposed path along the beach" and a "possible path to the beach." The Court did not allow the Commission to give a building permit conditioned on donating a path along the beach. Why might the court have allowed the Commission to give a building permit conditioned on donating a path to the beach?

> **QUESTION 5.44:** The Federal Government provides disaster insurance that helps people to build vacation homes in places subject to flooding, such as sand dunes. Assume the government wants to protect the environment by preventing construction of homes on a specific sand dune near the ocean. If the government takes private property on the sand dune, either by condemning it or by imposing regulations that forbid any construction, should compensation include or exclude the increase in the value of the land caused by government flood insurance?

F. Zoning and the Regulation of Development

Some goods, called *complements,* are better consumed together, such as hot dogs and sauerkraut, and other goods, called *substitutes,* are better consumed separately, such as ice cream and sauerkraut. A similar categorization may be made regarding the spatial separation of economic activities: it is best to locate restaurants near offices, and it is best to separate smokestack industries from residences. There is, however, an important difference between culinary and spatial separation: no law prohibits eating ice cream with sauerkraut, but zoning ordinances in most localities *do* prohibit locating industry in residential neighborhoods.

It is the element of compulsion in the segregation of economic activities by zoning laws that we here seek to explain. It is possible to make a case for zoning as a response to an important kind of market failure. When demand for a good increases, the price rises, and producers respond by supplying more of it. The rise in price is a signal for producers to devote more resources to producing the good. This signal is usually appropriate in the sense that society is better off when resources are shifted to producing goods whose price is rising. There are, however, special circumstances in which the signals get crossed. In these special circumstances, it would be better for society if producers of a certain good responded to a rise in the price of that good by supplying *less* of it; but in a free market, they will respond to the rise in price by supplying more of it.

To illustrate by a historical example, suppose that in 1900 industry locates on the shore of an undeveloped bay in California. Locating industry on the shore gave easy access to boats. By 1960, however, the manufacturers were supplied by truck rather than by boat. Moreover, the harbor now has great aesthetic and recreational appeal. Given the change in circumstances, efficiency requires gradually relocating industry into the interior and constructing residences or recreational parks on the harbor.

To cause factories to move out and residences to move in, residential developers should bid up the price of harbor land relative to land in the interior. There is, however, an obstacle to the unregulated market's accomplishing this end. The problem is that no one wants to live next door to a factory, so that residential developers are unwilling to pay much for harbor land as long as industry is present. Instead of factories' moving away from the harbor, the opposite may happen: as industry expands, residences may be driven farther away from the water. If the relative price of land near the water falls as residents flee to the interior to escape industry, the unregulated market in this situation gives the wrong signals.[67]

Conclusion

In Chapters 4 and 5 we developed an economic theory of property and applied it to a wide-ranging set of legal problems. Our theory views property as the institution that gives people freedom over resources; property law can encourage the efficient use of resources by creating rules that facilitate bargaining and exchange and that minimize the losses when bargaining fails. We organized our theoretical discussion of property rules around four questions that a system of property law must answer. In answering these questions, we revealed the economic logic underlying much of property law.

Suggested Readings

Cooter, Robert D., *Organization as Property: Economic Analysis of Property Law Applied to Privatization*, 2 J. Legal Econ. 77 (1992).

Epstein, Richard A., Takings: Private Property and the Power of Eminent Domain (1985).

---

[67] The explanation for why the market gives the wrong signals in this situation is somewhat technical. Our website contains the explanation.

FISCHEL, WILLIAM A., REGULATORY TAKINGS: LAW, ECONOMICS, AND POLITICS (1995).

GOLDSTEIN, PAUL, COPYRIGHT'S HIGHWAY: THE LAW AND LORE OF COPYRIGHT FROM GUTENBERG TO THE CELESTIAL JUKEBOX (1994).

HELLER, MICHAEL A., THE GRIDLOCK ECONOMY: HOW TOO MUCH OWNERSHIP WRECKS MARKETS, STOPS INNOVATION, AND COSTS LIVES (2008).

JAFFE, ADAM B., & MANUEL TRAJTENBERG, PATENTS, CITATIONS, AND INNOVATIONS: A WINDOW ON THE KNOWLEDGE ECONOMY (2002).

Lubet, Steven, *Notes on the Bedouin Horse Trade or Why Doesn't the Market Clear, Daddy?*, 74 TEX. L. REV. 1039 (1996).

MICELI, THOMAS J., & KATHLEEN SEGERSON, COMPENSATION FOR REGULATORY TAKINGS: AN ECONOMIC ANALYSIS WITH APPLICATIONS (1996).

Parchomovsky, Gideon, and Peter Siegelman, *Selling Mayberry: Communities and Individuals in Law and Economics*, 92 CAL. L. REV. 75 (2004).

Rapaczynski, Andrzej, *The Roles of the State and the Market in Establishing Property Rights*, 10 J. ECON. PERSP. 87 (1996).

6 An Economic Theory of Tort Law

The early law asked simply, "Did the defendant do the physical act which damaged the plaintiff?" The law of today, except in certain cases based upon public policy, asks the further question, "Was the act blameworthy?"

JAMES BARR ADAMS,
LAW AND MORALS, 22 HARV. L. REV. 97, 99 (1908)

Even if there is no negligence, public policy demands that responsibility be fixed wherever it will most effectively reduce the hazards to life and health inherent in defective products that reach the market.

JUDGE ROGER TRAYNOR,
ESCOLA V. COCA-COLA BOTTLING COMPANY, 150 P.2D 436 (1944)

PEOPLE OFTEN HARM each other by doing something wrong: Motorists collide on the highway; a patron in a bar punches the person standing next to him; an intrauterine birth control device causes infertility; a newspaper inaccurately reports the arrest of a businessman for soliciting a prostitute; a professor gives an unfair exam; and so forth. Some of these wrongs are accidental and some are intentional; some are serious and others are trivial; some are crimes and others are annoyances.

Suppose that the victim in each of these cases initiates a lawsuit. Under what body of law can the victim sue? Because the plaintiff and defendant are private persons (not the state), the suit belongs to "private law," as does contract and property law. The victim cannot sue under contract law (which we will discuss in later chapters) because a broken promise did not cause the injury in any of these cases. The victim cannot sue under property law for damage to body, reputation, or scholastic record because these things are not *property*. (You cannot transfer your body, bequeath your reputation, or sell your scholastic record.) Large losses can escape contract or property law, such as the explosion of British Petroleum's *Deepwater Horizon* oil rig in the Gulf of Mexico in 2010 that resulted in billions of dollars of losses (as well as dead birds, fish, and aquatic plants).

These facts demonstrate the need for a third major body of private law other than property and contracts. The third body of law concerns compensable wrongs that do not arise from breach of contract and cannot be remedied by an injunction against future interference. Here are some more detailed examples:

Example 1: Joe Potatoes has been driven to distraction by the escapades of his wife, Joan Potatoes. At the end of a hard night's work at the loading dock, Joe is approached by Jim Bloggs. Suspecting that Jim has been romancing Joan,

Joe insults and strikes him, breaking his nose. Bloggs subsequently sues for the injury to his reputation and his nose.

Example 2:   Three hunters go into the woods after pheasants. They are spread out in a straggling line about 25 yards apart, walking in the same direction. The hunter in the center flushes a bird that flies up, its wings pounding. The hunters to his left and right turn toward the bird in the middle and fire. The bird escapes, but the hunter in the middle is blinded by birdshot. One of the two hunters certainly caused the harm, but there is no way to determine which one of them it was. The victim sues both of them.

Example 3:   A manufacturer produces automobile fuel additives that demand careful control over quality. If quality control is maintained at a high level, the chemical mixture in the product is correct, and it never causes damage to automobile engines. If, however, quality control is relaxed and allowed to fall to a low level, some batches of the chemical mixture will be flawed. A few of the cars using the flawed batch will be harmed, specifically, the engine will throw a rod and tear itself to pieces. After a rod is thrown, an alert mechanic can detect the cause of the harm by examining the car's fuel and other signs. The manufacturer determines that a high level of quality control costs more than the harm to some automobile engines caused by a low level of quality control, so the manufacturer adopts a low level of quality control. The owner of a damaged car sues the manufacturer and asks for punitive damages.

In English-language countries, the name for the body of common law relevant for these cases is *tort* law. After the Normans conquered England in 1066, they soon lost the French language, but they retained a peculiar form of it for writing about law. *Tort* is "law-French," itself derived from the Latin word *tortus* (twisted). The common law of torts overlaps the law of "civil responsibility" in continental Europe. The continental Europeans use this phrase to refer to private suits over injuries, as opposed to criminal prosecutions. However, different legal traditions locate the boundaries of these broad areas of law somewhat differently and adopt somewhat different legal doctrines.

Example 1 illustrates an "intentional tort," so named because the injurer intentionally inflicted the harm on the victim. Many intentional torts are also crimes, such as assault, battery, false imprisonment, and intentional infliction of emotional duress. The person who commits such an act may be sued for damages under tort law by the victim and also prosecuted under criminal law by the state. Intentional torts are so much like crimes that we shall not discuss them here. Instead, we shall rely upon our analysis of crime in Chapter 12 to serve as an introduction to intentional torts.

Most of the wrongs that we shall consider in the two chapters on torts are *unintentional,* that is, inadvertent accidents. To illustrate, Example 2 describes a hunting accident. Example 3 is more complicated. The manufacturer's low level of quality control is deliberate, and the resulting harm to automobiles is statistically predictable, but the harm to particular cars is accidental. Example 3 also differs from the other two examples in that the injurer sold a product to the victim, so the two parties participated in a commercial transaction.

The law of accidents was one of the first bodies of private law successfully analyzed using formal economic models. Following the pattern throughout the book, this chapter focuses on general theory, and the next chapter turns to particular topics, including proposals to reform the tort liability system.

I. Defining Tort Law

We began this chapter by listing examples of harm for which the laws of contracts and property offer no remedy. The victim cannot use these laws to sue when there is no breach of contract, no damage to property, or no continuing harm to enjoin. This gap creates the need for tort law. Now we want to demonstrate that this gap in the law of property and contracts *necessarily* exists and, by doing so, we shall describe the economic essence of tort law.

A. Economic Essence of Tort Law

Bargaining enables people to cooperate over many kinds of harm that one person imposes upon another. Recall the examples that we discussed when explaining the Coase Theorem, such as the rancher's cows and the farmer's crop, or the electrical company's smoke and the laundry's white clothes, or the sparks from the railroad and the farmer's wheat fields. For some kinds of harm, however, the costs of bargaining are so high that the parties cannot cooperate together. The hunters in Example 2 could negotiate an agreement to allocate the cost of an accident before they begin shooting pheasants. However, the cost of negotiating (including the unpleasant atmosphere it creates) is large relative to the small probability of a hunting accident. Similarly, every driver cannot negotiate with every other driver and agree among themselves concerning how to allocate the costs of future automobile accidents.

In Example 1, Joe Potatoes was not in a frame of mind to negotiate when he broke the nose of Jim Bloggs. The obstacle to cooperation in Example 1 is emotions, not costs. In Example 3, where defective fuel additives destroy automobile engines, the manufacturer may think that most consumers will remain ignorant of the dangers caused by defective fuel additives. Consequently, the manufacturer of fuel additives may not want to alert consumers by mentioning the danger in the consumer contract or the product's warranty. The obstacle to cooperation in Example 3 is consumers' ignorance and the producer's strategic decision to keep information private.

Recall that the Coase Theorem treats all obstacles to bargaining—including bargaining costs, emotions, cognitive imperfections, private information, and strategy—as "transaction costs." We can use this idea to explain the boundary between the law of contracts and torts. Contract law concerns relationships among people for whom the transaction costs of private agreements are relatively low, whereas tort law concerns relationships among people for whom transaction costs of private agreements are relatively high. Economists describe harms that are outside private agreements as *externalities*. The economic purpose of tort liability is to induce injurers and victims to *internalize* the costs of harm that can occur from failing to take care. Tort law internalizes these costs by making the injurer compensate the victim. When potential wrongdoers internalize the costs of the harm that they cause, they have incentives to invest in safety at the efficient level. *The economic essence of tort law is its use of liability to internalize externalities created by high transaction costs.*

Tort liability is only one of several policy instruments available to internalize externalities created by high transaction costs. Alternative policy instruments include criminal statutes, safety regulations, and tax incentives. Each alternative has its advantages and disadvantages. This chapter will explain the strengths and weaknesses of tort liability as an instrument for internalizing externalities.

> **QUESTION 6.1:**   According to the conclusion to Chapter 4, ". . . property rights are part of the law that makes owners internalize the social costs and benefits of alternative uses of the goods that they own." Torts are also an essential part of that law. Explain why.

B. The Traditional Theory of Tort Liability

We described the essence of tort law in terms of its economic function. Before analyzing these functions, we describe a traditional legal theory of torts. In the early twentieth century, a legal theory specified the essential elements of a tort. This traditional theory of tort law enjoyed substantial acceptance in America 100 years ago. We discuss it now because the essential elements of a tort as stipulated by it serve as building blocks in the economic model of tort liability.

Three elements must be present for recovery by the plaintiff under the traditional theory of torts:

1. The plaintiff must have suffered *harm*;
2. The defendant's act or failure to act must *cause* the harm; and
3. The defendant's act or failure to act must constitute the *breach of a duty* owed to the plaintiff by the defendant.

We will explain each element in turn and develop an economic account of it.

1. Harm   The first element required for a plaintiff to sue in tort is that he or she must have suffered harm. Without harm, there can be no suit in tort, even if the act was dangerous. To illustrate, suppose that the manufacturer in Example 3 sold a batch of fuel additives that were harmless in cars with conventional carburetors and dangerous in cars with turbocharged carburetors. The owner of a car with a conventional carburetor might feel outrage when these facts become known, but outrage is not compensable. His car must have actually been damaged.

Harm has a simple economic interpretation: a downward shift in the victim's utility or profit function. To illustrate, Charlie's utility function in Figure 6.1 is defined over two goods—health (along the horizontal axis) and wealth (along the vertical axis). An indifference curve in that figure, such as u_0 or u_1, depicts all the combinations of health and wealth that give Charlie the same level of satisfaction. Higher indifference curves indicate more satisfaction. Thus, any combination of health and wealth that lies

FIGURE 6.1

Showing harm as a displacement from a higher to a lower indifference curve and the measures of compensation.

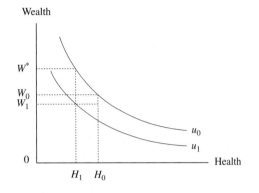

above u_0 is more desirable to Charlie than any combination that lies on or below u_0. The shape of Charlie's indifference curves indicates that he is willing to trade off one good to get more of the other and maintain overall well-being. To illustrate, as Charlie moves down u_0, his wealth decreases at a rate that exactly offsets his improving health. Similarly, as Charlie moves up u_1, his health declines at a rate that exactly offsets his increasing wealth.

Suppose that Charlie initially has health in the amount H_0 and wealth in the amount, W_0, which results in utility $u_0 = u(H_0, W_0)$. Now suppose that Amanda injures Charlie, causing his health to fall to H_1 and his wealth to fall to W_1. Charlie has been harmed in that he has been pushed from u_0 down to u_1 by Amanda. Perfect compensation requires Amanda to restore Charlie's satisfaction to level u_0. Money damages are the traditional means of doing this. Assume that costly medical treatment can restore Charlie's health. Typically, those damages would constitute a sum equal to $(W_0 - W_1)$ to compensate for the lost wealth and a sum equal to the cost of providing $(H_0 - H_1)$ units of health. This would restore Charlie to his original position before the wrong was done to him.

Suppose, however, that the accident did irreparable damage to Charlie's health, so that he is stuck at H_1 forever. Amanda could, nonetheless, restore his preaccident level of satisfaction by increasing his wealth, not to its preaccident level of W_0, but rather to level W^*. Because Charlie trades off wealth and health, Amanda can give him the monetary equivalent of his irreparable decline in health.

Figure 6.1 illustrates the ideal of perfect compensation. In reality, tort law limits the harms for which victims can receive compensation from their injurers. Traditionally, courts were willing to compensate for tangible losses that are easy to document, such as medical costs, lost income, the costs of replacing or repairing damaged property, and the like. By contrast, courts were traditionally reluctant to compensate for intangible losses or those that are difficult to measure, such as emotional harm, distress, loss of companionship, and "pain and suffering." Over the years, however, American courts have steadily expanded the list of compensable harms to include many intangibles. To illustrate by Example 1, Bloggs may receive compensation for the emotional distress of being reviled and struck by Potatoes. Other countries have also expanded the scope of compensable harms, but not so far as the United States.

Expanding the scope of compensable harm has advantages and disadvantages. On the one hand, this expansion allows compensation for real harms that would have gone unredressed, as illustrated by the following historical example. Suppose that a motorist accidentally kills one of the dependent children of a loving family. The death of the child entails no loss of income to the rest of the family; on the contrary, death saves the family the expense of raising the child. This fact once posed a difficult problem for courts: They wished to confine compensable damages to economic losses that are measurable, and yet no such losses follow from the death of dependent children. For the surviving members of the family to recover damages, courts had to allow compensation for emotional distress and loss of companionship.[1]

Expanding the scope of compensable harm also creates a vexing problem: How is the court to assign a dollar value to intangible (but real) losses? As explained, *perfect compensation* means a sum of money sufficient to make the victim of an injury equally well off with the money and the injury as he or she would have been without the money or the injury. Perfect compensation is the right goal for courts that are trying to internalize costs, but implementing the goal is difficult for intangible, but real, harms. Implementation is difficult because the court cannot observe and measure the plaintiff's subjective valuation of the loss of companionship, emotional distress, or pain and suffering. Even worse, the very idea of perfect compensation sometimes fails in court. Compensation for a child's death is not an amount of money such that the parents would just as soon have the money as their child.

Confusion over intangible damages contributes to *liability disparity,* which occurs when the same court awards different amounts of compensation to victims who suffered the identical injury. Similarly, court-awarded damages to victims with the same injury differ markedly across countries, with Americans giving higher damages than Germans, and Germans giving more damages than Japanese. Fairness and efficiency seem to require reducing liability disparity in each court and harmonizing damages across jurisdictions. Economics suggests how to reduce liability disparity by adopting better grounded and more predictable ways to calculate damages for intangible harms.

QUESTION 6.2:   Suppose that a person who is burned in an accident suffers intense pain for 1 week and then fully recovers. What does "perfect compensation" mean in principle as applied to the burn? Why do you expect actual compensation to be imperfect?

QUESTION 6.3:   Describe some difficulties in implementing perfect compensation for the destruction by fire of Blackacre, the estate of the Gascoyne-Stubbs family for 15 generations.

2. Cause   According to the traditional theory, the second element of a tort is "cause." In order for the plaintiff to sue, according to the traditional theory, the defendant must have *caused* the plaintiff's harm. To illustrate by modifying Example 1,

---

[1] In a similar vein, many legal systems used to hold that a person's legal causes of action died with him or her. So, if someone was killed in an accident, his estate could not, on this theory, bring an action against the injurer. We shall return to a discussion of this matter, as well as compensation for difficult-to-measure losses, in the next chapter.

suppose that just as Potatoes's fist was about to strike Bloggs's nose, the floor board broke under Bloggs, and he fell down, breaking his nose when he struck the ground. The fall enabled Bloggs to avoid Potatoes's fist, but he broke his nose anyway. In this new example, there is a wrong (throwing a punch), and there is damage (a broken nose), but the former did not cause the latter. Without causation, the wrongdoer who threw the punch is not liable in tort law for the harm.

The element of causation sharply differentiates torts from morality. To illustrate, suppose that in Example 2, both of the hunters were equally reckless when they discharged their guns at the pheasant. It was a matter of mere chance that one of the hunters actually blinded the victim and the other hunter missed. Because they were equally reckless, they are on the same plane morally. They may be equally blameworthy, but they are not equally liable. Under traditional rules of tort liability, only the hunter who actually *caused* the harm is liable; the hunter who missed is not liable.

The idea of causation may seem simple—perhaps an image comes to mind of billiard balls colliding with each other—but this impression is misleading. Causation is a notoriously difficult philosophical topic, and that difficulty carries over into law. The law distinguishes two types of causes. The first and more comprehensive is "cause-in-fact." Lawyers often use a simple criterion, called the "but-for test," to decide whether action A was the cause-in-fact of event B: "But for A, would B have occurred?" If the answer to this question is "no," then A is the cause-in-fact of B. If the answer to this question is "yes," then A is not the cause-in-fact of B.

To illustrate, we apply the but-for test to Example 3. An automobile owner cannot recover unless the defective fuel additive was the cause-in-fact of her engine's having thrown a rod. But for the defective fuel additive, would the car have thrown a rod? If the answer is "no," then the defective fuel additive is the cause-in-fact; if the answer is "yes," then the defective fuel additive is not the cause-in-fact.

The but-for test can determine causation in many legal cases, but in some cases it is useless or misleading. It is often useless in cases involving multiple causes of harm. To illustrate by changing Example 1 again, suppose that Potatoes takes a swing at Bloggs, who dodges the punch and lands on some rotten floorboards that collapse under him, and the fall breaks Bloggs's nose. But for Potatoes's trying to strike Bloggs, would Bloggs have broken his nose? The answer depends upon whether Bloggs would have stepped on the rotten floorboards even if he did not have to dodge the punch from Potatoes. It is unclear whether Potatoes's punch was the cause-in-fact of the broken nose. The punch might not have been a necessary condition for the harm to occur, although it was part of a sufficient set of conditions.[2]

Multiple causes can also increase the probability of harm, as when a person whose parents died from lung cancer lives in a house with asbestos siding, works in a factory with carcinogenic chemicals, and smokes. The courts have struggled to develop a workable theory to assign liability when probabilistic harms actually materialize. An economist might use a regression analysis to estimate the increase in probability of

---

[2] A famous article in philosophy argues that a cause is an Insufficient but Necessary part of an Unnecessary and Sufficient set of conditions (INU). See J. L. Mackie, *Causes and Conditions,* 2 AM. PHIL. Q. 245 (1965).

lung cancer caused by heredity, asbestos siding, chemicals at work, and smoking.[3] All variables with positive coefficients are contributing causes, and the variable with the largest coefficient is the most substantial cause. If the person develops lung cancer and sues someone, the court could assign full liability to the most substantial cause, apportion liability among the contributing causes, or find no liability.

Another problem arises when applying the but-for test to a sequence of events that precede an injury: The but-for test allows distant causes to have the same weight as proximate causes.[4] To illustrate, return to the original Example 1, in which Potatoes's fist breaks Bloggs's nose. The fist is the cause-in-fact of Bloggs's broken nose, but so are many other things. For example, but for having been born, Potatoes would not have broken Bloggs's nose; but for Joe's parents conceiving him, he would have not been born; so Joe's parents are a cause-in-fact of Bloggs's broken nose. The but-for test does not discriminate between the proximate cause (Joe's fist) and the remote cause (Joe's conception).

The defendant's act must not only be a cause-in-fact; it must be the *proximate* cause of the plaintiff's harm to establish legal liability under the traditional theory. Proximity is a matter of degree, so the question arises, "How close must the connection be in order for a particular cause to be 'proximate' in law?" One of the most famous cases addressing this problem is *Palsgraf v. Long Island Railway Co.* (248 N.Y. 399, 162 N.E. 99 [1928]). The relevant facts, as determined by the court, were these:

> Plaintiff [Mrs. Palsgraf] was standing on a platform of defendant's railroad after buying a ticket to go to Rockaway Beach. A train stopped at the station, bound for another place. Two men ran forward to catch it. One of the men reached the platform of the car without mishap, though the train was already moving. The other man, carrying a package, jumped aboard the car, but seemed unsteady as if about to fall. A guard on the car, who had held the door open, reached forward to help him in, and another guard on the platform pushed him from behind. In this act, the package was dislodged, and fell upon the rails. It was a package of small size, about fifteen inches long, and was covered by

---

[3] "Regression analysis" is a standard statistical technique that economists (and others) use to investigate correlations and causal relationships among variables. In a regression, the investigator seeks to investigate how a set of independent or explanatory variables correlates with or causes changes in a dependent variable. In the text example, the dependent variable would be the "probability of contracting lung cancer" (typically measured as the percentage of a particular group—say the residents of the United States in 1990—who have lung cancer. And the independent or explanatory variables would be such things as heredity, the presence of asbestos siding, exposure to chemicals, whether the subject smoked, age, annual income, and so on. The regression analysis produces values for the coefficients of the independent or explanatory variables and estimates of the statistical significance of those coefficient that allow the investigator to draw inferences about the relationship between each of the independent variables (and all of them collectively) and the dependent variable.

[4] A famous illustration of how great events can be said to be caused by remote causes comes from *Mother Goose:*

> For want of a nail, the shoe was lost;
> For want of a shoe, the horse was lost;
> For want of a horse, the rider was lost;
> For want of a rider, the battle was lost;
> For want of the battle, the kingdom was lost;
> And all for the want of a horseshoe nail.

a newspaper. In fact it contained fireworks, but there was nothing in its appearance to give notice of its contents. The fireworks when they fell exploded. The shock of the explosion threw down some scales at the other end of the platform many feet away. The scales struck the plaintiff, causing injuries for which she sues.

The New York court determined that the railroad was not liable for Mrs. Palsgraf's injuries because the railroad guard's actions in pushing the passenger were too remote in the chain of causes to be deemed the legal cause of the plaintiff's harm.[5] As this case illustrates, "proximity" in law is imprecise, although sometimes decisive, for liability.

A famous philosopher, Bertrand Russell, argued that science advances by replacing the imprecise concept of "cause" with the precise mathematical concept of a "function."[6] The idea of cause in tort law connects to functions in economic models. In economic models, the consumer's preferences are described by a utility function, and the producer's technology is described by a production function. The values of the variables in the utility function determine the consumer's level of utility, and the values of the variables in the production function determine the level of output. The consumer chooses the values of variables that he or she controls in the utility function to maximize it, and the producer chooses the values of the variables that he or she controls in the production function to maximize profits. One person harms another when the variables that he or she controls lower the utility or production of someone else. For example, the Long Island Railway Company controlled variables affecting its production that also affected Mrs. Palsgraf's utility. The functional representation of cause in tort law is a variable controlled by one person that appears in the utility or production function of someone else.

To illustrate, assume that Amanda enjoys smoking, which we indicate by the function $u_A = u_A(S, \ldots)$, where u_A denotes Amanda's utility, S denotes the amount that Amanda smokes, and "$\ldots$" indicates all the other variables affecting Amanda's utility. Charlie's utility depends upon his health and wealth, which we write $u_c = u_c(H, W)$. Assume that Charlie's health is a decreasing function of Amanda's smoking: $H = H(S)$. Amanda's utility function, $u_A = u_A(S)$, and Charlie's utility function, $u_c = u_c(H(S), W)$, both contain the variable S. The variable S that Amanda controls directly affects Charlie's utility. (By further complicating the preceding functions, we could represent a probabilistic relationship between Amanda's smoking and Charlie's health.[7])

When the same variable appears in different people's utility or production functions, the functions are "interdependent." Interdependent utility or production functions constitute an externality when obstacles prevent the parties from bargaining together and reaching an agreement to set the interdependent variable at the efficient value. "Cause" in tort law typically involves an externality created by interdependent utility or production functions.

---

[5] As is often true with famous cases, the facts are not as straightforward as generations of law students are led to believe. See JOHN NOONAN, PERSONS AND MASKS OF THE LAW 127 (1976).

[6] Bertrand Russell, *On the Notion of Cause,* 13 PROCEEDINGS OF THE ARISTOTELIAN SOCIETY (1912–1913).

[7] To illustrate, let $H = 1$ indicate "no cancer," and $H = 0$ indicate "cancer." Let p indicate the probability of cancer, where $p = p(S)$ is an increasing function. Charlie's expected utility can be written $p(S)u_c(0, W) + (1 - p(S))u_c(1, W))$.

QUESTION 6.4: Suppose that a car stalls on the railroad tracks because its carburetor is badly maintained. A train collides with the car because the train's brakes are badly maintained. What is the proximate cause of the accident? Did the train or the car have the "last clear chance" to avoid the accident? (A note in Chapter 3 discusses the doctrine of the last clear chance.)

3. Breach of a Duty

In some circumstances, the first two elements that we have just identified—harm and proximate cause—are sufficient to establish liability in tort for the defendant. A rule of liability based upon harm and causation is called "strict liability." For example, a construction company that uses dynamite to clear rocks from the path of a road is liable in common law for any harm caused by the blasting. In general, the common law applies a rule of strict liability to "abnormally dangerous activities" like blasting with dynamite.[8]

In the usual case, however, the victim must demonstrate more than harm and cause in order to recover damages from the defendant. In addition to these two elements, the plaintiff must usually demonstrate that the defendant breached a duty that he or she owed to the plaintiff, and that the breach caused the plaintiff's harm. To illustrate, Joe Potatoes in Example 1 breached a duty not to strike Bloggs. When an injurer breaches a legal duty, he or she is said to be "at fault" or to have been "negligent." For example, one or both of the hunters in Example 2 was at fault in handling a gun because one or both of them breached a duty of care that he or she or they owed to the victim.

A rule of liability requiring the plaintiff to prove harm, causation, and fault is a "negligence" rule. Unlike a rule of strict liability, a negligence rule permits the defense when the defendant is the proximate cause of the plaintiff's harm. Under a negligence rule, the defendant escapes liability if he satisfied the applicable standard of care to avoid the harm that he caused.

We want to develop an economic representation of fault. Some fault is binary (either-or, yes-no, on-off). For example, either a passenger fastens her seat belt or she does not fasten it; either a swimming pool has a lifesaving ring or it does not have one. Sometimes, however, the legal standard of care applies to a continuous variable. For example, a car can change speed continuously, and the trustee can vary continuously the proportion of the trust's portfolio in government bonds (a very safe investment). Economists often prefer to develop theory using continuous variables. Consequently, we denote precaution by the continuous variable x, with larger values of x corresponding to higher levels of precaution. The plaintiff in a tort suit must usually demonstrate that the defendant breached a duty owed to the plaintiff. A duty of care is a legal standard prescribing the minimum acceptable level of precaution. In Figure 6.2, $\tilde{x}$ denotes the legal standard. Precaution below $\tilde{x}$ breaches the duty of care, and precaution equal to $\tilde{x}$ or exceeding it satisfies the duty of care. Precaution $\tilde{x}$ partitions the line in Figure 6.2 and creates two zones—a permitted zone and a forbidden zone. Thus, $x < \tilde{x}$ implies that the actor is at fault, whereas $x \geq \tilde{x}$ implies that the actor is not at fault, where x indicates the actual amount of precaution taken by the injurer. Under a negligence

---

[8] RESTATEMENT (SECOND) OF TORTS §519(1) (1977).

FIGURE 6.2

Legal standard of care of continuous precaution.

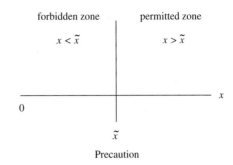

rule, decision makers who take precaution as great as or greater than the legal standard escape liability for another person's accidental harms. Those who take less precaution than the legal standard may have to pay compensatory damages for another person's accidental harms.

How is fault determined by law? In many nations, the government imposes precise safety regulations upon certain activities, such as speed limits on highways, whereas other legal duties are left vague, such as the legal definition of "reckless driving." For activities such as reckless driving, the law may draw upon unwritten social norms and community conventions, such as the "rules of the road." Moreover, what counts as "reckless driving" may depend on the weather conditions, the number of cars on the road, and other particularities of the context. Legal traditions differ in their reliance upon broad principles of care and their preferred language for expressing these principles. The common law in the English-language countries stresses the duty of *reasonable* care. This standard compares the defendant's actual care and the care that a *reasonable person* would have taken under the circumstances. The civil codes of Europe are not anchored by the concept of "reasonableness." (See the accompanying box in which Lord Herbert pokes fun at the notion of a "reasonable person.") Continental lawyers often feel discomfort toward a rule of reasonable care, which seems to give too little guidance to people and too much discretion to judges. Consequently, the civil codes often strive for greater specificity in prescribing duties. Civilian lawyers (that is, lawyers in civil law countries) sometimes invoke broad principles, such as "abuse of right" (for example, an owner exercises property rights in a way that harms others), or the "paterfamilias" (a person obligated to treat some other people much like the father treats his family), or "rationality" (choosing effective means to legal ends). As we shall see, economic analysis reveals similarities in behavior underlying these differences in legal language and traditions.

We have used Figure 6.2 to explain the meaning of "negligence." Under that liability rule, proof of negligence is a necessary condition for liability. In contrast, under a rule of strict liability, proof of causation is a necessary condition for liability, and proof of negligence is unnecessary. Some scholars detect a pattern of movement between these two rules over the history of liability law. (See the quote from Professor Adams at the beginning of this chapter.) Strict liability was the usual rule between clans in stateless tribes. Similarly, strict liability was the usual rule in much of Europe before the nineteenth century, but, according to legal historians, negligence became the usual rule by the beginning of the twentieth century. Thus, the requirement of fault as a condition for liability triumphed recently. The rule of strict liability, however, enjoyed a renaissance in the second half of the twentieth century, especially for the liability of manufacturers to American consumers. Manufacturers in America are now held liable for the harms caused by their defective products, regardless of whether the manufacturer was at fault. (See the quote from Judge Traynor at the beginning of this chapter.) To illustrate by Example 3, the manufacturer of a defective fuel additive is strictly liable for harm it causes to automobile engines.

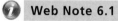

Web Note 6.1

There is some recent evidence of a discernible trend away from strict products liability—what some authors have described as a "quiet revolution" in products liability. On our website (and briefly in the next chapter) we discuss this evidence.

QUESTION 6.5: Adapt Figure 6.2 to represent the rule that motor vehicles must stay within a designated speed limit (say 90 kilometers per hour).

QUESTION 6.6: Offer an economic explanation for why the owner of a dog is liable for the harm it causes due to his negligence, whereas the owner of a tiger is strictly liable for any harm that it causes.

Conclusion to Part I

The three elements of tort liability fit neatly into a coherent picture of social life. We impose risks upon each other in our daily lives. Society has developed norms that prescribe standards of behavior to limit these risks. People sometimes cause harm by violating these standards of behavior. The cost of the harm must fall upon someone. The courts trace cause of the harm back to the violation of the standard and assign liability either to the party at fault or simply to the party who caused the harm.

Let Us Now Praise Reasonable Men

The following famous parody of the reasonable person standard is from an essay entitled "The Reasonable Man" by Lord A. P. Herbert:

"The Common Law of England has been laboriously built about a mythical figure—the figure of 'The Reasonable Man.' He is an ideal, a standard, the embodiment of all those qualities which we demand of the good citizen. . . . It is impossible to travel anywhere or to travel for long in that confusing forest of learned judgments which constitutes the Common Law of England without encountering the Reasonable Man. . . .

The Reasonable Man is always thinking of others; prudence is his guide, and 'Safety First' is his rule of life. He is one who invariably looks where he is going and is careful to examine the immediate foreground before he executes a leap or bound; who neither stargazes nor is lost in meditation when approaching trapdoors or the margin of a dock; who records in every case upon the counterfoils of checks such ample details as are desirable, who never mounts a moving omnibus, and does not alight from any car while the train is in motion; who investigates exhaustively the *bona fides* of every mendicant before distributing alms, and will inform himself of the history and habits of a dog before administering a caress; who believes no gossip, nor repeats it, without firm basis for believing it to be true; who never drives his ball till those in front of him have definitely vacated the putting-green which is his own objective; who never from one year's end to another makes an excessive demand upon his wife, his neighbors, his servants, his ox, or his ass; who in the way of business looks only for that narrow margin of profit which twelve men such as himself would reckon to be 'fair,' and contemplates his fellow-merchants, their agents, and their goods, with that degree of suspicion and distrust which the law deems admirable; who never swears, gambles, or loses his temper; who uses nothing except in moderation, and even while he flogs his child is meditating only on the golden mean. [He] stands like a monument in our Courts of Justice, vainly appealing to his fellow-citizens to order their lives after his own example. . . ."

Most torts correspond to this picture, which makes it useful as an introduction to the subject. The actual practices of the courts, however, have departed from the traditional theory of torts. Modern courts sometimes find liability in cases where one of the three elements of a tort is missing. Later we describe some of these departures from the traditional theory, and, in doing so, we sketch the frontiers of liability law in the United States.

QUESTION 6.7: Describe the three elements of a tort in the following situations:

a. Motorists driving on crossing streets come to an intersection with a stop light and collide.
b. The owner of Al's Donut Shop spreads the false rumor that patrons of Betty's Donut Shop got ptomaine poisoning from the jelly in her donuts.
c. The escalator in a store rips a customer's pant leg to shreds.

II. An Economic Theory of Tort Liability

Philosophy concerns meanings, and science concerns causes. Rather than defining "tort" by its essential elements, economic analysis models the effects of liability. We have explained that, when high transaction costs preclude private agreements, tort liability can induce injurers to internalize the costs that they impose on other people. Now we develop the simplest model of cost internalization by tort law, using the economic interpretations of harm, cause, and fault.

A. Minimizing the Social Costs of Accidents

The economic model of tort law builds from the simplest elements: the cost of harm and the cost of avoiding harm. We begin with some notation and simple functions.

The probability of an accident, which we denote p, decreases with increases in precaution, which we denote x. Thus, $p = p(x)$ is a decreasing function of x. If an accident occurs, it causes harm, such as lost income, damage to property, medical costs, and the like. Let A denote the monetary value of the harm from an accident. A multiplied by p equals the *expected* harm in dollars ("expected" because of the probabilistic element).

Like $p(x)$, the expected harm $p(x)A$ is a decreasing function of precaution x.[9] To depict this fact, the horizontal axis in Figure 6.3 indicates the quantity of the actor's precaution, x, and the vertical axis indicates dollar amounts, including the dollar amount of expected harm, $p(x)A$. The curve labeled $p(x)A$ in Figure 6.3 slopes down, indicating that expected harm decreases as precaution increases.

Taking precaution often involves the loss of money, time, or convenience. We assume that precaution costs \$$w$ per unit. To keep the analysis simple, we assume that w is constant and does not change with the amount of precaution x. Consequently, wx equals the total amount spent on precaution. The graph of wx in Figure 6.3 is a straight line through the origin whose slope equals w.

Figure 6.3 depicts two kinds of costs of accidents: the cost of precaution and the cost of expected harm. In the simplest model, we assume that accidents have no other social costs. This simplification, which may strike you as artificial at first, was the crucial step in Guido Calabresi's classic book *The Cost of Accidents* (1970), which systematically compared the incentive effects of alternative tort rules for the first time.

Consequently, we may add the costs of precaution and expected harm to obtain the expected social costs of accidents, which we denote SC:

$$SC = wx + p(x)A. \tag{6.1}$$

The expected social cost curve in Figure 6.3 is thus obtained by adding vertically the line wx and the curve $p(x)A$ at every level of precaution x. The result is the U-shaped curve, which is labeled $SC = wx + p(x)A$.

Because the expected-social-cost curve is U-shaped, a value of x exists that corresponds to the bottom of the U. This value, denoted x^* in Figure 6.3, is the level of

FIGURE 6.3

The expected social costs of accidents shown as the sum of precaution costs and the expected cost of harm.

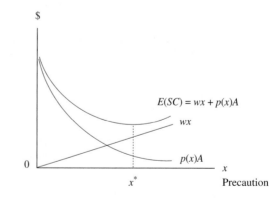

---

[9] To keep the graph simple, we assume that A is a constant. The analysis would not be changed by assuming that A is a decreasing function of x, so long as $p(x)A$ is a concave function.

precaution that minimizes the expected social costs of the accident. Efficiency requires minimizing social costs, so x^* is the socially efficient level of precaution or, simply, the efficient level of precaution.

Let us characterize x^* mathematically. The cost of a little more precaution (marginal cost) equals the price per unit w. A little more precaution reduces the expected cost of harm (marginal benefit). This reduction in the expected cost of harm equals the reduction in the probability of an accident, which we denote p', multiplied by the cost of harm A.[10] When precaution is efficient, the cost of a little more precaution (marginal cost) equals the resulting reduction in the expected cost of harm (marginal benefit). Thus, the efficient level of precaution x^* can be found by solving the following equation:

$$w \quad = \quad -p'(x^*)A.$$
$$\text{marginal social cost} \quad \text{marginal social benefit} \tag{6.2}$$

(Those of you who are familiar with calculus can obtain Equation 6.2 by setting the first derivative of Equation 6.1 with respect to precaution equal to zero.) This equation solves the problem, "choose precaution to minimize the cost of accidents and avoiding accidents."

If precaution is less than the efficient amount, then the marginal social cost of precaution is less than the marginal social benefit: $(x < x^*) \rightarrow (w < (p'[x^*]A)$. When the marginal social cost of precaution is less than the marginal social benefit, efficiency requires taking more precaution. In these circumstances, we say that more precaution is "cost-justified." Similarly, if precaution exceeds the efficient amount, then the marginal social cost of precaution exceeds the marginal social benefit: $(x > x^*) \rightarrow (w > (p'[x^*]A)$. In these circumstances, efficiency requires taking less precaution.

Figure 6.3 describes the effects of precaution on social costs. We have not said whose precaution is depicted in Figure 6.3. Sometimes the potential injurer can take precaution and the potential victim cannot, as when a surgeon operates on an unconscious person. Sometimes both the injurer and the victim can take precaution, as when the manufacturer assures the purity of a drug and the consumer takes the recommended dosage. Figure 6.3 can be taken to represent the relationship between social costs and precaution by the victim or the injurer. Remember that *precaution* refers to any behavior reducing the probability or magnitude of an accident. Table 6.1 gives some examples suggesting the range of possibilities.

B. Incentives for Precaution Under No Liability and Strict Liability

Having characterized the efficient level of precaution, we now consider the incentives needed to obtain it. Incentives for precaution in the simple model depend upon who can take precaution against accidents, and how the law allocates the costs of harm. To create efficient incentives, law should align the private benefits and costs of the

---

[10] The prime (′) after p indicates the slope of the graph of the function $p(x)$ at x. The slope is negative in Figure 6.3, so that minus sign in front of the p makes the expression $-p'(x)$ positive.

TABLE 6.1

Example of Accidents and Precaution

Accident	Injurer's Precaution	Victim's Precaution
Faulty electrical wiring causes house fire	Manufacture wiring more carefully	Fireproof house
Moving car hits parked car	Drive more safely	Park car in safer space
Car hits pedestrian	Drive more safely	Walk more safely
Software fails	Better design of software	Back up data at risk
Exploding coke bottle	Improve quality control by bottler	Handle bottles carefully
Medicine causes side effects	Improve warning on medicine	Study warning on medicine

actors with the social benefits and costs. We shall contrast the incentive effects of several different legal rules for allocating the costs of harm.

First, we consider the case in which there is no liability for accidental injuries. Let us consider first the decisions of the *victim* and denote her precaution by x_v.[11] The victim chooses precaution, which we indicate by placing subscript v on x and w. The victim pays the cost w_v for x_v units of precaution. Now consider the cost of harm A, which is suffered by the victim. Because there is no liability, the victim bears the expected harm $p(x_v)A$. The total costs that the victim expects to bear equal the cost of precaution plus the expected cost of harm: $w_v x_v + p(x_v)A$. The victim has an incentive to minimize the costs that he or she bears. Consequently, the victim chooses x_v to minimize $w_v x_v + p(x_v)A$. The minimum occurs at the level of precaution, denoted x_v^*, where the victim's marginal cost of precaution equals the resulting reduction in the expected cost of harm:

$$ w_v \qquad = \qquad -p'(x_v^*)A. $$

$$ \text{victim's marginal cost} \qquad \text{victim's marginal benefit} \qquad (6.2') $$

Equation 6.2′ corresponds to the efficiency condition given by Equation 6.2. Thus, we have shown that *the rule of no liability causes the victim to internalize the marginal costs and benefits of precaution, which gives the victim incentives for efficient precaution.* (We'll consider the incentive effect for injurers shortly.)

Now we repeat the analysis with a different legal rule. Consider the victim's incentives for precaution when the injurer is *strictly liable*. As before, the victim bears the cost of precaution, $w_v x_v$, and the victim also bears the expected cost of harm, $p(x_v)A$. In addition, the victim receives damages D when an accident occurs. Thus, total net costs that the victim expects to bear under the rule of strict liability are

$$ w_v x_v + p(x_v)A - p(x_v)D. $$

---

[11] Our exposition assumes that parties who engage in risky behavior know in advance which one will get hurt if an accident occurs. In reality, one usually—but not always—does *not* know *ex ante* whether one will be a victim or an injurer.

Further, assume that the damages compensate the victim perfectly: $D = A$. (Although unrealistic, the assumption of perfect compensation is very useful analytically.) With perfectly compensatory damages, total *net* costs reduce to the cost of precaution: $w_v x_v$. The victim has an incentive to minimize the costs that he or she bears. Consequently, the victim chooses x_v to minimize $w_v x_v$. Because x_v cannot fall below zero, the minimum occurs when precaution is zero: $x_v = 0$. Thus, we have shown that the rule of strict liability with perfectly compensatory damages gives the victim no incentive to take precaution.

This conclusion has a simple explanation. With a rule of strict liability and perfect compensation, the victim is indifferent between an accident with compensation and no accident. The victim pays the cost of his or her own precaution and gains no advantage from reducing the probability or severity of accidents. In other words, the victim internalizes the costs of precaution and externalizes the benefits. So, the victim has an incentive not to take any precaution.

We have analyzed the effects of the rule of no liability and the rule of strict liability on the victim's incentives for precaution. The first rule gives incentives for efficient precaution by the victim, and the second rule gives the victim no incentives for precaution.[12] Now we consider the effect of these two rules on the injurer's incentives for precaution. We denote the amount of precaution taken by the injurer as x_i. The injurer pays the cost w_i for x_i units of precaution. The harm A, however, is suffered by the victim. Unless the law reallocates the cost of the harm, the injurer will externalize it.

Assume that the rule of law is strict liability with perfect compensation. Thus, whenever an accident occurs, the injurer must pay damages equal to the cost of the harm: $D = A$. The injurer's expected liability equals the probability of an accident multiplied by the harm caused by it: $p(x_i)A$. The total costs that the injurer expects to bear under the rule of strict liability with perfect compensation equal $w_i x_i + p(x_i)A$. The injurer has an incentive to minimize the costs that he or she bears. Consequently, the injurer chooses x_i to minimize $w_i x_i + p(x_i)A$. The minimum occurs at the level of precaution, denoted, x_i^* where the injurer's marginal cost of precaution equals the resulting reduction in the expected cost of harm:

$$w_i \qquad = \qquad -p'(x_i^*)A.$$
(injurer's marginal cost) (injurer's marginal benefit) (6.2″)

Equation 6.2″ corresponds to the efficiency condition given by Equation 6.2. Thus, we have shown that *the rule of strict liability with perfect compensation causes the injurer to internalize the marginal costs and benefits of precaution, which gives him or her incentives for efficient precaution.*

Finally, we consider the effect of the rule of no liability on the injurer's incentives for precaution. Assume that precaution x_i is chosen by the injurer, so the injurer bears the cost of precaution $w_i x_i$. The harm A, however, is suffered by the victim, and, under the rule of no liability, A remains where it falls on the victim, and the injurer pays no

---

[12] Again we note our assumption—frequently not true—that *ex ante* an accident a party knows that he will be the injurer.

TABLE 6.2

Efficiency of Incentives Created by Liability Rules*

yes indicates efficient incentives;
no, inefficient incentives; and
zero, no incentive.

Legal Rule	Precaution		Activity Level	
	Victim	Injurer	Victim	Injurer
No liability	yes	zero	yes	no
Strict liability	zero	yes	no	yes
Simple negligence	yes	yes	yes	no
Negligence + contributory negligence	yes	yes	yes	no
Strict liability + contributory negligence	yes	yes	no	yes
Comparative negligence	yes	yes	yes	no

*assumes perfect compensation and legal standards equal to efficient precaution

damages: $D = 0$. The total costs paid by the injurer thus equal $w_i x_i$. The injurer has an incentive to minimize the costs that he or she bears. Consequently, the injurer chooses x_i to minimize $w_i x_i$. Because x_i cannot fall below zero, the minimum occurs when precaution is zero: $x_i = 0$. Thus, we have shown that *the rule of no liability gives the injurer no incentive to take precaution*. This conclusion has a simple explanation: With no liability, the injurer is indifferent between an accident and no accident. Thus, the injurer internalizes the costs of precaution and externalizes the benefits.

Table 6.2 summarizes many conclusions about the incentives of alternative tort rules. For now, focus on the first two rows and the first two columns of Table 6.2, which summarize our conclusions about the rules of no liability and strict liability. Notice the symmetry: The victim's incentives for precaution under "no liability" are the same as the injurer's under "strict liability," and vice versa. The table suggests how the law could create incentives for efficient precaution. If only the victim can take precaution, then a rule of no liability provides incentives for efficient precaution. If only the injurer can take precaution, then a rule of strict liability with perfect compensation provides incentives for efficient precaution.

C. Bilateral Precaution

We have explained that a rule of no liability causes the victim to internalize the cost of harm and the injurer to externalize it. Consequently, the victim has efficient incentives, and the injurer has inefficient incentives. Conversely, a rule of strict liability with perfect compensation causes the injurer to internalize the cost of harm and the victim to externalize it. Consequently, the injurer has efficient incentives, and the victim has inefficient incentives. We have arrived at a dilemma: *Neither the rule of strict liability nor the rule of no liability creates incentives for efficient precaution by both parties.*

We will restate this proposition in technical terms. *Unilateral precaution* describes circumstances in which only one party to an accident can take precaution against it.

Bilateral precaution describes circumstances in which the victim and the injurer can take precaution, and efficiency requires both of them to take it. (Bilateral precaution is also called "joint precaution.")

With bilateral precaution, the social cost function has the form

$$SC = w_v x_v + w_i x_i + p(x_v, x_i)A.$$

Under strict liability, the injurer chooses x_i to minimize SC, but the victim does not choose x_v to minimize SC. Under no liability, the opposite is true. *Under bilateral precaution, neither the rule of strict liability nor the rule of no liability creates incentives for efficient precaution by both parties.*

We cannot escape this dilemma by dividing the costs of harm between the victim and injurer. Dividing the costs of harm between them causes each of them to externalize part of it, so both of them have incentives for deficient precaution.[13] We call this fact the "paradox of compensation." We will resolve this paradox by the end of Section E.

QUESTION 6.8: Assume that you park your car in a legal parking space on a corner, and a driver who comes around the corner too fast rams the bumper of his truck into your car, damaging your car but not his truck. A rule of no liability gives the driver of the truck the same incentives to avoid such accidents as the incentives given to you to park your car in a safe place under a rule of strict liability with perfect compensation. Explain why.

QUESTION 6.9: Explain why the incentive problem in the previous question cannot be solved by a rule of strict liability with imperfect compensation (say, actual compensation equal to 50 percent of perfect compensation).

D. Incentives for Precaution Under a Negligence Rule

The solution to the paradox of compensation lies in a negligence rule. We shall now prove that a negligence rule can give efficient incentives to the victim *and* the injurer. A negligence rule imposes a legal standard of care with which actors must comply

---

[13] To see why, assume that the rule is strict liability with *deficient* compensation, by which we mean that actual compensation falls short of the amount required for perfect compensation ($D < A$). Under strict liability with deficient compensation, the injurer *internalizes* the fraction of harm *externalized* by the victim (specifically, D), and the injurer externalizes the fraction of harm internalized by the victim (specifically, $A - D$). Consequently, the rule of strict liability with deficient compensation does not provide incentives for efficient precaution by the injurer. To repeat the argument in notation, efficiency requires the injurer to choose x_i to minimize $w_i x_i + p(x_v, x_i) A$, whereas a rule of strict liability with compensatory damages D causes the injurer to minimize $w_i x_i + p(x_v, x_i) D$. If $D = A$, then the injurer's incentives are efficient; if $D < A$, then the injurer's incentives are deficient.

This same argument can be repeated for the victim.

in order to avoid liability. We assumed that courts apply a definite standard requiring a fixed amount of precaution, and this assumption permitted us to represent the legal standard, denoted $\tilde{x}$, as partitioning precaution into permitted and forbidden zones in Figure 6.2. Then, we developed the economic analysis of incentives to take care using Figure 6.3. Now, we combine these two ideas into a representation of a negligence rule in Figure 6.4.

The legal standard in Figure 6.2 is denoted $\tilde{x}$, and x^* denotes the efficient level of precaution in Figure 6.3. To combine the figures, we must say how $\tilde{x}$ relates to x^*. The simplest assumption, which we justify later, is that the legal standard equals the efficient level of care: $\tilde{x} = x^*$. This assumption permits us to combine the figures as represented in Figure 6.4. The forbidden zone $(x < \tilde{x})$ in Figure 6.4 corresponds to deficient precaution relative to the efficient level $(x < x^*)$, and the permitted zone $(x \geq \tilde{x})$ corresponds to excessive precaution relative to the efficient level $(x \geq x^*)$. Precaution at the boundary between the two zones equals efficient precaution $(x = x^*)$.

Consider the injurer's costs as a function of his level of precaution. In the permitted zone, injurers are not liable, so they bear the cost of their own precaution $w_i x_i$, but they do not bear the cost of the victims' harm. Thus, the injurer's costs in the permitted zone $(x_i \geq \tilde{x})$ are indicated by the straight line $w_i x_i$ in Figure 6.4. In the forbidden zone, injurers are liable, so they bear the cost of their own precaution $w_i x_i$ and the expected harm to the victim $p(x_i)A$. Thus, the injurer's expected costs in the forbidden zone $(x_i < \tilde{x})$ are indicated by the curve $w_i x_i + p(x_i)A$ in Figure 6.4. Thus, the injurer's costs under a negligence rule are indicated in Figure 6.4 by a smooth curve that jumps down at $x = \tilde{x}$ and then becomes a straight line.[14] The lowest point on this curve occurs when the injurer's precaution equals the legal standard: $x = \tilde{x}$. The injurer has an incentive to set precaution at this level in order to minimize costs. We have shown that *a negligence rule with perfect compensation and the legal standard equal to the efficient level of care gives the injurer incentives for efficient precaution.*

To illustrate the incentive effects of a negligence rule, consider how the injurer would find his or her preferred level of care. Assume the injurer sets his precaution equal to x_0 in Figure 6.4, in which precaution costs him $\$wx_0$ and he expects to pay $\$p(x_0)A$ in liability for accidents. The cost to the injurer of taking one more unit of precaution beyond x_0 is less than the resulting savings in expected liability because of the lower probability of an accident. Consequently, the rational injurer will take more precaution. He or she will continue taking more precaution until he or she reaches x^*, where liability falls to zero. Having reached x^*, the injurer has no incentive to increase precaution. If injurers' precaution exceeds x^*, they pay only for their own precaution,

---

[14] The jump occurs to the extent that the negligent injurer is held liable for the accidents that he caused, not just for the accidents that his negligence caused. To illustrate, if a railway negligently fails to install a filter to trap sparks emitted by the train, the railway will be held liable for fires caused by sparks emitted by the train, not just for fires caused by sparks that a filter would have trapped. Insofar as courts solve this problem and only find liability for accidents that nonnegligent behavior would have prevented, injurer's costs do not jump at the legal standard.

FIGURE 6.4

Expected costs with a discontinuity a x^*.

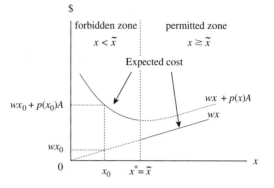

which costs w_i per unit, but their liability remains zero, so they will not take additional precaution beyond x^*.[15]

Recall that we began this section with a dilemma: How can a liability rule provide incentives for efficient precaution by the injurer and the victim? We have explained how a negligence rule can provide incentives for efficient precaution by the injurer. Now it is simple to explain how a negligence rule can provide incentives for efficient precaution by the victim. As explained, a rational injurer takes precaution at the legal standard $(x_i \geq \tilde{x})$ in order to avoid liability for the harm caused by accidents. When the injurer is not liable, the victim of an accident receives no compensation for accidental harm. Consequently, the victim responds as if the rule of law were no liability. We have already proved that a rule of no liability causes the victim to internalize the marginal costs and benefits of precaution, which gives incentives for efficient precaution. In general, a negligence rule that induces the injurer to escape liability by satisfying the legal standard provides incentives for efficient precaution by the victim.[16] Our conclusions about the incentives created by a negligence rule are summarized in the third line of Table 6.2.

---

[15] We can prove this more formally. Given a negligence rule with perfect compensation and the legal standard equal to the efficient level of care, the injurer faces the following cost function:

$$x < x^* \text{ (forbidden zone)} \quad \rightarrow \quad \text{injurer's costs} = w_i x_i + p(x_i)A;$$

$$x \geq x^* \text{ (permitted zone)} \quad \rightarrow \quad \text{injurer's costs} = w_i x_i.$$

In the forbidden zone, the injurer's costs approach a minimum as x approaches x^*. In the permitted zone, the injurer's costs are minimized when x equals x^*. Therefore, the injurer minimizes costs by setting x equal to x^*.

[16] Note that under our formulation the potential injurer and potential victim may both take precaution that may be efficient but *duplicative*. It is possible that the precaution of one or the other of them would have prevented the accident or minimized its severity so that the precaution by the other party adds nothing by way of marginal benefit. However, because of our (realistic) assumption that parties cannot negotiate before an accident takes place, they have no opportunity to discover that only one of them needs to take care. Suppose that A's marginal cost of precaution is $50 and that the expected marginal benefit of that precaution is $60. Further suppose that B's marginal cost of precaution is $53 and the expected marginal benefit is also $60. Each party, acting independently, will reckon that he or she should take care because the marginal cost of precaution is less than the anticipated marginal benefit. The total amount spent of precaution—$103—is, however, excessive. The same benefit could have been realized if only A had incurred a precautionary cost of $50 (or if only B had acted at a cost of $53). This duplicative investment in precaution seems wasteful but unavoidable, in light of our assumption that the transaction costs of the two parties' bargaining together are high.

QUESTION **6.10:**   A game is in equilibrium when no player can increase his or her payoff by changing strategy, so long as the other players do not change their strategies.[17] Prove that the simple liability game is in equilibrium when the injurer and the victim take efficient care.

E. Contributory Negligence and Comparative Negligence

The negligence rule has several different forms. We have been discussing its simplest form, which holds the injurer liable for accidents that he or she causes if, and only if, precaution is below the legal standard, regardless of the victim's level of precaution. Symbolically, we may describe simple negligence as follows:

simple negligence:

$$\text{injurer at fault, } x_i < x_i^* \quad \longrightarrow \quad \text{injurer liable;}$$
$$\text{injurer faultless, } x_i \geq x_i^* \quad \longrightarrow \quad \text{injurer not liable.}$$

Chapter 3 explained that English common law originally developed the simple negligence rule and later developed a more complex rule allowing a defense of contributory negligence. Under the rule of negligence with a defense of contributory negligence, the negligent injurer can escape liability by proving that the victim's precaution fell short of the legal standard of care. The defense of contributory negligence imposes a legal standard of care upon the victim. Symbolically, we may represent this form of the negligence rule as follows:

negligence with a defense of contributory negligence:

$$\text{injurer at fault, } x_i < x_i^*, \text{ and victim faultless, } x_v \geq x_v^* \quad \longrightarrow \quad \text{injurer liable;}$$
$$\text{injurer faultless, } x_i \geq x_i^*, \text{ or victim at fault, } x_v < x_v^* \quad \longrightarrow \quad \text{injurer not liable.}$$

Here's an example of the difference between (simple) negligence and negligence with a defense of contributory negligence. Someone dives into a swimming pool and strikes her head on the bottom. She sues the owner of the pool for failing to post signs warning that the pool was too shallow for diving. The pool owner admits that he posted no warnings, but he also asserts that the victim was negligent for diving without checking the depth of the water. If both parties are negligent, the pool owner is liable under a rule of simple negligence, and the pool owner is not liable under a rule of negligence with a defense of contributory negligence.

These two forms of the negligence rule, however, have been displaced by a new form of the negligence rule for most accidents in the United States. Under the rules of simple negligence or negligence with a defense of contributory negligence, one party is responsible for all the costs of accidental harm, even though both parties are at fault. The new form of the negligence rule, called "comparative negligence," divides the cost

---

[17] This is the definition of a *Nash equilibrium*.

of harm between the parties in proportion to the contribution of their negligence to the accident. For example, if the victim's negligence is 20 percent responsible for her accidental harm, and the injurer's negligence is 80 percent responsible for her accidental harm, then the victim may recover 80 percent of her losses from the injurer.

Symbolically, we may represent the rule of comparative negligence as follows:

comparative negligence:

injurer at fault, $x_i < x_i^*$, and victim faultless, $x_v \geq x_v^*$ $\rightarrow$ injurer bears 100 percent;

injurer faultless, $x_i \geq x_i^*$, and victim at fault, $x_v < x_v^*$ $\rightarrow$ victim bears 100 percent;

injurer at fault, $x_i < x_i^*$, and victim at fault, $x_v < x_v^*$ $\rightarrow$ bear cost in proportion to negligence.[18]

We have discussed the rules of simple negligence, negligence with a defense of contributory negligence, and comparative negligence. Other forms of the negligence rule exist. For example, the rule of *strict liability with a defense of contributory negligence* assigns the cost of accidental harm to the injurer, regardless of his or her level of precaution, unless the victim was at fault:

strict liability with a defense of contributory negligence:

victim at fault, $x_v < x_v^*$ $\rightarrow$ injurer not liable;

victim faultless, $x_v \geq x_v^*$ $\rightarrow$ injurer liable.

To illustrate, consumer products are sometimes subject to the rule of strict liability with a defense of contributory negligence. Under this rule, the manufacturer of a defective product is liable for the harm it causes to nonnegligent consumers and not liable for the harm it causes to negligent consumers.[19]

We have characterized four different forms of the negligence rule. The economic analysis of law proved a startling fact about the simple model of tort liability:

> Assuming perfect compensation and each legal standard equal to the efficient level of care, every form of the negligence rule gives the injurer and victim incentives for efficient precaution.[20]

---

[18] The extent of the injurer's negligence equals $\tilde{x} - x_i$. The extent of the victim's negligence equals $\tilde{x} - x_v$. The proportion of each party's negligence, which can be used to divide liability under a rule of comparative negligence, is given as follows:

$$\tilde{x}_i - x_i / [(\tilde{x}_i - x_i) + (\tilde{x}_v - x_v)] = \text{negligent injurer's proportion of liability};$$

$$\tilde{x}_v - x_v / [(\tilde{x}_i - x_i) + (\tilde{x}_v - x_v)] = \text{negligent victim's proportion of liability}.$$

To illustrate, if a car going 40 kph collides with a car going 35 kph on a street with a speed limit equal to 30 kph, then the two motorists divide liability in the proportions 2/3 and 1/3, respectively.

[19] The different forms of the negligence rule have an elegant mathematical symmetry, which we describe in the appendix to this chapter.

[20] This result is sometimes referred to in the professional literature as the "equivalence result."

It is easy to explain why. Recall that the simple negligence rule provides incentives for efficient precaution by both parties: A rational injurer takes precaution equal to the legal standard in order to escape liability, and, knowing this, a rational victim internalizes the harm from accidents, which gives incentives for efficient precaution. We can generalize this proof to every form of the negligence rule. Assume perfect compensation and each legal standard equal to the efficient level of precaution. Under every form of the negligence rule, *one* of the parties can escape bearing the cost of harm by satisfying the legal standard. This party will take efficient precaution in order to avoid the cost of harm. The *other* party will, consequently, internalize the cost of the harm from accidents, which creates incentives for efficient precaution. Table 6.2 summarizes our conclusions about liability rules and incentives for precaution.

We have been analyzing bilateral precaution, which we defined as a situation where efficiency requires the injurer and the victim to take precaution. Another possibility is *redundant precaution*, which we define as a situation where both parties can take precaution and efficiency requires only one of them to do so. To illustrate, the manufacturer and the homebuilder can check electrical wire for defects, but the manufacturer can check at less cost than the homebuilder. The preceding analysis of alternative legal rules applies to redundant precaution that is continuous, such as expenditure on quality control by a manufacturer of electrical wire.

The preceding analysis of alternative legal rules, however, can fail for technical reasons when redundant precaution is discontinuous. To illustrate, assume that the driver of a car can fasten a seat belt with less effort than the manufacturer can design a seat belt to fasten automatically. By assumption, efficiency requires the driver to fasten the seat belt and the manufacturer not to install automatic fasteners. However, a (simple) negligence rule might cause manufacturers to install automatic fasteners.[21]

Notice that buckling a seat belt is a discontinuous choice (yes–no). For discontinuous precaution, the relative efficiency of different rules depends upon particular facts. In general, discontinuous variables and cost functions yield messy results about optima, whereas continuous variables and cost functions yield clean results. It is usually best to build theory from clean results and then handle any messy results as exceptions.

QUESTION 6.11: Suppose that *B*'s faulty driving causes an accident that injures driver *A*. *A* was not at fault in her driving, but she was not wearing her seat belt, and this fact aggravated her personal injury. Discuss liability under

---

[21] Suppose that the manufacturer does not install an automatic fastener, the driver fails to fasten his seat belt, and an accident occurs. The driver sues the manufacturer and argues that the manufacturer was negligent for not installing an automatic fastener. (Installing an automatic fastener is cheaper than the harm from accidents). The driver might win the suit under a (simple) negligence rule. Foreseeing this fact, the manufacturers might install automatic fasteners. This is inefficient because it is cheaper for drivers to fasten their seat belts.

the rules of simple negligence, negligence with a defense of contributory negligence, and comparative negligence.

We have been discussing accidents in which one party, called the injurer, harms the other party, called the victim. Both parties can take precaution to reduce the probability and magnitude of an accident. In technical language, these accidents involve unilateral harm and bilateral precaution. We concluded that every form of the negligence rule can provide incentives for efficient precaution for both parties. In many accidents, however, both parties suffer harm, such as when two cars collide. These accidents involve bilateral harm and bilateral precaution. Does our major conclusion about incentives still apply when harm is bilateral?

With rare exceptions, the law allows the injured parties in an accident to sue each other. If, for example, my car collides with yours, you may sue me for the damage to your car, and I may counterclaim for the damage to my car. Such a suit can be factored into two parts and analyzed as if it were two separate accidents. Think of the damage to my car as one accident in which I was the victim and you were the injurer, and think of the damage to your car as another accident in which I was the injurer and you were the victim. Applying the analysis developed in this chapter to each accident separately usually reaches the same conclusions as would a more complicated analysis applied to both accidents simultaneously.[22]

QUESTION 6.12: Would the efficiency of a rule of simple negligence increase by imposing a standard of care on victims? Explain your answer by reference to the simple model.

F. Activity Levels

In the simple model, the rules of no liability and strict liability provide incentives for efficient precaution by the victim or injurer, but not both, whereas the various forms of the negligence rule create incentives for efficient precaution by the injurer and victim. Thus, the simple model provides a policy reason to prefer a negligence rule whenever precaution is bilateral. The simple model does not, however, provide a reason for preferring one form of the negligence rule to another. A complication of the model will provide an efficiency argument for distinguishing different forms of the negligence rule.

In the simple model, the injurer and victim choose precaution. Now we complicate the model by allowing them to make an additional choice. The probability of an automobile accident depends upon the level of precaution when driving, and the *amount* that one drives. By driving 10,000 miles a year, the probability that you will

---

[22] Any form of the negligence rule will induce efficient precaution by the injurer-victims when the legal standard is set by the Hand rule, which is discussed later in this chapter. See Jennifer H. Arlen, *Reexamining Liability Rules when Injurers as Well as Victims Suffer Losses*, 10 INTERNAT. REV. OF LAW & ECON. 233 (1990).

injure someone in an accident is approximately 10 times higher than it would be if you drove only 1000 miles per year. We shall compare the incentive effects of different liability rules on the amount of risky activities, such as driving, that people engage in.[23]

First, we contrast the rules of simple negligence and strict liability. Under a negligence rule, a driver can escape liability by conforming to the legal standard of care, no matter how much he or she drives. So, the driver can increase driving by tenfold, which increases the risk of harm to others by tenfold, without increasing his or her expected liability. Under a negligence rule the marginal risk of harm to others from more driving is externalized.

The incentive structure is quite different under a rule of strict liability. If a driver is strictly liable for the harm caused, then he or she internalizes the social costs of accidents from whatever source—whether from the activity level or a lack of precaution. Strict liability induces the potential injurer to set every variable affecting the probability of an accident at its efficient level. So, the rule of strict liability can induce both efficient precaution and an efficient activity level by drivers.[24]

We can generalize this conclusion to all activities and all liability rules. Some liability rules induce some actors to avoid liability by satisfying the legal standard of care. In the end, however, someone must bear the cost of accidental harm. We call that person the *ultimate* bearer of harm. To illustrate by the simple model, the victim is the ultimate bearer of harm under the simple negligence rule, whereas the injurer is the ultimate bearer of harm under the rule of strict liability with a defense of contributory negligence. In general, *the ultimate bearer of harm internalizes the benefits of any of his or her actions that reduce the probability or severity of accidents, including more precaution and less activity.*

We can use this generalization to expand Table 6.2. The last two columns show the effect of alternative liability rules on the incentives for the activity levels of the victim and injurer. Under each rule, the ultimate bearer of harm has incentives for an efficient activity level, whereas the party who escapes bearing the cost of accidental harm has incentives for an inefficient activity level.

Table 6.2 provides a useful guide for lawmakers to choose among liability rules. First, consider the problem of efficient incentives for precaution. If efficiency requires only one party to take precaution, then "no liability" and "strict liability" are just as efficient as a negligence rule. If efficiency requires bilateral precaution, then a negligence rule provides more efficient incentives for precaution than "no liability" and "strict liability." Second, consider the problem of efficient incentives for the activity level. Usually one party's activity level affects accidents more than the other party's activity level. Efficiency requires choosing a liability rule so that the

---

[23] See Aaron Edlin & Pinar Karaca-Mandic, *The Accident Externality from Driving,* 114 J. POL. ECON. 931 (2006).

[24] The original statement of this result is found in Steven Shavell, *Strict Liability Versus Negligence,* 9 J. LEGAL STUD. 1 (1980).

party whose activity level most affects accidents bears the ultimate costs of accidental harm.

Besides providing a useful guide, Table 6.2 shows some limits of liability law in creating efficient incentives. To illustrate, the different liability rules can provide incentives for an efficient activity level by either one of the parties but not by both of them. In other words, *bilateral activity levels* create a dilemma for lawmakers. In general, policymakers have difficulty hitting two targets with one policy variable. To hit two policy targets, two controls are usually required, just as two stones are usually needed to hit two birds. Thus, an additional control variable from outside liability law may be needed to control activity levels. For example, the number of miles driven by motorists can be influenced by a gasoline tax or an insurance policy whose premiums increase with the number of miles driven.

> **QUESTION 6.13:** Who is the ultimate bearer of the costs of harm under a rule of comparative negligence? Explain your answer.

> **QUESTION 6.14:** In Table 6.2, no liability and strict liability have the opposite incentive effects upon activity levels. Why?

> **QUESTION 6.15:** For purposes of the theory of accidents, how would you define the *activity level* of a railroad? An airline? For some activities, the *level* relevant to the probability of an accident is difficult to define. Can you define an activity level relevant to a homeowner's maintenance of her front steps? A pharmaceutical company's sale of a drug with dangerous side effects?

G. Setting Legal Standards: The Hand Rule

Our discussion of negligence rules assumes that the legal standard equals the efficient level of precaution ($\tilde{x} = x^*$). Now we want to explain how lawmakers can identify the efficient level of precaution when setting the legal standard. An American judge developed a famous rule to solve this problem in the case called *United States v. Carroll Towing Co.*[25]

The case concerned the loss of a barge and its cargo in New York Harbor. A number of barges were secured by a single mooring line to several piers. The defendant's tug was hired to take one of the barges out of the harbor. In order to release the barge, the crew of the defendant's tug, finding no one aboard in any of the barges, readjusted the mooring lines. The adjustment was not done properly, with the result that one of the barges later broke loose, collided with another ship, and sank with its cargo. The owner of the sunken barge sued the owner of the tug, claiming that the tug

---

[25] 159 F.2d 169 (2d Cir. 1947).

owner's employees were negligent in readjusting the mooring lines. The tug owner replied that the barge owner was also negligent because his agent, called a "bargee," was not on the barge when the tug's crew sought to adjust the mooring lines. The bargee could have assured that the tug's crew adjusted the mooring lines correctly. In deciding the case, Judge Learned Hand formulated his famous rule as follows:

L. HAND, J . . . It appears from the foregoing review that there is no general rule to determine when the absence of a bargee or other attendant will make the owner of a barge liable for injuries to other vessels if she breaks away from her moorings. . . . Since there are occasions when every vessel will break away from her moorings, and since, if she does, she becomes a menace to those about her; the owner's duty, as in other similar situations, to provide against resulting injuries is a function of three variables: (1) the probability that she will break away; (2) the gravity of the resulting injury, if she does; (3) the burden of adequate precautions. Possibly it serves to bring this notion into relief to state it in algebraic terms: if the probability be called *P*; the injury, *L*; and the burden, *B*; liability depends upon whether *B* is less than *L* multiplied by *P*, i.e., whether $B < PL$. . . . [Judge Hand subsequently applied the formula to the facts of the case and concluded that, because $B < PL$ in this case, the barge owner was negligent for not having a bargee aboard during the working hours of daylight.]

Judge Hand's statement of his rule is unclear as to whether the variables refer to marginal values or total values. If we assume that he was a good economist who had marginal values in mind, then we can translate his notation into our notation as used in the simple model of precaution:

Hand's name	Our name	Hand's notation	Our notation
Burden	Marginal cost of precaution	B	w_i
Liability	Cost of accidental harm	L	A
Probability	Marginal probability	P	p'

Substituting our notation into Hand's formula, we obtain the following rule:

marginal Hand rule: $w_i < -p'A \longrightarrow$ injurer is negligent.

The marginal Hand rule states that the injurer is negligent if the marginal cost of his or her precaution is less than the resulting marginal benefit. Thus, the injurer is liable under the Hand rule when further precaution is cost-justified. Further precaution is cost-justified when precaution falls short of the efficient level ($x < x^*$).

To escape liability under Hand's rule, the injurer must increase precaution until the inequality becomes an equality:

$$w \qquad = \qquad -p'(x^*)A.$$

marginal social cost　　　marginal social benefit　　　　　　　(6.3)

If the injurer's precaution is efficient ($x = x^*$), then the marginal social cost equals the marginal social benefit ($w_i = -p'A$). At this point, further precaution is not cost-justified.

American courts frequently use the Hand rule to decide questions of negligence.[26] Repeated application of the Hand rule enables adjudicators to discover the efficient level of care. In a series of cases, the adjudicators ask whether further precaution was cost-justified. If the answer is "yes," then the injurer has not satisfied the legal standard, and the injurer is liable. Injurers will presumably respond to this decision by increasing their level of precaution. Eventually a case will reach the adjudicators in which further precaution is not cost-justified. Just as a climber can reach the peak of a smooth mountain in a fog by always going up, so the court can discover the efficient level of care by holding defendants liable for failing to take cost-justified precautions. In fact, the Hand rule follows the same search pattern used by some computer programs to maximize a function.[27]

To apply the Hand rule, the decision maker must know whether a little more precaution costs more or less than the resulting reduction in expected accident costs. Calculating the expected accident costs, $p(x)A$, can be difficult. For example, if you increase your driving speed from, say, 40 mph to 50, will the average loss resulting from an accident increase by $1,000,000, or by $10, or something in between? Cost-benefit analysis demands a lot of information from anyone who uses it, whether an injurer, a court, a legislature, or an administrator. Liability law should take into account who is in the best position to obtain information about accidents.

Case-by-case application of the Hand rule is one way for courts to find an efficient legal standard. At trial, courts will hear expert witnesses give testimony on the relevant probabilities. If courts can obtain accurate information about accidents at moderate cost, this fact favors case-by-case adjudication. Another approach is to draft regulations or statutes specifying a legal standard that equals the efficient level of precaution. For example, highway officials may compute the efficient speed for motorists on a particular road, taking into account the value of the time of motorists and the reduction in accidents from driving more slowly. The officials can then declare the efficient speed to be the legal speed limit. Politicians and bureaucrats sometimes behave in this way. If a legislature or regulator can obtain accurate information about accidents at moderate cost and is willing to use it, these facts favor a system of public law for accidents, like workers' compensation for on-the-job injuries.

Another approach is for the law to enforce social customs or the best practices in an industry. In this approach, the lawmakers do not try to balance marginal costs and

---

[26] The Hand rule is enshrined in the definition of negligence offered by the American Law Institute in the RESTATEMENT (SECOND) OF TORTS.

[27] The maximum of a continuous, concave function can be found by going in the direction where the derivative is largest.

benefits. Rather, the lawmakers rely upon the community of people who created the norm, or the industry that engages in the practice, to balance costs and benefits. For example, a residential community has norms concerning the maintenance of steps leading to houses, and the accounting industry has practices concerning careful auditing. When enforcing these "community standards," the courts need much less information than when they compute the marginal costs and benefits of precaution. Before enforcing the community standard, however, the lawmakers should ascertain whether the community actually balances costs and benefits. In Chapter 11 we will return to this topic when we consider the evolution of social norms toward efficiency.

American courts have persistently erred in applying the Hand rule in a way that significantly affects results. In applying the Hand rule, the court must balance the injurer's burden against the *full* benefit of precaution. The full benefit includes the reduction in risk to plaintiff ("risk to others") and reduction in risk to injurer ("risk to self"). Courts have, remarkably, overlooked the reduction in self-risk and, consequently, set the standard too low. To illustrate, assume the bank robber injures a bank's customer during the robbery of an unguarded bank. The customer sues the bank alleging that the bank should have had a guard at the bank to deter robberies. If the court applies the Hand rule to determine whether the bank was negligent, the court must compare the cost of hiring a guard with the expected reduction in harm. The expected reduction in harm includes protecting customers from getting hurt ("risk to others") and protecting the bank from getting robbed ("risk to self"). The court will leave out more than half of the benefit of having a guard if it fails to consider the reduction in the bank's risk.[28]

As another example, assume that the court must determine whether the speed at which a driver took a curve was unreasonably dangerous. The court must balance slowing down and the benefit of reducing the risk of accidents to others and the driver. In applying the Hand rule, however, courts typically focus on reducing the risk to others and lose sight of the value of reducing the risk to the injurer. Losing sight of self-risk will cause the court to allow more speed than allowed by the correct application of the Hand rule.

Omitting self-risk is a logical error in applying the Hand rule. Instead of being logical, people often make predictable errors of which tort law ought to take account. Psychologists have investigated systematic biases that affect perception. Especially strong biases affect the perception of probabilities. One of these biases concerns the difference between foresight and hindsight estimates of probability. Assume that a citizen estimates in May that the probability equals 0.5 of a particular candidate's winning the presidential election in November. When November comes, the candidate wins. In December the citizen is asked what he thinks the candidate's probability of winning was back in May. The citizen says that it was 0.7. The hindsight estimate of 0.7 is higher than the foresight estimate of 0.5. Another example of the "hindsight bias" is the investor who observes an increase in the price of a stock and thinks that its rise was a "sure thing." In general, the hindsight-probability is higher than the foresight-probability for

---

[28] Robert Cooter & Ariel Porat, *Does Risk to Oneself Increase the Care Owed to Others?*, 29 J. LEGAL STUD. 19 (2000). We recognize that the principal goal of tort law is to induce the internalization of precaution that confers a benefit on another. Tort law does not generally seek to induce potential injurers to take care to minimize their own harms.

events that materialize. Applied to accidents, the hindsight bias may cause courts to overestimate the effects of untaken precaution on the probability of accidents that actually occurred. Hindsight probabilities can thus result in liability under the Hand rule in circumstances where foresight probabilities result in no liability. As a result, injurers may feel that they are being treated unfairly: They took what seemed to them, at the time, to have been sufficient care but were later deemed to have been at fault. If this result is widespread, it is possible that potential injurers will respond by taking more precaution than they really believe to be necessary. There is, thus far, no empirical evidence on this matter, but it is intriguing.

> **QUESTION 6.16:** Suppose that the sunken barge in *United States v. Carroll Towing Co.* and its cargo are worth $100,000. Assume that the probability that the barge would break loose if the bargee is not present equals 0.001. If the bargee is present, then the probability of the barge's breaking loose is reduced by half, to 0.0005. Paying the bargee to stay on the barge will cost the barge owner $25. If the barge owner does not incur this $25 expense, is his behavior negligent under the Hand rule?

> **QUESTION 6.17:** Courts have to decide whether to defer to community norms when setting a standard of negligence or to set a legal standard independently from the community norm. A community of homeowners has norms for maintaining the safety of steps leading to the front porch of a house. Similarly, hospitals and private companies that collect blood have norms for storing it safely. Make arguments for why a court might appropriately show more deference to community standards for porch steps than to a community standard for storing blood.

H. Errors

We have explained that a negligence rule can create efficient incentives for injurer and victim, whereas strict liability can only create efficient incentives for the injurer. Despite this fact, the twentieth century saw the scope of strict liability rules expand and the scope of negligence rules contract, especially with respect to consumer product injuries. What justifies this change? The answer concerns information. Proving causation is much easier than proving negligence. To illustrate, it is much easier to prove that an exploding Coke bottle harmed a restaurant worker than to prove that the manufacturer followed negligent bottling procedures. If liability requires the victim to prove negligence, as with a negligence rule, then many manufacturers will avoid liability, and they will take little precaution. Conversely, if liability only requires the victim to prove causation, as with a rule of strict liability, then few manufacturers will avoid liability, and most of them will take much precaution.

In tort disputes, mistakes are often made concerning the extent of harm, the cause of the accident, and the actor's fault. Such mistakes are unavoidable by courts and lawmakers because accidents are shrouded in a fog of uncertainty, interested parties such as the plaintiff and defendant provide biased information, and few people have expert information about risks and precaution. In this section we explain how courts and law-makers should take account of their own fallibility.

First, consider how a mistake by the court in estimating harm affects precaution. The effects are different under a rule of strict liability and a rule of no liability. The injurer's incentives for precaution are efficient under a rule of strict liability with perfect compensation. But suppose the court consistently estimates harm inaccurately and consistently fails to set damages equal to perfect compensation. If the damages actually awarded by the court consistently fall short of perfect compensation, then the injurer will externalize part of the cost of accidental harm; so, he or she will have incentives to take deficient precaution. Conversely, if the damages actually awarded by the court consistently exceed perfect compensation, then the injurer will have incentives to take excessive precaution. In general, *consistent court errors in setting damages under a rule of strict liability cause the injurer's precaution to respond in the same direction as the error.*

Second, consider mistakes in determining who caused an accident under a rule of strict liability. Specifically, assume that the court sometimes fails to hold someone liable who caused an accident. This kind of error lowers the expected liability of the injurer, just like awarding deficient damages. The effect of lowering the probability of liability is the same as the effect of lowering the amount of damages: Future potential injurers take less precaution. In general, *consistent court errors in failing to hold injurers liable under a rule of strict liability cause subsequent injurers to take less precaution.* (Conversely, consistent errors in the direction of holding a person liable for accidents that she did not cause may induce other persons to avoid activities where mistaken liability can occur.)[29]

The situation is different under a negligence rule. Under a negligence rule, the injurer is not liable if his precaution equals the legal standard, and he is liable if his precaution falls below the legal standard. Thus the injurer's expected costs jump up as his precaution falls below the legal standard $\tilde{x}$ as depicted in Figure 6.4. To the left of this discontinuity, the injurer's expected costs are $\$[wx + p(x)A]$; to the right of this discontinuity, the potential injurer's expected costs are $\$wx$. To escape liability and avoid the jump in costs, the injurer satisfies the legal standard $(x = \tilde{x})$. This is true whether the jump in costs is large or small. So, the injurer will want to satisfy the legal standard and escape liability even if the court makes errors in measuring damages. In general, *injurer's precaution does not respond to modest court errors in setting damages under a negligence rule.*[30]

This fact is illustrated in Figure 6.5, where lines *A* through *D* indicate different levels of expected accident costs. When the court awards perfectly compensatory damages, assume that the injurer's expected liability costs in Figure 6.5 are given by curve *B*.

---

[29] Thanks to Nick Tideman for correcting imprecision in an earlier formulation of this principle.

[30] Here is a more precise, and more technical, statement of the contrast: Many injurers respond a little to changes in damages under a rule of strict liability (response on the intensive margin), whereas a few injurers respond a lot to change in damages under a negligence rule (response on the extensive margin, with nonconvexity in the expected-cost function).

FIGURE 6.5

A single legal standard and different expected accident costs.

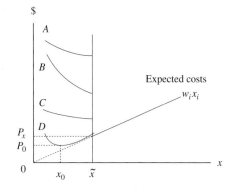

Above curve B, the courts award excessive damages, which results in an expected-cost curve such as A. Below curve B, the courts award deficient damages, which results in an expected-cost curve such as C. Regardless of these court errors, the injurer's expected costs jump down to when the injurer satisfies the legal standard; so, the injurer still minimizes expected costs by setting his or her precaution equal to the legal standard, $x = \tilde{x}$. To change the injurer's cost-minimizing precaution, the error made by the court in awarding damages must be very large, as illustrated by the curve labeled D. In that case, the cost-minimizing level of care will be less than the legal standard.

Rather than interpreting Figure 6.5 as depicting errors by courts, we can interpret the figure as depicting errors by injurers. For example, think of curves A, B, C, and D as depicting the expected costs of four different injurers. Curve B depicts the injurer who predicts court behavior accurately, curve A depicts the injurer who errs by overestimating court damages, and curve C depicts the injurer who errs by underestimating court damages. Regardless of these errors, the injurer's expected costs jump down to $w_i x$ when he or she satisfies the legal standard. So, each injurer still minimizes expected costs by setting precaution equal to the legal standard, $x = \tilde{x}$. To change the injurer's cost-minimizing precaution, the error in predicting damages must be very large, as illustrated by the curve labeled D. There the erring injurer perceives the cost-minimizing level of precaution to be x, far below the efficient level. In general, *injurer's precaution does not respond to injurer's modest errors in predicting damages under a negligence rule.*

We have interpreted the different expected-cost curves in Figure 6.5 as indicating an error by the court in computing damages or the injurer in predicting damages. Alternatively, the different expected-cost curves could be interpreted as indicating an error in determining who caused the accident. In general, *injurer's precaution does not respond to a court's modest errors in determining who caused an accident under a negligence rule.*

Having discussed errors in computing damages and determining causes, we turn to errors in setting the legal standard. By "errors," we mean situations in which lawmakers set the legal standard at a level different from the efficient level of precaution. Most injurers minimize their costs by conforming exactly to the legal standard, regardless of whether it exceeds or falls short of efficient precaution. Consequently, an excessive legal

FIGURE 6.6

Expected cost when the legal standard is less than the social optimum.

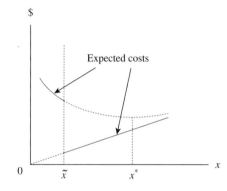

standard causes excessive precaution, and a deficient legal standard causes deficient precaution. In general, *injurer's precaution responds exactly to court errors in setting the legal standard under a negligence rule.*

To illustrate, Figure 6.6 depicts the injurer's expected costs under a negligence rule when the legal standard is less than the efficient level of precaution: $\tilde{x} < x^*$. The solid curves in Figure 6.6 indicate the injurer's costs as a function of the level of precaution. The injurer minimizes costs by setting precaution equal to the legal standard: $x = \tilde{x}$. His or her precaution is less than the efficient level: $x < x^*$. Consequently, too many accidents occur, and the harms they inflict are too severe.

QUESTION 6.18:   Use a graph to explain the efficiency consequences of a legal standard that exceeds the efficient level of care: $\tilde{x} > x^*$.

QUESTION 6.19:   "In general, the injurer's precaution responds to court errors in setting the legal standard under a negligence rule." Is this statement true for all forms of the negligence rule, or only for the simple negligence rule?

I.   Vague Standards and Uncertainty

We have analyzed precise rules—both precisely efficient rules and precisely inefficient rules—that are called "bright-line rules" because their meaning is as clear as a bright line. In reality, however, legal commands are often vague and unpredictable, frequently referred to as "standards." Vague and unpredictable tort standards leave people uncertain about the legal consequences of their acts. We shall discuss how people adjust their precaution in response to legal uncertainty.

Assume that the court makes purely random errors, or, what amounts to the same thing, assume that the injurer makes purely random errors in predicting what courts will do. By "purely random," we mean that excess is just as probable as deficiency, so that the average error is zero. (Technically, we assume that errors follow a random distribution with zero mean.) We shall consider purely random errors in damages and standards.

First, consider purely random errors by the court in computing damages or by the injurer in predicting damages. A purely random error in damages does not change the expected liability of the injurer. Expected liability remains unchanged because errors of excess offset errors of deficiency on average. Because expected liability remains unchanged, an injurer who minimizes expected costs does not change his or her precaution in response to purely random errors in damages.[31] This is true for every liability rule. In general, *the injurer who minimizes expected costs does not change his or her precaution in response to random errors in computing or predicting damages under any liability rule.*

The situation is different, however, for random errors concerning the legal standard in a negligence rule. To keep the analysis simple, consider the injurer's legal standard of care, $\tilde{x}_i$, under a rule of simple negligence. Assume that the court makes random errors in setting the legal standard $\tilde{x}_i$, or the court makes random errors in comparing the injurer's precaution x to the legal standard $\tilde{x}_i$, or the injurer makes random errors in predicting the legal standard $\tilde{x}$. Given any of these possibilities, injurers are uncertain about whether a particular level of precaution on their part will result in the court's finding them liable or not liable for accidents. If the court finds that their precaution exceeded the legal standard, then they will have taken unnecessary precaution. Unnecessary precautions cost them a little. Alternatively, if the court finds that their precaution fell short of the legal standard, then they will be liable. Liability costs them a lot. This asymmetry gives injurers an incentive to take more precaution in order to create a margin of error within which they will not be liable. In general, *small random errors in the legal standard imposed by a negligence rule cause potential injurers to increase precaution.*

Table 6.3, which summarizes our conclusions about precise errors and vague standards, suggests some prescriptions for lawmakers and courts. First, with a rule of strict liability, consistent errors by the court in computing damages distort precaution; so, the court should avoid these errors. Second, with a rule of negligence, consistent errors by the court in setting standards distort precaution more than consistent errors in computing

TABLE 6.3
Consequences of Errors of Excess

Liability Rule	Court's Error	Injurer's Error	Effect on Injurer
Strict liability	Excessive damages	Overestimates damages	Excessive precaution
Negligence	Excessive damages	Overestimates damages	None
Negligence	Excessive legal standard	Overestimates legal standard	Excessive precaution
Strict liability	Random error in damages	Random error in damages	None
Negligence	Random error in legal standard	Random error in legal standard	Excessive precaution

---

[31] In technical terms, the solution to Equation 6.2 does not change if we replace A with $E(A + \mu)$, where E is an expectation operator and μ is a random variable with zero mean and constant variance.

damages; so, the court should concentrate on avoiding errors in setting the standard of care. Given these two prescriptions, a court that assesses damages more accurately than standards for a given class of cases should favor a rule of strict liability, whereas a court that assess standards more accurately than damages for a given class of cases should favor a rule of negligence. Third, with a rule of negligence, vague standards cause excessive precaution; so, the court should apply vague standards leniently in order to avoid aggravating the problem of excessive precaution.

QUESTION 6.20:   "Excessive damages increase expected liability under a negligence rule, which results in excess precaution." Explain the mistake in this proposition.

QUESTION 6.21:   "If the legal standard of care in a negligence rule is necessarily vague, the court should set it below the level of efficient precaution." Explain the economic argument in favor of this proposition.

Rules V. Standards

A law can be precise like "The speed limit is 50 kilometers per hour," or a rule can be imprecise like "Drive at a reasonable speed." Law and economics scholars call precise laws "rules" and they call imprecise laws "standards."[32] Determining whether behavior complies with a precise rule is easier than an imprecise standard. Officials who enforce laws, and citizens who must obey them, appreciate the certainty and predictability of rules. The human imagination, however, cannot anticipate all of the circumstances in which a precise rule prescribes the wrong behavior, as when the policeman stops the car for speeding to the hospital with a passenger who is about to give birth to a baby. A system of rules tries to overcome inflexibility through exceptions, such as the rule that speed limits do not apply in emergencies. The exceptions to a rule, however, are an open set; so, no rule can enumerate all of them. As unforeseen circumstances arise, exceptions mount and a system of rules becomes increasingly complex. Conversely, a system of standards reaches precision through cases. When a case arises, its resolution precisely specifies the standard's application to the circumstances. The novel application of the standard in a case constitutes a precedent. Common law is a system of standards with many cases, whereas regulatory law is a system of rules with many exceptions. Civil codes also contain many imprecise standards.

Which is better, rules or standards? In Chapter 9 we will discuss precise contract terms like "Pay $100 for each day that delivery is late," and vague contract terms like "Make your best efforts to deliver on time." Our discussion of contracts will conclude that parties prefer precise terms when they can stipulate efficient behavior in advance, and they prefer imprecise terms when they want courts to decide whether behavior was fair and efficient after it occurs. Verifiable and unverifiable terms in contracts resemble rules and standards in tort law. Tort law should use rules when it can stipulate efficient and fair behavior in advance, and the law should use standards when courts can identify efficient and fair behavior in cases after disputes arise.

---

[32] See Louis Kaplow, *Rules Versus Standards: An Economic Analysis*, 42 DUKE L. J. 557 (1992). Note that instead of "standards," philosophers often use "principles" to refer to imprecise laws.

J. Administrative Costs and Tailored Rules

In the simple model, the economic goal of the tort liability system is to minimize the sum of the costs of precaution and the harm caused by accidents. A more complex model includes another important element of costs: administration. Administrative costs are incurred to allocate the costs of accidental harm. For example, a system of private law incurs the costs of lawyers, judges, and other officials involved in resolving legal disputes. Similarly, a public system to compensate workers injured on the job must collect taxes, decide claims, and pay benefits.

We begin by analyzing administrative costs in isolation from the costs of precaution and accidental harm. In private law, injurers compensate victims, whereas in public law, injurers pay fines to the state. Private law can lower administrative costs because the victims, who know a lot about the cause and extent of their injuries, sue the injurers. In contrast, public law requires an administrator to discover injurers who violate rules. For many injuries, but not all, private enforcement is more efficient than public enforcement. We postpone a more systematic comparison between public and private enforcement in order to focus on the administrative costs of three rules: no liability, strict liability, and negligence.

The rule of no liability leaves the costs of accidental harm where they fall, without attempting to reallocate them. Consequently, a rule of no liability eliminates the administrative costs of reallocating the costs of accidental harm. In contrast, the rule of strict liability and the rule of negligence reallocate the costs of accidental harm under certain conditions. Thus, a rule of no liability saves administrative costs relative to a rule of strict liability or a rule of negligence liability.

This fact has led reformers to advocate adopting the rule of no liability for most motor vehicle accidents. Under a so-called "no fault" rule, each of the parties to an automobile accident bears his or her own costs of accidental harm. In practice, this means that each accident victim recovers from his or her own insurance company, rather than recovering from the insurance company of the injurer.[33] The rule of no liability has the disadvantage that it gives injurers no incentive to take precaution. For example, the owners of trucks with steel cattle guards welded to the front of the vehicle may respond to a rule of no liability by driving aggressively. Thus, the no-fault systems presumably save administration costs and erode incentives for precaution.

Now we compare the administrative costs of a rule of strict liability and a rule of negligence. Recall that a rule of strict liability requires the plaintiff to prove harm and cause, whereas a rule of negligence requires the plaintiff to prove harm, cause, and fault. The additional element of proof in negligence requires an additional decision, which increases administrative costs. Thus, *a rule of strict liability lowers administrative costs relative to a rule of negligence by simplifying the adjudicator's task.*

This advantage of strict liability may be offset by a disadvantage. A rule of strict liability gives more victims the right to recover damages than a rule of negligence. Specifically, a rule of strict liability gives every victim who suffers harm caused by the

---

[33] There has been, in the recent past, discussion of implementing a no-fault regime for medical harms. We discuss this proposal in the next chapter.

injurer's *activity* the right to recover, whereas a rule of negligence gives every victim who suffers harm caused by the injurer's *fault* the right to recover. Thus, *a rule of negligence lowers the administrative costs relative to a rule of strict liability by reallocating the cost of harm in fewer cases.* In summary, a rule of strict liability results in more claims that are simpler to settle, whereas a rule of negligence results in fewer claims that are more complicated to settle.

We have contrasted the administrative costs of strict liability and negligence. Besides the form of the liability rule, administrative costs also depend upon the simplicity and breadth of the rules. Simple rules are based upon easily proven facts, and broad rules lump together many different cases. Conversely, complicated rules are based upon facts that are difficult to prove, and narrow rules apply to a few cases. We may characterize the extremes of simplicity and breadth as *wholesale* rules, and we may characterize the extremes of complicated and narrow as *case-by-case* adjudication. Wholesale rules are cheaper to make, enforce, and understand. However, wholesale rules distort incentives by treating people alike who have different utility and cost functions. In general, *wholesale rules save administrative costs and distort the relationship between the marginal cost of precaution and the marginal reduction in harm, whereas case-by-case adjudication has the opposite effects.*

Besides allocating the cost of accidental harm, the law also allocates the costs of administration. Different countries allocate administrative costs differently. To illustrate, an accident victim who successfully sues in the United States recovers damages for the harm suffered but does not usually recover costs of litigating. In contrast, many European countries require the loser of a lawsuit to pay the litigation costs of the winner. The allocation of administrative costs decisively affects the incentives of the victim to sue and the incentives of the parties to settle out of court. We shall analyze these incentives in a later chapter.

Because administrative costs are purely instrumental, reducing them without increasing accidents is a pure gain. To retain the same level of deterrence of injurers, the law can increase the magnitude of liability and reduce its probability. To illustrate, assume that negligent injurers must pay damages of 100. Now change the rules and assume that a flip of a coin will determine whether a negligent injurer pays damages of 200 or pays nothing. After randomizing, the expected liability remains 100, so deterrence will not change for many injurers. Administrative costs, however, should fall because damages are collected from half as many injurers. In general, increasing liability and reducing the frequency of trials can often save administrative costs without affecting the number of accidents. These facts suggest that efficiency requires a high magnitude and low probability of liability.

Increasing the magnitude of liability, however, encounters obstacles. Private law typically restricts the injurer's liability to the damages required to compensate the victim. Some theorists want to circumvent this obstacle by "decoupling" damages, so that the injurer pays compensation to the victim and also a fine to the state.[34]

---

[34]A. Mitchell Polinsky & Yeon-Koo Che, *Decoupling Liability: Optimal Incentives for Care and Litigation,* 22 RAND J. ECON. 562–570 (1991).

In principle, decoupling enables the law to save administrative costs by increasing the magnitude of liability and decreasing its probability. You will encounter this same principle in Chapter 12 when we analyze the optimal magnitude and certainty of criminal punishments.

QUESTION 6.22: Doctors are liable when their negligence injures patients. Suppose the rule was changed from negligence to strict liability. How would administrative costs change?

QUESTION 6.23: The rungs of ladders must be constructed to support the weight of the people who climb them. Compare the relative efficiency of a precise government standard for all ladders concerning the weight that the rungs must support, as opposed to the rule that the strength of the rungs should be determined as suits arise on a case-by-case basis using the Hand rule.

K. Consumer Product Injuries: Between Torts and Contracts

At the beginning of this chapter we explained that tort law uses liability to internalize externalities created by high transaction costs. The model of torts applies when transaction costs prevent the injurer and victim from dealing with each other before the accident, as with most automobile accidents. When the parties have a market relationship, however, the analysis must change, as we now show with an example of consumer product injuries.

Table 6.4 reproduces the numbers from a hypothetical example developed by Polinsky.[35] Consumers face a choice between buying soda in bottles or cans. Bottles are cheaper to produce than cans, as indicated by column 1, but bottles are twice as likely to cause an accident to the consumer, as indicated by column 2, and the accidents involving bottles are more severe, as indicated by column 3. The expected loss in column 4 equals the probability of an accident in column 2 multiplied by the loss in

TABLE 6.4

Cost of Soda

Behaviour of Firm	Firm's Cost of Production Per Unit	Probability of Accident to Consumer	Loss if Accident	Expected Accident Loss	Full Cost Per Unit
	(1)	(2)	(3)	(4)	(5)
Use bottle	40 cents	1/100,000	$10,000	10 cents	50 cents
Use can	43 cents	1/200,000	$4000	2 cents	45 cents

---

[35] A MITCHELL POLINSKY, AN INTRODUCTION TO LAW AND ECONOMICS (2d ed. 1989), Table 11, p. 98.

column 3. The full cost per unit, indicated by column 5, equals the sum of the cost of production in column 1 and the expected accident loss in column 4.

Notice that the full cost of bottles (50 cents) in this hypothetical example exceeds the full cost of cans (45 cents). Thus, efficiency requires the use of cans, not bottles. Let us consider whether consumers will actually use cans instead of bottles. The behavior of consumers depends upon the information that they possess, liability law, and the market for sodas. We assume that the market is perfectly competitive. Competition drives the price of a good down to its cost, as explained in Chapter 2. The cost of supplying soda depends upon production and liability. We assume that the price of a unit of soda equals the production cost plus the cost of the manufacturer's liability. Under a rule of no liability, the price of a unit of soda thus equals the production cost as shown in column 1: 40 cents per bottle and 43 cents per can. Under a rule of strict liability, the price of a unit of soda equals its full cost as shown in column 5: 50 cents per bottle and 45 cents per can.

First, consider the behavior of *perfectly informed* consumers under a rule of *no liability*. Being perfectly informed, the consumers know the expected accident costs and the fact that they must bear these costs. Consequently, consumers will prefer the soda whose full cost to them is lower, specifically, soda in cans. *Thus, perfectly informed consumers will choose the most efficient product under a rule of no liability.*

Second, consider the behavior of *imperfectly informed* consumers under a rule of *no liability*. Being imperfectly informed, the consumers do not know the expected accident costs. If consumers overestimate the greater danger associated with bottles, they will buy cans. If consumers underestimate the greater danger associated with bottles, or if they disregard the danger, they may buy bottles to obtain the (perceived) lower price of 40 cents per bottle, as opposed to the higher price of 43 cents per can. *Thus, imperfectly informed consumers will not necessarily choose the most efficient product under a rule of no liability.*

Third, consider the behavior of imperfectly informed consumers under a rule of *strict liability*. Strict liability and perfect competition cause the price of soda to equal its full cost, which is 50 cents per bottle and 45 cents per can. Consumers will prefer cans rather than bottles, regardless of whether they overestimate, underestimate, or disregard the greater danger associated with bottles. *Thus, imperfectly informed consumers will choose the most efficient product under a rule of strict liability.*

This example provides the basic rationale for holding manufacturers strictly liable for the harm that defective products cause consumers: The cost of liability will be captured in the price, thus directing consumers toward efficiency despite having imperfect information. This analysis, however, ignores many shortcomings of a system of strict liability for consumer product injuries, such as administrative costs, the lack of incentives for precaution by victims, and overinsurance of consumers by producers. We will discuss these shortcomings in detail in the next chapter.

QUESTION 6.24:   In effect, a rule of strict liability requires the seller to provide the consumer with a joint product: soda and insurance. What inefficiencies arise from such a compulsory purchase?

Conclusion

In communist countries like the former Soviet Union, planners could not get the information that they needed to manage an increasingly complex economy, which caused the economy to deteriorate. An increasingly complex economy must rely increasingly upon markets, which decentralize information. In this respect, making law resembles making commodities. As the economy grows in complexity, central officials cannot get the information that they need to make precise regulations. Instead of centralized lawmaking, the modern economy needs decentralized lawmaking analogous to markets. Tort liability removes many decisions about accidents from bureaucrats and politicians and allows judges to make laws, plaintiffs to decide when to prosecute violators, and courts to determine how much the violators must pay. Thus, the liability system decentralizes much of the task of internalizing externalities. In this chapter we developed the fundamental theory required to understand tort law. The next chapter refines the economic theory in order to address the problems that beset tort law everywhere in the world.

Suggested Readings

Brown, John P., *Toward an Economic Theory of Liability*, 2 J. LEGAL STUD. 323 (1973).

Grady, Mark, *A New Positive Economic Theory of Negligence*, 92 YALE L. J. 799 (1983).

LANDES, WILLIAM, & RICHARD A. POSNER, THE ECONOMIC STRUCTURE OF TORT LAW (1987).

SHAVELL, STEVEN, AN ECONOMIC ANALYSIS OF ACCIDENT LAW (1987).

Shavell, Steven, *Liability for Accidents*, in A. MITCHELL POLINSKY & STEVEN SHAVELL, EDS., HANDBOOK OF LAW AND ECONOMICS v. 1 (2007).

Liability and Symmetry

THE NEGLIGENCE RULE imposes a standard of care upon the injurer, which we depicted as partitioning the injurer's precaution into permitted and forbidden zones. The defense of contributory negligence imposes a legal standard of care upon the victim, which can be represented by partitioning the victim's precaution into permitted and forbidden zones.

Figure 6.7 shows the injurer's precaution on the horizontal axis and the victim's precaution on the vertical axis. The two legal standards partition Figure 6.7 into four quadrants. The following table summarizes the relationship between the four quadrants and the fault of the parties:

Quadrant	Injurer	Victim
I	fault	no fault
II	no fault	no fault
III	no fault	fault
IV	fault	fault

For example, in quadrant I, the injurer is at fault because $x_i < \tilde{x}_i$, and the victim is not at fault because $x_v > \tilde{x}$.

The following table summarizes the way different liability rules allocate the costs of accidental harm between the parties, depending upon their precaution by quadrant:

Liability rule	Injurer bears cost of harm	Victim bears cost of harm
Simple negligence	I, IV	II, III
Negligence with defense of contributory negligence	I	II, III, IV
Strict liability with defense of contributory negligence	I, II	III, IV
Strict liability with defense of dual contributory negligence	I, II, IV	III

FIGURE 6.7

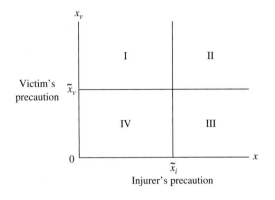

If we switch the labels of the axes in Figure 6.7 so that the injurer's precaution is on the vertical axis and the victim's precaution is on the horizontal axis, then compare how the liability rules allocate the burden of harm, we shall find some interesting relationships. "Simple negligence" is the mirror image of "strict liability with a defense of contributory negligence," and "negligence with defense of contributory negligence" is the mirror image of "strict liability with defense of dual contributory negligence."

QUESTION 6.25: Explain why the victim bears the costs of accidents under a rule of strict liability with a defense of contributory negligence in quadrant IV.

QUESTION 6.26: Explain why the injurer bears the costs of accidents under a rule of strict liability with a defense of contributory negligence in quadrant II.

7 Topics in the Economics of Tort Liability

T HE PRECEDING CHAPTER introduced the fundamental concepts of tort law and developed an economic analysis of tort liability. In this chapter we wish to advance the understanding of the economic analysis of the tort liability system in two ways. First, we relax some simplifying assumptions in order to bring the model closer to reality. Second, we shall examine some arguments that the tort liability system does not work well and needs thorough reform. In the course of this examination, we shall look at some recent evidence on how well the tort system minimizes the social costs of accidents.

I. Extending the Economic Model

The model that we introduced in the last chapter made some implicit simplifying assumptions. The grand tradition in economics would have us assert our intention to relax these simplifications but then forget to do so. But we aspire to do better. We turn immediately to the task of exploring the conclusions of our simple model when we relax our simplifying assumptions.

A. Relaxing the Core Assumptions

In the previous chapter we implicitly made five simplifying assumptions before we developed our economic analysis of tort law:

1. Decision makers are rationally self-interested.
2. There are no regulations designed to reduce external costs.
3. There is no insurance.
4. All injurers are solvent and pay damages in full.
5. Litigation costs are zero.

The purpose of this section is to relax these assumptions and to see the effect, if any, on the conclusions from the economic theory of tort liability.

1. Rationality   One of the central assumptions in economic theory is that decision makers are rationally self-interested. As a technical matter, this means (as we saw in our review of microeconomics in Chapter 2) that decision makers have stable, well-ordered preferences,[1] which implies something about the decision maker's cognitive

---

[1] Recall that such preferences are stable in the sense that they do not change too rapidly or quixotically and that they are well ordered in the sense that they are transitive, which means that if A is preferred to B and B is preferred to C, then A must be preferred to C.

and reasoning abilities. Specifically, it suggests that decision makers can calculate the costs and benefits of the alternatives available to them and that they choose to follow the alternative that offers the greatest net benefit.

There is a vital connection between the assumption of rationality and the economic model of tort liability in Chapter 6. We saw that the rules for assigning tort liability are, economically speaking, designed to send signals to potential victims and potential injurers about how they ought to behave. For the tort liability system to have this effect, it must be the case that those whose behavior the law is seeking to affect are rational: If they do not behave in the manner predicted by the assumption of rational self-interest, then we may need to amend the tort liability system in light of how people actually behave.

But do people really make decisions about potential liability in this way? Some people do, and others do not. Recent academic literature suggests that many decision makers commit predictable errors in making calculations of the sort that tort liability encourages them to make. For instance, Kahneman and Tversky report two disturbing conclusions.[2] First, they find that *most* people simply cannot accurately estimate low-probability events; they seem to deal with them by assuming that "low probability" means that the event will never happen—that the probability of the event's happening is zero. Second, they find that, for some well-publicized, potentially catastrophic outcomes—such as accidents from nuclear power plants—*most* people systematically exaggerate the probability of an accident's occurring, regardless of objective information to the contrary.

These opposite errors—underestimating most low-probability events and overestimating some low-probability events—apparently have a common cause: the frequency and vividness with which people are reminded of these risks. Infrequent and dull reminders of risk cause people to underestimate them, whereas frequent and vivid reminders cause people to overestimate them. Most low-probability events are seldom discussed or portrayed in the media; so, people tend to act as if their probability is close to zero, whereas potentially catastrophic events such as nuclear risks are much discussed and portrayed in the media, so people tend to overestimate their probability.[3]

These findings have implications for the economic model of tort liability. If many people do not accurately estimate risks, then they cannot make the appropriate calculations of net benefits and costs that the economic theory assumes that they make. Using the symbols of the previous chapters, some people may inaccurately set $p(x)$ equal to 0 for low-probability events and, therefore, take no precaution, when, in fact,

---

[2] See generally DANIEL KAHNEMAN & AMOS TVERSKY, EDS., JUDGMENT UNDER UNCERTAINTY: BIASES AND HEURISTICS (1981). For behavioral insights applied to law, see Russell Korobkin & Thomas S. Ulen, *Law and Behavioral Science: Removing the Rationality Assumption from Law and Economics,* 88 CAL. L. REV. 1051 (2000).

[3] A common example of this phenomenon arises from this question: "Which is more common—homicide or suicide?" Many people answer, "Homicide," largely because information about homicide is vivid and widely reported while that on suicide is typically not reported. In fact, suicide is approximately twice as common as homicide. The U.S. Centers for Disease Control and Prevention reports that in 2009 there were approximately 18,000 homicides in the United States and about 34,500 suicides.

that probability is positive, and they *should* take precaution. The inability of these decision makers to make accurate calculations may lead to too many or too severe accidents. In other cases, decision makers may *over*estimate $p(x)$—that is, they may think that an accident is far more likely than it, in fact, is—and may, therefore, take far too much precaution. As a result of these inabilities to calculate correctly, the tort liability system—to the extent that it presumes that people can and do calculate, may not induce people to take actions that minimize the social costs of accidents.

The economic theory of tort liability not only draws our attention to the importance of the rationality assumption in analyzing tort law, but it also suggests a corrective measure when that assumption is violated. Consider accidents involving power tools. One might suppose that precaution in such cases is bilateral: There is something that both the consumer and the producer can do to reduce the probability and severity of an accident. As a result, the economic theory would suggest that some form of the negligence rule should be used to induce efficient precaution by both consumers and producers. However, suppose that there is strong evidence that consumers do not accurately assess the risks associated with the use of power tools. They might presume that the tools are so safe that they need not take any particular care in how they are used. In short, consumers might mistakenly assume that the probability of an accident is zero and take very little precaution. That fact would make this a situation of *unilateral,* rather than *bilateral,* precaution: Only manufacturers could realistically be expected to take steps to reduce the probability and severity of an accident.[4] In these circumstances, manufacturers might be held liable for failing to design a product that would prevent foreseeable misuse by less than fully rational consumers.

Besides misperceived probabilities and other cognitive errors, many accidents result from tangled feet, quavering hands, distracted eyes, slips of the tongue, wandering minds, weak wills, emotional outbursts, misjudged distances, or miscalculated consequences. Described more abstractly, accidents result from clumsiness, inattention, misjudgment, misperception, or weakness of will. Occasional acts of this kind are called "lapses." Chapter 12 explains how lapses can cause crimes. Here we focus on lapses that cause unintended negligence, which in turn causes an accident. In these cases an actor aims for a given level of precaution and fails to achieve it. Negligence rules determine liability by comparing the legal standard to the injurer's actual level of care, not the injurer's intended level of care. So, actors are liable under a negligence rule for the harm caused by their lapses.

Here is an example.

Example 1:   *Unintended Negligence by a Motorist:* A motorist sets out on the long, straight drive from San Francisco to Los Angeles on Interstate 5. The road is uncongested, it is night, and the speed limit is 70 miles per hour. Under these conditions, a reasonable driver of a car with a mechanism to maintain constant speed ("cruise control") would set it at the speed limit of 70 miles per hour. The car, however, lacks such a mechanism. Not being a machine, the

---

[4] Note, further, that if the rationality assumption fails, then there is not a great deal to be said for a policy of better informing the parties about the objective values of the risks. They either discount or ignore that information.

driver cannot possibly go 70 all the time. The driver aims for 65. Occasional lapses in attention cause the driver to exceed or fall short of the intended speed of 65. Near the end of the trip, the driver has an accident while going 73 that he would have avoided if he had been going 70. Under a negligence rule, the motorist is liable for harm caused by the accident.

In this example, a safe driver is held liable for an accident that he caused by accidentally going too fast. Now consider the symmetrically opposite example.

> **Example 2:** *Intended Negligence by a Motorist:* The facts in the preceding example remain the same except that the driver aims for 75, so he intends to drive at an *un*reasonable speed. Occasional lapses in attention cause the driver to fall short of the intended speed of 75. Near the end of the trip, the driver has an accident while going 67. Under a negligence rule, the motorist is not liable for harm caused by the accident.

In this example, a dangerous driver is held *not* liable for an accident that occurred while he was accidentally going at a safe speed.

The first driver was intentionally nonnegligent most of the time and accidentally negligent part of the time. He had "bad moral luck": He accidentally went too fast at just the wrong time and caused an accident. The second driver, in contrast, was intentionally negligent most of the time and accidentally nonnegligent part of the time. He had "good moral luck" with respect to liability: He accidentally went too slow at just the right time and escaped liability.[5]

Allowing moral luck to determine liability may seem unfair to you. Fairness aside, reducing the role of moral luck in liability improves incentives and reduces inefficiencies. To see why, we construct a graph to represent the safe driver who had bad moral luck. The vertical axis in Figure 7.1 represents the probability of driving at a particular

FIGURE 7.1

Probability of a lapse causing negligent precaution.

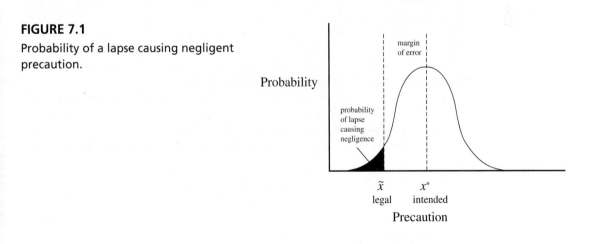

---

[5] Because he could not have avoided this accident by driving 67, speeding was not the cause of this accident, so he should not be held liable even if he had been speeding. In practice, however, the court may be unsure of these facts, and it is likely to find him liable if he were going 75 when the accident occurred.

speed. The horizontal axis represents precaution, which corresponds to driving slowly in the preceding example. We model a lapse as a probabilistic connection between intended and actual precaution. The actor in Figure 7.1 intends to achieve precaution level x^*. The actual level of precaution x the actor achieves depends on his intention x^* plus a random variable ε, so $x = x^* + \varepsilon$. To provide for a margin of error, the actor intends to exceed the legal standard, so $x^* > \tilde{x}$. An actor lapses when actual precaution falls below intended precaution, or $x < x^*$. In Figure 7.1, the probability of a lapse resulting in negligence is the shaded area under the probability density function that lies below the legal standard.

In Figure 7.1, the actor gains a private advantage by exceeding the legal standard, but social efficiency requires the actor *not* to exceed the legal standard. We already explained this fact in the preceding chapter, which we restate briefly. Recall that precaution is socially optimal when the cost of taking a little more equals the social benefit of fewer accidents. If the legal standard is set at the social optimum, then exceeding the legal standard of precaution has more social costs than benefits. For the actor, however, private benefits increase significantly when his precaution reaches the legal standard because he escapes liability. So the actor takes excessive precaution. (Moral luck also has another bad incentive effect that we cannot discuss here.[6])

We have explained that allowing moral luck to affect liability seems unfair and distorts incentives for precaution. Replacing a rule of liability for accidents caused by negligence with a rule of liability for accidents caused by *intentional* negligence would reduce the role of moral luck in determining liability. Unfortunately, this remedy is usually worse than the problem. Compared to a rule of liability for objective negligence, a rule of liability for intentional negligence requires the plaintiff to prove much more before recovering damages. If the plaintiff had to prove intentional negligence in order to recover damages, the burden of proof would be crushing, and recoveries would seldom occur. Thus, the victims of automobile accidents could seldom recover if they had to prove that the speeding driver *intended* to speed. Practical problems of information cause courts to condition liability on objective negligence rather than intentional negligence. (Consider, however, that global positioning systems or some other technological advance may someday provide a complete record of a driver's speed on any journey, which would often allow a driver to prove that his speeding was merely an unintended lapse.)

These thoughts raise concerns about whether tort liability induces the appropriate precautionary action by potential injurers and victims. We shall tentatively maintain the rationality assumption but shall be ready to amend our conclusions about efficient tort rules when there is sound evidence that the appropriate decision makers are not behaving rationally.

QUESTION 7.1: Wearing seat belts and shoulder harnesses is an efficient means of minimizing the costs of automobile accidents. Assuming that the

---

[6] While people cannot choose whether to lapse, they can control the frequency and magnitude of lapses through concentration, preparation, conditioning, and training. Moral luck causes excessive investment in these activities by a rational actor. We relegate this fact to a footnote, however, because irrational people who invest too little in cultivating self-control pose a greater danger to society.

benefits of these passive restraints exceed their costs, but that not all drivers and passengers use seat belts, how might the rules of tort liability be changed so as to induce a greater number of people to wear seat belts and shoulder harnesses?

Web Note 7.1

We have previously mentioned the burgeoning literature in behavioral law and economics. Much of that literature relates to the examination of the economics of tort liability. See our website for much more on the connections between behavioral law and economics and tort law.

---

2. Regulations

Fire regulations usually require a store to have a fire extinguisher. Inspectors will check from time to time to confirm that the store complies with the regulation. If it fails to comply, the regulators may impose a fine. Even if the store complies and a fire injures a customer, the store may be liable to that customer in a private cause of action. In this example, the store is subject to safety regulations and liability. In Chapter 6, the basic model assumed that injurers face liability but not regulations. The fact that injurers often face both liability and regulations poses the question, "Why have both safety regulation and liability?" If, in our example, liability law is adequate at inducing safety precaution, the store will presumably keep a fire extinguisher even without the regulation. And if the store complies with the regulation, perhaps the injured customer should seek compensation from his insurance company, not the store.

Comparing liability and regulation, sometimes one is more efficient than the other, and sometimes the two together are more efficient than either one by itself. A general theory of safety regulation and tort liability must distinguish these alternatives. Instead of attempting a comprehensive theory, we will sketch some determinants.[7]

Administrators have the power to order potential injurers to correct a hazard before an accident occurs, whereas courts have the power to order injurers to compensate victims after an accident occurs. Regulation is *ex ante* enforcement by administrators, and liability is *ex post* enforcement by victims. This difference determines many of the advantages and disadvantages of each.

Administrators and courts differ with respect to information. Administrators can often acquire technical knowledge needed to evaluate the safety of specialized industries, whereas courts of general jurisdiction have difficulty accumulating technical knowledge about specialized industries. In these circumstances, administrators may set standards better than courts, so the court may use a safety regulation as the standard of care for determining liability. By accepting safety regulations as defining the legal standard of care for tort liability, courts defer to administrators. If safety regulation and liability law impose the same standard of care, then potential injurers will conform to that standard in order to avoid both *ex ante* fines and *ex post* liability.

---

[7] See Steven Shavell, *Liability for Harm versus Regulation of Safety,* 13 J. LEGAL STUD. 357–374 (1984), and Charles Kolstad, Thomas Ulen, & Gary Johnson, *Ex Post Liability for Harm vs. Ex Ante Safety Regulation: Substitutes or Complements?*, 80 AM. ECON. REV. 888 (1990).

Sometimes, however, courts have better safety information than administrators do. For example, a trial may provide judges and juries with better information about the harm caused by an accident than administrators can predict. In addition, courts often have fewer political motives than administrators. Problems of information or motivation can cause a court to distrust the legal standard imposed by a safety regulation.

Courts may feel that the regulators set the standard too low in order to avoid liability for politically powerful businesses. In these circumstances, the standard of care imposed by the court for liability may exceed the safety regulation. If liability law imposes a higher standard than safety regulations, then most potential injurers will conform to the higher standard in order to avoid liability.

Alternatively, courts may feel that the regulators set the standard too high in order to reduce competition. For example, U.S. automobile manufacturers may seek high safety standards to increase compliance costs for foreign competitors. If safety regulations impose a higher standard than liability law, then most potential injurers will conform to the regulation in order to avoid fines.

Safety regulations provide a rich source of bribes for corrupt officials in many countries. Sometimes officials want tough regulations to guarantee that bribing an official is cheaper than conforming to the regulations. In countries where the administrators are more political and corrupt than judges, liability has a distinct advantage over regulation.

When tort liability exceeds an injurer's wealth, the injurer is bankrupt. Some risky activities attract undercapitalized firms that can escape liability through bankruptcy. Highly capitalized firms may avoid these same activities to avoid the risk of liability. In those industries where undercapitalized firms risk bankruptcy, safety regulations have an advantage over liability. By collecting fines before an accident occurs, officials can force an undercapitalized firm to comply with safety standards that it would violate if the only sanction were liability.

Finally, consider the administrative costs of regulations and liability. Sometimes accidents impose small harm on a large group of people. When the cost of trial for each victim exceeds his damages, making liability law work requires aggregating claims, as in a class action suit. Sometimes claims are easier to aggregate in an administrative proceeding than in a court trial. In general, safety regulations dominate liability as a remedy for accidents that impose small harm on a large group of people.

Web Note 7.2

The remarkable story of the attempts to regulate the harms from tobacco use and to hold the tobacco companies liable for those harms constitutes an instructive case study of the relationships between liability and regulation. See our website for a discussion of the tobacco cases and the settlement reached in the U.S. litigation.

3. Insurance   How does the availability of insurance affect our analysis of tort liability? So far, our analysis of alternative tort rules and institutions has proceeded as if no one were insured. In reality, insurance is pervasive for accidents and tort liability.

Now we need to discuss how insurance interacts with tort liability and consider whether insurance advances or retards the goals of tort law, which we formulated as minimizing the sum of the costs of precaution, accidental harm, and administrative costs.

A person who faces the risk of accidental harm may buy insurance. When an accident occurs, a victim with insurance files an insurance claim for compensation with his insurance company. In addition to recovering from his insurance company, the victim may have a right in tort law to recover from the injurer. In principle, the accident victim could recover twice—once from the insurance company and once from the injurer. The insurance contract, however, usually transfers the victim's recovery rights to the insurance company by means of what is called "subrogation": The insurance company stands in place of the insured in the tort suit for the harm covered in the insurance claim. To illustrate, the accident may cause the victim to lose $100 in medical costs and $200 in pain. The victim may have health insurance to cover the medical costs and no insurance to cover pain. So, the victim will recover $100 from the insurance company and $200 from the injurer, and the insurance company will recover $100 from the injurer.

Besides insurance against accidental harm, many people buy insurance against liability. In the preceding example, the injurer is liable for $300. If the injurer has full liability insurance, the injurer's insurance company will pay the injurer's liability of $300 ($200 to the victim and $100 to the victim's insurance company).

In the preceding example, the victim's insurance is *in*complete (it covers medical costs but not pain), and the injurer's insurance is complete (it covers medical costs and pain). As insurance becomes more complete, we approach a situation where victims recover all of their compensation from insurance companies, injurers recover all of their liability from insurance companies, and the insurance companies resolve disputes among themselves. In effect, insurance is a private system of liability law that reallocates the costs of accidents according to contracts between insurer and insured. As this private system becomes more complete, injurers and victims deal directly with their insurance companies, not with each other. In these circumstances, people care more about insurance rates and terms of coverage, and they care less about the underlying law of accidents (except insofar as the latter affects the former).

Insurance companies set premiums, which provide revenues. They also process claims and pay them, which are costs of doing business. In perfectly competitive markets, companies earn zero profits. Applied to insurance markets, this proposition implies that the premiums equal the claims plus administration costs. Earlier we formulated the goal of tort law as minimizing the sum of the cost of the harm from accidents, the costs of avoiding accidents, and the costs of administration. *In a system of universal insurance and competitive insurance markets, the goal of tort law can be described as minimizing the total cost of insurance to policyholders.*

To illustrate this proposition, we contrast no liability and the rule of strict liability. With a rule of no liability, potential victims buy accident insurance, and potential injurers have little need for liability insurance. In contrast, with a rule of strict liability potential injurers need liability insurance, and potential victims have little need for insurance against those accidents for which the injurers are liable. So, a rule of no liability causes victims to buy relatively more insurance, and a rule of strict liability causes injurers to buy relatively more insurance.

Which rule is more efficient? This policy debate is important historically. In the nineteenth century, consumers injured by defective products seldom recovered in court, so consumers who wanted insurance had to buy it themselves.[8] In the twentieth century, the emergence of strict products liability in tort law effectively caused manufacturers to insure consumers, and manufacturers often bought liability insurance for themselves. These facts provoked an argument about whether victims' insurance is more or less efficient than injurers' insurance. We cannot answer this question fully, but we can give the flavor of debate.

In general, insurance transfers risk from the insured party to the insurer. *Transfer* is another name for *externalize*. Externalizing risk gives the insured an incentive to reduce precaution. The insurance industry, which is old and has its own language, calls the reduction in precaution caused by insurance *moral hazard*. To illustrate moral hazard, a person who insures his car against theft may not be so careful about locking it.

Insurance companies employ various means to reduce moral hazard, notably coinsurance, deductibles, and experience rating. Under a deductible, the insured pays a fixed dollar amount of his accidental losses. Under coinsurance, the insured pays a fixed percentage of his accidental losses. Under experience rating, the insurance company sets the insured's rates according to the experience of the insured's claims. A claim in year two, for example, usually means a rate increase in year three. While these devices reduce moral hazard, they cannot eliminate it. Consequently, insurance inevitably undermines the insured's incentives for precaution.[9]

To combat this problem, liability insurers impose safety standards that policyholders must meet to remain covered by insurance. To illustrate, a fire insurance company may require a business to maintain fire extinguishers as a condition for writing an insurance policy. In the preceding section, we contrasted *ex ante* regulation and *ex post* liability. Insurance companies impose standards *ex ante*. Officials of the company may inspect for compliance. Insurance safety standards are private regulations imposed by contract and enforced by private parties, as opposed to public regulations imposed by law and enforced by state officials. On balance, legal scholars generally think that insurance promotes the goals of tort law and should be encouraged.[10]

Having discussed the incentive effects of insurance, we return to the question of whether no liability or strict liability is a better rule for consumer product injuries. The rule of strict liability has a distinct advantage over no liability in terms of the efficiency of insurance markets. As explained, insurance companies usually set rates according to the history of an individual's claims through the process of "experience rating." Many claims trigger a surcharge, and few claims trigger a discount. Under a rule of strict liability,

---

[8] Note, however, that many forms of insurance that we take for granted were unavailable in the nineteenth century. Insurance markets took time to develop.

[9] An additional problem for insurers is *adverse selection*, which we discuss in the section on insurance in Chapter 2 and also discuss below as a possible source of periodic insurance crises. Will adverse selection, if uncorrected, create efficiency issues in tort liability? Describe and contrast those problems in regimes of no liability and strict liability.

[10] Some states, however, prohibit liability insurance for punitive damages, presumably for the same reason that states prohibit insurance against criminal fines.

a company that produces many defective products makes many claims to its insurer and thus pays higher rates. This fact creates incentives for more precaution by the manufacturer to reduce its claims by reducing consumer accidents. However, these incentives for producers disappear under a rule of no liability, where consumers must buy their own insurance. One of the main arguments in favor of strict liability for consumer product injuries is that this rule causes liability insurers to monitor the safety of manufacturers.

Some scholars argue against the rule of strict liability on the ground that it provides consumers with unwanted insurance. By "unwanted" we mean that consumers would not voluntarily buy the insurance if they had to pay for it. To illustrate, a well-insured U.S. motorist who injures his knee when his car slips on ice and crashes will receive compensation from his insurance company for medical costs, lost wages, and damage to the car. If, however, the motorist suffers the identical injury due to the fault of another driver, the motorist will also receive additional compensation in tort for pain and suffering. In general, the tort liability system effectively provides consumers with insurance against pain and suffering that they would not buy for themselves. In personal injury cases, pain-and-suffering compensation can be relatively large, which implies that consumers have a lot of unwanted insurance. (Later we discuss how a market for tort claims can solve this problem by allowing potential accident victims to sell unwanted liability rights.)

We have introduced the complex interaction of tort liability rules and insurance markets. Before leaving the topic, we want to explain a problem with insurance markets. In 1985 and 1986 and again in the mid-1990s, a "crisis" over liability insurance—particularly with respect to medical malpractice insurance—occurred in the United States and elsewhere. During the crisis, insurance companies abandoned some lines of insurance, refused to renew policies for some persons and companies, lowered the limits on some insurance coverage, and sharply increased some premiums. The crisis poses the question, "Is the insurance industry inherently unstable?" Answering this question explains some fundamental characteristics of the insurance industry.

The answer may be "Yes" for two reasons. The first reason concerns the "reserves" held by an insurance company. Sound business policy and state regulations require insurance companies to hold a fraction of their revenue from premiums in reserve to cover future claims. For some risks, however, many claims can occur at once. To illustrate, earthquake insurance results in no claims in most years and vast claims when a large earthquake actually occurs. As a consequence, the insurance company must use the premiums in years with no claims to build up its reserves ("reserve funding"). Sometimes an insurance company has larger reserves than it needs to cover a risk. If an insurance company has excess reserves, it can expand the supply of insurance at little cost. At other times, insurance companies have no excess reserves, so they cannot write more insurance policies without increasing their reserves or liquidating the investments they have made with their other premium revenues. Changing the level of reserves can be very costly because of tax consequences.[11] One theory holds that insurance crises occur

---

[11] Capital removed from reserves becomes taxable as profit; so, insurance companies do not like to remove capital from reserves except in years when they have losses to offset their tax liability. Similarly, additions to reserves can reduce tax liabilities (especially under the U.S. tax law before the 1986 reforms), so insurance companies prefer to add to reserves in years when they have large profits from their other activities.

because insurance companies exhaust their reserves and must raise premiums relatively quickly to replace those reserves.

The second explanation is quite different in character. Suppose that insurance premiums rise, and some people stop purchasing insurance. The people who retain their insurance represent the worst risk, so the insurance company may have to increase its premiums again. To illustrate, suppose there is a 20 percent chance that I will suffer an accident costing $10,000 and only a 15 percent chance that you will suffer such an accident. If we are both insured, I expect to recover $2000 from the insurance company in claims, whereas you expect to recover $1500 in claims. Suppose the insurance company offers us the same insurance policy for the same premium, say $1500. It does not charge me more than you because it does not have enough information to tell us apart (or perhaps the regulators won't permit "price discrimination"). Both of us purchase the insurance because the premium is equal to or (in my case) less than the expected value of the claim, and we are both probably risk-averse. The insurance company collects $3000 in premiums from the two of us and expects to pay $3000 in claims, so it earns zero profits, as required in perfect competition.

Observe what would happen if the insurance company increased the rates to $1600. You are more likely than I am to decide to drop your policy. (Why?) But if you drop your policy, the insurance company loses a good risk (you) and retains a bad risk (me). Now the insurance company collects $1600 in premiums and it expects to pay out $2000 in claims, so it expects to lose $400. To overcome this loss, it must raise its rates again. (To what level does the company now need to raise its premium?) The rates have to be raised a second time because the first rate increase caused good risks to stop buying the policy while bad risks continued buying it.

This phenomenon, whereby an increase in insurance premiums drives out good risks while retaining bad risks, is called "adverse selection." The second explanation of the insurance crisis holds that increased claims set off a cascade of increased premiums due to adverse selection. Exhaustible reserves and adverse selection can create instability in the supply of insurance.[12]

> **QUESTION 7.2:**   Are subrogation clauses efficient? Be sure to review your answer in light of the section below about litigation costs and their effect on the efficiency of the tort liability system.

4. Bankruptcy   Under assumptions explained in Chapter 6, strict liability causes the firm to internalize the social costs of accidents, so it chooses the socially optimal activity and care levels. The possibility of escaping liability through bankruptcy changes this conclusion. When potential damages to tort victims exceed the firm's net worth, the firm externalizes part of the risk, thus eroding its incentives to take precaution and restrain its activity level. Limited liability can cause too little precaution and too much dangerous activity.

---

[12] See Ralph Winter, *The Liability Crisis and the Dynamics of Competitive Insurance Markets,* 45 YALE J. REG. 455 (1988); and Michael J. Trebilcock, *The Role of Insurance Considerations in the Choice of Efficient Civil Liability Rules,* 4 J. LAW, ECON. & ORG. 243 (1988).

Consider the example of a disposal company for hazardous waste. If such a company planned to remain in business indefinitely, it might use extreme care in dumping hazardous waste in order to avoid future liability. Alternatively, it might follow the strategy of dumping recklessly and accumulating potential tort liabilities that exceed its assets. Anticipating future liability and bankruptcy, the firm continually distributes profits and remains undercapitalized. When harm materializes and suits begin, the firm declares bankruptcy, and its tort victims take their place with other unsatisfied creditors.

This scenario suggests that firms in risky industries may have too many accidents and too little capital, thus lowering production and distorting the capital labor ratio. In addition, if tort liability causes bankruptcy and liquidation, the firm's nontransferable assets are destroyed, such as its reputation ("goodwill"), organization, and its employees' knowledge of how the company conducts business ("firm-specific human capital"). Thus, avoiding liability through insolvency causes significant inefficiencies.

A recent article, however, proposes that new judgment-proofing techniques enable corporations to avoid tort liability without being undercapitalized.[13] First, a corporation can place risky activities in a subsidiary, which is a separate company owned by the parent corporation. Courts seldom reach past a bankrupt subsidiary to the parent's assets. Some evidence exists that liability causes U.S. firms to divest and locate hazardous activities in smaller firms.[14] Some scholars urge U.S. courts to "pierce the corporate veil" and extend tort liability to the parent of a subsidiary, or even to people who own shares in bankrupt corporations. Research by Richard Brooks on the *Exxon Valdez*, which was an Exxon oil tanker whose wreck contaminated the Alaskan coast in spring 1989, demonstrates that the oil companies apparently believe that courts will pierce the corporate veil.[15] Specifically, large oil companies responded to massive liability by shipping more oil in their own tankers, which they control, rather than attempting to escape liability by contracting with tanker companies to ship their oil.

Second, in bankruptcy the secured creditors get priority over other, unsecured creditors, including tort victims. By lending a greater proportion of the corporation's debt to secure creditors, a firm can shield a larger portion of its assets from the claims of tort victims.

Third, firms often have expected income, such as future payments from buyers of the firm's products ("accounts receivable"). In a process called "securitization," firms convert expected income into securities and sell them to investors.[16] After securitizing, the future income belongs to the owners of the securities, so tort victims cannot tap this income as a source of compensation.

---

[13] Lynn M. LoPucki, *The Death of Liability,* 106 YALE L. J. 1 (1996).

[14] Al H. Ringleb & Steven N. Wiggins, *Liability and Large-Scale, Long-Term Hazards,* 98 J. POL. ECON. 574 (1990).

[15] Richard R. W. Brooks, *Liability and Organizational Choice,* 45 J. LAW & ECON. 91 (2002).

[16] The bonds allow the issuer to convert the stream of future income into a lump sum. One of the first to use the method of securitization was the rock singer David Bowie, who issued bonds that gave the bondholders a claim on Bowie's future income. In honor of this use, securitization bonds are sometimes called "David Bowie bonds."

The distortion of incentives for precaution caused by insolvency has no perfect solution. Imperfect solutions include compulsory insurance, posting bond, or replacing *ex post* liability with *ex ante* regulations. In addition, replacing rules of strict liability with negligence rules ameliorates the problem. A negligence rule allows a firm to escape liability by conforming to the legal standard of care. Having escaped liability, the firm has no need to shield assets from tort suits. In contrast, a rule of strict liability only allows a firm to escape liability by insolvency.[17]

5. Litigation Costs   The final core assumption of the economic theory of tort liability was that litigation is costless. Of course, nothing could be further from the truth: Litigation is expensive and sometimes ruinously so. A more complete analysis of the efficiency of the various liability rules we have discussed should introduce these costs explicitly.[18]

Costly litigation will have different effects on potential victims and potential injurers. Moreover, these different effects will have very different implications for the efficiency analysis of Chapter 6.

Consider, first, the impact of costly litigation on potential victims. If victims must incur a cost to assert their claims for compensation, then they may assert fewer claims. Consider an extreme case in which litigation costs exceed the expected compensatory damages. Victims will not bring suit, and so the potential injurers will not receive the signal from the tort liability system that what they are doing is unacceptable. They may, as a result, take less precaution than they should, with the consequence that there may be more accidents (and more severe accidents) than there should be.

However, costly litigation may have a contrary effect on the decisions of potential injurers. If it is expensive for an injurer to litigate, then it may make sense to take more precaution than would be the case if litigation were costless. By taking more precaution, the potential injurer makes an accident less likely or less severe; if the cost of this additional precaution is less than the cost of litigation, then we should expect potential injurers to take *additional* precaution when litigation is costly. Similarly, high litigation costs may cause investors to withdraw funds and reduce activities that risk lawsuits. As a result, there should be fewer and less severe accidents.

Because the effects of costly litigation on potential victims and on potential injurers pull in different directions (one suggests less precaution; the other suggests more precaution), we cannot be sure of the net effect of relaxing the assumption of costless litigation.

High litigation costs have an unsettling, counterintuitive implication, which we illustrate by contrasting two possible rules of legal procedure. Under the first procedure, assume that when a plaintiff complains that a wrongdoer caused harm of $100, the judge hears the case and awards damages of $100 whenever the plaintiff proves the

---

[17] For a detailed analysis of how bankruptcy impacts alternative tort rules, see Alexander Stremnitzer & Avraham Tabbach, *Insolvency and Biased Standards—The Case for Proportional Liability*, Yale Law School Faculty Papers, No. 24 (2009).

[18] See Janusz Ordover, *Costly Litigation in the Model of Single Activity Accidents,* 7 J. LEGAL STUD. 243 (1978); and A. Mitchell Polinsky & Daniel Rubinfeld, *The Welfare Implications of Costly Litigation in the Theory of Liability,* 17 J. LEGAL STUD. 151 (1988).

necessary facts. Under the second procedure, assume that when a plaintiff complains that a wrongdoer caused harm of $100, the judge flips a coin and dismisses the complaint without a trial whenever the coin shows "heads." If the coin lands "tails," however, the court decides the case and awards damages equal to 200 percent of the actual harm. The injurer's *expected* liability is the same for both procedures—1.0×100 under the old procedure, and $.5 \times 200$ under the new procedure. If potential injurers decide how much precaution to take based on expected liability, then the change in procedure will not affect their behavior, so the sum of the cost of harm from accidents and the cost of avoiding accidents apparently remains the same. However, the new procedure has reduced the number of trials by 50 percent, so administrative costs are much lower under the second procedure.[19]

Changing our legal system from the first to the second procedure would save costs, but this will not happen. A judge who actually decided a case by flipping a coin would provoke outrage and censure. Even so, our example makes this important point: A legal system can save administrative costs by reducing the probability of liability and offsetting this fall with an increase in damages. Chapter 13 returns to the equivalent point in criminal law when we discuss criminal fines rather than civil liability.

> **QUESTION 7.3:** Use the economic theory of bargaining to characterize the torts in which the transaction costs of settling disputes are likely to be large. (*Hint*: Recall the distinction between public bads and private bads.)

> **QUESTION 7.4:** For which liability standard would you expect the litigation costs to be greater—negligence or strict liability? Why? Is that an additional efficiency argument for preferring one standard to the other?

6. Conclusion Taken altogether, what is the ultimate result of relaxing the core assumptions for the conclusions of the previous chapter? Perhaps somewhat surprisingly, the conclusions of the economic model survive almost intact. We have seen that relaxing the rationality assumption may be warranted, and that where it is relaxed, the economic theory helps us to see how tort law ought to take into account the cognitive imperfections of those whose behavior it seeks to affect. We also saw that relaxing the assumption that there is no first- or third-party insurance does not change the results of the economic theory of tort liability. Coinsurance, deductibles, subrogation clauses, and the implied threat of higher premiums or of policy cancellations preserve the incentives of potential injurers to take optimal care and of potential victims (through their insurers) to bring actions in order to induce potential injurers to internalize the social costs of their carelessness. Nor does the presence of other social policies, such as safety regulation, necessitate our changing any of the economic conclusions. These alternative social policies require some account of how best to coordinate tort liability and safety regulation, and that coordination is likely to require an understanding of the economic tradeoffs involved. Finally, the fact that litigation is costly does not necessitate a change in our economic model. Rather, we have seen that costly litigation points in different

---

[19] See David Rosenberg & Steven Shavell, *A Simple Proposal to Halve Litigation Costs*, 61 VA. L. REV. 1721 (2005).

directions: On the one hand, it may induce potential victims not to file actions (thus allowing potential injurers not to bear the full costs of their carelessness and inviting them to take less care in the future), but, on the other hand, it may induce potential injurers to take more care (if taking additional care makes accidents less likely or less severe and is cheaper than the costs of litigating).

B. Extending the Basic Model

The economic model that we have been exploring in this and the previous chapter explains not just the broad questions of tort liability's purposes and the differences between negligence and strict liability, but it also helps us to understand some of the more special doctrines of tort liability. In this section we shall show how the economic theory applies to certain special cases—for example, the liability of employers for the torts of their employees—and to some issues at the frontiers of tort liability.

1. Vicarious Liability   There are circumstances in which one person may be held responsible for the torts committed by another. Where this happens, the third party is said to be *vicariously liable* for the tortfeasor's acts. Vicarious liability may extend from an agent to his or her principal or from a dependent child to a parent, but by far the most common instance of vicarious liability is that of employers' responsibility for the tortious wrongs of their employees under the doctrine of *respondeat superior* ("let the master answer"). The bare bones of this doctrine are that an employer will be held to answer for the unintentional torts of an employee if the employee was "acting within the scope of [his or her] employment." To illustrate, an employer tells an employee *never* to drive the company's truck faster than the speed limit. The employee speeds, and the truck has an accident. The employer is liable.

Does *respondeat superior* induce efficient behavior by employers and employees? The rule creates an incentive for the employer to take care in selecting employees, in assigning them various tasks, in deciding with which tools to equip them, in training them, in monitoring them, and more. This is efficient if it is the case—as it generally would seem to be—that employers are better placed than are employees to make precautionary decisions.[20]

In discussing tort liability, we often distinguish between two rules: strict liability and negligence. Our analysis of the difference applies to vicarious liability. Under a rule of strict vicarious liability, the employer is liable for harms *caused* by an employee. Under a rule of negligent vicarious liability, the employer is liable for harms caused by *negligent supervision* of an employee. A switch from negligence to strict liability lightens the plaintiff's burden of proof. To illustrate, a careless nurse employed by a hospital harms a patient. To recover damages from the hospital under a rule of strict vicarious liability, the patient must prove that someone in the hospital caused the harm, which is relatively easy. To recover damages from the hospital under a rule of negligent vicarious liability, the patient must prove that the hospital negligently supervised the nurse, which

---

[20] For a full discussion of the economics of this issue, see Alan Sykes, *The Economics of Vicarious Liability,* 93 Yale L. J. 1231 (1984).

is relatively hard. You already encountered this argument in favor of strict liability when we discussed consumer product injuries.

We have given an information-cost argument for favoring a rule of strict vicarious liability for employers rather than a rule of negligent vicarious liability. Another argument goes in the opposite direction. To illustrate, a sailor on a tanker might negligently discharge oil onto a public beach at night. Informing the authorities quickly about the accident will reduce the resulting harm and the cost of the cleanup. The captain of the ship might be the only person besides the sailor who knows that the harm occurred or who can prove that pollution came from its ship. Strict vicarious liability gives the captain an incentive to remain silent in the hope of escaping detection. In contrast, a rule of negligent vicarious liability gives the captain an incentive to reveal the harm to the authorities immediately. As long as the captain can prove that he carefully monitored the sailor, the rule of negligent vicarious liability allows the captain to escape liability. As compared to a rule of strict vicarious liability, a rule of negligent vicarious liability encourages employers to report more wrongdoing by employees.[21]

> **QUESTION 7.5:** What if an accident has occurred because an employee was performing a job for which he was not qualified after the employee had falsely told the employer that he *was* qualified? Should the employer still be liable for the victim's losses under *respondeat superior*?

> **QUESTION 7.6:** The common law did not hold parents liable for their children's unintentional torts unless the parents' negligent supervision led directly to the tort. But the common law did hold husbands vicariously liable for their wives' torts (a rule since abrogated by statute). Can you provide an efficiency explanation for these common law rules?

> **QUESTION 7.7:** In many states, a bartender (under so-called "dram shop laws"), friend, party host, or other person who serves liquor to an already-intoxicated person may be held vicariously liable for any damages that person subsequently inflicts on other people or their property. Does this form of vicarious liability make economic sense?

2. Joint and Several Liability With and Without Contribution

When several parties cause harm to someone, a question arises concerning whom the victim can sue and how damages should be allocated among them. To illustrate, suppose that you suffer a loss of $100 in an accident caused by two people called A and B. They are *jointly* liable if you can sue *both* of them at once, naming A and B as codefendants and receiving a judgment of $100 against them. They are *severally* liable if you can sue *either* A or B separately, naming each of them as a defendant in a distinct trial and recovering $100 from each.

---

[21] Jennifer Arlen & Reinier Kraakman, *Controlling Corporate Misconduct: An Analysis of Corporate Liability Regimes,* 72 NYU L. REV. 687 (1997).

Suppose that the plaintiff chooses to recover from only one of several injurers. May that defendant then force the other injurers to contribute to paying the damages? At common law for unintentional torts, the defendant did not generally have a right to *contribution*, as this is called, from other joint tortfeasors. This harsh rule against contribution has been abrogated, usually by statute but sometimes by judicial decision, in almost all the states.[22] The law usually subtracts the *contribution* of one party from the compensation owed by the other. For example, if A and B jointly cause you harm equal to $100 and you settle with A for $40, then the upper limit on a trial judgment against B is $60.

Defendants are said to be "jointly and severally liable" if each of them is liable for all the victim's full losses, not just a portion of them. The plaintiff may proceed jointly against all his injurers or may elect to recover all damages from only some of them or only one of them. (Typically, the plaintiff proceeds against the defendant or defendants who have "deep pockets," that is, the resources to compensate him.) In the United States, the actual law in most cases involving multiple injurers is "joint and several liability with contribution." Because liability is "joint and several," the plaintiff can sue the injurers jointly or separately, as he prefers. Because the law allows "contribution," the recovery is limited to 100 percent of the value of the harm. (The common law recognized two circumstances in which joint and several liability would hold.)[23]

There are several economic reasons for joint and several liability. One is that it relieves the victim of the potentially high costs of proving who caused her harm. The doctrine allows the victim to assert that one of these people, and perhaps many of them, caused her injuries without incurring the special costs of showing which one or more of them were responsible and in what proportion. In essence, the doctrine shifts the costs of establishing exactly what happened to the defendants. Imagine a situation in which a patient is anesthetized and taken into surgery. During the operation someone injures the patient. Later she sues all those who were in the operating room, but for obvious reasons she cannot tell who precisely caused her injury.

Another economic reason for joint and several liability is that it makes the victim's recovery more certain by allowing him to proceed against the defendant or defendants who have the most assets with which to pay damages. Suppose that an uninsured motorist is going at high speed, strikes a pothole in the road, loses control of his car, and hits another passenger car, seriously injuring its driver. Assume for the sake of argument that 90 percent of the fault is attributable to the speeding driver, and 10 percent of the fault is attributable to the city government for not filling the pothole. The victim will have difficulty recovering anything from the speeding driver because he lacks insurance and may have limited resources. However, if the law allows the victim to hold the

---

[22] This is true only for unintentional torts; for intentional torts, such as a violation of the antitrust statutes, there is still no right of contribution among joint tortfeasors.

[23] First, the defendants acted together to cause the victim's harm, as when two cars driven by A and B are racing down a street and one of them hits C, a pedestrian. The two drivers acted together by illegally racing each other. Second, the defendants acted separately, but victim's harm was indivisible between them. Thus, two hunters using identical ammunition fire at a pheasant and both of them accidentally hit a third person. They acted separately to cause the harm, but no one can disentangle the harm caused by one of them from the harm caused by the other.

motorist and the city jointly and severally liable, and if the victim can prove that the city was negligent in maintaining the road, then the victim can recover 100 percent of his losses from the city. The city then faces the hopeless task of trying to recover 90 percent of the damages it paid from the speeding driver who lacks insurance and resources.

Another economic issue concerns contribution and efficiency. Is a rule of contribution or no contribution more efficient? The no-contribution rule makes all defendants internalize the cost of accidents, thus creating incentives for optimal precaution by each of them. In contrast, the rule of contribution causes each defendant to internalize part of the cost of accidents and to externalize part of the cost. Because costs are partly externalized, the rule of contribution may not create incentives for optimal precaution by each defendant. To illustrate, in the example where A and B race their cars and strike C, optimal incentives require A to bear the full cost of the accident and B to bear the full cost of the accident.[24]

Although the rule of no-contribution creates efficient incentives for precaution by joint injurers, it can also, as we have noted, change reluctant victims into eager victims. For example, if C receives perfectly compensatory damages from A, then C is indifferent between no accident and an accident. If C receives perfectly compensatory damages from A and also from B, then C prefers an accident to no accident. Perhaps the phenomenon of eager victims explains why law favors contribution rather than no contribution.

Many states have reformed joint and several liability to reduce the ability of the victim to recover all the costs of the injurer from the injurer with the deep pockets. After these reforms, the victim must recover some damages from injurers with shallow pockets. A careful econometric study found that these reforms caused reductions in the accidental death rate in the United States. The authors' explanation is that reforms increase the incentives for precaution by injurers with shallow pockets, and their precaution reduces accidents the most.[25]

🛈 Web Note 7.3

When there are multiple defendants, it sometimes happens that one or more of the defendants make an agreement to settle their claims with the plaintiff and then keep the existence of that agreement secret from the other defendants. Such agreements are called "Mary Carter agreements" after the case in which they first arose. See our website for a history and economic analysis of Mary Carter agreements.

🛈 Web Note 7.4

We describe some recent empirical literature on "high-low agreements" between plaintiffs and defendants.

---

[24] See Landes & Posner, *Multiple Tortfeasors: An Economic Analysis,* 9 J. LEGAL STUD. 517 (1980); and Polinsky & Shavell, *Contribution and Claim Reduction Among Antitrust Defendants: An Economic Analysis,* 33 STAN. L. REV. 447 (1981).

[25] W. Bentley MacLeod, Janet Curry, & Daniel Carvell, *Accidental Death and the Rule of Joint and Several Liability,* BERKELEY LAW AND ECONOMICS WORKSHOP (October 29, 2009).

3. Evidentiary Uncertainty and Comparative Negligence[26]   In the previous chapter we discussed the several forms of the negligence rule: simple negligence, negligence with contributory negligence, and comparative negligence. For most of the last 200 years, negligence with contributory negligence has been not only the dominant form of the negligence rule but the dominant tort liability rule in the common law countries. However, within the last 40 years all this has changed. Today, all but a handful of the states in the United States have altered their law of accidents so that the prevailing liability standard is one of comparative negligence for non-product-related torts. The change has been effected principally by statute, with a minority of states adopting the rule by judicial decision. In most civil law jurisdictions of Europe, the principle of comparative negligence was adopted long before the United States made this change. In this section we shall explain briefly how the comparative-negligence rule works and how it differs from the rule of negligence with contributory negligence. Then we shall show how something called "evidentiary uncertainty" can give rise to an efficiency argument for comparative negligence.

The simple reason for the rise of comparative negligence is an increasing dissatisfaction with the rule of contributory negligence. Recall that a contributorily negligent plaintiff could not recover anything from the defendant, even from a negligent defendant. This rule struck most people as exceedingly harsh. To see why, imagine that an automobile accident has occurred; both the plaintiff and the defendant were driving. Suppose that violation of the speed limit constitutes negligence and that the evidence shows that the plaintiff was going 35 miles per hour in the 30 mile-per-hour zone and that the defendant was going 65 miles per hour in that same zone. Under the rule that bars recovery for a contributorily negligent plaintiff, the plaintiff will not be able to recover. This seems harsh in that the plaintiff's negligence was trivial in comparison to the defendant's.

To avoid this sort of harsh result, most jurisdictions found a means of limiting the scope of the rule of contributory negligence—for example, by means of the last-clear-chance doctrine.[27] But eventually these limitations on the application of the rule of contributory negligence gave way to comparative negligence.

The principal difference between comparative negligence and the rule of negligence with contributory negligence is that under comparative negligence the plaintiff's contributory fault is a partial but not a complete bar to recovery from a negligent defendant. Thus, under comparative negligence the negligent injurer usually owes something, but not full compensation, to the negligent victim.[28]

The equitable argument is the principal justification for the switch to comparative negligence. However, there are economic efficiency arguments that can be made on behalf of comparative negligence. To make these arguments requires relaxing at

---

[26] The material in this section draws on Cooter & Ulen, *An Economic Case for Comparative Negligence,* 61 NYU L. REV. 1067 (1986).

[27] Each of these limitations allowed an otherwise contributorily negligent plaintiff to recover *all* losses. Note how this differs from the result under comparative negligence described below.

[28] There are three different forms of comparative negligence: pure, modified, and slight-gross. These are extremely interesting but are not central to our economic analysis.

least one of the core assumptions that we made in the previous chapter. Recall that the basic economic theory of tort liability of Chapter 6 showed that *all* forms of the negligence rule (simple, contributory, and comparative negligence) were equally efficient. The only way we can draw efficiency distinctions among them is to relax one of the core assumptions. Suppose that, in a negligence case, we assume that litigation is costly in the sense that it is not certain how the court will evaluate the evidence developed at trial. Thus, neither the plaintiff nor the defendant can be certain whether the court will determine that their precautionary behavior was sufficient to absolve one of them of fault. It is possible, for example, that the court will determine that the precaution of one of the parties was insufficient, even though that party thought that he or she had complied with the relevant duty to take due care. Or the court may find one of the parties nonnegligent when in fact the party was violating the legal standard of care. We may call this condition "evidentiary uncertainty."

These possibilities of error may influence the precautionary decisions of a potential injurer. We assume, as seems realistic, that the probability that potential injurers will be found not liable increases as their precaution increases. Figure 7.2 shows the impact of this fact on expected costs. The effect of evidentiary uncertainty is to smooth the discontinuity in expected liability at the (presumed) legal standard that we developed in Chapter 6. Smoothing occurs because injurers' expected costs are a weighted average of their costs when liable and their costs when not liable, with the weights given by the probability that they will be found liable. The effect is indicated in Figure 7.2 by the sloping curve that connects the expected-cost curve and precautionary-cost line. Uncertainty about the court's assessment of a party's precautionary level with regard to the legal standard of care induces most injurers to take more precaution than is prescribed by the legal standard of care. In effect, they give themselves a margin of error to be sure that they avoid liability. This behavior is represented in Figure 7.2, which illustrates the fact that an injurer's costs are minimized on the smoothed curve at x^+, which is a higher level of precaution than the legal standard x^*.

FIGURE 7.2

Evidentiary uncertainty smooths the discontinuity at the legal standard of care and induces extra precaution by the potential injurer.

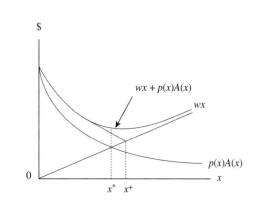

Evidentiary uncertainty causes potential injurers to go beyond the level of precaution that might just barely exonerate them.[29] That is, evidentiary uncertainty will cause overprecaution relative to the efficient level of precaution.

This result is true under any form of the negligence rule. What efficiency advantage, if any, does comparative negligence provide when there is evidentiary uncertainty? The overprecaution caused by evidentiary uncertainty is less under comparative negligence than it is under any other form of the negligence rule. The simple reason is that under comparative negligence, if either party makes a mistake in choosing the level of precaution that is necessary to satisfy the legal standard of care, the consequence of that mistake is not visited entirely on the person who made it, as it would be under any other form of the negligence rule, because, under comparative negligence, the losses are shared between the two parties rather than being concentrated on one party.

One frequent criticism that is made of comparative negligence is that its administrative costs are high. The rules to be used in apportioning fault are vague, it is said, even when the parties are engaged in the same activity: No one is quite sure how to apportion fault when A was going 45 in a 30 mile-per-hour zone and B was going 60. But things are even worse when the parties are engaged in different activities. How, for instance, would you have apportioned fault in *Butterfield v. Forrester,* the case in Chapter 3 involving an obstruction in the road left by Forrester and a negligent horseman, Butterfield, who crashed into the obstruction? Given this difficulty, it is alleged that litigants and juries will spend inordinately large amounts of effort trying to establish exact percentages of fault when such exactitude is impossible to achieve.

There may be some truth in the contention that comparative negligence has high administrative costs. If so, there is a balance to be struck between the efficiency gains of comparative negligence and these administrative costs. Until we can examine careful empirical studies, we cannot say whether there is a net efficiency gain from moving to this new liability standard.

i **Web Note 7.5**

There has been considerable writing about the economics of comparative negligence. We review that literature on our website.

QUESTION 7.8:   Admiralty law—the law that deals with controversies arising on navigable waters—used a rough-and-ready method of dealing with the problem of the administrative costs of comparative negligence. Rather than try to fine-tune the degrees of culpability between the contending parties, admiralty law simply split the losses 50-50 whenever there was negligence on the part of both parties. Comment on the efficiency of this method of reducing the administrative costs of comparative fault. Would you recommend that the admiralty rule be adopted in apportioning losses in, say, automobile accidents where both parties are at fault? Why or why not?

---

[29] This is an instance of the point we made earlier in this chapter—namely, that the prospect of costly litigation will induce potential injurers to take more precaution than they would otherwise. A little extra precaution makes an accident (and thus, a lawsuit) less likely.

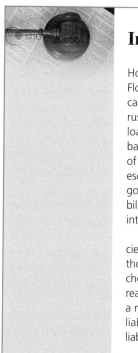

Incentives for Invisible Actors

How can authorities create incentives for someone who is invisible to them? The State of Florida has a clever solution. Florida farmers fertilize their fields with phosphorus, which rain carries into that massive, marvelous, fragile swamp called the Everglades. To control phosphorus, regulators have adopted a novel incentive system. Beginning in 1995–1996, phosphorus loadings are compared to a baseline derived from loadings recorded from 1979–1988. If basin-wide reductions in nutrient load into the Everglades do not meet statutory targets, all of the farmers in a designated area must pay the "Agricultural Privilege Tax." The farmers can escape the tax increase by exceeding an overall 25 percent basin-wide phosphorus reduction goal. Under this system, each farmer's abatement efforts reduce his own liability (and the liability of every other farmer) by the resulting reduction in pollution. Each farmer, consequently, internalizes the marginal benefits and costs of abatement, as required for efficiency.

This incentive system is remarkable in two ways. First, each farmer has incentives for efficient abatement *without the authorities knowing how much any one of them abates.* The authorities only need to know the total abatement by *all* farmers. Second, if the authorities have chosen the phosphorus reduction goal correctly, the farmers will continue abating until they reach it; so, *none of the farmers will actually pay the tax.* Theorists describe this approach as a rule of *total liability for excessive harm.* "Total liability" refers to the fact that each actor's liability depends on the harm that *all* actors cause. "Excessive harm" refers to the fact that liability applies to the amount by which the harm caused by all actors *exceeds* a baseline.[30]

4. Products Liability   Fifty years ago products liability was a minor part of tort law, but recently it has become a large and important specialty and the focus of much of the public dissatisfaction with the entire tort liability system. The liability standard in product-related accidents is called "strict products liability."[31] For a defendant-manufacturer to be held liable under this standard, the product must be determined to be defective. A defect can take three forms:

1. **A defect in design,** as would be the case if the design of automobile gas tanks made them liable to rupture and explode (see our website for more information);
2. **A defect in manufacture,** as would be the case if a bolt were left out of a lawn mower during its assembly, causing a piece of the mower to fly off and injure a user; and
3. **A defect in warning,** as when the manufacturer fails to warn consumers of dangers in the use of the product.

What liability standard would economic theory recommend for product-related accidents? Recall that our discussion of negligence and strict liability focused on whether precaution for reducing the likelihood and severity of the accident is unilateral or

---

[30] Robert Cooter & Ariel Porat, *Total Liability for Excessive Harm,* 36 J. LEGAL STUD. 63 (2007).

[31] RESTATEMENT (SECOND) OF TORTS (1965), §402A, published by the American Law Institute, lays out this standard.

bilateral. If it is bilateral (that is, if both parties can take precautionary action to reduce the probability and severity of an accident), then a form of the negligence rule is the appropriate standard. If precaution is unilateral (that is, if only the injurer can be looked to for actions to reduce the probability and severity of an accident), then strict liability is the appropriate liability standard. Using this economic analysis, which standard would modern products-liability law apply?

The more efficient standard would seem to be strict liability because in most instances of product-related harms, for clarity precaution lies unilaterally with the manufacturers. It is they who are in control of the design of the products and of the manufacturing process and who are most likely to be aware of any special dangers that their products present and, therefore, can most efficiently convey information about those dangers through warnings.

However, on further reflection, one finds elements of *bilateral* precaution in the product-accident situation. *Users* can also take precautions to reduce the probability and severity of accidents. For example, they can pay heed to the warnings and use the products only for their intended uses. There are stories about some consumers picking up their gasoline- or electric-powered lawn mowers and turning them sideways in order to trim their hedges, and being injured as a result. No manufacturer intends a lawn mower to be used in that fashion.

Products-liability law can steer a middle course between the view that precaution is unilateral (and, therefore, that strict liability is the appropriate standard) and the view that precaution is bilateral (and, therefore, that negligence is the appropriate standard). It can do so by holding defendant-manufacturers strictly liable for defective design, manufacture, or warning but allowing them to escape liability if the victim voluntarily assumed the risk of injury or misused the product. These defenses encourage the efficient allocation of risk of loss from product-related injuries between the consumer and manufacturer.

If the lawn mower manufacturer could not exclude liability for consumer misuse or for voluntarily assumed risk, it would be forced to insure each of its consumers. To cover the cost of this insurance policy, the manufacturer would have to raise the product price. The difficulty with this result is that *all* consumers must pay the higher price, not just those who are careless. Consumers who are careful would prefer to pay a lower price for the product and to purchase insurance against loss elsewhere.

We have discussed allowing manufacturers the defense of consumer misuse of defective products. In practice, a more decisive consideration is often the information that the court uses to decide whether a product has one of these defects. The court can either use the information available when the product was manufactured or when the case was tried. In the mean time, scientific progress uncovers much about risk that was previously unknown. Asbestos was originally celebrated as a lifesaver that miraculously protects people from flames, and later it was vilified as a deadly cause of lung cancer. A company that manufactured asbestos insulation for ships in 1947 did not produce a product known to be defective at the time, but the product was shown to be defective by 1977 when a worker brought suit. In the United States, courts have found asbestos to be defective by using the scientific knowledge available at the time of trial, thus holding the manufacturer liable for harm that it could not have foreseen by using the scientific knowledge available at the time of manufacture. Products liability is most "strict" when, besides disallowing manufacturers' defenses of reasonable care, the law also holds products to a standard of defect based on science available at trial and unavailable at manufacture.

QUESTION 7.10:   Some scholars discern a trend in modern products-liability law toward absolute liability or what is sometimes called "enterprise liability." Under that theory, manufacturers would be held liable for almost every injury resulting from the use of their outputs. Give an economic analysis of that liability standard for product-related harms.

II. Computing Damages

In the previous chapter we noted that the ability of liability rules to induce efficient precaution depends in part on the ability of the court to award truly compensatory damages to the victims of a tort. These damages accomplish two things simultaneously: First, they put the victim back onto the utility level or indifference curve occupied before the tortious act, and second, they are the "price" that the injurer must pay for having harmed the victim. In this section we elaborate the ways in which microeconomics can help to determine the appropriate amount of damages. Additionally, we use microeconomics to discuss the efficiency aspects of punitive damages in tort awards.

A. Hand Rule Damages

Compensatory damages are intended to "make the victim whole." In some circumstances, this is impossible. For example, when a child is killed in a tortious accident, damages cannot be computed on the formula, "find a sum of money such that the parents are indifferent between having the money and a dead child, and not having the money and having their child alive." The same difficulty arises in a more attenuated form for irreparable physical injuries, such as those resulting from a crippling accident.

There are, in fact, two distinct concepts of compensatory damages in tort law. One concept is the standard economic concept of indifference: Compensation is perfect when the victim is indifferent between having the injury and the damages, and having neither. Compensatory damages are thus perfect when the potential victim is indifferent about whether there is no accident or an accident with compensation. This concept is relevant for injuries in which a substitute for the lost good is available in the market. When a substitute is available, the market price of the substitute measures the value of the good to the plaintiff. This concept is also relevant for goods that are bought and sold from time to time but for which there is no regular, organized market. For example, a handwritten letter by James Joyce and a 1957 Chevy convertible are sold from time to time, but these items are so rare that a regular market for them does not exist. The owners of these rare goods usually have prices at which they are prepared to sell them, and these prices measure perfectly compensatory damages.[32]

---

[32] Economists use the term "reservation price" to refer to the minimum price at which the owner of a good is willing to sell it. Determining the owner's reservation price for a unique good is a difficult practical problem, but it is not a problem conceptually.

This concept of perfect compensation, based on indifference, is fundamental to an economic account of incentives. If potential injurers are liable for perfectly compensatory damages, then they will internalize the external harm caused by accidents. And this creates incentives for the potential injurers to take efficient precaution. Compensation of this kind is most easily computed for those losses for which there is a ready market substitute.

But for some tortious injuries there is no ready market substitute. For example, there is no price at which a good parent would sell a child. The idea that a person could be "indifferent" between a sum of money and a child is repugnant. And, for some people, there may be no price at which they would sell an arm or a leg.[33] So, for injuries involving the loss of a child or a limb, compensation simply cannot be perfect. Courts must, nevertheless, award damages for the wrongful death of a child or for grievous personal injuries. Our task, then, is to provide a more satisfactory understanding of their computation.

When U.S. courts award damages for incompensable losses, such as the death of a child, juries usually set the amount. Unfortunately, judges provide juries with no coherent instructions for how to compute damages. To illustrate, the recommended jury instruction for Massachusetts reads:

> Recovery for wrongful death represents damages to the survivors for the loss of value of decedent's life. . . . There is no special formula under the law to assess the plaintiff's damages. . . . It is your obligation to assess what is fair, adequate, and just. You must use your wisdom and judgment and your sense of basic justice to translate into dollars and cents the amount which will fully, fairly, and reasonably compensate the next of kin for the death of the decedent. You must be guided by your common sense and your conscience on the evidence of the case. . . .

It is common sense that money cannot compensate for a loved one's death, so how is common sense supposed to lead the jury to a dollar value? Rather than common sense, the California jury instructions refer to "reasonableness":

> Also, you should award reasonable compensation for the loss of love, companionship, comfort, affection, society, solace or moral support.

If no amount of money can compensate for loss of a loved one, then adding "reasonable" to "compensation" deepens the puzzle rather than clearing it up.

Besides courts, regulators must assign value to loss of life for purposes of cost-benefit analysis. Unlike court practice, the regulators have some clear methods developed by economists. We will describe such a method and explain its modification for use by courts.

A necessary part of living is being exposed to the risk of death or serious injury. For example, flying on an airplane or driving down the expressway involves such a risk. These risks can often be reduced, but doing so is costly. To illustrate, we may note that airplanes must be inspected and repaired at regular intervals, which is costly, but the

---

[33] For some people, there may be an amount of money at which selling an arm is an attractive bargain, but their concept of morality would not permit them to do it.

shorter the intervals, the fewer the accidents. Similarly, heavy cars with special safety features provide extra safety to passengers. But these cars are more expensive to produce and, therefore, more costly to consumers. When a parent decides what features of a car to buy or a commercial air carrier decides how frequently to inspect planes for safety, a decision is being made that balances the cost of additional precaution against reductions in the probability of injury.

A rational decision about these risks involves balancing the costs and benefits of precaution. By reasoning in this way, it is possible to compute damages for the loss of life. To illustrate, we may suppose that the probability of a fatal automobile accident falls by 1/10,000 when an additional $100 is spent on automotive safety. If expenditures on automotive safety are rational, then the reduction in the probability of a fatal accident, multiplied by the value of fatal risk, equals the marginal cost of care:

$$(1/10,000)(\text{value of fatal risk}) = 100,$$

or

$$(\text{value of fatal risk}) = 100/(1/10,000),$$

which suggests that the value of fatal risk is $1,000,000.

This method of computing damages for wrongful death, which is called the "value of a statistical life," takes actual market purchases as a guide to how much the purchaser values safety and, by implication, the value of being alive. For example, suppose that a consumer may purchase a safety device, such as an air bag, by paying extra to the retailer. If we know how much the safety device costs the consumer and by how much that device reduces the likelihood of death, then we may infer the consumer's valuation of safety, which implies a value of fatal risk. Using the figures from the previous paragraph, we may assume that the device costs $100 and that it reduces the likelihood of death by 1/10,000. (Remember that this implies a $1,000,000 value on being alive.) If consumers purchase the device, then they must value safety at a level that implies that the value of fatal risk equals at least $1 million.

To apply this method in a legal dispute, the court should consider those situations in which risk is "reasonable" and well known. In those circumstances, there will be some value p for the probability of a fatal accident, and some value B for the burden of precaution. Efficiency requires taking additional precaution until the burden equals the change in probability p multiplied by the loss L, or $B = pL$. (Notice that this is the Hand rule.) Thus, the court would compute the value of fatal risk by solving the equation for L, yielding $L = B/p$.

Notice that his method uses the Hand rule in an unusual way. In the usual way, the court uses the Hand rule to determine whether the injurer's precaution satisfied the legal standard. In its unusual use, the decision maker uses the accepted legal standard of care that an individual violated to determine his liability.

We have described two distinct methods for computing compensatory damages: the indifference method and Hand rule damages. The first method is appropriate for market goods—that is, for losses for which there is a market substitute; the second method is appropriate when there are legal and moral barriers to such markets. Only when the indifference method is appropriate can damages be perfectly compensatory.

However, both methods, when applied without error, provide incentives for an efficient level of precaution by potential injurers.

Empirical evidence suggests that Hand rule damages are several times higher than the U.S. average for damages that courts award in automobile accident cases involving loss of life.[34] For example, the National Highway Traffic Safety Administration (NHTSA) often values a traffic fatality at $2.5 million. Implementing Hand rule damages would, consequently, cause a significant increase in damage awards and insurance costs for some important kinds of accidents. Hand rule damages would also tend to smooth large differences in damages in individualized cases.[35] Besides bringing coherence to legal doctrine, implementing Hand rule damages would provide incentives for more rational safety expenditures and create a safer world.

The same accident results in larger damages in the United States than in Germany, and larger damages in Germany than in Japan. Damages cannot be different in similar countries for identical accidents and also be optimal in each country. Substantial reform seems to be required somewhere. Our view is that substantial reform is required everywhere. Creating a safer society by improving incentives for precaution begins by using economics to think more clearly about the problem. Hand rule damages suggest that damages for personal injuries are mostly too low to deter injurers, even in the United States. This is especially true for automobile accidents and other harms caused by ordinary people, as opposed to harms caused by corporations or governments, where damages are higher. A substantial increase in damages for personal injuries involving automobiles would increase insurance rates, which would reduce the amount of driving and make drivers more cautious. The lack of systematic calculation for damages in personal injury cases in the United States also means that damages vary randomly, which causes liability disparity. Liability disparity is even greater when corporate defendants are held liable for punitive damages, which is our next subject.

QUESTION 7.9: Victim V works at a job where he might be exposed accidentally to a chemical that increases the probability from .01 to .02 of dying from lung cancer in 20 years. V would pay $15,000 to avoid exposure to this risk, or he would accept $15,000 to expose himself to this risk. No matter how hard he tries, V cannot imagine any sum of money that he would accept in exchange for certain death by lung cancer. V's employer accidentally exposes him to the chemical. The risk materializes after 20 years, and V dies abruptly from lung cancer. How much are Hand rule damages for V's heirs? After exposure and before dying, V spent $1000 to move to another neighborhood with better air quality. Should $1000 be added to Hand rule damages, or is it already implicitly included?

---

[34] See Robert Cooter, "Hand Rule Damages," conference entitled "Theories of Compensation," Institute for Law and Philosophy, University of San Diego Law School, February 28, 2003.

[35] It is interesting to note that one of the first recorded legal codes, the Code of Hammurabi, stipulates the same amount of damages for the wrongful death of a free man or woman, whereas the individualized system in the United States awards higher damages on average for the wrongful death of a man than a woman.

Web Note 7.6

There is extensive literature on how regulators and other legal decision makers should place a value on a lost life—referred to as the "value of a statistical life" or VSL. We review that literature, with examples, on our website.

Web Note 7.7

Another difficult category of damage to evaluate for the purposes of compensation is "pain and suffering." (We saw earlier in this chapter that there is a principled argument to be made for not awarding pain-and-suffering damages. But most jurisdictions do so.) On our website we report on some recent empirical evidence that seeks to understand how jurors make decisions about how much money to award for "pain and suffering."

B. Punitive Damages

In 1984 Getty Oil allegedly agreed to sell itself to Pennzoil, but the Texaco oil company encroached on the deal and bought Getty. In a lawsuit a Texas jury awarded $7.53 billion in compensatory damages to Pennzoil and $3 billion in punitive damages. (In the end, the plaintiff settled out of court because the full judgment would have bankrupted the defendant.) Commentators on the case do not agree as to whether the defendant actually committed the wrong, which is unusual and has the name "tortious inducement to breach a contract." In any case, the award of punitive damages of $3 billion, which broke previous records, was unforeseeable. Earlier we mentioned the problem of *liability disparity* that arises when like cases result in different judgments. Punitive damages are a

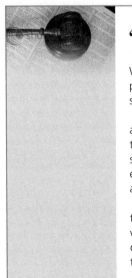

"Fortunately for My Client, the Victim Died."

Would you rather be dead or crippled? In most tortious accidents, victims and their families prefer the person alive and crippled rather than dead. It is, consequently, worse to cause someone's death in a tortious accident than to cause him or her to be crippled.

Yet, the death of the victim can be fortunate for the injurer, because the damages awarded by courts are often greater when the victim of a tortious accident is crippled than they are when he or she dies. Someone who is injured severely but has a relatively long life still ahead will require extraordinary compensation. The income that the victim can no longer enjoy must be replaced, and the fact that he or she may require constant, expensive medical attention every day must be taken into account in the assessment of damages.

By contrast, if the victim is killed, the family (or other dependents) will receive only what they would have received from the victim if he or she had been alive. Thus, if the decedent would have made $100,000 per year for the next 20 years and would have given his or her dependents two-thirds of that income each year, then the dependents are entitled to receive the two-thirds of $100,000 for 20 years, discounted to present value.

significant source of liability disparity. They cause much uncertainty and fear among corporate and government defendants. We will analyze punitive damages in the hope of understanding them better and seeing how to improve them.

Punitive damages are, by definition, damages given to the plaintiff as a way of punishing the defendant. We must begin our economic analysis of punitive damages by answering two questions:

1. Under what conditions might punitive damages be awarded?
2. How is the amount of punitive damages computed?

In most states there is a statute describing the conditions under which punitive damages may be awarded. These are usually attempts to state the common law practices actually followed by the courts. According to the usual formulation, punitive damages can be awarded when the defendant's behavior is malicious, oppressive, gross, willful and wanton, or fraudulent.[36] These statutes merely provide guidelines for awarding punitive damages. Because the guidelines have not been formulated into exact rules, there is much uncertainty about when punitive damages can be awarded. Studies in cognitive psychology demonstrate conclusively that people can order acts consistently according to how bad they are, but people cannot attach consistent numbers to the appropriate level of punishment.[37] Because moral orderings do not map consistently into dollar sanctions, the law must devise rules for computing dollar sanctions to avoid arbitrary disparity in the treatment of people.

There is much uncertainty concerning how to compute punitive damages under current laws. Statutes typically contain no specific instructions for computing punitive damages. Punitive damages are supposed to bear a reasonable relationship to compensatory damages and to the ability of the defendant to pay, but the courts have not specified what "reasonable" or "ability to pay" mean in this context. It is uncertain, for example, whether punitive damages may be only double the amount of compensatory damages or up to 1000 times compensatory damages. In several recent cases, described in Web Note 7.9, the United States Supreme Court held that punitive damages that are a double-digit multiple of compensatory damages will attract close scrutiny as possibly being unconstitutionally excessive. Judges apparently have an idea of how much is enough, and jury awards have often been reduced by judges, but there are no rules regarding the computation of punitive damages.[38] There is a compelling need in torts for a more coherent account of punitive damages, and economic analysis can provide guidelines for the development of this account.

---

[36] The following is the section on "Exemplary Damages" (which is another name for punitive damages) from the CALIFORNIA CIVIL CODE, §3294:

"For Oppression, Fraud or Malice.

(a) In an action for the breach of an obligation not arising from contract, where the defendant has been guilty of oppression, fraud, or malice, the plaintiff, in addition to the actual damages, may recover damages for the sake of the example and by way of punishing the defendant."

(b) That is not much detail to govern actions on which millions of dollars turn. Notice that nothing is said about how to compute punitive damages.

[37] Daniel Kahneman, Cass Sunstein, et al., *Assessing Punitive Damages,* 107 YALE L. J. 2071 (1998).

[38] See *State Farm Mutual Automobile Ins. Co. v. Campbell,* 123 S. Ct. 1513 (2003).

Organizations as Victims

Economists routinely impute utility functions to individual consumers and workers. But what if the victim seeking compensation is an organization, such as a partnership, a corporation, a government, or a club? Like individuals, organizations can be regarded as decision makers, and their choices can be regarded as revealing organizational preferences. Like those of an individual, the preferences of a rational organization can usually be represented by a well-ordered utility function. So the question arises, "Can the utility analysis of the idea of compensation be extended to organizations?"

In applied welfare economics, benefits or harms to institutions are traced to individuals, at least in principle. For example, the loss in profits suffered by a business is traced back to a loss in income to the business's owners. A common practice is to assume a one-to-one relationship between the loss in profits to the organization and the loss in income to individual owners, and to assume that the owners are interested in the business only for the sake of profits. Under these assumptions, the company's profits "stand in" for the utility of affected persons. Because the changes in profits to the business equal changes in income to its owners, compensating the organization is equivalent to compensating its owners.

In the case of business firms, the conventional assumption in economics is that they maximize profits. Thus, when a utility function is imputed to a business, it has a simple form: Profits are the only thing that the business cares about. For a business, the fall from a higher indifference curve to a lower indifference curve corresponds to a fall in profits that can be compensated for, when the fall results from another's wrongdoing, through an award of damages to the business equal to the lost profits.

In general, when there is a one-to-one relationship between the loss as measured by the institution's preferences and the losses to individuals, the institutional preferences can be used as a surrogate for the welfare of affected individuals. However, the extension of the utility analysis of compensation to organizations that are not profit-seeking, such as governments, clubs, and nonprofit corporations, is problematic because there is less agreement about the behavioral theories used in describing them. In the absence of an accepted behavioral theory, there cannot be agreement about how to trace the consequences of harm suffered by these organizations back to its effects on the welfare of individuals.

To begin the economic analysis of punitive damages, let us supply some numbers to the situation described in Example 3 of the preceding chapter.

FACTS: A manufacturer of a fuel additive for automobile engines is keeping a careful eye on costs. He can set quality control at a high or a low level. High-level quality control costs $9000 per year and guarantees that the fuel additive is pure and never causes damage to automobile engines. Low-level quality control is costless (thus saving $9000) but results in some batches of the fuel additive's being flawed. A few of the cars using the flawed batch will be harmed; specifically, the expected damage to cars is $10,000 per year ($1000 in expected damages to each of 10 cars).

From an economic viewpoint, efficiency requires the manufacturer to make the quality-control expenditures because the company can expect to save consumers $10,000 per year by spending $9000 per year on quality control.

Will making the manufacturer strictly liable for compensatory damages produce this result? The answer is "yes" if the tort liability system is perfect, but "no" if it is imperfect. Suppose that the tort liability system is perfect in the sense that disputes between the manufacturer and consumers can be resolved without cost and error, and damages are perfectly compensatory. With a perfect tort liability system and a rule of strict liability, every car owner harmed by the product will recover from the manufacturer without having to spend anything to resolve the dispute. The manufacturer thus faces $10,000 in expected liability if he does not take precautions costing $9000. A rational manufacturer maximizes profits net of expected tort liability, so our manufacturer will set quality control at the high level.

But suppose we make the more realistic assumption that the tort liability system works imperfectly. Specifically, let us suppose that for every two consumers whose cars suffer damage, only one actually brings suit and recovers. The other consumer does not sue because she does not know that the fuel additive caused the harm, or she knows and cannot prove it. Call the ratio of compensated victims to total victims, which is 1/2 in this example, the "enforcement error." Given an enforcement error of 1/2 and assuming the successful plaintiff only receives compensatory damages, the manufacturer's expected liability will be $5000 if he adopts the low level of quality control. He can, however, save $9000 by reducing his quality control from high to low. So, enforcement error in this example creates a situation in which a profit-maximizing manufacturer, whose expected liability is limited to compensatory damages, will choose low-level quality control, which is inefficient.

The efficiency loss due to enforcement error can be offset by augmenting compensatory damages with punitive damages. Suppose, as above, that the actual damages are $1000 per car but that the court doubles this compensatory amount so that total damages are $2000 per car. If we call the amount in excess of compensation "punitive damages," then the punitive damages are $1000 per car. We might also refer to the multiplicative factor by which we adjusted the compensatory damages in order to offset the enforcement error as the "punitive multiple." In our example, a punitive multiple of two exactly offsets the enforcement error of 1/2 and restores the manufacturer's liability to the level that would have prevailed under perfect enforcement.[39]

---

[39] Implicit in this argument is the assumption that the rate at which consumers successfully bring suit against the manufacturer does not change when punitive damages are added to compensatory damages. This is a strong and unrealistic assumption. When damage awards are high, victims and their attorneys have stronger incentives to bring action against those who have injured them. This then causes a second-round effect, in that, as the number of actions increases, the enforcement error falls, and therefore the punitive multiple should fall. It is an open question whether the existence of a punitive multiple can increase the number of actions just enough to correct for the inefficiency caused by enforcement error or whether it leads to overenforcement.

We can state this method of computing punitive damages more abstractly by using some notation. Without punitive damages, decision maker's liability L is limited to compensatory damages, A, which are imposed with enforcement error e in the event of an accident. Thus,

$$L = Ae.$$

To offset the error, impose the punitive multiple m, so that liability is given by the equation

$$L = Aem.$$

By mathematical definition, the "reciprocal" of any value x equals $1/x$. Set the punitive multiple equal to the reciprocal of the enforcement error: $m = 1/e$. Thus, the punitive multiple exactly offsets the enforcement error, and the decision maker's liability reduces to $L = A$.

The law might adopt as a rule that, when punitive damages are awarded, the punitive multiple should equal the inverse of the enforcement error. If such a rule were written into the law, either by statute or by judges, juries would have some guidance in setting the punitive multiple. For example, if there were proof that an injurer had failed to take the appropriate amount of care, because she suspected that only a fraction of those injured would bring an action against her, the court could impose punitive damages in an amount determined by application of a punitive multiple equal to the inverse of the enforcement error.[40]

Web Note 7.8

In addition to the Kahneman, Sunstein, et al. piece cited in footnote 36 on page 258, there has been much additional interesting literature on the economics of punitive damages, including an important article by Polinsky and Shavell. We review that literature on our website.

Web Note 7.9

The United States Supreme Court has handed down several important recent decisions on the constitutionality of punitive damages. We describe these holdings and relate them to the material of this section on our website.

III. An Empirical Assessment of the U.S. Tort Liability System

How well does the tort liability system achieve its economic goal of minimizing the social costs of accidents? Many people—including some legislators and other leading decision makers—believe that the U.S. tort liability system is chaotic, unfair, and inefficient.

---

[40] A recent opinion by the United States Supreme Court—*Philip Morris v. Williams* (2007)—seems to suggest that the instrumental use of punitive damages that we suggest in this section may be unconstitutional. See Web Note 7.9.

Their evidence is largely anecdotal, not systematic, but those anecdotes are striking. For example, many people are aware that in the mid-1990s a woman who was scalded when she spilled coffee from a drive-through window at McDonald's recovered $640,000 in compensatory damages and $2.9 million in punitive damages for her injuries.[41] And many municipalities are said to have removed play structures and swing sets from their public parks and diving boards from the public swimming pools because of the fear of liability. Congress and many state legislatures consider numerous tort reform bills each year, all motivated by a desire to reduce high liability insurance costs (triggered, it is said, by adverse liability judgments).

Anecdotes should not be the basis for assessing something as complex as the U.S. tort liability system. Such an assessment requires quantitative empirical evidence, which is quickly improving but still remains at an early stage of development. We will review the evidence and show that the U.S. tort liability system performs better than its harshest critics claim. We begin with some descriptive number and then briefly consider the empirical literature on products liability, medical malpractice, and mass torts.[42]

A. Some General Facts About the U.S. Tort Liability System

Over the past 150 years the most numerous controversies in federal and state courts arose under contract law. However, some time in the mid-1990s tort cases became the most common form of adjudicated controversy.[43]

In the United States, tort law, like contract and property law, is largely state law. And as we have indicated at several points in the text, there are some significant differences among the states in these substantive areas of law. In one of the most recent assessments of the civil justice system, there were, in 1994, slightly more than 41,000 tort cases resolved in federal district courts (some of which were in federal court on the ground of diversity but were resolved by the federal court by the application of state law). During the same time period there were more than 378,000 tort cases resolved by state courts in the largest 75 counties in the United States.

Of these state and federal tort cases, 94 percent involve an individual plaintiff. This is in clear contrast to contract cases, where a significant fraction involve multiple plaintiffs.

Slightly more than 60 percent of the tort cases in the 75 largest counties in the United States deal with accidents involving automobiles. The next most common type of tort dispute (accounting in 1992 for just over 17 percent of all tort cases) is

---

[41] See *Libeck v. McDonald's Restaurants, P.T.S., Inc.*, No. D-202 CV-93-02419, 1995 WL 360309 (Bernalillo County, N.M. Dist. Ct. Aug. 18, 1994).

[42] We have relied on Daniel Kessler & Daniel Rubinfeld, *Empirical Study of the Civil Justice System*, in A. MITCHELL POLINSKY & STEVEN SHAVELL, EDS., HANDBOOK OF LAW AND ECONOMICS, v. 1 (2007). Also see our website for some additional material on the empirical assessment of the tort liability system.

[43] See our discussion of other trends in litigation in the last part of Chapter 11.

that arising from "premises liability" for, say, slips and falls or other injuries at residences, governmental offices, or commercial establishments. The third most common form of tort case is medical malpractice, accounting for just under 5 percent of all torts. And the fourth is products liability, accounting for 3.4 percent of the total.[44]

Critics of the tort liability system in the United States contend that juries award punitive damages too often and too liberally and that judges do little to restrain these punitive awards. However, punitive damages are extremely rare. In all product-liability cases between 1965 and 1990 there were only 353 punitive awards, and those averaged $625,000 (in 1990 dollars). Appellate panels reduced many of these punitive awards so that, after appeal, the average fell to $135,000. More than 25 percent of those 353 awards involved asbestos. Over the entire period there was an average of 11 punitive-damages awards per year in product-liability cases in all state and federal courts. A careful study of punitive damages in product-liability cases found that at the trial level the ratio of punitive to compensatory damages was 1.2 to 1; in more than one-third of the cases in which punitives were awarded, compensatory damages were larger than the punitives.[45] More than half the states prohibit or cap punitive damages or raise the evidence standard that must be met before they can be awarded.[46] Recall that the usual standard in civil actions is "preponderance of the evidence," which is generally taken to mean 51 percent believability. The "clear and convincing" evidence standard is more demanding, but not as demanding as the criminal law's standard of "beyond a reasonable doubt."

The theme of much of the empirical literature is that the tort liability system (perhaps in conjunction with the administrative agency regulatory system) works reasonably well at deterring accidents. In most situations in which accidents might happen, the recent trend in the United States has been toward fewer and less severe accidents. For instance, the number of motor vehicle deaths and injuries peaked around 1970 and has declined ever since. The death and injury *rate* per capita has shown a dramatic drop.

Web Note 7.10

A central issue for the economic analysis of tort law is the extent to which exposure to tort liability induces parties to behave in an efficient manner. In the last few years there has been an outpouring of scholarship designed to explore this matter with careful empirical studies. We review this literature on our website.

---

[44] We will see in Chapter 11 that there is evidence to suggest that the total number of trials of all kinds has been declining in the United States. We will also consider some additional facts about litigation, such as the success rate of plaintiffs in different kinds of actions. To the extent that there is specific information about success in torts cases, we will describe it in the next two sections of this chapter.

[45] Michael Rustad, *Demystifying Punitive Damages in Products Liability Cases: A Survey of a Quarter Century of Verdicts,* The Roscoe Pound Foundation (1991).

[46] Twelve states require a "clear and convincing" evidence standard for punitive damages but do not limit the amount. Another twelve states cap the amount of damages and require the "clear and convincing evidence" standard. Seven states require a portion of the punitive award to be paid to the state. Four states prohibit punitive-damages awards.

B. Medical Malpractice

Even though disputes about iatrogenic injuries (those arising in the course of health care delivery) are a relatively minor portion of all tort cases (accounting for about 5 percent of the total), there has been a great deal of concern about medical malpractice litigation. And with some justification. The Institute of Medicine reported in 2000 that medical errors are the "leading cause of accidental death in the United States."[47] Exact figures are hard to pin down, but estimates made in 1997 range from 44,000 to almost 100,000 deaths per year. "Medication errors alone account for approximately 7000 deaths per year, exceeding the number of deaths due to workplace injuries."[48] A comprehensive study of hospital admissions in New York State during 1 year in the 1980s found that 1 percent of admissions involved serious injury due to negligent care.[49]

The most careful studies of medical malpractice litigation indicate that the "number of malpractice claims per physician and the award paid per claim increased rapidly in the United States from the 1960s to the 1980s. Claim frequency increased at more than 10 percent per year, reaching a peak of 17 claims per 100 physicians in 1980s. Awards paid per claim increased at roughly twice the rate of inflation."[50] There is some evidence to suggest that in at least some jurisdictions the rate of increase of both claims against physicians and award levels ceased or slowed significantly in the 1990s and remained at those lower levels through the early 2000s, perhaps as a result of statutory reform, which we will discuss at the end of this section.

The tort liability system should provide an incentive for physicians and other health care professionals to take precautions against injuries. Are the incentives currently provided by the system deficient, efficient, or excessive? With current evidence, we can only speculate. Physicians have monetary incentives to be careful when they bear the cost of the accidents that they cause. Liability insurance transfers the cost of accidents caused by physicians to the insurer. The insurance rates paid by individual physicians respond only weakly to the history of tort claims against them, so physicians may bear only a fraction of the costs of patient injury.[51] Furthermore, a study of New York State hospital patients by Weiler found that only about 10 percent of those who were injured—even seriously—filed a complaint against their health care provider. These facts suggest that monetary incentives for care by physicians are deficient.

Evidence about "defensive medicine" can be interpreted as implying the opposite conclusion. This phrase refers to procedures and treatments motivated by reducing liability

---

[47] Janet Corrigan, Linda T. Kohn, & Molla S. Davidson, To Err is Human: Building a Safer Health System (2000).

[48] See Daniel Kessler in the Winter 2000 edition of the *NBER Reporter*, available at http://www.nber.org/reporter/winter00/kessler.html.

[49] See Paul C. Weiler, Howard Hiatt, Joseph P. Newhouse, William G. Johnson, Troyen A. Brennan, & Lucian L. Leape, A Measure of Malpractice: Medical Injury, Malpractice Litigation, and Patient Compensation (1993).

[50] Patricia Danzon, *Liability for Medical Malpractice*, in A. J. Culyer & Joseph P. Newhouse, Eds., Handbook of Health Economics, v. 1B (2000).

[51] See Frank Sloan, *Experience Rating: Does It Make Sense for Medical Malpractice Insurance?*, 80 Am. Econ. Rev. 128 (1990).

more than by medical needs. Thus, doctors and hospitals take too much care in the hope of forestalling injury or demonstrating in later litigation that they did "everything possible" to prevent harm. Patients have little reason to resist unnecessary procedures that do no harm so long as insurance companies pay the bill. In 2005, U.S. health care spending was 16 percent of gross domestic product, or $6697 per person.[52] Plausible estimates suggest that defensive medicine accounts for, at most, 5 percent of total health care costs. If these figures are right order of magnitude, then defensive medicine costs each American around $300 per year.

Societal concerns about the cost and availability of health care and the possible link between medical malpractice and those concerns have motivated many states to reform their medical malpractice systems.[53] Those reforms have taken two particular forms—limitations on the total amount and kind of damages available in medical malpractice actions and abrogation of the collateral source rule in medical malpractice.

These reforms may sometimes have perverse results. In the mid-1980s, Indiana capped medical-malpractice awards at a maximum of $500,000 for all damages and instituted a professionally administered patient-compensation fund to decide all losses above $100,000. The unexpected result was that malpractice awards in Indiana became one-third higher than those in Michigan and Ohio, which had kept the traditional method of compensation. Perhaps the reason for the Indiana result was that the professional administrators were better able than lay jurors to calculate damages and, therefore, came closer to the "true," higher losses of the victims.

The intended effect of the limitation on damages for medical malpractice is, we hope, obvious. Some states limited the total amount that could be recovered in any tort action, while others capped noneconomic damages, such as those on pain and suffering. Some state supreme courts, such as that in Illinois, have struck down those limitations. But most caps have survived litigation and attempts at legislative reform.[54]

---

[52] Aaron Catlin, Cathy Cowan, Stephen Heffler, & Benjamin Washington (the National Health Expenditure Accounts Team), *National Health Spending in 2005: The Slowdown Continues*, 26 HEALTH AFFAIRS, 142 (2007).

[53] Health care costs in the United States in 2009 account for almost 18 percent of the $13 trillion Gross Domestic Product, and in late 2009 there were approximately 47 million uninsured people (of a total population slightly greater than 310 million), two-thirds of whom are low income.

[54] At least one state, Florida, sought to reduce malpractice litigation by abrogating the American rule in favor of the English rule for attorney's fees in some malpractice actions. (The American rule, which we will discuss in Chapter 11, calls for each party to pay its own attorney's fees. The English rule calls for the losing party to pay not only for its attorney but also for the winning party's attorney.) The thought was that there would be less incentive to bring a speculative cause of action under the English rule. Florida abandoned the experiment after only five years, 1980–1985. See James W. Hughes & Edward A. Snyder, *Litigation and Settlement under the English and American Rules: Theory and Evidence,* 38 J. LAW & ECON. 225 (1995) (which found that plaintiff success rates, average jury awards, and the size of out-of-court settlements all increased under the English rule, perhaps because the average quality of those claims brought forward increased under the English rule), and A. Mitchell Polinsky & Daniel Rubinfeld, *Does the English Rule Discourage Low-Probability-of-Prevailing Plaintiffs?*, 32 J. LEGAL STUD. 517 (1998) (which argues that, taking the settlement process into account, the English rule encourages *more* litigation by low-probability-of-prevailing plaintiffs).

In an earlier discussion of insurance, we explained that an accident victim's compensation from an insurance company does not reduce the tort damages owed by the injurer. Suppose that the plaintiff seeks $100,000 in damages from the defendant-injurer and has already been paid $80,000 from her insurer for her injuries. According to the legal principle called the "collateral source rule," the plaintiff does not have to reduce the amount she seeks from the defendant—to, say, $20,000—by deducting the collateral benefits. Some states changed this rule, mandating deduction of collateral benefits for injuries received in the course of health care delivery. The thought was that the collateral source rule created an incentive for plaintiffs to litigate on the theory that they could recover more than their actual losses. So, removing the rule would, all other things equal, reduce the incentive to bring medical malpractice complaints.

Both types of reform seek to reduce health care costs by reducing medical malpractice awards. Were the reforms responsible for the slowdown in the number of malpractice actions in the 1990s and early 2000s and the cessation in the rate of increase of the average malpractice award? Or were there other factors—such as an increase in the technology of treatment and levels of precaution—that explain these effects? The evidence is still not clear. There is some evidence to suggest that reforms in the 1980s reduced defensive medicine expenditures by 5 to 9 percent and that the supply of physicians was about 12 percent greater in those states with caps on noneconomic damages, by comparison to the supply in states without those caps.[55] But other evidence suggests that the medical malpractice problems observable in the United States are not specific to the structure of the U.S. civil justice system but are happening worldwide, perhaps because the great advances in medical technology have made a much wider range—a perhaps a *riskier* range—of medical interventions possible.

Web Note 7.11

Some prominent legal scholars have been using a remarkable data set from the State of Texas to explore many issues in medical malpractice. We summarize their work on our website.

Web Note 7.12

Product liability might be triggered by a design defect, a manufacturing defect, or a failure to warn consumers (and intermediaries) of risk of harm. On our website we discuss some economics of the duty to warn and some recent empirical evidence on the effectiveness of that duty.

---

[55] See Kessler & Rubinfeld, supra n. 42, for citations.

C. Reforming Products Liability

Products liability law is the focus of much of the public dissatisfaction with the entire tort liability system. A survey of chief executive officers by the Conference Board (a business interest group) found that liability concerns caused 47 percent of those surveyed to drop one or more product lines, 25 percent to stop some research and development, and 39 percent to cancel plans for a new product. In some instances, insurers have decided that the products liability area is so uncertain that they have withdrawn from the market entirely. Some of the manufacturers and others who have been left without insurance coverage have decided to stop making their products, or they have raised prices to cover the cost of additional risks of liability. Since the early 1980s in the United States there has been a powerful political interest in reforming products-liability law both at the federal and state level. But until very recently no reform occurred.

Manufacturers have long argued for reform at the federal level for two reasons. First, they contend that a uniform federal products-liability law would save costs, with consequent savings to consumers. Second, many manufacturers believe that the products-liability law that has become the norm in the states is seriously flawed. Specifically, they believe that plaintiffs win too easily, and that juries are overly generous to successful plaintiffs (as evidenced, they believe, by the example of the award against McDonald's for a hot coffee spill). The argument that the manufacturers make is that these inefficiencies could be corrected by Congress enacting a sensible uniform federal products-liability law. Although reform measures have been introduced in Congress for many years, they have never been passed by both houses.

At the state level, there was a spate of reforms in the mid-1980s and a second round in the mid-1990s. The reform movement has not revived in the early 2000s. State reform has typically been limited to putting a cap or upper limit on the amount and kind of damages that victims can recover. Sometimes the states place this cap only on what is perceived to be the offending element in damage awards, such as pain-and-suffering or punitive damages. For example, Illinois' 1995 Civil Justice Reform Act put a cap on noneconomic damages of $500,000 and limited punitive damages to three times compensatory damages.[56]

We should note, in light of the material at the beginning of this chapter, that federal regulatory agencies do a significant job of promoting product safety. For example, the Consumer Product Safety Commission, the National Highway Transportation Safety Administration, the Occupational Health and Safety Administration, the Federal Aviation Administration, the Food and Drug Administration, and the Environmental Protection Agency issue and enforce product safety regulations for a wide variety of products.[57] An important issue is whether this joint system of *ex ante* safety regulation and *ex post* liability exposure achieves the socially optimal amount of care. Or does it do too little or too much?

As was the case with medical malpractice, the effects are unclear. The empirical literature on the effects of products liability, regulations, and the reforms instituted in

---

[56] The Illinois Supreme Court found this act to be unconstitutional in 1997.

[57] See CONGRESSIONAL BUDGET OFFICE, THE ECONOMICS OF U.S. TORT LIABILITY: A PRIMER (2003), available at http://www.cbo.gov/showdoc.cfm?index=4641&sequence=0. Recall, too, that in Web Note 7.2 we described the story of liability for harms arising from cigarette use.

the 1980s and 1990s is still young and has not yet reached a consensus. There is some evidence to suggest that the reforms eased the liability pressure on manufacturers, and thereby caused liability insurance premiums to stop their long pattern of increase. And there is some evidence that accidental injuries and deaths have declined in the early 2000s, although how much of that decline is due to law is not clear.

> **QUESTION 7.11:** Analyze caps and limitations on litigation awards using the analysis of rent control in Chapter 2.

> **QUESTION 7.12:** Use the graphical analysis of liability of the previous chapter to show the effect on the precautionary decisions of a potential injurer when the amount of compensatory damages that a victim may receive is capped.

> **QUESTION 7.13:** Suppose that any punitive damages awarded to the plaintiff were to be paid, not to the plaintiff, but rather to, say, a charity designated by the plaintiff. How might plaintiffs' incentives to seek punitive damages be affected by such a scheme? How might the jury's disposition to award punitive damages be affected?

Notwithstanding specific problems, there are other indications that the system is working reasonably well. Products-liability actions in the United States increased in the mid and late 1980s, but the vast majority of those cases involved asbestos. If we exclude asbestos claims, the number of products-liability cases in the federal courts between 1985 and 1991 *decreased* by 40 percent and has remained at that low level through the early 2000s. Another interesting recent change regards plaintiff success rates. Between 1981 and 1987 the defendant won 51 percent of the verdicts in products-liability cases. Between 1988 and 1994 defendants won 64 percent of the cases. The best recent figures for the early 2000s suggest a retreat to a roughly 50 percent success rate for defendants. Finally, products-liability insurance costs amount to one-quarter of one cent for each dollar of product purchase price—an insignificantly small amount.[58]

Web Note 7.13

In a recent article in the *Harvard Law Review*, Professors Polinsky and Shavell discuss the "Uneasy Case for Product Liability." We discuss that article and several comments on it in this web note.

D. Mass Torts

A "mass tort" is not a formal legal term but rather a term used to describe a situation in which a large number of tort claims arise from a single incident or use of the same product.[59] An example might be the Bhopal disaster in 1984 in India in which a

---

[58] See James A. Henderson & Theodore Eisenberg, *The Quiet Revolution in Products Liability: An Empirical Study of Legal Change,* 37 UCLA L. REV. 479 (1990). The figures cited in this study are for actions filed in federal courts. Most tort actions are filed in state courts, but the authors feel that the federal statistics also reflect trends in state courts.

[59] Mass torts are related to but distinct from class actions, which may be an administratively tractable method of dealing with mass torts. We will discuss the economics of class actions in Chapter 11.

cloud of a highly toxic chemical escaped from a Union Carbide plant and killed between 15,000 and 20,000 people and injured thousands more. Dealing with an incident of this sort may overwhelm the normal institutions and practices of the tort liability system. As a result, the law has increasingly tried to deal with the problems of mass torts through novel arrangements.

Consider the problems arising from asbestos. Asbestos has remarkable fire-retardant properties, which made it a valuable construction material. It was used extensively in the United States from the 1930s through 1979, when use virtually ceased. The cessation occurred because it became increasingly obvious that asbestos could be extremely dangerous to one's health, including killing some of those who inhaled asbestos fibers. Inhaling asbestos causes cancer, but the gap in time between exposure to asbestos and the appearance of cancer can be 20 years. During the 50 years of asbestos use and the decade or so during which removal of asbestos was a common practice (before being suspended as causing more harm than good), more than 25 million U.S. workers were exposed to ambient asbestos fibers and could, therefore, contract a debilitating disease or die. It is estimated that more than 225,000 premature deaths occurred between 1985 and 2000 because of exposure to asbestos fibers. And estimates are that an additional 10,000 people will die each year for the next decade or more because of exposure to asbestos. Much larger numbers of people have been injured but not killed by exposure to the fiber.

Naturally, when these health risks became widely known, a large number of claimants stepped forward to seek compensation from the asbestos manufacturers and others. Indeed, 600,000 claimants had come forward by the year 2000 to proceed against 6000 defendants representing 75 out of 83 possible industries (suggesting that this problem touches almost every branch of the U.S. economy). Several important firms have filed for bankruptcy because of earlier or reasonably anticipated adverse judgments involving asbestos.

A large number—perhaps a majority of claimants—may never develop an asbestos-related disease. Liability law does not compensate for *exposure* to risk, as opposed to the *realization* of a risk. A person exposed to asbestos must wait until she actually develops an asbestos-related disease before suing. However, the victims who develop such a disease must assert their claims without delay. Every jurisdiction in the United States has a statute of limitations that requires all those who seek compensation to come forward within a relatively short time to assert their claim against others.[60] Failing to do so may cause the victim's cause of action to lapse. In light of these statutes, claimants who think that they may develop an asbestos-related disease come forward as soon as they can. They sue when X-rays are consistent with the early stages of disease, even though disease may not develop fully. This uncertainty makes the claimants extremely uneasy but also creates an incentive for the defendants to contest liability (and to delay settlement as long as possible in the hope that asbestos-related diseases will never become manifest).

---

[60] Every legal system has a similar set of rules for encouraging those with legal claims to come forward. The period during which a victim must assert her claim or lose it is called a "prescriptive period" in the civil law systems. The law also uses the phrases "statute of repose" and *laches* to describe situations similar to those covered by a statute of limitation.

Dealing with this litigation has been extremely expensive. One estimate suggests that more than $50 billion has been spent on asbestos litigation. More than half of that amount has, it is alleged, gone to pay for transaction costs, rather than redounding to the benefit of victims. There are plausible estimates that total litigation costs have reached more than $250 billion, with almost all asbestos cases resolved, as of late 2009.

To deal with mass torts, the courts and legislatures have been willing to entertain novel practices. One reason for these novelties is a fear that relying upon standard tools of tort liability might lead to injustices. The slow development of asbestos-related diseases creates a conflict between the timeliness of claims required by statutes of limitation and the need to get compensation to deserving plaintiffs. To address this and other perceived problems with resolving the large number of asbestos claims through private litigation, Congress has proposed (in "The Fairness in Asbestos Injury Resolution Act" (2005)) for several years (but not enacted, as of July, 2010) the creation of a trust fund to provide limited compensation to victims of asbestos-related diseases and to limit liability of defendants.

Consider one more example—problems of proving causation arising in a mass tort having to do with the drug DES (diethylstilbestrol). DES was administered to pregnant women in the 1950s to prevent miscarriages. However, the drug caused genital diseases, including cervical cancer, in some of the adult women whose mothers had taken DES 20 or more years ago. By the time the connection between the adult diseases and the DES was discovered, it was all but impossible for the plaintiffs to produce evidence about which manufacturer had produced the DES taken by their mothers 20 years or more before. Standard theories of causation in tort required the plaintiff to demonstrate by a preponderance of the evidence that the defendant was responsible for the plaintiff's harm. In these instances, plaintiffs had been harmed by one of the manufacturers of DES, but they could not demonstrate which one or ones. Rather than allow the plaintiffs to leave the court empty-handed, the California Supreme Court fashioned a novel theory of liability—"market share liability"—according to which all the manufacturers who might have been selling DES to the plaintiff's mother would share liability for the plaintiff's damages in proportion to their market shares in the market for DES at the time of the mother's having taken the drug.[61]

 Web Note 7.14

The tragic events of September 11, 2001 gave rise to mass torts. See our website for a discussion of the methods by which the federal government put together an administered compensation package for those who lost relatives and others in the tragedy.

QUESTION 7.14: Explain how a potential victim's waiving a future claim (that is, an employee's agreeing not to seek compensation from his employer if he is injured on the job) is like a transaction in a UTC (which we explain in the box on pp. 272–73).

---

[61] See *Sindell v. Abbott Laboratories,* 26 Cal. 3d 588, 607 P.2d 924, 163 Cal. Rptr. 132, *cert. denied,* 101 S. Ct. 285 (1980).

Vaccines and Products Liability

Many recent products-liability cases involve the duty of pharmaceutical manufacturers and doctors to warn those taking drugs of the potential risks involved.

One such case involved two polio vaccines. The first vaccine against this crippling disease was the Salk vaccine or IPV, which is a so-called killed-virus vaccine. The killed-virus vaccine prevents polio in the person who receives it without presenting the risk that the recipient will contract polio. The second vaccine was the Sabin vaccine or OPV, a "live-virus" vaccine. The recipient retains the live virus in his or her system and can pass it to others, who are themselves immunized against polio. This external benefit is so considerable that public-health authorities strongly recommended that young children take the Sabin vaccine instead of the older Salk vaccine. When only the Salk vaccine was available, there were 2500 cases of polio a year. After the development of the live-virus vaccine, polio virtually disappeared.

However, the live-virus presents a risk.[62] Approximately one of every 4 million people who take the vaccine or come in close contact with those who have taken OPV contracts polio.

The law should require vaccine manufacturers to warn recipients of the risk from the live-virus vaccine. That is precisely what the U.S. Court of Appeals for the Fifth Circuit held in *Reyes v. Wyeth Laboratories,* 498 F.2d 1264 (1974). After *Reyes,* it became standard practice for vaccine manufacturers to include package inserts warning of the risks of the OPV vaccine.

However, that resolution was only temporary. The more general trend toward absolute or enterprise liability for product-related harms has been felt in this market, too. In many recent cases, children, whose parents had been warned in accordance with *Reyes* but who, nonetheless, took the live-virus vaccine and developed polio, sued the manufacturers and received large awards. Without the defense of assumption of the risk after an adequate warning, the manufacturer cannot avoid liability. Therefore, the company must build this higher expected-liability cost into the costs of production.

Pharmaceutical manufacturers are so fearful of products-liability awards that they have become reluctant to manufacture and distribute beneficial drugs. In 1976, after an outbreak of swine flu, a dangerous illness, manufacturers of a swine flu vaccine refused to market it because private insurers, fearful of the product-liability consequences of 100 million or more injections, would not issue liability insurance. The companies offered the inoculations only after the federal government agreed to be the exclusive defendant in any actions for harms arising from the vaccine.[63] The DPT vaccine against whooping cough is in short supply in this country because the largest manufacturer, Eli Lilly & Company, has stopped producing the drug due to its fear of adverse products-liability judgments. Currently the following vaccines that were once manufactured by a number of firms in the United States are now produced by a single firm: measles, mumps, Sabin polio, Salk polio, and rabies. Worse still, the threat of product-liability suits may reduce the incentive of pharmaceutical companies to invest in research and development of potentially beneficial new drugs.

---

[62] See Edmund Kitch, *Vaccines and Product Liability: A Case of Contagious Litigation,* REGULATION (May/June 1985).

[63] The vaccine's manufacturers proved particularly astute in this matter. The vaccine seems to have caused a potentially paralyzing or fatal disease called Guillain-Barré syndrome in a small fraction of those who were inoculated. Numerous plaintiffs brought actions against the federal government, as the sole defendant, on a theory of inadequate warning. The federal government relatively quickly stopped the program of inoculation for swine flu.

Contractual Solutions to the Tort Liability Crisis[64]

A victim's right to compensation for accidental harm is a form of insurance. Victims buy these rights from insurance companies by contract and the tort system gives these rights to potential victims by law. The tort system, however, gives people far more rights to compensation than they buy from insurers. Critics of the tort liability system complain that it gives people insurance that they do not buy when they have to pay for it themselves. Thus, parents seldom insure their children's lives, and few people buy insurance against emotional distress or pain and suffering.

It is easy to see why people do not buy insurance for some kinds of harm that tort law compensates. Insurance transfers money from the uninjured state (the premiums paid by the customers for insurance policies) to the injured state (the claims made by the injured policy-holders). For some tort claims, the cost of the transfer is very high. Thus, claims for nonpecuniary damages are very costly to assess and administer, and negligence is costly to prove in, say, medical malpractice cases. For other tort claims, the transfer is inappropriate because money is *not* more useful in the injured state than in the uninjured state. Thus, the death of a dependent child reduces the parents' need for money.

In principle, allowing potential victims to sell unwanted tort rights can solve the problem of unwanted insurance caused by tort liability. Here is how sales would work. A potential victim's right to damages in the event of a future accident is an "unmatured tort claim" (UTC). Imagine a market for UTCs. Potential tort victims could sell their right to recover and could include in the sale whichever of their tort rights they chose to sell and retain others for their own use. For example, a victim might sell the right to recover her nonpecuniary losses in an automobile accident but retain her right to recover her major pecuniary losses. Or she might sell the right to recover in the event of medical malpractice but keep the right to recover in the event of a product-related injury. If someone had sold her tort claims to a third party and was later injured, she could not recover from the injurer; she could, however, recover from an insurance company if she had bought insurance.

A market for UTCs could be extremely flexible. Consider, for example, how a regime of no-fault automobile insurance could result from a market in UTCs. Suppose that drivers sell some of their rights to recover for tortious injuries in automobile accidents to their own insurance companies. Their own insurers might then waive these rights in exchange for payment from the insurance companies of other drivers.

If it were legal to sell and buy UTCs, potential victims would probably substitute first-party insurance for the current method of compensation through the tort liability system. This first-party insurance would probably be a cheaper means of compensating victims than is the tort liability system. But what about the deterrence function of tort law? How will the creation of a market for UTCs induce potential victims and injurers to take care? Interestingly, there might be no significant difference in deterrence from the current system, and there might be an improvement. There will, after all, be someone proceeding against the injurer for recovery in the event of an accident; it just might not be the victim. Indeed, the deterrence effect under UTCs may be better than under the current system: Third parties who have purchased UTCs may have a strong incentive to monitor the behavior of potential victims and injurers for optimal precaution.

---

[64] The material in this box is based on Robert D. Cooter, *Towards a Market in Unmatured Tort Claims*, 75 VA. L. REV. 383 (1989). See also PAUL RUBIN, TORT REFORM BY CONTRACT (1993).

Current American law prohibits victims from selling tort claims to lawyers. Thus, the plaintiff cannot contract with her lawyer to receive a fixed fee before the trial in exchange for giving the lawyer all, or almost all, of the damages eventually awarded by the court. Current law, however, does not prohibit nonlawyers from buying some matured tort claims, and a small market has already developed on the Internet.

QUESTION 7.15: Imagine a system of contractual or elective no-fault with respect to product-related injuries. Manufacturers would offer with their products schedules of benefits that they would pay if consumers should be injured while using the products. In the event of an injury, there would be no inquiry into the product's defect or the user's fault; benefits would simply be paid to the injured consumer according to the contractual schedule. Pain and suffering would not be compensable; collateral benefits would be deducted; and a few other restrictions would apply. Those manufacturers who chose not to offer elective no-fault would still be strictly liable for product-related injuries under the current system. Explore the efficiency of this elective no-fault system. (See J. O'CONNELL, ENDING INSULT TO INJURY (1975).)

Workers' Compensation

The most prominent form of no-fault liability in the United States is the system for dealing with employee accidents that occur on the job, which are common. In any given year approximately 3 percent of all industrial workers will be injured while on the job sufficiently to result in lost work time. This risk of on-the-job accidents is slightly higher than the risk of accidents off the job—for example, in the home.

Through the late nineteenth century, the common law of job-related accidents made it extremely difficult for plaintiff-employees who had been injured on the job to recover from their employers or from anyone else.[65] Early in the twentieth century, most industrialized countries, including the United States, adopted an alternative to tort liability for dealing with on-the-job accidents—namely, a system of compulsory compensation of injured employees without regard to fault. Today all but three states in the United States have a compulsory system for nearly all workers, and more than 90 percent of the United States labor force is covered by workers' compensation systems. The systems typically work in the following way. Employers contribute sums to the state workers' compensation system based on the dollar amount of their payroll. When an employee is injured, he

(Continued)

---

[65] There were three defenses available to the employer: (1) common employment (also known as the "fellow servant rule"), under which the employer could escape liability by claiming that the proximate cause of the plaintiff's harm was the negligence of another employee; (2) assumption of the risk, under which the employer could argue that the employee willingly assumed the risk of a job-related injury (on the economics of job-related risks, see KIP VISCUSI, RISK BY CHOICE (1983); and (3) contributory negligence, under which the employer could escape liability by showing that the employee's own negligence had contributed to the harm.

files a claim with the state governmental agency that administers the system. If the agency determines that the harm is job related, then it awards the employee compensation according to a statutory schedule of benefits. For example, the compensation for a lost finger may be $5000. For other injuries, the benefits may be determined in a relatively brief evidentiary hearing. For example, the victim may be awarded two-thirds of the lost wages and full compensation of medical and rehabilitation expenses. In the event of a dispute between the employee and the workers' compensation commission, a process of appeal and adjudication is available.

In the workers' compensation system, workers relinquished their right to sue their employers in tort law for on-the-job injuries and, in exchange, employers assumed strict liability for injuries suffered on the job. Is this an improvement? Almost all states in the United States compel employers to participate in the workers' compensation system, but Texas allows employers to opt out. Texas generates some data to compare a workers' compensation system and a system of tort liability. When large Texas firms opt out, they create their own system for compensating injured workers. If injured workers do not want to accept compensation offered under the employer's plan, then they must sue the employer in tort law and prove that the employer's negligence caused the injury.

Morantz investigated the claims for on-the-job injuries by employees of two large companies. These two companies opt out of workers' compensation for the retail outlets inside Texas, and they must remain inside this system for their retail outlets outside Texas. Morantz found a lower frequency of indemnity claims in Texas than outside of it, and she also found lower average per-claim costs. While she demonstrated cost savings to employers, the welfare effects on workers remains to be determined by future research.[66]

Conclusion

The tort liability system plays a significant role in reducing the frequency with which we accidentally lose our property, health, and lives. By allocating the cost of accidents, the tort liability system provides incentives for precaution, much as markets allocate costs and provide incentives for production. Improving the efficiency of the tort liability system can make the world safer at no more cost. Observers note various signs of inefficiency in tort liability law, such as significant differences in the level of compensatory damages for the same injury in different countries of similar wealth, unpredictable decisions about liability and damages from one case to another ("liability disparity"), defensive medicine, and vaccine shortages. Moving beyond anecdotes requires careful statistical studies that remain in short supply. The statistical knowledge that we do possess at this time, which we reviewed, is enough to debunk some myths about the tort liability system.

---

[66] For a report on work in progress, see Alison Morantz, *Rethinking the Great Compromise: What Happens When Large Companies Opt Out of Workers Compensation?*, Berkeley Law and Economics Workshop, 14 April 2008.

Suggested Readings

BAKER, TOM, THE MEDICAL MALPRACTICE MYTH (2005).

Bar-Gill, Oren, & Omri Ben-Shahar, *The Uneasy Care for Comparative Negligence,* 5 AM. LAW & ECON. REV. 433 (2003).

Black, Bernard, Charles Silver, David A. Hyman, & William M. Sage, *Stability, Not Crisis: Medical Malpractice Claim Outcomes in Texas, 1988-2002,* 2 J. EMP. LEGAL. STUD. 207 (2005).

DEWEES, DONALD, DONALD DUFF, & MICHAEL J. TREBILCOCK, EXPLORING THE DOMAIN OF ACCIDENT LAW (1996).

GAWANDE, ATUL, COMPLICATIONS: A SURGEON'S NOTES ON AN IMPERFECT SCIENCE (2002).

Hyman, David A., *Medical Malpractice: What Do We Know and What (If Anything) Should We Do About It?,* 80 TEX. L. REV. 1639 (2002).

PORAT, ARIEL, & ALEX STEIN, TORT LAW UNDER UNCERTAINTY (2002).

Schwartz, Gary T., *The Beginning and the Possible End of the Rise of Modern American Tort Law,* 26 GA. L. REV. 601 (1992).

Shavell, Steven, *Liability for Accidents*, in A. MITCHELL POLINSKY & STEVEN SHAVELL, EDS., HANDBOOK OF LAW AND ECONOMICS, v. 1 (2007).

SUNSTEIN, CASS R., REID HASTIE, JOHN W. PAYNE, DAVID A. SCHKADE, & W. KIP VISCUSI, PUNITIVE DAMAGES: HOW JURIES DECIDE (2002).

8

An Economic Theory of Contract Law

[T]he movement of the progressive societies has hitherto been a movement from Status to Contract.

HENRY MAINE,
ANCIENT LAW 170 (1861)

Whoever offers to another a bargain of any kind, proposes to do this: Give me that which I want, and you shall have this which you want, is the meaning of every such offer; and it is in this manner that we obtain from one another the far greater part of those good offices which we stand in need of. It is not from the benevolence of the butcher, the brewer, or the baker, that we expect our dinner, but from their regard to their own interest.

ADAM SMITH,
THE WEALTH OF NATIONS 22 (5TH ED. 1789)

A promise invokes trust in my future actions, not merely in my present sincerity.

CHARLES FRIED,
CONTRACT AS PROMISE 11 (1981)

PEOPLE CONTINUALLY MAKE promises: sales people promise happiness; lovers promise marriage; generals promise victory; and children promise to behave better. The law becomes involved when someone seeks to have a promise enforced by the state. Here are some examples:

Example 1: The Rich Uncle. The rich uncle of a struggling college student learns at the graduation party that his nephew graduated with honors. Swept away by good feeling, the uncle promises the nephew a trip around the world. Later the uncle reneges on his promise. The student sues his uncle, asking the court to compel the uncle to pay for a trip around the world.

Example 2: The Rusty Chevy. One neighbor offers to sell a used car to another for $1000. The buyer gives the money to the seller, and the seller gives the car keys to the buyer. To her great surprise, the buyer discovers that the keys fit the rusting Chevrolet in the backyard, not the shiny Cadillac in the driveway. The seller is equally surprised to learn that the buyer expected the Cadillac. The buyer asks the court to order the seller to turn over the Cadillac.

Example 3:   The Grasshopper Killer. A farmer, in response to a magazine advertisement for "a sure means to kill grasshoppers," mails $25 and receives two wooden blocks by return post with the instructions, "Place grasshopper on Block A and smash with Block B." The buyer asks the court to require the seller to return the $25 and to pay $500 in punitive damages.

Should the courts enforce the promises in these examples? A promise is enforceable if the courts offer a remedy to the victim of the broken promise. Traditionally, courts have been cautious about enforcing promises that are not given in exchange for something. In Example 1, the promise of a trip around the world is a gift to the nephew. The rich uncle does not receive anything in exchange; so, according to the traditional analysis, the courts should not enforce the uncle's promise. In Example 2, money exchanges for a promise, but the seller thought that he gave a different promise than the buyer thought she received. Courts often refuse to enforce confused promises. In Example 2, the courts would probably require the seller to return the money and the buyer to return the car keys. Example 3 involves deception, not confusion. A "sure method to kill grasshoppers" means something more than what the seller delivered. The courts ordinarily offer a remedy to the victims of deceptive promises.

If an enforceable promise was broken, what should the remedy be? One remedy requires the promise breaker to keep the promise. For example, if the court decided that the seller in Example 2 broke his promise, then the court might order the seller to deliver the Cadillac to the buyer. This kind of remedy is unavailable in Example 3 because the seller cannot exterminate grasshoppers as promised. Instead, the remedy in Example 3 must involve the payment of money damages as compensation for the failure to provide an effective grasshopper killer.

Our examples illustrate the two fundamental questions in contract law: "What promises should be enforced?" and "What should be the remedy for breaking enforceable promises?" Courts face these questions when deciding contract disputes and legislatures face these questions when making statutes to regulate contracts. A theory of contract law must guide courts, legislatures, and private parties (and their lawyers) who make contracts.

I. Bargain Theory: An Introduction to Contracts

In the late nineteenth and early twentieth centuries, Anglo-American courts and legal commentators developed the *bargain theory of contracts* to answer the two fundamental questions of contract law. The bargain theory held that the law should enforce promises given in a bargain. To implement this answer, theorists isolated and abstracted the minimal elements of a typical bargain, and these distinctions remain fundamental to the way lawyers think about contracts. We will explain the bargain theory and use its elements in an economic theory of contracts.

A. What Promises Should Be Enforceable at Law?

"What promises should be enforceable at law?" The bargain theory has a clear answer to this question, which, following Professor Mel Eisenberg, we call *the bargain principle: A promise is legally enforceable if it is given as part of a bargain; otherwise, a promise is unenforceable.* The bargain theory makes enforcement hinge upon classifying promises as "bargains" or "nonbargains." Consequently, the theory requires an exact specification of the necessary and sufficient conditions for the court to conclude that a bargain occurred.

Bargaining is a dialogue on value to agree on a price. The bargain theorists distinguished three elements in the dialogue: offer, acceptance, and consideration. "Offer" and "acceptance" have the same meaning in this theory as they do in ordinary speech: One party must make an offer ("I'll take that rusty Chevy over there for $1000"), and the other must accept it ("Done"). Sometimes business practices and social conventions prescribe the signals for making and accepting offers. For example, a buyer at an auction may signal an offer to buy by raising his or her hand, and the auctioneer may signal acceptance by shouting "Sold!" Sometimes contract law and statutes specify procedures for offer and acceptance. For example, most states require written contracts and registration for sales of land.

The "promisor" refers to the person who gives a promise, and the "promisee" refers to the person who receives a promise. In a bargain, the promisee induces the promisor to give the promise. The inducement may be money, as when the farmer pays $25 for the promise of a device that kills grasshoppers. The inducement may be goods, as when an automobile dealer delivers a car in exchange for the promise of future payment. The inducement may be a service, as when a painter paints a house in exchange for the promise of future payment. Or the inducement may be another promise, as when a farmer promises to deliver wheat to a wholesaler in the fall, and the wholesaler promises to pay a certain price upon delivery. The forms of a bargain thus include money-for-a-promise, goods-for-a-promise, service-for-a-promise, and promise-for-a-promise.

Regardless of form, each bargain involves *reciprocal inducement*: The promisee gives something to induce the promisor to give the promise, and the promisor gives the promise as inducement to the promisee. Common law uses the technical term *consideration* to describe what the promisee gives the promisor to induce the promise. Thus, the farmer's payment of $25 is consideration for the promise to supply a device that kills grasshoppers. The delivery of a car, the painting of a house, or a promise to deliver crops may be consideration for a promise of future payment.

According to the bargain theory, the contract remains incomplete until the promisee gives something to the promisor to induce the promise. When completed, the contract becomes enforceable. In other words, *consideration makes the promise enforceable.* The bargain theory holds that promises secured by consideration are enforceable and promises lacking consideration are unenforceable.

Let us illustrate the bargain theory by applying it to the three examples at the beginning of this chapter. In Example 1, the nephew apparently did not give anything as inducement for his rich uncle's promise of a trip around the world. Apparently there was no consideration, so the promise is unenforceable. In general, the promise to give a pure gift, which is not induced by the promise of something in return, is not enforceable under the bargain theory.

In contrast, consideration was given in Example 2 in exchange for the promise to supply the used car. The question raised in Example 2 is whether there was offer and acceptance. The seller thought they were discussing the rusty Chevy and the buyer thought they were discussing the immaculate Cadillac. The seller offered to sell one good and the buyer agreed to buy another good. There was no "meeting of the minds." Without a meeting of the minds, there is no offer and no acceptance, just a failure to communicate.

In Example 3, the seller offered a sure method for killing grasshoppers in exchange for $25, the buyer accepted the offer, and consideration took the form of the payment of $25. Therefore, the promise is enforceable according to the bargain theory. The remaining question is whether the seller did what he promised.

We conclude this section by relating bargains to fairness. Most people have beliefs about fair bargains. In a fair bargain, each party gives equivalent value. In the language of law, a contract is fair when the value of the promise is proportional to the value of the consideration. Conversely, in an unfair bargain, the value of the promise is disproportional to the value of the consideration. To illustrate an unfair bargain, the elder brother (Esau) in a famous Bible story promised to give his inheritance rights to a younger brother (Jacob) in exchange for a bowl of soup.

According to bargain theory, a court should enforce promises induced by consideration, regardless of whether the consideration was equivalent in value to the promise. It is enough for enforceability under the bargain theory that the promisor found the consideration adequate to induce the promise. Bargain theory holds that courts should determine whether a bargain occurred, not inquire into whether the bargain was fair. Consequently, the doctrine of consideration requires courts to enforce some unfair promises, such as exchanging one's inheritance for a bowl of soup.[1]

An alternative theory would limit courts to enforcing fair bargains. To apply such a theory, a court would have to ask whether the value of the promise was equivalent to the value of the consideration. People often disagree about the value of goods, and litigants often disguise values from courts. Supervising all bargains for fairness would burden the courts and inhibit commerce. Consequently, most people want the courts to enforce bargains, not to supervise them. Perhaps this fact explains why courts do not routinely examine bargains for fairness. However, some bargains are so one-sided that most people require little information to condemn them as unfair. Modern U.S. courts sometimes refuse to enforce extremely one-sided bargains. (See the discussion of "unconscionability" in the next chapter.)

In most English-speaking countries, traditional common-law doctrine requires "consideration" for a promise to be enforceable. (See accompanying box entitled "Humpty-Dumpty Jurisprudence.") Instead of relying upon "consideration" to identify the essential element of an enforceable promise, however, the civil law tradition that prevails in continental Europe sometimes invokes the equally mysterious idea of "cause." Just as the bargain theory attempts to explain "consideration," so various theories have been advanced to explain "cause," such as the will theory. According to the will theory, a binding contract requires an intention by the parties to be bound. When each party intends the promise to bind, their wills meet, which creates the contract. The meeting of minds resembles Pareto efficiency, as we will explain.

---

[1] If Esau were starving to death when he promised his inheritance for a bowl of soup, the contract might not be enforceable under the bargain doctrine because of an exception, discussed in the next chapter, called the "necessity defense."

Humpty-Dumpty Jurisprudence: The Life History of the Word "Consideration"

"When I use a word, it means just what I choose it to mean—neither more nor less."
—Humpty-Dumpty in Lewis Carroll, Through the Looking-Glass

In the bargain theory of contracts, "consideration" means something the promisee gives the promisor to induce the promise. According to the bargain theory, consideration makes the promise enforceable. Anglo-American courts accepted the bargain theory in the early years of the twentieth century and adopted the legal principle that consideration makes a promise enforceable. Then, as the years passed, exceptions to the principle accumulated. Courts, however, are slow to discard the abstract principles that they adopt. Instead of renouncing the principle of consideration, the courts did something characteristic of them: They changed the meaning of "consideration." Instead of meaning "something the promisee gives the promisor to induce the promise," the word "consideration" as used by the courts came to mean "the thing that makes a promise enforceable."

A tautology is a proposition that is true by definition of the words, such as "All husbands are married." When the courts changed the meaning of "consideration," they reduced the legal principle of consideration to a tautology. If "consideration" means "the thing that makes a promise enforceable," then the principle "consideration makes a promise enforceable" has no bite. When reduced to a tautology, a legal principle merely draws our attention to the meaning of a word, rather than telling us something about the legal consequences of our actions. Having made the principle of consideration into a tautology, the courts could assert its truth without fear of being wrong. Hence, we have an example of Humpty-Dumpty jurisprudence.

QUESTION 8.1: People often change the form of a promise in an attempt to increase their certainty that courts will enforce it according to its terms. For example, suppose the rich uncle in Example 1 wanted to assure his nephew of the enforceability of the promise of a trip around the world. He might do this by changing the form of the promise from a gift to a bargain. According to tradition, the uncle would solemnly offer to give his nephew a trip around the world in exchange for a peppercorn from the dinner table, and the nephew would solemnly give the uncle a peppercorn. Will this charade make the uncle's promise enforceable under the bargain theory? Answer this question by using the doctrine that courts inquire into the presence of consideration but not its adequacy. Also answer this question using the doctrine that courts should refuse to enforce extremely unfair bargains.

B. What Should Be the Remedy for the Breach of Enforceable Promises?

The bargain theory also had an answer to the second fundamental question of contract theory: "What should be the remedy for the breach of enforceable promises?" According to the bargain theory, the promisee is entitled to the "benefit of the bargain"—that is, to the benefit he or she would have obtained from performance of the promise. Computing compensation under this formula involves answering the counterfactual question "How well off would the promisee have been if the promise had been kept?" The counterfactual question concerns the benefit that the promisee could reasonably expect from performance. Consequently, the damage measure under the bargain theory is called *expectation damages.*

Note the connection between the answers to the questions "What promises should be enforced?" and "What should be the remedy for breach of enforceable promises?" Promises should be enforced, according to the bargain theory, if they are part of a bargain, and the remedy for the breach of an enforceable promise is an award of the value expected of the bargain. The fact of a bargain establishes enforceability, and the expected value of a bargain measures damages.

Assume that the promises are enforceable in the three examples at the beginning of the chapter. What measures expectation damages? The student's expectation damage in Example 1 equals the value to him of a trip around the world. The buyer's expectation damage in Example 2 equals the difference in the value that she places on the rusty Chevy and the value that she places on the immaculate Cadillac. In Example 3, the farmer's expectation damage equals the value of the crops destroyed by grasshoppers.

Counterfactual values are difficult to compute. The cost of a trip around the world, as in Example 1, depends on the route taken and, among other things, whether the traveler goes first class or economy class. The value of a unique, old Cadillac, as in Example 2, depends upon, among other things, the buyer's subjective preferences. The value of killing the grasshoppers in Example 3 depends upon the value of the crops that would have been harvested if they had not been destroyed by insects.

C. A Criticism of the Bargain Theory

The answer that the bargain theory gives to the first question of contract law is clear. Unfortunately, as a description of what courts actually do (and what they ought to do), the answer is also wrong. Sometimes the person who makes a promise wants it enforced and so does the person who receives it. Contract law should enforce such a promise in order to help the people get what they want. However, the bargain theory denies enforcement when the promise did not arise from a bargain.

For example, assume that a buyer begins her search for a car by taking a new Chevrolet for a test drive. After the test drive, the buyer plans to continue her search by visiting other car dealers. The seller wants to induce the buyer to consider carefully the purchase of the new Chevrolet. Consequently, the seller promises to sell the new Chevrolet to the buyer for a stated price, provided that the buyer accepts within 1 week. In other words, the seller makes a "firm offer" and promises to "keep it open" for 1 week. The buyer does not want to waste her time by considering the offer carefully and then finding that the seller has reneged. Consequently, the buyer wants the promise to be enforceable. The seller knows that the buyer is more likely to consider the offer carefully if the promise is enforceable, so the seller wants the promise to be enforceable. Thus, both the promisor and the promisee want the promise to be enforceable. Despite the wishes of both parties, the bargain theory withholds enforcement of the promise because the buyer gave nothing to the seller in exchange for the seller's promise to keep the offer open ("no consideration").

As another example, assume that a prominent alumna promises to give Old Siwash University the funds to construct a new building. The university wants to begin construction immediately. The alumna also wants the university to begin construction immediately. To obtain cash for the donation, the alumna must liquidate assets, which will take some time. The university dare not begin construction without an enforceable promise. In this example, both parties want the promise to be enforceable, but the bargain theory withholds enforcement of this promise.[2] Gift-promises are not induced by the prospect of gain, so they always lack consideration.

In the two preceding examples, both parties to the promise want it to be enforceable, yet the bargain theory withholds enforcement. A legal theory that frustrates the desires of the people affected by the law can be called *dogmatic.* In contrast, a legal theory that satisfies the desires of the people affected by the law can be called *responsive.* In general, a responsive theory maximizes the well-being of people, whereas a dogmatic theory sacrifices the well-being of people in favor of other ends. Contemporary courts in America prefer to be responsive rather than dogmatic. Consequently, contemporary courts in America often enforce firm offers and gift-promises.[3] As a result of such facts, the bargain theory is typically regarded as wrong.[4]

There is a second problem with the bargain theory—it calls for the routine enforceability of *any* bargain, just so long as it is a bargain and regardless of how outrageous the terms may be. As we saw earlier in this chapter, the farmer and the seller of a "sure means to kill grasshoppers" have, according to the bargain theory, a bargain. Enforcing this promise against the farmer leaves a bad taste in one's mouth. There is deception and trickery by the seller. And although one could argue that "buyers should beware," the seller's behavior here violates widespread community norms of fair dealing. Indeed, most modern courts would *not* enforce this contract against the farmer, precisely because it is deceptive. (We discuss fairness in the following chapter.)

The bargain theory sharpened the distinctions among offer, acceptance, and consideration, which theorists still use in analyzing the formation of contracts. However, the bargain theory of contract is not a good theory of contracting because it is both overinclusive (in arguing for the enforceability of contracts that, on most other grounds, ought not to be enforced) and underinclusive (in not arguing for the enforceability of promises that both parties truly want enforced). Consequently, the theory fails to describe what courts actually do.

---

[2] The original *Restatement of Contracts,* when issued in 1932, generally embraced the bargain theory in Section 75. Section 90 of the *Restatement* rejected the bargain theory and established enforceability of gift promises upon which a reasonable person had detrimentally relied without consideration.

[3] The *Uniform Commercial Code* Section 2-205 allows for some firm offers to be enforceable for a period not exceeding three months, but not all. (The *UCC* is described in a box at the beginning of Chapter 9.) American courts generally enforce gift-promises to the extent of reasonable reliance. Where the promisee is a nonprofit organization like a university, American courts sometimes enforce gift-promises to the full extent of the promise. We discuss the economics of gift promises on our website.

[4] One famous commentator on the history of contract theory—GRANT GILMORE, THE DEATH OF CONTRACT (1974)—believed that the classical or bargain theory was dead almost as soon as it was born.

II. An Economic Theory of Contract Enforcement

We want to replace the bargain theory with a better answer to the two fundamental questions in contract law. The enforceability of a contract usually makes the parties better off, as measured by their own desires, without making anyone worse off. Making someone better off without making anyone worse off is a "Pareto-efficient" change. *Economic efficiency usually requires enforcing a promise if the promisor and promisee both wanted enforceability when it was made.* We will develop this central idea in the economic theory of contracts to answer the first question of contract law, "What promises should be enforced?"

A. Cooperation and Commitment

Many exchanges occur instantly and simultaneously, as when a shopper pays cash for goods in the grocery store. In a simultaneous, instantaneous exchange, there is little reason to promise anything. The making of promises, however, typically concerns *deferred exchanges*—that is, transactions that involve the passage of time for their completion. For example, one party pays now and the other promises to deliver goods later ("payment for a promise"); one party delivers goods now and the other promises to pay later ("goods for a promise"); or one party promises to deliver goods later, and the other promises to pay when the goods are delivered ("promise for a promise").

The passage of time between the exchange of promises and their performance creates uncertainties and risks. Thus, the seller asks the buyer to pay now for future delivery of goods. The cautious buyer wants a legal obligation of the seller to deliver the goods, not just a moral obligation. The buyer may be willing to pay now for an *enforceable* promise, but not for an unenforceable promise. Recognizing these facts, both parties want the seller's promise to be enforceable at the time it is made. The seller wants enforceability in order to induce the buyer to make the purchase, and the buyer wants enforceability to provide an incentive for seller's performance and a remedy for seller's breach. By enforcing such promises, the court gives both parties what they want and facilitates cooperation between them.

To develop these insights, we describe a situation called the "agency game" that often arises in business. In this game, the first player decides whether to put a valuable asset under the control of the second player. The first player might be an investor in a corporation, a consumer advancing funds to purchase goods, a depositor at a bank, the buyer of an insurance policy, or a shipper of goods, to list some possibilities. If the first player puts the asset under the second player's control, the second player decides whether to cooperate or appropriate. Cooperation is productive, whereas appropriation is redistributive. Productivity could take the form of the profit from investment, the surplus from trade, or the interest from a loan. The parties divide the product of cooperation between them, so both of them benefit. In contrast, appropriation redistributes from the first player to the second player.

We depict these alternatives in Figure 8.1 and attach numbers to them. The numbers indicate the difference in the wealth of the two players before playing the agency game and after playing it. The first player to move in Figure 8.1 decides whether to

FIGURE 8.1

Agency game without contract.

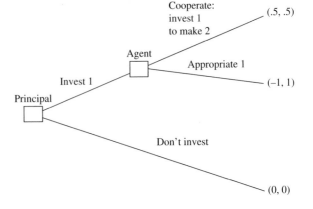

make an investment of 1. If no investment is made, the game ends, and the players receive nothing. If an investment is made, the second player decides whether to cooperate or appropriate. Cooperation produces a total payoff of 1. The players divide the total payoff equally: The first player recovers the investment of 1 and also receives a payoff of .5, and the second player receives a payoff of .5. Thus, the two players benefit equally from playing the agency game. Alternatively, the second player can appropriate. Appropriation enables the second player to acquire the first player's investment, while producing nothing: The first player loses 1, and the second player gains 1.

Consider the best moves for each player to make in Figure 8.1. If the first player invests, then the second player receives more from appropriating than cooperating. Consequently, the second player's best move is to appropriate.[5] The first player may anticipate that the second player will appropriate. Consequently, the first player's best move is "don't invest." We have shown that the solution to the agency game in Figure 8.1 is "don't invest."

The payoffs to the agency game in Figure 8.1 assume that the parties cannot make an enforceable contract. The barrier to an enforceable contract might be unprovable behavior, costly litigation, or bad judges.

Now consider how the payoffs change if we assume that the parties can make an enforceable contract. We assume that the second player offers to cooperate in exchange for an investment by the first player, and the first player accepts the offer by investing. The first player's investment is consideration for the second player's promise. We assume that the law will hold the second player liable for compensatory damages if he breaks the promise and appropriates.

Figure 8.2 depicts the revised payoffs in the agency game when the first player offers to invest in exchange for an *enforceable* promise by the second player to cooperate. Consider the payoffs to the first player. If the first player invests and the second player performs, the first receives a net payoff equal to .5. If the first player invests

---

[5] Game theorists describe a move that is best against *any* possible move by the other side as a "dominant strategy." In Figure 8.1, the second player has a dominant strategy. The first player does not have a dominant strategy, but the first player has a best reply to the second player's dominant strategy.

FIGURE 8.2

Agency game with contract.

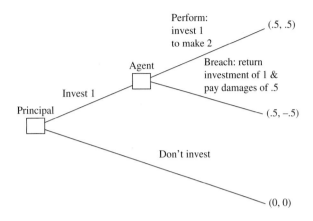

and the second player breaches, the first player receives compensatory damages. We assume that compensatory damages restore the first player's payoff to the level that he or she would have enjoyed if the second player had performed. If the second player had performed, the first player would have recovered the investment of 1 and received a payoff of .5. Thus, the first player receives a net payoff of .5 from investing, regardless of what the second player does. Alternatively, the first player can receive a payoff of 0 from not investing. Faced with these two alternatives, investing is the first player's best move.

Assume that the first player invests and consider the payoffs to the second player. The second player receives a payoff of .5 from performing as promised (cooperating). In contrast, breaching the contract (appropriating) yields a payoff of 1 to the second player, from which the second player must pay compensation to the first player. As compensation, the first player must receive 1 that he or she invested and .5 that was expected in profits. Consequently, liability of 1.5 must be subtracted from the second player's payoff of 1, yielding a net payoff of −.5 for breaching the contract. So, the best move for the second player is to cooperate.

Figure 8.1 shows that the first player does not invest when promises are *un*enforceable. Figure 8.2 shows that the first player invests and the second player cooperates when promises are enforceable. Thus, an enforceable contract converts a game with a non-cooperative solution into a game with a cooperative solution. *The first purpose of contract law is to enable people to cooperate by converting games with non-cooperative solutions into games with cooperative solutions.*

Modern business activity provides countless examples of the agency game. Thus, an innovator in Silicon Valley asks a venture capitalist to invest $1 million in a start-up company to develop a new computer chip. By developing the chip, the innovator can turn $1 million into $2 million. The innovator promises to develop the chip and share the profits of $1 million equally with the investor. Instead of developing the chip, however, the innovator might try to appropriate the investor's $1 million. An enforceable promise to develop the chip will prevent the innovator from appropriating the money; so, the investor will trust the innovator and invest the money.

We have shown that the unique solution of the agency game with a contract is "invest" and "perform" (cooperate). So far, we have discussed the best move for each player from that player's viewpoint. Now consider the sum of the payoffs to both players. The numbers sum to 1 when the first player invests and the second player cooperates. Otherwise, the numbers sum to zero. Investing and cooperating are productive, whereas "don't invest" changes nothing and "appropriate" merely redistributes money from the first player to the second player. Given these facts, we could restate the preceding conclusion: *The first purpose of contract law is to enable people to convert games with inefficient solutions into games with efficient solutions.*

The language of game theory clarifies how enforceable contracts promote cooperation. In game theory, a *commitment* forecloses an opportunity. To illustrate from a classical book on the art of war, the Chinese philosopher Sun Tzu writes, "When your army has crossed the border [into hostile territory], you should burn your boats and bridges, in order to make it clear to everybody that you have no hankering after home."[6] Burning the boats and bridges commits the army to attack by foreclosing the opportunity to retreat. Similarly, making a contract commits the second player in Figure 8.2 to cooperate. Commitment is achieved by foreclosing the opportunity to appropriate. The opportunity to appropriate is foreclosed by the high cost of liability for breach. A commitment is *credible* when the other party observes the foreclosing of an opportunity.

The chef at the resort asks whether you would prefer a menu of chicken or beef for dinner, or a menu of chicken or beef or fish. Perhaps you think to yourself, "A wider choice cannot make me worse off, and it might make me better off." This is true for many restaurant choices, but it is false for coordinating with others in situations like the agency game. You may need to commit *not* to make certain choices in order to induce the other party to cooperate with you.

Here's how we answered the first question of contract law: *A promise usually should be enforced if both parties wanted it to be enforceable when it was made.* The agency game shows why both parties usually want enforceability: So the agent can credibly commit to performing and the principal has sufficient trust to put an asset under the agent's control.

QUESTION 8.2: Explain why the economic theory of contracts would enforce a firm offer to sell a Chevrolet and the promise of a gift to Old Siwash University.

QUESTION 8.3: Explain why the numbers in Figure 8.2 indicate that the second player is liable for *expectation* damages in the event of breach.

QUESTION 8.4: In Figure 8.2, both parties desire enforceability of the second player's promise when the promise is made, but when the time comes to perform, the promisor may not want enforceability. What do these facts say about the Pareto efficiency of enforcing the second player's promise? (Hint: Distinguish between the Pareto efficiency of enforceability when the

---

[6] SUN TZU, THE ART OF WAR, section IX, part 3. This is the oldest written treatise on war, dating back to the sixth century B.C.E.

promise is made, which can be called *ex ante* Pareto efficiency, and the Pareto efficiency of actually enforcing the promise when the time comes to perform, which can be called *ex post* Pareto efficiency.)

QUESTION 8.5: As an exercise in legal vocabulary, let us modify the facts about the contract in Figure 8.2 and describe it differently. Assume that the first player offers to invest in exchange for the second player's promise to co-operate, and the second player accepts by promising to cooperate. What is the "consideration" in this contract?

QUESTION 8.6: Figure 8.2 describes a game based upon a bargain. Construct a similar figure to describe a game based upon a firm offer.

Web Note 8.1

Our website describes some recent literature on liability for precontractual bargaining costs and the economics of gift promises.

III. An Economic Theory of Contract Remedies

We have outlined the answer to the question, "What promises should be enforced?" Now we turn to the second question of contract law: What should be the remedy for breaking enforceable promises?

> **Example 4:** Yvonne owns a restaurant for economists that is called the Waffle Shop. Her business prospers, and she needs a larger facility. She contracts with Xavier, a builder, who promises to expand the restaurant and complete the work by September 1. Her restaurant will remain closed while he builds. Xavier knows that events could jeopardize completing the construction on time. He is especially concerned that city officials may delay issuing the permits needed to begin construction. With good luck, he will get the permits early enough to complete construction on time at low cost. With bad luck, he will suffer a delay in getting the permits, and he will have to choose between completing construction on time at high cost, or breaching the contract and delaying completion of the building.

Figure 8.3 depicts the Waffle Shop in numbers. The contract requires Yvonne to pay 1 to Xavier in advance and to pay .5 on timely completion of the construction. If completed on time, the construction will be worth 2 to Yvonne. Thus, Yvonne stands to gain .5 from the construction project. With good luck, officials issue construction permits on time and Xavier does the work for the low cost of 1, so he gains .5. (Remarkably, these numbers for the "good luck" branch in Figure 8.3 are the same as in Figure 8.2!) With bad luck, officials delay issuing the permits. Xavier can complete construction on time at the high cost of 2.5, so he will lose 1 and she will gain .5. Alternatively, Xavier can breach the contract and complete construction late at a cost of 1, in which case Xavier will owe Yvonne .5 in damages; so, he will lose .5 and she will gain .5.

FIGURE 8.3

Contract with luck affecting
performance.

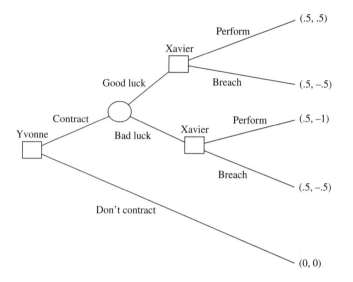

Figure 8.3 shows Xavier's perform-or-breach choice. Given good luck, Xavier is better off to perform with payoff .5 than to breach with payoff −.5. Given bad luck, Xavier is better off to breach with payoff −.5 than to perform with payoff −1. Since Yvonne is fully compensated for breach, she is no worse off for breach.

Modern business activity provides countless examples where the promisor prefers to breach and pay damages, rather than to perform at a loss. Thus, a venture capitalist in Silicon Valley pays $1 million for preferred stock in a start-up company that promises to develop a new computer chip. According to the contract, the startup company must develop and market the chip within three years. If the startup fails to do so, it must pay damages of $1.5 million. The innovator subsequently discovers a technical problem that vastly increases the cost of developing the chip. Instead of continuing to develop it, the innovator abandons the project and pays $1.5 million to the venture capitalist.

The parties to a contract sometimes take a short-sighted view of their self-interest, especially in one-time transactions or transactions with large stakes. Traveling carnivals, used-car salespersons, and ordinary people who buy or sell a house often deal sharply with each other. With sharp dealing, the promisor may not care about the harm that breach causes the promisee or his own reputation, but he still cares about legal liability. He will perform if his net benefits from performing exceed his net benefits from breaching minus his liability; otherwise he will breach.

To formalize the sharp-dealing promisor's behavior, let N_{px} and N_{bx} denote Xavier's net benefits from performing and breaching respectively. Let L_{bx} denote Xavier's liability for breaching. Xavier follows this decision rule:

$$N_{px} \geq N_{bx} - L_{bx} \Rightarrow \text{perform}$$
$$N_{px} \leq N_{bx} - L_{bx} \Rightarrow \text{breach.}$$

Thus, when Xavier has good luck in Figure 8.3, $N_{px} = .5$ and $N_{bx} - L_{bx} = -.5$, so Xavier performs. Conversely, when Xavier has bad luck in Figure 8.3, $N_{px} = -1$ and $N_{bx} - L_{bx} = -.5$, so Xavier breaches.

This formula concerns the promisor's *actual* commitment to perform. Consider his *ideally efficient* commitment. Assume that the contract only affects the parties to it; so, efficiency requires maximizing the sum of their payoffs. In notation, $N_{px} + N_{py}$ denotes the sum of the net benefits to Xavier and Yvonne from performance, and $N_{bx} + N_{by}$ denotes the sum of the net benefits to Xavier and Yvonne from breach. Efficiency requires Xavier to follow this decision rule:

$$N_{px} + N_{py} \geq N_{bx} + N_{by} \Rightarrow \text{perform}$$
$$N_{px} + N_{py} \leq N_{bx} + N_{by} \Rightarrow \text{breach.}$$

As mentioned above, contract law frequently awards "expectation damages" as compensation for breach. Awarding perfect expectation damages restores the promisee to the position that he or she would have enjoyed if the promisor had performed. In notation, perfect expectation damages equal the difference in Yvonne's net benefits between performance and breach: $L = N_{py} - N_{by}$. Substitute this value for L in Xavier's decision rule, and it is identical to the decision rule for efficiency. (Prove it for yourself.) We have established the following proposition: *When a contract only affects the parties to it, liability for perfect expectation damages gives the promisor efficient incentives to perform or breach.*

What should be the remedy for breaking enforceable promises? This is the second fundamental question of contract law. The preceding proposition, which eluded contact theorists for decades, suggests an answer: expectation damages. This is the right answer to cause people who make promises to take the efficient level of commitment to keeping them. It is also the right answer to compensate fully the victims of breach.

In fact, expectation damages are the most common remedy for breach of contract in the United States. Perfect expectation damages are apparently the legal ideal, but the actual remedy often differs from the perfect one. Damages below the perfect level cause the promisor to breach too often, and damages above the perfect level cause the promisor to perform too often, as explained in the next chapter.

QUESTION 8.7: Assume that the high costs of performing cause the promisor to breach a contract and pay perfect expectation damages to the promisee. Would the promisee have preferred that the promisor perform?

QUESTION 8.8: Explain the gain in total payoffs from allowing the promisor to breach and pay expectation damages when performing is inefficient.

A. Precaution Against Breach

In the Waffle Shop contract, Xavier has good luck and performs, or else he has bad luck and breaches. Viewed realistically, however, Xavier can affect his luck. To increase the probability of getting a building permit on time, he can hire a lawyer, meet with the restive neighbors, and telephone politicians. We call these acts "promisor's precaution against breach" because they reduce the probability of breach, rather like the injurer's precaution reduces the probability of an accident as discussed in Chapter 6.

The preceding section proved that when a contract only affects the parties to it, liability for perfect expectation damages gives the promisor efficient incentives to perform or breach. The same proposition is true for the promisor's incentives to take precaution against breach. *When a contract only affects the parties to it, liability for perfect expectation damages gives the promisor efficient incentives to take precaution against breach.*

B. Reliance

Now our focus shifts to the choices of the promisee, specifically to her reliance on the contract. In Figure 8.3, Yvonne can decide whether to contract, but after contracting she cannot affect her payoffs. This is a simplifying assumption. Viewed more realistically, Yvonne can increase her gain from performance or reduce her loss from breach. She can increase her gain from performance by ordering more food in advance, accepting more dining reservations, and leasing more parking spaces for her guests. Alternatively, she can reduce her loss from breach by the opposite—order less food in advance, accept fewer dining reservations, and leasing fewer parking spaces for her guests.

In general, reliance is a change in the promisee's position induced by the promise. The change increases the benefit of performance and the cost of breach, which makes the contract riskier. Recall the rich uncle's promise to give his nephew a trip around the world. The trip is more valuable to the nephew if he purchases the necessary items in advance—luggage, snowshoes, a pith helmet, and so on. But he must sell them at a loss if his uncle breaches his promise.

Are Yvonne's actual incentives for reliance efficient? Not if she receives perfect expectation damages for breach. When Yvonne receives perfect expectation damages, reliance increases her benefits from performance, and her reliance also increases Xavier's costs of breach. With perfect expectation damages, Yvonne bears none of the risk of breach, and Xavier bears all of it. *Perfect expectation damages thus cause Yvonne to overrely relative to the efficient reliance.*

In notation, when Xavier has good luck and performs, Yvonne's reliance y *increases* her net benefit N_{gpy} according to the function $N_{gpy} = N_{gpy}(y)$. When Xavier has bad luck and breaches, Yvonne's reliance y *decreases* her net benefit N_{bby} according to the function $N_{bby} = N_{bby}(y)$. When Xavier breaches, Yvonne receives compensation equal to his liability L_{bx}. Let w_y denote the price of reliance y. The expected value of the contract to Yvonne thus equals

$$(1 - p)N_{gpy}(y) + p(N_{bby}(y) + L_{bx}) - w_y y.$$

Perfect expectation damages equal the difference in Yvonne's net benefits between performance and breach: $L_{bx} = N_{gpy}(y) - N_{bby}(y)$. Substitute this value for L_{bx} in the expected value of the contract to Yvonne and it reduces to

$$N_{gpy}(y) - w_y y.$$

The risk of loss has disappeared from this expression. When Yvonne chooses y to maximize this expression, she only considers her increase in net benefits from performance, not the increase in Xavier's liability from breach.

We have shown that liability for perfect expectation damages gives efficient incentives to the promisor to take precautions against breach, but the promisee has no incentive to restrain her reliance. This proposition should look familiar to you, because you encountered its equivalent in Chapter 6 on torts: A rule of strict liability with perfect compensation for accidents gives efficient incentives to the injurer to take precaution, but the victim has no incentive to take precaution. Perfect damages have the same effect in contracts and torts: The injurer internalizes the harm and the victim externalizes it. This is only one of the remarkable symmetries hidden in liability law.

The simple answer to the second question of contract law—What should be the remedy for breaking enforceable promises?—is "perfect expectation damages." This remedy is perfect for the promisor's incentives, but imperfect for the promisee's incentives. Contract law has developed various doctrines to modify expectation damages and reduce overreliance on contracts. The next chapter analyzes some of these doctrines.

> **QUESTION 8.9:** Explain why compensating the victim of breach for expectation damages causes efficient performance and breach, whereas compensating the victim of breach for excessive reliance may cause inefficient performance and breach.

IV. Economic Interpretation of Contracts

Enforcing a contract frequently involves interpreting it, which often poses conundrums. A contract says, "Exceptions are allowed," when the parties meant to say, "Exceptions are not allowed." Should the court interpret the contract according to its plain meaning or the intent behind the words? The contract says "Two exceptions are allowed," but the parties would have allowed a third exception if they had thought of it. Should the court interpret the contract to allow a third exception? When uncle promised to pay for his nephew's trip around the world, did the promise mean business class or economy class airfare? When a child signs an unfavorable contract, should the court replace the actual terms with terms favorable to the child? Instead of immersing ourselves in these conundrums—that's for a law school class on contracts—we will elaborate some economic principles for interpreting contracts.

Perfect Contracts   According to the Coase Theorem, given zero transaction costs, rational parties will allocate legal entitlements efficiently. This proposition applies to contracts. When transaction costs are zero, the contract is a perfect instrument for exchange. Every contingency is anticipated; every risk is internalized; all relevant information is communicated; no gaps remain for courts to fill; no one needs the court's protection from deceit or abuse; nothing can go wrong. Perfect contracts pose no conundrums of interpretation. The parties need the state to enforce a perfect contract according to its plain meaning, but nothing more is required.

Why contemplate such an absurdity? Because perfect contracts connect law to economics. In microeconomics, students learn the theory of perfect competition and then use departures from it to analyze actual markets, such as oligopolistic markets. By this approach, microeconomics sorts different kinds of market imperfections according to their causes. We will use the theories of market imperfections that students learn in microeconomics to analyze contract imperfections.

Unlike perfect contracts, real contracts allocate risks imperfectly. Suppose that Mr. McGuire signs a contract with the Wabash Construction Company to build a house for his family. Floor plan, construction materials, style of carpets, landscaping, compliance with zoning codes—all of this and more is specified, as well as the price to be paid and the date for completing the house. Now imagine some of the things that can go wrong. Mr. McGuire might die, and his family might no longer want the house. The court may make the estate of Mr. McGuire pay for the house after his death, thus enforcing the contract as written. Or zoning officials in the local government might reject the construction plan. The court may decide that the contract is void because law forbids its construction. Here the court fills a gap in the contract by supplying terms of its own that do not contradict the contract's explicit terms. Or Mr. McGuire might discover that the contract calls for Wabash to install grossly inadequate pipes. The court may decide that Wabash, the builder, must install adequate pipes, in spite of what the contract says. Here the court sets aside explicit terms in the contract and replaces them with its own terms.

We described three possible responses of courts to contract imperfections: (i) enforce the explicit terms as if the contract were perfect; (ii) fill a gap in the contract without contradicting its explicit terms; or (iii) replace the contract's explicit terms. Courts should usually tolerate contract imperfections and enforce the terms as written, just as officials should usually tolerate market imperfection and allow business to proceed without regulation. Tolerance is usually required because the state cannot fix most imperfections in private transactions, just as it cannot fix most imperfections in marriages. When courts attempt to improve on a contract's explicit terms, two instruments are available to them: default rules to fill gaps and mandatory rules to replace explicit terms.

A. Default Rules

Gaps in contracts may be inadvertent. The construction contract may not mention the possibility of zoning officials rejecting the construction plan because neither Mr. McGuire nor Wabash thought about this possibility. Alternatively, gaps may be deliberate. The construction contract may not mention the possibility of zoning officials rejecting the construction plan because Mr. McGuire and Wabash both believed that this possibility was remote. Remote risks do not justify the cost of negotiating and drafting terms to allocate them. Or a deliberate gap may be left in a contract for psychological reasons, as when a couple promises to marry and remains silent about dividing property in the event of divorce.

Consider the calculations that might lead rational parties to leave gaps deliberately in contracts. "*Ex ante* risks" refer to the risks of future losses faced by the parties when they negotiate a contract. "*Ex post* losses" refer to losses that actually materialize after making the contract. In general, the parties to a contract must choose between allocating *ex ante* risks and allocating *ex post* losses. The parties expect to save transaction costs by leaving gaps in contracts whenever the actual cost of negotiating explicit terms exceeds the expected cost of filling a gap. The *expected* cost of filling a gap in the contract equals the probability that the loss materializes multiplied by the subsequent cost of allocating it. The following rule summarizes these facts:

minimizing transaction costs of contracts

allocating a risk $>$ allocating a loss $\times$ its probability $\Rightarrow$ leave gap,

allocating a risk $\leq$ allocating a loss $\times$ its probability $\Rightarrow$ fill gap.

When a court imputes terms to fill a gap in a contract, the implicit terms apply by *default,* which means "in the absence of explicit terms to the contrary." The parties are free to alter default terms by mutual consent. If the parties allocate the risk explicitly, the court enforces the explicit terms even though they contradict the default terms that the court would have used to fill a gap. Thus, the court might enforce a term in the construction contract that requires the McGuires to pay compensation to Wabash if zoning officials prevent construction, even though the court would have voided the contract if it did not mention zoning disapproval and zoning officials prevented construction.

Courts supply default terms to contracts by following rules. These "default rules" can be efficient or inefficient. How much harm can inefficient default rules do? That depends on the cost of transacting around them. When a default rule is inefficient, the parties can gain by replacing it with explicit terms that are efficient, but they have to bear the transaction costs of negotiating the explicit terms. Conversely, when default rules are efficient, the parties cannot gain by replacing the default rule with explicit terms. When the courts supply efficient default rules, the parties save the cost of negotiating explicit terms. The fewer the terms requiring negotiation, the cheaper is the contracting process. In general, all parties to a contract can benefit when lawmakers replace inefficient default terms with efficient default terms, and the size of the benefits depends on the cost of transacting around the default rule.

Economic analysis offers a simple rule for courts to follow in order to identify efficient rules: *Impute the terms to the contract that the parties would have agreed to if they had bargained over all the relevant risk.*[7] This is the method of filling gaps by a

---

[7] See David Charny, *Hypothetical Bargains: The Normative Structure of Contract Interpretation,* 89 MICH. L. REV. 1815 (1991).

hypothetical bargain. The actual bargain consists in the terms negotiated by the parties. The hypothetical bargain consists in the terms the parties would have reached if they had filled the gaps in the contract by negotiation. For maximum gain, the parties would have reached an efficient bargain. To discover the hypothetical bargain, the court must establish the most efficient form of cooperation. (The court may or may not have to adjust prices in the contract.[8]) When courts fill gaps by imputing terms of the hypothetical bargain, the parties receive their preferred contract from the court. Further negotiations between them cannot improve it.

> **QUESTION 8.10:** "Default rules save transaction costs in direct proportion to their efficiency." Explain this proposition.

> **QUESTION 8.11:** Suppose that Wabash completes the house one month later than promised. Inclement weather, which was no one's fault, caused the tardiness. Explain how the court might compute efficient damages.

> **QUESTION 8.12:** Doctors who form a partnership may say nothing in the partnership agreement concerning its future dissolution. The parties may deliberately avoid discussing dissolution for fear of breeding distrust. Provide some other examples of gaps left in contracts for strategic reasons.

B. Mandatory Rules

Besides gaps, imperfect contracts sometimes contain explicit terms that courts set aside. The court may disregard a consumer's waiver of the right to sue for injuries caused by a defective product, or the court may substitute its own terms for the actual terms in a contract made by a child. Unlike default terms, these terms are mandatory. The parties to a contract cannot waive or remove or replace mandatory terms by mutual agreement.

By imposing mandatory terms, the law *regulates* the contract. The economic theory of contract regulation resembles the economic theory of market regulation. Textbooks in microeconomics usually describe a perfectly competitive economy that requires no regulation and subsequently describe imperfections that may require

---

[8] When the efficient risk-bearer *actually* foresaw a risk, or *ought* to have foreseen a risk, the court should presume that the negotiated price included compensation for bearing the risk. Whether someone actually foresaw a risk is a question of fact, and whether someone ought to have foreseen a risk is a question of good business practices. Sometimes, however, neither party to a contract foresees a risk and neither party ought to have foreseen it. Allocating an unforeseen loss can dramatically change the cost of the contract to one of the parties, so the court may also need to alter the price by applying the Nash bargaining solution (splitting the surplus) as explained in Chapter 4. Allocating risk and adjusting prices put such great demands on courts that they should seldom make the attempt.

regulation, such as an electric company's monopoly in supplying power to households in a town. Similarly, we described a perfect contract that requires no regulation and now we describe imperfect contracts that require mandatory rules. Categories of market failure often found in microeconomics can be used to categorize legal doctrines that impose mandatory rules. A brief sketch of those categories prepares for their detailed discussion in the next chapter.

Individual Rationality   Our review of microeconomics in Chapter 2 identified three assumptions about rational choice by individuals. First, a rational decision-maker can rank outcomes in order from least preferred to most preferred. In order to rank outcomes, decision makers must have stable preferences. If the promisor's preferences are sufficiently unstable or disorderly, then he or she is legally *incompetent* and cannot conclude an enforceable contract. For example, children and the insane are legally incompetent.

Second, the rational decision makers' opportunities are moderately constrained so that they can achieve some, but not all, of their objectives. Dire constraints destroy freedom of action. Two major contract doctrines excuse promise breaking on the ground that the promisor faced dire constraints. If the beneficiary of the promise extracted it by threats, then promise breaking is excused by reason of *duress*. For example, in a famous movie the "godfather" of a criminal syndicate makes contract offers that "cannot be refused" because the victim signs the contract with a gun held to his head. No court would enforce such a contract.

Similarly, if a promise is extracted from a desperate promisor, the court may excuse nonperformance on the ground of *necessity*. For example, suppose a surgeon runs out of gas on a lonely desert road where she might perish. A passerby offers to sell her five liters of gas for $50,000. Even if the surgeon accepts the offer, the court will not enforce her promise to pay. The court will not enforce the promise because it was given out of necessity.

Notice that *duress* and *necessity* both apply when the promisor is in dire circumstances, but the cause is different. The cause of necessity is usually the promisor's bad judgment, bad luck, or a third person. For example, the surgeon may have run out of gas in the desert because she did not check the gas gauge, a hidden defect caused the gas gauge to fail, or her enemy secretly punctured the gas tank. In contrast, the cause of duress is usually the promisee. For example, the godfather held the gun to the promisor's head. Thus, duress can be regarded as necessity caused by the promisee.

In these examples, the dire constraint *preceded* the promise. Sometimes a dire constraint *follows* the promise. A dire constraint that follows a promise can prevent the promisor from performing. For example, a surgeon may promise to operate and then break her hand before the scheduled operation. If a promise is made in good faith and fate intervenes to make performance impossible, then promise breaking may be excused by reason of *impossibility*. For example, a manufacturer may be excused from fulfilling his contracts because his factory burned down. In general, the impossibility doctrine applies to unlikely events that prevent performance. In the next chapter we discuss the optimal allocation of the risk of such events.

i   **Web Note 8.2**

Much research has been done recently on deviations from individual rationality. See our website for a discussion of some of that literature as it applies to the theory of contracts.

Spillovers   Sometimes transaction costs prevent people from participating in negotiations that affect them. An electric utility generates power by a dirty process such as burning soft coal, and the smoke harms the neighbors. The contracts between the buyers of electricity and the electric utility affect its neighbors. Although contracts often have external effects, the legal remedy seldom involves *contract* law. In most cases, the plaintiff in a suit for breach of contract must be the person to whom the promise was made (the promisee) or the person to whom the promisee's rights were transferred (the transferee). People affected by a contract who are not parties to it—"third parties"—cannot find relief in contract law except under special circumstances. Instead of suing for relief under contract law, third parties must usually seek relief under the law of torts, property, crimes, or regulations. If a private contract to purchase goods from a polluting manufacturer causes more pollution, the public victims must sue under nuisance law or under an environmental regulation, not contract law.

Sometimes contract law protects third parties by refusing to enforce a contract between the first and second party. The courts may refuse to enforce such a contract when it *derogates public policy*. An example is the promise of a victim of a crime to reward a policeman for solving it. A policeman's job is to catch criminals. Allowing victims to pay rewards for this service might distort police efforts. Rewards would make the police focus on crimes whose solution recovers valuable assets that victims will pay to get back, such as stolen cars. The police might neglect crimes where deterrence is urgently needed and the victim has nothing economic to recover, such as rape.

Some important kinds of business contracts are unenforceable for reasons of public policy. Companies often wish to make contracts not to compete with each other. Agreements not to compete enable cartels to exploit buyers by charging monopoly prices. Courts in England and America were reluctant to enforce nineteenth-century contracts to create cartels. Such contracts derogated public policies aiming to foster competition. Subsequent antitrust statutes outlawed cartels in the United States and the nations of Western Europe. For example, contracts to create a cartel are void in Europe by the law of the European Union (European Union Treaty, Section 85, paragraph 2).

These are examples where the law will not enforce a contract whose performance is illegal or derogates public policy. Many examples of the opposite also exist—cases where the law *will* enforce a contract whose performance is illegal or derogates public policy. Thus, a married man may be liable for inducing a woman to rely on his promise of marriage, even though the law prohibits him from marrying without first obtaining a divorce. Similarly, a company that fails to supply a good as promised may be liable even though producing the good is impossible without violating an environmental regulation.

Economic analysis suggests when the law should enforce or not enforce a contract whose performance violates law or public policy. Liability should rest with the party who knew, or had reason to know, that performance is illegal or derogates public policy. Liability should rest with the informed party because he knew that he should not make the contract.

Asymmetric Information   Sometimes one or more of the parties to a contract lacks essential information about it. Several doctrines in contract law excuse promise breaking on the ground that the promise resulted from bad information. If the beneficiary of the promise extracted it by lies, then breaking the promise is excused by reason of *fraud*. For example, the seller of the "sure method to kill grasshoppers" defrauded the farmer. Fraud violates the duty not to misinform the other party to a contract.

Besides this negative duty, parties sometimes have the positive duty to disclose information. In most sales contracts, a seller must warn the buyer about hidden dangers associated with the use of the product, even though this information may cause the buyer not to buy it. For example, the manufacturer of a drug must warn the user about side effects. In these circumstances, common law finds a duty to disclose. In the civil law tradition, your contract may be void because you did not supply the information that you should have. Civil law calls this doctrine *culpa in contrahendo*.

Sometimes disguised defects lower the value of a good without making it dangerous or unfit for use. Common law apparently contains no general duty to disclose such disguised defects. Common law does not require a used-car dealer to disclose the faults in a car offered for sale (only a duty not to lie about those faults). The law is different for new goods, including new cars.[9]

People often trade because they have different expectations about whether the price of a good will rise of fall, as in stock markets. In such circumstances, at least one of the parties is misinformed. If people make contracts premised upon misinformation that they gathered for themselves, then the fact that the contract is based on misinformation does not excuse them from their contractual duties. For example, a stock trader who promises to supply 100 shares of Exxon in six months at a predetermined price cannot escape his obligation just because the price of the stock rose when he expected it to fall.

Most of the preceding examples concern a misinformed party and a well-informed party. Another possibility is that *both* parties are misinformed. This is the basis of a legal excuse for breaking a promise known as *frustration of purpose*. English law provides some famous examples known as the Coronation Cases. In the early years of the twentieth century, rooms in buildings situated along certain London streets were rented in advance for the day on which the new king's coronation parade would pass by. However, the heir to the throne became ill, and the coronation was postponed. Postponing the parade made the rental agreement worthless to the renter. Some owners of the rented rooms tried to collect the rent anyway. The courts refused to enforce the contracts on the ground that the change in circumstances frustrated the purpose of the contracts.

---

[9] For new goods, the law in most states in the United States imputes a "warranty of fitness," which is a guarantee that the court reads into the contract, even though the actual contract did not explicitly contain such a guarantee. According to the implied warranty of fitness, the seller of a new good promises that it is fit to use for its intended purposes. The seller of a new car breaches this warranty and must return the purchase price if a fault in the car's design prevents its use for transportation." See *UCC* Sections 2-314 and 2-315.

Yet another possibility is that both parties premise the contract upon different misinformation. If promises are exchanged on the basis of contradictory, but reasonable, conceptions of what is promised, then the contract is said to rest upon what is called a *mutual mistake*. To illustrate using our Example 2, the seller genuinely believed that he was negotiating to sell his rusty Chevrolet in the backyard, and the buyer genuinely believed that she was negotiating to purchase the immaculate Cadillac in the driveway. Like frustration of purpose, mutual mistake justifies the court's setting the contract aside. In our example, the court might order the buyer to return the car keys, and the seller to return the money.

Monopoly   Competitive markets contain enough buyers and sellers that each person has many alternative trading partners. In contrast, oligopoly limits the available trading partners to a small number, and monopoly limits the available trading partners to a single seller. When trading partners are limited, bargains can be very one-sided. Under the bargain theory, the courts enforced bargained promises and did not ask if the terms are fair. Consequently, the common law historically contains weak protection against exploitation by monopolies. Instead of common law, statutes supply most protections against monopolies.

In recent years, however, a new common law doctrine has evolved that allows judges to scrutinize the substantive terms of contracts. When a contract seems so unfair that its enforcement would violate the conscience of the judge, it may be set aside according to the doctrine of *unconscionability*. For example, assume a consumer signs a contract allowing a furniture seller to repossess all the furniture in her house if she misses one monthly payment on a single item of furniture. The court may find the repossession term "unconscionable" and refuse to enforce it. We discuss this elusive doctrine in the next chapter. The civil law tradition contains a concept—"lesion"—similar to unconscionability. "Lesion" refers to a contract that is too unequal to have legal force.

Table 8.1 associates the leading doctrines for regulating contracts with the market failure that they attempt to correct. Given low transaction costs, rational people will make contracts that approach perfection. A perfect contract has no gaps for courts to fill or market failures to regulate. If a contract approaches perfection, the court should simply enforce its terms. As transaction costs increase, however, people leave gaps in

TABLE 8.1

Rationality, Transaction Costs, and Regulatory Doctrines of Contract Law

Assumption	If Violated, Contract Doctrine
Individual Rationality	Incompetency; incapacity; coercion; duress; necessity; impossibility
Spillovers	Unenforceability of contracts derogating public policy or statutory duty
Information	Fraud; failure to disclose; frustration of purpose; mutual mistake
Monopoly	Necessity; unconscionability or lesion

contracts. Courts should fill the gaps with efficient default terms. Transaction costs can also cause externalities, misinformation, or monopolies. Serious imperfections can cause markets to fail and create a need to regulate contracts. *The farther the facts depart from the ideal of perfect rationality and zero transaction costs, the stronger the case for judges' regulating the terms of the contract.*

V. Relational Contracts: The Economics of the Long-Run

If you break your promise to come to family dinner on Sunday evening, your mother can punish you in a thousand small ways. The same is true in repeated business transactions, where the preferred remedy for a broken promise is some form of retaliation, but not a lawsuit. To secure cooperation in long-run relations, the parties often rely upon informal devices, rather than enforceable rules. An overbearing partner may be brought back into line by a warning rather than a lawsuit. Or a businessman who oversteps the ethical boundaries of his profession may be chastened by gossip and ostracism. The most common problems of contracting are nonpayment of bills, late delivery, and poor performance. For nonpayment, a typical retaliation is suspension of supply; for late delivery, it is delayed payment; and for poor performance, it is partial payment.

These informal devices usually operate within enduring relationships. Contracts often create relationships. In addition, contracts create legal duties that are not part of the contract. For example, when a customer opens a checking account with a U.S. bank, she signs a contract called a "depository agreement," which creates a "fiduciary relationship." This relationship imposes many duties upon the bank that are not stated in the depository agreement. As another illustration, a "franchisee" (local investor) may sign a contract with the "franchisor" (parent corporation) to operate a local fast-food restaurant. The franchise relationship creates many legal duties that the contract does not mention. Economists have studied how enduring relationships affect behavior. We will explain some of their central conclusions by repeating the agency game.

A. Repeated Game

In the agency game, the principal (first player) invests by placing some funds under the control of the agent (second player). To depict cooperation in an enduring relationship, assume that the agency game in Figure 8.1 is repeated indefinitely, thus transforming a "one-shot game" into a "repeated game." In any round of the repeated game in which the principal invests, the agent enjoys an immediate advantage from appropriating. An enforceable promise can solve this problem, as depicted in Figure 8.2. But suppose the promise is unenforceable for some reason—breach is unprovable, trials are too expensive, or courts are corrupt. To solve the problem without law, the principal can retaliate in subsequent rounds of the game.

Figure 8.4 illustrates an effective strategy for the principal to deter appropriation by retaliating against it. Assume that the agent appropriates in round n of the game. The agent receives a payoff of 1 in round n. However, the principal retaliates by not investing in round $n + 1$ and in $n + 2$. The agent receives a payoff of zero in rounds $n + 1$ and $n + 2$. Thus, the strategy of appropriation yields a total payoff to the agent equal to 1 in rounds n through $n + 2$. These facts are summarized in the first row of Figure 8.4.

FIGURE 8.4

Payoffs to second player (agent) when first player (principal) plays tit for tat.

Strategy of second player	round	$n-1$	n	$n+1$	$n+2$	$n+3$	$n+4$	$n+5$	$n+6$
	appropriate	...	1	0	0	1	0	0	...
	cooperate	...	.5	.5	.5	.5	.5	.5	...

Alternatively, assume that the agent could follow the strategy of cooperating in each round of the game. When the agent cooperates, the principal responds by investing. The agent's payoffs in rounds n, $n+1$, and $n+2$ thus equal .5, .5, and .5. The strategy of cooperating yields a total payoff to the agent equal to 1.5 in rounds n through $n+2$.[10] These facts are summarized in the second row of Figure 8.4.

Figure 8.4 shows that the agent's payoff in rounds n through $n+2$ is higher from cooperating than appropriating. This will be true for any three rounds of the game, provided that the principal continues playing the same strategy. For example, the total payoff to the agent who appropriates in rounds $n+3$ through $n+5$ equals 1, whereas the total payoff for cooperating equals 1.5. The agent thus benefits in the long run from cooperating rather than appropriating. The principal's strategy of retaliation can teach this lesson to the agent. If the agent follows the strategy of appropriating in round n, he or she will probably learn a lesson by receiving zero payoff in rounds $n+1$ and $n+2$. After learning the lesson, the agent will probably switch to the strategy of cooperating in round $n+3$.

We have described a strategy in which the principal repays the agent's cooperation by investing, and the principal retaliates against the agent's appropriation by not investing. Rewarding cooperation and punishing appropriation has been called "tit for tat."[11] When the principal plays the strategy of tit for tat, the agent maximizes payoff by cooperating. What about the principal? Does he or she maximize payoff by playing tit for tat? Experimental evidence indicates that tit for tat comes very close to maximizing the principal's payoff in a variety of circumstances, and these empirical findings are generally supported by theory.[12] Thus, the strategy of tit for tat is an efficient equilibrium to a repeated agency game.[13]

---

[10] Figure 8.4 assumes no discounting for time. Strictly speaking, payoffs should be discounted to present value from the date of receipt.

[11] R. Axelrod, The Evolution of Cooperation (1984).

[12] Id.

[13] Maskin and Fudenberg have proved that in any game in which (1) players maximize the discounted sum of single period utilities, (2) the discount rate is not too high, and (3) the players can observe the past history of moves in the game, any pair of payoffs that Pareto-dominate the minimax can arise as average equilibrium payoffs of the repeated game. This theorem, however, still leaves unexplained why the probability of a Pareto-efficient solution is as high as empirical studies suggest it to be. See Drew Fudenberg & Eric Maskin, *The Folk Theorem in Repeated Games with Discounting, or With Incomplete Information,* 54 Econometrica 533 (1986). If the players are willing to settle for a strategy that is very close to the self-interested maximum, but a little short of it, the endgame problem can be solved and the players will cooperate. In general, see Avinash Sixit & Barry Nalebuff, Thinking Strategically: The Competitive Edge in Business, Politics, and Everyday Life (1991), and Drew Fudenberg & Jean Tirole, Game Theory (1991). Exceptional games without cooperative solutions need not concern us here. See Glenn W. Harrison & Jack Hirshleifer, *An Experimental Evaluation of Weakest Link/Best Shot Models of Public Goods,* 97 J. Pol. Econ. 201 (1989) and Jack Hirshleifer & Juan Carlos Martinez Coll, *What Strategies Can Support the Evolutionary Emergence of Cooperation?,* 32 J. Conflict Resolution 367 (1988).

Long-run relationships require commitment, which can facilitate economic cooperation without state protection. Traditional forms of commitment include friendship, kinship, ethnicity, and religion. They often dominate economic life in communities with weak state protection of contracts. Business communities with weak state protection include international merchants, businesses in countries with weak or corrupt governments, businesses caught in civil wars, and foraging tribes that remain unsubordinated to states. Our model predicts, correctly, that traditional forms of commitment will flourish in these circumstances and decline if the state imposed effective contract law.

Similarly, traditional forms of commitment often dominate economic life in communities that face the state's hostility. Businesses facing state hostility include organized crime and some private businesses in socialist states. Our model predicts, correctly, that traditional forms of commitment should flourish in these circumstances.

Long-run relations can arise from commitments to institutions. For example, Japanese employees show a high level of commitment to the corporation, as evidenced by low rates of labor mobility. Our theory predicts correctly that long-run relationships will cause Japanese corporations to rely less on enforceable contracts as compared to American or European corporations. Long-run relations in the Japanese economy create more order and less law than in other countries.

B. Endgame Problem

Even long-run relationships end eventually. Near their end, business relationships often deteriorate. To see why, return to our example of tit for tat as depicted in Figure 8.4. Recall that when the agent appropriates, the principal retaliates by not investing for several rounds. However, the principal has no power to retaliate on the *last* round of the game. Thus, the final round of the agency game has the same logic as a one-shot agency game.

To illustrate, assume that the repeated game in Figure 8.4 has an end and both parties know it. To be concrete, assume that both parties know the game will end after round $n + 3$. The agent does not fear retaliation for appropriating in round $n + 3$, because the agent knows that there will not be any more rounds. In round $n + 3$, the agent will receive a payoff of 1 from appropriating and a payoff of .5 from cooperating. Consequently, the agent maximizes his or her payoff in round $n + 3$ by appropriating. Knowing this, the principal will refuse to invest in round $n + 3$. Thus the players cannot cooperate in round $n + 3$. The last round in a repeated agency game has the same logic as a one-shot game. Consequently, the players in the agency game cannot cooperate in the last round without enforceable contracts.

Worse still, the players could fail to cooperate in *every* round of the game. To see why, consider the strict logic of the situation. The principal follows the strategy of tit for tat, which rewards cooperation by subsequent investing and punishes appropriation by not investing in subsequent rounds. However, the principal will not invest in the last round, which is round $n + 3$. Consequently, the principal cannot use round $n + 3$ to reward cooperation or punish appropriation by the agent in round $n + 2$.

Knowing this fact, the agent can appropriate in round $n + 2$ without fearing retaliation in round $n + 3$. Knowing this, the principal will refuse to invest in round $n + 2$. The same logic now applies to round $n + 1$ and so forth back to the first round. In general, the demonstration that the players cannot cooperate in any given round leads to the conclusion that they cannot cooperate in the preceding round. If strictly rational parties know the round in which the repeated agency game ends, then the whole game unwinds, and the players fail to cooperate in any round. The phrase "the endgame problem" describes the unwinding of cooperation as a repeated game approaches its final round. Eastern Europe provides a dramatic example of the endgame problem after 1989 when communism collapsed and central planning ended, as discussed in the accompanying box.

People in long-run relationships develop social norms to coordinate their behavior without bargaining, which businessmen call "customs in trade." Lisa Bernstein discovered a peculiar fact: Customs in trade often contradict the explicit provisions of written contracts.[14] In the Memphis textile exchange, the seller weighs the cotton to ensure that he ships the amount specified in the contract. The contract stipulates that the buyer must also weigh the cotton when accepting delivery from the seller so that the buyer will not have cause for complaint later. The custom, however, is for the buyer to accept the weight as stated by the seller, thus saving the bother of weighing it a second time.

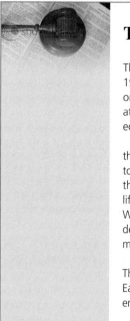

The Endgame Problem of Eastern Europe in 1989

The disintegration of communist governments in Eastern Europe accelerated dramatically in 1989. Central planning failed irreparably, and markets rapidly replaced central planning as the organizing economic principle. Unfortunately, production declined throughout Eastern Europe at this time. Why did the shift to markets immediately produce economic decline rather than economic growth?

The "endgame problem" provides the key. Under communism, much production occurred through long-run relations. For example, a truck driver would haul goods for "free" as a "favor" to his friend who operated a gas station, and the gas-station operator would supply petrol for the trucker when supplies ran short. The demise of communism massively disrupted political life, which caused people to doubt the persistence of their long-run economic relationships. With the end of relationships in sight, cooperation failed. For example, the trucker lost confidence that the gas-station operator could continue to supply petrol (the gas-station operator might lose her job), so the trucker stopped hauling the gas-station operator's goods for free.

The failure of cooperation caused production to decline all over Eastern Europe after 1989. This situation could be corrected by effective legal protection for property and contracts. Some Eastern European states have made the correction. In other states, however, entrepreneurs still enjoy higher profits from stealing property (especially state property) than from producing goods.

---

[14] Lisa Bernstein, *Private Commercial Law in the Cotton Industry: Creating Cooperation Through Rules, Norms, and Institutions*, 99 MICH. L. REV. 1724 (2001).

This contradiction between the written contract and the custom is easy to understand. The custom arises from buyers and sellers in long-run relationships who trust each other. As long as the relationship remains firm, the parties have little need for the contract. The contract, however, is written for deteriorating relationships. When the parties cannot rely on their relationship, they turn to the written contract. We have a long-run custom in trade and an endgame contract.

This fact complicates using customs in trade to interpret contracts. Assume that the seller purports to deliver a ton of cotton to the buyer. The buyer accepts delivery without weighing the cotton. Later the buyer discovers that the cotton weighs less than a ton. The buyer stops dealing with the seller and sues the seller for "short-weighting." The seller defends in court by saying that the contract obligated the buyer to weigh the cotton on delivery, which the buyer did not do. Having failed to complain when the cotton was delivered, the buyer is precluded by contract from complaining later. The seller replies that, contrary to what the contract says, the custom in trade is for the buyer not to weight the cotton when it is delivered. Should the court follow the explicit terms of the contract and decide for the seller, or should the court set the the contract aside and decide for the buyer? Presumably the court should recognize that the parties wrote the contract for the dissolution of a relationship, which is what has occurred, so the court should enforce the written contract.

So far we have discussed commitment to enduring relationships. However, most business relationships are tentative: They can persist indefinitely or end unexpectedly as circumstances change. With tentative relationships in the agency game, the players often follow the strategy tit for tat: The principal retaliates against the agent's appropriation by dissolving the relationship. This strategy by principals presents agents with a choice between two alternatives. The first strategy is for the agent to cooperate, in which case the relationship continues, and the agent receives a payoff of .5 in each round. The second strategy is to appropriate, thus provoking the first player to dissolve the relationship. By following the second strategy, the agent receives a payoff of 1.0 in the few rounds when he or she finds a principle to invest, and a payoff of zero in the other rounds when the search for a partner is unsuccessful. In brief, the agent chooses between cooperating and receiving a modest payoff in most rounds of the game or appropriating and receiving a large payoff in a few rounds of the game.

Notice that these two strategies in the agency game correspond to familiar facts about business. Some businesses try to make modest profits on many transactions. These businesses focus on long-run relationships with repeat customers. Other businesses try to make large profits on few transactions. These businesses focus on attracting new customers for one-time sales. In a competitive equilibrium, both strategies must earn the same payoff. In other words, the strategy of cooperating in long-run relationships must yield the same payoff as the strategy of appropriating in one-shot relationships.

This account corresponds to the dynamics of real markets. To illustrate, consider the market for trial lawyers. Most trial lawyers realistically assess their clients' prospects at trial and use this assessment as the basis for a settlement out of court. These lawyers correspond to cooperators in the agency game who attract repeat customers and maintain long-run relationships with their clients. However, some lawyers provide unrealistically optimistic assessments of their clients' prospects at trial and use these assessments to induce their clients to engage in costly litigation. These lawyers correspond to appropriators in the agency game who attract relatively few repeat customers and maintain short-run relationships with most clients. The proportion of lawyers of each type adjusts in response to the profitability of the two strategies. If the bar finds ways to reduce the profitability of trials relative to settlements, then more lawyers will try to settle cases, and fewer lawyers will provoke trials.

Businesses must expect the unexpected. Accommodating unforeseen changes requires flexible business relationships, not rigid rules. Formal rules do not tightly control very much business behavior. In a business relationship as in a marriage, enforcing the rights of the parties differs from repairing their relationship. When businesses in enduring relationships come to court, the judges sometimes adopt a different style of adjudication by, say, requiring the parties to attempt mediation before proceeding to trial.

Web Note 8.3

For more on relational contracts, see our website.

How to Exchange Hostages

Medieval kings used to guarantee the peace among themselves by exchanging hostages. Ask yourself this question: Suppose that a king wants to exchange hostages with another monarch to guarantee the peace. Assume that the king likes diamonds as much as he likes his children. That is, he values a diamond ring just as much as—neither more nor less than—he values his own son. Which would make a better hostage: the king's diamond ring or his son?

The better hostage is the one that deters both the hostage-giver and the hostage-taker from starting a war. By assumption, the king values the diamond ring and his son equally; the fear of losing the ring by starting a war equals the fear of losing his son. They are equally good deterrents against the hostage-giver's starting a war. However, they are not equally good deterrents against the hostage-*taker's* starting a war. The hostage-taker would presumably like to have the diamond ring but presumably places little intrinsic value on having the son of the neighboring king. The hostage-taker, therefore, is more inclined to start a war and keep the hostage if he holds the diamond ring rather than the king's son. That is why the king's son is a better hostage than the diamond ring.

In general, a good hostage is something that the hostage-giver values highly and the hostage-taker values little. Asymmetrical valuation makes a good hostage. (See Oliver Williamson, *Credible Commitments: Using Hostages to Support Exchange*, 83 AM. ECON. REV. 519 (1983).)

QUESTION 8.13: What sorts of things can corporations give as hostages in long-run contractual relations? Does hostage giving in long-run relationships serve the same or a different function as consideration in a short-run contract?

"Please, It's My Turn to Pay."

Assume that two computer companies consider merging. To discuss the possible merger, the CEOs decide to have dinner together twice a week for two months. Each can pay for his own meal, or they can take turns paying the whole bill. If each pays for his own meal, neither of them has an incentive to overeat. Conversely, if they take turns paying the bill, then each of them has an incentive to order very expensive items when the other one is paying. "Each-pays-for-his-own-meal" is apparently the better practice.

On further consideration, however, this is a mistake. The risk of overeating is trivial compared to the risk of a bad merger. A merger will require trust between them. They might try to establish trust in the small matter of lunch before going to the large matter of merging. "Take-turns-paying-the-whole-check" is a better practice for building trust. If you find out that someone over-orders whenever you pay for lunch, do you really want to merge your company with his?

Conclusion

Let us summarize our theoretical conclusions. Figure 8.1 describes a problem of cooperation: The principal will not invest unless the agent has an incentive to cooperate. Figure 8.2 depicts a legal solution to the problem. The legal solution is to make an enforceable contract. By enforcing promises, contract law enables people to make credible commitments to cooperate with each other. They maximize the gain from cooperation when law creates efficient incentives for performance and reliance. The law can also reduce the cost of negotiating contracts by supplying efficient default terms, and correct some market failures by supplying mandatory terms.

The legal solution to cooperation presupposes an effective state to enforce contracts. The machinery of state law is expensive in the best circumstances and ineffective in the worst circumstances. Figure 8.4 depicts a nonlegal solution to the problem of cooperation: Form an enduring relationship, which enables the principal to retaliate when the agent appropriates. Long-run relationships succeed in repeated transactions of small value and fail in one-shot transactions of large value.

Suggested Readings

Bernstein, Lisa, *Opting Out of the Legal System: Extralegal Contractual Relations in the Diamond Industry*, 21 J. Legal Stud. 115 (1992).

Eisenberg, Melvin A., *The Limits of Cognition and the Limits of Contract*, 47 Stan. L. Rev. 211 (1995).

———, *The Bargain Principle and Its Limits*, 95 Harv. L. Rev. 741 (1982).

Hermalin, Benjamin E., Avery W. Katz, & Richard Craswell, *The Law and Economics of Contracts*, in A. MITCHELL POLINSKY & STEVEN SHAVELL, EDS., HANDBOOK OF LAW AND ECONOMICS, v. 1 (2007).

Posner, Eric A., *Economic Analysis of Contract Law After Three Decades: Success or Failure?*, 112 YALEL L. J. 829 (2003). See also the responses to Posner's article: Ian Ayres, *Valuing Modern Contract Scholarship,* 112 YALE L. J. 881 (2003), and Richard Craswell, *In That Case What Is the Question?: Economics and the Demands of Contract Theory,* 112 YALE L. J. 903 (2003).

TREBILCOCK, MICHAEL J., THE LIMITS OF FREEDOM OF CONTRACT (1993).

9 Topics in the Economics of Contract Law

I N THE PRECEDING chapter, we explained that a theory of contracts must answer two questions: "What promises should be enforced?" and "What should be the remedy for breaking an enforceable promise?" We summarized the economic theory developed to answer these questions. Cooperation is productive: It creates value and typically benefits both parties. Enforcing promises enables people to make their commitments credible. Courts should enforce promises when the parties want enforceability in order to make a credible commitment to cooperate. Enforcement ideally induces optimal performance and reliance at low transaction costs. Optimal performance and reliance maximize the expected value of cooperation to both parties.

This economic theory allowed us to develop a framework for analyzing contracts in the preceding chapter. In this chapter we add texture and detail to the economic framework. In the first part of this chapter we focus on remedies for breach of contract. The best remedy for breach secures optimal commitment to the contract, which causes efficient formation, performance, and reliance.

Explicit terms in a contract may require interpretation, gaps may require filling, and inefficient or unfair terms may require regulation. We developed a general theory in the preceding chapter for optimal interpretation, gap-filling, and regulation of contracts. According to this theory, legal doctrines should perfect contracts by minimizing transaction costs and correcting market failures. We analyze the relevant legal doctrines in detail in the second part of this chapter.

I. Remedies as Incentives

When a party to a contract fails to perform as promised, the victim may ask the court for a remedy. Remedies fall into three general types: party-designed remedies, court-imposed damages, and specific performance. First, the contract may *stipulate* a remedy. The contract stipulates a remedy when it contains explicit terms prescribing what to do if someone breaches. For example, a construction contract may stipulate that the builder will pay $200 per day for late completion of a building. Instead of stipulating a specific remedy, the contract may stipulate a remedial process. For example, the contract may specify that disputes between the parties will be arbitrated by the International Chamber of Commerce, which has its own rules about remedies.

Because negotiating and drafting are costly, an efficient contract will not explicitly cover every contingency. In fact, most contracts do not specify remedies for breach. When the contract omits a remedy, the court must supply one. Second, the courts may supply a remedy in the form of damages. And third, the courts may order the breaching party to specifically perform the contractual promise.

Damages and specific performance are the two general types of court-designed remedies for breach of contract. Different legal systems in different countries disagree about the preferred remedy. In common law countries and in France, courts say that damages are the preferred remedy, whereas German and most other European courts say that specific performance is the preferred remedy. The difference between alternative legal traditions, however, is greater in theory than in practice. In practice, each legal system prescribes damages as the remedy in some circumstances and specific performance as the remedy in other circumstances. Furthermore, the prescriptions largely overlap in many different legal systems. Presumably, the prescriptions overlap because different systems of law respond to the same economic logic. Common law and civil law traditions both tend to specify the efficient remedy for breach of contract.

The Uniform Commercial Code, Restatements of Contracts, and Statute of Frauds

In the civil law countries, which include the nations of continental Europe, committees of scholars have formulated contract law into codes that legislatures enacted. In common law countries, which include the United States, judges have formulated contract law in deciding cases. This contrast, however, can be overstated. Americans have actually codified much of the common law of contracts in three important documents: the *Uniform Commercial Code*, the American Law Institute's *Restatements of Contracts*, and statutes revising the old English *Statute of Frauds*.

The National Conference of Commissioners on Uniform State Laws was founded in the 1890s to unify common law in the American states. The Conference and the American Law Institute (described below) adopted the *Uniform Commercial Code* in 1952, extensively revised it in 1956, and have periodically revised portions of the code since then. Forty-nine states (all but Louisiana, which has a civil law tradition) have adopted the *Uniform Commercial Code*. It consists of nine articles covering all aspects of commercial transactions. For example, Article 1 sets out the general provisions of the code; Article 2 covers the sale of goods (services are not covered); and Article 9 covers secured transactions.

The *Restatements* of the law are a project of the American Law Institute, a private group of judges, lawyers, and law professors founded in 1923, whose purpose "is to state clearly and precisely in the light of the decisions the principles and rules of the common law." The Institute's first project was the *Restatement of Contracts*, which was published in 1932 and subsequently revised in 1979. The ALI has also sought to restate the common law in property, contracts, torts, and other subjects.

The *Statute of Frauds* ("An Act for Prevention of Frauds and Perjuries") was passed by the English Parliament in 1677. The purpose of the act was to prevent fraud in the proof of contracts, deeds to land, trusts, and wills. To guarantee a trustworthy record, the statute required a signed writing in certain contractual transactions, possibly supplemented by witnesses. The requirement of a written record for contracts whose value exceeds a certain minimum has become the most important feature in the modern revisions of the statute, which every American state has adopted.

A. Alternative Remedies

Different remedies create different incentives for the parties to a contract. We will develop models to compare the incentive effects of different remedies on investment in performance and reliance. Before turning to their incentive effects, however, we must use economics to distinguish the different forms of remedies given by courts.

1. Expectation Damages Damages for breach of contract compensate the promisee for the injury caused by the nonperforming promisor. In a contract setting, the term "injury" has several different meanings. First, the promisee is worse off than if the contract had been performed. Performance provides a baseline for computing the injury. Using this baseline, the courts award damages that place the victim of breach in the position he or she would have been in if the other party had performed.

The promisee expects to gain from performance. Consequently, the common law tradition refers to damages based on the value of expected performance as "expectation damages."[1] The civil law tradition refers to these damages as "positive damages" (*lucrum cessans*) because the damages replace income that would have accrued in the future. If expectation damages or positive damages achieve their purpose, the potential victim of breach is equally well off whether there is performance, on the one hand, or breach and the payment of damages, on the other hand. We say that *perfect expectation damages* leave potential victims *indifferent* between performance and breach.

We will illustrate expectation damages by three examples:

> **Example 1:** Seller's Breach. O Ticket Agency offers opera tickets at the price p_O. K Ticket Agency offers equivalent opera tickets at the lower price p_K. Consumer orders x_K tickets from K at the contract price p_K and promises to pay when he picks up the tickets on the day of the performance. Close to the day of the performance, K announces that it will breach and not deliver the tickets to Consumer. In the meantime, the show has succeeded and the price of tickets has risen; so, Consumer pays the higher price, p_S, for substitute tickets purchased from a third ticket agency.

Replacing the promised performance with a perfect substitute puts the consumer in the same position that he would have been in if the promisor had performed. In this example, "substitute performance" consists in buying tickets at the price p_S. Accordingly, perfect expectation damages equal $x_K(p_s - p_K)$.[2] We will restate this formula in the language of contract law. The contract was made for future delivery of a good ("futures market"). After breach, the consumer bought substitute goods for delivery on the spot ("spot market"). The price had risen, so the spot price exceeded the contract price. To put the consumer in the same position as if the seller had delivered the goods, the seller

---

[1] The distinction between expectation and reliance damages, which is old in European jurisprudence, is neither as old nor as clear-cut in Anglo-American jurisprudence.

[2] This specific formula for damages is called the "substitute-price formula." The substitute-price formula awards the victim of breach the cost of replacing a promised performance with a substitute performance. If a commodity is homogeneous, the substitute performance may be identical to the promised performance. In that case, the substitute-price formula awards perfect expectation damages. However, if the commodity is differentiated rather than homogeneous, the substitution is imperfect.

must pay compensation equal to the difference between the contract price p_s and the spot price p_K.

Now we turn from seller's breach to buyer's breach.

> **Example 2:** Buyer's Breach. K Ticket Agency offers opera tickets for sale at the price p_K. Consumer orders x_K tickets and promises to pay when he picks up the tickets on the day of the performance. In reliance on Consumer's promise, K purchases x_K tickets at the wholesale price p_W. If Consumer had not ordered the tickets, K could have contracted to sell them to an agency named O at the lower price p_O. Close to the date of the performance, Consumer announces that he will not pick up or pay for the tickets. In the meantime, the show has flopped and the price of tickets has fallen; so, K resells the tickets at the lower price, p_S, to another consumer.

To put K in the same position as if Consumer had performed in Example 2, damages must equal $x_K(p_K - p_s)$. In other words, perfect expectation damages for buyer's breach equal the difference between the contract price p_K and the spot price p_s.

In Examples 1 and 2, many seats in the opera are close substitutes for each other. Our third example involves breach with an imperfect substitute.

> **Example 3:** Buyer's Breach with Unique Good. Seller builds custom boats, and Buyer retails boats, to consumers. Seller offers to build Buyer a custom boat with any one of three compass systems for navigation, which are named K, O, and A. Buyer estimates correctly that the market value at which he can retail the boat, depending on which compass is installed, will be v_K, v_O, or v_A, respectively. These values are net of the cost of the compass. Because $v_K > v_O > v_A$, Buyer maximizes profits by ordering the boat built with the K compass. However, Seller actually delivers a boat with an A compass. Replacing the compass after installation is prohibitively expensive, so Buyer subsequently retails the boat for v_A.

To put Buyer in the same position as if Seller had performed in Example 2, damages must equal $v_K - v_A$.[3] In other words, perfect expectation damages for Seller's breach equal the difference between the value of a performed contract and the actual value of what was delivered.

Table 9.1 summarizes these facts about expectation damages from our three examples. We will explain the entries for "reliance damages" and "opportunity cost" shortly.

TABLE 9.1

	Example 1: Seller's Breach with Substitute	Example 2: Buyer's Breach	Example 3: Seller's Breach with no Substitute
Expectation damages	$x_K(p_S - p_K)$	$x_K(p_K - p_S)$	$v_k - v_A$
Reliance damages	0	$x_K(p_W - p_S)$	0
Opportunity cost	$x_K(p_S - p_O)$	$x_K(p_O - p_S)$	$v_O - v_A$

---

[3] This is called the "diminished-value formula." When performance of a contract is partial or imperfect, the diminished-value formula awards the victim of breach the difference between (1) the post-breach value of a commodity that was to be received or improved under the contract, and (2) the value the commodity would have had if the contract had been properly performed.

2. Reliance Damages   Now we consider the second meaning of "injury" in a contract setting. The promisee may invest in reliance on the promise. Breach usually diminishes or destroys the value of the investment in reliance. So, reliance increases the loss resulting from breach. Breach makes promisees who rely worse off than if they had not made contracts. "No contract" provides a baseline for computing the injury. Using this baseline, the courts may award damages that place victims of breach in the position that they would have been in if they had never contracted with another party.

Damages computed relative to this baseline are called "reliance damages" in the common law tradition. The civil law tradition refers to these damages as "negative damages" because the damages replace income that was actually lost. If reliance damages or negative damages achieve their purpose, the potential victim of breach is equally well off whether there is no contract, on the one hand, or breach of contract and payment of damages, on the other hand. We say that *perfect reliance damages* leave potential victims *indifferent* between no contract and breach.[4]

To illustrate by Example 1, after K breached, Consumer had no opera tickets and faced a spot price of p_s to buy them. This is the same position that Consumer would have been in if Consumer had not contracted to buy opera tickets from anyone. Consequently, Consumer did not change his position in reliance on the contract and reliance damages in Example 1 are zero. (Can you think of a reliance investment that Consumer might reasonably have made?)

To illustrate by Example 2, in reliance on Consumer's promise, K bought x_K opera tickets at the wholesale price p_w. After Consumer breached, K sold the tickets at the spot price p_s. Assuming the wholesale price exceeds the spot price, reliance on the contract caused K to lose $x_K(p_w - p_s)$,[5] which equals perfect reliance damages.

Turning to Example 3, Buyer did not change his position in reliance on Seller's delivering the boat with a K compass rather than another kind of compass. Because the contract did not cause Buyer to change his position, reliance damages are zero. The row labeled "Reliance Damages" in the preceding table summarizes these facts.

3. Opportunity Cost   Now we consider the third meaning of "injury" in a contract setting. Making a contract often entails the loss of an opportunity to make an alternative contract. The lost opportunity provides a baseline for computing the injury. Using this baseline, the courts award damages that place victims of breach in the position that they would have been in if they had signed the contract that was the best alternative to the one that was breached. In other words, damages replace the value of the lost opportunity.

---

[4] Recall our discussion in the previous chapter of the subtle relationship between money damages and optimal reliance.

[5] This specific formula is called the "out-of-pocket-cost" formula. The out-of-pocket-cost formula awards the victim of breach the difference between (1) the costs incurred in reliance on the contract prior to breach, and (2) the value produced by those costs that can be realized after breach.

Damages computed relative to this baseline are called "opportunity-cost" damages. If opportunity-cost damages achieve their purpose, the potential victim of breach is equally well off whether there is breach of contract, on the one hand, or the best alternative contract, on the other hand. We say that *perfect opportunity-cost damages* leave potential victims *indifferent* between breach and performance of the best alternative contract.

Previously we discussed the fact that the promisee may invest in reliance on a contract. Similarly, the promisee may forego an opportunity in reliance on a promise. Consequently, the common law tradition considers opportunity-cost damages to be a form of reliance damages. This form of reliance damages takes into account the opportunity lost from relying on a promise, not merely the promisee's investment in reliance. Similarly, the civil law tradition considers opportunity-cost damages a form of negative damages (*damnum emergens*).

To illustrate opportunity-cost damages by Example 1, if Consumer had not contracted to buy opera tickets from K at price p_K, then Consumer would have purchased the tickets from O at price p_O. By relying on K's promise, Consumer lost the opportunity to buy from O and instead had to pay the spot price p_s. Consequently, the difference between these prices measures the lost opportunity: $x_K(p_s - p_O)$. In other words, perfect opportunity-cost damages for seller's breach equal the difference between the best alternative contract price and the spot price.

To illustrate by Example 2, in reliance on Consumer's promise, Agency K bought x_K opera tickets at the wholesale price p_w and lost the opportunity to sell them to Agency O at price p_O. After Consumer breached, K sold the tickets at the spot price p_s. Assuming the wholesale price exceeds the spot price, perfect compensation for K's lost opportunity equals $x_K(p_O - p_s)$.[6] In other words, perfect opportunity-cost damages for buyer's breach equal the difference between the best alternative contract price and the spot price.

Turning to Example 3, contracting for a K compass caused Buyer to lose the opportunity to purchase the boat with an O compass. The difference between the boat's retail market value with an O compass and its retail value with the actual compass equals perfect opportunity-cost damages: $v_O - v_A$. The row labeled "Opportunity Costs" in Table 9.1 summarizes these facts.

We have been discussing a contract for opera tickets with a close substitute that is available in the event of breach. The parties make the contract to hedge against future changes in prices. Thus, the buyer makes the contract to hedge against having to pay "scalpers" a high price for the tickets to a successful show at the time of performance. Conversely, the seller makes the contract to hedge against the possibility of having to sell tickets cheaply for an unsuccessful show at the time of performance. In markets for stocks and commodities, the parties often hedge against price changes by buying and selling options. An option is the right to buy a good in the

---

[6] In general, if breach causes the injured party to purchase a substitute performance, the opportunity cost formula equals the difference between the best alternative contract price available at the time of contracting and the price of the substitute performance obtained after the breach.

future at a price specified in the contract, or, equivalently, the obligation to sell a good in the future at a price specified in the contract. It is straightforward to show that a contract for goods with close substitutes is equivalent to a contract for an option. In both cases, the material consequence of the contract is to hedge against price changes.[7]

4. Problem of Subjective Value: *Hawkins v. McGee*   In the preceding examples of expectation, reliance, and opportunity-cost damages, the victim of breach values performance according to market prices. Now we turn to a famous case in which the victim of breach valued performances differently from the market. The famous case of *Hawkins v. McGee,* 84 N.H. 114, 146 A. 641 (N.H., 1929), dramatically illustrates the distinction between the three forms of damages when subjective value does not equal market value. The plaintiff, George Hawkins, suffered a childhood accident that left a permanent scar on his hand. When Hawkins was 18 years old, his family physician, McGee, persuaded him to submit to an operation that the doctor asserted would restore the hand to perfection. In the operation, skin from the plaintiff's chest was grafted onto his hand. The result was hideous. The formerly small scar was enlarged, covered with hair, and irreversibly worse. (Generations of American law students know *Hawkins v. McGee* as "the case of the hairy hand.") Hawkins prevailed against McGee in a suit alleging that the doctor had broken his contractual promise to make the hand perfect.

The question on appeal was "What damages should be awarded to Hawkins?" This issue is illustrated in Figure 9.1. The horizontal axis in this figure indicates the range of possible conditions of the hand, which vary from perfection to total disability. The vertical axis indicates the dollar amount of damages. The curved lines on the graph indicate the relationship between the extent of the disability and the amount of money needed to compensate for it.

Courts compute compensatory damages for physical injuries every day. Juries typically make the computation in America, whereas judges typically make the computation in Europe. Doubt remains as to exactly how courts make, or should make, the computation. The idea that money compensates for a serious physical injury perplexes some people. Please set aside your perplexity for the moment and consider an economic theory of compensation.

Assume that welfare or utility remains unchanged while moving along any curve in Figure 9.1. Welfare or utility remains unchanged because a change in compensation

---

[7] To prove equivalence, we will formulate a contract to sell a good in the future (an executory sales contract) as an option. At time 0, buyer *A* promises to pay $x to seller *B* for delivery of a widget at time 1. If buyer *A* breaches by refusing to pay $x and refusing to accept delivery of widget, then *A* owes damages $e to seller *B*. $e may be damages stipulated in the contract or default damages such as expectation damages. In this contract, *A* must either pay $e at time 1 and not receive the widget, or else *A* must pay $x and receive the widget. This is materially equivalent to the proposition "*A* pays $e to *B*, and then *A* chooses between paying nothing additional and getting nothing, or paying an additional $x − $e and getting the widget." This proposition is the following call option: At time 0, *A* promises to pay $e at time 1 for an option to buy a widget from *B* at the price $x − $e.

FIGURE 9.1

Expectation, opportunity cost, and reliance measures of damages in *Hawkins v. McGee.*

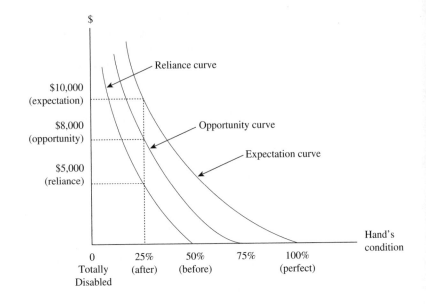

exactly offsets a change in the patient's condition when moving from one point to another on the same curve. Therefore, the curves are analogous to indifference curves in the microeconomic theory of consumer choice. (See Chapter 2.)

Now we can use Figure 9.1 to contrast damages based on expectation, reliance, and opportunity cost. First, consider expectation damages in *Hawkins v. McGee* as represented by the curved line labeled "expectation." The physician promised to make the boy's hand perfect. If the physician had performed, Hawkins would have a 100 percent perfect hand and no compensation. Assume that after the operation the patient's hand was 25 percent perfect. Expectation damages are the amount of money needed to compensate for the shortfall between the 100 percent perfect hand that was promised and the 25 percent perfect hand that was achieved. To measure these damages, locate the 25 percent point on the horizontal axis, move vertically up to the curve labeled "expectation," and then move horizontally over to the vertical axis to determine the corresponding dollar amount of damages—$10,000. By assumption, the patient is as well off with $10,000 in damages and a 25 percent perfect hand as with no damages and a 100 percent perfect hand.

Now consider reliance damages, which are graphed by the curve labeled "reliance." Under the reliance conception, the uninjured state is the condition in which the patient would have been if he had not made the contract with the breaching party. Assume that if there had never been a contract, the patient would have had a 50 percent perfect hand, whereas after the operation the hand was 25 percent perfect. Reliance damages are the amount of money needed to compensate the deterioration of the hand from 50 percent to 25 percent. Like the expectation curve, the reliance curve represents the relationship between the extent of the disability and the amount of money needed to compensate for it. The only difference is that the reliance curve touches the horizontal axis at the point where the hand is 50 percent perfect, rather than 100 percent perfect. By following the same steps as in expectation damages, we find that the patient is equally well off with $5,000 in damages and a 25 percent perfect hand as with no damages and a 50 percent perfect hand. Thus, reliance damages equal $5,000.[8]

Finally, consider the opportunity-cost measure of damages. Perhaps the operation performed by Dr. McGee caused Hawkins to lose the opportunity of having another doctor perform the operation successfully. If such an opportunity were lost, its value provides another baseline for computing damages. The value of the foregone opportunity depends on how close to perfection the hand would have been after an operation by another doctor. To illustrate, suppose that another doctor would have restored the hand to the 75 percent level. The injury from relying on Dr. McGee equals the difference between the 75 percent level that the other doctor would have provided and the 25 percent level achieved by Dr. McGee.

To measure opportunity-cost damages, consider the opportunity-cost curve in Figure 9.1. The opportunity-cost curve touches the horizontal axis at the 75 percent point, corresponding to the (speculated) condition of the hand after an operation by the best alternative doctor. As with the other two curves, the opportunity-cost curve is constructed so that every point on it represents the same level of welfare. Consequently, a change in the hand's condition represented by a move along the new curve is exactly offset by the corresponding change in damages. The value of the lost opportunity is read off the graph by moving vertically from the 25 percent point on the horizontal axis up to the "opportunity curve," and then horizontally to the intersection with the vertical axis. Following these steps, the opportunity-cost measure of damages equals $8000, which is less than expectation damages ($10,000) and more than reliance damages stripped of the opportunity cost ($5,000).

Figure 9.1 shows that expectation, reliance, and opportunity cost damages differ according to the baseline for measuring the injury, where "baseline" refers to the uninjured state. For measuring expectation damages, the uninjured state is the promisee's position if the actual contract had been performed.[9] For measuring reliance damages, the uninjured state is the promisee's position if no contract had been made. For measuring opportunity-cost damages, the uninjured state is the promisee's position if the best alternative contract had been performed.

In general, *perfect compensation* means a sum of money sufficient to make the victim of an injury equally well off with the money and with the injury as he or she would have been without the money and without the injury. The curves in Figure 9.1 depict perfect expectation, opportunity-cost, and reliance damages.[10] When this book speaks about damages measures such as "expectation damages" or "reliance damages," we mean an idealized measure of damages that we call "perfect."

---

[8] In fact, Hawkins received $3,000 from the original jury; subsequently, after the appellate court ordered a new trial, the plaintiff settled for $1,400 plus lawyer's fees.

[9] This proposition implicitly assumes that the rate of breach is low. When the rate of breach is high, it can be anticipated to some extent, and so the promisee can plan for breach, just as airlines and hotels plan for "no-shows." The phenomenon of statistically predictable breach creates a special set of problems for expectation damages.

[10] Note that the curves in Figure 9.1 illustrate the logic of compensation, not the actual computation of damages in this case.

Performance of the actual contract would make the promisee at least as well off as performance of the next best alternative. Consequently, perfect expectation damages are at least as high as perfect opportunity-cost damages. Performance of the next best alternative would make the promisee at least as well off as no contract. Consequently, perfect opportunity-cost damages are at least as high as perfect reliance damages. The following inequalities typically hold when courts measure damages perfectly:

$$\text{expectation damages} \geq \text{opportunity-cost damages} \geq \text{reliance damages}$$

Why do these three measures of damages usually have this rank by size? The promisee ordinarily chooses the best available contract; his loss from breach of the contract that he actually made is usually greater than his gain would have been from making the best alternative contract. Consequently, expectation damages typically exceed opportunity-cost damages.[11] Furthermore, the promisee expects to gain from making a contract rather than making no contract, so expectation damages usually exceed reliance damages. (See if you can explain why it is the case that opportunity-cost damages are, therefore, usually greater than reliance damages.)

Sometimes, however, the three damages measures do not have their standard order. One reason for this is that courts award imperfect damages, and sometimes the imperfection is so large that, say, imperfect reliance damages exceed imperfect expectation damages. To illustrate, assume that the promisor contracts to deliver a glass diamond that belonged to the promisee's grandmother. In reliance on the contract, the promise, for sentimental reasons, commissions an expensive ring to hold the glass diamond. The fact that sentiment motivated the promisee's commissioning of the ring means that the market value of the ring, with or without the glass diamond, is less than its cost. Suppose that the promisor fails to deliver the glass diamond, and the promisee sues. Perfect expectation damages equals the promisee's subjective value of the ring with the jewel. However, the court refuses to compensate the promisee for loss of subjective value. Instead, the court asserts that "expectation damages" equal the *market value* of the ring with the jewel in it. As explained, the market value of the ring is less than its cost. In this case, perfect reliance damages equal the cost of the ring. So reliance damages exceed what the court calls "expectation damages."

So, imperfections in damages awarded by courts can cause departures from the ordering of perfect damages. In addition, perfect damages can depart from their usual order because the promisee makes a mistake when contracting. In these circumstances, the actual contract may make the promisee worse off than no contract or an alternative contract. To illustrate, assume that a speculator who expects the market price of a good to rise signs a contract to pay now for its future delivery. If he is mistaken and the price falls, then he might be better off from having no contract rather than having this contract. In that case, his reliance damages will be higher than his expectation

---

[11] These two damage measures approach equality as markets approach perfect competition. The reason is that every contract has a perfect substitute in perfectly competitive markets; so, the actual contract is identical to alternative contracts that were not made.

damages. In fact, this seldom happens because the promisor almost never breaches such a contract.[12]

We have distinguished three damages measures and illustrated their calculation. Question 9.1 provides a good test of your ability to distinguish and calculate these damages. To attack this problem, we suggest that you first compute the expected profit from the contract. (You should get $900.) Then calculate the actual loss. (You should get $11,100.). Finally, calculate the profit from the best alternative contract. (You should get $400.) You should immediately see the expectation, reliance, and opportunity-cost damages.

> **QUESTION 9.1:** Buyer B pays $10,000 to New Orleans grain dealer D in exchange for D's promise to deliver grain to buyer B's London office on October 1. As a result of signing this contract, B decides not to sign a similar contract with another dealer for $10,500. D contracts with shipping company S to transport the grain. Buyer B agrees to resell the grain on arrival in London for $11,000 to another party. B pays $100 in advance (nonrefundable) as docking and unloading fees for the ship's projected arrival in London.
>
> The ship begins taking water several days out of New Orleans and returns to port. Inspection reveals that the grain is badly damaged by salt water, and D sells it as cattle fodder for $500. D conveys the news to B in London, who then purchases the same quantity of grain for delivery on October 1 at a price of $12,000.
>
> a. How would you measure expectation damages for D's breach of contract with B?
> b. How would you measure reliance damages?
> c. How would you measure opportunity-cost damages?

> **QUESTION 9.2:** The actual choice of a damage measure often depends on practical problems, not theory. Give some examples of breached contracts in which opportunity-cost damages are easier to implement than expectation damages. Give some examples of breached contracts in which reliance damages are easier to implement than opportunity-cost damages.

---

[12] To illustrate concretely, assume that A, who produces oil, promises to deliver x barrels to B next month. In exchange, B promises to pay A the contract price p_c per barrel on delivery. B is a speculator who buys for resale and does not change his position in reliance on the contract. At the end of the month, a fire in A's refinery prevents him from delivering his oil; so, A must breach or buy oil at the spot price p_S to deliver to B.

Consider two possible situations. First, assume that the contract price p_c exceeds the spot price p_S. As a result, B expects to gain $(p_c - p_S)x$ from A's performance. If A breaches, the expectation damages equal $(p_c - p_S)x$ and the reliance damages equal zero. This is the usual ordering of damage measures. Second, assume that the spot price p_S exceeds the contract price p_c. As a result, B expects to lose $(p_c - p_S)x$ from A's performance. If A breaches, the expectation damages are *negative* and reliance damages are zero. This is *not* the usual ordering of damage measures. In the second case, however, A will not breach. Instead of breaching, A will purchase oil at the price p_S and deliver it to B, thus performing on the contract and earning a profit of $(p_c - p_S)x$.

QUESTION 9.3: Perfectly competitive markets contain many buyers and sellers of the same contract; so, the best alternative contract is identical to the actual contract signed. What does this fact imply about the relationship between perfect expectation damages and perfect opportunity-cost damages for breach in perfectly competitive contract markets?

QUESTION 9.4: Airlines routinely sell more tickets for flights than the number of seats on the plane. "Overbooking" seldom causes problems because a statistically predictable number of ticketholders fail to show up for flights. In contrast, each retailer of hearing aids typically has the capacity to sell many more hearing aids per week than it actually sells. "Excess capacity" is routine for retailers of hearing aids. Contrast the effects of overbooking and excess capacity on profits lost by the seller when the buyer breaches a contract to buy.[13]

QUESTION 9.5: Here is a timeline for breach of contract that leads to litigation.

On Jan. 1, *A* contracts to deliver a widget to *B* on June 1 at a price of $2 to be paid on delivery.

On April 1, *A* renounces the contract. At that time, *B* can buy a widget for immediate delivery for $3, or *B* can contract with *C* to deliver a widget on June 1 at a price of $3.25. *B* does not buy a widget for immediate delivery or contract for future delivery.

On June 1, *B*'s suit against *A* succeeds. The court finds that *A* breached the contract on April 1. The court wants to give *B* perfect expectation damages. On June 1, *B* can buy a widget for $4.

Question: Should the court give damages of $1.25, $2, $3, $3.25, $4, or $5?

Question: Should the award depend on whether *B* bought a widget on April 1, or signed a contract with *C* on April 1, or bought a widget on June 1?

5. Restitution   In a deferred exchange, one party often gives something in exchange for the other party's promise to do something later. In these circumstances, a remedy for breach is to require the breaching party to return what was given. For example, the buyer of a car often makes a "down payment" before receiving the car. If the seller breaches the contract to deliver the car, the court may order the seller to return the down payment. This remedy is called "restitution," because it requires the injurer to give back what he or she took from the victim.[14] Restitution simply reverses the transfer that took place. Restitution is a minimal remedy in contracts. It does not compensate the victim of breach for expectation, opportunity, or reliance. Each of these three

---

[13] This question concerns what is called the "lost-volume" problem.

[14] See E. Allan Farnsworth, *Your Loss or My Gain?: The Dilemma of the Disgorgement Principle in Contract Damages*, 94 YALE L. J. 1339 (1985); and Robert Cooter & Bradley J. Freedman, *The Fiduciary Relationship: Its Economic Character and Legal Consequences*, 66 N. Y. U. L. REV. 1045 (1991).

measures is typically larger than restitution damages. Although minimal, restitution often has the advantages of simplicity and enforceability. (Common law and civil law contain a larger concept of restitution, especially in the law of property, but we cannot discuss it here.)

6. Disgorgement

Perfect compensation is a sum of money that substitutes for the injury and leaves the victim indifferent about its occurrence. The victim who receives perfect compensation has no basis to complain about the injury. Consequently, the law often does not punish people who compensate perfectly for the injuries that they cause.

We can restate this argument in economic terms. Perfect compensation completely internalizes the external costs of an injury. When costs are completely internalized, efficiency requires freedom of action, not deterrence. Given cost internalization and freedom, a rational person injures others whenever the benefit is large enough to pay perfect compensation and have some left over, as required for efficiency.

Perfect compensation is impossible in principle for some kinds of injuries. For example, vague promises create uncertainty about the value of performance. When the value of performance is uncertain, perfect compensation is impossible. Compensation for breaking vague promises is inevitably imperfect.

Vague promises are often made in long-run relationships. Although vague, the promises can be important for sustaining the relationship. Consequently, the parties may want vague promises to be enforceable, but they may want a different remedy than compensatory damages.

To illustrate, consider the relationship between stockholders and directors of a corporation. Instead of promising the stockholders a definite rate of return on their investment, directors make vague promises to be loyal and do their best. Even if directors make no such promises, the common law tradition requires directors to be loyal to stockholders and to act in the best interests of the corporation.[15] Sometimes, however, directors behave disloyally, and stockholders sue. To illustrate, assume that a corporate director learns about valuable minerals on the company's land. Before anyone else finds out, the director induces the company to sell her the land. The director violates her duty of loyalty by taking valuable minerals for herself that belong to the corporation.

The relationship between directors and stockholders involves trust. Trust would be undermined by allowing a director to take assets that belong to the corporation. The law deters disloyalty by various means, including requiring the injurer to give the profits of wrongdoing to the victim. "Disgorgement damages" are damages paid to the victim to eliminate the injurer's profit from wrongdoing. To illustrate, assume that the director who purchased the corporation's mineral-bearing land resold it to a third party at a high price. The director might be required to "disgorge" her profits from the sale by giving them to her corporation.

---

[15] The common law tradition holds directors to a "duty of loyalty" by virtue of the fiduciary relationship. Furthermore, the common law tradition applies the "business-judgment rule" to their decisions. The business-judgment rule holds directors responsible for making their best efforts to gather information and deliberate on decisions affecting the company, but excuses directors whose best efforts result in bad outcomes from liability to shareholders for any losses.

When disgorgement is perfect, the injurer is indifferent between doing right, on one hand, or doing wrong and paying disgorgement damages, on the other hand. Thus, perfect disgorgement is identical to perfect compensation, with the roles of injurer and victim reversed. The injurer achieves no gain from the wrongdoing net of perfect disgorgement damages, just as the victim suffers no harm from the injury net of perfectly compensatory damages.

Web Note 9.1

For more on cases illustrating the difficulties of computing damages and further discussion, see our website.

***

7. Specific Performance[16]   Instead of damages, the court may order the breaching party to perform a specific act as a remedy. "Specific performance" usually requires the promisor to do what he or she promised in the contract.[17] As mentioned, specific performance is the traditional remedy for breach of contract in some civil law countries, and damages are the traditional remedy in common law countries, but in practice, most legal systems use similar remedies in similar circumstances.

The typical case in which courts adopt specific performance as the remedy involves the sale of goods for which no close substitute exists. Examples include land, houses, antiques, works of art, and specialized labor contracts. In contrast, when breach involves the sale of goods for which close substitutes exist, courts typically award damages as the remedy. The victim can use the damages to purchase substitute performance. Examples include new cars, wheat, televisions, and stock in public companies.

To understand the role of substitution, consider two contrasting examples. First, the K ticket agency breaks its promise to supply a pair of opera tickets, so the customer has to pay more to purchase equivalent tickets from a "scalper" on the night of the performance. The tickets are equivalent, so the difference in their price perfectly measures the expectation damages. Second, assume that a dealer in rare books breaks his promise to sell the only manuscript copy of William Faulkner's *The Sound and the Fury* to a wealthy collector. The value of this unique manuscript is highly subjective, an amount that the court cannot determine accurately. The computation of expectation damages in this case is highly imperfect. Consequently, the court may order the dealer to deliver the manuscript to the collector.

In general, the error in the court's estimation of expectation damages decreases as the ease of substitution increases for the promised performance. The error decreases because the court can award damages at a level enabling the victim to purchase a substitute for the promised performance. When a good has a close substitute that is readily available in the market, no one is likely to value the good at much more than the price of the available substitute.

***

[16] This section is based on material in Ulen, *The Efficiency of Specific Performance: Toward a Unified Theory of Contract Remedies*, 83 Mich. L. Rev. 358 (1984).

[17] Sometimes the court orders the promisor to do something similar to what was promised, and sometimes the court forbids the promisor from performing with anyone other than the promisee.

In contrast, the remedy of specific performance entitles the promisee to the good itself, rather than its value. By adopting the remedy of specific performance for breach of promise to deliver unique goods, courts avoid the impossible task of determining the promisee's subjective valuation. Later we compare the advantages and disadvantages of damages and specific performance.

8. Party-Designed Remedies: Liquidated Damages

Contracts often specify the remedy for breaching one of their terms. The contract might stipulate a sum of money that the promise-breaker will pay to the innocent party ("liquidated damages"). Alternatively, the parties may leave valuable assets on deposit with a third party and specify that the assets should be given to the victim in the event of a breach ("performance bonds"). Or the parties may specify a process for resolving disputes between them, such as arbitration by the International Chamber of Commerce applying the law of New York.

Courts examine terms specifying remedies more skeptically and critically than other terms in contracts. Instead of enforcing terms specifying remedies, courts sometimes set the terms aside and substitute court-designed remedies. To illustrate, sellers in America frequently present buyers with a form contract stipulating that disputes will be resolved by arbitration in the seller's home city. Thus, a manufacturer in New York City offers a contract to a buyer in Los Angeles specifying that disputes will be resolved by the American Arbitration Association in New York City. If the buyer sues the seller in a California court, the court will be reluctant to concede jurisdiction to the arbitrator in New York City (although this reluctance appears to be changing so as to give the parties greater flexibility in specifying where a dispute arising from their agreement will be heard and according to what law it will be decided).

The common law and civil law traditions differ with respect to enforcing penalty clauses in contracts. A common law tradition prevents courts from enforcing terms stipulating damages that exceed the actual harm caused by breach. Courts call a term a "penalty" when it stipulates damages exceeding the actual harm (or a reasonable prior estimate of that harm) caused by breach. Courts call a term "liquidated damages" when it stipulates damages that do not exceed the actual harm (or are a reasonable prior estimate of that harm) caused by breach. The common law tradition enforces liquidated damages and withholds enforcement of penalties. In contrast, courts in civil law countries tend not to object to penalties as such. Courts in civil law countries show more willingness to enforce contract penalties or to reduce them without setting them aside.

Some economists now believe that the civil law countries are right to enforce penalty clauses. Stipulation of damages exceeding the requirements for compensation can serve three functions. First, the punitive element may be considered as payment on an insurance contract written in favor of the innocent party by the breaching party.[18]

---

[18] See Charles Goetz & Robert Scott, *Liquidated Damages Penalties and the Just Compensation Principle: Some Notes on an Enforcement Model of Efficient Breach*, 77 COLUM. L. REV. 554 (1977). For a sophisticated economic argument in favor of the traditional view, limiting stipulated damages to a reasonable approximation of what a court would have awarded in damages, see Eric L. Talley, *Contract Renegotiation, Mechanism Design, and the Liquidated Damages Rule*, 46 STAN. L. REV. 1195 (1995). Talley argues that the traditional view facilitates Coasean bargaining in the event that the parties modify the contract.

This situation arises when one party to the contract places a high subjective valuation on performance of the contract, and the other party is the best possible insurer against its loss.

To illustrate, consider Professors Goetz and Scott's delightful example of the Anxious Alumnus. An alumnus of the University of Virginia charters a bus to carry his friends to the site of an important basketball tournament where his college team will play. The alumnus is anxious about mishaps. Suppose the bus breaks down; suppose inclement weather prevents the bus from proceeding; or suppose traffic is so heavy that the fans do not arrive in time. He values performance of the contract to deliver him to the game at far more than the price he has paid to hire the bus, yet the subjective value is too speculative for courts to measure accurately. So, the bus company agrees to pay the alumnus a stipulated penalty in the event of the bus company's breach. In exchange, the alumnus agrees to pay the bus company a price for renting the bus that exceeds the usual price. The difference between the contract price and the usual price represents the premium on an insurance policy written by the bus company in favor of the alumnus. The insurance policy compensates the alumnus for his subjective losses in the event that the bus company's fault prevents him from attending the basketball game.

A second reason for enforcing penalty clauses is that they often convey information about the promisor's reliability. To illustrate, consider a contract that specifies the date for completing a construction project. Perhaps the builder is certain of her ability to complete performance by the specified date, but the buyer doubts the builder's ability to meet the deadline. If the builder promises to pay a large penalty for late construction, she signals her certainty about finishing on time. A penalty clause may be the cheapest way for the builder to communicate credibility to the buyer.

A third reason to enforce penalty clauses, as explained by Avery Katz, is that most penalties can be restated as bonuses. To illustrate, assume that Seller receives $90 from Buyer for a promise to deliver in one month goods that Buyer values at $100. Further assume that the parties would like to stipulate that Seller pays Buyer damages of $125 for breach of contract. This stipulation, however, creates a penalty of $25 for breach, so the courts might not enforce the penalty. The first row of Table 9.2 summarizes the numbers for the penalty contract. With performance of the penalty contract, Buyer's net payoff equals $100 - 90 = 10$, and Seller's net payoff equals $90. With breach of the penalty contract, Buyer's net payoff equals $125 - 90 = 35$, and Seller's net payoff equals $90 - 125 = -35$.

TABLE 9.2

	Price	Performance Bonus	Seller's Payoff from Performance	Actual Harm from Breach	Penalty for Breach	Seller's Loss from Breach	Buyer's Gain from Breach
Penalty contract	90	0	90	100	25	−35	+35
Bonus contracts	65	25	90	100	0	−35	+35

Web Note 9.2

For the representation of Table 9.2 as a decision tree, see our website.

To increase the probability of enforcement by the court, the parties can reword the contract so that a bonus for performance replaces a penalty for breach in the language of the contract, but the two contracts have identical material outcomes. To achieve this end, the alternative contract stipulates that Buyer pays Seller $65 on signing the contract, and Buyer pays Seller $25 as a bonus for performance. Buyer's net payoff from performance thus equals $100 - 65 - 25 = 10$ and Seller's net payoff equals $65 + 25 = 90$, which is the identical outcome as with the penalty contract. In the event that Seller breaches the bonus contract, Seller pays Buyer's actual damages of 100. Thus, Buyer's net payoff from breach equals $100 - 65 = 35$, and Seller's net payoff equals $65 - 100 = -35$, which is the identical outcome as with the penalty contract. The penalty contract apparently contains an illegal penalty and the bonus contract apparently contains a legal bonus, even though the contracts are materially identical. The point of this example is that not enforcing penalties creates incentives to redraft identical contracts with bonuses.

QUESTION 9.6: Earlier we explained that specific performance is the usual remedy for breach of a contract to deliver goods for which no close substitutes exist, whereas damages are the usual remedy when close substitutes exist. Use the "closeness of substitutes" to explain why the death of an artist releases his estate from any contracts that he signed to paint portraits, whereas the death of a house painter does not release her estate from contracts that she signed to paint houses.

QUESTION 9.7: Restitution is usually inadequate to compensate the victim. What practical reasons do courts have for using restitution as a remedy?

QUESTION 9.8: Assume that a swindler must disgorge her profits if she gets caught. In order to make swindling unprofitable (expected value of swindling equals zero), how high must the probability of getting caught be?

QUESTION 9.9: Can you describe conditions when specific performance is an impossible remedy? Can you describe conditions when specific performance is an unfair remedy to a third party? (Hint: Suppose the dealer in New York breached his contract and sold Faulkner's manuscript to someone else.)

QUESTION 9.10: Construction company C and landlord L negotiate to build an office building for occupancy on September 1. Landlord L wants to sign up commercial renters to occupy the building on September 1. Unforeseeable causes often delay construction projects. C is willing to take this risk. C proposes a price of $10 million and a liquidation clause requiring C to pay L

$1,500 per day for completing the building late. You are a lawyer hired by *L* to help on the contract. *L* tells you in private that he will actually lose $1,000 per day of delay, not $1,500 per day. How would you explain to *L* that he might benefit from proposing to reduce liquidated damages from $1,500 to $1,000 per day?

 Web Note 9.3

Our website discusses some further issues having to do with stipulated damages, includes an excerpt from a decision by Judge Posner in which he had to determine the enforceability of a penalty clause, and of other remedies.

Liquidated Damages and Efficient Breach

Until late 2001, the Boston Fire Department allowed its employees unlimited sick leave. During 2001 firefighters took a total of 6,432 days of sick leave. Then, as part of a program to increase professionalism within the department, the Fire Department announced that beginning in 2002 firefighters could take only 15 sick days of leave per year. Any additional days of sick leave would be unpaid. In 2002, firefighters took a total of 13,431 sick days—more than double the amount they had taken in the previous year when sick leave was unlimited and compensated. What happened?

One possibility, suggested by Professor Tess Wilkinson-Ryan of the University of Pennsylvania School of Law, was that when the new employment contract formalized the sick leave policy and imposed an explicit sanction for breaching the limit, that very fact encouraged breach.[19] This possibility that replacing informal norms with explicit laws might have unexpected results has been noticed before. Uri Gneezy and Aldo Rustichini did a famous study of Israeli day-care centers that found a similar effect.[20] Parents were supposed to pick up their children in day-care centers by 4 p.m. Failure to do so required the center to pay aides to remain on duty to supervise the children who had not been picked up. So many parents failed to pick up their children, despite pleas to be on time and warnings about the adverse consequences of being late, that some of the day-care centers introduced an explicit fine on parents who were 10 minutes or more late in picking up their children. The surprising result was that parental tardiness *increased* in the day-care centers that imposed the fine while remaining constant in those that did not impose the fine. This was precisely the opposite of what was expected: Fines are supposed to deter, not encourage, the sanctioned activity.

Following the examples of the Boston firefighters and the Israeli day-care parents, Professor Wilkinson-Ryan hypothesized that making the price of contract breach explicit by including a liquidated-damages clause might encourage breach. Moreover, she speculated

---

[19] *Do Liquidated Damages Encourage Breach?: A Psychological Experiment*, 108 MICH. L. REV. 633 (2010).

[20] *A Fine Is a Price*, 29 J. LEGAL STUD. 1 (2000).

that because general considerations of morality might discourage breach even when it was efficient, liquidation clauses might further efficient breach.

In a series of carefully designed web-based experiments, Professor Wilkinson-Ryan confirmed her hypotheses. She wrote:

> [W]hen interpersonal obligations are informal or underspecified, people act in accordance with shared community norms, like the moral norm of keeping promises. However, when sanctions for uncooperative behavior are specified or otherwise formalized between the parties, behavior becomes more strategic and more self-interested.

Does this conclusion suggest that to encourage efficient breach the law ought to encourage liquidated damages clauses?

B. Models of Remedies

Having described the remedies for breach of contract, we now analyze them. An economic analysis of remedies models their effects on behavior. Remedies affect many kinds of behavior, but we cannot model all of them.[21] Our analysis concentrates on these three:

1. The promisor's decision to breach or perform,
2. The promisor's investment in performing, and
3. The promisee's investment in reliance on the promise.

1. Efficient Breach and Performance When circumstances change, not performing a promise can be more efficient than performing. In these circumstances, nonperformance occurs in two ways. First, the promisor can *breach* the contract by breaking his promise. Second, the parties can renegotiate and modify the contract to allow nonperformance of the original obligation.

To illustrate, assume that *A* promises to build a custom widget and deliver it to *B* on September 1. On August 1, *A* learns that building the widget will cost more than anticipated and more than it is worth to *B*. This is an unfortunate contingency. Alternatively, *A* may learn that *C* values the widget far more than *B*, so delivering it to *C* creates more value than delivering it to *B*. This is a fortunate contingency. In either case, performing the promise to build and deliver the widget to *B* is inefficient. To avoid inefficiency, *A* can breach the contract and suffer the consequences, such as paying damages to *B*. Alternatively, *A* can renegotiate the contract with *B* and obtain a release from its terms, which usually involves *A* giving *B* something that *B* values more than performance.

---

[21] Here is a partial list of affected behaviors: (1) searching for trading partners; (2) negotiating exchanges; (3) drafting contracts (explicitness); (4) keeping or breaking promises; (5) taking precaution against events causing breach; (6) acting in reliance on promises; (7) acting to mitigate damages caused by broken promises; and (8) resolving disputes caused by broken promises.

When nonperformance is more efficient than performance, what determines whether *A* will breach the contract or renegotiate it? According to the Coase Theorem, the parties will renegotiate whenever transaction costs are low. In renegotiating, the parties will divide the surplus from substituting a more efficient contract for the original one. The terms of the renegotiated contract will depend on the bargaining power of the parties, which in turn depends on the legal remedy in the event that bargaining fails. The next two sections explain how the legal remedy (damages) or the equitable remedy (specific performance) affects bargaining power when there is an unfortunate or a fortunate contingency.

2. Unfortunate Contingency   We modeled an unfortunate contingency in the preceding chapter by using the agency game. In the relevant version of the agency game, the agent (second player) promises to cooperate with the principal (first player). When making the promise, the future cost of cooperating remains uncertain. The cost of cooperating might be low or high. Low costs are likely and high costs are unlikely. High costs of performing are an unfortunate contingency that makes breach efficient.

Figure 9.2, which reproduces numbers used to construct Figure 8.3 from the preceding chapter, depicts these payoffs in a matrix. With good luck, performance is cheap for Xavier, so Xavier performs and the payoffs to Yvonne and Xavier are (.5, .5). With bad luck, performance is expensive for Xavier, so Xavier breaches and compensates Yvonne by paying her expectation damages. In that case, the payoffs to Yvonne and Xavier are (.5, –5).

Figure 9.2 assumes the Xavier must pay expectation damages to Yvonne. Now consider the remedy of specific performance. This remedy gives the principal a right to the agent's performance, regardless of its cost. If the principal asserts this right, then the agent will be forced to perform even when the costs of performance are high. If the

FIGURE 9.2

Contract with luck affecting performance.

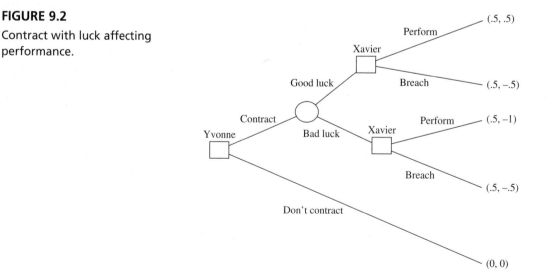

principal in Figure 9.2 forces the agent to perform at high costs, the agent receives –1.0 and the principal receives .5.

Instead of exercising this right, however, the principal might respond to the unfortunate contingency by renegotiating the contract. If renegotiation succeeds, the principal will agree to accept damages in exchange for allowing the agent to breach. When the agent breaches, the joint payoffs equal zero in Figure 9.2. Alternatively, if renegotiations fail, the principal will exercise his or her right to performance. The joint payoffs for performing at high cost equal (–1.0 + .5) or –0.5 in Figure 9.2. The difference in joint payoffs between performing at high cost and breaching equals the surplus from successful renegotiations. The surplus from successful renegotiation in Figure 9.2 thus equals $0 - (-1.0 + .5) = .5$.

Successful renegotiation allows the parties to share the surplus of .5. We discussed the division of a bargaining surplus at length in Chapter 4. Rationality, alone, does not generally prescribe a division of the surplus. Consider a reasonable way to divide the surplus. Without renegotiating the contract, the principal can force the agent to perform, which yields a payoff of .5 to the principal. The principal must receive at least .5 in order to benefit from renegotiating the contract. In addition to .5, the principal will want a share of the surplus. A reasonable division of the surplus gives half of it, or .25, to each player. Consequently, a reasonable renegotiation of the contract gives the principal ($.5 + .25 = .75$). The agent pays .75 to the principal in exchange for not exercising his or her right to specific performance. (Can you demonstrate that this solution also gives the agent the payoff that he or she can get independently plus half the surplus from cooperation?[22])

Efficiency requires the players to choose the actions that maximize the sum of the payoffs to the principal and agent. The sum of the payoffs is found by adding the two numbers at the end of each branch of Figure 9.2. It is easy to see that to perform at low cost is more efficient than breaching, whereas breaching is more efficient than performing at high cost. We have shown that the remedy of damages causes the agent to perform at low cost and to breach rather than to perform at high cost. In contrast, the remedy of specific performance causes the agent to perform at low cost, and the agent sometimes breaches and sometimes performs at high cost. The agent performs at high cost when renegotiation fails. Consequently, the damage remedy is always efficient, whereas specific performance is sometimes inefficient.[23]

The difference in efficiency between the two remedies is easy to understand. The remedy of damages gives the promisor the choice of performing or breaching and paying damages. The promisor can choose the cheaper alternative.[24] In contrast, the remedy of specific performance gives the promisee the right to performance, regardless of its costs. Exercising this right in the wrong circumstances causes the inefficiency.

---

[22] Without renegotiation, the agent will be forced to perform at high costs, which yields the agent a payoff equal to –1.0. A reasonable renegotiation gives the agent half the surplus, or .25. Therefore, the agent's payoff after renegotiation should equal $-1.0 + .25 = -.75$.

[23] Somewhat awkwardly, the law could preclude specific performance if the innocent party has become a monopolist and has an unfair bargaining advantage over the breacher.

[24] Recall that perfect expectation damages internalize the full cost of breach to the promisor. Consequently, the promisor chooses the cheaper alternative based on *social costs*, as required for efficiency.

To avoid the inefficient exercise of the right to specific performance, the parties must succeed in renegotiating the contract. Successful renegotiation can restore efficiency to the decision to breach. As long as the principal and agent can renegotiate successfully and very cheaply, both the legal and equitable remedies affect distribution but not efficiency.

You should already know this conclusion about renegotiation from studying the positive Coase Theorem in Chapter 4, especially the example of the laundry and the electric company. According to the positive Coase Theorem, private bargaining under zero transaction costs always succeeds in allocating resources efficiently. Given zero transaction costs, the law influences distribution but not efficiency. We have just applied the Coase Theorem to contracts. We found that the agent will breach efficiently, regardless of the rule of law, provided that renegotiation succeeds. Given costless renegotiations, the legal and equitable remedies for breach of contract influence distribution but not efficiency. Given costly renegotiations, however, the damage remedy for breach of contract has an advantage over specific performance, just as compensation has an advantage over injunction in nuisance cases with high negotiations costs.

ⓘ Web Note 9.4

Does a focus on efficient breach slight the moral basis of promising? In this web note we consider some recent experimental and theoretical articles on the morality of completing one's promises.

3. Fortunate Contingency
The preceding discussion explained that when an unfortunate contingency makes performance uneconomical and the promisor wants to avoid performing, the injunctive remedy increases the promisee's bargaining power in the ensuing negotiations relative to a damages remedy. Now we apply this line of argument to a fortunate contingency. A fortunate contingency is typically an alternative contract that is even more profitable than the original contract. When a fortunate contingency makes the promisor want to avoid performing on the original contract in order to profit even more from an alternative contract, the injunctive remedy increases the promisee's bargaining power in the ensuing negotiations relative to a damages remedy. With increased bargaining power, the promisee can extract a larger share of the surplus created by the fortunate contingency.

To demonstrate this fact, assume that person A values living in his house at $90,000, and person B values living in A's house at $110,000. A promises to sell the house to B for $100,000, which will create a surplus of $20,000. Before completing the sale, however, person C appears on the scene and offers to buy the house from A. C values the house at $126,000. C offers to pay $118,000 for the house. C's appearance creates a new, more profitable alternative to the original contract. Transferring the house from A, who values it at $90,000, to C, who values it at $126,000, creates a surplus of $36,000. Figure 9.3 summarizes these numbers in the first column, which is labeled "Value placed on house."

Assume that the appearance of C causes A to breach the contract by refusing to sell the house to B. B sues A. Consider the payoffs to the three parties when the law gives B

FIGURE 9.3

Remedies.

	Value placed on house	Distribution of surplus if no remedy	Distribution of surplus if remedy is specific performance	Distribution of surplus if remedy is expectation damages
Person A	$90,000	$28,000	$10,000	$18,000
Person B	$110,000	$0	$18,000	$10,000
Person C	$126,000	$8,000	$8,000	$8,000
Total		$36,000	$36,000	$36,000

no remedy, thus allowing A to sell the house to C. A's payoff equals the difference between the value of the house to him ($90,000) and the sale price to C ($118,000), or $28,000. B's payoff equals zero. C's payoff equals the difference between the purchase price ($118,000) and the value of the house to her ($126,000), or $8,000. Figure 9.3 summarizes these numbers in the second column, which is labeled "Distribution of surplus if no remedy."

Now assume that the courts respond to B's suit against A's breach by the remedy of specific performance. Specific performance is an order from the court for A to sell the house to B for $100,000 as promised. A's payoff equals the difference between the value of the house to him ($90,000) and the sale price to B ($100,000), or $10,000. B will presumably resell the house to C for $118,000. B's payoff equals the difference between her purchase price ($100,000) and her sale price ($118,000), or $18,000. C's payoff equals the difference between the purchase price ($118,000) and the value of the house to her ($126,000), or $8,000. Figure 9.3 summarizes these numbers in the third column, which is labeled "Distribution of surplus if remedy is specific performance."

Finally, assume that the courts respond to B's suit against A's breach by the remedy of damages. A breaches the contract with B and sells the house to C for $118,000. A's payoff equals the difference between the value of the house to him ($90,000) and the sale price to B ($118,000), or $28,000. Having obtained a surplus of $28,000, A must now pay damages to compensate B for breaching the contract. The extent of the damages will determine the division of the surplus of $28,000 between A and B. Assume that the damages have been designed by the court to put B in the position she expected to be in if A had delivered the house and B had kept it. B expected to get a house that she values at $110,000 for a price of $100,000, yielding an expected surplus of $10,000. By this calculation, B's expectation damages equal $10,000. Expectation damages produce the result that A gets $18,000 in surplus, B gets $10,000 in cash, and C gets a surplus of $8,000 on purchasing the house. Figure 9.3 summarizes these numbers in the fourth column, which is labeled "Distribution of surplus if remedy is expectation damages."

Now let us compare the remedies of specific performance and expectation damages. Economic efficiency requires allocating resources to their highest-valued use. C values the use of the house more than A or B. Thus, an efficient remedy requires that C get the house. With specific performance, C buys the house from B, and B gets more of the surplus than A. With expectation damages, C buys the house from A, and A gets more of the surplus than B. Either court-designed remedy creates efficient incentives for allocating the house, but the remedies differ in the pathway of the sale and the distribution of the surplus from exchange. As we showed in the previous section and in

Chapter 4, given zero transaction costs, the law affects distribution but not efficiency. Figure 9.3 expresses this result. As long as *A*, *B*, and *C* can bargain successfully at zero transaction costs, the choice of remedy affects distribution but not efficiency.

The remedy of expectation damages gives the promisor a choice between performing or breaching and paying damages. The distribution of the surplus favors the promisor when the remedy for breach is damages. In contrast, when the remedy is specific performance, the distribution of the surplus favors the promisee.

The Coase Theorem implies that court-designed remedies differ with respect to efficiency only when transaction costs are positive. When transaction costs are positive, the most efficient court-designed remedy minimizes the transaction costs of moving the good to its highest-valued use. Applied to our example, the most efficient court-designed remedy minimizes the transaction costs of moving ownership of the house from *A* to *C*. Figure 9.3 assumes the move can be made with zero transaction costs, which implies that both remedies are equally efficient (but differ in distributional consequences).

Earlier we explained that the consequences of protecting an entitlement by a damage remedy or an injunctive remedy are much the same in property and contract law. When property owners can negotiate at little cost, or the parties to a contract can renegotiate at little cost, the injunctive remedy strengthens the bargaining position of the entitled party without affecting the outcome's efficiency. When negotiations are costly, however, the remedy may affect their magnitude. As in property disputes, contract renegotiation may be simpler when the remedy is specific performance.

To see why, consider the task faced by the court when computing damages for *A*'s breach of contract with *B*. To determine compensatory damages, the court must estimate the value that *B* places on the house. The subjective valuation of the buyer is difficult for courts to estimate. The buyer's subjective valuation must exceed the sale price, but by how much? Lawyers could use up a lot of money arguing about whether *B* valued the house at $105,000, $110,000, or $125,000.[25] This uncertainty clouds negotiations by the parties to settle the dispute out of court.

Unlike damages, the remedy of specific performance does not present courts with a problem of valuation. When the court applies this remedy, the court orders *A* to sell the house to *B* at the *contract price*. The court does not have to set a price. Nor does a transfer of the house to *B* have to occur. Bargaining may replace performance. In bargaining, each side will be uncertain about the other's valuation of the house. Many advantages exist to having markets, not courts, resolve price uncertainty. Some economists think that the problem of valuation by courts is so severe that contract law should adopt specific performance more widely as a remedy.[26]

QUESTION 9.11: Assume that *A* values his house at $90,000. *B* is willing to pay $110,000 for *A*'s house in order to relocate closer to work. (Forget about person *C* for purposes of this question). After signing a contract, *B*'s employer

---

[25] Determining the extent of damages in litigation is a specific form of what economists call the "problem of preference revelation." The general problem is to close the gap between objective prices and subjective values. Economists have had limited success trying to solve this problem.

[26] See Ulen, supra n. 16.

announces that the company will move to another city. In view of this fact, the value of the house to B is reduced to $75,000. From an efficiency viewpoint, who should own the house, A or B? How will the parties achieve efficiency in allocating the house if the court enforces the contract?

QUESTION 9.12: Give examples of unfortunate and fortunate contingencies that could make breach of contract more efficient than performance. Give reasons why the parties might not insert explicit terms in the contract to deal with these contingencies, such as a term excusing breach when performance is very costly.

QUESTION 9.13: State the Coase Theorem as applied to remedies for breach of contract.

QUESTION 9.14: Assume that a fortunate contingency makes breach efficient for a sales contract, and assume that the parties cannot renegotiate the contract. Explain why the remedy of damages can save transaction costs by reducing the number of sales required to move the good to the person who values it most. Explain why the remedy of specific performance enables the court to avoid the problem of subjective valuations of the good.

C. Investment in Performance and Reliance

We have compared the incentive effects of two different remedies (expectation damages and specific performance) on one kind of decision (performance or breach). Now we consider the incentive effects of several different remedies on two kinds of decisions (investment in performance and reliance). Our analysis of property law revealed a paradox when we compared state actions that require compensation of private property owners for reductions in their property values ("takings") and state actions that require no compensation ("regulations"). Specifically, requiring compensation gives efficient incentives for state action and inefficient incentives for private owners to invest, whereas *not* requiring compensation has the opposite effect. We encounter the same paradox in contract law when we consider incentives effect on two kinds of decisions, investment in performance and reliance.

1. Paradox of Compensation We begin by explaining the paradox of compensation in contracts. A contract imposes obligations on the promisor that are typically costly to perform. To perform or to increase the probability of performing, the promisor must invest. The promisor has an incentive to invest more on performing when liability for breach is higher. Conversely, the promisee can increase the value of performance by relying, but relying also increases the loss from breach. The promisee has an incentive to rely more when liability for breach is higher.

The following example illustrates the situation.

Example 4: The Waffle Shop. Yvonne owns a restaurant for economists that is called the Waffle Shop. Her business prospers so that she needs a larger facility. She enters into a contract with Xavier, a builder, who promises to construct the new restaurant for occupancy on September 1. Xavier knows that events could jeopardize completing the building on time, such as striking plumbers, recalcitrant city inspectors, or foul weather. He can reduce the probability of late completion by working overtime before the plumbers' contract expires, badgering the city inspectors, or accelerating work on the roof.

Yvonne anticipates a surge in business when she opens the new facility. To accommodate the surge in business, she needs to order more food than she can use in her old restaurant. She would like to order supplementary food for delivery on September 1 to assure continuous service, but she risks disposing of the supplementary food at a loss if the building is not completed on time.

Increasing the damages that Xavier must pay Yvonne for late completion of the building increases the incentives for Xavier to invest in performing and also increases the incentives for Yvonne to rely.

Earlier we compared perfect damages measures and concluded that expectation damages are at least as great as opportunity-cost damages, which are at least as great as reliance damages. So promisors' incentives to invest in performing diminish as the basis of damages changes from expectation to opportunity-cost to reliance. The same is true of Yvonne's incentives to invest in reliance.

What level of damages gives efficient incentives to invest, so that the promisor does not over- or underperform? For efficient incentives, the promisor must fully internalize the loss that the promisee suffers from breach. Perfect expectation damages cause the promisor to internalize the loss fully, as required for efficiency. Because perfect expectation damages are at least as great as perfect opportunity cost damages, the latter must often allow the promisor to externalize part of the cost of breach. Similarly, because perfect opportunity-cost damages are at least as great as perfect reliance damages, the latter must often allow the promisor to externalize even more of the cost of breach.

Turning to the promisee, what level of damages gives efficient incentives to rely, so that the promisee does not over- or under-rely? For efficient incentives, the promisee must fully internalize the loss from breach, which means that the promisee should receive no damages. As the measure of damages increases from reliance to opportunity-cost to expectation damages, the promisee externalizes an increasing fraction of the loss from breach. Perfect expectation damages cause the promisee to externalize 100 percent of the loss. Applied to contracts, the paradox of compensation is that, starting from perfect expectation damages, decreasing damages worsens the promisor's incentives and improves the promisee's incentives.

To illustrate the paradox of compensation, return to the example of Xavier and Yvonne. If Xavier is liable for the actual loss that late completion of the building causes, then Xavier fully internalizes Yvonne's benefits from timely completion. Consequently, he has efficient incentives to balance his cost of performing and the resulting benefit to Yvonne. Unfortunately, Xavier's liability distorts Yvonne's incentives. If Xavier is liable for the actual loss that late completion of the building causes, then Yvonne externalizes the cost of relying. In effect, Xavier will provide her with complete insurance against late completion. Consequently, she will have an incentive to act as if timely completion were certain and to order enough food for delivery on September 1.

FIGURE 9.4

Promisee's entitlement to receive damages.

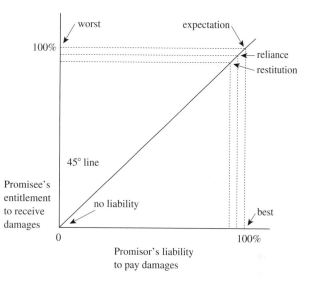

Conversely, if Xavier is not liable for late completion, then Xavier externalizes the cost that late completion imposes on Yvonne, which gives inefficient incentives to Xavier and efficient incentives to Yvonne.

Figure 9.4 summarizes these facts. The horizontal axis measures the promisor's liability to pay damages, and the vertical axis measures the promisee's entitlement to receive damages. Along the 45-degree line, the promisor's liability to pay damages equals the promisee's entitlement to receive damages. With expectation damages, the promisor internalizes 100 percent of the cost of breach, so he has efficient incentives, but the promisee internalizes 0 percent of the cost of breach; so, she has inefficient incentives. Conversely, at the graph's origin, where damages are zero, the promisor internalizes 0 percent of the cost of breach; so, he has inefficient incentives. But the promisee internalizes 100 percent of the cost of breach; so, she has efficient incentives. In between these extremes lie opportunity-cost damages and reliance damages, which cause both parties to internalize less than 100 percent and more than 0 percent of the cost of breach. So, neither one has incentives that are fully efficient.

Here is the general form of the *paradox of compensation*: (1) In order for the injurer to internalize costs, he must fully compensate the victim. (2) In order for the victim to internalize costs, she must receive no compensation for her injuries. (3) In private law, compensation paid by the injurer equals compensation received by the victim. (4) Therefore, private law cannot internalize costs for the injurer and the victim as required for efficiency.

This paradox afflicts all areas of private law. You met the paradox of compensation in Chapter 4 when we discussed compensation for the taking of property by the state, and you met the paradox again in Chapter 6 when we considered compensation for accidents. In contract law, this paradox takes the following form: (1) In order for the promisor to internalize the benefits of precaution, he must fully compensate the promisee for breach. (2) In order for the promisee to internalize the costs of reliance, she must receive no compensation for breach. (3) In contract law, compensation paid by the promisor for breach equals compensation received by the promisee. (4) Therefore, contract law cannot internalize costs for the promisor and promisee as required for efficiency.

2. Unverifiable Acts and Anti-insurance   According to Figure 9.4, liability for perfect expectation damages gives efficient incentives to the promisor and inefficient incentives to the promisee. Why not solve the paradox of compensation by having everyone promise to act efficiently all of the time? This solution fails because the promises are enforceable. To enforce a promise, a court must verify whether it was performed or broken. Many promises to act efficiently are unverifiable by courts.

To appreciate the problem, consider the example of the Waffle Shop in which Xavier promises to complete a building for Yvonne on September 1. To finish construction on time, Xavier needs Yvonne to use her political influence to obtain construction permits from city officials. The parties cannot foresee the exact assistance that Xavier needs from Yvonne, such as lobbying a council member or calling the mayor. Given this uncertainty, the parties insert an indefinite term into the contract. Yvonne promises to make her "best efforts" to assist Xavier in obtaining construction permits. The "best efforts" clause is largely unenforceable because the level of Yvonne's assistance is unverifiable in court. (Later we discuss why parties so often write contracts with indefinite terms like "best efforts.")

In general, when two people cooperate to supply inputs to a joint venture, some of the inputs are unverifiable. To maximize the value of cooperation, the parties try to write a contract that will induce them to supply the efficient combination of inputs. But promises concerning unverifiable inputs are unenforceable.

Instead of promises about unverifiable inputs, the parties should try to solve the problem by focusing on liability for the output. Anyone who is 100 percent liable for the output internalizes the benefits and costs of the inputs, including the unverifiable inputs, as required for efficiency. Thus, the contract may stipulate that the builder must pay $1,000 per week to the buyer for late completion of the building. If the buyer's actual cost of delay equals $1,000 per week, the builder internalizes the benefits of completing the project on time. The buyer, however, is indifferent between timely completion of the building and receiving damages of $1,000 per week for late completion; so, the buyer externalizes the costs of late completion of the building. To make the buyer internalize the costs of late completion, the buyer must receive *no* compensation for the harm caused by late completion of the building. With zero compensation, the buyer bears 100 percent liability of the costs of late completion. If the buyer received no compensation for the builder's late performance, then the buyer would have strong incentives to assist the builder with the construction permits.

To make the builder 100 percent liable for the output and to make the buyer receive 0 percent compensation for the builder's breach, the contract must involve a third party. The contract should stipulate that the promisor who breaches must pay damages to the third party, not to the promisee. Thus, the builder promises to pay $1,000 per week for late completion of the building *to a third party* so that the builder is 100 percent liable and the buyer bears 100 percent of the loss caused by the builder's breach of contract.

Total liability of the builder and the buyer adds up to 200 percent. *In general, the efficient supply of unverifiable inputs requires each of the two parties to be liable for 100 percent of the output so that their total liability adds up to 200 percent.*

This kind of three-party contract is called *anti-insurance?*[27] To understand its name, consider three possibilities in the preceding example: no insurance, liability insurance, and anti-insurance. With no insurance, the builder pays 100 percent of the cost of breach to the buyer, so the builder and the buyer bear a total of 100 percent of the harm. With liability insurance, the insurer pays 100 percent of the damages from breach owed by the builder to the buyer; so, the builder and the buyer bear a total of 0 percent of the harm. With anti-insurance, the builder pays 100 percent of the cost of breach to the third party; so, the builder and the buyer bear a total of 200 percent of the harm. At this point in history, anti-insurance is mostly a theoretical idea, but a person who understands anti-insurance also understands the incentive problem of unverifiable acts.

3. Contract Solutions to the Paradox of Compensation
We have been discussing incentives for the promisee to assist the promisor, such as Yvonne's helping Xavier with the construction permits, which increases the *probability* of performance. Now we return to incentives for the promisee to rely on the promise, such as Yvonne's ordering food for delivery on the day when the new restaurant is supposed to be ready, which increases the *value* of performance. In some contracts both parties want the promisee to rely fully, as if performance were certain. In other contracts both parties want the promisee to restrain reliance in light of uncertainty about performance. In the latter case, the paradox of compensation predicts that compensating the victims of breach will cause them to overrely.

Before discussing legal mechanisms to avoid the promisee's overreliance, we will explain a general strategy for solving the paradox of compensation. Efficient incentives often require internalization of *marginal* costs but not internalization of *total* costs. One way to achieve this goal is to base compensation on the hypothetical harm caused by breach, not the actual harm. *Hypothetical* expectation damages equal the gain that the promisee would have obtained from performance if the promisee had relied efficiently. Hypothetical expectation damages thus restore the promisee to the position that she would have enjoyed if the promise had been kept and she had relied efficiently. Hypothetical expectation damages do not compensate for *actual* harm. The promisee bears the actual losses caused by the promisee's overreliance.

To illustrate, assume that breach causes the promisee who relies efficiently to lose $100, and breach causes the promisee who overrelies to lose $125. Hypothetical expectation damages equal $100. If the court awards hypothetical expectation damages, then the promisee who overrelies and suffers a loss of $125 from breach bears the additional loss of $25. Thus, the promisee internalizes the marginal cost of his actual reliance, as required for efficient incentives.

---

[27] Robert Cooter & Ariel Porat, *Anti-Insurance*, 31 J. LEGAL STUD. 203 (2002). Note that the third party, called the "anti-insurer," gains $1,000 from breach in our example and loses nothing from performance, so the contract is very profitable for the anti-insurer. Competition among anti-insurers would cause them to pay the first two parties for the right to perform this profitable service.

Liability for hypothetical expectation damages can arise in two ways. First, the contract can stipulate damages at the level required for hypothetical expectation damages. In the preceding case, the parties could give themselves efficient incentives by inserting a liquidation clause into their contract that stipulates damages of $100 for breach. Second, if the parties fail to stipulate damages, the court might decide not to compensate for harm caused by overreliance. In the preceding case, the court would deduct $25 from the actual harm of $125 caused by breach and set damages equal to $100.

Instead of approaching the problem directly and deducting damages from overreliance, courts actually approach the problem indirectly through the doctrine of *foreseeability*. The reliance that the promisor could reasonably expect the promisee to take in the circumstances is foreseeable. In contrast, unforeseeable reliance exceeds the amount that the promisor could reasonably expect the promisee to take in the circumstances. The foreseeability doctrine in common law compensates for foreseeable reliance and does not compensate for unforeseeable reliance. The foreseeability doctrine thus imposes a cap on damages. If "foreseeable reliance" equates with "efficient reliance," then the foreseeability doctrine caps damages at the level required for efficient incentives.

The famous case of *Hadley v. Baxendale* established the principle that overreliance is unforeseeable and noncompensable. To summarize the facts of this case, Hadley owned a gristmill; the main shaft of the mill broke; and Hadley hired a shipping firm where Baxendale worked to transport the shaft for repair. The damaged shaft was the only one in Hadley's mill, which remained closed awaiting return of the repaired shaft. The shipper did not deliver the shaft expeditiously. After the tardy return of the repaired shaft, Hadley sued for breach of contract and asked for damages equal to his profits lost while his mill remained closed awaiting the return of the shaft. The defendant claimed that the measure of damages (if there was a breach) should be much less. The shipper assumed that Hadley, like most millers, kept a spare shaft. The shipper contended that Hadley did not inform him of the special urgency in getting the shaft repaired.[28] The shipper prevailed in court on the damages issue, and the case subsequently stands for the principle that recovery for breach of contract is limited to foreseeable damages.[29]

Consider the connection between a cap on damages and marginal reliance. As long as the actual harm is below the cap, additional reliance that increases the actual harm also increases the damages received by the promisee. When the actual harm rises to the level of the cap, however, additional reliance that increases the actual harm does not increase the damages received by the promisee. Once the cap is reached, damages are invariant, and the promisee bears the marginal cost of additional reliance. The rule of *Hadley* is not the only way to make damages invariant with respect to reliance. Liquidated damages are also invariant with respect to reliance. Stipulating an exact amount of damages in the contract is a common mechanism used to prevent overreliance.

According to the doctrine of *Hadley,* a promisee who faces unforeseeable damages can *inform* the promisor in advance so that the promisor foresees the actual damages. In principle, informing the promisor makes him liable for the actual harm caused by

---

[28] Hadley contended that he did inform the shipper that repairs were urgent because this was his only shaft.

[29] The rule in *Hadley v. Baxendale* may be found in RESTATEMENT (SECOND) OF CONTRACTS § 351(1) (1979).

breach, including the harm that an uninformed promisor would not foresee. Thus, the *Hadley* doctrine provides a powerful incentive for the promisee to disclose information to the promisor when they make the contract.

Theorists have developed useful language to describe these facts: The *Hadley* doctrine forces disclosure of information by creating a "penalty default rule." The default rule, which applies if the promisee does not inform the promisor about extraordinary harm from breach, penalizes the promisee by disallowing recovery of unforeseeable harms.[30]

A clever game theorist might note that, under certain circumstances, a market mechanism reveals the facts about reliance even without the law's forcing this result. Consider a world with many low-reliance promisees and a few high-reliance promisees. Without the rule *of Hadley*, each low-reliance promisee will want to reveal this fact to the promisor and then negotiate a lower price for the contract. The promisor can infer that any promisee who does not negotiate a lower price must be a high-reliance promisee. Like the rule of *Hadley*, this market mechanism causes the promisor to learn all of the facts about harm to the promisees from nonperformance. The difference is that the *Hadley* rule causes the high-reliance promisees to make the revelation, whereas the market mechanism causes the low-reliance promisees to make the revelation. It is cheaper for the few to reveal their special circumstances than for the many to reveal their ordinary circumstances. Compared to the market mechanisms, the *Hadley* rule reduces the transaction costs of revealing the facts about the promisee's expected damages from breach.

QUESTION 9.15: Explain the difference between foreseeable events and foreseen events.

QUESTION 9.16: Assume that you have taken some very valuable photographs. You want to inform the developer so that he will be liable for extraordinary damages in the event that he harms the film. Instead, the developer makes you sign a contract stipulating damages at the ordinary level. If the developer subsequently loses the photographs, would you expect to recover damages at the extraordinary or the ordinary level?

QUESTION 9.17: Restraining reliance before breach reduces the harm that it causes. "Mitigating" damages after breach also reduces the harm that it causes. In the Waffle Shop case, for example, Yvonne can mitigate harm by reselling the supplemental food order to another restaurant. The common law requires the promisee to mitigate damages. Specifically, the promisee must take reasonable actions to reduce losses from the promisor's breach. Describe the efficient amount of mitigation. How could the mitigation requirement create an incentive for efficient mitigation?

---

[30] The term "penalty-default rule" is due to Ian Ayres & Robert Gertner, *Filling Gaps in Incomplete Contracts: An Economic Theory of Default Rules*, 87 YALE L. J. 87 (1989).

4. Time   We have discussed the incentive effects of liability for breach without explicitly discussing the timing of contractual acts. Contracts often follow a sequence like this one:

> Time 0: Seller promises to deliver a good at time 2 and Buyer promises to pay for it on delivery.
> Time 1: Buyer begins to rely. Seller begins to make the good.
> Time 2: Buyer finishes relying. Seller delivers the good and Buyer pays for it.

$$0 \dots\dots\dots\dots\dots\dots 1 \dots\dots\dots\dots\dots\dots 2$$

| pay and promise | begin relying and performing | finish relying and performing |

If the seller breaks the promise and fails to deliver the good at time 2, then the seller must pay damages to the buyer. Expectation damages equal the price increases at which a close substitute can be bought at time 2.

To illustrate concretely, assume that the buyer promises to pay 100 for the seller's promise to deliver good g at time 2. If the seller breaches at time 2 and good g is selling for 125 at time 2, then expectation damages equal 25.

Sometimes the seller decides at time 1 that he will breach the contract at time 2. The seller, consequently, renounces the contract at time 1 and tells the buyer that he will not perform as promised. Renouncing the contract is called "anticipatory breach." Expectation damages for anticipatory breach have two possibilities in principle, although the law is unclear about the distinction. First, the buyer can purchase a substitute at the time of anticipatory breach and ask for damages equal to its price. In our example, assume that a contract costs 110 at time 1 to deliver good g at time 2. When the seller renounces the contract at time 1, the buyer pays 110 for the substitute contract and immediately asks for compensation of 10 from the seller. Second, the buyer can wait until time 2, purchase a substitute for 125, and ask for damages equal to 25. Either approach puts the buyer in the same position as if the seller had performed the contract; so, the buyer has no reason to prefer one instead of the other.

In the preceding example, the price of the promised performance rises with time from 100 at time 1, to 110 at time 1, and to 125 at time 2. Alternatively, consider the consequences when the buyer pays in advance, and the price falls. Assume that the buyer pays 100 at time 0 for the seller's promise to deliver good g at time 2. If the seller breaches at time 2 and good g is selling for 80, then the seller can earn a profit of 20 by buying the good from someone else and delivering it to the buyer.

Paying now for delivery on the spot is called a "spot contract." Paying for a promise to deliver a good in the future is called a "futures contract." We can restate the preceding conclusions in this language. Expectation damages for anticipatory breach equal the futures price at the time of renunciation or the spot price at the promised time of delivery. Either damage measure puts the promisee in the same position as if the promisor had performed the contract.

The promisor usually breaches or renounces the contract because his costs of performing rise unexpectedly. Instead of breaching or renouncing the contract in these circumstances, the promisor can buy the good from someone else and deliver it to the promisee. By purchasing and delivering a substitute, the promisor would perform as promised instead of breaching the contract. Given a market for substitute perform-ance, it makes little difference whether the promisor buys a substitute and delivers it (performs), or the promisee buys a substitute and obtains reimbursement from the promisor (nonperformance and compensation).

The main difference is transaction costs. Performance is more efficient than nonper-formance when the promisor can purchase a substitute at lower cost than the promisee. Conversely, nonperformance is more efficient than performance when the promisee can purchase a substitute at lower cost than the promisor. In the latter case, nonperformance can take the form of renegotiating the contract, in which case the promisor agrees to pay the promisee the price of buying the substitute, and the promisee agrees to release the promisor from the original contract. Alternatively, nonperformance can take the form of the promisor's breaching the contract and paying damages to the promisee.

We have explained that a market for substitute performance and low transaction costs enable the seller to perform at the same cost as paying damages for breach. Because the seller can avoid breach at no extra cost, the seller can avoid paying dam-ages in the event that courts set damages too high. Specifically, the seller is indifferent whether courts set expectation damages for anticipatory breach equal to the futures price at the time of renunciation or the spot price at the promised time of delivery.[31]

We have explained that expectation damages for breach of a futures contract equals the market price of a close substitute. Sometimes, however, a good does not have a close substitute, as with a customized computer program, a house designed by a partic-ular architect, or a performance by an opera star. When goods are differentiated, the price of the nearest substitute imperfectly reflects the value of performance to the promisee. With differentiated goods, difficulty in computing expectation may cause the courts to award reliance damages. We have already explained that reliance damages for breach of contract to deliver differentiated goods creates an incentive problem: The promisor does not fully internalize the cost of breach to the promisee; so, the promisor will repudiate too soon and too often.

In our example, assume that the buyer invests 5 in reliance at time 1 and 10 in re-liance at time 2. Reliance damages for breach at time 2 equal the buyer's investment in reliance at time 1 and 2, or 15. Reliance damages for anticipatory breach at time 1 equal the buyer's investment in reliance at time 1, or 5. One reason why the seller tries to renounce the contract at time 1 is to reduce his liability for reliance damages. In any case, the buyer values performance more than her investment of 5 or 15 in reliance. Liability for reliance damages causes the seller to repudiate too soon and breach too often because the cost to the seller, which is 5 or 15, is usually less than the cost to the buyer, which is the value of performance.

---

[31] If the seller thinks that the price of good *g* will rise, then the seller who breaches prefers for the buyer to purchase the substitute sooner rather than later. If the seller thinks that the price of good *g* will fall, then the seller who breaches prefers for the buyer to purchase the substitute later rather than sooner. In either case, if the seller fears that the buyer will not act as the seller prefers, then the seller can simply purchase the substitute himself and not breach the contract. With a market for substitute performance and low trans-action costs, little is at stake.

We mentioned that the promisor usually breaches or renounces the contract because his costs of performing rise unexpectedly. When a promised performance has no close substitutes, a rise in its cost usually causes the parties to enter new discussions about the contract. The success of renegotiation often depends on the clarity of the party's rights and duties. Unfortunately, the common law of anticipatory breach is unclear, which causes inefficiencies and other problems.[32] To appreciate these facts, we will explain the elements of a theory of renegotiation.

The preceding chapter developed the fundamental economic principle of contract law: Enforce promises when both parties wanted enforceability at the time the promises were given. This principle achieves Pareto efficiency by giving the parties what they want (enforceability) at the time that they want it. A renegotiated contract arises from an earlier contract and supersedes it. The fundamental principle for enforceability of renegotiation is the same as for any contract: Enforce renegotiated contracts when both parties wanted enforceability at the time of the renegotiation.

According to this principle, the court should enforce a renegotiated contract when both parties expect to benefit more from the new contract than from the persistence of the old contract. When circumstances change and the promisor must breach a contract without close substitutes, a renegotiated contact can often benefit both parties. Both parties benefit because the promisor and the promisee often remain better partners for their cooperative venture than anyone else; so, they need to continue collaborating but on different terms. We will return to the theory of renegotiation when we consider contracts made under duress.

> **QUESTION 9.18:**   At time 0, the buyer pays for the seller's promise to deliver good *g* at time 2. The seller renounces the contract at time 1. Perfect substitutes for good *g* exist in the market. A futures contract at time 1 for a substitute costs 110. The buyer, however, does not buy a substitute at time 1. Instead, the buyer waits until time 2 and purchases a substitute on the spot market, which turns out to cost 125. The buyer sues for expectation damages of 125, and the seller responds that expectation damages equal 110. The court must decide which level of damages to apply. Explain why the choice between these two damage remedies matters little to the future behavior of parties like this buyer and seller.

> **QUESTION 9.19:**   At time 0, the buyer pays for the seller's promise to deliver good *g* at time 2, where *g* is a differentiated good. Assume that the numbers given in the preceding question indicate the price of the closest substitute (which is not very close) and the extent of the buyer's reliance. The seller's costs of performing rise unexpectedly; so, the seller and the buyer bargain in

---

[32] Here are some complexities that make the law unclear: After partial performance, the promisor can repudiate the contract, in which case the promisee will receive no compensation for subsequent reliance. Until the promisee responds to repudiation by changing his position (for example, by obtaining alternative performance from a third party), the promisor can "repudiate the repudiation" under some circumstances, and reestablish the contract. In addition, the promisee may be able to "resist repudiation for a commercially reasonable time." For an economic analysis of anticipatory repudiation, see George Triantis & Jody Kraus, *Anticipatory Repudiation Reconsidered*, 6 VIRGINIA J. 54 (2003).

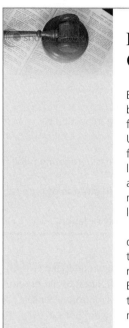

Formal and Informal Methods for Contractual Compliance

Businesses from hamburgers to gas stations often organize as franchises. The relationships between franchisors and franchisees involve such issues as supplies, cleanliness, advertising, franchisee-employment relations, and territorial exclusivity. Adam Badawi of Washington University School of Law researched contracting in franchises.[33] He hypothesized that the franchisor could induce the franchisee to comply with their agreement through the threat of legal sanctions, which Badawi calls "damages." Alternatively the franchisor could use rewards and punishments that the contract does not specify, which Badawi calls "relational governance." Examples of the latter include returning more profits to the franchisee (reward) or allowing a competing franchise to open near the franchisee's business (punishment).

To induce compliance with agreements, Badawi hypothesized that franchisors will use damages or relational governance, depending on which one is cheaper. The relative cost in turn depends on market conditions. Thus, the promise of an additional outlet is an effective reward if the market for the produce is rising, but not if the market is constant or falling. When Badawi collected data from formal contracts and informal compliance practices, he concluded that damages and relational governance are, indeed, substitutes in enforcing franchise agreements, and that different industries use them in ways that depend upon their relative cost.

an attempt to renegotiate the contract. Explain why the seller would rather renegotiate in circumstances in which the court gives reliance damages for breach rather than those in which the court gives expectation damages for breach.

II. Formation Defenses and Performance Excuses

The first part of this chapter concerned the question, "What should be the remedy for breaking an enforceable promise?" The second part of this chapter concerns the question, "What promises should be enforced?" Our answer develops the prescription from the preceding chapter, in which we divided contractual obligations into default rules and regulations. Default rules fill gaps in contracts in order to reduce transaction costs. Regulations prescribe terms for contracts in order to correct market failures. The remainder of this chapter analyzes some of the major doctrines that fill gaps and regulate contracts. We will analyze selected doctrines in the order in which they appear in Table 9.3, which categorizes contract regulations as forms of market failure. (Table 9.3 reproduces Table 8.1 in the preceding chapter.)

---

[33] Adam Badawi, *Relational Governance and Contract Damages: Evidence from Franchising*, 7 J. EMP. LEGAL STUD. 743 (2010). Badawi's study builds on empirical research on informal contracting practices such as Stewart Macaulay, *Non-Contractual Relations in Business: A Preliminary Study*, 28 AM. SOC. REV. 55 (1963); David Charny, *Non-Legal Sanctions in Commercial Relationships*, 104 HARV. L. REV. 373 (1990); and Benjamin Klein, *The Economics of Franchise Contracts*, 2 J. CORP. FIN. 9 (1995).

TABLE 9.3

Regulatory Doctrines of Contract Law

Assumption	If Violated, Contract Doctrine
A. Individual Rationality	
1. Stable, well-ordered preferences	1. Incompetency; incapacity
2. Constrained choice	2. Coercion; duress; necessity; impossibility
B. Transaction Costs	
1. Spillovers	1. Unenforceability of contracts derogating public policy or statutory duty
2. Information	2. Fraud; failure to disclose; frustration of purpose; mutual mistake
3. Monopoly	3. Necessity; unconscionability or lesion

When defendants invoke these doctrines in contract disputes, they can make two different claims. First, defendants can claim that they have no legal obligation to the plaintiff because no contract exists between them. These claims rely on "formation defenses." A formation defense asserts that the conditions for creating a contract were not satisfied. To illustrate, a man can argue that his promise to give a gift did not create a legal obligation.

Alternatively, defendants can concede that a contract exists, and then claim that they were excused from performing under the circumstances. These claims rely on "performance excuses." A performance excuse admits the existence of a contract and denies liability for breach. Liability is typically denied because unusual contingencies prevented performance. To illustrate, a manufacturer may argue that she is excused from delivering the promised goods because her factory burned down. Imperfect procedures provide formation defenses, and unusual contingencies provide performance excuses.

A. Incompetence

A rational decision maker can rank outcomes in order from least preferred to most preferred. In order to rank outcomes, the decision maker must have stable preferences. If the decision maker's preferences are unstable or disorderly, then he or she cannot make competent judgments about his or her own interests. Such a person is legally incompetent. For example, children, the insane, and some mentally disabled adults are legally incompetent.

In special circumstances, a competent person may suffer temporary incompetence. For example, ingesting a prescription drug can incapacitate. A temporarily incapacitated person may be unable to make legally enforceable promises. To illustrate, if a seller uses high-pressure tactics to confuse a consumer into signing an unfavorable contract, the consumer's lawyer may allege "transactional incapacity," which means an incapacity to make *this* transaction under *these* circumstances.

Most people look after their own interests better than anyone else would do for them. However, incompetent people cannot look after themselves; so, others must look after them. Law assigns responsibility for protecting incompetent people from harmful contracts to the competent people with whom they deal. *Competent people must protect the interests of incompetent contractual partners or assume liability for failing to do so.* Thus, law interprets a contract between a competent person and an incompetent person so as to serve the best interests of the latter. For example, the law will excuse a legally incompetent promisor from performing a contract that he signed against his interests, whereas the law will require a legally competent person to perform a contract that serves the interests of an incompetent promisee.

Competent contractual partners are usually better situated than anyone else to protect incompetent people from harmful contracts. In other words, *competent contractual partners can usually protect incompetent contractual partners from harmful contracts at less cost than anyone else.* Thus, the law assigns liability for harm suffered by incompetent contractual partners to the competent people who can avoid the harm at least cost. In this matter, the law follows the general principle of tort law, according to which liability for accidents should fall on the party who can avoid them at least cost.

> **QUESTION 9.20:** A young girl found an attractive stone in the woods and sold it to a jeweler for $1. Later, her family discovered that the stone was a rough diamond worth $700. Her family asked the court to void the contract for incompetency. Who was situated to protect the young girl in this transaction at least cost?

> **QUESTION 9.21:** Suppose that excessive drinking causes temporary incompetence, and suppose that someone who has drunk too much alcohol seeks to enter into a contract with someone who is sober. Contrast the incentive effects of enforcing and not enforcing such contracts.

B. Dire Constraints and Remote Risks

We proceed down Table 9.3 from incompetence to constrained choice. Most bargains occur under conditions of moderate constraint, but sometimes one of the parties to a bargain faces a *dire* constraint. A dire constraint leaves the decision maker with little or no choice. Contract law treats dire constraints differently from moderate constraints. A dire constraint can provide the promisor with a defense or an excuse for breaking a promise. We will discuss several relevant doctrines.

1. Duress   Law prohibits people from making threats such as, "Work for me if you want your sister to come home safely from school," or "I'll ruin your business unless you sell it to me for $3,500." If a person extracts a promise by using such a threat, the promise is called a "contract made under duress" and is unenforceable.

Unlike threats, law permits people to make demands such as "Pay me $10 per hour, or I'll work for your competitor," or "My final offer for your car is $3,500; take it or leave it." Demands occur routinely in bargaining. The fact that a person extracted a promise by making such a demand does not provide a defense or excuse for not keeping the promise.

A theory of duress must distinguish between improper threats and proper demands. We will use bargaining theory to draw the distinction. First, we review the fundamentals of bargaining as explained in Chapter 4. In a bargaining situation, the parties can produce more by cooperating ("surplus") than they can on their own. In order to cooperate, they must agree to divide the cooperative product. In dividing the cooperative product, both parties must receive at least as much as they can get on their own ("threat value"). Bargaining often involves exchanging demands and offers in an attempt to agree on the price of cooperation.

It is easy to see why the law permits people to make demands when bargaining. People know more about their own interests than anyone else, and people protect their own interests more persistently than anyone else. Most people can decide for themselves which cooperative ventures to join far better than anyone else can decide for them. The state can help people to make their own decisions by enforcing private bargains. Conversely, the state can prevent people from making their own decisions by prohibiting private bargains. Efficiency requires the state to facilitate private bargains, not to prohibit them.

Insofar as the law forbids private bargains, a third party must decide who should cooperate with whom. Third parties typically lack the information and motivation to make such decisions. For example, the most complete prohibition of private bargains occurred under central planning in communist countries. Many planning officials cared for personal power more than efficiency, and those who cared about efficiency lacked the information to make decisions for other people. Central planning collapsed under the weight of its own inefficiency.

Many modest attempts by the state to restrict private bargains have failed. For example, most wealthy nations have abandoned attempts by the state to set prices for consumer goods. As an alternative to state planning or price-setting, the law typically enforces promises given in response to demands.

Bargaining, which involves demands and offers, is the opposite of coercion, which involves threats. A contract usually involves a bargain in which one party gives something to induce the other party to make a promise. The bargain facilitates cooperation, which is productive. Both parties usually expect to gain from the bargain. Both parties usually want enforceability to secure a credible commitment to cooperate.

In contrast, a contract made under duress has the opposite traits. Duress usually involves extracting a promise by an improper threat. Enforcing the promise usually redistributes wealth from one person to the other. One party expects to gain from a coerced promise, and the other party expects to lose. One party wants enforceability of a coerced promise, and the other party does not.

To illustrate, contrast voluntary and coerced exchange of goods. When exchange is voluntary, the parties agree to trade because they both perceive an advantage. Ownership usually passes from someone who values a good less to someone who values it more. Allocative efficiency requires moving a good from someone who values it less to someone who values it more. In contrast, when exchange is involuntary, one party may be coerced into selling a good for less than it's worth to him or her. Consequently, ownership may pass from someone who values it more to someone who values it less, and that, of course, is allocatively inefficient.

Another important difference between bargains and coerced contracts concerns the consequence of a failed attempt to form a contract. If bargaining fails, the parties do not cooperate or create a surplus. Suppose I say, "Pay me $10 per hour, or I'll work for your competitor." You offer $9 per hour; so, I go to work for your competitor at $8 per hour. My best alternative bargain is apparently less productive than the proposed bargain.

In contrast, if coercion fails and the injurer acts on the threat, he or she destroys something valuable to the victim. To illustrate, suppose I say to you, "Work for me if you want your sister to come home safely from school." If you refuse to be coerced and if I act on my threat, a tragic crime ensues. In general, *failed bargains do not create, whereas failed coercion can destroy.*

Even unexecuted threats cause waste by inducing their victims to invest in defense. To illustrate, suppose that the local bully "buys" bicycles in exchange for $10 and the promise not to thrash the owner. The owners of bicycles will try to protect themselves from the bully. Protecting themselves against the bully uses resources. The state can often provide protection against threats more cheaply than anyone else. By providing protection against threats, the state channels resources from defense to production.[34]

We have explained that involuntary contracts usually redistribute wealth. The modern state suppresses private, involuntary redistributions of wealth, such as theft and fraud. The modern state reserves for itself the power to redistribute wealth involuntarily through such means as progressive taxation.

Economic analysis suggests the following rule for duress: *A promise extracted as the price to cooperate in creating value is enforceable, and a promise extracted by a threat to destroy value is unenforceable.* To illustrate the rule, consider this example. The captain of a boat in Seattle contracts with the crew to make a fishing voyage to Alaska. After the boat reaches Alaska, the crew demands a bonus to finish the voyage. The captain cannot find replacements for the crew in Alaska; so, he agrees. After the ship returns to Seattle, the captain refuses to pay the bonus on the ground of duress.

This example illustrates the form of duress called the *holdup problem*. When negotiating the original contract, the crew faced competition from other crews. After the boat reached Alaska, the crew no longer faced competition from other crews. The captain's reliance on the contract caused him to forego the opportunity of contracting with another crew in Seattle. Furthermore, the captain made investments in reliance on the contract, such as purchasing fuel and supplies. The absence of competition and the captain's reliance on the crew increased the crew's bargaining strength. So, the crew tried to renegotiate the price.

Notice that this example fits our distinction between proper demands and improper threats. If the parties failed to agree on the original contract, they would not cooperate together. By failing to cooperate, they would not create a surplus. Renegotiation is different. After making the contract, the captain relied by foregoing the opportunity to hire an alternative crew and outfitting the boat for the voyage to Alaska. In the renegotiation, the crew threatened to destroy the value of the captain's reliance. The destructive

---

[34] We already made this point in Chapter 4 when we discussed a lawless world in which people divide their time between growing, protecting, and stealing corn. State security ideally diverts effort from protecting and stealing corn to producing it.

threat to breach a contract after reliance constitutes coercion in renegotiating the price. In general, courts do not enforce contract renegotiation motivated by the increase in the promisor's bargaining strength that results from the promisee's reliance.

In the example of the fishing crew, duress arose in renegotiating a contract. We have already discussed the general principle that courts should enforce renegotiated contracts when both parties wanted enforceability at the time of the renegotiation. Notice that in this case, the captain of the ship presumably wanted the renegotiated contract to be *un*enforceable. If the renegotiated contract is unenforceable, the crew's only choice is to continue fishing under the original contract or to return to port without any fish. The best interests of the crew would be served by continuing to fish. So, the captain prefers for the law not to allow him to make a renegotiated contract that is enforceable.

In addition, when both parties signed the original contract, they had reason to prefer that the law not enforce revisions in the contract based on renegotiation like the one that occurred. This fact is easy to see: If the crew had demanded a term in the original contract giving them the right to renegotiate its wage terms once the boat reached Alaskan waters, the captain would not have hired them. The doctrine of duress is thus important to making this labor market work for captain and crew.

Alternatively, change the facts in this case to produce the opposite result. Assume that the contract calls for the crew to fish for two weeks, and after one week the crew receives a radio message that makes them prefer to return to port immediately to pursue a better opportunity. In these changed circumstances, the crew would rather breach and pay damages to the captain than continue the voyage on the present terms. To induce them to complete the voyage and not to breach, the captain offers a more favorable contract. The crew will only accept the offer and continue fishing if it is enforceable. In this case the captain and crew both want the renegotiated contract to be enforceable when made, so the court should enforce it.[35]

We explained earlier that courts often say that a promise has "consideration" as a way of announcing that they will enforce it, and courts often say that a promise has "no consideration" as a way of announcing that they will not enforce it. Similarly, courts may say that a contract was renegotiated under "changed circumstances" as a way of announcing that it will enforce the modified contract, and courts may say that a contract was renegotiated under "duress" as a way of announcing that it will not enforce the modified contract. Or the court may announce that it will not enforce the modified contract by saying that one party had "no reasonable alternative" or "no adequate remedy" other than agreeing to the other side's demand. Our economic analysis provides a guide for how to use these words. According to our principle for enforcing renegotiated contracts, a radio message increasing the crew's opportunity cost for continuing the voyage should count as "changed circumstances," whereas the crew's demands without this change should count as "duress."

---

[35] In the first case the crew's threat to breach the contract is not credible, and in the second case the crew's threat is credible. For the argument that the threat's credibility should determine the promise's enforceability in contract renegotiation, see Oren Bar-Gill & Omri Ben-Shahar, *The Law of Duress and the Economics of Credible Threats*, 33 J. LEGAL STUD. 391 (2004).

QUESTION 9.22:   Suppose that person *A*, while aiming a gun at person *B*, invites *B* to write a check. Explain the efficiency argument for allowing *B* to cancel the check later.

QUESTION 9.23:   Suppose that a baseball star signs a five-year contract for $1 million per year. In the third year of the contract, the player hits more home runs than anyone else in the league. Now he demands to renegotiate his salary. Does efficiency require the law to enforce the original contract or set it aside?

Web Note 9.5

The opinion in the fishing-crew case described above is available on our website with some additional questions.

---

2. Necessity   The following example illustrates the next doctrine, called "necessity." A surgeon runs out of gas on a lonely desert road. A passerby offers to sell the surgeon five gallons of gas in exchange for a promise to pay $50,000. The surgeon makes the promise and uses the gas to escape from the desert, but later the surgeon refuses to pay $50,000. The surgeon asserts that "necessity" forced him to make the promise.

Like duress, necessity is a promise given under a dire constraint. As explained, *duress* concerns a dire constraint imposed on the promisor by the promisee. In contrast, necessity concerns a dire constraint imposed on the promisor by someone other than the promisee. The cause of the dire constraint could be the promisor, a third party, or bad luck. For example, the surgeon might run out of gas on a lonely desert road because he neglected to fill the tank, someone gave him false directions, or a rock punctured the fuel line.

In cases of duress and necessity, the promisee makes a destructive threat, and the promisor responds by making a one-sided promise. The nature of the threat, however, differs for the two doctrines. With duress, the promisee threatens to destroy by *acting*. With necessity, the promisee threatens to destroy by *not* acting, specifically by not rescuing. For example, the passerby threatens to leave the surgeon stranded on a desert road unless he promises to pay $50,000 for five gallons of gas.

In a biblical parable, the "good Samaritan" saved the life of a man attacked by thieves and nursed him back to health, without expectation of reward. In the necessity cases, a "bad Samaritan" extracts the promise of an extravagant reward in exchange for a rescue. Rescue deserves an appropriate reward, not an extravagant reward. An appropriate award provides efficient incentives for rescue. Efficient incentives for rescue induce enough investment in rescue so that the cost equals the expected benefit. The expected benefit equals the probability of a rescue multiplied by its value.

To illustrate, return to the example of the surgeon who ran out of gas on a lonely desert road. The rescue cost the passerby at least five gallons of gas, plus inconvenience and delay. In order to provide incentives for rescue, the rescuer should recover the cost of the rescue. In addition to costs, the rescuer should receive sufficient reward so that future rescuers will perform eagerly, not reluctantly.

We distinguish three kinds of rescues by their cost. First, a *fortuitous* rescue uses resources that were on hand by chance. For example, the passerby happens to have extra gas in her tank when she happens to encounter the stranded surgeon; so, the passerby siphons five gallons of gas from the tank of her car to the tank of the surgeon's car. Second, an *anticipated* rescue uses resources set aside in case they are needed for a rescue. For example, the passerby always carries a five-gallon can of gas in the trunk of her car just in case she happens to encounter someone stranded. Third, a *planned* rescue occurs when the rescuer searches for people who need rescuing. For example, a professional rescuer patrolling the desert comes on the stranded surgeon.

The difference in costs affects the difference in rewards required to create incentives for the three kinds of rescue. Fortuitous rescue uses resources that just happen to be available. Incentives for fortuitous rescue require a modest reward to compensate for resources actually consumed in the rescue. Anticipated rescue uses resources set aside for emergencies. Incentives for anticipated rescue require sufficient reward to compensate for preparations against emergencies. Preparations use more than the resources consumed in an actual rescue. Planned rescue uses resources invested in searching for people in distress. Incentives for planned rescue require sufficient reward to compensate for search. Searching uses more than the resources consumed in preparing for emergencies or rescuing. In general, incentives for planned rescues require larger rewards than for anticipated rescues, and incentives for anticipated rescues require larger rewards than for fortuitous rescues.

The reward should be adjusted by law to induce investment in rescue at the efficient level. When jeopardy is rare and its consequences are slight, investment in fortuitous rescue may be sufficient. For example, if people seldom run out of gas in the desert and the consequences are temporary discomfort, then a trivial reward may be sufficient. As probability and seriousness increase, efficiency may require anticipated or planned rescue. If people occasionally run out of gas in the desert and the consequences are serious, then an extra reward should be given to rescuers for carrying extra gas. Finally, if people often run out of gas in the desert and the consequences are life-threatening, then an even larger reward should be given to planned rescuers in order to induce them to form a "desert patrol."[36]

QUESTION 9.24:   Explain why professional rescuers should typically receive a larger reward than anticipated rescuers, and anticipated rescuers should typically receive a larger reward than fortuitous rescuers.

QUESTION 9.25:   A house catches on fire. The fire is extinguished by the combined efforts of (1) professional firefighters, (2) volunteer firefighters who help the professionals, and (3) passersby who spontaneously help the professionals and volunteers. The owner of the house makes various promises to induce the help of the three groups. Use economics to explain why a court should not enforce the promises, but the court should require the homeowner to pay (1) more than (2), and to pay (2) more than (3).

---

[36] Free entry in the market for rescuing, like open-access fishing, has an incentive problem due to congestion, but this is a technical detail.

QUESTION 9.26: In *Post v. Jones*, 60 U.S. (19 How.) 150 (1857), the whaling ship *Richmond* ran aground on a barren coast in the Arctic Ocean and began to sink with a full cargo of whale oil. A few days later three other whaling ships came on the *Richmond*. The three captains, while agreeing to save the crew, threatened not to take any of the *Richmond*'s whale oil unless the captain of the *Richmond* agreed to an auction. One of the three captains bid $1 per barrel for as much as he could take; the other two took as much as they could hold at $0.75 per barrel. Both prices were well below the competitive price of whale oil. When the three vessels returned to port with the *Richmond*'s oil and crew, the owners of the *Richmond* sued, asking the court not to enforce the sale of the whale oil at the low auction prices. Did the captains who purchased the oil make destructive threats? Should the court set aside the auction on efficiency grounds? What compensation should the rescuers receive? (Note: Sea captains have a legal duty to rescue ships and cargo in distress.)

3. Impossibility   With duress and necessity, the dire constraint *precedes* the promise. Sometimes a dire constraint *follows* the promise and prevents performance. For example, a surgeon may promise to operate and then break her hand before the scheduled operation. Although the surgeon cannot perform, she can pay damages. If the surgeon cannot physically perform, the law can either excuse her or require her to pay damages. In general, when a contingency makes performance impossible, should the promisor be excused or held liable? The "impossibility doctrine" answers this question.

As discussed in the preceding chapter, perfect contracts contain terms that explicitly allocate all risks. Explicit allocation of risk requires costly negotiating. The cost of negotiating must be balanced against the benefit from explicit allocation of risk. On balance, the cost of negotiating over remote risks may exceed the benefit. Consequently, efficient contracts have gaps concerning remote risks.

Sometimes the explicit terms in the contract provide guidance to filling a gap. To illustrate, assume that a company promises to drill a well for a landowner, but the drill runs into impenetrable granite rock. If the contract remains silent about this contingency, the court must decide whether the driller owes damages to the landowner. If the price in the drilling contract exceeds competing offers, perhaps the driller implicitly guaranteed success to the landowner. If the driller gave an implicit guarantee, he should be held liable. Or perhaps the industry custom requires drillers to bear the cost of breach whenever the contract remains silent. If industry custom holds drillers liable, the court should apply the custom to the case.

In other instances, however, the terms of the contract and the custom of the industry provide no guidance to the allocation of risk. When the contract does not allocate the risk explicitly or implicitly to one of the parties, the law must do so. In contract law, the promisor is typically liable for breach, even though the breach was not his or her fault. In other words, contractual liability is *strict*. For example, a construction company is liable for late completion of a building, regardless of whether the construction company did its best to meet the deadline. Similarly, when the contract was silent about the contingency causing breach, the promisor is typically liable, even though the breach was not the promisor's fault. In the typical case, the promisor is liable for breach caused by a remote contingency that was not mentioned in the contract.

In some circumstances, however, physical impossibility of performance excuses non-performance.[37] For example, the estate of a famous portrait painter is not liable if death prevents the artist from completing a contract to paint someone's picture.[38] Similarly, a manufacturer may be excused from fulfilling its contracts to deliver goods because lightning ignited a fire that destroyed her factory.[39] The burning of the factory is an "act of God" or *force majeure*. Also, breach is excused if performance became illegal before it could occur. For example, a shipping company is excused from its contract to carry civilian cargo in time of war if the government commandeers its ships to carry military cargo.

These examples concern physical impossibility. In other cases, performance is *physically* possible and *economically impractical*.[40] Thus, the driller may be excused for not completing the well as promised to the landowner because the drill could only penetrate granite at ruinous cost.

What underlies and unifies these cases? According to a traditional legal theory, a contingency destroyed a "basic assumption on which the contract was made" in each case.[41] For example, the contract with the portrait painter assumed that he would live, the contract with the factory assumed that it would not burn down, and the contract with the shipping company assumed that the government would not commandeer its ships. According to this theory, breach of a contract made in good faith is excused whenever events destroy one of its basic assumptions.

How do we decide whether an assumption is basic or dispensable? Economics can clarify this vague distinction or dispense with it. The impossibility doctrine concerns contingencies that make performance impossible. These contingencies represent a risk, much like the risk of pneumonia or an automobile accident. Economics has a theory of efficient risk-bearing. To apply it to contract law, assume that transaction costs preclude a bargain to allocate a risk among the people who affect it. Assume that one person can eliminate the risk at lower cost than anyone else or any combination of people. Or, to be more precise, assume that efficiency requires only one person to take action against accidental harm (unilateral precaution). Then hold the person liable who can eliminate the risk at least cost. If the impossibility doctrine in contract law were efficient, under the preceding assumptions, it would *assign liability to the party who can bear the risk that performance becomes impossible at least cost.*

---

[37] *L.N. Jackson & Co. v. Royal Norwegian Govt.,* 177 F.2d 694 (2d Cir. 1949), *cert. den.,* 339 U.S. 914 (1950).

[38] Note that this exception, as in the example given, most typically involves the promise to provide personal services. The law, both common and statutory, has frequently been reluctant to compel performance of personal service contracts under any circumstances.

[39] RESTATEMENT (SECOND) OF CONTRACTS §263 (1979).

[40] Sometimes the defense of "impracticability" or "commercial impracticability" concerns the absolute cost of performance, and sometimes the defense concerns the cost of performance relative to the promisor's assets (for example, performing bankrupts the promisor).

[41] See Chapter 11, RESTATEMENT (SECOND) OF CONTRACTS (1979).

Several factors determine who can bear risk at least cost. First, people can often take steps to decrease the probability that performance becomes impossible or to reduce the losses from breach. For example, an elderly and ailing painter might delay other work in order to complete a portrait as commissioned. The ship's owner might alert the customer to the need for alternative supplies in the event that war causes the government to commandeer ships. The factory owner might install a sprinkler system to reduce the damage caused by fire. These considerations suggest that a risk should be assigned to the party who can take *precautions* to reduce it at least cost.

Second, even if no one can take precautions to reduce risk, someone can usually *spread* it. For example, assume that an earthquake prevents a seller from delivering goods on time. No one can prevent earthquakes, but people can insure against them. Insurance companies specialize in spreading risk. Even without insurance, an individual may be able to spread risk by other means. For example, the investors in a factory subject to an earthquake hazard can spread risk by purchasing stocks from companies in different locations ("portfolio diversification"). Risk is cheaper to bear when spread than when concentrated. These considerations suggest that risk should be assigned to the party who can spread it at least cost, by insurance or other means.

A person's ability to reduce and spread risk determines his or her cost of bearing it. Efficiency requires allocating risk to the people who can bear it at least cost. Thus, efficiency requires interpreting the impossibility doctrine as follows: *If a contingency makes performance impossible, assign liability to the party who could reduce or spread the risk at least cost.*

The concept of "lowest-cost risk-bearer" provides a clear interpretation of the impossibility doctrine in many difficult cases. To see how, consider two versions of the example of the commandeered ship. In the first version, the shipping company has easier access to alternative transportation than does the owner of civilian goods. Consequently, the shipping company can bear the risk of its ship's being commandeered at lower cost than the owner of civilian goods; so, the shipping company should be held liable for breach of contract. In the second version, the owner of civilian goods has easier access to alternative transportation than does the shipping company. Consequently, the owner of civilian goods can bear the risk of commandeering at lower cost than can the shipping company, so the shipping company should be excused for breaching the contract. (To see the improvement made by economic analysis, try to distinguish these two versions of the case of the commandeered ship using the "basic assumption" theory of traditional contract doctrine.)

Similar analysis applies to the other examples. The portrait painter can bear the risk of breach at least cost if he can easily rearrange his schedule to paint commissioned pictures first, whereas the person who ordered the portrait can bear the risk of breach at least cost if he can easily obtain a portrait from another artist with equal talent. The factory owner can bear the risk of fire at least cost if she can easily purchase fire insurance whose coverage includes liability for not delivering goods, whereas the customer can bear the risk at least cost if he can easily obtain substitute goods from another factory.

Interpreting the impossibility doctrine to assign liability to the lowest-cost risk-bearer minimizes the cost of remote risks. Minimizing the cost of remote risks maximizes the surplus from the contract, which the parties can divide between them. Both parties stand to gain from the economic interpretation of the impossibility doctrine. We presume that, if the parties had explicitly allocated the risk, they would have assigned it to the party who can bear it at least cost. Thus, the economic principle can be defended as a rational reconstruction of the will of the parties. Moreover, the economic principle, if applied as a default rule, helps future parties to lower their costs of forming contracts or alerts them to assign liability differently from the default rule if they so prefer. (Note, however, that identifying the least-cost avoider of risks gets tricky when both the promisor and the promisee need to take precaution.[42])

QUESTION 9.27: Lightning is an "act of God." Describe some of its incentive effects on people.

QUESTION 9.28: In the famous case of *Taylor v. Caldwell*, 3 B. & S. 826, 122 Eng. Rep. 309 (K.B. 1863), the plaintiff, Taylor, leased the defendant's concert hall for four nights at 100 pounds sterling to be paid to Caldwell after each performance. Shortly after the first performance, the concert hall was destroyed by fire. Taylor sued Caldwell for breach of contract and asked the court to award him as damages the expenses he incurred in preparation for the last three performances. The defendant sought to be excused from performing on the ground that it was literally impossible for him to perform the contract after the fire.

a. What factors enable one party to prevent a risk better than another?
b. What factors enable one party to insure against a risk better than another?
c. Do these factors tend to converge or diverge, or is their association merely coincidental?
d. How would you decide this case in light of economic analysis?

QUESTION 9.29: In the mid-1970s, the Westinghouse Corporation persuaded electric companies to purchase nuclear reactors, and Westinghouse agreed to supply purchasers with uranium at a fixed price of $8–10 per pound. By mid-1975 Westinghouse had commitments to supply 40,000 more tons of uranium than it held in inventory or forward contracts, and the market price of uranium had risen to more than $30 per pound. To cover its shortage, Westinghouse would have incurred losses of nearly $2 billion, which would have led to its bankruptcy. In September 1975, the company announced that it would not honor its contracts. It sought to be excused on the ground that performance was economically impossible ("commercial impracticability").

---

[42] When two parties should take precaution against a risk, incentives are efficient. Both of them internalize 100 percent of the reduction in risk caused by their own marginal precaution. We called this fact "the paradox of compensation"—the promisor must pay damages for breach and the promisee must not receive compensation. With "bilateral precaution," efficient incentives require *full risk for all avoiders* at the margin, not all risk for the cheapest avoider.

Most of the utilities sued Westinghouse. What considerations do you think should have been used by courts to determine whether Westinghouse was excused from supplying the uranium?[43]

4. Frustration of Purpose

Having discussed a contingency that prevents performing, we now consider a contingency that destroys the contract's purpose. A coronation parade was planned for June 1902, in London. Many owners of property along the parade route leased rooms for the day to people wishing to observe the ceremony. When the king's illness caused the parade to be postponed, many people refused to pay the rent, and some of the property owners sued to enforce the contracts. The courts held that the contracts were unenforceable because their purpose was destroyed by postponing the ceremony.[44]

As explained, the impossibility doctrine provides a default rule to allocate losses caused by remote contingencies that make performance impossible. Similarly, the frustration doctrine provides a default rule to allocate losses caused by contingencies that make performance pointless. Pointless performance does not serve the purpose that induced the parties to make the contract. For example, the scheduled coronation parade induced the parties to make a contract for viewing it. Efficiency requires allocating risk to the party who can bear it at least cost. Thus, efficiency requires interpreting the doctrine of frustration of purpose as follows: *If a contingency makes performance pointless, assign liability to the party who could bear the risk at least cost.*

As explained, a person's ability to reduce and spread risk determines his or her cost of bearing it. Returning to our example, the property owners who rented rooms could completely eliminate their losses caused by postponement of the coronation parade by renting the rooms a second time for the rescheduled parade. Bearing the risk of postponement was probably costless to the owners. Alternatively, the people who rented the rooms to view the parade face the risk of having to pay the rent twice. Efficiency apparently requires allocating the risk of postponement to the property owners, not the renters of the rooms.

> **QUESTION 9.30:** We divided the doctrines of contract law into default rules that fill gaps and regulations that restrict promises. Classify the following doctrines as default rules or regulations: incompetence, duress, necessity, impossibility, and frustration of purpose.

5. Mutual Mistake About Facts

We discussed a contingency that materializes after the parties sign the contract and makes performance of a contract pointless. Another possibility is that the contingency materializes *before* the parties sign the contract, without their knowing it. To illustrate, assume that the buyer contracts to buy a tract of timber land from the seller. Both the seller and the buyer believe that the land

---

[43] See Paul Joskow, *Commercial Impossibility, the Uranium Market, and the "Westinghouse" Case,* 6 J. LEGAL STUD. 119 (1976). All of the lawsuits were settled out of court.

[44] See, for example, *Krell v. Henry,* 2 K.B. 740 (1903).

has timber, but in fact a forest fire has destroyed it. The parties have made a mutual mistake about a fundamental fact concerning the object of sale.

In analyzing frustration of purpose, we proposed the following principle: *If a contingency makes performance pointless, assign liability to the party who could bear the risk at least cost.* The law should assign liability in such cases to the party who can take precaution to prevent the contingency at least cost, or to the party who can insure against the contingency at least cost. The same principle applies to a mutual mistake concerning a fundamental fact about the object of sale. To illustrate, if the seller can prevent forest fires or insure against them more cheaply than the buyer, then the seller should be *unable* to enforce the contract for the sale of timber against the buyer. The owner at the time of the accident is usually the cheapest avoider of it.

6. Mutual Mistake About Identity   Now we turn from mutual mistakes about facts to mutual mistakes about identity. A mutual mistake about identity occurs when the buyer and seller have different objects in mind so that their "minds do not meet." Recall the example of the rusty Chevy, in which the seller and buyer agreed to a price of $1,000 for a car, but the seller intended to sell a rusty Chevy and the buyer intended to buy a shiny Cadillac. In the example, the buyer was mistaken about what the seller proposed to sell, and the seller was mistaken about what the buyer proposed to buy.

When the parties make a mutual mistake about identity, there is no true agreement to exchange. If the courts were to force an exchange, it would be involuntary. Involuntary exchange can destroy value rather than create it. Involuntary exchange destroys value by transferring ownership from someone who values the good more to someone who values it less. To illustrate, the buyer may value the shiny Cadillac at $2,000, and the seller may value it at $2,500. Forcing the Cadillac's transfer of ownership destroys $500 ("negative surplus"). By setting aside contracts based on mutual mistake, courts preclude the destruction of value by involuntary exchange. We propose this principle: *If reasonable parties disagreed about the identity of the performance offered and accepted, the contract is void.*

QUESTION 9.31:   In *Raffles v. Wichelhaus*, 2 Hurl. & C. 906, 159 Eng. Rep. 375 (Ex. 1864), the plaintiff sold the defendants 125 bales of cotton to arrive "ex *Peerless* from Bombay," that is, by way of the ship *Peerless* sailing from Bombay, India. A ship by that name sailed from India in December, but when it arrived, the defendants refused to take delivery of the cotton on the ground that they had meant a second ship named the *Peerless* that had left Bombay in October. The Court of Exchequer gave judgment for the defendants on the argument that there had been no meeting of the minds. How would you analyze this case?

C. Information

We have been discussing contract doctrines that allocate risk. Now we consider contract doctrines that allocate information. Doctrines that allocate information are different from doctrines that allocate other economic goods. The difference in doctrines is caused by a difference in the goods themselves. Information is discovered and transmitted, whereas most other goods are made and consumed. Unlike the makers of goods, the discoverers of information have difficulty appropriating its value, which creates a need for patents. Unlike consuming commodities, using information does not diminish the amount that remains for others. Consequently, information can be transmitted to many people without diminution. These facts make information different from most other goods. (Recall the discussion of public goods in the section on information economics in Chapter 5.)

What special problems exist in defining property rights and establishing markets in information? Everyone with a television or computer buys information, but information differs from other commodities like oranges or razor blades. Buyers cannot determine the value of information until they have it, and having it removes their willingness to pay for it. To illustrate, a banker recently received a letter that read, "If you pay me $1 million, I'll tell you how your bank can make $2 million." This letter illustrates a pervasive problem in computer software: Small companies often invent software that only large companies can market. To assess the value of the product, a large buyer like Microsoft must understand how it works. After learning how the product works, however, the large company may produce its own version of the product rather than paying royalties to the small company.

We will explain how contract doctrines contribute to the efficient discovery and transmission of information. Economists say that *public* (or *common*) information is known to both parties in a bargain, whereas *private* (or *asymmetric*) information is known to one party and unknown to the other. Private information often motivates exchange. To illustrate, assume that someone knows how to get more production from a resource than does its owner. To increase production, knowledge must be united with control. To unite knowledge with control, the owner of the resource must acquire the information, or else the informed person must acquire ownership of the resource. In general, the transmission of information and the sale of goods unites knowledge and control over resources. *Efficiency requires uniting knowledge and control over resources at least cost, including the transaction costs of transmitting information and selling goods.*

The parties can usually solve the problem of private information through private bargaining. For example, the informed party may offer to buy the resource and pay more than the uninformed owner can earn from using it. Or the informed party may offer to share the information with the uninformed owner of the resource in exchange for a proportion of the resulting increase in profits. Private bargaining usually solves the problem of asymmetrical information much better than any alternative, such as having the state dictate a solution. Consequently, the law usually enforces contracts based on asymmetrical information.

Instead of uniting knowledge and control, however, some contracts separate them. Separating knowledge and control reduces efficiency in the use of resources. Contracts that separate knowledge and control should be suppressed for the sake of efficiency. In subsequent sections, we will discuss three such doctrines: mistake, failure to disclose, and fraud.

1. Unilateral Mistake   Each of the parties to a bargain usually knows something that the other does not know. Sometimes one of the parties knows that the other party has a mistaken belief. For example, the seller of a car may think that it is merely old, whereas the buyer may know that it is a classic. Although the seller was mistaken about the car's value, the buyer was not; so, mistake is unilateral. When one party to a bargain knows the truth and the other party does not, the exchange is based on a "unilateral mistake," according to the language of the law. Courts usually enforce contracts based on unilateral mistakes. For example, if the owner promises to sell a classic car for less than its market value, the law will usually enforce the promise. Indeed, trades occur on the stock exchange when one party believes the price of a company's stock will rise and the other believes that the price will fall. One of them is (unilaterally) mistaken.

When the buyer acquires the classic car in this example, knowledge and control are united, which typically increases efficiency. For example, the buyer will probably take better care of the car because he or she knows its worth. The contract also increases efficiency in another way. Discovering information often requires investing time and resources, which requires a reward. In this example, the buyer may have searched long and hard to find a seller who does not know that he or she owns a classic car. The profit from buying the classic car at a low price rewards the buyer for the search.

We explained above that a mutual mistake about facts or identity is a valid formation defense in common law, whereas unilateral mistake is not. Consequently, a party who seeks performance of a contract may say that mistake was unilateral, and a party who seeks release from a contract may say that mistake was mutual.[45] Economic efficiency provides a criterion for making this distinction. Mutual mistake converts a contract into an involuntary exchange, which can destroy value. In contrast, a contract based on a unilateral mistake usually promotes efficiency by rewarding discovery and uniting knowledge with control. We propose the following principle to improve the legal distinction underlying the doctrines of unilateral and mutual mistake: *Withhold enforcement from contracts involving involuntary exchange, and enforce contracts that reward discovery and unite knowledge with control.*

We apply this principle to the famous case of *Laidlaw v. Organ*, 15 U.S. (2 Wheat.) 178 (1815). During the War of 1812 between Britain and the United States, the British blockaded New Orleans, which depressed the price of export goods like tobacco. Organ, a buyer of tobacco, received private information that the war had ended by treaty; so, he called on a representative of the Laidlaw firm and offered to buy tobacco. The representative of the Laidlaw firm was ignorant about the peace treaty; so,

---

[45] We are drawing attention here to the evidentiary problem of determining what the parties truly believed at the time the contract was formed. It is possible that there is credible contemporaneous evidence about those beliefs. However, in the absence of that evidence the parties have adverse incentives to recount their beliefs. The party for whom the terms seem to be favorable has an incentive to contend that he or she was not mistaken about the terms of the contract and that if there was a mistake, it was made by the other party; the party for whom the terms are unfavorable has an incentive to assert that there was a mutual misunderstanding.

a contract was concluded between them at the depressed price. The next day public notice was given in New Orleans that peace was concluded, and the price of tobacco soared. The mistake in this contract was obviously unilateral, not mutual—Organ knew about the treaty, and Laidlaw did not. Even so, the contract was apparently set aside by the court after a trial.[46]

This outcome can be defended on economic grounds. According to the preceding principle, the contract should be enforced if doing so rewards discovery and unites knowledge with control. The evidence suggests that Organ discovered fortuitously that peace was concluded, rather than investing time and resources in making the discovery. Furthermore, the contract merely accelerated by one day the uniting of knowledge and control, which did not contribute to production of tobacco. So, enforcing the contract would probably not increase efficiency.

To sharpen this analysis, distinguish between *productive* information and *redistributive* information. Productive information can be used to produce more wealth. It is information that allows existing resources to be moved to more productive uses (such as information that farmland contains valuable mineral resources) or discovers new methods of organizing resources for more productive uses (such as double-entry bookkeeping methods). The discovery of a vaccine for polio and the discovery of a water route between Europe and China were productive. Efficiency demands giving people strong incentives to discover productive facts. Transmitting information is so easy that the person who discovers productive information seldom captures its full value. Consequently, the state must take special measures to reward people who discover productive information. For example, the state must subsidize basic scientific research and provide patents to inventors.

In contrast, redistributive information creates a bargaining advantage that can be used to redistribute wealth in favor of the informed party. To illustrate, knowing before anyone else where the state will locate a new highway conveys a powerful advantage in real-estate markets. Investment in discovering redistributive information wastes resources. In addition, investment in redistributive information induces defensive expenditures by people trying not to lose their wealth to better-informed people. Defensive expenditures prevent redistribution, rather than produce something. Thus, investment in redistributive information wastes resources directly and indirectly.

The state should not create incentives to discover redistributive information. Instead, the state should discourage investment in discovering redistributive information. For example, the state should punish officials who leak information about the location of a new highway before the public announcement. Such leaks encourage real-estate dealers to devote resources to gaining privileged information from officials.

To further sharpen this complicated issue, let us also distinguish the methods by which people acquire information. One can acquire information either *actively*—that is, by investing resources in the acquisition of information—or *fortuitously*—that is, by

---

[46] A verdict at trial for the buyer was appealed to the U.S. Supreme Court, which remanded it for retrial, but it is not entirely clear what happened on retrial. See Anthony T. Kronman, *Mistake, Disclosure, Information and the Law of Contracts*, 7 J. LEGAL STUD. 1 (1978).

TABLE 9.4

Information in Contracts

		Method by Which the Information Was Acquired	
		Acquired by investment	*Acquired by fortuity*
Nature of the Information	*Productive*	Enforcement	No enforcement
	Redistributive	No enforcement	No enforcement

chance. As we argued at some length in Chapter 5, there is a strong social interest in encouraging the investment of resources in acquiring valuable, productive information. That, recall, is the premise upon which intellectual property law rests. Fortuity is different, and there is nothing that society gains from more-or-less chance occurrences.

We can bring together our concerns about the nature of the information—whether it is productive or redistributive—and about the method by which it was acquired—whether by active investment of fortuity—in order to make a proposal about encouraging the efficient exchange and use of information in contracts. Consider the two-by-two chart shown in Table 9.4.

Note that the only combination of the nature of the information and the method by which it was acquired for which there is a strong efficiency argument for enforcement is the one in the upper left-hand corner of Table 9.4—productive information that is the result of an active investment of resources. There is no efficiency case to be made for enforcing any of the other combinations in the chart. Indeed, we can go further than that and say that there is probably an argument to be made in favor of actively discouraging the investment of resources in acquiring redistributive information, such as investing in eavesdropping or establishing personal connections with powerful people so as to be the first to discover the route of the new major highway.

These considerations prompt another formulation of the economic principle for improving the legal distinction underlying the doctrines of unilateral and mutual mistake: *Contracts based upon one party's knowledge of productive information—especially if that knowledge was the result of active investment—should be enforced, whereas contracts based upon one party's knowledge of purely redistributive information or fortuitously acquired information should not be enforced.* This principle rewards investment in discovering productive information and discourages investment in discovering redistributive information.[47]

In our discussion of information economics in Chapter 5, we explained that most information is both productive and redistributive, what we might call "mixed" information. To illustrate, the invention of the cotton gin in 1792 by Eli Whitney increased cotton production and promoted speculation in land suitable for growing cotton.

---

[47] In his article cited in the previous footnote, Professor Kronman asserts that the contract between Organ and Laidlaw should have been set aside because the facts known to Organ were acquired *fortuitously*, rather than through *deliberate* investment.

The example of the informed buyer who purchased a classic car from an uninformed seller also illustrates mixed information, that is, information that is both productive and redistributive. The information was productive because the informed buyer knew that the car deserved special care. The information was redistributive because the informed buyer's gain from buying the car probably exceeded the increase in value from taking special care of it. We argued that private bargains usually succeed in rewarding discovery and uniting knowledge with control. Consequently, most bargains based upon differences in information affecting production and distribution should be enforced. In other words, most bargains based upon mixed information should be enforced.

We have arrived at three economic principles to govern the analysis of contract cases in which the formation defense of mistake is raised:

1. Enforce contracts based on differences in productive information, especially if that information was acquired by investment;
2. Enforce most contracts based on differences in mixed information (productive and redistributive); and
3. Set aside contracts based on differences in purely redistributive information or if the information was acquired fortuitously.

These normative principles clarify the principle underlying the legal doctrines of mutual and unilateral mistake.

QUESTION 9.32: Return to the case of *Laidlaw v. Organ.* List the ways in which Organ's information might be productive. Explain how Organ's information might be redistributive. What do you conclude about whether or not efficiency requires enforcing the contract?

QUESTION 9.33: A large number of cases involve a dispute about whether a mistake was mutual or unilateral concerning the quality of the object or its value. In a famous case, *Sherwood v. Walker;* 66 Mich. 568, 33 N.W. 919 (Mich. 1887), the seller (Walker) promised to deliver a cow to the buyer (Sherwood). The seller, who apparently believed that the cow was incapable of becoming pregnant, learned before the delivery was to take place that the cow was pregnant. A pregnant cow is far more valuable than a barren cow. The seller refused to deliver the cow to the buyer as promised. He contended that the contract was premised on the mutual mistake that the cow was barren. The buyer denied that he had made such a mistake.

a. The knowledge that a cow is fertile, rather than barren, is productive, rather than merely redistributive. Why?
b. Suppose the law imposed on Sherwood (the plaintiff-buyer) the duty to disclose to Walker (the defendant-seller) any evidence that the cow is fertile. Would there be an objection to such a duty on efficiency grounds?
c. Should it matter in this case that Walker was a professional cattle rancher and that Sherwood was a banker?

2. The Duty to Disclose   In the preceding section, we discussed productive and redistributive information. Now we consider another kind of information. *Safety information* helps people to avoid harm. For example, the safety information on an electrical appliance helps consumers to avoid fires. Conversely, the absence of safety information increases the probability and magnitude of accidents.

The law treats safety information differently from productive and redistributive information. As explained, contracts are often motivated by a difference in information between the parties. The law does not generally require an informed person to disclose productive or redistributive information to uninformed people. However, the law typically requires informed people to disclose safety information to uninformed people. For example, manufacturers must provide safety information concerning their products or assume liability when accidents occur. Regulatory law imposes most duties to disclose safety information. In this section we discuss the duty to disclose imposed by contract law.

The case of *Obde v. Schlemeyer*, 56 Wash.2d 449, 353 P.2d 672 (1960), provides an example of the common law duty to disclose. In this case, the seller of a building knew that it was infested with termites. The seller deliberately withheld the information about the termites from the buyer. The seller did not lie to the buyer, who never inquired about termites. Not long after the sale, the buyer discovered the termite infestation and sued the seller.[48]

To minimize termite damages, the termites should have been exterminated as soon as they were discovered. By not disclosing the infestation, the seller gave the termites the opportunity to cause further destruction. The court in the *Obde* case departed from tradition and imposed a duty to disclose.[49] By enforcing a duty to disclose, the court avoided future harms caused by the failure to disclose safety information, and the court diminished the need for future buyers to be wary or to undertake defensive expenditures against this sort of concealment by sellers.

The seller knew about the termite infestation, and the buyer did not know about it. Thus, the sale of the termite-infested house separates knowledge from control. A contract *separates* knowledge from control when the seller fails to disclose information needed by the buyer to prevent the good's destruction. Earlier we explained that contract law seeks to *unite* knowledge and control. Thus, contracts based on the failure to disclose safety information undermine one purpose of contract law. These considerations suggest a fourth economic principle for contract cases involving information: *When bargaining to a contract, the parties should divulge safety information.*

> **QUESTION 9.34:**   Suppose that a seller has not bothered to investigate whether her house has termites; so, she does not know. When asked by a buyer if it does, she says, "I guess not." On efficiency grounds, should this statement be enough to void the contract?

---

[48] In the case, the buyer asked not for invalidation of the contract but rather for damages for the costs that correcting the termite infestation imposed on him.

[49] The common law tradition held that sellers had no duty to disclose. The old rule was *caveat emptor*; "Let the buyer beware!" Sellers did, however, have the duty not to lie. See the discussion of fraud in the next section. Note that regulations in many parts of the United States now require the seller of real estate to provide the buyer with a certificate from a licensed exterminator that the house is free of termite infestation.

QUESTION 9.35: Professor Schmidt, a geologist, has agreed to purchase McDonald's farm for a price of $2,000 per acre, which corresponds to the price of good quality farmland in the vicinity. However, Schmidt, on the basis of his own geological studies, is convinced that McDonald's farm contains valuable mineral deposits, which make the property worth $25,000 per acre. Schmidt's true motive is discovered by McDonald before Schmidt takes possession, and McDonald refuses to hand over the property. Schmidt sues for breach of contract. McDonald defends on the ground that Schmidt had a duty to disclose the results of his studies. According to our economic principles, who should win?

3. Fraud and Misrepresentation
The seller in *Obde v. Schlemeyer* failed to disclose safety information, but he did not claim that the property was free from termites. If the seller in *Obde* had actually claimed that the property was free from termites, the claim would have been fraudulent. Fraud at common law requires a lie—a false assertion made with the intention to deceive. Under the traditional common law doctrine, the victim of fraud is entitled to damages for harm caused by fraud.

The economic reason for not enforcing a promise elicited by fraud is straightforward. If parties to a contract know that fraud is a ground for voiding the agreement, then they can rely on the truthfulness of the information developed in negotiations for the contract. This saves the parties the costs of verifying material statements. This, in turn, lowers the costs of concluding cooperative agreements—furthering one of the economic goals of contract law.

Many misleading statements lie between fraud and nondisclosure, and these cases cause the most disputes. Courts and legislatures in the United States have recently broadened the circumstances in which a contract may be voided for nondisclosure. For example, lenders are now required by law to divulge the annual percentage rate of interest on all consumer loans. Used-car dealers are required in many states to reveal any major repairs done to their cars. Sellers of homes in most states are required to reveal latent defects, such as a cracked foundation. Producers of food are required to list ingredients. Manufacturers of some appliances must notify consumers about the appliance's energy use. Like the traditional common law rules on fraud, these regulations aim to improve the exchange of information in private contracts. Enforcing these regulations can be costly. Consequently, legislation directed at a real abuse can end up costing consumers more than the harm they suffer in the absence of regulation.

QUESTION 9.36: Suppose that the seller is very attached to her home and wishes to sell only to someone who will maintain the property as a single-family dwelling. A prospective buyer says that he, too, wants to use the property as a single-family dwelling. The sale is completed, and the seller moves out. However, several days later, she learns that the buyer intended all along to demolish the house in order to open a commercial establishment. Does efficiency commend enforcing the contract or rescinding it?

4. Indefinite or Vague Promises
People often make informal promises that they do not want the law to enforce. People also make formal contracts containing indefinite

language that courts do not know how to enforce. Thus, one person may promise to make his "best efforts" to accomplish some end on behalf of another person, or to make "reasonable efforts," or to bargain "in good faith." The parties recognize that courts cannot interpret these indefinite terms in a precise way. But these terms are inexpensive to include: being more precise might be very costly.

Should courts do their best to give precise meaning to these terms, or should courts refuse to enforce them? We have stressed the fundamental principle that courts should enforce promises when the parties want enforceability at the time the promise was made. Similarly, the courts should enforce vague terms in contracts to the extent that the parties wanted them to be enforceable when they were made.

The problem for courts is to determine what the parties actually wanted. Earlier we discussed "penalty default rules" that force a party to reveal information to the other party in a transaction. Similarly, courts penalize the parties for writing excessively vague terms into contracts by refusing to enforce them. Common law doctrine allows courts to set aside vague terms in contracts by applying the principle of "indefiniteness" or "void for vagueness"—the principle that courts will not enforce a term in a contract that is too indefinite or too vague. By applying this doctrine and leaving breach of informal promises to informal remedies, courts give incentives for parties to be more precise.

When the contract is formed, however, the parties often want vague terms to be enforceable as best the courts can do. The parties often cannot foresee future contingencies well enough to describe them explicitly in the contract. Thus, most business ventures can fail for so many reasons that no one could list all of them in advance. When the parties cannot be precise *ex ante*, they may want courts to apply vague principles *ex post*. If no one can say in advance exactly what would constitute "best efforts" in managing a business asset, the parties may want the court to decide after the fact. While the court probably cannot distinguish "best efforts" from "second-best efforts," the court can probably distinguish "best efforts" from "minimal efforts." Similarly, if the parties cannot say in advance all the circumstances that would require modifying the contract, they may foresee a likely need for modification. As a result, the parties may specify in the contract that they should renegotiate "in good faith." Although the court cannot distinguish "good faith" from "pretty good faith," it may be able to distinguish them from "bad faith." The "good faith" provision may cause the court to reverse the burden of proof. Thus, a party under an obligation to bargain in good faith may have the burden of proving that it had a good reason for breaking off negotiations.

In general, courts can refuse to enforce indefinite terms in contracts, or courts can enforce the terms roughly or use vague terms to change presumptions and procedures. Making good decisions in such cases requires the courts to understand thoroughly the purpose of the contract. Understanding the contract's purpose allows the courts to discern the extent that the parties wanted enforceability of an indefinite promise when they made the contract. Economic analysis is a valuable tool for judges and lawyers to understand the business purposes of contracts.[50]

---

[50] For a discussion of the purposes of indefinite contracts, see Robert Scott & George Triantis, *Anticipating Litigation in Contract Design*, 115 YALE L. J. 814 (2006). Also see Lewis Kornhauser & W. Bentley MacLeod, *Contingency and Control: A Theory of Contracts,* Berkeley Law and Economics Seminar, 2 Feb 2005.

D. Monopoly

We discussed dire constraints that leave the promisor with no choice. A less extreme situation occurs when a monopolist controls a product valued by many people. Strictly defined, a *monopolist is the only seller of a product for which no close substitutes exist.* A monopolist can dictate the price and nonprice terms of the contract offered to many buyers. The buyer must respond by accepting the monopolist's offer or doing without the good.

Monopoly contrasts with its polar opposite, *perfect competition*, in which many buyers and sellers substitute perfectly for each other. In perfect competition, no one can dictate the price or nonprice terms of contracts. No one has power over the contractual terms because each buyer or seller who dislikes a contractual partner can get an alternative contract from someone else. Perfect competition shades into monopoly as the availability of substitutes decreases.

Monopolists set prices too high, which distorts the economy. A price is too high when it exceeds the marginal cost of producing the good. When price exceeds marginal cost, some consumers, who would be willing to pay more for it than its cost of production, do not purchase the good. If producing a good costs less than people would be willing to pay for it, then *not* supplying the good is inefficient ("allocative inefficiency"). In addition to high prices, monopoly depletes the drive and dynamism of entrepreneurs ("dynamic inefficiency"). Consequently, economists condemn monopoly as inefficient.

Lawyers often condemn monopoly as unfair. In monopoly, the seller faces many potential buyers, whereas the buyers face only one potential seller. This asymmetry between seller and buyer constitutes the unfairness of monopoly. The law, consequently, looks on monopoly contracts with skepticism. Earlier we explained that a dire constraint can provide a defense or excuse for breaking a promise. Now we discuss whether monopoly provides a defense or excuse for breaking a promise.

Under the bargain theory, the courts enforce bargained promises and do not ask if the terms are fair. Consequently, the common law historically contains weak protection against monopolies. Most protections against monopolies come from statutes, not common law. Similarly, the "mercantilist" tradition in continental Europe favors monopolies protected by the state. The civil codes of Europe originally provided little protection against monopolies. To illustrate, companies often wish to keep prices high by promising not to compete with each other. Agreements not to compete enable cartels to extract monopoly prices from buyers. The courts in England and America were reluctant to enforce nineteenth-century contracts to create cartels. However, the common law did nothing beyond not enforcing cartel contracts to undermine cartels. Cartels were finally outlawed by antitrust statutes, not common law.

Besides contracts to create cartels, two common law doctrines sometimes lead courts not to enforce monopoly contracts. We will explain and critique two doctrines that provide performance excuses for monopoly contracts. For these doctrines, the healthy skepticism of courts concerning monopoly combines with confusion about the underlying economics.

QUESTION 9.37: Explain the relationship between the availability of substitutes and the elasticity of demand for a good.

QUESTION 9.38: I want to build a garage in my backyard. My neighbor's driveway offers the only practical way to reach the proposed garage. I offer to purchase an easement from my neighbor, thus giving me the right to share her driveway. Economists describe the relationship between my neighbor and me as "bilateral monopoly." Explain why this phrase is appropriate.

1. Fill in a Form: Contracts of Adhesion

Most written contracts use standard forms. Some terms in a standard-form contract are fixed; others may be variable. For example, the legal staff of an automobile manufacturer may provide its salespersons with form contracts that stipulate the warranty (fixed terms) and leave the price open for negotiation (variable term). Some standard forms do not allow the parties to vary any terms. In an extreme situation, one party makes a take-it-or-leave-it offer, meaning that the other party must sign the standard form or not make a contract.

Many fixed terms in standard-form contracts are uniform throughout an industry. For example, many automobile manufacturers promise to repair certain problems with their new cars within the first five years or 50,000 miles of the car's life. When terms are uniform, sellers do not compete over them. Narrowing the scope of competition can reduce its intensity.

To see why, consider cartels. The members of a cartel agree to keep prices up, which profits the members as a group. Each individual member, however, profits even more by undercutting the cartel's price and luring buyers away from other members. To prevent such "cheating," the cartel must punish members who undercut the cartel's price. Uniform, fixed terms in contracts prevent sellers from offering special concessions to buyers. Consequently, the cartel can focus on determining whether all members charge the cartel's price. Monitoring "cheating" in the cartel is much easier when all sellers use the same contract with fixed terms.

In an influential article, Friedrich Kessler called take-it-or-leave-it agreements "contracts of adhesion."[51] This term suggests that standard-form contracts indicate the existence of a monopoly, which deprives buyers of bargaining power. Consequently, courts sometimes use "contract of adhesion" as a term of opprobrium to undermine the enforceability of a contract.

This court practice can be justified when sellers use standard-form contracts to reduce competition. However, this court practice is unjustified when sellers use standard-form contracts to increase the efficiency of exchange. Standard-form contracts narrow the scope of bargaining, which can promote efficiency in two ways. First, standard-form contracts can promote price competition by reducing product differentiation. To see why, consider an analogy. Toothpaste comes in different sizes, shapes, colors, textures, tastes, and smells. Manufacturers tinker with these differences in an attempt to attract customers by differentiating their product. Product differentiation complicates price comparisons. Price competition would be more intense if all toothpaste were the same. Similarly, uniformity reduces differences among contracts and intensifies the competition over price.

---

[51] Friedrich Kessler, *Contracts of Adhesion: Some Thoughts About Freedom of Contract*, 43 COLUM. L. REV. 629 (1943).

Second, standard-form contracts reduce transaction costs. The parties can bargain over variable terms, such as the price, and the parties cannot bargain over fixed terms. Instead of bargaining, buyers choose among standardized contracts with different price and nonprice terms. Sellers may build an actual contract by plugging "modules" of language into a universal form. Thus, standard forms reduce the number of terms requiring drafting, bargaining, and agreement.

One of the usual assumptions of a perfectly competitive market is that transaction costs are zero. Standard-form contracts can move a market closer to the perfectly competitive ideal by reducing transaction costs. The availability of substitutes in perfectly competitive markets prevents anyone from bargaining over price. Similarly, the availability of substitutes in perfectly competitive markets prevents anyone from bargaining over contracts. In general, substitutes turn everyone into "takers" of the price. The fact that many firms use the same standard form may indicate a high level of competition among them. Take-it-or-leave-it contracts can indicate perfect competition rather than monopoly.

Because standard-form contracts can increase competition and efficiency in exchange, the phrase "contract of adhesion" should not be applied to standard-form contracts. Rather, the phrase should be reserved for monopoly contracts. The relevant question is whether a market is competitive or monopolistic. The fact that a contract was made on a standard form does not establish a presumption in either direction.

What should courts do with the terms in monopoly contracts? In monopoly contracts, the price is too high. Courts, however, usually do not think that adjusting the prices in a contract is their job. Courts are more willing to adjust the nonprice terms. Should they?

To answer this question, we first ask whether the nonprice terms of monopoly contracts are efficient or inefficient. The abstract answer given by economic theory is simple. The nonprice terms of a contract typically create incentives that affect the size of the surplus from exchange, and efficient nonprice terms maximize the surplus from exchange and thereby maximize its profits. In contrast, the price terms typically distribute the surplus between the parties. Sometimes the monopolist can use its power to extract the entire surplus from each exchange and thereby maximize its profits. In brief, a monopolist who can extract all of the surplus from each exchange by controlling the price will choose efficient nonprice terms.

In contrast, a monopolist who cannot extract all of the surplus from exchange by controlling the price may adopt inefficient nonprice terms in order to increase its control over the price terms. (These propositions can be restated in familiar jargon for economists.[52]) For example, a monopoly supplier of software may increase its power to over-price by contracts that prohibit resale.

---

[52] In economic jargon, a perfectly discriminating monopolist sets efficient nonprice terms in its contract. Otherwise, a monopolist may use inefficient nonprice terms to increase price discrimination. To illustrate the latter, assume that buyers who are willing to pay a lot for a product also prefer a strong warranty, whereas buyers who are willing to pay a little prefer a weak warranty. Recognizing this fact, the monopolist might offer two contracts: a high-price-strong-warranty contract and a low-price-weak-warranty contract. The difference in warranties helps to separate the two consumer groups so the monopolist can charge them different prices. Without the two nonprice terms, the monopolist cannot tell the two groups apart.

Besides monopoly, another defect in markets can cause inefficient standardization of contracts. Lawyers often use the term "contract of adhesion" when a seller takes advantage of a buyer's ignorance. Thus, contracts often stipulate a process for resolving future disputes that favor sellers, such as compulsory arbitration before a board organized by the association of sellers. The buyer often fails to read the contract with sufficient care to be aware of such terms, or the buyer is aware but does not appreciate the term's significance. When such a contract results in a legal dispute, the buyer's lawyer will argue that the court should void the contract because the standardized form prevented the buyer from bargaining. (Remember that according to the bargain theory of contract, which many judges accept in some form, "no bargain" implies "no contract.") This argument, however, misleads. If buyers are informed and markets are competitive, the standardized terms in form contracts will be efficient, not biased against buyers, without any bargaining. The real problem with this kind of contract is the buyer's ignorance, not the absence of bargaining.

QUESTION 9.39: Explain how uniformity can reduce price competition by strengthening cartels or increase price competition by reducing product differentiation.

QUESTION 9.40: Competition drives prices down to costs, whereas monopolies price above cost. California banks have paid large damages for allegedly charging fees greater than the cost of certain services that they provide. Suppose a car manufacturer charges an additional $450 for an automatic transmission in a new car. What inefficiencies would result if the consumer could sue the manufacturer and make the company prove that $450 is not disproportionately above the actual cost of the automatic transmission?

QUESTION 9.41: Monopoly distorts contracts by making prices too high. Why would a monopolist ever want to distort the nonprice term by, say, limiting liability for harm caused by defective products?

QUESTION 9.42: Assume that two kinds of buyers purchase contracts from a monopolist who promises to deliver goods in the future. One kind of buyer values the good more highly than the other. The monopolist would like to charge a higher price to the buyers who value the good more highly, but he cannot identify who they are. To overcome this problem, he offers two different contracts. One contract charges a high price and offers to pay high damages in the event that the seller fails to deliver the goods. The other contract charges a low price and offers to pay low damages in the event that the seller fails to deliver the goods. Explain why the two kinds of buyers might prefer different contracts. Explain why the monopolist might gain from offering two kinds of contracts. (In economic jargon, the "menu" of contracts "separates" the "pool" of buyers and permits "price discrimination.")

Buying Souls by Using Standard-Form Contracts

By one estimate, 99 percent of all commercial contracts are made on standard forms.[53] While most commercial contracts rely on standard forms, researchers know little about how consumers respond to them. A British software company forcefully demonstrated how little we pay attention to online contract-term disclosures earlier this year. On April Fool's Day, the GameStation company in Britain added an "immortal soul clause" to the standard form contract for users of its software. The clause read in part:

> By placing an order via this Web site on the first day of the fourth month of the year 2010 Anno Domini, you agree to grant Us a non-transferable option to claim, for now and forever more, your immortal soul. Should We wish to exercise this option, you agree to surrender your immortal soul, and any claim you may have on it, within 5 (five) working days of receiving written notification from gamstation.co.uk or one of its authorized minions.

The company included a simple tick box for any purchaser to opt out of the clause, which would also give the purchaser a £5 voucher good on the current purchase. Almost no one ticked the opt-out box.

Florencia Marotta-Wurgler of the New York University School of Law has examined thousands of contracts relating to computer and software information.[54] She finds that almost all end-user licenses are biased in favor of the software company that wrote them. Vigorous competition in the computer industry, fails to generate more buyer-friendly terms because too few consumers read the standard forms. When we install a new software program on our computers, most of us scroll down to the "Accept" button without bothering to read the license. Why do we do this? Perhaps we hope that an "informed minority" reads the contracts closely and raises complaints if the terms are unfair.[55] If so, then the rest us might assume that whatever terms are presented to us in a standard form are the result of a process that has filtered out the one-sided terms. But Marotta-Wurgler and her coauthors have found that they "can plausibly rule out an informed minority mechanism being important in this market." The problem is clear, but its remedy is not.

---

[53] David Slawson, *Standard Form Contracts and Democratic Control of Law Making Power*, 84 HARV. L. REV. 529 (1971).

[54] Florencia Marotta-Wurgler, *What's In a Standard Form Contract?: An Empirical Analysis of Software License Agreements*, 4 J. EMP. LEGAL STUD. 677 (2007); Marotta-Wurgler, *Competition and the Quality of Standard Form Contracts: The Case of Software License Agreements*, 5 J. EMP. LEGAL STUD. 447 (2008); Yannis Bakos, Florencia Marotta-Wurgler, & David R. Trossen, *Does Anyone Read the Fine Print?: Testing a Law and Economics Approach to Standard Form Contracts* (2009), available at www.ssrn.com; and Marotta-Wurgler, *Does Disclosure Matter?* (2010) available at www.ssrn.com.

[55] This was the contention in Alan Schwartz & Louis Wilde, *Intervening in Markets on the Basis of Imperfect Information: A Legal and Economic Analysis*, 127 U. PA. L. REV. 630 (1979).

2. Unconscionability   When a contract seems so one-sided that its enforcement would violate the conscience of the court, it may be set aside according to the common law doctrine of *unconscionability*. The civil law tradition contains a concept similar to unconscionability. "Lesion" refers to a contract that is too unequal to enforce in civil law. It is easy to see why judges do not want to use their power to enforce unconscionable contracts. It is difficult, however, to create legal doctrine about what shocks, or ought to shock, the conscience of a judge.[56] We will use economics to dispel some of the obscurity in the unconscionability doctrine.

Lacking generally accepted definitions, the analysis of unconscionability must proceed from cases. We briefly discuss the famous case of *Williams v. Walker-Thomas Furniture Co., 350 F.2d 445 (D.C. Cir. 1965)*, to show how economics can contradict common sense. *Williams* concerns the purchase of a durable good from a retailer on credit. When a retailer loans the money for a consumer to buy a good, the lender-retailer wants a guarantee of repayment. The borrower offers something valuable that he or she owns (collateral). The lender acquires a right to the valuable object through what is known as a "security interest." If the borrower defaults on the loan, the lender can take possession of the valuable object, sell it, and use the proceeds of the sale to discharge the debt.[57]

In theory, the borrower can offer anything valuable as a guarantee, but in practice the borrower usually offers the item that he or she is buying with the borrowed money, such as a refrigerator or an automobile. The lender-retailer obviously knows the market for that item and can easily resell it. However, consumer durables typically lose value faster than the purchase price is paid off. Consequently, the right to repossess the item being purchased will not fully protect the lender-retailer from loss due to default by the borrower. For example, assume that a car dealer lends $20,000 to a consumer to buy a new car. The instant the car leaves the dealership, it becomes a "used car" and falls in value to, say, $16,000. If the consumer-borrower defaults on the $20,000 loan, the most that the dealer can recover by repossessing the car and reselling it is $16,000. Consequently, consumer-borrowers need additional guarantees in order to borrow money to purchase consumer durables. The best alternative is a cash payment, called a "down payment," equal to the

---

[56] Both the *Uniform Commercial Code* and the *Restatement (Second) of Contracts* have attempted definitions of unconscionability, but neither is precise. Here is what they say:

> UNIFORM COMMERCIAL CODE, §2–302 comment 1 (1977): "The basic test [of unconscionability] is whether ... the clauses involved [in the contract] are so one-sided as to be unconscionable under the circumstances existing at the time of the making of the contract. . . . The principle is one of the prevention of oppression and unfair surprise. . . . "

> RESTATEMENT (SECOND) OF CONTRACTS, §208 (1979): "c. Overall imbalance. Inadequacy of consideration does not of itself invalidate a bargain, but gross disparity in the values exchanged may be an important factor in a determination that a contract is unconscionable. . . . Such a disparity may also corroborate indications of defects in the bargaining process . . . gross inequality of bargaining power, together with terms unreasonably favorable to the stronger party, may confirm indications that the transaction involved elements of deception or compulsion, or may show that the weaker party had no meaningful choice, nor real alternative, and hence did not in fact assent or appear to assent to the unfair terms."

[57] Most jurisdictions have statutes that limit the repossessor to recovering the debt and the cost of its collection. See Alan Schwartz, *The Enforceability of Security Interests in Consumer Goods*, 26 J. LAW & ECON 117 (1983).

difference between the purchase price and the amount of the loan. But some consumers do not have the cash to make a down payment. Their problem can be solved by an "add-on clause," which specifies that any goods that the borrower has previously purchased on credit from the lender-retailer will serve as additional security for the current purchase.

To illustrate, assume that *A* bought a refrigerator from *B*'s store two years ago for $800. *A* borrowed $600 from *B* to make the purchase, and *A* promised to repay the loan at $10 per month for five years. *A* has made payments each month for the past two years and still owes $360 on the refrigerator. Now *A* decides to purchase a television set for $500. *A* does not have the cash for a down payment. Instead, *B* suggests an add-on clause, by which *A* offers the refrigerator and the television as a guarantee. Thus, if *A* should default on the payments for the television, *B* may repossess the television *and* the refrigerator to discharge *A*'s debt on the television.[58] (The refrigerator is "cross-collateral" for the loan to buy the television.)

The *Williams* case involved such an add-on clause. Mrs. Williams was a single mother of seven children and had a limited education. When she missed several payments on the most recently purchased goods, the Walker-Thomas Furniture Company laid claim to most of the household goods she had purchased from it under 14 contracts over a five-year period. In such individual cases, the consumer's situation is desperate, and the impulse to provide legal relief is powerful. The *Williams* court held the add-on clause to be unconscionable.

Lawyers focus on individual cases, whereas economists focus on statistics. Statistically, the paternalistic protection of Mrs. Williams by legal restrictions on the credit market imposes high costs on poor consumers as a class.[59] The add-on clause presumably represents the cheapest way for some poor consumers to obtain credit. Denying them this instrument for borrowing will either force them to borrow at higher costs, or prevent them from borrowing to purchase needed goods. The poor as a class will borrow at higher cost and purchase fewer consumer goods than they otherwise would. Those retailers who offered the add-on clause in an attempt to lower the costs of consumer credit may also be made worse off by the holding. Their sales may decline or their costs may rise; in either case their profits are likely to fall.

We have suggested that Mrs. Williams deserved protection as an individual, and that refusing to enforce add-on clauses harms poor consumers as a class. The courts need a finer analysis to distinguish between consumers who need paternalistic protection and those whom it harms. Some consumers do not understand the complexities of

---

[58] *B* cannot realize a profit on this repossession. Of the proceeds from the resale of the repossessed items, *B* may only keep the amount of the unpaid loan. Anything more that comes from the resale must be turned over to *A*.

There is more to the add-on clause. It also provides, typically, that the lender may use discretion in applying each installment payment made with respect to *any* item purchased from the lender-retailer against whatever outstanding balance the lender-retailer chooses. This may allow the creditor to keep the security interest in the refrigerator alive after the five years for which the original loan was to run. By adroit accounting, the creditor can keep this security interest in all previously purchased goods until all the loans have been paid off.

[59] See Richard Epstein, *Unconscionability: A Critical Reappraisal*, 18 J. LAW & ECON. 293 (1975).

the add-on clause. Perhaps they think that if they fail to make their payments on the most recent purchase, the lender-retailer will repossess only their most recent purchase. Such people undertake an additional loan without fully appreciating the risks and consequences of default. In cases like *Williams,* the court might require proof that the buyer understood the add-on clause as a condition for enforcing it. The courts would require the contractual process to contain protections against ignorance about add-on clauses. The unconscionability doctrine might protect people from their own ignorance, but otherwise let them make their own decisions.

Courts frequently distinguish between *substantive* and *procedural* unconscionability. Substantive unconscionability usually refers to a price that is utterly disproportionate to market value. In contrast, procedural unconscionability consists of circumstances and procedures present at the formation of the bargain that violate widely accepted norms of fairness. Substantive and procedural unconscionability are often combined in actual cases because an unfair procedure frequently results in an unfair price. Violation of these norms undermines the quality of consent to the contract.

> **QUESTION 9.43:**   A 21-year-old songwriter signed a contract in 1966 with a music publisher. The standard-form contract assigned the copyrights of all the plaintiff's output to the defendant company in return for the defendant's agreement to pay 50 percent of the net royalties to the plaintiff. The contract was to run for five years, with automatic renewal for another five years if the plaintiff's royalties during the first term exceeded 5,000 pounds sterling. The defendant company could terminate the contract on one month's notice and could assign the contract and any copyrights held under it without the plaintiff's consent. For signing the contract, the plaintiff received 50 pounds as an advance against future royalties. The plaintiff became a successful songwriter and sought to be released from the contract on the ground that it was unconscionably one-sided in the music publisher's favor. *Macaulay v. Schroeder Publishing Co. Ltd.* (1974) 1 W.L.R. 1308 (H.L.). Use economics to analyze this case.

---

i **Web Note 9.6**

There is much more to be said about the troubling and troubled subject of unconscionability. We discuss some additional literature and cases involving that doctrine and pose additional questions about them on our website.

---

i **Web Note 9.7**

There is an increasing amount of interesting empirical work on contract law. We discuss that literature—especially that on unfair contract terms in new car deals by Professor Ian Ayres of Yale and a summary of that literature by Professor Russell Korobkin of UCLA—on our website.

TABLE 9.5

Defenses and Excuses

Legal Doctrine	Fact Triggering Legal Doctrine Problem	Incentive Solution	Legal
Incompetence	Incompetent person makes promise	Protect incompetents at least cost	Interpret contract in incompetent's best interests
Duress	Promisee threatens to destroy	Deter threats	No enforcement of coerced promises
Necessity	Promisee threatens not to rescue	Reward rescue	Beneficiary pays cost of rescue plus reward
Impossibility	Contingency prevents performance	Encourage precaution and risk-spreading	Liability for the least-cost risk-bearer
Frustration of purpose	Contingency destroys purpose of performance	Encourage precaution and risk-spreading	Liability for the least-cost risk-bearer
Mutual mistake about facts	Buyer and seller make same mistake about facts	Encourage precaution and risk-spreading	Liability for the least-cost risk bearer
Mutual mistake about identity	Buyer and seller have different object in mind	Prevent involuntary exchanges	Unwind contract
Unilateral mistake	Buyer or seller mistaken about facts	Unite knowledge and control; encourage discovery	Enforce contract
Duty to disclose	Promisee harms by withholding information	Induce supply of true information	Liability for harm
Fraud	Promisee supplies false information knowingly	Deter supply of false information	No enforcement of contract and liability for harm
Adhesion contracts	Cartel uses standard forms to promote collusion	Destabilize cartels	Deny enforcement to contracts of cartels
Procedural unconscionability	Consumer ignorant of critical terms in retailer's contract	Create incentive to communicate meaning of contract terms	Deny enforcement unless bargaining process communicates crucial information

A. Conclusion to Part II

We summarize our analysis of excuses and defenses. The doctrine of incompetence is triggered when an incompetent person makes a promise. The law provides incentives to protect incompetent people at least cost by interpreting contracts in their best interests. The doctrine of duress gets triggered when the promisor threatens destruction in order to induce the promisee to make a one-sided promise. The law creates incentives to deter threats by not enforcing coerced promises. The doctrine of necessity gets triggered when the promisor threatens not to rescue the promisee in order to induce a one-sided promise. The law creates incentives for efficient rescue by requiring the beneficiary to pay the rescuer the cost of rescue plus a reward, and by refusing to enforce the one-sided promise. The doctrine of impossibility gets triggered when a contingency prevents performance. The law encourages efficient precaution and risk-spreading by allocating liability to the party who can bear the risk of the contingency at the least cost.

A contract can separate information and control when both of the parties make a mistake, or when the seller fails to disclose information needed by the buyer to prevent the good's destruction, or when the promisee supplies false information to the promisor.

Turning to monopoly, standard-form contracts can be used to promote collusion in a cartel. The law should not enforce such "contracts of adhesion." More typically, standard-form contracts increase competition by reducing product differentiation and lowering transaction costs. Finally, "unconscionability" covers a confusing array of doctrines, including bargaining processes that leave consumers ignorant of important terms. If events trigger these terms, the consumers are "unfairly surprised." The remedy is to require a process that communicates the information as a condition of enforceability. Table 9.5 on the previous page encapsulates our analysis.

Suggested Readings

Eisenberg, Melvin A., *The Bargain Principle and Its Limits*, 95 HARV. L. REV. 741 (1982).

Eisenberg, Melvin A., *The Limits of Cognition and the Limits of Contract Law*, 47 STAN. L. REV. 211(1995).

Eisenberg, Melvin A., *Actual and Virtual Specific Performance: The Theory of Efficient Breach and the Indifference Principle in Contract Law*, 93 CAL. L. REV. 975 (2005).

GOLDBERG, VICTOR E., FRAMING CONTRACT LAW: AN ECONOMIC PERSPECTIVE (2007).

GOLDBERG, VICTOR E., ED., READINGS IN THE ECONOMICS OF CONTRACT LAW (2006).

Katz, Avery W., *The Option Element in Contracting*, 90 VA. L. REV. 2187 (2004).

Katz, Avery W, *The Economics of Form and Substance in Contract Interpretation*, 104 COLUM. L. REV. 496 (2004).

Posner, Richard A., *The Law and Economics of Contract Interpretation*, 83 TEX. L. REV. 1581 (2005).

SALANIE, BERNARD, THE ECONOMICS OF CONTRACTS: A PRIMER, (2d ed. 2005).

Schwartz, Alan, & Robert E. Scott, *Contract Theory and the Limits of Contract Law*, 113 YALE L. J. 541 (2003).

Scott, Robert E., & George G. Triantis, *Anticipating Litigation in Contract Design*, 115 YALE L.J. 814 (2006).

Shavell, Steven, *Specific Performance Versus Damages for Breach of Contract: An Economic Analysis*, 84 TEX. L. REV. 831 (2006).

Mathematical Appendix

T O DEVELOP the model of performance and reliance more formally, we will apply math and graphs to the example of the Waffle Shop. Figure 9.5 depicts the relationship between Xavier's expenditure and the probability that he will perform as promised. The variable x denotes Xavier's expenditure on performing; the variable p denotes the probability of performing; and $p = p(x)$ denotes the functional relationship between the variables. The probability of performing increases when Xavier spends; thus, p is an increasing function of x.

Now, we turn from Xavier's performance to Yvonne's reliance. Figure 9.6 graphs the relationship between the size of Yvonne's food order and her profits in September. By definition, profits in September equal total revenues minus total variable costs. Food orders are one cost that Yvonne can vary on short notice. To keep the example simple, we assume that she cannot vary any other costs in September. So the variable y, which denotes Yvonne's expenditure on food orders, also indicates her total variable costs for the month.

Total revenues equal Yvonne's income from selling meals in September. Her income from selling meals depends on whether she occupies the new building or the old building. If Xavier performs, then Yvonne occupies the new building on September 1 and she enjoys high revenues, as indicated in Figure 9.6 by the curve labeled $R_p(y)$. If Xavier does not perform, then Yvonne remains in the old building on September 1 and she enjoys low revenues, as indicated in Figure 9.6 by the curve labeled $R_{np}(y)$.

Figure 9.6 depicts profits, which equal the difference between total revenues and total variable costs, as the vertical distance between the appropriate total revenue curve and the total-cost curve. The appropriate total-revenue curve depends on the probability that Xavier finishes the building on time. If Xavier is certain to finish the building on time, then $R_p(y)$ is the appropriate total-revenue curve. Conversely, if Xavier is certain to finish the building late, then $R_{np}(y)$ is the appropriate total-revenue curve.

Yvonne maximizes profits by maximizing the vertical distance between the appropriate total-revenue curve and the total-cost curve. When $R_p(y)$ is the appropriate total-revenue curve, the high level of reliance denoted y_1 in Figure 9.6 maximizes Yvonne's profits. When $R_{np}(y)$ is the appropriate total revenue curve, the low level of reliance denoted y_0 in Figure 9.6 maximizes Yvonne's profits. (At both levels of reliance, the marginal cost of reliance (given by the constant slope of the line through the origin) equals the marginal revenue from reliance (given by the slope of either $R_p(y)$ or $R_{np}(y)$).)

Increasing the food order above y_0 is risky. The farther y rises above y_0 (up to the maximum y_1), the more Yvonne's profits increase if Xavier performs, and the more Yvonne's profits decrease if Xavier breaches.

FIGURE 9.5

The direct relationship between levels of precaution and the probability of performance.

FIGURE 9.6

How a promisee's reliance depends on the probability of a promisor's performance.

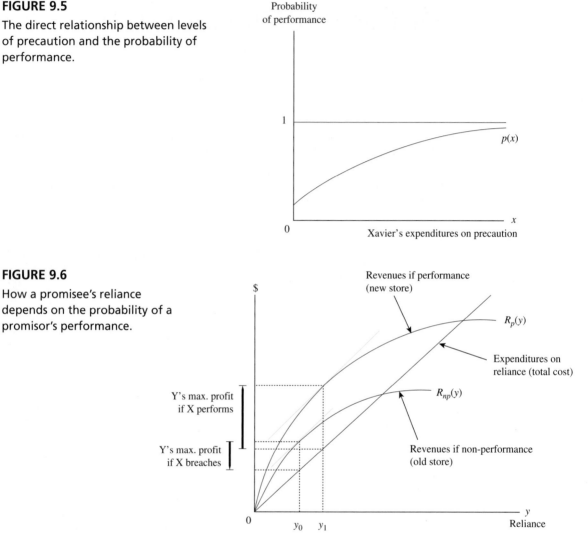

The concrete example of the Waffle Shop captures two general truths. First, the promisor can take costly precautions that increase the probability that he or she will perform as promised. Second, the more the promisee relies on the promise, the greater the profits if the promise is kept, and the lower the profits if the promise is broken.

1. Efficiency   Efficiency requires choosing x and y so as to maximize Yvonne's expected profits minus Xavier's expenditures. First, consider Xavier's expenditure on performance. More expenditures by Xavier increases his costs and Yvonne's expected profits, which efficiency requires Xavier to balance. Second, consider reliance. Yvonne's expenditures on reliance increase her profits if Xavier performs and decrease her profits if Xavier breaches. Efficiency requires Yvonne to balance the expected gains and losses of reliance.

We restate this verbal account of efficiency in notation. Efficiency requires choosing x and y to maximize Yvonne's expected profits minus Xavier's costs of precaution:

$$\text{maximize } p(x)R_p(y) + [1 - p(x)]R_{np}(y) \qquad - \qquad y \qquad - \qquad x$$
$$x, y$$

| Y's expected revenues | Y's food orders | X's expenditure |

Y's expected profits   (9.1)

We will explain how to choose x and y to maximize the preceding function. First, consider Xavier. He spends x, which increases the probability $p(x)$ that Yvonne enjoys high revenues equal to $R_p(y)$, rather than low revenues equal to $R_{np}(y)$. Efficiency requires the last dollar that Xavier spends to increase Yvonne's expected revenues by a dollar, which we write

$$1 \qquad = \qquad p'(x)[R_p(y) - R_{np}(y)]$$

marginal expenditure   marginal expected revenues   (9.2)

(If you know calculus, note that setting the partial derivative of equation (9.1) with respect to x equal to zero yields equation (9.2).)

Second, consider Yvonne. Increasing her expenditure y beyond y_0 increases her revenues $R_p(y)$ with probability p and decreases her revenues $R_{np}(y)$ with probability $(1 - p)$. Efficiency requires the last dollar that Yvonne spends in reliance to increase her expected revenues by a dollar, which we write

$$1 \qquad = \qquad pR_p'(y) \qquad + \qquad (1 - p)R_{np}'(y)$$

| marginal reliance expenditure | expected increase in revenues | possible decrease in revenues |

                                                                  (9.3)

(If you know calculus, note that setting the partial derivative of equation (9.1) with respect to y equal to zero yields equation (9.3).)

Equations (9.2) and (9.3) determine the values of x and y that maximize equation (9.1). These values, denoted x^* and y^*, are the efficient levels of precaution and reliance. The magnitude of y^* depends on the probability p that Xavier will perform. If performance is unlikely, then little reliance is efficient; so, the efficient value of y is close to y_0. If performance is likely, then heavy reliance is efficient, so the efficient value of y is close to y_1. If the probability of performance is greater than zero and less than 1, then y^* is in between y_0 and y_1.

2. Damages Measures

Consider several different damages measures. Expectation damages D_e put Yvonne in the same position as if Xavier performed. Thus, expectation damages equal the difference between Yvonne's profits if Xavier performs, $R_p(y) - y$, and her actual profits when he breaches, $R_{np}(y) - y$. Thus, we define expectation damages:

$$D_e \qquad = \qquad R_p(y) - R_{np}(y)$$

expectation damages   performance revenues minus actual revenues   (9.4)

Opportunity-cost damages D_o put Yvonne in the same position after breach as if she had signed the best alternative contract. Yvonne signed the actual contract because she found its terms at least as good as the best alternative contract. To keep the model simple, we will say nothing explicit about the best alternative contract.

Reliance damages D_r put Yvonne in the same position after breach as if she had not signed a construction contract with Xavier or anyone else. If she had not signed a construction contract, she would have spent y_o on food and sold it in the old restaurant, thus receiving profits equal to $R_{np}(y_o) - y_o$. She actually spent y on food, Xavier breached, and she received profits equal to $R_{np}(y) - y$. The difference in profits equals her reliance damages:

$$D_r \quad = \quad [R_{np}(y_o) - y_o] \quad - \quad [R_{np}(y) - y]$$

$$\text{reliance damages} \qquad \text{profits if no contract} \qquad \text{actual profits} \qquad (9.5)$$

Now we compare the three damages measures. Performance on the contract that she actually signed is at least as good for Yvonne as performance on the best alternative contract. So, expectation damages are at least as high as opportunity-cost damages: $D_e \geq D_o$. The best alternative contract is at least as good for Yvonne as no contract. So, opportunity-cost damages are at least as high as reliance damages: $D_o \geq D_r$. In summary we have:

$$D_e \geq D_o \geq D_r \qquad (9.6)$$

3. Incentives for Efficient Precaution

We described efficient behavior in words and notation, and then we described alternative measures of damages. Now we consider which measure of damages creates incentives for the promisor and promisee to behave efficiently.

Xavier bears the full cost of his own precaution x. Xavier also bears liability for damages D with probability $[1 - p(x)]$. The sum $(x + [1 - p(x)D])$ equals Xavier's expected costs. Xavier chooses x to minimize his expected costs:

$$\text{minimize} \qquad x \qquad + \qquad [1 - p(x)D]$$

$$x \qquad \text{precaution} \qquad \text{expected liability} \qquad (9.7)$$

Figure 9.7 depicts Xavier's problem. As the figure illustrates, Xavier's costs are high if he takes no precaution because his expected damages are large. His costs are also high if he takes excessive precaution, because the precaution costs more than it saves in liability. Xavier minimizes his costs by taking precaution at an intermediate level, denoted x^* in Figure 9.7, where the expected cost curve falls to its lowest point. This occurs

FIGURE 9.7

A promisor's expected costs of precaution and of breach.

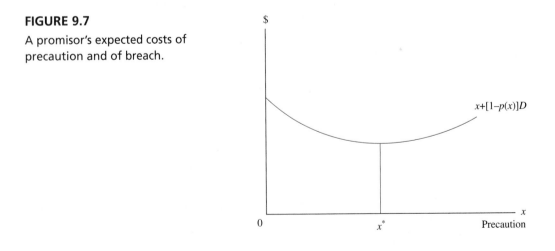

where an additional dollar spent on precaution reduces his expected liability by a dollar. In other words, his costs are minimized when the marginal cost of precaution equals the marginal reduction in expected liability:

$$\underset{\substack{\text{marginal cost} \\ \text{of precaution}}}{1} = \underset{\substack{\text{marginal reduction} \\ \text{in expected liability}}}{p'(x)D} \tag{9.8}$$

(If you know calculus, note that setting the partial derivative of equation (9.7) with respect to x equal to zero yields equation (9.8).)

We can compare the incentive effects of alternative measures of damages by substituting their definition for D into equation (9.8). First, consider expectation damages D_e as defined by equation (9.4). Substitute this definition of D_e for D in equation (9.8) to obtain

$$\underset{\substack{\text{marginal cost of} \\ \text{precaution}}}{1} = \underset{\substack{\text{marginal expected revenues}}}{p'(x)[R_p(y) - R_{np}(y)]} \tag{9.9}$$

This equation is identical to the efficiency condition in equation (9.2), which proves that expectation damages cause Xavier to take socially efficient precaution in order to minimize his expected costs.

It is easy to see why expectation damages create incentives for efficient precaution by the promisor. Promisors bear the full cost of their precaution. Their incentives are efficient when they also enjoy the full benefit. The full benefit equals any benefit that they receive plus the benefit that the promisees expect to receive. The benefit that promisees expect to receive equals the promisor's liability under expectation damages. Therefore, expectation damages cause promisors *to internalize the benefits of their precaution against breach*, which creates incentives for efficient precaution.

Now consider opportunity-cost damages and reliance damages. According to equation (9.6), expectation damages are at least as high as opportunity-cost damages, and opportunity-cost damages are at least as high as reliance damages. If the three damages are equal, then each of them provides incentives for efficient precaution by the promisor. If expectation damages exceed an alternative measure, then the alternative provides incentives for deficient precaution by the promisor. "Incentives for deficient precaution" means that the promisor minimizes expected costs by taking precaution below the efficient level. We summarize our conclusions as follows.

Promisor's Incentives for Precaution Against Breach

expectation		opportunity-cost		reliance
D_e	$=$	D_o	$=$	D_r
efficient		efficient		efficient
D_e	$>$	D_o	$>$	D_r
efficient		deficient		deficient

Figure 9.8 depicts these facts. Increasing the expected damages D increases Xavier's incentive to take precaution against events that cause him to breach. As damages increase from D_r to D_o, and from D_o to D_e, Xavier's cost-minimizing level of precaution increases from x_r to x_o and from x_o to x_e.

FIGURE 9.8

How precaution varies with the size of damages for breach of contract.

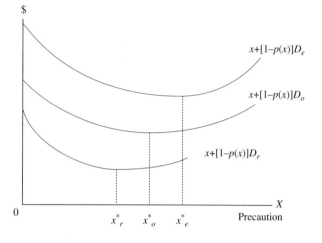

It is not hard to understand why awarding less than expectation damages provides incentives for deficient precaution. As explained, expectation damages cause the promisor to internalize the expected benefits of precaution. Consequently, awarding less than expectation damages causes the promisor to externalize part of the expected benefits of precaution. For example, opportunity-cost damages externalize the part of the promisee's benefit from performance of the actual contract that the promisee could not obtain from the best alternative contract.

QUESTION 9.44: Explain why perfect expectation damages generally create incentives for efficient precaution by the promisor. Explain why perfect opportunity-cost or reliance damages do not generally create incentives for efficient precaution by the promisor.

QUESTION 9.45: Assume that the remedy for breach is specific performance.

a. Use Figure 9.8 to find the amount of precaution that Xavier would take if specific performance costs the promisor the same as expectation damages.

b. Use Figure 9.8 to describe the amount of precaution that Xavier would take if specific performance costs the promisor more than expectation damages. (What are you implicitly assuming about renegotiation between the promisor and promisee?)

QUESTION 9.46: Assume that disgorgement damages are the remedy for breach, and assume that disgorgement damages exceed expectation damages. Use Figure 9.8 to describe the amount of precaution that Xavier would take.

4. Incentives for Efficient Reliance   We explained that the efficiency of the promisor's incentives for precaution depend on the level of damages ("total damages"). Expectation damages provide incentives for efficient precaution by the promisor

FIGURE 9.9

Promisee's expected net profits.

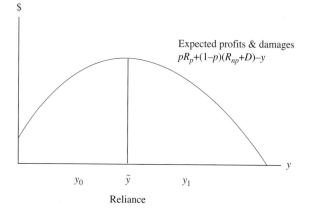

against breach, whereas opportunity-cost damages and reliance damages provide deficient incentives. Now we explain how the law creates incentives for efficient reliance by the promisee. We will show that the efficiency of the promisee's incentives for reliance depends on changes in damages caused by reliance ("marginal damages").

Yvonne invests y in reliance; she receives revenues $R_p(y)$ with probability p; and she receives revenues $R_{np}(y)$ and damages D with probability $(1 - p)$. The probability-weighted sum equals her expected net profits. Yvonne chooses y to maximize her expected net profits:

$$\underset{y}{\text{maximize}} \quad \underbrace{pR_p(y) + (1 - p)(R_{np}(y) + D)}_{\text{expected revenues and damages}} \quad - \quad \underbrace{y}_{\text{reliance}} \qquad (9.10)$$

Figure 9.9 depicts Yvonne's maximization problem. Yvonne's expected net profits are low if she does not rely ($y = 0$), because she does not order enough food in advance. Her expected net profits are also low if she relies excessively, because she orders too much food in advance. Yvonne maximizes her expected net profits by relying at an intermediate level, denoted $\tilde{y}$ in Figure 9.9, where the expected-net-profits curve reaches its highest point. This occurs where an additional dollar spent in reliance increases her expected revenues and damages by a dollar. In other words, her net profits are maximized when the marginal cost of reliance equals the marginal increase in expected revenues and damages:

$$\underbrace{1}_{\substack{\text{marginal cost} \\ \text{of reliance}}} = \underbrace{pR'_p(y) + (1 - p)R'_{np}(y)}_{\substack{\text{expected marginal} \\ \text{revenues}}} + \underbrace{(1 - p)D'}_{\substack{\text{expected marginal} \\ \text{damages}}} \qquad (9.11)$$

(If you know calculus, note that setting the partial derivative of equation (9.10) with respect to y equal to zero yields equation (9.11).)

We can compare the incentive effects of alternative measures of damages by substituting their definition for D into equation (9.10). Recall that expectation damages restore the promisee to the position that he or she would have enjoyed if the promise had been kept. In the preceding chapter we defined *perfect* expectation damages as enough money to restore the promisee to the position that he or she would have enjoyed if the promise had been kept and if reliance had been *optimal*. Applied to the Waffle Shop, perfect expectation damages equal the difference between Yvonne's revenues when Xavier performs and her revenues when he breaches, *assuming optimal reliance ($y = y^*$):*

$$D_e^* \qquad = \qquad R_p(y^*) - R_{np}(y^*)$$

perfect expectation damages   expected revenues minus actual revenues, given optimal reliance   (9.12)

Notice that equation (9.12) does not contain Yvonne's actual reliance, y. It contains her optimal reliance, y^*. When reliance equals y^*, Yvonne's expected recovery of damages does not vary with her actual reliance. An additional dollar of reliance y by Yvonne does not change the damages that she receives. "Marginal damages," denoted D', means the increase in damages when Yvonne spends another dollar in reliance. Thus, if Yvonne had relied optimally, her marginal damages would equal zero: $D' = 0$. Substitute $D' = 0$ into equation (9.11) to obtain

$$1 \qquad = \qquad pR'_p(y) \qquad + \qquad (1 - p)R'_{np}(y)$$

marginal reliance expenditure   expected increase in revenues   expected decrease in revenues   (9.13)

Equation (9.13) is identical to the efficiency condition in equation (9.3), which proves that perfect expectation damages cause Yvonne to rely at the socially efficient level.

It is easy to see why perfect expectation damages create incentives for efficient reliance by the promisee. Efficiency requires the person who increases risk to bear it. The promisee's reliance increases risk, specifically the risk that breach will destroy the value of the promisee's investment. Perfect expectation damages remain constant when the promisee relies more than is optimal. Thus, the risk caused by more reliance remains with the promisee. In brief, perfect expectation damages cause the promisee to internalize the risk of more than optimal reliance.

To illustrate, we contrast perfect and imperfect expectation damages in Figure 9.10. The curve labeled "no damages" indicates Yvonne's expected net profits when $D = 0$. Shift this curve up by the amount of perfect expectation damages, $D = D_e^* = D(y^*)$, to obtain the curve labeled "perfect damages." Perfect damages remain constant as reliance increases, so $D' = 0$. The curve labeled "perfect damages" in Figure 9.10 achieves its high point when Yvonne relies optimally: $y = y^*$.

FIGURE 9.10

How reliance varies with marginal damages for breach of contract.

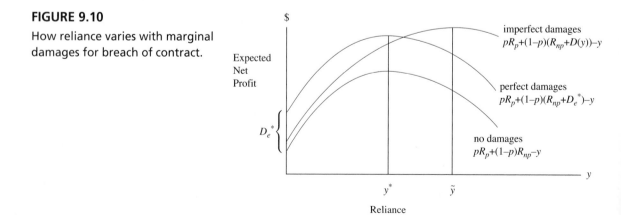

Finally, the curve labeled "imperfect damages" in Figure 9.10 indicates Yvonne's expected net profits when damages change as a function of reliance: $D = D(y)$.[60] Notice that imperfect damages $D(y)$ increase as Yvonne's reliance y increases, so marginal damages exceed zero: $D' > 0$. This fact causes Yvonne's expected-net-profit curve to shift to the right for values of y above y^*, as depicted in Figure 9.10. As a result of the shift to the right, Yvonne's expected-net-profit curve achieves its maximum at a level of reliance, denoted $\tilde{y}$, that exceeds the efficient reliance y^*.[61] In brief, Figure 9.10 illustrates that positive marginal damages ($D' > 0$) cause overreliance ($y > y^*$).

QUESTION 9.47: Why does the "no-damages" curve achieve its maximum in Figure 9.10 for the same value of y as the "perfect-damages" curve? Explain why "no damages" provides efficient incentives for reliance by Yvonne and inefficient incentives for precaution by Xavier.

QUESTION 9.48: The "imperfect-damages" curve in Figure 9.10 lies below the "perfect-damages" curve for values of y smaller than y^*. The opposite is true for values of y larger than y^*. Consider a composite consisting of the imperfect-damages curve for values of y less than y^* and the perfect-damages curve for values of y greater than y^*:

$$D = D(y) \text{ for } y, y^*;$$
$$D = D(y^*) \text{ for } y > y^*.$$

Assume that Yvonne's expected profits correspond to this composite curve. Thus, Yvonne receives compensation for actual damages up to a maximum value of $D(y^*)$. Given this composite measure of damages, what level of reliance y maximizes Yvonne's expected profits?

QUESTION 9.49: Assume that the parties cannot renegotiate after breach. Also assume that the remedy for breach is specific performance. Specific performance guarantees that Xavier will perform. Will Yvonne set her reliance y equal to y_0, y^*, or y_1 in Figures 9.6 and 9.10? Explain your answer.

QUESTION 9.50: Assume that disgorgement damages are the remedy for breach. Disgorgement damages depend on the profits earned by the promisor as a result of breaching. Consequently, disgorgement damages do not vary with the promisee's reliance ($D' = 0$). Use Figure 9.10 to explain the incentive effects of disgorgement damages on Yvonne's reliance.

---

[60] Three facts explain the shape of the imperfect-damages curve as depicted in Figure 9.10. (1) Perfect damages exceed imperfect damages at deficient levels of reliance: $D_e^* > D(y)$ for $y < y^*$; (2) perfect damages equal imperfect damages at the efficient level of reliance: $D_e^* = D(y)$ for $y = y^*$; (3) imperfect damages exceed perfect damages for excessive levels of reliance: $D(y) > fD_e^*$ for $y > y^*$.

[61] To prove that Yvonne's reliance increases when D increases from zero to a positive number, notice that $D' > 0$ implies that the right side of equation (9.11) exceeds the efficiency condition given by equation (9.3) (and repeated in (9.13)) for any given value of y.

10 An Economic Theory of the Legal Process

The first thing we do—let's kill all the lawyers.

WILLIAM SHAKESPEARE,
HENRY VI, PART II, ACT IV, SCENE II

If you think that justice is expensive, try injustice.

ANONYMOUS
(Adapted from Derek Bok's famous comment
about education and ignorance.)

THE CLIENT SAID, "I want justice." His lawyer replied, "How much justice can you afford?"

The law and facts in a case usually require a court to reach a specific decision. Resolving a dispute on different terms from those required by the law and the facts usually amounts to injustice. Developing the law and facts in court, however, gets expensive fast. To the parties in a legal dispute, the procedures sometimes seem so clumsy and unnecessary that they feel Dick the Butcher's urge to kill all the lawyers. From the lawyer's viewpoint, however, the procedural law makes exquisite sense; justice is expensive, but it's worth it, like a fine automobile.

Is the intricacy and expense of the legal process the unavoidable cost of justice, or is it the tribute extracted from the public by a powerful legal profession? A theory of the incentives created by the legal process can help to answer this question. This chapter applies economics to the *procedural* aspects of civil disputes, whereas the preceding chapters applied economics to the *substantive* law of property, torts, and contracts. The procedural aspects concern the process from the filing of a complaint to the resolution of the dispute through dismissal, settlement, or litigation.

Although different countries follow different legal procedures, broad similarities exist. Consider some stages in the following legal dispute as it would develop in almost any country. Joe Potatoes suspects that Jim Bloggs has been romancing his wife, Joan Potatoes; Potatoes insults Bloggs and breaks his nose. Bloggs consults a lawyer, who files a legal complaint against Potatoes. Potatoes also consults a lawyer, who contacts Bloggs's lawyer, and the two lawyers try to settle the dispute. If the attempted settlement fails, the dispute proceeds through a series of legal steps, including the reply by Potatoes's lawyer to the complaint, a pretrial hearing with a judge, and the exchange of information about the case between the lawyers. If further negotiations fail to settle the dispute, a trial occurs, and, after the trial, either party may decide to appeal the decision

FIGURE 10.1

Stages in a legal dispute.

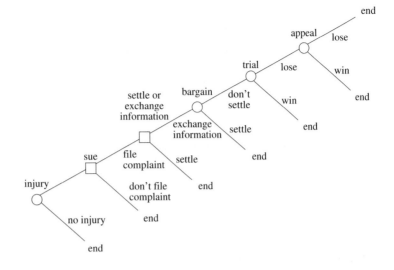

to a higher court. This example suggests that a full-blown legal dispute has the stages depicted in Figure 10.1, regardless of the substantive issues.

We will give examples of each of the stages in Figure 10.1.

> **Example 1:**   In response to a magazine advertisement for "a sure means to kill grasshoppers," a farmer mailed $25 and receives by return post two wooden blocks with the instructions, "Place grasshopper on Block A and smash with Block B." Filing a legal complaint will cost the farmer more than the $25 that he lost. The farmer consults a lawyer to determine whether he has a legal remedy that is economically viable.

In order to bring suit, the plaintiff must have a "cause of action," which usually consists of harm caused by the defendant for which the law provides a remedy. In Example 1 (the grasshopper killer), the injury is the loss of $25, plus any additional losses from relying upon the misleading advertisement. Not every plaintiff with a cause of action can sue profitably. Example 1 raises the question, "When does it pay to file a suit?" We will answer this question soon by computing the plaintiff's expected value from asserting a legal claim.

> **Example 2:**   Some consumers file suit alleging that the engines in their cars were destroyed by a defective fuel additive. The manufacturer of the fuel additive would like to settle the dispute before it goes to trial and newspapers learn about it. In order to decide how much money to offer as a settlement, the manufacturer's lawyer asks the judge to require the consumers' lawyer to disclose all available evidence concerning the cause and extent of damage to the cars.

Most legal systems require the parties to disclose some of their *private information* (facts known by one party to the dispute and unknown by the other) prior to trial. In the American legal system, the parties exchange extensive information before trial in a process known as "pretrial discovery." In the system used in Germany and other European countries, the parties exchange information in the "giving of proofs" at the first stage of a trial.

Example 2 (defective fuel additive) suggests that compulsory disclosure of private information promotes settlements. We will use game theory to test this proposition.

> **Example 3:**   Joan Potatoes wants to divorce her husband, Joe. They disagree over how to divide the value of their house. After bargaining between their lawyers fails, the judge considers whether to require them to consult a professional mediator before proceeding to trial.

Critics often complain that the formality of trials increases the cost of resolving disputes. Example 3 (divorce) raises the question of whether informal processes, like compulsory mediation, could improve upon formal legal procedures. To answer this question, we will use game theory to explain why bargaining sometimes succeeds and sometimes fails.

> **Example 4:**   A Los Angeles manufacturer faces large liabilities for dumping hazardous waste in 1965. The manufacturer files a claim with the London insurer that supplied its policy in 1965. The insurer denies that the insurance policy covers the loss. The manufacturer has the option of suing the insurer in Los Angeles or London. In Los Angeles, each side pays its own legal costs, whereas in London the loser pays the legal costs of the winner. The manufacturer asks its counsel how the allocation of legal costs should influence its choice of the place to file suit.

Different legal systems allocate the costs of trials differently. The polar opposite rules are "each-pays-his-own" legal costs (the "American rule") and "loser-pays-all" legal costs (the "English rule"). Example 4 (hazardous wastes) asks whether one of these rules especially favors defendants. To answer this question, we will consider the incentives created by alternative allocations of legal costs.

> **Example 5:**   Someone dives into a swimming pool and strikes her head on the bottom. She sues the owner of the pool for failing to post signs warning that the pool was too shallow for diving, and the pool owner replies that the victim should have checked the depth of the water before diving. At trial, the court applies the rule of negligence with a defense of contributory negligence, and the pool owner escapes liability. The plaintiff wonders whether to appeal the case and ask the court to depart from past precedent and apply the rule of comparative negligence.[1]

Finally, Example 5 raises the question of whether judges should create new rules to decide cases. Later we explain that this question relates closely to whether or not the common law evolves toward economically efficient rules.

I.   The Goal of the Legal Process: Minimizing Social Costs

Is the legal process, as some critics contend, unnecessarily complicated and expensive? Evaluating different procedural rules and practices requires a measure of social costs. In Chapter 6, we found that a simple measure of the social costs of accidents provided a useful guide to the analysis of tort law Similarly, a simple measure of the social

---

[1] Comparative negligence would require the pool owner to pay damages in proportion to the harm caused by the negligence.

costs of the legal process provides a useful guide to the analysis of procedural laws. To develop a simple measure, think of procedural laws as instruments for applying substantive laws. Using the instruments costs something, which, following Chapter 6, we call "administrative costs." Administrative costs are the sum of the costs to everyone involved in passing through the stages of a legal dispute, such as the costs of filing a legal claim, exchanging information with the other party, bargaining in an attempt to settle, litigating, and appealing. In addition, the legal process sometimes makes errors in applying substantive law. For example, the wrong party may be held liable, or the right party may be held liable but for the wrong amount. Errors distort incentives and impose a variety of costs on society. Our simplest measure of social costs, denoted SC, combines administrative costs, denoted c_a, and costs of errors, denoted $c(e)$. *We assume that the economic objective of procedural law is to minimize the sum of administrative costs and error costs.*

$$\min SC = c_a + c(e) \tag{10.1}$$

To illustrate, assume that the parties settle out of court on the same terms that a trial would have produced. Because the results of settlement or trial are the same by assumption, the error costs (*if* there is an error) of settlement equal the error costs of trial. The administrative costs of the settlement, however, are much lower than those of a trial. Consequently, the settlement saves social costs. In general, settlements that replicate the results of trials reduce the social costs of resolving disputes.

In comparison to administrative costs, error costs are more difficult to understand and measure, because measuring an error requires a standard of perfection. To obtain a standard of perfection, consider the information possessed by courts. In reality, courts have imperfect information, which causes them to make mistakes when applying substantive law. As information improves, however, courts make fewer mistakes. As a thought experiment, imagine a court that possesses *perfect* information about the facts and the law for every case it decides. Such a court never makes mistakes. It never finds that the plaintiff caused the harm when the plaintiff did not cause it, or that the plaintiff did not cause the harm when the plaintiff caused it; it never finds that the plaintiff was negligent when the plaintiff was nonnegligent, or that the plaintiff was nonnegligent when the plaintiff was negligent; and it always awards the correct amount of damages. In brief, the court gives ideal decisions relative to existing law and the actual facts. We will call such a decision the *perfect-information judgment*, which we denote j^*.

The difference between the perfect-information judgment, j^*, and the actual judgment, j, *equals the extent of the court's error concerning damages* $e = j^* - j$. To illustrate by Example 2, the perfect information judgment j^* might award the owner of an automobile the exact cost of replacing the engine destroyed by a defective fuel additive, which equals, say, $2500. If the actual judgment equals $2000, then the extent of the error equals $j^* - j = \$500$. (As we noted, there are deviations from a perfect-information judgment other than an error in the computation of damages. Many of those other deviations can be expressed as errors in damages. For instance, if the defendant should have been found not liable but *was* found liable and assessed damages, then $j^* = 0$, and the error costs are equal to $-j$. And if the plaintiff should have won and received j^*, but the court mistakenly excused the defendant from liability and, therefore, gave the plaintiff no damages, then the error costs are equal to j^*.)

The *extent* of the error, however, does not necessarily equal its *social cost.* The social cost of an error depends additionally upon the distortions in incentives caused by the error. To illustrate, if perfect compensation equals $2500 and actual compensation equals $2000, the error of $500 may cause the manufacturer of fuel additives to lower quality control. Lowering quality control saves the manufacturer, say, $1000 and causes, say, an additional $10,000 in losses to the owners of automobiles. In this example, the social cost of the error $c(e)$ equals the *net* loss of $9000 from lower quality control: $c(\$500) = \$9000$.

In the rest of this chapter, we will model each stage in the legal process, show the incentive effects of different procedural rules and practices, and evaluate the alternatives in terms of social costs. In general, the social costs of errors are difficult to measure. Consequently, we will avoid conclusions that rely upon precise measurements of error.

> **QUESTION 10.1:** Assume that the following legal rule applies to Example 1 (the "grasshopper killer"): "Breach of contract arising from false or misleading advertising results in liability equal to two times the consumer's out-of-pocket expenditures in reliance on the promise." Given this rule, what is the perfect-information judgment?

> **QUESTION 10.2:** Why is a trial economically inferior to a settlement on the same terms as the expected trial judgment?

 Web Note 10.1

Lawyers often experience a great deal of criticism. We shall deal very briefly with some of those criticisms later in the chapter. For a review of some interesting literature on the actual costs of justice in the United States and lawyers' compensation, see our website.

II. Why Sue?

Most private disputes remain outside the courts. (A frequent estimate is that less than 5 percent of all legal disputes go to trial.) The courts typically get involved when the injured party asks them for a remedy. The filing of a suit marks the beginning of this formal process. These facts raise the question, "Why sue?" We will explain game theory's answer to this question.

A. Decision Trees

A client asks a lawyer to take his case and offers to pay the lawyer 30 percent of the court's judgment as the lawyer's fee. If the plaintiff wins and the court's judgment is *j*, then the lawyer gets .3*j*. Assume that the probability that the plaintiff will win, if there is a trial, is .5. If the plaintiff loses, the lawyer gets 0. The lawyer estimates that the time he will spend on the case is worth 15. What is the lowest value of the court's judgment at which the lawyer expects to gain by taking the case? The answer is 100.

Perhaps you can intuit the answer or perhaps not. In either case, the correct answer is easy to compute by using the decision tree in Figure 10.2:

FIGURE 10.2

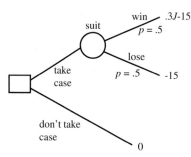

By convention, the circles in the tree represent probabilities, and the squares represent decisions. The expected value of taking the case equals $.5(3j - 15) + .5(-15)$. The lawyer should take the case if the expected value of doing so is positive. The tipping point for taking the case is the judgment that makes the expected value zero: $.5(3j - 15) + .5(-15) = 0$. Solving this equation yields $j = 100$. So, the lawyer should take the case if he expects the judgment to equal or exceed 100.

Here is a slightly harder example of a decision tree. A business allegedly causes a consumer to suffer harm of 100. The consumer offers to settle the dispute for 50. If the business refuses, it will face a suit that will cost it 10 to litigate. If it loses at trial, the business will have to pay the consumer 100. What is the lowest probability of the consumer winning at which the business expects to gain by settling the case?

If the parties don't settle, they go to trial, and the plaintiff either wins or loses (Figure 10.3). If p indicates the probability that the plaintiff wins, then the probability that the plaintiff loses must equal $(1 - p)$. The expected payoff to the business from "don't settle" thus equals $-10p - (110)(1 - p)$, and the payoff from settling equals -50. To find the probability of winning at trial that is the tipping point for settling the case, set the former equal to the latter and solve for p:

$$-10p - (110)(1 - p) = -50 \Rightarrow p = .6.$$

The business should reject the settlement if it expects to win with probability at least as high as .6.

In many circumstances, using a decision tree significantly helps to clarify the right choice, especially when the decision gets more complicated, as in the next section.

FIGURE 10.3

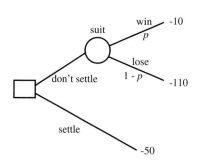

B. Computing the Value of a Legal Claim

To file a complaint, the plaintiff must usually hire a lawyer and pay filing fees to the court. Filing a complaint creates a legal claim. To decide whether to initiate a suit, a rational plaintiff compares the cost of the complaint and the expected value of the legal claim. The expected value of the legal claim (*EVC*) depends upon what the plaintiff thinks will occur after filing a complaint. Figure 10.1 depicts the possible events. To decide whether to file a complaint, the rational plaintiff must attach probabilities and payoffs to these events. Let us assume that the plaintiff, with the help of a lawyer, attaches the probabilities and payoffs to these events as depicted in Figure 10.4a. (We scaled down the numbers in Figure 10.4a below realistic levels to simplify the arithmetic.)

Before making the computations, we must explain our assumptions about who pays for legal costs. In America, each side usually pays his own legal costs. In Europe (and much of the rest of the world), the loser usually pays most of the winner's legal costs.[2] Simplifying, the American rule is "each pays his own," and the European rule (also called the "English rule") is "loser pays all." In general, the two rules require two slightly different ways of computing the value of a legal claim. The European rule is more complicated analytically because it makes the distribution of costs contingent on who wins. Consequently, we will first develop our example assuming that each side pays its own legal costs, and consider later the consequences of the loser's paying the legal costs for both sides. However, in order not to distract readers from situations in which the loser pays all, we contrive the numbers in our particular example so that "each pays his own" and "loser pays all" yield exactly the same decisions. The particular numbers in the following example are constructed so that both rules give the same answers, although they often give different answers in fact.

FIGURE 10.4a

Expected value of a legal claim to the plaintiff.

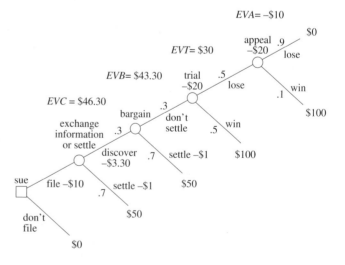

---

[2] We are grateful to Raoul Meier of Switzerland for pointing out an error in how we stated this rule in previous editions.

In order to compute expected values in a sequence of events, one begins with the last possible event, which is "appeal" in Figure 10.4a, and works toward the first event, which is the decision to file a complaint.[3] We will take this approach to computing the expected value of the legal claim at each step in the legal process. Assume that each side pays his own legal costs. According to Figure 10.4a, the plaintiff who has lost at trial must pay $20 to appeal the case. On appeal, the plaintiff stands to win $100 with probability .1 and to lose with probability .9. Thus, the expected value of the appeal (*EVA*) equals −$10:

$$EVA = .1(\$100) + .9(\$0) - \$20 = -\$10.$$

Because the expected value of appeal is negative, the rational plaintiff who loses at trial will not appeal the case. (Notice that if the rule were changed from "each pays his own" to "loser pays all," the expected value of trial would fall even further; so, the decision not to appeal is the same under the American rule and the European rule.)

Having computed the expected value of appeal (second trial), we can now compute the expected value of the first trial. According to Figure 10.4a, the plaintiff who failed to settle out of court by bargaining must pay $20 to go to trial. At trial, the plaintiff stands to win $100 with probability .5 and to lose with probability .5. If the plaintiff loses, he will not appeal the case and so will receive a payoff equal to $0. We combine these numbers to obtain the expected value of the first trial (*EVT*):

$$EVT = .5(\$100) + .5(\$0) - \$20 = \$30.$$

(Confirm for yourself that, assuming defendant's litigation costs are the same as plaintiff's litigation costs, *EVT* is the same under the European rule and the American rule.[4])

Having computed the expected value of the trial, we can now compute the expected value of bargaining to a settlement before beginning the trial. According to Figure 10.4a, the plaintiff who completed the process of exchanging information with the defendant can bargain to a settlement out of court with probability of success equal to .7. If bargaining succeeds, the plaintiff settles for $50 and pays settlement costs of $1. Bargaining fails to reach a settlement with probability .3, in which case the plaintiff proceeds to trial, whose expected value equals $30. We combine these numbers to obtain the expected value of the settlement bargain (*EVB*):

$$EVB = .7(\$50 - \$1) + .3(\$30) = \$43.30.$$

Because the expected value of the settlement bargain is positive, the plaintiff who reaches this stage will bargain.

---

[3] This is called, in game theory, "backward induction" or the process of "looking forward and reasoning backward" or solving a game "recursively."

[4] Under the American rule, the plaintiff pays his own litigation costs of $20 with certainty, whereas under the European rule, the plaintiff pays no litigation costs with probability .5 and the plaintiff pays the litigation costs of both parties ($20 + $20) with probability .5. Thus, the plaintiff faces certain litigation costs of $20 under the American rule and expected litigation costs of $20 under the European rule. Remember that we are computing expected *values,* not expected *utilities.* (If you are not clear about the difference, see the relevant section of Chapter 2.)

Having computed the expected value of the bargain, we can now compute the expected value of the legal claim when the complaint is filed. After the complaint is filed, the parties may settle. According to Figure 10.4a, the plaintiff who files a suit settles immediately with probability .7, in which case he or she receives $50 and pays $1 in settlement costs. Alternatively, the plaintiff fails to settle immediately with probability .3 and proceeds to exchange information with the defendant, which costs $3.30. After exchanging information, the parties continue to bargain. We already computed the expected value of the bargain, which equals $43.30. We combine these numbers to obtain the expected value of the legal claim when the plaintiff initiates the suit by filing the complaint (*EVC*):

$$EVC = .7(\$50 - \$1) + .3(\$43.30 - \$3.30) = \$46.30.$$

In Germany and other European countries, discovery does not occur before the beginning of a trial. Rather, the first phase of a trial concerns the "giving of proofs" (*beweisverfahren*), in which the parties present evidence supporting the basic facts of the case. For purposes of computing the value of a claim from the decision tree, discovery and the giving of proofs are the same. (Some important differences between them must be taken into account in a more specific analysis.[5])

The filing costs (*FC*) include the costs of hiring a lawyer, drafting the complaint, and paying the filing fee assessed by the court. According to Figure 10.4a, the filing costs equal $10. After filing, the plaintiff expects to receive the value of the claim at the time of filing (*EVC*), which equals $46.30. Therefore, the expected net payoff from filing equals $46.30 − $10 = $36.30. The rational plaintiff files a complaint if its expected net payoff is positive:

$$\begin{aligned} EVC \geq FC &\rightarrow \text{file legal complaint;} \\ EVC < FC &\rightarrow \text{do not file legal complaint.} \end{aligned} \qquad (10.2)$$

Thus, the rational plaintiff in Figure 10.4a files a legal complaint.

What about the defendant? When the plaintiff files a complaint, the defendant must respond to it. To compute the best response, a rational defendant must solve a decision problem similar to the plaintiff's problem depicted in Figure 10.4a. The defendant's decision problem is to minimize the expected cost of his or her legal liability. Because the decision problem of the defendant parallels the decision problem of the plaintiff, we will not explicitly analyze it here.[6]

---

[5] At least four important differences exist. First, discovery does not take place before the judge or jury, whereas the giving of proofs occurs before the judge, who takes an active role. Second, in discovery one party can compel the other to reveal information, whereas compulsory revelation is limited or impossible in the giving of proofs. Third, discovery permits the examination and cross examination of witnesses, whereas in the giving of proofs the witnesses are named but not examined. Finally, in the giving of proofs the judge decides whether the alleged facts warrant proceeding to the next stage of the trial, whereas the judge in the American system usually decides this issue in a separate hearing that may occur before or after discovery when the plaintiff moves for summary judgment.

[6] You should note that the two parties may not agree about the amounts at stake or the probabilities of success at each stage. We will assume for the time being that the amounts and probabilities are similar. Later we will relax that assumption.

FIGURE 10.4b

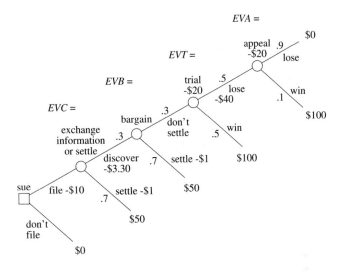

QUESTION **10.3:**   The tree in Figure 10.4b is identical to that in Figure 10.4a, except that a trial costs the plaintiff $40 instead of $20, and settlement is for $51 instead of $50. Solve recursively for the expected values of the legal claim by filling in the blanks at each stage in the following tree. What is the plaintiff's expected net profit from filing a legal complaint?

QUESTION **10.4:**   In Europe, the party who loses at trial pays the litigation costs of the winner. Assume that the plaintiff in the preceding figure pays litigation costs of $40 if she loses at trial, and the plaintiff pays litigation costs of $0 if she wins. Recompute the expected values of the legal claim under this assumption.

III.   Exchange of Information

Having analyzed the filing of a complaint, we now consider the next stage in a legal dispute, as depicted in Figure 10.1—the exchange of information between the parties.

A. Bad News Is Good for Settlements

After the plaintiff complains and the defendant responds, the two parties try to resolve their dispute before it leads to a trial. Why do some complaints end up being tried rather than settled? It might seem on first impression that trials, being so costly, would not occur unless someone behaves irrationally. Like many first impressions, this one is wrong. Game theory explains why rational bargainers sometimes fail to settle their disputes and end up in trial. Although there are several strands of the argument, the simplest explanation is that trials occur because the parties have different expectations about its outcome: The plaintiff expects liability and a large judgment, and the defendant expects no liability or a small judgment. In these circumstances, the parties are *relatively optimistic.* Given relative optimism, the plaintiff demands a large settlement, and the defendant offers a small settlement, so the parties cannot agree on the terms for settling out of court.

To illustrate concretely, assume that a bus collides with a pedestrian. The bus company admits fault, but the parties disagree over damages. The bus company, which believes that the pedestrian suffered minor injuries, predicts that a trial will cost it $1,000 and result in a judgment of $1,500, thus costing a total of $2,500. The pedestrian, who actually suffered a serious injury requiring surgery, predicts that a trial will cost $1,000 and result in a judgment of $15,000, thus resulting in a net gain of $14,000. *If the plaintiff's expected value of the judgment at trial exceeds the defendant's expected value of the judgment at trial, we say that the parties are relatively optimistic.*

The bus company's false optimism about trial will cause it to reject any settlement on terms acceptable to the pedestrian. In general, the plaintiff usually rejects an offer by the defendant that falls short of the expected value of the legal claim.[7] In the preceding example, the plaintiff will reject an offer to settle for less than $14,000. (We can develop this argument futher by using the Nash Bargaining solution from Chapter 4.[8])

Turning from the plaintiff to the defendant, the defendant's offer reflects the expected value of his or her legal liability. The defendant usually rejects a demand by the plaintiff that exceeds the expected value of the legal liability. To illustrate by the preceding example, the defendant will reject a demand to settle for more than $2,500.

As explained, relative optimism about trial makes settlement out of court difficult. Conversely, relative pessimism makes settlement easy. We revise the numbers in the bus-pedestrian example to reflect relative pessimism. Assume as before that a bus collides with a pedestrian, the bus company admits fault, and the estimates of damages by the two parties diverge to reflect pessimism about trial. The bus company, which knows that the pedestrian had surgery, believes that a trial will cost it $1000 and result in a judgment of $15,000, thus costing a total of $16,000. The pedestrian knows that the surgery corrected a preexisting condition, not an injury caused by the accident Therefore, the pedestrian predicts that a trial will cost $1,000 and result in a judgment of $1,500, thus resulting in a net gain of $500 The bus company's false pessimism about a trial will cause it to accept a settlement offer of, say, $10,000, which far exceeds what the pedestrian believes can be had at trial As long as the bus company remains ignorant of the facts, the case should settle out of court.

---

[7] We say "usually" because, recall, we are talking about expected *values,* not expected *utilities.* It is possible that a risk-averse plaintiff will accept a settlement offer that is less than the expected value of the legal claim. Similar reservations may be made about the defendant's behavior.

[8] A reasonable party in a bargain will demand to receive his or her threat point T plus an equal share of the surplus from cooperating. In bargaining to avoid a trial, the threat position of the plaintiff T_p is what he or she expects to gain (the "expected value of the legal claim" as depicted in Figure 10.2) if they do not settle out of court. Similarly, the threat position of the defendant T_d is what he or she expects to lose if they do not settle out of court. The cooperative value of the game C equals the sum of the value of a settlement to the plaintiff and the defendant. The reasonable amount for the plaintiff to demand to settle the case is $T_p + \frac{1}{2}(C - T_p - T_d)$. The reasonable amount for the defendant to offer to settle the case is $T_d + \frac{1}{2}(C - T_p - T_d)$. If T_p is much greater than T_d, the defendant will reject the reasonable plaintiff's demand. Equivalently, the plaintiff will reject the reasonable defendant's offer.

In many suits, the defendant knows less than the plaintiff about the extent of the injury, and the plaintiff knows less than the defendant about the extent of the defendant's precautions against the accident. If the defendant overestimates the plaintiff's injury, and the plaintiff overestimates the defendant's precaution, then both parties are relatively pessimistic; so, settlement is easy. Conversely, if the defendant underestimates the plaintiff's injury, and the plaintiff underestimates the defendant's precaution, then both parties are relatively optimistic; so, settlement is difficult.

The expected value of the legal claim diverges for the parties because of *private information,* which means valuable information (what lawyers call "material information") possessed by one party and not possessed by the other. When relative optimism initially prevents the parties from settling out of court, they may be able to correct the relative optimism before trial by exchanging information. To correct relative optimism, one party gives the other some "news"—information previously unknown to the recipient. The news is "bad" if it causes the recipient to expect a worse result at trial. Transmitting bad news is good for settlements.

B. Bad News Is Free

The parties to a legal dispute exchange some private information voluntarily, without the law's requiring it. Voluntary pooling of information occurs informally through discussions between the parties, and it also occurs formally, as when the judge holds a pretrial conference in which the parties are asked to discuss their positions in the dispute. In the first stage of a European trial, where the plaintiff gives proofs to support the complaint, and the defendant replies to the alleged proofs, the parties exchange information before the judge. In the United States, the exchange of information between the parties prior to trial does not usually occur before the judge.

In addition to the voluntary exchange of information, some pooling of information is compulsory. For example, the law may require the party making a complaint to tell the other side what it will prove in court in the event that a trial occurs. In the United States, the law compels each side to answer questions about the case asked by the other side. This practice is called *discovery,* because one party has the right to discover certain facts known to the other party. In contrast, in Europe the judge can ask the parties for any relevant information, but the parties are limited in their ability to ask questions on their own.

We will ask two questions about the relationship between voluntary and involuntary pooling of information. First, "Does the voluntary pooling of information promote settlements out of court?" Second, "Does involuntary pooling of information promote more settlements beyond the number achieved by voluntary pooling?"

In general, *the parties tend to disclose information voluntarily before trial to correct the other side's relative optimism, thereby promoting settlements.* In other words, bad news is free. To see why, return to the example in which a bus collides with a pedestrian, the bus company admits fault, and the bus company mistakenly believes that the pedestrian suffered a minor injury. The bus company predicts inaccurately that a trial will cost it $1000 and result in a judgment of $1500, and the pedestrian predicts accurately that a trial will cost $1000 and result in a judgment of $15,000. A settlement could save each party $1000 in trial costs. However, the bus company's false optimism about a trial will cause it to reject any settlement on terms acceptable to the pedestrian. Knowing these facts, the pedestrian has an incentive to correct the bus company's false optimism by revealing the extent of the injuries. By doing so, the pedestrian can probably enable the parties to settle and save the costs of a trial, which will benefit both of them. Thus, the pedestrian might voluntarily provide medical records to prove to the bus company that the accident caused serious injuries.

We will state the conclusion of this example more abstractly. As explained, trials occur when the parties are relatively optimistic about their outcome, so that each side prefers a trial rather than settlement on terms acceptable to the other side. When the parties are relatively optimistic, at least one of them is uninformed. Pooling of information before trial that reduces relative optimism promotes settlements. Furthermore, by revealing private information to correct the other side's false optimism, the party making the disclosure increases the probability of settling on more favorable terms. Thus, efficiency (through saving the costs of trial) and redistribution (through strengthening your bargaining position) provide incentives to voluntarily disclose facts correcting the other side's false optimism.

Similarly, *the parties tend to withhold information that would correct the other side's relative pessimism, thereby promoting settlements.* To see why, return to the preceding example, but assume that the bus company's mistaken belief is falsely pessimistic. The bus company, which knows that the pedestrian had surgery and mistakenly attributes its cause to the bus accident, believes that a trial will cost it $1000 and result in a judgment of $15,000, whereas the pedestrian, who knows that the surgery corrected a pre-existing condition, predicts that a trial will cost $1000 and result in a judgment of $1500. The bus company's false pessimism about a trial will cause it to accept a settlement offer that far exceeds what the pedestrian would win at trial. As long as the bus company remains ignorant of the facts, the case should settle out of court. Knowing these facts, the pedestrian has an incentive to withhold information about the true extent of the injury.

We have explained that voluntary pooling of information tends to correct false optimism and to leave false pessimism uncorrected, both of which promote settlements out of court. We speak of "tendencies" and not "certainties," because expectations are partly logical and partly psychological. The parties to a dispute must guess at what information the other has withheld, and various possibilities can occur in fact.

Now we turn to involuntary disclosure, which occurs when one party discovers information withheld by the other party. As explained, the information withheld is the mirror image of the information voluntarily disclosed: Parties withhold information that would correct the other side's false pessimism. Being compulsory, discovery tends to uncover the information that was withheld, thus correcting false pessimism. Correcting false pessimism decreases the likelihood that someone will make unnecessary concessions when bargaining. In general, *the parties tend to discover information that corrects their relative pessimism, thereby causing them to demand better terms to settle out of court.*

To illustrate, return to the example of the bus company that believes incorrectly that a trial will result in a large judgment, whereas the pedestrian knows that a trial will result in a small judgment. The bus company's false pessimism about a trial will cause it to accept a settlement offer that far exceeds what the pedestrian would get at trial. If the bus company discovers the truth, it will save itself a lot of money by demanding better terms to settle out of court. The pedestrian, therefore, will not voluntarily correct the bus company's false pessimism, although the bus company may discover the truth by asking questions that the pedestrian is legally required to answer.

Discovering information that causes someone to demand better terms presumably makes settling out of court less likely. (There may be an effect in the opposite direction that we do not discuss.[9])

We summarize our conclusions about the exchange of information before a trial:

voluntary disclosure ⟹ corrects false optimism ⟹ causes settlement

involuntary disclosure ⟹ corrects false pessimism ⟹ causes trials.

Loss Aversion, Regret Aversion, and Trials

An alternative (or supplemental) explanation to our relative optimism explanation for litigation is the presence of "loss aversion." This is a view of behavior under uncertainty developed by Daniel Kahneman and Amos Tversky on the basis of empirical research.[10] In making decisions about choices involving risk, people tend to "frame" results as gains or losses from their current situation. They tend to be risk-averse with respect to gains and risk-seeking with respect to losses. Suppose that someone is put to the following choice:

1. A sure gain of $50, or
2. A gamble in which there is a .5 probability of gaining $100 and a .5 probability of gaining nothing.

Both choices have an expected value of $50, and most people prefer the sure gain to the gamble.

However, suppose that someone is put to a choice between the following:

1. A sure loss of $50, or
2. A gamble in which there is a .5 probability of losing $100 and a .5 probability of losing nothing.

Both choices have an expected value of –$50, and many people prefer the gamble to the sure loss.

Applying these ideas to litigation, Jeff Rachlinski has argued that plaintiffs may frame the choice between trial and settlement as one between the certain gain of a settlement and the probabilistic gain of a successful trial. If most plaintiffs are risk averse, then they will prefer settlement to litigation. However, defendants may view the choice as

(Continued)

---

[9] The knowledge that discovery can force revelation of all materially relevant information may increase trust between the two parties, which makes settling out of court easier. Empirical research is needed to decide whether, on balance, discovery increases or decreases settlements relative to voluntary disclosure.

[10] See Daniel Kahneman & Amos Tversky, *Prospect Theory: An Analysis of Decision Under Risk,* 47 ECONOMETRICA 263 (1979). Professor Kahneman won the Nobel Prize in Economics in October 2002.

one between the certain loss of a settlement and the probabilistic loss from a trial. To the extent that most defendants are loss averse—that is, risk-seeking with respect to losses—they will prefer litigation to settlement.[11]

Chris Guthrie has suggested a psychological reason why settlements might occur more often than logic might suggest. Litigants who settle will never know what they might have obtained at trial; so, they will feel no regret. Litigants who proceed to trial, however, might feel regret if they reject a settlement offer that proves better than the trial outcome. He predicted, consequently, that many litigants will choose settlement over trial so as to avoid feelings of regret. (See *Better Settle Than Sorry: The Regret Aversion Theory of Litigation Behavior*, 1999 U. ILL. L. REV. 43.)

He tested this hypothesis in two empirical studies in which participants had to decide whether to settle or sue. One group made their choice in a "traditional" jurisdiction, defined as one in which "the litigant will not learn what would have happened at trial if she settles the case." In a traditional jurisdiction, settlement thus precludes the possibility of regret. The other group made their choices in a "regret jurisdiction," defined as one in which "the judge is required, upon learning that the parties have reached an out-of-court settlement, to inform the parties of what he would have awarded" had they gone to trial. In a regret jurisdiction, the parties can feel regret regardless of whether they settle or litigate. Dean Guthrie predicted, and his statistics confirmed, that litigants in a traditional jurisdiction would settle more often than litigants in a regret jurisdiction.

C. United States vs. Europe

Different countries and jurisdictions have different rules about discovery. The most extensive and elaborate discovery occurs in the United States. Long before a trial begins in America, each side must reveal the basic arguments that it plans to use in trial, the evidence supporting these arguments, the names of witnesses, and the general nature of the testimony that witnesses will supply. The failure to disclose arguments or evidence may cause the judge to prevent their use in a trial. Further, the American rules of procedure entitle each side to discover any evidence possessed by the other side that has material relevance to the case, such as inspecting physical objects, reading documents, and deposing expert witnesses. The discovery of new facts can radically alter the course of the legal dispute.

Unlike the United States, most European countries have little or no discovery. Several practical reasons account for this difference in procedures. In America, a party to a suit has a constitutional right to request a trial by jury. Serving on a jury takes its members away from their jobs and other activities. The court tries to minimize the disruption of jurors' lives by making the parties prepare extensively before the trial, and then proceeding from beginning to end of the trial without interruption. In contrast, European countries seldom use juries to decide civil cases. Delays and interruptions in proceedings inconvenience judges less than juries; so, European trials often pause and

---

[11] *Gains, Losses, and the Psychology of Litigation*, 70 SO. CAL. L. REV. 113 (1996).

resume several times before reaching an end. American trials are like performing a play from the first act to the final act, whereas European trials are like filming a movie in segments with pauses in between.

Another difference concerns the role of the judge. In the civil tradition of Europe, the judge takes an active role in developing arguments and exploring evidence (called an "inquisitorial procedure"). Indeed, the judge may not allow the lawyers to examine witnesses or scrutinize certain evidence before the trial. Unprepared witnesses are more candid and reveal many facts inadvertently (they may "lapse into candor," as lawyers say). In the common law tradition, however, the judge takes a more passive role. Instead of directing the case, the common law judge referees a contest between opposing attorneys (called an "adversarial procedure"). In America, the judge expects the lawyers to develop the arguments and explore the evidence *before* the case comes to trial. Preparation improves the quality of the argument, and a prepared witness goes directly to the point of his or her testimony.

D. Minimizing Social Costs

Now we relate our contrast between voluntary and involuntary pooling of information to the objective of minimizing the sum of administrative costs and error costs. The voluntary pooling of information avoids trials, and avoiding trials saves administrative costs. Furthermore, the voluntary exchange of information corrects some miscalculations that cause the terms of a settlement to diverge from the expected trial judgment. Narrowing the gap between the terms of the settlement and the expected trial judgment usually reduces error costs. (More on this later.) Therefore, *the voluntary pooling of information usually reduces both components of social costs—administrative costs and error costs.*

The effects of *compulsory* pooling of information on social costs are more ambiguous. First consider the effect of discovery on administrative costs. As explained above, game theory does not generally predict whether discovery encourages or discourages settlements. In the event of a trial, discovery prior to trial often simplifies the arguments and proofs made during trial. However, it is uncertain whether discovery reduces the cost of trials by an amount commensurate with the cost of discovery itself.[12] Current research does not permit us to conclude whether discovery reduces administrative costs.

Now we turn to error costs. Discovery, as we saw above, corrects some miscalculations that cause the terms of a settlement to diverge from the expected trial judgment. Because discovery narrows the gap between the terms of settlement and the expected trial judgment, we conclude that *discovery usually reduces error.*

In summary, the involuntary pooling of information reduces one component of social costs (error costs) but may not reduce the other (administrative costs).

---

[12] Discovery is a cheaper process than litigation; therefore, discovering facts prior to trial is cheaper than finding the same facts in trial. However, discovery is more certain to occur than trials. Consequently, postponing the compulsory disclosure of facts until trial implies the possibility that a settlement will completely avoid this cost.

Discovery Abuse: The Process is the Punishment

Suppose that you had the legal power to require someone to bear the expense of supplying you with enough documents to fill a railroad boxcar. In complex legal disputes in America, the legal right to discovery sometimes gives such powers to one of the parties. One party can require the other to deliver a boxcar of documents, provided that they are materially relevant to the suit and compliance is not unduly burdensome [FEDERAL RULES OF PROCEDURE, Rule 26(b)(1)].

Unlike current federal law, economics provides a clear account of discovery abuse and its remedy. From an economic perspective, abuse occurs when the cost of making and complying with a discovery request exceeds the expected value of the information to the requesting party. The cost of making and complying with a request for documents equals the cost of formulating the request, finding the documents, examining all of them, and reproducing and delivering some of them. The expected value of the information to the requesting party equals the expected increase in the value of the legal claim caused by the evidence obtained from the documents.

Under current U.S. law, the plaintiff pays most of the cost of *making* a discovery request, and the defendant pays much of the cost of *complying* with it. Externalizing compliance costs provides an incentive for discovery abuse. To illustrate, assume that the plaintiff spends $500 to make a discovery request, and the defendant spends $2000 to comply. The total cost of the request to both parties equals $2500. Assume that the plaintiff expects the request to produce evidence increasing the value of the legal claim by less than $1500. Because the plaintiff pays $500 to obtain an expected payoff of $1500, the plaintiff has a strong incentive to make the request. Because the cost ($2500) exceeds the expected benefit ($1500), the request is abusive. Thus, current U.S. law gives strong incentives for discovery abuse.

Notice that the incentive for abuse would disappear if the plaintiff had to pay the defendant's cost of compliance, thus internalizing the full cost of the discovery request. Discovery illustrates a general proposition: *People can use legal procedures to abuse others whenever one party has the right to request a procedure and the other party must bear part of the cost of complying with the request. Furthermore, shifting the cost of compliance to the party making the request eliminates the incentive for abuse.*

QUESTION 10.5: Example 4 at the beginning of this chapter concerns whether a judge should order a divorcing couple to attempt mediation before beginning a trial. Assume that false optimism causes trials and predict whether compulsory mediation would cause more disputes to be settled without trial.

QUESTION 10.6: Assume that discovery increases the optimism of plaintiffs and thus increases the value of their legal claims. Explain the consequences for the number of claims filed.

QUESTION 10.7: Trial procedures are formal and involve a lot of people, whereas discovery procedures are relatively informal and involve relatively few people. Consequently, discovering a fact before trial is cheaper than finding it during trial. Most trials, however, are averted through an out-of-court settlement. As a result, if the parties postpone finding a fact until trial, they may avoid the cost completely. To appreciate this trade-off between cost and certainty, consider a numerical problem. Let x denote the ratio of the cost of finding a fact during the trial and the cost of discovering the fact before trial. Assume that the probability of a settlement out of court equals .9. How large must x be in order for the expected cost of finding the fact at trial to exceed the cost of discovering it before trial?

QUESTION 10.8: Discovery increases deliberation, which improves the quality of argument. However, discovery reduces spontaneity, and spontaneous answers by witnesses are sometimes more revealing than considered answers. ("When desperate, tell the truth.") A complete economic theory of discovery would thus model the trade-off between deliberation and spontaneity in revealing the truth. Describe some considerations that you think would go into modeling this trade-off.

IV. Settlement Bargaining

Having analyzed the exchange of information, we move to the next stage in Figure 10.1, which concerns bargaining to attempt to settle out of court. Unlike the other stages, procedural law does not prescribe a time for bargaining to settle disputes. Rather, bargaining can occur at any time in the legal process. We place bargaining at the stage just before trial in Figure 10.1 because bargaining often intensifies before the beginning of an expensive legal process in an attempt to avoid it. However, bargaining may well continue after a trial has begun and even while the jury is deliberating.

Most disputes are resolved without resorting to trial. Estimates suggest that less than 5 percent of civil disputes filed actually require the commencement of a trial in order to resolve them.[13] Bargaining is more important than trials for the resolution of most disputes. However, bargaining occurs *in the shadow of the law.* In other words, expectations about trials determine the outcomes of bargains.

A. Settlements Replicating Trials

We begin by reviewing the elements of bargaining theory as developed in Chapter 4. In a bargaining situation, the parties can cooperate, or each party can act on its own without the other party's cooperation. The joint payoff from cooperating exceeds the sum

---

[13] See Galanter, *Reading the Landscape of Disputes: What We Know and Don't Know (and Think We Know) About Our Allegedly Contentious and Litigious Society,* 31 UCLA L. REV. 40, 44 (1983). However, a more careful disaggregation of data reveals a complicated picture. Erhard Blankenberg found that the ratio of settlement to judgment in Germany was 10 to 1 for traffic accidents, but only 2.7 to 1 for debt collection, 2.4 to 1 for disputes over service contracts, and 1.7 to 1 for disputes about rental contracts. See Blankenberg, *Legal Insurance, Litigant Decisions, and the Rising Caseloads of Courts: A West German Study,* 16 LAW & SOC. REV. 619 (1981–1982).

of individual payoffs from not cooperating. In order to induce someone to cooperate, the party must receive at least as much as can be obtained by not cooperating, which is called a *threat value* by economists. (A better term to use in court is "go-it-alone" value or "concession limit.") The sum of the threat values equals the *noncooperative value* of the game. The difference between the joint payoff from cooperating and the noncooperative value of the game equals the *cooperative surplus*. In order to cooperate, the parties must agree about dividing the cooperative surplus. An equal division of the surplus is *reasonable*. The rational pursuit of narrow self-interest, however, does not guarantee that the parties will be reasonable; so, they may not agree, or they may reach an unreasonable agreement.

Now we apply these concepts to settlement bargaining in a civil dispute. (We already did so briefly in the box in Chapter 4 titled "A Civil Dispute as a Bargaining Game.") In a civil dispute, an agreement to settle out of court can replicate any judgment that the court would have reached after a trial. To illustrate by a divorce, suppose the court concludes after a trial that the parties should sell the house and divide the proceeds equally, and custody of the children should be divided between husband and wife in the proportions 40 percent and 60 percent. If the parties had agreed to these terms without a trial, the judge would have accepted the agreement and enforced it. Thus, a settlement could achieve the same outcome as a trial, and the parties would save the cost of litigation. The savings in the cost of a trial could have been divided between the parties, making both of them better off. For any trial, a settlement usually exists that makes both parties better off; so, trials are usually inefficient.

Exceptions to this generalization about efficiency sometimes occur, as when one side wants the publicity of a trial, or when one side wants to create a generally accepted precedent by winning on appeal. We need not concern ourselves with these exceptions now.

A settlement out of court is a cooperative solution, and a trial is the noncooperative solution. The difference between the joint payoffs from a settlement and the sum of the individual payoffs from a trial equals the cooperative surplus. A reasonable settlement divides the cooperative surplus equally. We show how to calculate these values using Figure 10.4a. According to that figure, the plaintiff expects to win $100 at trial with probability .5, and to lose with probability .5. Win or lose, the trial will cost the plaintiff $20. If the plaintiff loses, he will not appeal, because the expected value of an appeal is negative, according to Figure 10.4a. Therefore, the plaintiff's expected value of trial equals $30. Because a trial requires no cooperation from the other party, the plaintiff's expected value of trial equals his threat value.

To develop this example into a bargaining problem, we must also describe the defendant's expected value of trial. Assume that the defendant is the mirror image of the plaintiff so that the defendant expects to lose $100 at trial with probability .5, and to win with probability .5. Win or lose, the trial will cost the defendant $20. If the defendant loses, she will not appeal, because we assume that the expected value of an appeal is negative. We compute the defendant's expected value of trial as follow:

$$.5(-\$100) + .5(\$0) - \$20 = -\$70.$$

Because a trial requires no cooperation from the other party, defendant's expected value of trial equals her threat value.

The sum of the threat points equals the noncooperative value of the game:

$$\text{noncooperative value} = \$30 - \$70 = -\$40.$$

If the parties settle out of court, the plaintiff will receive the settlement, denoted S, and the defendant will lose S. In addition, each side will pay settlement costs equal to $1. Thus, we compute the cooperative value of the game as follows:

$$\text{cooperative value} = +\$5 - \$1 - \$5 - \$1 = -\$2.$$

Finally, the cooperative surplus equals the difference between the noncooperative value of the game and its cooperative value:

$$\text{cooperative surplus} = -\$2 - (-\$40) = \$38.$$

Notice that the cooperative surplus equals the difference between the joint costs of settling (−$2) and the joint costs of litigating (−$40). Thus, the savings in transaction costs from settling creates the cooperative surplus.

Now let us compute the reasonable settlement of this dispute. A reasonable settlement gives each party a payoff equal to his or her threat value plus an equal share of the surplus. The plaintiff's threat value equals $30. Half of the surplus equals $19. Therefore, a reasonable settlement gives the plaintiff a payoff equal to $49. To achieve this payoff, the defendant should pay $50 to the plaintiff, and then the plaintiff must pay settlement costs equal to $1, leaving the plaintiff with a net gain of $49.

Now we repeat this computation for the defendant. The defendant's threat value equals −$70. Half of the surplus equals $19. Therefore, a reasonable settlement gives the defendant a payoff equal to $-\$70 + \$19 = -\$51$. To achieve this payoff, the defendant should pay $50 to the plaintiff, and then the defendant must pay settlement costs equal to $1, leaving him with $49.

Now we relate the reasonable settlement to the expected judgment. The *expected judgment* from a trial equals the actual judgment multiplied by its probability. In Figure 10.4a, the expected judgment from the trial equals $(.5)(\$100) = \$50$. The reasonable settlement also equals $50. Thus, the reasonable settlement replicates the expected judgment in this example.

Recall our simple measure of social costs as the sum of administrative costs and error costs. When the settlement replicates the expected judgment, a settlement uses lower transaction costs to achieve the result as expected at trial. Thus, the administrative costs are lower, and the error costs are the same. Therefore, *a settlement that replicates the expected judgment at trial usually reduces social costs.* Given this fact, the law should encourage settlements that replicate the expected judgment. By doing so, the law can achieve the same results as trials while lowering social costs.

This important conclusion raises the question, "When does the reasonable settlement equal the expected judgment at trial?" The preceding example produces this result because the defendant is the mirror image of the plaintiff. In general, *the reasonable settlement equals the expected judgment at trial when (1) the plaintiff and defendant have the same expectations about the trial, and (2) the plaintiff and defendant bear the same transaction costs to resolve the dispute.* We will develop an example to show the truth of this proposition, which is fundamental to the analysis and design of legal procedures.

B. No Settlement

Earlier we explained that relative optimism causes trials. Let us use bargaining theory to develop this argument. Consider how the reasonable solution changes in the preceding example if the expectations about trial diverge for the two parties. To keep the example simple, assume that the plaintiff expects to win at trial with probability .8. Consequently, the plaintiff's subjective threat value equals

$$.8(\$100) + .2(\$0) - \$20 = \$60.$$

The defendant's expectations remain unchanged, so she expects to lose $70 at trial. We compute the cooperative surplus as follows:

$$
\begin{aligned}
\text{cooperative surplus} &= \text{cooperative value} - \text{noncooperative value} \\
&= +\$5 - \$1 - \$5 - \$1 - (\$60 - \$70) \\
&= \$8.
\end{aligned}
$$

A reasonable settlement gives the plaintiff a payoff equal to his threat value plus an equal share of the surplus: $60 + $4 = $64. For the plaintiff to receive a net payoff of $64, the defendant should settle for $65, from which the plaintiff will pay $1 in settlement costs. (Can you show that $65 is also a reasonable settlement from the defendant's viewpoint?[14])

In this example, the plaintiff expects to win at trial with probability .8, whereas the defendant expects to lose at trial with probability .5, so the plaintiff is relatively optimistic. In bargaining together, the parties may agree to disagree on these probabilities, and to compute resulting gain from cooperation. The computation of the surplus from cooperation as perceived by the parties can be called the "putative cooperative surplus"—that is the surplus that they impute to cooperating, given that they do not agree about their prospects at trial. Notice that the plaintiff's relative optimism reduced the putative cooperative surplus from $40 to $8. *If relative optimism reduces the putative cooperative surplus below zero, then settlement cannot occur.*

To illustrate this fact, assume that the plaintiff expects to win at trial with probability 0.95. Consequently, the plaintiff's *subjective* threat value equals

$$.95(\$100) + .05(\$0) - \$20 = \$75.$$

The defendant's expectations remains unchanged; so, he expects to lose $70 at trial. We compute the putative cooperative surplus as follows:

$$
\begin{aligned}
\text{putative cooperative surplus} &= \text{cooperative value} - \text{noncooperative value} \\
&= +\$5 - \$1 - \$5 - \$1 - (\$75 - \$70) \\
&= -\$7.
\end{aligned}
$$

Because cooperation produces a negative putative surplus, both parties prefer a trial. Settlement cannot occur because each party expects to gain more from a trial than he

---

[14] The defendant's subjective threat value equals −$70; half the surplus equals $4; so the defendant's payoff when settling should equal $66. To achieve this payoff, the defendant pays $65 to the plaintiff, and he pays settlement costs of $1.

could gain by a settlement acceptable to the other side. (Can you compute the "reasonable settlement" from the plaintiff's viewpoint, and show that the defendant would not agree to it?[15])

This example illustrates that relative optimism about trial can overwhelm the savings in the cost of litigating. We can state the relationship precisely. Relative optimism is measured by the difference in the expected judgment of the two parties, which we write ΔEJ. By settling, the parties save the difference in costs between litigating and settling, which we write $LC - SC$. *The expected surplus from settling becomes negative, making trial inevitable, when relative optimism exceeds the difference in costs between litigating and settling*:

$$\Delta EJ > LC - SC \rightarrow \text{trial.}$$

QUESTION 10.9:   Assume that litigation will cost the plaintiff $100 and the defendant $100. Assume that settling out of court is free ($SC = \$0$). What is the largest value of relative optimism (ΔEJ) at which the parties can still settle out of court?

V. Trial

Having analyzed bargaining to settle out of court, we move to the next stage in Figure 10.1 and analyze trials. Different countries organize trials differently. For example, as we have noted above, the judge serves as a neutral referee in common law countries ("the adversarial process"), whereas the judge actively develops the case in European countries ("the inquisitorial process"); European countries have specialized courts (civil, administrative, labor, social, constitutional), whereas the common law countries rely more on courts of general jurisdiction; American civil trials usually involve juries, whereas civil trials in most other countries do not; American lawyers prepare their witnesses, whereas some countries limit the contact between witnesses and lawyers before the trial; and European countries sometimes allow evidence that American courts exclude.[16]

These are just some of the many differences in trials in various countries. Most differences in trials have not been analyzed as yet using economic models. Consequently, we can only sketch the contours of some differences and then consider a few formal models.

Before we analyze trials, consider alternatives to them. Trials are very expensive everywhere. The notorious cost of litigation has generated countless lawyer jokes that

---

[15] A reasonable settlement gives the plaintiff a payoff equal to his threat value plus an equal share of the surplus: $75 - \$3.50 = \$71.50$. Therefore, the defendant must settle for $72.50, from which the plaintiff will pay $1 in settlement costs and receive a net payoff of $71.50. However, the defendant expects to lose $70 at trial. The defendant will never agree to a settlement that makes her worse off than a trial.

[16] For a fascinating comparison to the status and practices of judges in the United States. and Europe, see J. MARK RAMSEYER & ERIC B. RASMUSEN, MEASURING JUDICIAL INDEPENDENCE: THE POLITICAL ECONOMY OF JUDGING IN JAPAN (2003).

circulate on the Internet (Q: Why don't sharks attack lawyers? A: Professional courtesy. See the Cooter/Ulen website for more jokes like this one.) Costs come in three kinds:

Fees—Lawyers command high fees in many countries, partly because of the bar's monopoly power, its specialized training and licensure, and its privileged access to legal officials. Legal fees increase further where corruption makes bribery a routine part of the legal process.

Delays—Chinese courts dispose of most cases within a year; in Los Angeles it takes around three years to bring a case to the Superior Court, and resolving a court case in India can take a decade. (Besides trials, waiting in long lines plagues many services that the state supplies below cost, such as lines of commuters on the highway and lines of people to get government permits to drive or emigrate.)

Uncertainty—Lack of clarity in law and uncertainty about how a court might resolve an issue imposes unpredictable costs on people caught in legal disputes.

Given these costs, being drawn into a legal suit is a punishment in itself for the parties, but not their lawyers.[17]

To avoid this punishment, many lawyers earn their living by keeping people out of legal disputes. Thus, commercial lawyers pride themselves on writing tight contracts that anticipate all contingencies and provide for them explicitly and clearly; so, the contract is performed flawlessly, and no one litigates the contract. Unfortunately, even the best contracts sometimes result in litigation. Anticipating this possibility prompts many businesses to search for alternatives to trials and to specify in the contract how future disputes will be resolved. The specified procedures characteristically bypass the public courts and substitute streamlined alternatives. The alternative procedures have the name "alternative dispute resolution" or ADR, which includes various types of mediation and arbitration. The contract, for example, may call for resolving any dispute by arbitration in a particular city, following the rules of a particular arbitration association. For instance, the International Chamber of Commerce in Paris organizes arbitrations for many international businesses. Compared to litigation, arbitration procedures have fewer formalities, weaker procedural rights, and tighter restrictions on appeals. These factors make arbitrations simpler and quicker than trials. Arbitration is also usually secret rather than public, which business prefers.

The Visa credit card corporation offers another interesting example. Visa provides a network connecting banks that issue cards and enrolling merchants to accept Visa cards as payment for goods. Consumers sometimes refuse to pay a disputed bill ("The goods were never delivered"). When this happens, the bank that issued the card to the consumer will try to charge the item's cost back to the bank that enrolled the merchant who sold the disputed goods. This action could result in a legal dispute between the two banks about the responsibility for the item's cost. Such disputes are handled by Visa's Arbitration Committee. The plaintiff has to pay a fee for originating a complaint, and

---

[17] Joke: Litigating is like wrestling with a pig: You both get dirty, and the pig enjoys it.

both parties submit written accounts of the facts. The committee decides on the basis of these documents, without ever meeting with the disputants. When the committee announces its decision, the loser pays the judgment and also the costs of arbitration. There are no lawyers, no detailed legal procedures, and no face-to-face encounters between disputants.

The burdensome procedures followed by public courts are designed to ferret out the truth while protecting the rights of the parties. The Visa members could have adopted these public-court procedural rules for resolving their disputes but chose not to. The fact that Visa members voluntarily abandon most procedural rights suggests that the rights' costs exceed their benefits to Visa members.

When both parties to the contract are businesses, as with the banks in the Visa system, terms calling for the arbitration of disputes are relatively unproblematic. More problems arise, however, when one party is a business and the other is a consumer. Health maintenance organizations in the United States sometimes stipulate that disputes between patients and doctors will be resolved by compulsory arbitration. The apparent aim is to reduce the cost of medical malpractice insurance. Similarly, many contracts for the delivery of goods specify that disputes will be resolved by compulsory arbitration according to the rules of the American Arbitration Association, and that arbitration will occur in the home city of the seller. This is an attempt by sellers to avoid the high cost of defending themselves in remote places. Until a dispute arises, however, the consumers who sign these contracts are often unaware of the arbitration clause or unappreciative of its significance. Given ignorant consumers, businesses can often stipulate arbitration procedures and arbitration organizations that favor business (the repeat customer) and disfavor consumers (one-shot buyers).

Web Note 10.2

See our website for a summary of the burgeoning literature on the economics of mediation and arbitration.

A. Independence vs. Alignment

Now we begin to analyze trials. First, let us contrast the role of a judge who actively develops the case in an attempt to find the truth with the role of a judge who passively referees the dispute. Our aim is to determine the optimal activism of judges. The difference in the role of the judge parallels a difference in the role of lawyers. When the judge actively develops the case, the lawyers must respond to the judge, a practice that reduces the scope of lawyers to develop their own arguments. In contrast, when the judge passively referees the dispute, the lawyers have more scope to develop their own arguments. So, the difference between the inquisitorial and adversarial systems partly concerns the allocation of effort between judges and lawyers.

We will evaluate the role of judge and lawyer in terms of the incentives faced by each. Like other professionals, lawyers pursue their self-interest by selling their services. In one of social science's most famous metaphors, Adam Smith described the participants in a competitive market, who consciously pursue their private interests, as directed by an "invisible hand" to serve the public good. According to Smith, competitive markets align private and public interests. The market for lawyers ideally works this way. Within the context of law, professional ethics, and morality, self-interest ideally directs lawyers to pursue the best interests of their clients. By pursuing the best interests of their clients, lawyers help courts to reach toward an ideal outcome of disputes, which we described as the "perfect-information judgment."

As explained, the incentive structure for lawyers ideally aligns self-interest and the public interest. In the old phrase, lawyers can "do good by doing well." The incentive structure for judges, however, is very different from that of lawyers. Bargains among lawmakers yield laws, and bargains among citizens yield contracts. To facilitate cooperation, the parties involved in bargaining need an independent interpreter of their agreements. To achieve independence, the interpreter's wealth and power must be unaffected by the interpretation. The state can supply an independent interpreter of laws and contracts by creating an independent judiciary. Instead of aligning public and private interests, independence severs the link between the judges' decisions and their own wealth or power. Independence requires shielding the judge's promotion, tenure, transfer, salary, and budget.

Different countries secure the independence of judges by different means. In civil law countries, judges are civil servants in a hierarchical bureaucracy. Their hiring and promotion prospects depend upon the evaluation of their performance by their superiors, who are senior judges and other senior civil servants, who often constitute judicial counsels or judicial commissions. Thus, the independence of the judiciary in Europe and Latin America depends upon the insulation of the judicial bureaucracy from private disputes in society. In contrast, American judges in federal courts and most higher state courts are political appointees, not civil servants.[18] Promotion to a higher court in America is extremely unpredictable. Once appointed to a high court, however, American judges enjoy long and secure tenure (life tenure for federal judges), and politicians are prohibited from communicating with sitting judges. Appointment to the bench is usually the capstone of a lawyer's career. Thus, the independence of American judges rests upon the fact that, after they have been appointed, politicians and administrators have no continuing influence.[19]

With judicial independence, the outcome of a case decided by a judge does not affect his or her wealth or power. It costs judges no more to do what they think is right than to do what they know is wrong. Consequently, independent judges might just as well follow their own inner lights concerning the right and the good. (English judges changed their behavior in the late eighteenth century when they began to receive a

---

[18] Different states have different rules for selecting high court judges. For example, in California, the governor appoints judges to the California Supreme Court, but, after being appointed, a judge must be confirmed by a majority of Californians voting in the next regularly scheduled general election. In Illinois, justices of the intermediate appellate courts and of the supreme court are elected from districts determined by the state legislature. In approximately half of the states, judges at all levels are elected to office, and in the other half, they are appointed by the state's governor, often with the advice and consent of the upper house of the state legislature and then later subject to retention elections.

[19] For a fascinating comparison to the status and practices of judges in the United States. and Japan, see Ramseyer & Rasmusen, supra n. 16.

salary from the state instead of being paid by fees collected from the litigants.[20]) In addition, independent judges gain nothing material from devoting more effort to a case. Thus, we expect judges to use their independence to make their lives easy and pleasant.

As a glib summary, we could say that judges have incentives to do what is right and easy, whereas lawyers have incentives to do what is profitable and hard. This perspective suggests how to analyze the optimal activism of judges. Transferring responsibility for developing the case from lawyer to judge increases independence and decreases motivation. The greater activism of the judge in the inquisitorial system brings more independence to finding facts and interpreting laws, whereas the increased scope for lawyers in the adversarial system brings more vigor to the search for facts and arguments. The box below restates this argument in the language of statistics.

An analysis of juries resembles an analysis of judges. As with judges, the legal system tries to make jurors independent, so that they do what is right. Unlike judges, jurors are *required* to serve and their compensation is nominal. According to data from the National Center for State Courts, jury compensation varied across states from a high of $42.20 per day in New Mexico to $0 in several states. (When Robert Cooter was called to jury duty in California, the summons recommended parking in the official parking lot, where the daily fee exceeded the per diem paid to jurors!) As with most forced labor, the U.S. system is extremely wasteful with the time of jurors. Other legal systems use jurors or something similar within a different institutional framework. For example, the juvenile courts in Munich, Germany, include "lay judges" without legal training who serve for several years at modest pay and decide cases in panels

Information Theory Applied to Judging

Let x denote a variable relevant to a legal dispute. Let x^* denote the true value of the variable x. The court seeks the truth, but the court observes x^* with error ϵ, where ϵ is a random variable. Thus, the court observes $x^* + \epsilon$. The expected value of the court's observation is denoted $E(x) = x^* + E(\epsilon)$, where $E(\epsilon)$ equals the average or mean error. If the mean error is zero, $E(\epsilon) = 0$, then the court's expected observation is accurate: $E(x) = x^*$. If the expected error is not zero, say, $E(\epsilon) = 10$, then the court's expected observation is biased. If the variance of ϵ is large, then the court's observation is *erratic*.

The self-interest of lawyers causes them to conduct a diligent, biased search for information, whereas the independence of judges causes them to conduct a lax, unbiased search. Thus, lawyers tend to make biased observations of x with low variance, whereas independent judges tend to make unbiased and erratic observations of x.

---

[20] The fee system incentivized judges to attract cases to their courts by deciding them in favor of plaintiffs. Replacing fees with a salary from the state resulted in fewer pro-plaintiff decisions and more pro-defendant decisions. Daniel Klerman, *Jurisdictional Competition and the Evolution of the Common Law*, 74 U. Chi. L. Rev. 1179 (2007).

with professional judges. Jurors and lay judges tend to give more weight to social norms, which they know, and less weight to formal law in deciding cases. (Later in this chapter we discuss the role of social norms in the evolution of law.) In addition, a large jury affords some protection against corruption because bribes and threats are more likely to succeed when concentrated rather than dispersed.

> **QUESTION 10.10:**   Compare the incentives of the judge and the lawyers with respect to the time allocated to a trial.

> **QUESTION 10.11:**   Bribing or intimidating the court is a persistent worry in trials. The use of juries is often justified on the ground that corrupting the jury is more difficult than corrupting a judge. Why might this be true?

B. Should the Loser Pay All?

In Britain, fewer disputes go to trial than in the United States. And in Britain, the loser of a lawsuit must pay the litigation costs of the winner, whereas in the United States, each party ordinarily pays its own litigation expenses. Some people believe that the British rule of "loser pays all," which is also the rule in much of Europe, causes fewer trials than the American rule of "each pays his own." However, other important differences between British and American trial practices could account for the difference in litigation rates in the two countries.[21] To evaluate the claim that "loser pays all" causes less litigation than "each pays his own," we contrast the incentive effects of the two rules.[22]

Most civil disputes involve two issues: liability and damages. The expected judgment equals the probability of liability multiplied by the damages. For example, in a medical malpractice case, the plaintiff may expect to lose with probability .9 and to win $10 million with probability .1, thus yielding an expected judgment of $1 million. In this example, the rule of "each pays his own" causes the plaintiff to pay his or her own legal costs in all cases. In contrast, the rule of "loser pays all" causes the plaintiff to pay no legal costs with probability .1 and to pay the legal costs of both parties with probability .9. In suits with low probability that the plaintiff will win, a rule of "loser pays all" increases the expected costs of the plaintiff relative to a rule of "each pays his own." In general, *the rule of "loser pays all" discourages suits with low probability that the court will find liability.* (Suits discouraged by this rule include nuisance suits and also suits where the plaintiff has uncertain proof of a legitimate grievance.)

---

[21] For example, the British bar (and other national legal professions) is split into solicitors and barristers, contingency fees are not allowed in Britain, and civil trials in Britain have no juries (except in libel cases). The first two of these distinctions are disappearing.

[22] For a different view from ours about the effect of these fee shifting rules, see John J. Donohue III, *Opting for the British Rule, or If Posner and Shavell Can't Remember the Coase Theorem, Who Will?*, 104 HARV. L. REV. 1093 (1991). Professor Donohue argues that the rule for attorney fee compensation is a default rule away from which the parties can bargain as part of a settlement. So, it does not really matter, he argues, to efficiency whether the default rule is the American rule or the English rule. The parties will bargain to whatever assignment of fees is mutually satisfactory.

Now consider cases in which the probability of liability is closer to .5. Earlier we explained that the simplest cause of trials is relative optimism of the parties. For example, settlement out of court will be difficult if the plaintiff believes the court will find liability with probability .6, whereas the defendant believes the court will find liability with probability .4. From this example, it is easy to see that the rule of "loser pays all" aggravates the problem of relative optimism. Under a rule of "each pays his own," each party in this example expects to bear its own litigation expenses in the event of a trial. In contrast, under a rule of "loser pays all," each party expects to escape bearing any litigation expenses in the event of a trial with probability .6. *When the parties' estimated probability that the court will find liability for the plaintiff is not low, the rule of "loser pays all" generally encourages trials caused by false optimism.*

We have been discussing suits over liability. In some disputes, liability is conceded by the defendant, and the parties contest damages. In these cases, both parties agree that the plaintiff will win something at trial, but they disagree about how much the plaintiff will win. When applying the rule "loser pays all" to these cases, the plaintiff does not automatically "win" just because the defendant concedes liability. Instead, the definition of the "winner" depends upon how much the plaintiff wins. To illustrate, consider an example: Suppose Joan Potatoes demands $600 as her share of the car valued at $1000 in her divorce with her husband, Joe. Some American courts recognize an institution called "offers to compromise," which, in effect, adopts the loser-pays-all rule.[23] Under this institution, Joan's offer to settle for $600 will be recorded at the courthouse. If Joe rejects the offer, and a trial occurs, the winner is determined by whether the court awards Joan more or less than $600. Joe will pay most of Joan's court costs if the court awards Joan more than $600, whereas Joan will pay most of Joe's court costs if the court awards Joan less than $600. *In disputes that concede liability and contest damages, the "winner" can be defined by the difference between the last offer to settle and the court judgment.*

Notice that the effect of this institution is to penalize hard bargaining. Under the rule of "loser pays all," demanding more increases the probability that she will pay the litigation costs of the other party. To see why, assume that Joan increases her demand from $600 to $601. As a result, she gains an additional $1 in the event of a settlement, but she increases the risk that she will pay all of Joe's litigation costs in the event of a trial. *In disputes that concede liability and contest damages, the rule of "loser pays all" discourages trials by penalizing hard bargaining.*[24]

QUESTION 10.12: Assume that the plaintiff demands $1000 to settle, the defendant rejects the offer, and the jury awards $900 at trial. Who "won" for purposes of the rule "loser pays all"?

---

[23] Each state has its own rules. In federal court in the United States, Rule 68 prescribes a form of "offers to compromise," although it is "asymmetrical" as opposed to the "symmetrical" form that we describe above. In general, the American forms of "loser pays" do not shift *all* the costs of litigation.

[24] Note that in disputes that concede liability and contest damages, the rule of "loser pays all" encourages trials caused by false optimism.

QUESTION 10.13: Assume that the plaintiff demands $1000 to settle, the defendant offers $600, and the jury awards $900 at trial. Extend the definition of "winner" and "loser" to this case for purposes of applying the rule "loser pays all."

QUESTION 10.14: Recall that, according to one definition, a nuisance suit has no merit in the sense that the plaintiff's expected judgment is zero. Will there be more nuisance suits under the rule of "each pays his own" or "loser pays all"?

QUESTION 10.15: The parties to a suit may dispute the fact and extent of liability. Disputes over whether the defendant was liable often have no scope for compromise, whereas disputes over the magnitude of damages have scope for compromise. Explain why the rule of "loser pays all" may cause parties to resolve most disputes over the extent of liability but not the fact of liability.

QUESTION 10.16: Assume that both parties to a legal dispute are averse to the risk of losing at trial. Would risk-averse parties be more inclined to settle out of court under a rule of "each pays his own" or "loser pays all"?

QUESTION 10.17: Suppose "loser pays all" is more efficient than "each pays his own." In a jurisdiction that follows "each pays his own," the Coase Theorem would predict that the two parties would sign a contract requiring the loser to reimburse the winner, thus adopting the more efficient rule by private agreement. Give some economic reasons why this does not occur in fact.

VI. Appeals

Many court systems consist of a hierarchy of courts in which a discontented litigant can appeal the decision of a lower court and request a hearing before a higher court. Sometimes the higher court *must* accept the appeal and hear the case (the parties may appeal "as of right"), and sometimes the higher court can *choose* whether to accept the appeal or reject it (the court has "discretionary review"). For example, U.S. federal courts consist of three levels in which the highest court (the U.S. Supreme Court) can decide whether to accept or reject most appeals from the intermediate court (a circuit court of appeals), and the intermediate court must accept appeals from the lowest court (a district court). In some countries (but not in federal or state courts in the United States) the appeals courts can hear the entire case from the beginning ("trial de novo"). For example, appeals courts in continental Europe often hear cases from the beginning, considering matters of fact and law. Sometimes, however, the appeals court considers some issues but not others. For example, the appeals courts in common law countries usually limit consideration to matters of law, accepting without reviewing all the facts found by lower courts.

Appeals courts have two distinct functions. First, they correct mistakes in decisions made by lower courts. Second, they make law, either directly as in common law or indirectly through the interpretation of statutes. We will consider each function of appeals courts in turn.

A. Correcting Mistakes

Hierarchical court systems enable the highest judges to monitor the performance of lower judges and correct their mistakes at low cost. The system of appeals keeps monitoring costs low because litigants typically appeal when the lower court makes a mistake. Thus, a system of appeals enables the highest judges to draw upon the private information of litigants about whether a mistake was made by a lower court. By using this information, a system of appeals can reduce the sum of administrative costs and error costs in deciding disputes.

To illustrate, consider a numerical comparison of a system without appeal and a system with appeal. Assume that a trial costs the plaintiff and defendant $500 each, for a total of $1000 in administrative costs. Assume the probability of an error by the trial court in deciding the case equals .2 and the social costs of an error equal $25,000. Thus, the social cost of deciding the dispute in the trial court is

$$\text{Social cost} = \underset{\text{administrative costs}}{\$1000} + \underset{\text{expected error costs}}{.2(\$25,000)} = \$6000.$$

Now consider how the creation of an appeals court affects social costs. Assume for now that the case is appealed if, and only if, the trial court made an error. Assume that an appeal costs each party $1000, for a total of $2000 in administrative costs. The appeals court is likely to reverse the trial court when the latter made an error. Specifically, let .9 equal the probability of reversal conditional on an error by the trial court, which implies that the probability of the appeals court's sustaining an error made by the trial court equals .1. The social cost of deciding the dispute in a court system with the possibility of appeal is

$$\text{Social cost} = \underset{\substack{\text{administrative}\\\text{cost of first trial}}}{\$1000} + \underset{\substack{\text{probability}\\\text{of appeal}}}{.2} \underset{\substack{\text{admin. cost}\\\text{of 2nd trial}}}{[\$2000} + \underset{\substack{\text{expected}\\\text{error cost}}}{.1(\$2,000)]}$$
$$= \$1900.$$

In this example, the existence of an appeals court causes social costs to fall from $6000 to $1900.

A rational litigant does not appeal a case unless the expected value of appealing exceeds its cost. The expected value of appealing is high when the appeals court is likely to reverse the decision of the trial court. The appeals court is likely to reverse when the lower court makes an error. Thus, appeals courts are most likely to lower social costs (1) when the appeals court is more likely to reverse an error by the lower court than to reverse a correct decision, and (2) when this behavior by the appeals court causes litigants to appeal errors with higher probability than the probability of appealing correct decisions by the lower court.

QUESTION 10.18:   By setting fees for appealing, the state can discourage appeals with low probability of success. Construct a numerical example to illustrate this fact.

QUESTION 10.19:   Appeals are often subsidized in the sense that the state bears part of the litigation costs. Use the preceding theory to construct a justification of state subsidies for appeals.

QUESTION 10.20:   Assume that delay is more costly to the plaintiff than the defendant. How does the possibility of appealing an adverse court decision, which delays resolution of the case, affect bargaining between the parties to settle the dispute out of court?

B. Efficiency of the Litigation Market

Now we turn from correcting mistakes to making law. A trial imposes substantial costs on the state, including the cost of the court building and the salaries of the judge, court stenographer, bailiff, and various assistants. Unfortunately, courts keep poor accounts, and we know of no authoritative estimate of the cost to the state of an hour spent on a trial in an American court (although we will propose one in the second part of the next chapter). Apparently no one knows how much of the state's cost of a trial is a subsidy and how much is recouped from the parties to the dispute in the form of court fees assessed against them.

While no one knows how large the subsidy is, we can say something about how large it ought to be. Deciding disputes and making laws differ in this respect: A decision mostly affects the plaintiff and defendant, whereas a new, generally accepted precedent affects many people. This difference is fundamental to the economics of trials. When an appeals court decides a matter of law, the precedent affects many people other than the parties to the dispute. Because the parties to the dispute do not internalize most of its effects, they should not pay most of its costs. The state should subsidize appeals on matters of law because of the public value of precedent. This argument does *not* apply to deciding disputes that mostly affect the plaintiff and defendant. When the law is settled and the dispute concerns the facts, the effects of its resolution do not go beyond the parties. Consequently, the case for subsidizing trials to resolve private disputes is much weaker than the case for subsidizing trials to make law.

How beneficial to the public is judge-made law? We will discuss some theories that try to answer this question by focusing on whether legal precedents evolve toward efficiency. Some social goals can be achieved without government's pursuing them. Recall that Adam Smith argued that competitive markets often cause people who consciously pursue their private interests to serve the public good. A competitive market is a kind of social machine whose laws of operation allocate resources efficiently without anyone's consciously striving for that goal. Litigation has some elements of a competitive market; specifically, plaintiffs and defendants compete with each other to advance their own ends. Are courts like competitive markets in the sense that judge-made law tends toward efficiency without anyone's consciously striving for this goal?

The economic analysis of law has investigated the inspiring possibility that litigation can make the law more efficient without the conscious help of judges. This might occur through what is called *selective litigation*. Assume that inefficient laws are litigated more than efficient laws. (In a moment we shall explain why that might occur.) By assumption, inefficient laws are repeatedly challenged in court, whereas efficient laws are challenged less frequently. If efficient laws are not favored or disfavored by judges, the probability of a law's surviving a court test is independent of whether it is efficient or inefficient. But we are assuming that inefficient laws are challenged in court more often than efficient laws. These two assumptions—that efficiency is negatively correlated to the probability of a court test and that efficiency is not negatively correlated to the probability of a law's surviving such a test—are sufficient to cause the law to evolve toward efficiency.

Under these assumptions, selective litigation works like a strainer that catches inefficient laws while allowing efficient laws to slip past. The law, being repeatedly sieved, becomes more efficient with the passage of time. The process of filtering out inefficient laws could operate without judges' consciously favoring efficiency; indeed, it is sufficient for judges not to disfavor efficiency. In order for selective litigation to cause the law to evolve toward efficiency, selection must be biased against inefficient laws.

Is there any reason to think that inefficient laws will be challenged in court more often than efficient laws? The answer is "yes," but this is not a strong yes—more like a "probably." To see why, consider that inefficient laws allocate entitlements to the wrong parties. Return to Example 3 from the beginning of this chapter, which concerned the division of property in a divorce. Suppose that Joan Potatoes and Joe Potatoes place different valuations upon their house. Joan values it at $150,000, and Joe values it at $100,000. Efficiency requires the allocation of legal entitlements to the parties who value them the most; so, efficiency requires Joan to get the house. If Joan gets the house, the value to Joe of overturning that allocation equals $100,000. In contrast, if Joe gets the house, the value to Joan of overturning that allocation equals $150,000. Because Joan has more at stake than Joe, Joan would be more likely than Joe to challenge an unfavorable legal allocation. In general, the party who values a legal entitlement the most will spend more on a suit to obtain it than anyone else. So, an inefficient allocation of an entitlement will provoke more expenditure on litigation than will an efficient allocation.

More money will be spent challenging inefficient laws than challenging efficient laws. More will be spent extensively and intensively; more extensive litigation means more frequent challenges in court; more intensive litigation means that the plaintiffs hire more expensive lawyers and spend more on preparing the case. Insofar as expenditures improve the quality of the argument in court and insofar as courts are influenced by arguments of higher quality; litigation against inefficient laws will tend to be more successful than litigation against efficient laws.

We have argued that litigation selects against inefficient laws, resulting in more frequent court challenges and better preparation of plaintiffs' cases. Thus, a mechanism in the common law works similarly to the "invisible hand" in markets. Unfortunately, the invisible hand guides courts weakly compared to its guidance on markets. To understand why, consider an analogy between legal precedents and scientific discoveries. Some scientific advances, including the discovery of basic principles, are unpatentable. Insofar as scientific advances are unpatentable, investors in research cannot capture its full value to society. Part of the value spills over, which constitutes an externality. Markets for basic scientific discoveries may fail because value spills over, unlike, say, the market for bananas, where the grower captures the product's full value.

Trials have more in common with basic scientific research than with the market for bananas. A law is, by its nature, general in the scope of its application; so, challenging a law affects everyone who is subject to it. The effects of a new, more efficient precedent spill far beyond the litigants in the case in which the precedent is set. Consequently, most plaintiffs appropriate no more than a fraction of the value that a new precedent creates and redistributes. Other beneficiaries free-ride on this plaintiff's success. Consequently, litigation selects against rules whose costs are internalized by a single plaintiff. Free-riding is more powerful than inefficiency in channeling litigation pressure.

QUESTION 10.21:   The plaintiff who brings a suit to establish a more efficient precedent enjoys only a fraction of its social value. Does this fact show that the government should subsidize lawsuits by paying part of the cost of litigation?

QUESTION 10.22:   What features of the inquisitorial system might attenuate the pressure of selective litigation as compared to the adversarial system?

C. Enacting Social Norms

We have asked whether competition in the litigation market drives judge-made law toward efficiency. Apparently, competitive pressures toward efficiency are present but weak in the litigation market. Economic analysis of law has demonstrated more consistency between the common law and efficiency than anyone anticipated when the intellectual enterprise first began in the 1960s. The degree of consistency far exceeds what could be expected from competitive pressure in the litigation market. Besides litigation pressure, another possible cause of efficiency is competition among "social norms," by which we mean norms that arise outside of the legal system. Norms arise in communities where people interact repeatedly. Social norms compete for peoples' allegiance, and, under certain conditions, the more efficient norms win the competition. Judges sometimes enforce social norms. If judge-made law evolves in the same direction as social norms, then competition in the "market for norms" will drive judge-made law toward efficiency.

The traditional account of the "law merchant" provides an example. Medieval merchants engaged in a variety of commercial practices, such as paying each other with bills of exchange.[25] These practices sometimes competed against each other,

---

[25] A "bill of exchange" is, in essence, a formal enforceable promissory note. These bills, originally given by a debtor to his creditor, might then be passed on by the creditor to *his* debtors in settlement of obligations. In some communities these bills became a *de facto* currency.

and the more efficient ones prevailed. A practice that prevailed was raised to the level of an obligation among merchants. These obligations constituted the social norms of the community of medieval merchants. The merchants in the medieval trade fairs of England developed their own courts to regulate trade. As the English legal system became stronger and more unified, English judges increasingly assumed jurisdiction over disputes among merchants. The English judges often did not know enough about these specialized businesses to evaluate alternative rules. Instead of making rules, the English judges then tried to find out what rules already existed among the merchants and selectively enforced them. Thus, the judges dictated conformity to merchant practices, not the practices to which merchants should conform. The law of notes and bills of exchange in the eighteenth century especially exemplifies this pattern.[26]

The model of the law merchant once enjoyed a special place in the philosophy of law. According to an old theory of jurisprudence, courts should *find* the common law, not *make* it. Judges find the common law by identifying social norms and selectively raising them to the level of law. When judges follow this pattern, the common law has the authority of custom behind it. This philosophy is not limited to common law. The makers of legal codes often follow this philosophy. For example, Karl Llewellyn, the scholar who directed the creation of America's most successful code, *The Uniform Commercial Code,* explicitly identified the best business practices and wrote them into the code. Similarly, the creators of the great European codes often tried to identify and enact the best business practices of the day.

We now live in an age of a new law merchant. The modern economy creates many specialized business communities and norms arise in them to coordinate the interaction of people. The formality of the norms varies from one business to another. Self-regulating professions, like law and accounting, and formal networks like Visa promulgate their own rules. Voluntary associations, like the Association of Home Appliance Manufacturers, may issue guidelines. Informal networks, such as the computer software manufacturers, may have inchoate ethical standards. All of these social norms provide a rich source for decentralized law making by judges. As the economy develops and becomes more complex, social norms should become more important as a source of law.

We stated that social norms compete for people's allegiance, and, under certain conditions, the more efficient norms win the competition. Economists have begun to study social norms in an attempt to understand when they evolve toward efficiency. A short answer is that social norms evolve toward efficiency when they coordinate the

---

[26] The extent to which the medieval law merchant was substantive, rather than procedural, is disputed, and its relationship with common law and admiralty law is difficult to reconstruct. The process of assimilating bills of exchange and negotiable instruments into the common law, which occurred in the eighteenth century, is well documented. The traditional theory is developed by JAMES W. HOLDEN, HISTORY OF NEGOTIABLE INSTRUMENTS IN ENGLISH LAW (1993). Holden is criticized by John Baker in *The Law Merchant and the Common Law Before 1700,* 38 CAMBRIDGE L. J. 295 (1979).

behavior of people in long-run relationships and when the effects of the norms do not spill over to other people.

QUESTION 10.23:   Central planning was the method used in the communist system for making commodities. It failed because the planners lacked the information and motivation to direct an increasingly complicated economy. Instead of being inevitable, socialism proved to be impossible. Making laws is not so different from making commodities. Contrast centralized and decentralized ways of making laws.

Web Note 10.3

There is now a large and fascinating literature on the relationship between social norms and law. For references, links, and summaries, see our website.

D. Efficiency as a Judicial Motive

We have asked whether judge-made law tends toward efficiency without anyone's consciously striving for it. We found a weak pressure toward efficiency in the litigation market and a stronger pressure in the market for norms. What about more conscious forces? Do judges consciously adopt efficiency as a goal? Philosophers disagree about whether a judge can properly decide a case on the ground of efficiency. It can be argued, for example, that judges should allocate legal entitlements fairly and that the fair allocation has no systematic connection to an efficient allocation. Despite such arguments, judges often prefer more efficient rules, but their own descriptions employ terms other than "efficiency." The law embeds efficiency principles under other names.

We cannot develop this theory systematically, but we can provide some suggestive examples. We have argued repeatedly that efficient incentives require the internalization of costs and benefits by the private decision maker. That is, private decision makers face efficient incentives when they bear social costs. The law often prescribes the internalization of costs. To illustrate, recall our analysis of tort law in Chapter 6. An injurer can avoid harming someone else by taking precaution against accidents. Internalization requires injurers to proceed as if the harm were their own (that is, as if the harm were part of their expected costs). When injurers internalize the cost of the harm, they will balance it against the cost of precaution, as required for economic efficiency. Thus, tort law requires injurers to take precaution as if accidental harm to others were their own. Judges may call this "a requirement that injurers show equal concern for the harms suffered by others as for themselves." But this is simply cost internalization under another name.

Here is another example of courts' using alternative terminology when they decide cases on efficiency grounds: Each dollar the plaintiff receives in a lawsuit must be paid by the defendant, so the immediate effect of the judgment is pure redistribution. Self-interested litigants may have diametrically opposite preferences concerning the distribution of the stakes. But suppose they look beyond the immediate division of the stakes and consider the future effects of the legal rule that applies to their dispute. Even though they disagree about this case, they may agree over the rule that they would like to use to resolve new disputes that arise in the future.

Consider an example. Negligence rules as they used to operate in the common law countries (when contributory negligence was a complete bar to recovery) were all-or-nothing: Either the plaintiff was entitled to full compensation for the injury, or the defendant was not liable. In recent years many jurisdictions have abandoned all-or-nothing rules in favor of comparative negligence. Under the rule of comparative negligence, each party is responsible for accident costs in proportion to the harm she caused or to her fault. Thus, if the defendant was twice as negligent as the plaintiff, the defendant is liable for two-thirds of the harm.

Suppose that everyone who lives in a jurisdiction governed by an all-or-nothing rule favors changing to comparative negligence. Further, suppose that someone is injured under circumstances in which the current rule puts all the costs on the other party, whereas comparative negligence would split the costs between them. The accident victim will want this dispute resolved by using the current law, even though he, and everyone else, favors resolving future disputes by the new rule of comparative negligence.

In a common law system, a court may take such a case as the occasion to change the law from the old all-or-nothing rule to the new rule of comparative negligence. Good arguments can be made that judges have the power to abandon a rule in favor of an alternative that makes everyone better off in the future. Certainly a court that made such a change would justify it by pointing to the future benefits that everyone will enjoy. The retrospective application of the new rule can be defended on the ground that everyone prefers its prospective application.

An important normative standard in economics is Pareto efficiency. An improvement by this standard makes someone better off without making anyone worse off. When an appeals court adopts a new precedent, one party to the dispute wins and the other loses. A change in which there are some losers is not an improvement by the Pareto standard. So, the Pareto standard in its simplest interpretation does not provide a guide to adjudicating disputes. We have explained, however, that people who disagree about the best rule for resolving their current dispute may yet agree about the best rule for resolving future disputes. If the prospective application of a new rule makes some people better off and no one worse off, we will say that the new rule is an improvement by the *ex ante* Pareto standard.

This modified concept of Pareto efficiency is very valuable in the economic analysis of law. When an appeals court adopts a new rule whose prospective application is better for everyone, the court may be arguing in different language that the new precedent is *ex ante* Pareto efficient.

> **QUESTION 10.24:** In Chapter 6 we explained the Hand rule for determining whether an injurer was negligent. Does the Hand rule require that "injurers show equal concern for the harms suffered by others as for themselves"?

Conclusion

This chapter developed a general theory of the legal process. We defined a simple measure of social costs; we distinguished the stages of the legal process and modeled the incentive effects of different rules at each stage. The next chapter examines more specific topics concerning the legal process and attempts to evaluate its efficiency and fairness.

Suggested Readings

BONE, ROBERT, THE ECONOMICS OF CIVIL PROCEDURE (2002).

Cooter, Robert, & Daniel Rubinfeld, *Economic Analysis of Legal Disputes and Their Resolution,* 27 J. ECON. LIT. 1067 (1989).

Daughety, Andrew F., & Jennifer Reinganum, *Economic Theories of Settlement Bargaining,* 1 ANN. REV. LAW & SOC. SCI. 35 (2005).

Hadfield, Gillian K., *Bias in the Evolution of Legal Rules,* 80 GEO. L. J. 583 (1992).

Hay, Bruce, & Kathryn Spier, "Settlement of Litigation," in PETER NEWMAN, ED., THE NEW PALGRAVE DICTIONARY OF ECONOMICS AND THE LAW (1998).

11 Topics in the Economics of the Legal Process

THE LEGAL PROCESS is an incentive system that evolved over centuries of tinkering. Its basic logic reduces the injustice from resolving disputes on terms different from those required by the law and the facts. Reducing these legal errors requires costly procedures. The previous chapter developed a simple measure of social costs—the sum of the costs of legal errors and the administrative costs of avoiding them—and applied it to the stages of the legal process. On balance, is the legal process the best instrument for justice or is it unnecessarily cumbersome and expensive?

Most lawyers want to do justice and make money. Lawyers often profit from rules that impose costly procedures, just as the firms in an industry profit by forming a cartel. How can we tell the difference between procedural rules of the legal process that promote justice at reasonable cost and those that increase the earnings of lawyers? To tell the difference, this chapter proceeds through the stages of the legal process and considers specific topics. In Part I, we attempt to assess the consequences of particular process rules for social costs. Then, in Part II, we report on various empirical studies of aspects of the legal process.

I. Complaints, Lawyers, Nuisances, and Other Issues in the Legal Process

This section elaborates on some of the topics that we introduced in the last chapter. We begin with a discussion of what determines the decision to file a legal complaint and proceed through a discussion of the market for legal services, nuisance suits, unitary v. segmented trials, and other issues.

A. Filing Complaints

A lawsuit begins with the filing of a complaint. How does an individual determine whether to file a complaint? What determines the total number of complaints that get filed? Filing of legal complaints should increase with increases in underlying events that cause them, such as accidents, broken promises, invasion of property, and so forth. Filing of legal complaints should also increase with decreases in the cost of filing a complaint, including the cost of hiring a lawyer. Finally, filing of legal complaints should increase with increases in the expected value of the claims. We have identified three immediate causes of the filing of legal complaints:

1. Injuries that trigger disputes,
2. The costs of filing complaints, and
3. The expected values of the claims.

To see these causes at work, consider how an increase in the money damages awarded at trial to successful plaintiffs would affect the filing of legal complaints. An increase in money damages awarded at trial increases the expected value of a trial (*EVT*), which increases the expected value of the legal claim and leads to more claims being filed. To illustrate, assume that an accident victim must pay $501 to go to trial, where he expects to lose with probability .5 and to win $1000 with probability .5; so, the expected value of trial equals $-\$501 - .5(\$0) + .5(\$1000) = -\$1$. The plaintiff is unlikely to file a complaint in this case. If, however, the damages awarded to a successful plaintiff increase to $2000, then the expected value of the trial equals $499, and the plaintiff is likely to file a complaint.

An increase in damages awarded to successful plaintiffs tends to increase the filing of legal complaints by increasing the expected value of trial, but it also has an effect in the opposite direction. Potential defendants can often avoid disputes by avoiding the injuries that cause them. Assume that the damages awarded to successful plaintiffs increase, or if the likelihood of plaintiffs' winning increases, or both, which we summarize by saying that the plaintiffs' *expected damages* increase, potential defendants will take more precaution and thus give potential plaintiffs less opportunity to file legal complaints. Thus, a manufacturer may increase quality control to reduce the number of defects that would expose the company to liability claims by injured consumers.

These considerations suggest a prediction about the connection between the magnitude of damages awarded to successful plaintiffs and the number of legal complaints filed. If damages equal zero, then the expected value of trial is so low that potential plaintiffs seldom file complaints. As damages increase, more potential plaintiffs file complaints. As damages increase further, however, potential defendants respond by giving fewer potential plaintiffs cause for legal action. Eventually a point is reached where the number of complaints begins to decrease as damages increase. Figure 11.1 depicts these facts. The number of suits, which is read off the vertical axis, is largest when the expected judgment, which is read off the horizontal axis, equals a value denoted $\tilde{d}$. The effect of a small increase in damages upon the filing of complaints depends upon whether the starting point is below or above $\tilde{d}$. Below $\tilde{d}$, a small increase in damages increases the number of lawsuits filed. Above $\tilde{d}$, a small increase in damages decreases the number of lawsuits filed.

B. Filing Fees and the Number of Legal Complaints

In the United States, courts charge fees for filing a claim and for each subsequent stage in the legal process. The fees paid by litigants, however, fall short of the total cost

FIGURE 11.1

Suits as a function of damages.

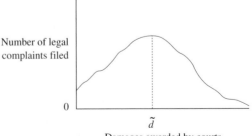

to the state. The taxpayers must make up the difference. As with so many other state subsidies, the extent of this subsidy is unknown because courts do not keep the requisite accounts. In theory, the subsidy could range from almost 100 percent to 0 percent.

Some civil law countries, including Mexico and Chile, interpret the rights of citizens to mean that the state should charge no significant fees for using its courts in civil suits, including fees for filing a claim. In these countries, the subsidy is closer to 100 percent than to 0. Where the litigants pay low fees, the court often spends little on deciding a case, relying primarily on written documents rather than hearing testimony. Also, low fees exacerbate congestion in courts. Conversely, lawyers allege that some jurisdictions set fees to recover the actual cost to the state of using its courts to resolve private disputes, but we cannot find data to confirm these claims.

Here is how a court would use economic principles to set filing fees. The horizontal axis in Figure 11.2 indicates the expected value of the legal claim at the time of filing (*EVC*), and the vertical axis indicates the corresponding number of potential plaintiffs. Some potential plaintiffs have valuable legal claims and others have worthless legal claims. The line indicating filing costs (*FC*) partitions the distribution of potential plaintiffs into two groups. For those plaintiffs to the left of *FC*, the filing cost exceeds the expected value of the legal claim; so, these plaintiffs do not sue. For those plaintiffs to the right of *FC*, the expected value of the legal claim exceeds the filing cost; so, these plaintiffs sue. Thus, filing costs act as a filter for disputes. High-value disputes pass through the filter and result in lawsuits, whereas low-value disputes are caught by the filter and do not result in suits.

By changing filing costs, officials move the partition in Figure 11.2. Raising the fees charged by the court for filing a legal complaint shifts the boundary in Figure 11.2 to the right and causes the filing of fewer complaints. The minimum value of suits rises. Alternatively, lowering the fees charged by the authorities shifts the boundary in Figure 11.2 to the left and causes the filing of more complaints. The minimum value of suits decreases.

How does the filing of complaints relate to social efficiency? The authorities should set the fees charged by the court for filing a legal complaint to minimize the sum of administrative costs and error costs: $\min[c_a + c(e)]$. The authorities can make calculations to determine whether they should raise or lower the fees for filing a complaint. When making these calculations, the authorities should focus on the marginal case, which is on the boundary between "don't sue" and "sue" in Figure 11.2. For the marginal case, the filing costs equal the expected value of the legal claim, $FC = EVC$.

FIGURE 11.2

Number of suits filed.

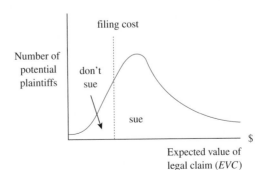

A small increase in the fees charged by courts for filing a legal complaint will cause the marginal plaintiff to drop the suit. Thus, the marginal plaintiff will receive 0 instead of receiving *EVC*. The authorities must compare the resulting savings in administrative costs and the costs of the resulting legal error.

Many constitutions give citizens the right to have a trial to resolve their disputes. In some countries this right is interpreted to mean that trials should be free to the parties. In other countries, however, the constitutional right to a trial has been interpreted to allow assessing "court costs" against the parties to the dispute. Our model predicts that free trials will result in the filing of more claims than a system with court costs. Later we explain that court costs paid by the parties to disputes in America and elsewhere fall short of the full cost to the state of a trial. Ending this subsidy would presumably result in fewer trials in America.

Similarly, the constitutional right of Americans to a jury trial is interpreted to mean that no extra fee will be charged for a jury trial. American citizens are drafted to serve on juries for nominal compensation. If the true cost of the jury were included in the court fees assessed against the parties, then fewer parties would request a jury trial and more of them would be content to let the judge decide the facts of the case.

QUESTION 11.1: Assume that breach of business contracts strongly influences production, whereas property disputes in divorces affect distribution (but not production). Explain the consequences of these assumptions for setting filing fees at the efficient level in disputes involving business contracts and property disputes in divorces.

C. Supply of Legal Services

Here is a lawyer's joke from the cowboy days in the old West: "When I first moved to Shinbone, I was the only lawyer in town, and I almost starved. Now there are two of us, and we're both building new houses." The joke suggests that the market for legal services works in the opposite direction from the market for other goods. In economic theory, an increase in the supply of a good or service causes a fall in its price. In the joke about Shinbone, more lawyers cause higher prices for legal services by creating more legal disputes.

In fact, the number of lawyers in the United States has increased rapidly in recent years. What has happened, as a result, to the price of legal services—have they risen or fallen? Who is right, the joke about Shinbone or economic theory? Let's consider more carefully how an increase in the number of lawyers affects the filing of legal claims. The effect of an increase in the number of lawyers depends upon the organization of the market for legal services, which the bar regulates in all countries. As a benchmark, first consider the effects of an increase in the number of lawyers in a country with relatively lax regulation of the market for legal services. By "lax regulation" we mean that lawyers enjoy much freedom in creating contracts with their clients, as in the United States, and that certification and regulation of who may call themselves a lawyer is not strict. In a free market, where supply and demand determine prices, an increase in the number of lawyers shifts the supply curve out, as depicted in Figure 11.3. The shift in the supply curve from *S* to *S'* should cause the price of lawyers' services to fall from

FIGURE 11.3

The effects of more lawyers on the market for lawyers' services.

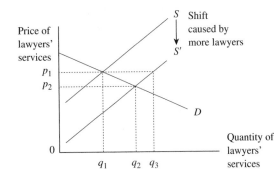

p_1 to p_2. Thus, the increase in the supply of lawyers should lower the cost of filing suits. A fall in the price of lawyers' services from p_1 to p_2 causes the demand for the services of lawyers to increase from q_1 to q_2. We conclude that an increase in the number of lawyers may cause more suits to be filed.

To illustrate, the plaintiff's lawyer in some tort cases in the United States receives compensation in the form of a "contingency fee," which means that the lawyer gets a share of the judgment if his client wins and nothing if his client loses.[1] Suppose that the plaintiff expects to win $1000 with probability .5, and the contingency fee equals .3. Then the expected value of the case to the plaintiff's lawyer equals $1000(.5)(.3) = \$150$. If the case takes 2 hours to prepare and try, then the lawyer's expected remuneration equals $75 per hour. Thus, a profit-maximizing lawyer will take the case so long as he or she does not have an alternative that pays more than $75 per hour. As the number of lawyers increases, the opportunities available to the average lawyer decrease. When the number of lawyers increases, some of them take cases that no lawyer would previously have taken.[2]

Some American attorneys say, "Law was a profession, and now it's a business." Increased pressure from market forces has certainly reduced intimacy and comfort among attorneys. As a group, however, lawyers are not passive victims of markets. Like other professional associations, the bar in every country attempts to control the portals of the profession in order to keep the supply of legal services low and the price high. The bar exercises this power primarily by setting high professional qualifications for the right to argue in court or supply other legal services.[3]

The bar is not immune from the law of supply and demand, but the bar in many countries has insulated itself from market pressures. For example, in many countries,

---

[1] Most plaintiffs' lawyers use a sliding scale for contingency fees. A common practice is for the lawyer to take one-third of the plaintiff's award if the case is settled without trial; 40 percent if the plaintiff wins at trial; and 50 percent if a judgment for the plaintiff is affirmed on appeal. The fee scheme may vary from place to place and over time.

[2] Unlike the United States, many legal systems do not allow lawyers to take cases on a contingency-fee basis.

[3] The standard reason publicly given for regulating lawyers is to ensure their high quality—not to feather the nests of lawyers. See the Web Note referenced at the end of this section for a summary of some interesting literature on the reasons for and effects of the regulation of the legal profession in a number of different countries.

the law prescribes the minimum price that lawyers can charge for their legal services. This is approximately true in Germany, although actual practices are complex. When the law prescribes a schedule of fees for legal services, and the fee schedule is enforced effectively, an increase in the supply of lawyers cannot change the fees for legal services. Instead, an increase in lawyers causes more unemployment among them.

To demonstrate this fact, assume that the price of legal services is set at p_1 in Figure 11.3 by law. If the supply curve for lawyers is given by S, then the legal price p_1 has no effect, because it merely confirms the market price. Suppose, however, that the supply curve for lawyers shifts from S to S', while the price of legal services remains equal to p_1. The demand for lawyers at this price equals q_1, but after the shift in supply from S to S', the supply of lawyers at price p_1 equals q_3. The expression $(q_3 - q_1)$ measures the amount by which supply exceeds demand ("excess supply"), which correlates closely with the number of lawyers who want to work at the price p_1 and cannot find employment.

In fact, young German lawyers sometimes complain of unemployment or underemployment, and the law forbids them to attract clients by charging lower fees. To circumvent the prohibition, young German lawyers may try to attract business by spending more hours on the same legal task that a senior German lawyer would complete quickly, or by supplying extra services for "free." In general, the prohibition of price competition promotes quality competition and secret discounting.

Besides prescribing prices, the law can increase the earnings of lawyers by restricting entry to the bar. In some countries like Brazil, many students study law, and they can join the bar after graduating from the university. In other countries like the United States, joining the bar requires special training in a law school after completing university and success in a rigorous examination—the "bar exam."[4] In a few countries like Japan, membership in the bar is very tightly restricted by an exceedingly difficult state examination. Unlike in Brazil, even smart Japanese students who study law for years fail to pass the bar exam. We can interpret Figure 11.3 to predict the effects of these restrictions. An increase in the difficulty of the bar exam reduces the supply of members of the bar. The supply curve shifts up from S' to S, which causes legal services to fall from q_2 to q_1, while their wages rise from p_2 to p_1.

QUESTION 11.2: Price regulation prevents some people from buying a good who value that good more than it costs to supply it. Apply this proposition to Figure 11.3, assuming that the state sets the price at p_1 and S' gives the supply.

QUESTION 11.3: If most litigation is a costly form of redistribution, then public policy should discourage it for the sake of economic efficiency. Compare the efficiency of the following restrictions on the market for legal

---

[4] In fact, until relatively recently, when Japan and South Korea partially reformed their legal education systems, the United States was the only country in the world in which legal education was graduate education.

services: (a) low damages awarded as compensation for injuries; (b) high fees charged by the court for the filing of a legal complaint; (c) lawyers' fees set by the state at a high level.

QUESTION 11.4: Litigation insurance shifts the legal costs of plaintiffs or defendants to insurers. How do you think this insurance would affect the number of suits filed?

Web Note 11.1

Please see our website for a summary of some recent literature on the legal profession. We discuss and compare how different countries educate, organize, and regulate lawyers.

Class Actions

Did you ever write a check for more money than was in your account? Such a check usually "bounces," and your bank charges you a fee called an "NSF charge" (not-sufficient-funds charge). In California in 1975, Mr. Perdue was charged $6 by Crocker Bank for writing an NSF check. He sued the bank in a case that eventually went to the California Supreme Court. It costs a lot more than $6 to pursue a case that far. Mr. Perdue and his lawyers pursued this case because the stakes far exceeded $6. In fact, Mr. Perdue brought this action not merely on his own behalf but also on behalf of all those account holders at Crocker Bank who paid NSF charges. If successful, Mr. Perdue would recover his $6 and all the other alleged overcharges made by Crocker Bank against its customers.

When a plaintiff attempts to bring an action on behalf of a class of plaintiffs, the court must decide whether to "certify" a "class" and permit someone like Mr. Perdue to sue on behalf of himself and everyone else in the alleged class. This is a delicate problem because a successful suit by Mr. Perdue will extinguish everyone else's claims. Once a class action succeeds, the members of the class, most of whom were not even consulted about the case, will have lost their right to sue.

When should a class be certified? Economics suggests that class actions are appropriate when the stakes are large in aggregate and small for any individual plaintiff. In our example, the sum of NSF charges to all account holders at Crocker Bank roughly measured the stakes in dispute, and the stakes for each individual account holder roughly equaled $6. So, the certification of a class seems appropriate.

Once a class is certified, if the plaintiff who represents the class agrees to a settlement, or if that plaintiff succeeds at trial, damages will be paid by the defendant. These damages must be distributed in such a way that the whole class of plaintiffs benefits, rather than merely the active plaintiff and his or her lawyers, who are naturally inclined to grab a large share for themselves. The courts must decide whether a proposed distribution in a class action is fair. For example, should the active plaintiff's lawyers, who are often responsible for organizing and initiating the suit, be compensated at their standard billing rate? Or should they

(Continued)

receive more than their usual fee in order to compensate them for taking the high risk of losing the suit? Distributing small sums of money to everyone in the class is usually prohibitively expensive. Sometimes the court approves a distribution to some members of the class and the donation of the remaining recovery to a charity that benefits people similar to the members of the class.

In technical terms, class actions ideally consolidate litigation to achieve economies of scale and provide a legal remedy for small injuries that are large in aggregate. (Additionally, class actions are sometimes used to reduce total litigation costs in mass torts, as with asbestos victims or, as we saw in a Web Note in Chapter 9, those harmed by tobacco consumption.)

The potential economic benefits of class actions are clear. But recently, some have raised the possibility that there are economic costs as well. The thrust of the concern is that there are some circumstances in which the court certifies a class of plaintiffs to proceed against a defendant even though the merits of each individual claim are very small (so that the objective likelihood of each individual's prevailing is small). But the risk to the defendant if the class should prevail is so catastrophic that the defendant is, in essence, blackmailed into settling a class action, even though it might have won each individual contest with members of the class.

These are precisely the arguments made by Judge Richard A. Posner in *In the Matter of Rhone-Poulenc Rorer, Inc.*, 51 F.3d 1293 (7th Cir. 1995). The litigation in that case involved a group of about 300 hemophiliacs who alleged that they had become HIV-positive as a result of taking AHF, a clotting agent made by Rhone-Poulenc Rorer, Inc. in the early 1980s. The 300 plaintiffs all had similar enough claims that they sought and received certification as a class from the federal district court. Judge Posner, on appeal, was reluctant to certify the class. Of the 13 individual cases that had been brought at the time of this appeal, 12 had been won by the defendant, and Judge Posner speculated that the defendant would have probably won the vast majority of the remaining individual cases. Nonetheless, he suggested that if the class were to be certified, many more plaintiffs would present themselves, perhaps in the thousands. And in that circumstance Rhone-Poulenc Rorer might be facing $25 billion in potential liability and, as a result, bankruptcy. "They may not wish to roll these dice. That is putting it mildly. They will be under intense pressure to settle." Judge Posner quoted Judge Henry Friendly as saying, "settlements induced by a small probability of an immense judgment in a class action [are] 'blackmail settlements.'" That is, there are circumstances in which the mere act of certifying a class may be enough to convert low-merit claims into such a high risk of catastrophic failure that the defendant will be impelled to settle.

These concerns about class actions creating settlement pressure may be overblown. See CHARLES M. SILVER, *"We're Scared to Death": Class Certification and Blackmail*, 78 N.Y.U. L. REV. 1357 (2003). But Congress found the concerns compelling enough to pass the Class Action Fairness Act of 2005, which expanded federal jurisdiction in class certifications and imposed restrictions on attorneys' fees in class actions.

Most other countries, including those of the European Union, have not allowed class action litigation. That may be changing; the EU appears to be poised to allow class action litigation.

QUESTION 11.5: Explain the effects of class actions on the number of suits, using our distinction of causes, into (1) injuries, (2) filing costs, and (3) expected value of the legal claim.

D. Agency Problem

Recall that we built the theory of contracts in Chapter 8 upon the "agency game." In that game, the principal decides whether to put a valuable asset under the control of the agent, and the agent decides whether to cooperate or appropriate. In a legal dispute, the plaintiff puts a legal claim under a lawyer's control. The lawyer can serve or exploit the client. The lawyer serves the client by providing good advice and devoting effort to winning the case. Consequently, the market for legal services is an agency game.

We will analyze the lawyer's incentives in this game to provide information and effort to his clients. First, consider the lawyer's incentives to work on a case. As explained in Chapter 8, the agency relationship is efficient from the viewpoint of the principal and agent when the parties maximize their joint payoffs. To maximize the joint payoffs, the lawyer should work on the case until the marginal cost equals the marginal benefit for both parties. The marginal cost of the lawyer's time spent on a suit equals its value in the best alternative use ("opportunity cost"). If the lawyer represents the plaintiff, the marginal benefit to the client equals the resulting increase in the expected value of the client's legal claim. If the lawyer represents the defendant, the marginal benefit to the client equals the resulting decrease in the expected value of the client's legal liability.

Devising a contract to achieve this ideal is notoriously difficult. Contracts with lawyers usually focus upon three variables: (1) time spent working, (2) services performed, and (3) outcome of the dispute.[5] In many cases, the lawyers bill by the hour (or rather the minute[6]). Hourly billing causes lawyers to externalize the cost of working on a case, which gives them an incentive to devote too much time to it. Lawyers also bill by the service performed (x dollars for filing a complaint, y dollars for arguing the case in court, z dollars for an appeal, and so forth). Fee-for-service contracts cause lawyers to internalize the cost of additional time spent on the service and to externalize the benefit, which gives lawyers an incentive to devote little time to performing many services. With contingency fees, the plaintiff's lawyer receives a share of the outcome, such as one-third of the settlement or judgment. When working for a contingency fee of one-third, the lawyer internalizes the cost of additional time spent on the service and internalizes one-third of the resulting benefit. Thus, each of the three methods of remuneration distorts the lawyer's incentives away from the client's best interests, but each method distorts in a different direction.

Second, consider the lawyer's incentive to provide information. Imagine that a plaintiff consults a lawyer to find out whether the cost of filing a complaint exceeds the expected value of the resulting legal claim, as depicted in Figure 11.2. A truthful answer may not maximize the lawyer's expected payoff. A lawyer who is paid by the hour, or a lawyer who is paid for services performed, may exaggerate the expected value of the legal claim in order to induce the client to pay for filing a complaint.

---

[5] Other alternatives that we do not discuss are to hire a full-time lawyer ("in-house counsel") or to purchase liability insurance.

[6] Joke: A businessman receives a bill from his lawyer that reads: "Crossed street to see client. Thought it was you. $50."

Joke: A sociologist studying longevity found that the average lawyer lives twice as long as the average doctor and three times as long as the average school teacher. Life span for lawyers was computed using billing hours.

Alternatively, a lawyer who is paid a contingency fee has an incentive to mislead in the opposite direction. Imagine that a plaintiff consults a lawyer to find out whether he will take the case on a one-third contingency. Under this contract, the lawyer internalizes all the cost of filing the complaint, and the lawyer internalizes one-third of the expected value of the claim. Therefore, the lawyer may refuse to take the case, even though the expected value of the claim exceeds the filing costs.

Notice that this incentive problem would be solved if the lawyer took the case on a "100 percent contingency." With a 100 percent contingency, the lawyer internalizes the cost of working on the case and the lawyer also internalizes 100 percent of the payoff from a settlement or judgment. A "100 percent contingency" means that the lawyer keeps the full value of a settlement or judgment; in effect, the client sells the claim to the lawyer. A competitive market for the sale of legal claims would solve many incentive problems for lawyers, but the law prohibits such transactions everywhere.[7]

In markets with lax regulation like the United States, lawyers and their clients have scope to design their own contracts. Thus, the plaintiff's lawyer might charge by the hour for some activities, charge fixed fees for other services, and also take a contingency. In more tightly regulated legal markets like Germany, the state may prescribe the fees for services performed, limit additional fees for time spent on the case, and prohibit contingency fees. In addition, some countries like Britain have a "split bar," which means that the client deals with one lawyer (the "solicitor"), and the client's lawyer chooses another lawyer (the "barrister") to argue the case in court.[8] The wide variation in solutions to the agency problem by different countries reflects its difficulty, as well as reflecting the political power of an ancient profession.

In general, the agency problem between lawyer and client has two causes: asymmetric information and randomness. The lawyer knows much more about the law than the client. Furthermore, the case's outcome depends on random events such as the assignment of a judge and the availability of a witness. Randomness prevents the client from inferring the lawyer's performance from the cases' outcomes.

To overcome these problems, people often choose lawyers based upon reputation and long-run relationships. (Recall the demonstration in Chapter 8 that long-run relationships solve agency problems.) Reputation explains why established law firms command a premium for their services. The growing importance of reputation may also explain the steady increase in the size of law firms in many countries. Large firms are the "brand names" that stand for quality in legal services. However, many countries create obstacles to retard the growth of "brand names" in law. For example, some countries prohibit law firms from naming themselves after anyone not currently working in the firm; so, the firm's name has to change with the retirement of senior partners. Furthermore, most countries restrict or prohibit advertising by lawyers; so, lawyers cannot build a reputation by broadcasting their accomplishments.[9]

---

[7] The common law prohibition is called "champerty." We discussed a market for unmatured tort claims in a box in Chapter 7.

[8] England is in the process of abolishing this distinction.

[9] One of the authors was in the People's Republic of China in the late 1980s when the government authorized the first private law firms in Shanghai in 40 years. Those firms were named "Shanghai People's Law Firm Number 1," "Shanghai People's Law Firm Number 2," and so on. Today law firms in the PRC frequently bear the names of the founders.

QUESTION 11.6:   From an economic viewpoint, restrictions on advertising by lawyers look like a device used by the bar to limit competition. (Such advertising restrictions broke down in America, not because they violated antitrust laws, but because the courts found them to violate the constitutional right of free speech.) From an economic viewpoint, is advertising by lawyers any different from advertising by other professionals, such as accountants or insurers?

QUESTION 11.7:   Contingency fees:

a. If the plaintiff is more averse to risk than his or her lawyer, would this fact incline the client to prefer a contingency fee or an hourly fee?
b. Under a contingency fee, the plaintiff bears none of the lawyer's costs of a trial. Consequently, the plaintiff can take a hard position in bargaining over a settlement. Explain why the plaintiff's lawyer might also benefit from this commitment to hard bargaining.
c. Contingency fees are common for the plaintiff's lawyer in America, but not for the defendant's lawyer. Under a contingency fee contract, the defendant would pay a fixed amount to a lawyer at the beginning of the legal process and the lawyer would receive a fraction of the trial judgment. Are the incentive effects of contingency fees the same for the plaintiff's lawyer and the defendant's lawyer?

Web Note 11.2

For more on the economics of contingency fees, the statistical pattern of legal incomes in the United States, and additional information about recent trends in "Big Law" (large law firms with national and international clients and time-honored reputations), see our website.

E. Nuisance Suits

The preceding chapter demonstrated that the reasonable settlement equals the expected judgment at trial when (1) the plaintiff and defendant have the same expectations about the trial, and (2) the plaintiff and defendant bear the same transaction costs. Litigation costs are a form of transaction costs. Now we show how divergent litigation costs distort settlements.

Assume that litigation will cost one party far more than the other. For example, assume that a trial will disrupt the defendant more than the plaintiff. The cost of disruption increases the burden imposed on the defendant by a trial. Consequently, the defendant's bargaining position is relatively weak. Given these facts, a reasonable settlement favors the plaintiff.

To illustrate using an extreme example, developers in New York City sometimes avoid construction delays by settling suits that have no merit. In such a "nuisance suit," the plaintiff files a complaint solely to delay the construction project and extract a settlement. The plaintiff stands to gain nothing from trial. Instead of winning at trial, the plaintiff expects the defendant to "buy him off" in a settlement. The defendant "buys off" the plaintiff in order to avoid the high cost of delaying construction.

What conditions make a nuisance suit possible? Our bargaining theory can easily answer this question. First, we describe an example in which a nuisance suit fails, and then we change the numbers to show a nuisance suit that succeeds.

Suppose that litigating would cost the plaintiff and the defendant $1000 each, and a trial would result in victory for the defendant ($EJ = \$0$). The plaintiff's threat value is $-\$1000$. It is easy to see that a reasonable settlement (the "Nash bargaining solution") requires the defendant to pay the plaintiff $\$0$.[10] If the plaintiff files suit and demands a settlement, the defendant should call the plaintiff's bluff and refuse to settle.

Now change the numbers. Suppose a trial would cost the plaintiff $1000 and the defendant $5000, and the plaintiff expects to win $0 at trial. The large cost of the trial to the defendant could be due to the fact that she is a developer in New York City. The $5000 cost of the trial includes the indirect costs to her of delaying construction until the trial ends. Under these new numbers, a reasonable defendant should pay off the plaintiff and settle the nuisance suit. (Can you demonstrate that a reasonable settlement—the Nash bargaining solution—equals $2000?[11])

This account of nuisance suits leaves out the potentially important fact that one party may incur costs before the other. To illustrate by modifying the preceding example, assume that most of the plaintiff's costs of $1000 involves gathering facts before the trial, whereas most of defendant's costs of $5000 involves time spent in the trial. In effect, the plaintiff must spend $1000 first, after which the plaintiff will have the power to impose $5000 in costs on the defendant at no further cost to himself. Before spending any money on the case, the plaintiff asks the defendant to settle for $2000. Should the defendant accept or refuse? The answer depends on whether the defendant thinks that the plaintiff is prepared to spend $1000 on the case. Perhaps, if he thinks that the plaintiff will not spend $1000 first, then the defendant will reject the threat as not credible. Or perhaps, if he thinks that the plaintiff will spend $1000 first, then the defendant should settle before it gets more expensive.

QUESTION 11.8: Make a small change in the numbers in Figure 11.2. Assume that litigation costs the plaintiff $20, and the plaintiff wins $40 (not $100) at trial with probability .5. Define a nuisance suit as one in which the expected value of trial is nonpositive ($EVT \leq 0$). Demonstrate that this is a nuisance suit.

---

[10] The cooperative surplus (here, the total amount that the parties would save from not going to trial) is $2000. In a settlement, the plaintiff should receive his threat value plus half the cooperative surplus, or $-\$1000 + 0.5(\$2000) = \$0$.

[11] The plaintiff's threat value equals $-\$1000$. The cooperative surplus of not going to trial now equals $6000 (the plaintiff's savings of $1000 plus the defendant's savings of $5000). The defendant's payoff to the plaintiff should equal the plaintiff's threat value plus half the cooperative surplus, or $-\$1000 + 0.5(\$6000) = \$2000$.

QUESTION 11.9: The preceding question assumed that the plaintiff expects to win $40 at trial with probability .5, and that the trial costs the plaintiff $20. Assume that litigation costs the defendant $60 (not $20). Demonstrate that a reasonable settlement is for the defendant to pay the plaintiff $40.

QUESTION 11.10: Use the numbers in the preceding question, but assume that the total litigation costs of $80 ($60 for defendant, $20 for plaintiff) are paid by the *losing* party (European rule of loser pays all). Demonstrate that a reasonable settlement is for the defendant to pay the plaintiff $20.

QUESTION 11.11: Use the analysis of this section to explain why "blackmail settlements" might occur in some class action lawsuits (See the box above on "Class Actions").

F. Offers as Filters

Relative optimism can cause wasteful trials. Sometimes, however, wasteful trials occur between parties who are *not* optimistic. Such trials occur because of the strategic nature of bargaining. In the 1990s the Dalkon Shield Claimants Trust paid out billions of dollars to hundreds of thousands of women who used this intrauterine contraceptive device (IUD) and allegedly suffered medical harm. The Trust's problem was to distribute money to accident victims without trying each case to determine the extent of the claimant's injury. We model this problem to show how the defendant can use settlement offers to filter plaintiffs and determine the true extent of their injuries.

Assume that the defendant's defective product has injured people who sue for compensatory damages. If a dispute goes to trial, the plaintiff will receive damages equal to the true cost of the injury. The defendant, however, cannot determine the true extent of the plaintiffs' injuries *before* trial. Consequently, the defendant cannot make a settlement offer to each plaintiff that equals the individual's injury. Instead, the defendant contemplates making the same offer to every plaintiff. The plaintiffs with minor injuries will accept the offer, and those with major injuries will reject it.

To be concrete, assume the defendant offers $10,000 to each plaintiff to settle out of court. If a plaintiff refuses the offer and goes to trial, litigating will cost the plaintiff $1000 and the court will award damages equal to the true cost of the injury. Consequently, each plaintiff accepts the offer to settle for $10,000 if the true cost of the injury does not exceed $11,000. Thus, the defendant offers to pay more than plaintiffs who have minor injuries would demand to settle. In contrast, each plaintiff rejects the offer if the true cost of the injury exceeds $11,000. Thus, the defendant offers to pay less than plaintiffs who have major injuries demand to settle.

In this example, the offer to settle for $10,000 *filters* plaintiffs according to whether the severity of their injuries exceeds $11,000. Raising the offer to $10,100 would filter plaintiffs according to whether the severity of their injuries exceeds $11,100. Conversely, lowering the offer to $9900 would filter plaintiffs according to whether the severity of their injuries exceeds $10,900.

How much should the defendant offer in order to minimize the total cost of her legal liability? The more she offers, the more she pays in settlements and the less she pays in judgments and litigation costs. The less she offers, the less she pays in settlements and the more she pays in judgments and litigation costs. She minimizes her liability by balancing these considerations.

To illustrate, assume that 50 plaintiffs settle when the defendant offers $10,000, and 55 plaintiffs settle when she offers $10,100. Raising the offer by $100 requires her to pay the original 50 plaintiffs an extra $100, for a total increase in costs of $5,000. By raising the offer, she settles with five more plaintiffs and litigates with five fewer plaintiffs, which saves the defendant $1000 each in litigation costs, or a total of $5,000. Also, by settling with five additional plaintiffs, she pays $10,100 to each of them and avoids paying a judgment to them. If the judgment were paid, it would be more than $11,000 per person and less than $11,100, for an average of approximately $11,050.[12] In summary, increasing the offer by $100 causes the defendant's costs to change as follows:

$$\$100(50) \quad - \$1000(5) \quad + \$10,100(5) - \$11,050(5) \ = \ -\$4750.$$

$100(50)	− $1000(5)	+ $10,100(5)	− $11,050(5)	= −$4750.
inframarginal settlements	administrative costs	marginal settlements	marginal judgments

Increasing her offer by $100 saves the defendant $4,750; so, the defendant should increase her offer. Furthermore, the defendant should continue increasing the offer until her costs stop falling.

Sometimes the defendant can save costs by randomizing offers. For example, assume the defendant offers $10,000 to 80 percent of the plaintiffs who file a complaint and offers $0 to 20 percent of them. Randomizing can save costs by discouraging nuisance suits. To see why, consider that the 20 percent of plaintiffs who receive no offer to settle go to trial or drop the case. At this point, any nuisance suits among the 20 percent will be dropped, because the plaintiffs' expected value of trial is negative in a nuisance suit. In effect, a nuisance suit is a bluff, and we are assuming that the defendant calls the bluff in 20 percent of the cases. When players sometimes bluff in a game, their opponents usually benefit from calling the bluff a proportion of the time, but not 100 percent and not 0 percent of the time.[13]

---

[12] These five plaintiffs reject an offer of $10,000 and accept an offer of $10,100 to settle out of court. The judgment at trial must be more than $11,000 or else these defendants would have accepted the offer of $10,000. The judgment must be less than $11,100, or else these defendants would reject the offer of $10,100.

[13] Developing the example further shows the value of calling bluffs at random. Assume as before that the defendant offers a percentage (p) of plaintiffs $10,000 to settle, and the defendant refuses to settle with $(1 - p)$ of the plaintiffs. Also assume that potential plaintiffs must spend $3000 to develop and file a complaint. By definition, a nuisance suit is brought only to extract a settlement; so, assume that the expected value of litigation for the plaintiff in a nuisance suit equals $0. Thus, a person who brings a nuisance suit spends $3000 in order to file a complaint with expected value $10,000p + $0(1 − p). A rational plaintiff who maximizes expected value (as will a risk-neutral decision maker) will file a nuisance suit when the following condition is satisfied:

$$\$10,000p \ + \ \$0(1 \ - \ p) \ > \ \$3000 \ p \ > \ .3.$$
$$p \ > \ .3.$$

Thus, the defendant in our mathematical example eliminates all nuisance suits by randomizing and offering to settle with no more than 30 percent of plaintiffs.

With more information, the defendant could develop a better strategy to deal with nuisance suits. If the defendant had enough information to identify plaintiffs who are more likely than the others to bring nuisance suits, then the defendant could offer to settle with them at low probability and offer to settle with all of the other plaintiffs with high probability.

G. Unitary vs. Segmented Trials

A trial usually involves several issues, most prominent of which are whether the defendant is liable, and, if liable, the extent of the damages. The issues can be bundled together in a single trial or distinguished from each other and tried separately. For example, liability and damages are decided in the same trial in most tort suits in the United States, but sometimes separate trials are held on liability and damages. Furthermore, European trials often proceed in small segments in which separate issues get decided in a series of exchanges between the judge and the parties to the dispute. These facts raise at least two interesting questions: Are the transaction costs of resolving disputes lower under unitary or segmented trials? Does segmenting trials favor plaintiffs or defendants?

Economists have begun to address these questions, for example, through the use of the notion of "economies of scope." "Economies of scope" refers to reductions in cost from combining two different activities. Sometimes the questions of liability and damages are bound together. As explained in Chapter 6, showing negligence under the Hand rule typically requires demonstrating fault and also measuring the extent of damages. When the issues are bound together, deciding them simultaneously is cheaper than deciding them sequentially. Thus, economies of scope favor unitary trials. In contrast, sometimes the question of liability is easily separated from the question of damages. In patent law, the question of whether a new innovation infringes a prior patent is often completely distinct from the harm the new innovation caused to the owner of the prior patent.

In any event, a finding of "no liability" in the first trial precludes having a second trial on damages. Sequential ordering can save costs by precluding subsequent trials— a "preclusive disposition." Thus, minimizing the transaction costs of resolving disputes requires balancing economies of scope and the savings from preclusive dispositions. Large economies of scope favor unitary trials. Frequent preclusive dispositions favor segmented trials.[14]

In the United States, judges have discretion over whether trials should be unitary or segmented. In choosing between these processes, judges probably weigh economies of scope and the probability of a preclusive disposition, along with other factors. Defendants often ask the judge for segmented trials, whereas plaintiffs often seek a unitary trial. This pattern occurs when the facts about liability and damages often reinforce each other. For example, a graphic account of damages can create sympathy in the jury for the plaintiff and predispose it to find liability. Alternatively,

---

[14] See William M. Landes, *Sequential Versus Unitary Trials: An Economic Analysis,* 22 J. LEGAL STUD. 99 (1993).

a graphic account of negligence can create hostility in the jury for the defendant and predispose it to find large damages. The jury may behave this way even though, strictly speaking, the formal law prescribes independent grounds for finding liability and setting damages.

In addition to these facts about the psychology of juries, there is a rational reason why defendants might favor segmented trials. Segmenting trials has an advantage over unitary trials in sorting out plaintiffs and forcing them to reveal the strength of their cases, as we illustrate by a hypothetical example. Assume that consumers who suffer an injury allege that a certain company is liable. Plaintiffs can be divided into two types according to how they would fare at trial. The first type ("uninjured plaintiffs") would lose on liability, and the second type ("injured plaintiffs") would win on liability and receive substantial damages. Plaintiffs know their type when they commence legal proceedings, but the defendant does not. In technical terms, individual plaintiffs have private information about their type that becomes public after trial. Consequently, the defendant cannot distinguish between the two types of plaintiffs when making settlement offers.

In these circumstances, a segmented trial has a big advantage over a unitary trial for the defendant. First, assume a unitary trial and consider the efforts of the defendant to settle out of court. Before the trial begins, the defendant can make a settlement offer. A settlement offer is pointless unless the injured plaintiffs accept it. If the defendant makes a single settlement offer to everyone and that induces the injured plaintiffs to accept, then the uninjured plaintiffs will also accept. Thus, the only successful settlement offer available to the defendant is one that every plaintiff accepts. Under unitary trials, the defendant will probably settle with everyone.

Second, consider a segmented trial. If the defendant refuses to make a settlement offer before the first trial, all of the uninjured plaintiffs will drop their claims, rather than lose at trial. In contrast, the injured plaintiffs will proceed to trial. Thus, the first trial sorts injured plaintiffs and uninjured plaintiffs. After liability has been decided in the first trial, the defendant can make a settlement offer to the injured plaintiffs alone. Thus, segmenting the trial enables the defendant to sort plaintiffs by their injuries for purposes of making an offer to settle.[15] *In general, segmenting trials enables defendants to overcome asymmetric information and separate types of plaintiffs according to the strength of their claims.*

> **QUESTION 11.12:** In the preceding example, we contrasted unitary and segmented trials from the viewpoint of the defendant's costs. Analyze the example from the viewpoint of social costs, defined as the sum of administrative costs and error costs.

---

[15] In technical terms, the "bifurcated equilibrium is separating" (injured and uninjured plaintiffs receive different payoffs), whereas the "unitary equilibrium is pooled" (injured and uninjured plaintiffs receive the same payoff). Notice that in this example, the defendant saves money from segmented trials rather than unitary trials if the cost of litigating liability with injured plaintiffs is less than the cost of settling with uninjured plaintiffs.

🕐 **Web Note 11.3**

The behavioral law and economics literature has investigated a phenomenon known as "hindsight bias" that may have a profound effect on the ability of trials to reach a desirable social result. For a summary of that literature and a suggestion of how it might impact the discussion above about unitary versus segmented trials, see our website.

H. Multiple Injurers: Joint and Several Liability

In Chapter 7 we explained the U.S. law for accidents involving multiple injurers. The usual rule is "joint and several liability with contribution." Under this rule, if A and B jointly caused harm of 100 to C, then C can sue A for 100 and not sue B, or C can sue B for 100 and not sue A, or C can sue A for 60 and then sue B for 40. Joint and several liability with contribution allows C to sue A and B separately or jointly for any amounts whose sum does not exceed 100, and then, depending on what C did, for A and B to sue one another to recover a portion of the 100 paid to C. In brief, the victim can recover the full cost of his injury (and no more) from whichever of the joint injurers is easier to sue. Typically the victim goes after the richest injurer who can pay the damages in full.

While "joint and several liability" is the usual U.S. rule, "joint liability" is an alternative. Under joint liability, the plaintiff must sue all of the injurers jointly, rather than suing them separately. Thus, C would have to sue A and B for 100.

Which liability law results in more trials? Legal theorists have often presumed that the rule of joint and several liability with contribution results in fewer trials and more settlements than does joint liability, because the plaintiff can stampede the defendants into settling, like a herd of cows in danger of running from a fire. To see why, assume that A and B jointly caused harm of 100 to C. Under joint and several liability with contribution, C can threaten to sue B for 70 unless B settles out of court for 50, and C can also make the identical threat to A. The fear of disproportionate liability allegedly causes defendants to stampede to settle the case. In contrast, settling under joint liability requires both of the defendants to agree to its terms, which might be difficult and cause a trial.

This reasoning, however, is flawed, because it fails to consider the uncertainty of trials.[16] Assume that the probability is .5 of C's winning 100 in a suit against A or B. C adopts this strategy: Sue A for 100; if the suit succeeds, then do not sue B; if the suit fails, then sue B for 100. C's expected payoff from this strategy is

$$(.5 \times 100) + .5(.5 \times 100) = 75$$

In effect, several liability with contribution gives the plaintiff an insurance policy against the risk of trial. Insurance consists in the fact that he can try to win several suits,

---

[16] Lewis A. Kornhauser & Richard E. Revesz, *Sharing Damages Among Multiple Tortfeasors*, 98 YALE L. J. 831 (1989).

rather than trying to win only one suit. Being insured against loss at trial, the plaintiff is not so eager to settle. Joint and several liability causes C's expected value of litigating to increase from 50 to 75. As a consequence, C will demand more to settle out of court, which may make settlement more difficult and trial more likely.[17]

We have explained reasons for the old belief that several liability with contribution results in more settlements and fewer trials than does joint liability. We also explained the newer belief that several liability with contribution results in more trials and fewer settlements than does joint liability. While the theory is clear, which effect is stronger remains an unanswered empirical question.

> **QUESTION 11.13:** In the preceding discussion, we contrasted joint and several liability (with contribution) from the viewpoint of the number of trials. Compare the two rules from the viewpoint of social costs, defined as the sum of administrative costs and error costs.

I.   Burden of Proof and Standard of Proof

Economic theory has developed a precise calculus for making decisions under uncertainty, such as investing in the stock market, insuring an automobile, or gambling in Las Vegas. As explained in Chapter 2, this calculus is called "maximizing subjective expected utility (SEU)." Actors who contradict its rules frustrate themselves and give strategic advantages to their competitors. A trial is an uncertain event that requires a decision by the court. Do court procedures conform to the logic of economic decision making under uncertainty? If the answer is "yes," then courts are economically rational. If the answer is "no," then courts are irrational by the standards applicable to economic behavior.

The law imposes constraints on behavior that some individuals would not impose on themselves. Many injurers would not voluntarily compensate the victims of accidents or breaches of contract, even when ordinary morality and economic efficiency require compensation. Similarly, the rules of evidence impose constrains on the use of information by judges and juries that many individual decision makers would not voluntarily impose on themselves. For example, American courts do not allow witnesses to testify about rumors reported to them by other people (the rule against hearsay), whereas rational investors often let rumors affect their decisions to purchase stock. In general, American courts prevent rumors, hearsay, and other second-hand information from affecting judgments of liability or guilt much more than a rational person would prevent them from affecting her personal judgments.

---

[17] To complete the proof, consider A's expected losses. A expects to lose at trial with probability .5 and to pay 100. If A loses at trial, then A will sue B for equal contribution and win with probability .5. Thus A expects litigation to cost

$$-.5 \times (100 - .5 \times 50) = 37.5.$$

Thus, A will not settle for more than 37.5, and B is in the identical situation as A. However, C will not settle for less than 75. Settlement is impossible unless A and B cooperate together and offer to settle with C for 75. So, a trial is likely.

Procedural rules impose constraints on decision making under uncertainty. Within these constraints, judges and juries presumably strive to reason like rational decision makers. What else could they strive for? The law constrains the rules of inference, but it does not ask people to abandon their practical reason. Within the constraints of procedural rules whose justification is not necessarily economic, the economic logic of choice under uncertainty presumably applies to courts. Consequently, broad areas of agreement exist between legal procedures and economic rationality.

Within certain constraints of fairness, the rules of statistical reasoning provide an appealing standard of rationality to which courts should aspire. Consequently, these rules can provide a reconstruction of the aspirations for rationality by courts, even though the language of the courts seldom invokes the statistical rules. In this respect, the economic analysis of decision making is similar for courts and businesses. A good model of business behavior assumes the maximization of profits, even though businessmen untrained in economic theory do not use its language to reason about their choices. Similarly, a good model of court behavior assumes consistency with statistical rules, even though courts seldom use the language of probabilities and statistics.

An economically rational decision maker begins with some prior beliefs and updates them in light of new evidence by conforming to certain rules of inference. Evidence is ideally processed in much the same way in trials. A rational gambler begins with prior beliefs based upon experience, hunches, and instincts, and whatever information can be gleaned about the event in question. The judge instructs the jurors at the beginning of a trial to rid themselves of all prior beliefs concerning the case. They should begin as if they knew nothing factual pertaining to this dispute. A potential juror with knowledge of facts about the case may be excluded from the jury—he should be a witness, not a juror. In effect, a juror is asked by the judge to construct a probability estimate (called a "prior probability estimate" or a "prior" by statisticians) of the defendant's liability or guilt. This constructed estimate of probability assumes no knowledge of particular facts pertaining to the case.

Starting without prior evidence, the jury should revise their beliefs exclusively in light of the evidence admitted during the trial. Further, the judge explains that one of the parties has the burden of producing evidence to prove its position in the dispute. In common law countries, the plaintiff must prove the case by a preponderance of the evidence in civil disputes, and the plaintiff must prove the case beyond a reasonable doubt in criminal cases. (The standards are formulated differently in civil law countries.[18]) The constructed probability estimate favors the defendant, because the plaintiff has the burden of proof.

The jury updates the constructed probability estimate in light of the evidence allowed to enter the trial, called a "posterior distribution."[19] At the trial's end, the legal

---

[18] Lawyers in civil law systems sometimes say that there is one standard of proof in criminal and civil law cases: Sufficient evidence to produce a clear conviction in the judge's mind. However, a "clear conviction" is a psychological state, which does not describe the standard of proof that produces such a conviction. When training judges, should you teach them that a conviction is "clear" when supported by the preponderance of the evidence or when it is beyond a reasonable doubt?

[19] Joke: A statistician is the only person who can safely comment on someone else's posterior distribution.

decision maker, whether juror or judge, will have a posterior probability estimate of the defendant's liability probability formed after hearing the evidence presented and admitted at the trial. If the posterior probability exceeds 50 percent, the plaintiff has proved the case by the preponderance of the evidence and deserves to win; otherwise, the plaintiff deserves to lose. Reasoning in the courtroom may thus be described as constrained rational choice under uncertainty, where the constraints are formed by rules of evidence.[20]

As noted, this is an idealized reconstruction of actual reasoning in court, which provides a standard for evaluating the court's decision making. In this light, the actual behavior of courts often seems puzzling or irrational, as we show by the *gate crasher's paradox.*

> A rock concert is sold out. The auditorium holds 1000 people. Ticket holders file through the front doors and occupy 400 seats. Then, before any more legitimate ticket holders can get in, some rude youths break down a back door and crash in, occupying all 600 of the remaining seats. There are so many gate crashers that the concert's organizer cannot eject them; so, he proceeds with the music.
>
> The concert organizer photographs the crowd and succeeds in identifying 100 persons who were in the audience. Of the 100, he does not know which ones bought tickets and which ones crashed the gate; so, he names all of them in a lawsuit. By the time the suit is brought, ticket stubs have been discarded; so, few defendants can prove that they purchased tickets. At trial the plaintiff's lawyer points out that civil suits are decided according to the preponderance of the evidence. Further, he shows that 600 out of 1000 people in the audience were gate crashers and that, therefore, the chances are at least .6 that any defendant is a gate crasher. According to the plaintiff's lawyer, the preponderance of the evidence favors liability for each defendant; so, his client deserves to win.

This use of probabilistic reasoning is sound for betting on whether any particular defendant crashed the gate, but it is unacceptable in court. Let us change the facts to make the evidence more acceptable:

> One of the guards at the back door purportedly recognized 100 of the gate crashers. The concert organizer sues them and the guard testifies in court that he saw them crash the gate. Tests performed on the guard show that he remembers and correctly identifies defendants' faces 60 percent of the time. The plaintiff's lawyer points out that civil suits are decided according to the preponderance of the evidence and that the guard's eyewitness identifications are more likely to be correct than incorrect. Therefore, the lawyer argues, the plaintiff deserves to win.

---

[20] The decision-making process described here is an example of "Bayesian inference." For more along these lines, see Dale Nance, *Evidential Competition and the Burden of Proof,* 49 HASTINGS L. J. 621 (1998).

The first example of evidence was based upon mere probabilities (what is called in the literature "naked statistical evidence"), which courts view unfavorably. The second example of evidence was based upon eyewitness reporting, which courts view favorably (but with caution). This example was constructed so that the probabilistic evidence equals the reliability of the eyewitness testimony. Even so, the former evidence would probably be excluded in an American court, and the latter evidence would be allowed, so that the plaintiff would be likely to lose the case under the first set of facts and win under the second set of facts. However, a rational gambler would give equal weight to probabilistic evidence and eyewitness testimony having the same reliability. When betting whether the defendant crashed the gate, the rational gambler regards a 60 percent likelihood as just as good as eyewitness testimony that is 60 percent reliable. Insofar as naked statistical evidence results in no more errors than eyewitness testimony, excluding the latter from court and including the former seems puzzling and inconsistent but that is what courts often do in the U.S.

Instructions in court for combining evidence often obscure or contradict the rules of probability theory, as illustrated by a recent trial from Oakland, California. A man went to the hospital for a hernia operation. Before the operation, the anesthesiologist gave the patient a medical exam. Having completed the exam, the anesthesiologist put the patient to "sleep." In an ordinary case, the anesthesiologist would keep the patient "sleeping" until the surgeon repaired the hernia, the patient would wake up, and the patient would leave the hospital and go home the same evening. In this case, however, the patient stopped breathing, suffered cardiac arrest, and died. An autopsy revealed that the victim's heart muscles were excessively thick and scarred, which is a condition commonly called a "heavy heart." This condition makes a person susceptible to a heart attack. Until the autopsy after his death, no one knew that the patient had a heavy heart. The strain of the operation, which is unproblematic for a normal heart, caused cardiac arrest in this patient.

When the patient died, his descendants sued the anesthesiologist. Plaintiff made two accusations of negligence by the anesthesiologist. First, plaintiff alleged that the anesthesiologist had not given adequate tests before the operation to determine if the patient had a condition such as a heavy heart. Second, plaintiff alleged that when the patient began to have trouble breathing during the operation, the anesthesiologist responded too slowly and incorrectly.

Consider the rules of evidence the court used to weigh the facts. The plaintiff had to prove by a preponderance of the evidence that the defendant's negligence caused the victim's death. We will focus on the legal rules for combining evidence to construct such a proof.

Figure 11.4 depicts the court's problem as a decision tree. The first branch indicates that the anesthesiologist may have been negligent or nonnegligent in the pre-operation screening. "Preponderance of the evidence" will be interpreted as a probability of .5 or greater. According to Figure 11.4, the evidence indicates that the probability is .4 that negligence in pre-operation screening caused the patient's death. Consequently, the plaintiff has not proved negligence in the pre-operation screening by a preponderance of the evidence.

FIGURE 11.4

Anesthesiologist's decisions.

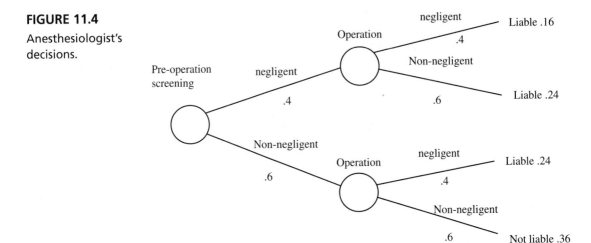

In the second branch of the tree, the anesthesiologist may have been negligent or nonnegligent in the operation. According to Figure 11.4, the evidence indicates that the probability is .4 that negligence in the operating procedure caused the patient's death. Consequently, the plaintiff has not proved negligence in the operating procedure by the preponderance of the evidence.

We have shown that independent and sequential application of the standard of the preponderance of the evidence leads to the conclusion that the anesthesiologist was not negligent. What about combining probabilities to reach an overall judgment? If the probabilities on each branch of the tree are independent,[21] the laws of probability theory prescribe a simple rule to combine them: the multiplication rule. Applying this rule to Figure 11.4, the probability that the anesthesiologist was *not negligent* in the pre-operation screening and also not negligent in the operating procedure is $.36 (= .6 \times .6)$, as indicated on the decision tree. The probability that the anesthesiologist was *negligent* in the pre-operation screening or in the operating procedure is $1 - .36$, which equals .64. Thus, the preponderance of the evidence indicates that the defendant's negligence caused the patient's death one way or the other.

The decision tree clarifies the fact that independent and sequential application of the preponderance of the evidence standard sometimes gets a different result from an overall judgment. The latter approach is more nearly correct from the viewpoint of probability theory. The court in Oakland, California, gave ambiguous instructions to the jury that did not distinguish between these two ways of reasoning. This case illustrates that

---

[21] From the plaintiff's argument, it seems that the alleged negligence was the result of a lapse in judgment by a generally sound physician, which is consistent with our assumption of independent probabilities. The plaintiff did present an argument that linked negligence in the two acts. For example, the plaintiff did not argue that the anesthesiologist suffered from a temporary case of inattention (for example, a hangover), or a permanent case of bad judgment (for example, bad training).

courts have formulated rules of reasoning with insufficient striving for consistency with probability theory.[22]

Much remains to be done to reconcile the rules of legal procedure with sound statistical reasoning. Some of that research is underway, such as explaining the interaction between the burden of proof, the standard of proof, and the severity of the legal sanction.[23] Perhaps the rules of procedure will get rewritten in the future to achieve a higher degree of economic and statistical rationality.

Rent-A-Judge

In the Soviet Union, people stood in long lines to buy bread from state bakeries. In many countries, citizens wait in long lines to litigate their disputes in state courts. In Los Angeles, as in most major cities, it can take several years before disputes are decided in a public trial. In Los Angeles, unlike most other places, a private alternative exists that is a close substitute for a public trial. The parties can agree to "rent" a retired judge to decide their case. The resulting private trial is usually held in a mutually convenient place, such as a hotel suite. The retired judge usually conducts the trial in an informal manner, without the concern for procedure shown in public trials. The case is decided by application of the relevant state law. The judge's final decision is, furthermore, registered with the state court and has the full effect of a decision in a public court.

Critics say that "rent-a-judge" is unfair to the poor because only the rich can use it. Proponents say that everyone benefits: People who rent judges benefit from a speedy trial, and others benefit indirectly from relieving the congestion in the public courts. Notice that renting a judge changes judicial motivation. Suppose you were a retired judge who decided to participate in a rent-a-judge program. In your former role as a public judge, you were supposed to be "independent." That is, the income that you enjoyed as a public judge was unrelated to how you decided cases. Now that has changed. Your income is directly determined by how often you are "rented." To be rented, you must be chosen by both parties to a potential dispute.

QUESTION 11.14: In what ways do you think a "rent-a-judge" who sought to maximize income might decide cases differently from an independent public judge?

---

[22] A more detailed discussion of this actual case, including its psychological dimension, is in Robert Cooter, *Adapt or Optimize: Psychology and Economics of Evidence Law*, in GERD GIGERENZER & CHRISTOPH ENGEL, EDS, HEURISTICS AND THE LAW (2006).

[23] Preliminary research by Louis Kaplow is exploring this connection. Here is an example of the kind of clever argument that he has made: Increasing the burden of proof or the standard of proof results in more wrongdoers escaping the sanctions that they deserve. It also results in more rightdoers escaping sanctions that they did *not* deserve. The optimal burden of proof trades off the social cost from less deterrence of wrongdoing and the social benefit from less deterring of rightdoing. Instead of merely lowering the burden of proof, however, suppose the authorities also increase the sanction for wrongdoing. The authorities could increase the sanction just enough to hold the level of wrongdoing constant. However, the amount of rightdoing might remain higher, thus producing a net social gain. If high sanctions are cheap, then net social benefits are maximized by a high burden and a high standard of proof, and a severe sanction.

QUESTION 11.15:   Rules of evidence can change behavior, as shown by this example used by philosophers. Forty percent of the buses in a town are operated by the Red Bus Company, and 60 percent are operated by the Blue Bus Company. A bus unknowingly injures a bicyclist at night and the victim sues the Blue Bus Company. An eyewitness testifies that he saw a bus hit the bicyclist, but darkness prevented him from telling whether the bus was red or blue. If recovery on the probabilities is not allowed by the court, what will be the effect on incentives for precaution by the bus companies? If recovery on the probabilities is allowed, what will be the effect on the Red Bus Company's incentives to merge with the Blue Bus Company?

QUESTION 11.16:   Assume that you are one of the people contemplating "crashing the gate" at the rock concert as described previously. Are you more likely to be deterred if the court accepts or rejects probabilistic reasoning? If the court accepts probabilistic reasoning and you are not deterred, would you rather crash the gate alone or recruit others to join you?

QUESTION 11.17:   The probability of flipping a coin two times and getting all heads is $.5^2 = .25$. Suppose that liability in a tort case requires the plaintiff to prove that the defendant caused the injury and that the defendant's behavior was negligent. The plaintiff presents evidence proving each proposition with probability .7. Thus, the probability that both propositions are true equals $.7^2 = .49$. Apparently, the preponderance of the evidence supports each proposition separately but not jointly. How should the court decide the case?

II. An Empirical Assessment of the Legal Process

Does the legal system minimize the sum of administrative costs and error costs? We developed some theories relevant to this question by analyzing the stages of the litigation process. Now we turn to the relevant empirical research, beginning with some basic facts about the United States.

In 2009 in the federal judiciary there were almost 260,000 civil complaints filed, about 240,000 civil cases terminated, and just over 300,000 civil cases pending. These figures represent a 5 percent increase in filings over those in 2008, a 0.2 percent increase in terminations over those in 2008, and a 7.1 percent increase in civil cases pending over those in 2008.[24] With respect to federal criminal cases filed, terminated, and pending in

---

[24] There are some terms of art in this section that bear comment. A "legal complaint" is a submission to a court asking for adjudication of a grievance or resolution of an allegation of criminal conduct. The legal system then "disposes" of the complaints submitted to it in a variety of different ways. Some complaints are dropped; some are resolved by settlement bargaining among the parties; some are resolved by pretrial motions and summary judgment; some are dismissed; some are pending (that is, awaiting resolution); some are in the process of being transferred to other courts; and some go to trial for litigation to a judgment. In the ideal world, 100 legal complaints result in 100 dispositions. As we will shortly see, of those 100 complaints somewhere between 3 and 5 of them result in trial. The vast majority of legal complaints are disposed of by means other than trial.

2009 the figures are 75,000 filed, 74,000 terminated, and about 74,000 pending. Those are increases of 7.9, 9.3, and 0.8 percent over comparable figures for 2008.

The figures for civil and criminal complaints, terminations, and pending cases in state courts are not readily available for 2009 on a national basis. Rather, there are 50 separate state court reports, typically for earlier years. We know, on the basis of past comparisons, that the state courts deal with many more civil and criminal legal disputes in any given year than do the federal courts. To illustrate, note that in 2008 the courts in the State of Illinois alone had more than 750,000 civil filings (almost three times the total number of civil complaints in all federal courts in 2009).[25]

How were these cases disposed of? We have good figures for the disposition of legal complaints for cases in the federal courts and good reasons for believing that the figures for dispositions of complaints filed in state courts follow a similar pattern. The last time that we had comparable figures for both sets of courts was in 2000, and we have good reason for believing that the ratios are the same today as they were then. In 2000 we know that the federal courts disposed of almost 260,000 civil cases. Of that total slightly less than 2 percent were disposed of by means of a trial. (Only about 3100 or 1.2 percent of those cases were tried to a jury verdict, and about 1500 or 0.6 percent resulted in a bench verdict.) So, the federal courts disposed of 98.2 percent of the civil complaints in some other way. More than half (53.3 percent) were dismissed for lack of jurisdiction, voluntary dismissals, settlements, or other causes of dismissal. About 20 percent (18.5 percent) were transferred to another court for further proceedings, remanded to state courts, resulted in judgments on an award by arbitrators, fresh trials following arbitral judgments, or other judgments. Another 13 percent were resolved through pretrial motions, and slightly more than 8 percent were disposed of by default judgments.[26]

What about the trend over time? Total dispositions of all criminal and civil disputes in the U.S. state and federal courts increased by a factor of three between 1981 and 1992, but have fallen significantly since then. The long-term pattern of civil disputes resolved by trial during the twentieth century has been one of slow, steady increase through the first half of the century, followed by a slow (and then accelerating) turn away from litigation, a trend that continues through the early twenty-first century. Contract disputes have, until recently, been far more numerous than any other kinds of civil disputes in the courts. Beginning sometime in the mid-1990s, however, tort disputes surpassed contract disputes as the leading form of civil litigation. The number of property disputes is far behind both tort and contract disputes.

---

[25] In 2002 there was a total of 20 million civil complaints filed in all federal and state courts, of which approximately 250,000 were filed in all federal district courts. So, as a rough approximation, there are about 80 times as many civil complaints filed in state as in federal courts. That is, about 98 percent of all civil complaints are filed in state courts. A slightly higher percentage of all criminal complaints is filed in state courts.

[26] A "default judgment" occurs when one of the parties fails to appear or contest the complaint, so that the other party wins "by default." The remaining (roughly) 5 percent of dispositions are either not recorded or were pending resolution. The figures come from Chris Guthrie, *Procedural Justice Research and the Paucity of Trials,* J. DISP. RES. 127 (2002). Guthrie notes that approximately 35 percent of legal complaints are resolved by means of pretrial motions or summary judgment.

A. Lawyers

Giving legal advice, filing legal complaints, and disposing of them requires lawyers. Different countries have substantially different numbers of lawyers per capita. The American Bar Association estimated in 2005 that there were 1.1 million lawyers in the United States, or one lawyer for every 275 people. (In 2009 the figure was 1.2 million, or one lawyer for every 260 people.) For comparison, Germany in 2005 had one lawyer for every 622 people, the United Kingdom had one lawyer for every 496 people, and Japan had one lawyer for every 5,800 people.[27]

Is having more lawyers per capita a good thing? Most lawyers are "transaction cost engineers"—to use Ron Gilson's phrase[28]—who mostly remove impediments to cooperation among private parties (as we argued in Chapter 4's Normative Coase Theorem). Without them, people would have more difficulty establishing businesses organizations, hiring employees, setting up trusts, or dissolving marriages, to name a few activities requiring legal support for cooperation.[29] Legal education and the bar should ideally supply competent lawyers without artificially constraining their numbers or controlling prices. In these conditions of fair competition, the people who hire lawyers are the best ones to judge their own needs for legal services. Unfortunately, everywhere the history of the bar is a story of constrained supply and monopoly practices. Recent U.S. history, fortunately, is a new story of overcoming some of these constraints and dismantling some monopoly practices, especially by allowing lawyers to advertise their services in various ways.

B. Trials

In this section we consider three topics regarding trials—their costs, which disputes go to trial and who wins, and what explains the fact that trials are becoming increasingly rare.

1. The Costs of Trials   No one is sure of the total or average costs of all civil disputes in the United States, but we do know something about the costs of various parts of the trial process.[30] For example, we know something about "filing fees," the cost of asking a court to resolve a dispute. Those fees differ according to the jurisdiction and the amount in controversy. In Cook County, Illinois—that is, Chicago—the cost to

---

[27] In 2005 Germany had approximately 130,000 lawyers in a total population of 82.5 million, in 2004 the United Kingdom had 121,000 lawyers in a total population of 60.2 million, and in 2005 Japan had 22,000 lawyers in a total population of 128 million. Japan has recently embarked on a reform of its legal education system to increase the number of lawyers.

[28] Ronald Gilson, *Value Creation by Business Lawyers: Legal Skills and Asset Pricing*, 94 YALE L. J. 239, 301–2 (1984).

[29] Some empirical evidence suggests a positive causal relationship between the number of lawyers per capita and a nation's growth rate, which is consistent with the proposition that lawyers are principally transaction cost engineers. See Frank B. Cross, *The First Thing We Do, Let's Kill All the Economists: An Empirical Evaluation of the Effects of Lawyers on the United States Economy and Political System*, 70 TEX. L. REV. 645, 689 (1992).

[30] Charles Silver, *Does Civil Justice Cost Too Much?*, 80 TEX. L. REV. 2073 (2002).

initiate a civil action is scaled according to the stakes at issue in the action: $244 if the controversy involves less than $15,000, and $114 if under $250. In Champaign County, Illinois, the fees are not scaled by the size of the controversy; they are a flat $215. But there are additional charges for such matters as appearance fees; confession of judgment and Law Library fees; counterclaim, third-party action, and contribution fees; jury fees (depending on whether the size of the jury is 6 or 12 persons); garnishment-of-wages fees; fees for issuing a summons; and more.[31] These costs for a routine civil action can mount into the thousands of dollars quickly.

We also have cost figures on pretrial discovery. The Civil Litigation Research Project examined about 1600 cases from federal and state courts and found that there was no discovery in more than half of those cases. Where there was discovery, there were no more than five "discovery events." A RAND study concluded, "Discovery is not a pervasive litigation cost problem for the majority of cases. The empirical data show that any problems that may exist with discovery are concentrated in a minority of the cases."[32] That same RAND study found that discovery typically consumes "about one-fourth to one-third of total lawyer work hours per litigant. Discovery accounted for less than half the lawyer work hours in all the subsets of general civil cases that we examined." The amount of discovery tends to increase with the stakes in the trial, but even when the stakes were more than $500,000, discovery rarely accounted for more than 30 percent of the lawyers' work hours on the case. Lawyer hours are the biggest component of litigation costs.

Charles Silver concluded that about 3 percent of legal complaints are resolved by trial and 97 percent are settled out of court (or resolved in some other manner). By comparison to litigation, settlement is much cheaper. Samuel Gross and Kent Syverud found that a typical trial lasted nine days, and a typical negotiation to resolve a similar matter lasted nine hours.[33]

We can use these numbers to make back-of-the-envelope estimates of the cost of each. An American trial usually involves a prosecutor, or plaintiff and his lawyer, a defendant and his lawyer, a judge, a 12-person jury, a court stenographer, and a court guard. There are usually witnesses—one testifying and others waiting to testify. That adds up to roughly 20 people, whose labor or opportunity costs vary widely. Lawyers may bill their trial time at $250 per hour, so that an hour of a trial costs $500 in lawyers' fees. (That does not include any time outside of court preparing for trial.) If the trial takes four hours per day, then the trial cost of the lawyers is $2000 per day. The judge is paid on an annual basis whether there are trials or not. Nonetheless, let us impute to the judge's time a figure comparable to that of the lawyers ($250 per hour) and assume that the cost of the judge's time is $1000 per day of trial. Jurors are usually compensated at a rate of something like $10 per day, which is far below the opportunity cost of their time.

---

[31] In more rural counties of Illinois those filing fees are less. For example, in relatively sparsely populated Monroe County in the southwestern portion of Illinois, the filing cost for a civil action is $173.

[32] Silver, supra n. 30, at 2095.

[33] See Samuel Gross & Kent Syverud, *Getting to No: A Study of Settlement Negotiations and the Selection of Cases for Trial,* 90 MICH. L. REV. 319 (1991).

There are usually 12 of them (although not all civil trials are jury trials) for a total cost of $120 per day. If we estimate the average value of the labor of the additional participants at, say, $40 per hour, then the labor value of the additional five participants amounts to $200 per hour or $800 per day of trial. That gives us a total social cost per day of trial equal to slightly less than $4000.

Now we convert these daily costs into costs per trial. If we use the estimate that a civil trial takes nine days on average (as Gross and Syverud found), then the total social cost of the average civil trial would be $36,000.

These numbers underestimate the social cost of trials because they exclude the time spent preparing for trial, the cost of the administrative and support staff for the judge and the lawyers, the opportunity cost of the time spent by the jury and witnesses, and the implicit rental value of the court room.

On the other side of the ledger, we have not attempted to estimate the social benefits of trial, which include the benefit to the private parties of resolving their dispute, setting a baseline for bargaining in the cases that settle without a trial, deterring wrongdoing and harm by potential defendants, and improving laws by the evolution of new precedents. In any case, full trials are not worthwhile socially unless the stakes are substantial. This fact provides an incentive to avoid trials by alternative resolution of disputes, or to simplify trials as in small claims courts.

2. The Selection Effect and the 50-Percent Rule

Earlier in this chapter we developed a theory of how a rational party would decide between litigation and settlement. We concluded that the major cause of trials is relative optimism—each side expects to do better at trial than the other side believes it will do. Put differently, the major cause of trials is the parties' private information that makes them disagree about the trial's likely outcome. As a result, disputes that result in trials rather than settlements must have characteristics that produce relative optimism. The disputes that go to trial are a biased set of all disputes with respect to the characteristics that cause expectations to diverge. Because of this "selection effect," the distribution of characteristics of disputes resolved by trial differs from the distribution of characteristics of all disputes.

In 1984 George Priest and Benjamin Klein published an influential paper on these matters.[34] They conjectured that each party is equally likely to make the mistake resulting in false optimism that causes a trial. Because each party is equally likely to be mistaken, they inferred that each party is equally likely to win at trial. Moreover, where both parties agree that the likelihood of a plaintiff victory is relatively high or that a defendant victory is relatively high, the parties are likely to settle. On average, the likelihood that plaintiffs will win at trial is, consequently, the same as the probability that the defendant will win, approximately 50 percent.

If each party is equally likely to be mistaken, does it follow that each party is equally likely to "win," as this word is understood in legal disputes? We need to look carefully at whether theory justifies this strikingly simple conclusion. At trial, a "win" for the plaintiff

---

[34] George L. Priest & Benjamin Klein, *The Selection of Disputes for Litigation,* 13 J. LEGAL STUD. 1 (1984). Priest and Klein also held that there is no simple set of characteristics that distinguishes litigated from settled cases.

usually means that the court awards damages to the plaintiff. There is no reason why the plaintiff should win half of the time by this definition. To see why, consider that the defendant in many disputes concedes liability and contests damages. Thus, the defendant may concede that his negligence caused a dent in the plaintiff's car but denies that his negligence caused the broken headlight. In these circumstances, the definition of a plaintiff "win" at trial cannot mean that the plaintiff wins *something,* which occurs with 100 percent certainty. Rather, the definition of a plaintiff "win" must mean something like "the court awards the plaintiff higher damages than the defendant expected to pay."[35]

Another possible definition of "winning" occurs in the symmetrically opposite case, where the defendant concedes damages and contests liability. To illustrate, assume that the defendant concedes the plaintiff's claim that damages equal $1000 but vigorously contests that he is responsible for those damages.

Steve Shavell has argued that the Priest-Klein prediction makes very special assumptions—namely, that the "parties obtain very accurate information about trial outcomes" and the "information that each receives is statistically identical." Shavell notes that these assumptions rule out such likely situations as one or both parties' not having accurate information about trial outcomes or one party's having "substantially superior information to the other." As a result, Shavell shows that "it is possible for the cases that go to trial to result in plaintiff victory with any probability. Moreover, given any probability of plaintiff victory at trial, the probability of plaintiff victory among settled cases (had they been tried) may be any other probability."[36] So, the case for 50 percent victory by plaintiffs at trial is weak in theory.

The question remains whether the 50 percent rule is true in fact. Perloff and Rubinfeld examined antitrust cases in the late 1970s and early and mid-1980s and found that defendants won about 70 percent of those cases.[37] Donald Wittman examined a sample of rear-end automobile collision cases in California and concluded that the data set did not confirm the 50 percent rule.[38] Theodore Eisenberg found that plaintiff win rates were approximately 50 percent in products liability cases but were less than 40 percent for medical malpractice cases in federal court.[39] Jeremy Waldfogel

---

[35] In civil law systems of Europe, where the loser pays the winner's legal costs, the defendant in such a case will have to pay the plaintiff's legal costs if the court's judgment exceeds the defendant's settlement offer.

[36] Consideration of differences in the costs of litigation to the two parties further undermines the 50 percent rule. Steven Shavell, *Any Frequency of Plaintiff Victory at Trial Is Possible,* 25 J. LEGAL STUD. 493 (1996).

[37] Jeffrey Perloff & Daniel Rubinfeld, *Settlement in Private Antitrust Litigation,* in STEVEN SALOP & LAWRENCE WHITE, EDS., PRIVATE ANTITRUST LITIGATION (1987). See also Perloff, Rubinfeld, & Paul Ruud, *Antitrust Settlement and Trial Outcomes,* 78 REV. ECON. & STAT. 401 (1996).

[38] Donald Wittman, *Is the Selection of Cases for Trial Biased?,* 14 J. LEGAL STUD. 185 (1985). George Priest responded by examining a set of rear-end auto collision cases in Cook County, Illinois, and found support for the 50 percent rule in that data set.

[39] See Theodore Eisenberg, *Testing the Selection Effect: A New Theoretical Framework with Empirical Tests,* 9 J. LEGAL STUD. 337, 349 (1990). "The 50 percent hypothesis may be rejected while the basic selection effect is retained." In a later study with Kevin Clermont, Eisenberg found the somewhat puzzling result that plaintiff win rates were substantially higher when the dispute was tried to a judge rather than to a jury, which is puzzling because they choose to try their complaint before a jury in 90 percent of all cases. Kevin Clermont & Theodore Eisenberg, *Trial by Jury or Judge: Transcending Empiricism,* 77 CORNELL L. REV. 1124 (1992).

tested the 50 percent rule for a selection of contracts, intellectual property, and tort cases from the mid-1980s from the Southern District of New York. He found that when relatively few cases within a category go to trial, the plaintiff win rate tends to be close to 50 percent. When the trial rate increases, however, plaintiff success rates diverge from 50 percent—in some instances higher and in others, lower.[40]

Finally, Kessler, Meites, and Miller, focusing on appellate cases rather than those from trial courts, sought through regression analysis of more than 3000 cases to find causes for deviations from the 50 percent rule. Taking into consideration differences in stakes, information, settlement, and litigation costs, and four other dispute-specific characteristics, they found that these characteristics affect win rates in statistically significant ways. Furthermore, these effects are consistent with predictions by the models in this and the preceding chapter.[41]

So, the empirical evidence on the 50 percent rule is mixed: Some studies find it to be borne out by the evidence; others suggest that it is not; some find the rule to be true only in certain kinds of disputes but not true in other kinds of disputes; and some find that the evidence supports the hypothesis but only in the restrictive circumstances in which Priest and Klein suggested that it would hold.

3. Vanishing Trials?   The United States has a reputation as a highly litigious society, but that view is not consistent with the facts that less than 5 percent of legal disputes are resolved by trial and that civil trials have declined in the United States over the last 40 years. That is the heart of an important article by Professor Marc Galanter.[42] Galanter shows that even though the total number of dispositions of disputes has increased by fivefold between 1962 and 2002, the number of civil trials in all courts in the United States in 2002 was more than 20 percent lower than in 1962. Not lower per capita—relative to the number of people in the United States—but lower in absolute numbers. Disposition of disputes by trial in 2002 "was less than one-sixth of what it was in 1962—1.8 percent, as opposed to 11.5 percent in 1962." The decline in trials is recent and steep, not slow and steady over the course of the 40-year period. In fact, the number of civil trials in federal courts increased from 1962 to 1985 and then dropped by more than 40 percent from 1985 to 2002.[43] At the same time as the number of civil trials has been falling, the percentage of trials that are before juries, rather than bench trials, has been increasing. By 2002 two-thirds of all civil trials were jury trials.[44] Since

---

[40] Joel Waldfogel, *The Selection Hypothesis and the Relationship between Trial and Plaintiff Victory,* 103 J. POL. ECON. 229 (1995).

[41] Daniel Kessler, Thomas Meites, & Geoffrey Miller, *Explaining Deviations from the Fifty-Percent Rule: A Multimodal Approach to the Selection of Cases for Litigation,* 25 J. LEGAL STUD. 233 (1996).

[42] Marc Galanter, *The Vanishing Trial: An Examination of Trials and Related Matters in Federal and State Courts,* 1 J. EMP. LEGAL STUD. 459 (2004). That issue of the *Journal* also contained responses to Galanter's article by a distinguished group of legal scholars.

[43] Galanter says that the trends in state courts, where, recall, almost 98 percent of all litigation takes place, reflect those in the federal courts.

[44] It is not clear that these same trends with respect to bench and jury trials are true for the reduced number of state court trials over the 1962–2002 period.

Forum Shopping

Lawyers frequently have a choice about where to file a complaint—a decision called "forum shopping." Thus, the plaintiff may search for the most favorable jurisdiction to file a complaint, and the defendant may respond by requesting removal of the case from the state court for decision in a federal court. (The defendant can ask for such a change when the plaintiff and defendant reside in different states.) Forum shopping has increased significantly over the last 30 years. In 1970, 15 percent of state court cases were removed to federal courts, presumably by defendants who asked for removal after plaintiffs filed their complaints. In 2000, more than 30 percent of state court cases were removed to federal courts.

As a theoretical matter, it is not clear whether forum shopping is efficient. If litigants can choose among jurisdictions in deciding where to have a trial, then that may create an incentive for jurisdictions to compete among themselves in the provision of better litigation services. They may, for instance, offer clearer substantive law, more rapid decisions, and specialized services. Delaware, according to this theory, has made itself a particularly attractive venue in which to try matters of corporate law. But this jurisdictional competition may have a dark side, too. States might compete not by offering better justice but by promising cheaper justice or justice tailored to noncorporate clients or for corporate clients. Some jurisdictions, for instance, have in the past decade or so become famous as venues friendly to plaintiffs. It is not yet clear whether, on balance, forum shopping is a good thing (a "race to the top") or a bad thing (a "race to the bottom").[45]

Why has there been an increase in forum shopping? Kevin Clermont and Ted Eisenberg examined more than 3000 cases in which diversity of citizenship would have allowed the plaintiff to file the complaint in the plaintiff's state, the defendant's state, or federal court.[46] They reasoned that the plaintiff would seek out a plaintiff-friendly jurisdiction in which to file suit, and the defendant would seek to remove the case to a more defendant-friendly jurisdiction. Consequently, Clermont and Eisenberg predicted that the plaintiff would be more likely to win those cases that remained in the jurisdiction originally selected by the plaintiff, than in those cases in which the defendant successfully removed the dispute to a federal court. And that is precisely what they found. Plaintiffs were successful in just over 70 percent of all the cases, but in only 34 percent of those removed to federal court. An important implication of this study is that the initial ability to shop for a forum favors the plaintiff, and the ability to remove the case to a federal court favors the defendant.

1962 the number of bench trials has fallen by almost 50 percent, and the number of jury trials has increased by almost 9 percent.

The change in the types of litigation has also been significant. For instance, in 1962 tort cases made up 55 percent of all civil trials and 81 percent of all civil jury trials. By 2002 torts had dropped to just 23.4 percent of all civil trials and 26 percent of all civil jury trials. By contrast, in 1962 contract disputes made up almost 20 percent of all civil trials. Almost 75 percent of those trials were tried before a judge without a jury.

---

[45] See Daniel Kessler & Daniel Rubinfeld, *An Empirical Study of the Civil Justice System*, in A. MITCHELL POLINSKY & STEVEN SHAVELL, EDS., HANDBOOK OF LAW AND ECONOMICS, V. 1 (2007).

[46] Kevin Clermont & Theodore Eisenberg, *Litigation Realities*, 88 CORNELL L. REV. 119 (2002).

In 2002 contracts counted for about 15 percent of all civil trials with 53 percent of them tried to a jury. In the 1980s there were more contract than tort cases filed in the federal courts. Taken together, contract plus tort trials fell from being 74 percent of all civil trials in 1962 to being 38 percent in 2002. What trials took their place?

In 1962 civil rights trials accounted for less than 1 percent of all civil trials. In 2002 they accounted for 33 percent of all trials and for 41 percent of all jury trials. Among other controversies, the two categories that stand out are labor cases and IP cases. The same overall trends apply to them—namely, a rise and then a recent fall in the number of trials; an ever-decreasing percentage of dispositions by trial; and a shift from a small to a substantial portion of jury trials.

Do the same trends apply to criminal trials? The short answer is, "Yes." Criminal caseload in the federal courts has risen from 33,110 in 1962 to 76,827 in 2002, and then to about 75,000 in 2009, about half the rate of increase on the civil side. Today there is a smaller percentage of criminal dispositions by trial—less than 5 percent in 2002 compared with 15 percent in 1962. The absolute number of criminal trials has diminished by 30 percent between 1962 and 2002.

One possible explanation for the decline in criminal trials is the implementation of determinate sentencing in the federal courts. The sentencing guidelines offer an incentive to avoid trial in the form of a criminal offense level reduction for "acceptance of responsibility." Since implementation of the guidelines in November, 1987, the number of criminal trials has declined. From 1962 to 1991 the percentage of trials in criminal cases was relatively steady between 13 and 15 percent. However, since 1991 the percentage of trials in criminal cases has steadily decreased (with the exception of a 0.06 percent increase in 2001) from 12.6 percent in 1991 to less than 4.7 percent in 2002. As we shall see in Chapter 13, this decline is consistent with the significant decline in the number of crimes in the United States that began in the early 1990s.

Why has there been this dramatic decline in the number of trials? Galanter canvases a wide variety of possible explanations. For example, he rejects the possibilities that there has been some significant change in procedural law, that class actions have replaced individual causes of action, and that there is a dearth of judges to hear cases.[47]

There are three related explanations for the phenomenon that deserve further study. First, the relative cost of trials may have increased significantly (perhaps because controversies have become more complex, requiring more lawyering, more specialized lawyers, more expert witnesses, more jury consultants, and so on).

Second, this increase in relative costs might induce disputants to substitute away from trials and toward alternative methods of dispute resolution. In one of our earlier Web Notes we have shown that one of the attractions of arbitration and mediation is that it is much cheaper and less time-consuming than litigation. Even so, there is some casual evidence to suggest that the rise in ADR has not been sufficient to replace the large number of "vanished trials." We know that ADR increased significantly in the 1990s but probably not by enough to account for the 300,000 contracts cases that have "disappeared" from the federal courts since the 1980s. As late as 1992 arbitration

---

[47] See our website for more information on Galanter's article.

accounted for only 1.7 percent of contract dispositions and 3.5 percent of tort dispositions in the state courts in the nation's 75 largest counties.

Third, it might be the case that there are fewer trials because there are fewer disputes and that there are fewer disputes because there is better lawyering today that was the case in the past. If lawyers, acting as transaction cost engineers, have grown increasingly sophisticated at anticipating problems and either providing for their peaceful resolution *ex ante*, urging their clients to take more precaution so as to reduce the likelihood of injury, or more successfully negotiating solutions, then lawyers deserve some credit for the vanishing trial. There is some casual evidence against this proposition. Recall that dispositions increased fivefold between 1962 and 2002. The population of the United States increased from approximately 187 million in 1962 to 310 million in 2010. So, disputes per capita increased significantly over the period. But that could have been due to the increasing complexity of individual and economic life. There needs to be much more empirical work on this possible explanation before we dismiss the possibility that better lawyering is responsible for the vanishing trial.

C. Appeals

Sometimes the judgment in a trial is not the end of the story. One of the parties—even the winner—may feel that the trial court erred and that the result was unjust or inadequate. As a matter of right in the common law system, either party may appeal the trial court judgment to a higher court.[48]

An appeal is costly. The filing fees for docketing an appeal in the federal courts is $450 per party. There are additional fees for certifying the results and the record from the court below, for reproducing records from the trial court, certifying documents, and so on—all of which can add hundreds of dollars to the costs of appeal. Because appellate litigation is a specialty among attorneys, the hourly costs of hiring a lawyer to pursue an appeal are almost certainly higher—and possibly much higher—than the lawyers' fees for the original trial. For instance, in a contingent fee arrangement it is customary for the plaintiff's lawyer to receive 33 percent of an award at the trial court and 40 percent if the matter goes to an appeal and is successful. The higher percentage awarded the successful attorney at the appellate level suggests that there is more intense lawyering involved in an appeal.[49]

The economic theory of bringing an appeal is analogous to the decision to proceed to trial but with the cost difference noted above. However, for an appellate court to grant a "leave to appeal," there must be an error of law in the proceedings at the trial court. Because lawyers and trial court judges know this and because trial court judges are generally competent, there are relatively few errors of law that would warrant the costs of appeal. We can predict that these errors are so rare (and the additional costs of appeal so high) that the vast majority of trial judgments will not be appealed. And the statistics bear this out.

---

[48] See the discussion of the appellate process in Chapter 3.

[49] There are no new witnesses or evidence to be presented in an appeal; so, filing and lawyers' fees are the principal expenses to the appellant and appellee.

We can begin to get a glimpse of the work of appellate courts by looking at some recent trends in appellate caseload for the State of Illinois and the federal judiciary. The table below gives important statistics on cases filed in circuit courts (the trial courts) and the appellate courts of Illinois between 2001 and 2005.

Year	Total Circuit Filings	Civil Circuit Filings	Appellate Filings	% of cases appealed
2004	4,240,300	685,557	8,060	0.0020
2005	4,213,700	672,731	8,153	0.0020
2006	4,220,121	706,836	7,838	0.0019
2007	4,455,546	773,204	7,631	0.0017
2008	4,305,551	753,569	7,630	0.0018

Note: The total caseload includes traffic, felony, dissolution of marriage, chancery, and other categories.

It is striking that such a small percentage—one-fifth of 1 percent—of all cases is appealed. Approximately half of all appeals are on criminal matters, and approximately half on civil issues.

Comparable figures on appeals for the federal judiciary come from the Administrative Office of the United States Courts for fiscal year ending September 30, 2009. The figures indicate that in the prior year the 13 federal Circuit Courts of Appeal dealt with 57,740 filings. During that same year, the U.S. District Courts dealt with a total of approximately 276,000 civil filings and 87,000 criminal filings for a total of 365,000 filings in 2009.

As a result, the rate of appeal in federal courts was approximately 16 percent, a much higher rate than was the case for the State of Illinois.

Is the rate of appeal too high or too low? Recall that in the United States, the trial court decides matters of fact and the appeals court decides matters of law. A decision about the law can lead to a new precedent, which is a new legal rule. The effects of a new precedent spill far beyond the litigants in the case in which the precedent is set. The litigants, consequently, internalize a small proportion of the value of a new precedent that resolves their dispute. Because appeals lead to changes in the rule that benefit many people, perhaps the judges should be able to pay more of the litigation costs of the parties when an appeal results in a new precedent. Thus, the full cost should be assigned at the trial level to all cases, not a fraction of the cost as is the usual practice, but a successful appeals that results in new precedents should be subsidized by the state.

Conclusion

Is the legal process a sharp instrument for deciding cases according to the law and the facts, or is it an unwieldy instrument to burden litigation with high costs that profit lawyers? The answer is complicated, like the architecture of an ancient building built and rebuilt over centuries. A combination of economic theory and facts suggests that the basic logic of the legal system serves to reduce injustice and errors, but a powerful legal profession has also influenced the rules to its own advantage.

Suggested Readings

Cooter, Robert, *Structural Adjudication and the New Law Merchant: A Model of Decentralized Law,* 14 INT. REV. LAW & ECON. 215 (1994).

Ginsburg, Tom, & Glenn Hoetker, *The Unreluctant Litigant?: An Empirical Analysis of Japan's Turn to Litigation,* 35 J. LEGAL STUD. 31 (2006).

Posner, Richard A., FRONTIERS OF LEGAL THEORY, Chs. 10 ("Testimony"), 11 ("The Principles of Evidence and the Critique of the Adversarial Process"), and 12 ("The Rules of Evidence") (2001).

Posner, Richard A., *What Do Judges and Justices Maximize? (The Same Thing Everyone Else Does),* 3 SUP. CT. ECON. REV. (1993).

Spier, Kathryn, *Tied to the Mast: Most-Favored-Nation Clauses in Settlement Contracts,* 32 J. LEGAL STUD. 91 (2003).

12 An Economic Theory of Crime and Punishment

The true measure of crimes is the harm done to society.

CESARE BECCARIA,
ON CRIMES AND PUNISHMENT 64 (1764)

ANY THEORY OF crime must answer two questions: "What acts should be punished?" and "To what extent?" The first question asks for the distinguishing criteria of a crime, and the second question asks to calibrate punishments. In the next two chapters we will develop an economic theory of crime, contrast it with a particular moral theory, and discuss some implications and empirical findings of that economic theory. The economic theory, we argue, gives more convincing and precise answers to these two general questions.

Instead of seeing crime as a challenge to theory, however, most people see crime as a threat to life and property. In the United States, crime directly affects nearly one in three households each year. Inconsistencies in crime reports make international comparisons difficult, but, compared to the United States, violent crime is apparently more frequent in Latin America and Africa, less frequent in Europe and Japan, and probably less frequent in China and India.[1] The rates of theft are apparently similar in the United States and Europe, but the rates are substantially lower in Japan and Korea. Crime, which once seemed rare to many people, is pervasive in many countries. As a result, people argue passionately for reforms to make punishment more certain, swift, and severe. Conversely, people argue equally passionately that more punishment will victimize some people without reducing crime. When U.S. crime rates subsided recently, the proponents of harsh punishments claimed credit for the improvement, whereas their opponents claim that the decline in crime is attributable to other factors and another reason to get rid of harsh punishments.

To advance these disputes, the next two chapters use economic theory to define crimes, distinguish them from civil wrongs, develop models of behavior by criminals and police, examine statistics on crime rates, and survey such important issues as capital punishment, handgun control, illegal drugs, and the deterrent effect of criminal sanctions. Here are some examples of particular issues in criminal law that we will address:

Example 1: Jim Bloggs is convicted of assault for striking and breaking the nose of Joe Potatoes. As punishment, the judge has discretion to choose a stiff fine or a short jail sentence. If the judge believes that each punishment would deter future crime equally, which punishment should the judge use?

---

[1] See ROBERT COOTER AND HANS BERND SCHAEFER, SOLOMON'S KNOT Ch. 11 (2011).

Example 2: Bloggs is sentenced to jail, but the jail is full and the jailer cannot legally add any more inmates. The state could build another jail or release some current inmates to make room for Bloggs. Which response will lead to the right amount of deterrence of criminals and minimize the social costs of crime?

Example 3: A thief shatters a car window costing $100 and steals a radio worth $75. Is the social cost of the crime $175 (the victim's loss), $100 (the victim's loss minus the injurer's gain), or some other number?

Example 4: Yvonne wishes to increase the security of her home against burglars. She considers three alternatives: (1) install bars on her windows; (2) install a loud burglar alarm; or (3) buy a gun. How will each alternative affect burglaries of her house and of *neighboring* houses? For example, will bars on Yvonne's windows reduce crime in the neighborhood or merely redirect it to other houses? Will an alarm alert neighbors? Will burglars know that she has a gun? Which alternative should the state encourage Yvonne to adopt?

I. The Traditional Theory of Criminal Law

The economic theory of torts in Chapter 6 distinguished between the harm caused by accidents and the cost of preventing it. Law should ideally minimize the sum of the costs of accidental harm and preventing it, thus yielding the "optimal number of accidents." Similarly, the economic theory of crimes distinguishes between the harm caused by crime and the cost of preventing it. Law should minimize the sum of the costs of crime and its prevention, which yields the "optimal amount of crime." This language sounds odd, but it helps answer the two primary questions of a theory of crime: What acts should be punished and to what extent? The central strand of economic analysis focuses on social costs, whose simple measure equals the sum of the cost of the harm from crime and its prevention. An act should be treated as a crime and punished if doing so reduces social costs. The severity of the punishment should be calibrated to minimize social costs.

These answers place the economic theory of crime in the long tradition of utilitarian thought. This tradition contrasts with a moral theory of crime called "retributivism," which gives different answers to the two primary questions of a theory of crime. According to retributivism, criminal law and policy should do what is morally right, regardless of whether doing so minimizes social costs. The right thing to do is to punish people who commit crimes by intentionally harming others, and the wrong thing to do is to punish people who are innocent. Punishment's extent should be proportional to the seriousness of the crime, or to how morally wrong it is. Disproportionate punishment is wrong, even if it reduces social costs.[2]

The usual way that philosophers contrast utilitarian and retributivist theories is by posing hypothetical examples that pit one against the other in a kind of mental tug-of-war. If you could only imprison one person for life, would you choose the one whose

---

[2] See the book by Michael S. Moore noted at the conclusion of this chapter for the best modern statement of retributivism.

imprisonment would prevent the most harm, such as deterring murders, as suggested by utilitarianism? Or would you imprison the person who committed the worst crime, such as the most heinous murder, as suggested by retributivism? Or suppose that prisoner *A* committed a horrible murder and would never harm anyone again (he's too weak and repentant), whereas prisoner *B* committed manslaughter and would commit crimes again if released (he's strong, hot-tempered, and unrepentant). Would you parole person *A* as suggested by utilitarianism, or would you parole *B* as suggested by retributivism?

Pursued to their logical extremes, utilitarianism and retributivism yield puzzles and paradoxes. Instead of exploring those, we develop the economic theory of crime and apply it to practical questions of criminal law and policy.

In England much of the criminal law was originally part of the common law, but over many decades criminal statutes replaced the common law of crimes. In common law and civil law countries, criminal law is now codified in statutes. This body of law embodies what we might call a traditional theory of crimes, according to which criminal law differs from civil law by the following characteristics:

1. The criminal *intended* to do wrong, whereas some civil wrongs are accidental.
2. The harm done by the criminal was public as well as private.
3. The plaintiff is the state, not a private individual.
4. The plaintiff has a higher standard of proof in a criminal trial than in a civil suit.
5. If the defendant is guilty, then he or she will be punished.

We will describe these characteristics and then show that economic theory provides a useful framework to explain them, whereas retributivism begs the important questions or gives the wrong answers.

Web Note 12.1

The retributivist theory has a long and honorable tradition and deserves further elaboration than we can give it here. On our website, however, we give a much more complete account of retributivism and draw sharper contrasts between that theory and the economic account of crime and punishment.

A. Criminal Intent

A careful driver is not at fault and imposes moderate risk on others, whereas a careless driver is negligent and imposes excessive risk on others. Negligent drivers must compensate those they have harmed. Even careless drivers, however, do not disregard the safety of others or intentionally impose excessive risk on them. A driver who intentionally imposes excessive risk on others is reckless. As we saw in Chapter 7, recklessness can oblige the injurer in some countries to pay punitive damages in addition to compensatory damages.

FIGURE 12.1

Culpability scale.

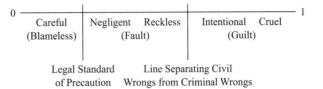

A driver who disregards the safety of others does not intentionally run into some-one. Beyond recklessness lies intentional harm. "Even a dog knows the difference be-tween being stumbled over and kicked," and so does the law. The law makes much over the distinction between accidental and intentional harm. Tort law mostly concerns acci-dental harm, and criminal law mostly concerns intentional harm.

Mens rea (Latin for "a guilty mind") is the legal term for criminal intent. To de-velop this idea of *mens rea,* we must draw the boundary between accidental and inten-tional harm.

Consider the ranking of acts along a continuum in Figure 12.1. Starting at the left side of the scale, the injurer is careful and blameless. Moving to the right, the injurer's behavior becomes negligent, then reckless, and then criminal. Careful behavior is less culpable than negligent behavior; negligent behavior is less culpable than intentional harm. According to this continuum, the line separating fault from *mens rea* lies between recklessness and intentional harm. As actors cross this boundary line, they pass from fault to guilt.

Further gradations in criminal intent are sometimes relevant to determining pun-ishment. To illustrate, harming someone intentionally to gain a personal advantage is not as bad as harming someone cruelly and taking pleasure in the victim's pain. There is, thus, a continuous gradation in the moral evaluation of the actor from blameless on the good end to cruel on the bad end.[3] Developing these distinctions has long engaged philosophers and social scientists. Later in this chapter we will describe some contribu-tions of economists when we distinguish between full and diminished rationality, which relates to the distinction between intentional and unintentional harms.

> **QUESTION 12.1:**   We defined crime as "intentional harm to persons or prop-erty." In communist countries, "crime" was often defined as "socially danger-ous" behavior. Can you relate the difference in definitions to the continuum depicted above?

B. Public Harm and Public Prosecution

Proceeding down our list, the second distinguishing feature of a crime is the nature of the harm. In the areas of the law we have examined to this point—property, contract, and torts—most of the harm has been private. In criminal law much of the harm is public. So, a murder threatens the peace and security of society at large and thus puts others besides the victim in fear for their lives. The great eighteenth-century commentator on

---

[3] We could, of course, extend the line and fill in the gaps with fine distinctions found in criminal law. To il-lustrate, off the scale to the left lie meritorious acts, and off the scale to the right lie sadistic acts.

the laws of England, William Blackstone, said that "in these gross and atrocious injuries [which we call crimes] the private wrong is swallowed up in the public: We seldom hear any mention made of satisfaction to the individual; the satisfaction to the community being so great."[4]

Later we will connect this traditional discussion of public harm to the economic theory of public goods. Our discussion will criticize the traditional view, expressed by Blackstone, that crime harms the public whereas torts merely cause private harm. For now, however, we explain the traditional view that crime harms the public—a view understood by generations of lawyers.

The idea that crimes harm the public has several implications. First, it justifies the difference between the plaintiffs in civil and criminal suits. In a civil suit the plaintiff is a private individual (the victim). In a criminal prosecution the plaintiff is society as represented by the public prosecutor or attorney general.

Second, the idea that crimes harm the public implies the possibility of "victimless" crimes, such as gambling, prostitution, and the sale of illegal drugs. The parties to these crimes often engage in voluntary sales for mutual advantage. However, the traditional theory of criminal law holds that these transactions have victims—namely society, whose peace and security are threatened.

Third, the traditional theory of public harm justifies punishing *attempts* to cause harm, even when they fail. When potentially harmful behavior causes no actual harm, the victim's injury is nil, so the victim usually has no cause for a civil suit. However, failed attempts at crime, a so-called *inchoate* crime, cause fear and other harm to the public. The traditional theory of criminal law holds that a person who tries to injure another and fails should be punished.

QUESTION 12.2:   Explain why counterfeiting money is a crime. Who is the victim? Is there a private victim as well as public victims?

QUESTION 12.3:   Distinguish between (1) imposing risk on others by driving carelessly without an accident actually occurring, and (2) inspiring fear in others by attempting to commit a crime and failing.

C. Standard of Proof

The fourth characteristic of a crime is the high standard of proof imposed upon the prosecution. In a criminal case the prosecutor must satisfy a higher standard of proof than the plaintiff in a civil case. In a civil case in common law countries, as we saw in the last chapter, the plaintiff must prove the case by a preponderance of the evidence— that is, the plaintiff's account must be more believable than the defendant's. In a criminal action in common law countries, the prosecutor, to secure a conviction, must prove the case *beyond a reasonable doubt.*

---

[4] WILLIAM BLACKSTONE, COMMENTARIES ON THE LAWS OF ENGLAND, v. IV. p. 6 (1776, reptd. 1977).

The traditional theory gives three reasons for imposing this high standard on the prosecution. First, convicting an innocent person seems worse than failing to convict a guilty person. Criminal law strikes the balance between these two errors—which statisticians call Type II (a false positive—that is, convicting an innocent person) and Type I errors (a false negative—that is, exonerating a guilty person), respectively—in favor of the defendant. Second, the prosecution can bring the full resources of the state to bear on winning. Imposing a heavy burden of proof on the prosecution diminishes this advantage. Third, citizens may need protection from overzealous prosecutors who seek bureaucratic and political advancement.

Compared to common law countries, some civil law countries encourage an intimate relationship between judges and the state prosecutor. In Germany, for example, officials often work as prosecutors before becoming judges, or alternate between these two jobs. One rationale for intimacy is reduction of errors by judge and prosecutor. Knowing the judge's perspective helps prosecutors avoid wasting court time. Also, compared to common law countries, the judge in civil law countries plays a more active role in developing arguments during the trial. Judges are more effective in developing arguments when they have had experience as prosecutors. Reducing mistakes is especially important in criminal cases because the process of prosecution for a crime involves embarrassment and expense for the accused, even if the final verdict is "not guilty." Note that people from common law countries sometimes exaggerate the intimacy of judge and prosecutor in civil law countries by saying that a person accused of a crime in an inquisitorial system is guilty until he proves his innocence. This is strictly false.[5]

QUESTION 12.4: Explain how the confidence of the public in the prosecutor influences the standard of proof in criminal trials.

QUESTION 12.5: Most jurisdictions have two possible verdicts in criminal trials: guilty or not guilty. Scottish criminal trials have three possible verdicts: guilty, not proven, or not guilty. Explain the difference between binary and trinary verdicts, with reference to the standard of proof.

D. Punishment

People who commit crimes expose themselves to the risk of punishment. Punishment can take several forms: confinement to prison, restriction of activities by probation (now called "supervisory release" in U.S. federal law), or monetary fines. These three—imprisonment, probation, and fines—are by far the most common forms of punishment. Other forms of punishment, such as forced labor ("community service"), occur in some jurisdictions. In some jurisdictions, the defendant still faces the possibility of being beaten, mutilated, or executed by the state. Capital punishment is

---

[5] Article 6 (2) of the *Convention for the Protection of Human Rights and Fundamental Freedoms,* which the European Union requires its members to approve as a condition of joining, asserts the presumption of innocence—anyone charged with a crime is innocent until proven guilty.

prohibited in countries belonging to the European Union, but it persists in other countries such as China, and it was restored by the U.S. Supreme Court in many U.S. states in 1976 after that Court had found it to be unconstitutional in 1972.

Punishment in criminal law is different from compensation in civil law. Compensation in civil law aims to restore the victim's welfare at the expense of the injurer. Punishment in criminal law makes the injurer worse off without directly benefiting the victim. Because the motivation is different, the issues of compensation and punishment are often independent of each other in a given instance. This is easy to see for torts that are also crimes, such as assault. Punishment may be imposed on top of compensation, as when criminal prosecution follows recovery in tort for assault. Alternatively, punishment may be imposed in lieu of compensation, as when the state imprisons a pauper for assault, and the victim does not sue in tort because the injurer could not pay compensation.

In cases involving money, a strict definition illuminates the difference between compensation and punishment. *Perfect compensation* is a sum of money that leaves the *victim indifferent* between the injury with compensation or no injury. In Chapter 7, we defined the parallel concept of *perfect disgorgement,* which is a sum of money that leaves the *injurer indifferent* between the injury with disgorgement or no injury. By definition, punishment goes beyond disgorgement. *Monetary punishment* is a sum of money that makes the *injurer prefer no injury* rather than the injury with payment of the money. To illustrate by Example 3, if a thief shatters a car window costing $100 and steals a radio worth $75, then perfect compensation equals $175, perfect disgorgement equals $75, and punishment is a sum of money exceeding $75. Thus, the criminal might be required to pay $175 as compensation to the victim and also to pay the state a fine of $100.

> **QUESTION 12.6:** For burglary, the victim's loss usually exceeds the injurer's gain, but the opposite is true for breach of contract. Why? What are the implications for relative dollar values of compensation and punishment?

II. An Economic Theory of Crime and Punishment

The traditional theory of criminal law offers reasons for the characteristics of a crime and distinguishes criminal prosecutions from civil disputes, but it does not offer a predictive model of criminal behavior or propose a clear goal for criminal law. The economic theory of crime, which we develop in this chapter, does all of this and more. We begin by distinguishing criminal prosecutions from civil disputes and offering reasons for the characteristics of a crime. Next we develop a predictive model of criminal behavior based upon a theory of the rational choice to commit a crime. Finally, we propose a clear goal for criminal law and policy: It should minimize the social costs of crimes. Using this standard, we identify optimal criminal justice policies.

A. Inadequacy of Tort Law, Necessity of Criminal Law

In Chapters 6 and 7, we discussed how tort law achieves efficient incentives by making injurers—and, in some cases, victims—internalize the cost of accidents. Most crimes are also torts, which means that most criminals are vulnerable to civil suits. If civil suits made the injurer internalize the costs of crimes, then criminal law would be unnecessary from an economic viewpoint. For several reasons, however, civil suits cannot internalize the costs of crimes. We will explain these reasons in order to justify the existence of criminal law.

The first reason concerns some inherent limitations on compensation. In Chapter 6, we said that compensation is perfect when potential victims are indifferent about accidents in the sense that they would just as soon have the injury and the damages as have no injury and no damages. Perfect compensation internalizes the harm caused by injurers. In Chapter 7 we argued, however, that perfect compensation is impossible for some injuries, such as when someone loses a leg or a child. In those cases, courts awarding damages deter unreasonable risks, but they do not compensate for actual harm. It would be better if these incompensable harms did not occur.

Similarly, criminal punishment aims to deter intentional harms, not to compensate for them. Consider a thought experiment regarding a crime. How much money would you require in order to agree to allow someone to assault you with a hammer? This question does not make much sense. The concept of indifference is difficult to apply to crimes like assault. Consequently, the relevant law cannot take as its goal the perfect compensation of victims and the internalization of costs by injurers. Rather than pricing crime, the goal of punishment is to deter it. The state prohibits people from intentionally harming others and backs this prohibition by punishment. Thus, criminal law is a necessary supplement to tort law when perfect compensation is impossible.

Even if perfect compensation *is* possible in principle, it may be impossible in fact. Let us suppose, for example, that a level of compensation exists that makes Jonny indifferent about whether Frankie lops off Jonny's arm. It would be impossible to prove this level in court. The obstacle to proof is that arms are not bought and sold in a market; there is no objective way to know how much the loss is worth to Jonny. If the court asks Jonny what amount he feels would compensate for the loss, he may not know the answer, or he may answer by exaggerating. When there is no market to induce people to reveal their subjective valuations, economists say that there is a "problem of preference revelation." When perfect compensation is possible in principle, it may be impossible in fact because of the problem of preference revelation.

We have justified criminal law where compensation is imperfect. But suppose that perfect compensation *is* possible. Can private law accomplish efficiency without the need for criminal law? The answer is no. To see why, we must consider another argument. In Chapter 4 on property, we distinguished between protecting an interest and protecting a right. Recall that if the law allows trespass on the condition that the trespasser compensates the owner for any harm caused, the law protects the interest of the owner in the property. But the law does not protect the owner's right to use the property as he or she chooses without interference from others. Similarly, if the victims of car accidents were perfectly compensated, their interests in their persons and property would be protected, but their right to go about their business without interference from others would be infringed. Going about your business without interference from others is part of liberty. Protecting interests secures wealth, and protecting rights secures liberty.

There are good economic arguments for protecting rights more vigilantly than interests. In earlier chapters we saw that society is, in general, better off when goods are acquired through voluntary exchange, because such exchange guarantees that goods move to those who value them the most and, in doing so, makes both parties better off. Goods that change hands without the consent of both parties—as by theft—do not carry this same guarantee. The stolen good may be more valuable to its owner than to the thief. The thief need not pay the owner's asking price. Thus, remedies in criminal law should, in part, be set so as to protect and encourage voluntary exchange through markets.

We have argued that two obstacles prevent substituting compensation for punishment: First, perfect compensation may be impossible, and, second, even if perfect compensation were possible, the law may seek to protect the rights of potential victims rather than their interests.

There is a third reason to supplement liability with punishment in some circumstances: Punishment is often necessary for deterrence. To illustrate, assume that a thief is considering whether to steal a $1000 television set. Assume that the probability of the thief's being apprehended and convicted equals 0.5. Assume that the thief is liable in property law but not punishable in criminal law. The expected cost of the theft to the criminal equals the expected liability: .5($1000) = $500. The benefit to the thief equals $1000. Thus, the *net* expected benefit to the thief equals $1000 − $500 = $500. In this example, civil liability without punishment makes theft profitable.

In general, thieves cannot be deterred by the requirement that they return what they have stolen whenever they happen to get caught. In order to deter thieves, the law must impose enough punishment so that the expected net benefit of crime to the criminal is negative. In the preceding example, deterring the thief requires the return of the television set, or its value of $1000, plus an additional fine.

According to the preceding discussion, tort law often aims to internalize costs, such as the risk of accidents. Once costs are internalized, actors are free to do as they please, provided that they pay the price. Internalization, however, is not the proper goal when perfect compensation is impossible in principle or in practice, or when people want law to protect their rights instead of their interests, or when enforcement errors systematically undermine liability. In these circumstances, law's proper goal is deterrence. When deterrence is the goal, actors are not free to pay the price and do as they please. Instead, punishments are calibrated to deter those actors who prefer to do the act in spite of its price.

The connection between the sanction and the actor's psychology tips off the observer as to whether the law aims for internalization or deterrence. As the actor's psychological commitment to the act increases, deterring the actor requires a larger sanction. When the goal is deterrence, a more severe punishment goes with greater psychological commitment to the act. For example, deterrence requires a deliberate act to receive harsher punishment than the same act done spontaneously. Similarly, deterrence requires harsher punishment for a repeated crime than a first offense.

In contrast, the actor's psychological commitment to the act does not affect the goal of internalization. Internalization concerns those costs the actor imposes on others. The cost to others depends on the harm caused by the act, not the actor's commitment to doing it. As the actor's psychological commitment to the act increases, internalization does not require the sanction to increase. For example, internalization does not require stronger sanctions for the same act done deliberately rather than spontaneously, or for a repeated act rather than a one-time act.

Now we return to the first of our fundamental questions, "What acts should be punished?" Acts should be punished when the aim is deterrence, whereas acts should be priced when the aim is internalization.[6] The law should aim for deterrence when perfect compensation is impossible in principle or in practice, when people want law to protect their rights instead of their interests, or when enforcement errors systematically undermine liability.

> **QUESTION 12.7:** We gave three reasons for having criminal punishments
> instead of tort liability. Give a concrete example illustrating each reason.

B. Rational Crime

We have offered some economic reasons why criminal law is needed to supplement tort law. Now we develop a predictive theory of criminal behavior, first by explaining how a rational, amoral person might decide whether to commit a crime. (Later we consider the relationship between diminished rationality and crime.) By a "rational, amoral person," we mean someone who carefully determines the means to achieve illegal ends, without restraint by guilt or internalized morality.

Crimes can be ranked by seriousness. Let x denote the seriousness of a crime, where $x = 0$ indicates no crime and $x > 0$ indicates a serious crime. More serious crimes often have a larger payoff for the criminal. Let y denote the criminal's payoff, where $y = y(x)$ and $y(x)$ increases in x. To be concrete, consider the crime of embezzlement by an accountant in a small company. The seriousness of embezzlement is partly measured by the amount stolen. The accountant can embezzle nothing, in which case $y = x = \$0$, and there is no crime. Alternatively, the accountant can embezzle a lot, say $10,000, in which case $y = x = \$10,000$ and the crime is serious.

Punishment can be ranked by severity. Let f denote the severity of the punishment, where $f = 0$ indicates no punishment and $f > 0$ indicates severe punishment. More severe punishments attach to more serious crimes, so $f = f(x)$, and $f(x)$ increases in x. To be concrete, consider a fine to punish embezzlement. To punish, the fine must exceed the criminal's payoff: $f(x) > y(x)$.

Figure 12.2 depicts these assumptions. The horizontal axis indicates the seriousness of the offense as measured by the amount embezzled, x. The payoff to the criminal, denoted $y(x)$ and measured on the horizontal axis, also equals the amount embezzled. Hence, $y(x)$ slopes up at 45 degrees. The curve denoted $f(x)$ and labeled "punishment" shows the severity of the punishment prescribed by law as a function of the seriousness of the offense. The punishment is assumed to be a fine. The curve $f(x)$ slopes up to indicate that the punishment becomes more severe as the crime becomes

---

[6] See Robert Cooter, *Prices and Sanctions,* 84 COLUM. L. REV. 1523 (1984).

FIGURE 12.2

Payoff and punishment.

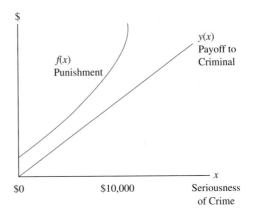

more serious, and $f(x)$ lies above the payoff $y(x)$ because the sanction is a *punishment*—that is, it exceeds the criminal's payoff.

If every crime were punished with certainty, committing crime would not pay. Hence, the criminal would choose x to equal zero.

Criminal Corporations?

Corporations regularly commit torts. For example, much of the law of consumer-product liability concerns torts by corporations. When a corporation commits a tort, liability is imposed upon the organization. But what about crimes? Can a corporation commit a crime? There is a legal obstacle to convicting corporations of crimes: *mens rea*. An individual can have a guilty mind, but it is not clear that organizations can. *Mens rea* requires the intention to do wrong and cause harm. Presumably, organizations lack minds, so they also lack intentions (except metaphorically).

So long as it was thought that organizations could not have criminal intent, the crimes that corporations could commit were limited to so-called *strict liability crimes*. Strict criminal liability does not require intending to do anything wrong. Examples of strict liability crimes are selling uncertified drugs or transporting explosives by forbidden routes. Other crimes, like manslaughter, fraud, or assault, could be committed by the members of the corporation, but not by the corporation itself.

The ability to prosecute corporations for strict liability crimes gives regulators and other officials an additional method for deterring corporate wrongdoing. In a civil suit, the prosecutor only needs to establish liability by the preponderance of the evidence, but damages are limited to compensation for the harm actually caused by the wrongdoing (and, possibly, punitive damages). In a criminal suit, the prosecutor has to prove his case beyond a reasonable doubt, which is harder to do. However, a successful criminal prosecution results in punishment, not just liability.

QUESTION 12.8: Assume that a corporation commits a tort that is also a strict liability crime. How should the state decide whether to bring a civil action or a criminal prosecution?

QUESTION 12.9: What does it mean to say that a corporation intends to do something? Can corporations be punished beyond the value of their assets?

FIGURE 12.3

Payoff, sanction, expected sanction.

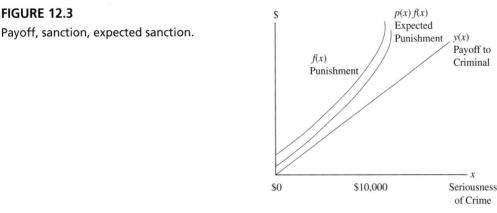

In reality, punishment is probabilistic, not certain. The offender may escape detection, apprehension, or conviction. A rational decision maker takes the probability of punishment into account when contemplating the commission of any crime. The *expected* punishment equals the probability p of punishment times its severity: pf. To illustrate, if the fine for embezzling $1000 equals $2000, and the probability that an offender will be caught and convicted equals .75, then the expected punishment equals .75($2000) = $1500. The expected punishment curve pf in Figure 12.3 necessarily lies *below* the actual punishment curve f, because the probability p is less than 1.

Efforts to detect, prosecute, and convict criminals normally increase with the crime's seriousness. Thus, the probability p of a sanction is a function of the crime's seriousness, $p = p(x)$, and $p(x)$ increases in x. Also the punishment $f(x)$ increases with the crime's seriousness. Thus, the expected sanction $p(x)f(x)$ increases with the crime's seriousness, as depicted in Figure 12.3.

The difference between the criminal's payoff $y(x)$ and the expected punishment $p(x)f(x)$ equals the criminal's expected net gain from crime. The expected punishment curve $p(x)f(x)$ in Figure 12.3 lies above criminal's payoff $y(x)$ for all values of x, which means that crime does not pay for a person facing the expected punishment as depicted in Figure 12.3.

Most people are in the situation most of the time in which crime does not pay. However, sometimes a person is in circumstances in which crime pays. Crime pays, for example, when a person has the opportunity to commit the crime with little chance of getting caught. Crime also pays in circumstances where the criminal suffers relatively little from the punishment. Figure 12.4 depicts someone in circumstances where crime pays. The criminal's payoff function $y(x)$ lies above the expected punishment $p(x)f(x)$ for some values of x. Consequently, embezzling low amounts of money yields an expected net gain. As the seriousness of the crime increases, the actual payoff increases more slowly than the expected punishment. Consequently, embezzling large amounts of money yields an expected net loss.

Exactly how much will a criminal embezzle? We can read off Figure 12.4 exactly how serious the most profitable offense is. The expected profit from the offense equals the difference between the payoff $y(x)$ and the expected punishment $p(x)f(x)$, which is

FIGURE 12.4

Rational crime.

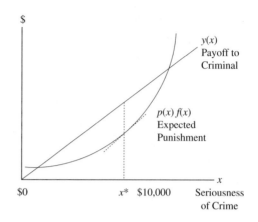

represented on the graph by the vertical distance between these two curves. The vertical distance is maximized when the seriousness of the offense equals x^*. Consequently, the rational criminal embezzles x^*.

This conclusion can be expressed in marginal values. So x^* solves

$$\max y(x) - p(x)f(x).$$

The marginal benefit to the criminal from increasing the seriousness of the offense by a small amount is given by the slope of a tangent line to the payoff curve, which we denote y'. The marginal expected cost to the criminal is equal to the expected increase in punishment from increasing the seriousness of the offense by a small amount, which is given by the slope of a tangent line to the expected punishment curve, which we denote $p'f + pf'$. The criminal maximizes the net benefits of the crime by embezzling an amount of money up to the point at which the marginal benefit of an additional amount embezzled equals the marginal expected punishment:

$$y' \quad\quad\quad = \quad p'f + pf'.$$

criminal's	criminal's marginal
marginal benefit	expected cost of punishment

For values of x below x^*, the marginal benefit exceeds the marginal expected cost to the criminal, so the criminal will increase the seriousness of the offense. For values of x above x^*, the marginal expected cost exceeds the marginal benefit, so the criminal will decrease the seriousness of the offense. For x equal to x^*, the marginal benefit equals the marginal expected cost, so the criminal maximizes his net payoff by not changing the seriousness of the offense.

The marginal expected punishment for embezzling an additional dollar has two components: the change in the probability of punishment, p', multiplied by the fine; and the change in the severity of punishment, f' multiplied by the probability of punishment. We can attach signs to these two components. More serious crimes attract greater enforcement effort by the authorities, so the probability of punishment usually increases with the seriousness of the crime. Thus, p' is usually a positive number. Furthermore, the severity of the punishment almost always increases with the seriousness of the crime, so f' is a positive number. Because p' and f' are usually positive, the expected-punishment curve in Figure 12.3 slopes up.

We can use this analysis to predict the response of criminals to changes in marginal costs and benefits. An investment of more effort in enforcing criminal law can increase the marginal probability p' of punishing the criminal. Similarly, an investment of more effort in punishing criminals, such as improving the system of collecting fines, can increase the marginal severity f'. According to the preceding equation and graphs, an increase in p' or f' will decrease the seriousness of the offense committed by the rational criminal. More certain and severe punishment reduces the seriousness of crime.

Now consider a change in the opportunity to commit crimes like embezzlement. The marginal benefit of crime falls when the opportunities to commit lucrative crimes diminish. According to the preceding equation, a decrease in the marginal benefit of crime, y', will decrease the seriousness of the offense committed by the rational criminal. Conversely, when the opportunity to embezzle increases, the rational criminal increases the seriousness of his offense until the risk of punishment rises to a level commensurate with his improved opportunities for crime.[7]

> **QUESTION 12.10:** How do Figures 12.3 and 12.4 change if the police become more efficient and catch a larger proportion of criminals? What does the change in the figures indicate about a change in criminal behavior?

> **QUESTION 12.11:** Assume that the punishment function $f(x)$ increases by a constant k, so that $f(x)$ becomes $f(x) + k$. What is the effect on the criminal's behavior?

> **QUESTION 12.12:** Assume that the payoff function $y(x)$ increases by a constant k, so that $y(x)$ becomes $y(x) + k$. What is the effect on the criminal's behavior?

C. Applying the Model of Rational Crime to Public Policy

Our discussion has focused on the crimes' seriousness, not the number of crimes committed. With a slight adjustment, our model of the seriousness of crimes can become a model of the quantity of crimes. Instead of interpreting x as the seriousness of a crime that someone commits, we interpret x as the number of crimes of given seriousness that someone commits. In the case of embezzlement, instead of x's indicating the amount of money embezzled in a single crime, let x represent the number of times that a single criminal embezzles a given amount of money. Thus, x might represent the number of times that an accountant steals $1,000 from the monthly payroll.

---

[7] See if you can explain why there might be systematic variations in the opportunities to commit, say, embezzlement. What effect might improvements in the technology of tracking a firm's resources have on the opportunities for crime? Also, explain how opportunity costs influence the decision to commit a crime.

Reinterpreting x as the number of crimes of given seriousness, rather than the seriousness of the crime, does not change the shape of the curves. For crimes of given seriousness, the criminal's payoff y is an increasing function of the number of crimes that he or she commits, $y = y(x)$; the criminal's punishment f is an increasing function of the number of crimes that he or she commits, $f = f(x)$; and the probability of punishment p is an increasing function of the number of crimes that he or she commits, $p = p(x)$. As before, the criminals commits the number of crimes x^* that maximizes the net payoff $y(x) - p(x)f(x)$.

Summing the number of crimes of a particular type committed by each criminal gives the aggregate number of these crimes in society, denoted X where $X = \Sigma x$. Aggregate crime responds to punishment just like the response of the underlying individuals. An increase in the marginal probability or seriousness of punishment causes a decrease in the aggregate number of crimes. Thus, Figure 12.5 depicts aggregate crime as a decreasing function of expected punishment.

The demand curve for goods slopes down because, when the price rises, some people buy less of the good and others stop buying it. Similarly the crime curve in Figure 12.5 slopes down because, when the expected punishment rises, some criminals commit fewer crimes and other criminals stop committing them. The proposition that the demand curve for goods slopes down bears the august title, the "First Law of Demand." Similarly, the proposition that an increase in expected punishment causes a decrease in crimes is the "First Law of Deterrence."

Perhaps you think that the First Law of Deterrence is false because people commit crimes passionately, irrationally, or ignorantly. In laboratory experiments, even rats obey the First Law of Deterrence, and people at their worst are more rational than rats at their best. Economists have a lot of confidence in the First Law of Deterrence, just as they have a lot of confidence in the First Law of Demand.

The interesting question for economists is not whether people commit less crime when the expected punishment increases. Rather, the interesting question is "How much do crime rates respond to increases in expected punishment?" In other words, the interesting question concerns the *elasticity* of the supply of crime. (See the discussion of price elasticity in Chapter 2.) When the supply of crime is elastic, policymakers can reduce crime significantly by moderate increases in expected punishment. When the supply of crime is inelastic, however, the variables encompassed by the economic model of rational

FIGURE 12.5

Aggregate Crime.

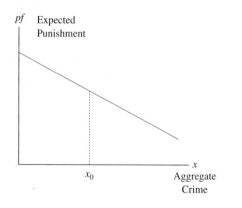

crime are less important than other variables, such as employment rates, family configuration, drug addiction, quality of schooling, and so on.

We have explained how the rational, amoral criminal responds to changes in a few variables—the probability of punishment, the severity of punishment, and opportunities to commit crimes. Our model of rational crime simplifies reality in various ways in order to reason carefully about causes and effects. Empirical research requires a more complicated analysis. Crime has multiple causes, so empirical research on crime should especially rely on multiple variable analysis. We cannot develop more complex models here, but we will briefly discuss some of our simplifying assumptions.

We assume an informed criminal, who knows the costs, benefits, and probabilities associated with the crime; we assume a risk-neutral criminal; and we assume that all the criminal's costs and benefits are monetary. Most criminals are imperfectly informed about the benefits of crime and the probabilities and magnitudes of punishment. Criminals are unlikely to be neutral toward risk. Most people are risk-averse, although criminals may be unusually risk-loving. (Later we discuss more about risk.) Many crimes have nonmonetary punishments and rewards, such as disapproval in the larger society and prestige within the society of criminals. These remarks indicate some complications to the simple model required for empirical research.

D. Criminal Behavior and Criminal Intent

Economists usually describe the economic model of decision making as an account of behavior, not as an account of subjective reasoning processes. Thus, consumers are said to act *as if* they were computing marginal utilities. Similarly, criminals are said to act *as if* they were comparing marginal benefits of crime and expected punishments. The commission of most crimes, however, requires criminal intent. To commit crimes, it is not enough for people to act *as if* they had criminal intent. They must actually have it. So, criminal law concerns reasons, not just behavior.

Notwithstanding its focus on behavior rather than reasons, the economic model of rational choice remains useful as an account of the criminal mind. Criminal intent is often distinguished according to the level of deliberation. To illustrate, a crime may be committed spontaneously in the sense that the criminal did not make any plans in advance. Spontaneous criminals do not search out opportunities to commit crimes, but when opportunities come their way, they avail themselves of them. At the opposite extreme, crimes may be carefully planned out in advance and all the possibilities weighed. Thus, a premeditated crime shows a greater degree of deliberation than a spontaneous crime.

The economic model may be understood as an account of the deliberations of a rational, amoral person when deciding in advance whether to commit a crime. In the case of premeditated crimes, the economic model may correspond to the actual reasoning process of the criminal. In the case of spontaneous crimes, where there is no deliberation, the economic model may nevertheless be understood as an account of the criminal's behavior but not of his reasoning. For spontaneous crimes, criminals may not actually reason as in the economic model, but they may act as if they had. By saying that criminals act "as if they had deliberated," we mean that when presented with the opportunity to commit crimes, they respond immediately to benefits and risks as if they had weighed them. If they respond in this way, their behavior can be explained by the economic model, even though their reasoning processes are only a fragment of it.

Much of criminal law focuses on criminal trials, which concern individual defendants and their alleged intent when committing particular crimes. The focus on individuals committing particular crimes, however, is not the only perspective in criminal law. General policies toward crime must be set by legislators and officials in the criminal justice system. For example, police have to decide where to send patrols in a city, and prosecutors have to decide which crimes to prosecute. Such general policies must be formulated with an eye to their aggregate effects, such as the social costs of crime.

We have asserted that the economic model of choice describes the deliberation of rational criminals when their crimes are premeditated, and we have asserted that rational criminals behave as if guided by the economic model when they commit spontaneous crimes. If this assertion is true, empirical investigations should demonstrate that crime rates respond to the considerations identified in our model, specifically, that crime rates respond in the predicted manner to punishments and payoffs. This is an empirical question to be answered by facts, not logic. Fortunately, there is a great deal of evidence on this matter, and we shall present a summary of the literature on deterrence in the next chapter. Now we turn to crime that is not so rational.

> **QUESTION 12.13:**   Why should the law punish a person more severely for committing the same crime deliberately rather than spontaneously?

> **QUESTION 12.14:**   Laboratory experiments demonstrate that rats respond in an economically rational way to punishment, yet rats cannot legally commit crimes. Why not?

E. Diminished Rationality—Saturday Night Fever[8]

The economic theory of behavior begins with super-rationality, but it need not end there. Many crimes and torts occur under conditions of diminished rationality, which economists have begun to model. For example, many crimes result from *lapses,* which are temporary aberrations in behavior that we discussed in Chapter 7. Thus, young people often commit crimes when they temporarily lose control of their emotions and act impulsively. We call this behavior "Saturday Night Fever." The proof of Saturday Night Fever is that a person wakes up on Sunday morning and thinks, "I can't believe what I did last night!"

In this section, we develop an economic model for this type of lapse. Prudence involves giving reasonable weight to future events, whereas imprudence involves giving unreasonably little weight to future events. Occasional imprudence is a kind of lapse in which the actor temporarily discounts the future consequences of his or her behavior at a much higher level than ordinarily would be the case. When the act in question is illegal, a high discount rate prevents the actor from giving as much weight to future punishment as he or she would ordinarily give.

---

[8] Robert Cooter has developed this model in several papers, most recently *Models of Morality in Law and Economics: Self-Control and Self-Improvement for the Bad Man of Holmes,* 78 B. U. L. REV. 903 (1998).

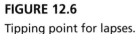

FIGURE 12.6

Tipping point for lapses.

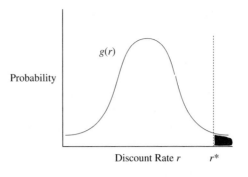

To formalize this idea, imagine that a person draws his discount rate for future costs and benefits from a probability distribution. Most of the time, the person draws a moderate discount rate from the center of the distribution, so he acts prudently and does not commit crimes. From time to time, however, he draws a very high discount rate from the tail of the distribution. In this situation, the person may lapse and commit a crime.

To express this argument in notation, assume that wrongdoing yields an immediate benefit at time 1, denoted b_1, risks future punishment at time 2, denoted c_2 for cost. Let r denote the rate at which the actor discounts costs for futurity and uncertainty.[9] The "tipping point," denoted r^*, is the discount rate at which the immediate benefits equal the expected future costs. Thus, an actor whose discount rate exceeds r^* commits the wrong, and an actor whose discount rate falls short of r^* does not commit the wrong.

As moods shift, a person may discount the future at different rates. The horizontal axis in Figure 12.6 depicts possible values of the discount rate r depending on the actor's mood. The vertical axis depicts the probability distribution $g(r)$ that the actor will have different values of r at any point in time. If the actual value r drawn from the distribution $g(r)$ equals or exceeds r^*, the actor commits the wrong. The small shaded area in the right tail of the distribution represents the probability that the actor commits the wrong. Conversely, if the actual value drawn from the distribution $g(r)$ is less than r^*, the actor does not commit the wrong. The unshaded area in the distribution represents the probability that the actor does not commit the wrong.

Mood, which determines the actor's discount rate for uncertainty and futurity, obeys a mysterious chemistry. In effect, Figure 12.6 assumes that mood is unpredictable at any point in time but distributes predictably over time. With low probability, the actor draws a value of r greater than r^* and commits the wrong. With high probability, the actor

---

[9] The discount rate r exceeds 1. To illustrate, the discount rate might be, say, $r = (1 + 0.07)$. Thus, the rational actor follows this rule:

$$b_1 - \frac{c_2}{r} < 0 \Rightarrow \text{do not commit the wrong.}$$

The tipping point occurs where the actor is equally poised between committing the wrong and not committing it. The tipping point value of r, denoted r^*, is found by solving the preceding equation, which implies

$$r^* = \frac{c_2}{b_1}.$$

draws a value of r smaller than r^* and does not commit the wrong. These characteristics of the distribution correspond to the proposition that crime is unusual.

An increase in the variability of moods increases the probability of wrongdoing by the actor. In terms of Figure 12.6, spreading the distribution by shifting density into the tails increases the area to the right of r^*. Greater probability density to the right of r^* implies an increase in the probability of wrongdoing.[10] Having volatile emotions, which corresponds to high variance in the distribution $g(r)$, causes young people to commit disproportionately many crimes. Conversely, a decrease in the variability of moods decreases the probability of wrongdoing. Maturation stabilizes the emotions, which reduces the variance in the discount rate and causes older people to commit fewer crimes.

Will increasing punishment c cause crime to decrease? Whenever the actor draws a discount rate close to the tipping value r^*, a small change in punishment c can tip the decision one way or another. For example, a small increase in punishment causes the actor to decide against committing the wrong, whereas a small decrease in punishment causes the actor to decide in favor of committing the wrong. Thus, punishment deters.

Earlier we explained that the issue for economists, however, is *how much* punishment deters. The probability that the actor draws a discount rate close to r^* is low, whereas the probability that the actor draws a discount rate much smaller or larger than r^* is high. When r is not close to r^*, a small change in punishment cannot tip the decision one way or another.

Insofar as imprudent lapses cause crime, more severe punishment is not a very effective deterrent. Severity is ineffective because the cause of crime is unreasonable discounting of future punishment. In these circumstances, increasing the punishment's severity gets discounted too much to have a large effect on behavior. Alternatively, increasing the certainty and immediacy of punishment may be more effective for deterring crime. For example, if teenagers in the school yard sometimes commit violence against each other, having a disciplinarian present to administer certain and swift punishment may prevent violence more effectively than increasing the severity of future punishment.

Moods are more variable for youth than adults. In terms of Figure 12.6, aging reduces the variance in $g(r)$. Deterrence of youth crime may require certain and swift punishment, whereas severe punishment that is uncertain and remote may deter many kinds of adult crime, such as embezzling. In general, the state should punish differently youthful crime due to lapses and deliberative crime by adults. Certainty of punishment is relatively important for impulsive youths, and severity is relatively important for deliberative adults.

A recent empirical study confirms that young criminals are undeterred by severe, rather than certain, punishments. The severity of punishments prescribed by law jumps up for many crimes when an adolescent turns 18 years old and becomes a legal adult. If severity deters, then people should commit more crimes as they approach their eighteenth

---

[10] To be precise, the probability of wrongdoing may increase, and cannot decrease, with a mean-preserving spread in $g(r)$.

birthday, and they should commit fewer crimes once they turn 18. Contrary to this prediction, economic analysis of Florida arrest data shows no decrease in the probability of committing a crime when a person turns 18. Youth who become legal adults are undeterred by the discontinuous increase in the punishments that they face. Although longer sentences do not deter, more certain punishment may deter, which suggests that redirecting money away from prisons and toward police might significantly reduce youth crime.[11]

Besides punishment, this model predicts that social policies can reduce crime by reducing variability in moods. To illustrate, chemical stimulants or depressants, such as alcohol and drugs, increase variability in moods. Social policies that reduce episodic use of alcohol and drugs will decrease crime. Psychological testing and counseling and the use of new families of medicinal drugs can help adolescents to stabilize their moods. A regular rhythm to life, such as holding a steady job, presumably reduces variability in moods for most people.

We have explained that emotions cause actors to discount the future unreasonably from time to time. In addition, research suggests that some people—especially some young people—systematically discount the future unreasonably. The most important empirical finding is that people are more consistent about their trade-offs between two future choices than between a present and future choice. To illustrate, assume that a child must choose between a promise to receive one candy on Saturday or two candies on Sunday. He prefers the two candies when he chooses on Monday, Tuesday, Wednesday, Thursday, or Friday. When Saturday arrives, however, the child may switch and choose to receive one candy immediately rather than two candies the next day. Notice that the child's preference for trading one future choice against another conflicts with his preference for trading a present choice against a future choice.[12] The child's trade-off between a present and future choice seems unreasonable compared to his trade-off between two future choices. When people discount the future unreasonably in this way, the immediate gain from doing something wrong attracts them more strongly than the threat of a future punishment. Increasing the severity of the future sanction has little effect on their behavior because the future has little effect on their behavior.

Unreasonable discounting of the future, whether probabilistic or systematic, is a form of diminished rationality that afflicts many people. When rationality diminishes too far, a person becomes insane. An insane person is legally incapable of committing a crime. The insanity defense against a criminal charge in the United States basically follows the nineteenth-century M'Naughten rule: An actor is insane who does not know the difference between right and wrong. A criminal knows the difference and makes the wrong choice, whereas an insane person cannot choose properly because he does not know the difference. While an insane person cannot be punished legally, he can be confined until his insanity no longer threatens other people.

---

[11] David S. Lee & Justin McCrary, *Crime, Punishment, and Myopia*, NBER Working Paper 11491 (2006).

[12] Economists call this behavior "time-inconsistent preferences," philosophers call it "akrasia," and psychologists call it "hyperbolic discounting." For a policy application, see Jonathan Gruber & Botond Koszegi, *Tax Incidence when Individuals Are Time Inconsistent: The Case of Cigarette Excise Taxes*, 88 J. PUB. ECON. 1959 (2004).

The set of people who cannot tell right from wrong presumably is not identical to the set of people who cannot be deterred. The threat of confinement presumably deters some people who are legally insane from harming others. Perhaps psychologists and economists will someday improve our ability to distinguish between the insane who can and cannot be deterred. Special policies might be devised to deter the former, just as we recommend special policies for young criminals that emphasize the certainty and not the severity of punishment.

F. The Economic Goal of Criminal Law

Crime imposes various costs on society, which we reduce to two basic kinds. First, the criminals gain something, and the victims suffer harm to their persons or property. The resulting social harm, according to the standard view among economists, equals the net loss in value. To illustrate by Example 3 at the beginning of this chapter, if a thief shatters a car window costing $100 and steals a radio worth $75, then the criminal gains $75 and the victim loses $175, for a net social loss of $100. The net loss equals value destroyed, not value redistributed. Second, the state and the potential victims of crime expend resources to protect against it. For example, homeowners install bars on their windows, and the city employs police officers to patrol the streets.

We described two basic kinds of social costs: the net harm caused by crime and the resources spent on preventing it. The optimal amount of crime, or efficient deterrence, balances these costs. We propose the following simple goal for analyzing criminal law: *Criminal law should minimize the social cost of crime, which equals the sum of the harm it causes and the costs of preventing it.*

These two basic kinds of social costs often suffice for purposes of analysis. When analysis requires more complexity, we can refine and expand the types of social costs. To illustrate, criminal activities divert the efforts of criminals from legal to illegal activities, which imposes an opportunity cost. For example, an accountant who devotes herself to embezzling funds has less time for legitimate bookkeeping. Furthermore, while in prison, an accountant cannot audit books for clients. The opportunity cost of crime among accountants may be large enough to affect the optimal deterrence of embezzlement. From time to time, we will expand the definition of social costs to include such losses as the criminal's opportunity cost, as required by our analysis.

Another complexity concerns the criminal's perceived benefit from crime. According to the standard view among economists, as mentioned, the criminal's benefit partly offsets the victim's cost. Moralists, however, might say that the criminal's illicit gain should not count as a social benefit. Ordinarily people reach different conclusions depending on the details of the case. To illustrate, most people agree that the benefit enjoyed by a person who steals food from an unoccupied cabin to save his life when lost in the wilderness should count as a social gain, and most people agree that the pleasure felt by a rapist (if there is such a pleasure) should not count as a social gain commensurate with the victim's pain.

Unfortunately, many important examples that confront policymakers do not provoke a consensus, even among economists, about the social value of the criminal's gain. To illustrate, some government regulations on industry promote efficiency by correcting market failures, such as prohibitions against dumping toxic chemicals in rivers, whereas other regulations profit politically favored groups by making competition a crime, such as restrictions on agricultural production. A dramatic example of disagreement over regulations concerns the United States' most creative and profitable financier in the 1970s, Michael Milken, who used high-risk bonds ("junk bonds") to finance leveraged buyouts and hostile takeovers of corporations. He was sentenced to prison for violating technical regulations in security laws. Some economists believe that he did much to help modernize American industry, and other economists believe that he undermined the stock market by engaging in fraud.

When policymakers disagree about the social benefits of crime, a good strategy for economists is to clarify the issues without trying to resolve the dispute. Following this strategy, we will avoid arguments whose conclusions require taking sides in such debates.

> **QUESTION 12.15:** What are some ways to measure the social costs of the harm caused by murder? (Recall our discussion in Chapter 7 of how to assign value to a life lost in an accident.)

> **QUESTION 12.16:** Compare the simple economic goals of criminal law and tort law.

G. Optimal Amount of Crime Deterrence and of Efficient Punishment

Figure 12.7 depicts how to strike the balance between the net cost of the harm caused by crime and the cost of preventing it. In the figure, the horizontal axis measures reductions in the amount of criminal activity, ranging from no reduction at the origin up to a complete absence of crime at the amount 100 percent. Dollar amounts are measured along the vertical axis. The curve MSC_D represents the marginal social costs of achieving a given level of crime reduction. MSC_D slopes upward because officials

FIGURE 12.7

The efficient level of deterrence.

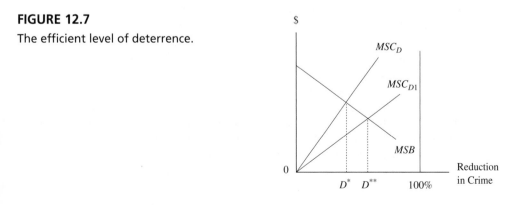

undertake easy deterrence before resorting to harder deterrence. Consequently, achieving additional reductions in crime becomes increasingly costly. For example, reducing crime by an additional 1 percent is easier when crime has already been reduced 5 percent than when crime has already been reduced 95 percent.

The curve labeled *MSB* measures the marginal social benefit of achieving various levels of crime reduction or deterrence. *MSB* slopes downward because the benefit to society of a small reduction in the amount of crime declines as the total amount of crime declines. Thus, the reduction from, say, 5 percent to 7 percent benefits society more than the reduction from 95 percent to 97 percent.

Socially optimal deterrence occurs at the point where the marginal social cost of reducing crime further equals the marginal social benefit. In Figure 12.7 the social optimum occurs at the level of deterrence marked D^*. Notice that for any level of reduction in crime less than D^*, the marginal social benefit of a further reduction exceeds the marginal social cost, so society should reduce crime further. Similarly, for any level of reduction in crime greater than D^*, the marginal social costs of a further reduction exceed the marginal social benefit, so society should allow more crime to go undeterred.

Notice that changes in MSC_D and MSB can change the optimal level of deterrence. For example, suppose that the opportunity cost of resources devoted to deterring crime falls, and the marginal social benefit of deterrence remains the same; MSC_D would fall to MSC_{D1} and the optimal level of deterrence would increase to D^{**}.

As long as deterrence is costly, the optimal amount of crime is positive. Costly deterrence precludes a rational society from entirely eliminating crime. If deterrence costs rise, the optimal amount of crime rises. If, however, the net harm from crime rises, the optimal amount of crime falls.

In the next chapter, we describe efforts to determine whether marginal deterrence costs more or less than the resulting savings in the cost of crime in the United States; in other words, these studies try to determine whether the value of D for the United States is above, below, or equal to the optimal value of D^*.

Note that this mathematical representation simplifies the computation of optimal deterrence in several ways. One important simplification is that we have not modeled an optimal schedule of punishments for related crimes. Rather than standing alone, criminal penalties form part of an integrated schedule, which influences their optimal values. Using powerful deterrents on less serious crimes often precludes using them on more serious crimes.

To illustrate, assume that life imprisonment is the maximum punishment available in a society and that the law prescribes life imprisonment for embezzling. Now assume that a policeman runs after an embezzler who has a gun. If the policeman apprehends the embezzler, the criminal will be imprisoned for life as required by the harsh law. So, the embezzler might as well try to shoot the policeman. If he succeeds in killing the policeman, he will escape. If he fails, there will be no additional punishment because the punishment for embezzling is already the maximum. In this example, harsh penalties for minor crimes undermine the deterrence of serious crimes. Unfortunately, taking such facts into account when calibrating punishments requires mathematics beyond the scope of this book.

Harsh penalties may violate the moral and constitutional rights of criminals. For example, a law imposing the death sentence for embezzling petty cash would create a large disparity between the severity of the punishment and the seriousness of the offense. Most people would regard the law as immoral, and U.S. judges would probably declare it unconstitutional. Such noneconomic considerations can operate as constraints upon the computation of optimal deterrents.

QUESTION 12.17: Assume the acquisition of computers by the police increases the force's efficiency. How would Figure 12.7 change?

QUESTION 12.18: Assume the acquisition of computers by criminals increases their elusiveness. How would Figure 12.7 change?

H. Mathematics of Optimal Means of Deterrence

Having shown how to determine the optimum amount of deterrence, we next turn to an analysis of the optimal *means* of deterring crime. There are many allocation decisions to be made, such as the choice between foot patrols and car patrols by police, the choice between more police and more prosecutors, and the choice between more fines and more incarceration. We shall examine several of these choices to bring out some underlying principles.

First, consider a choice between allocating resources to make punishment more certain or more severe. For example, allocating more resources to police makes punishment more certain (in that it makes deterrence, detection, and conviction more likely), and allocating more resources to prisons permits longer—more severe—sentences. Recall that the expected punishment equals the probability of punishment multiplied by its extent. For example, the four rows in Table 12.1 represent combinations of a punishment f, which might be a fine denominated in dollars, and a probability p, that result in expected punishment $p \times f$ equal to 10.

When the probability of punishment is multiplied by its severity, the result is the expected punishment. To keep the analysis simple, assume that the amount of crime is constant when the expected punishment is constant. By assumption, all four combinations of fines and probabilities in the preceding table result in the same amount of crime. Consequently, the socially efficient combination is the one that costs less. The one that costs less is almost certainly the fine of $100 applied with probability 0.10. The reason

TABLE 12.1

Expected Punishment for Crimes

f(Punishment)	p(Probability)	$p \times f$(Expected Punishment)
10	1.00	10
20	.50	10
40	.25	10
100	.10	10

Insurance for Criminals?

We explained that the state should deter crimes through fines rather than imprisonment whenever possible. The inability of the criminal to pay a fine limits its use. The criminal's bankruptcy forces the justice system to resort to imprisonment. Insurance can overcome the bankruptcy constraint. For example, a $100,000 insurance policy against criminal fines would enable a person with only $10,000 in wealth to pay a $50,000 fine.

It might seem, then, that the state would encourage insurance against criminal fines. In fact, the law in the United States and elsewhere typically forbids writing insurance policies to cover criminal fines. Apparently, officials fear that insurance, because of moral hazard, will cause criminals to commit more crimes because the punishment will fall upon the criminals' insurers. According to this argument, insurance blunts deterrence. If insurance against criminal fines were allowed, however, the insurance companies would want to monitor policyholders to make sure that they do not commit crimes. Thus, private enforcement by insurance companies would supplement public enforcement by the police. Private enforcement by insurance companies might be effective in deterring crime. This body of law needs rethinking.

is that a higher probability requires more expenditures on police and prosecutors, whereas a large fine costs not much more to collect than a small fine. Indeed, fines are so cheap to administer that they yield a profit to the state, at least so long as the fine is not too large relative to the offender's wealth. Because certainty of punishment is costly for the state to achieve relative to severity of punishment by a fine, large fines with low probability are typically more efficient than low fines with high probability.

So far, our discussion assumed that criminals have the ability to pay fines. Many criminals are too poor to pay a fine commensurate with the seriousness of their crimes. These circumstances require punishment by incarceration. In economic jargon, we say that the incarceration enables the sanction to escape the criminal's bankruptcy constraint. However, fines are cheap for the state to collect and incarceration is very expensive. This fact has an important consequence for the optimal combination of fines and jail sentences: It seldom makes sense to put someone in jail until the state first exhausts its ability to collect a fine from the criminal. If the state violates this rule and incarcerates someone with the ability to pay a fine, the state could have saved taxpayers' money and held deterrence constant by increasing the fine to the maximum and reducing the prison sentence by an offsetting amount. The optimal combination of fines and incarceration includes the maximum fine that the criminal can pay. This fact prompts policymakers to look for ways to increase the capacity of criminals to pay fines. In the next chapter we describe a system developed in northern Europe, called the "day fine," which attempts to overcome the criminal's bankruptcy constraint that limits his ability to pay a fine.

Our earlier discussion explained that unreasonably high discounting between present and future weakens the ability of the threat of future punishment to deter. We apply this insight to incarceration. When the punishment in question is incarceration, a more severe punishment means longer incarceration. With unreasonably high discounting, adding time at the end of the prison sentence has little deterrence value.[13]

Does America have the combination of police and prisons that roughly minimizes the sum of the harm caused by crime and the cost of preventing it? In America the cost of one additional policeman roughly equals the cost of incarcerating someone for three years. If hiring an additional policeman and reducing average prison sentences by three years results in less crime, then America could reduce the amount of crime at no additional cost to taxpayers by hiring more police and shortening prison sentences. Some states like California have sharply increased lengths of prison sentences for repeat felons—the policy of "three strikes and you're out." The fact that young criminals discount the future unreasonably suggests that more police and shorter prison sentences would reduce the cost of violent crime committed by youths in California.[14]

QUESTION 12.19: Explain in words when efficiency requires severe punishments with low probability, and when efficiency requires mild punishments with high probability.

QUESTION 12.20: How does full employment reduce the cost of deterring crime?

I. Private Deterrence

Private individuals, not public officials, deter much crime. Thus, Example 4 at the beginning of this chapter concerns whether Yvonne should protect herself by (1) installing bars on her windows, (2) installing a loud burglar alarm, or (3) buying a gun. The example raises the question of whether private citizens have incentives to invest optimally in deterring crime. In general, the answer is "no." Private citizens are mostly concerned with private costs and benefits, which do not necessarily align with public costs and benefits.

To illustrate, suppose that Yvonne installs a brand X double-bolt lock on her front door. Installing the lock has private value for her if it prevents the burglary of her house. Call this effect *private deterrence* because it benefits the private investor in precaution. Installing the lock has public value for Yvonne's neighbors if burglars tend to avoid neighborhoods in which some houses have brand X double-bolt locks. Call this effect *public deterrence* because it benefits the public. Installing the lock has little social value if it prevents the burglary of Yvonne's house by causing a burglar to rob the house next door. Call this effect *redistributing crime*. Redistributing crime has no net social benefit.

---

[13] We report on some additional empirical evidence on these matters in the next chapter.

[14] Space does not allow us to discuss the relationship between discounting future events and discounting uncertain events. Unreasonable discounting of the future may go with unreasonable discounting of uncertainty. These two forms of unreasonable discounting reinforce each other with respect to deterrence in that each one requires a large increase in the length of incarceration to offset a small decrease in the certainty of punishment.

Modern Bounty Hunters?

People complain about increasing crime. Would privatizing enforcement help? Consider this privatization plan: Whoever apprehends a criminal receives the fine the criminal owed to the state. Instead of relying on police, society would rely upon bounty hunters to apprehend criminals whose crimes are punishable by fines. To keep the bounty hunters under control, they would be bonded and held liable for any harm that they cause by apprehending the wrong person.

This system has a defect much like open-access fishing, which results in overfishing the sea. Giving the full fine to a private bounty hunter might attract too many bounty hunters. To eliminate the defect and prevent excessive bounty-hunting, the state could retain part of the fine and pay the remainder to the bounty hunter. By continually adjusting this "tax," the state could induce optimal private-enforcement effort. This system could work well, for example, in apprehending people who flout parking and motor vehicle laws.

Private investment in preventing crime usually has all three effects: private deterrence, public deterrence, and redistribution. The state should encourage private investments that contribute to public deterrence. The state need not encourage private investments that contribute to private deterrence. The state should not encourage private investment that only redistributes crime.

A simple condition determines whether the redistributive effect is small or large. Before committing a crime, the criminal can observe some private precautions. For burglary, examples of *ex ante observable precautions* include lights on walkways, bars on exterior windows, and exterior alarms. *Ex ante* observable precautions tend to redistribute crime—the mugger avoids lighted streets, and the burglar avoids houses with barred windows and visible alarms. Criminals cannot observe other private precautions until they begin committing the crime. For burglary, examples of *ex post observable precautions* include locks on interior doors, interior alarms, identification marks on valuable objects, and guns owned by residents. *Ex post* observable precautions promote public deterrence by reducing the average profitability of crime. These facts lead to a definite prescription about private investment in preventing crime: *The state should encourage* ex post *observable precautions, and the state need not encourage* ex ante *observable precautions.* (We will discuss the special case of guns—including whether they should be encouraged as an *ex post* observable precaution—in the next chapter.)

> **QUESTION 12.21:** Classify the following precautions against crime into *ex ante* observable and *ex ante* unobservable, and explain your answer: private guards in stores, auto alarms, "quick-dial" emergency phone systems (911 numbers in the United States), hidden cameras, and plainclothes detectives.

> **QUESTION 12.22:** Assume that burglars correctly believe that many people in your neighborhood keep guns. How might this fact increase your security? How might this fact endanger you?

J. Bad Crimes and Good People

Much legal thinking concerns deterring bad people from committing crimes. The law's success in deterring bad people, however, depends on the support of good people to help the police and other legal officials. Civic acts such as helping the police to solve a crime often involve personal sacrifice of time, effort, convenience, or safety. Unless good people make the sacrifice, the police and other officials become ineffective and crime rates soar. The reluctance of citizens to support the police perpetuates high crime rates in some neighborhoods and encourages gang activities. Understanding the prevention of bad crimes requires analyzing the behavior of good people.

The vertical axis in Figure 12.8 represents the amount a person would sacrifice to do his or her civic duty. Sacrifice is measured by the amount the citizen would be willing to pay, which is the money equivalent of time, effort, opportunity, inconvenience, or risk. The horizontal axis represents the proportion of citizens willing to pay the price. According to the graph, roughly 80 percent of the citizens will pay something to do their civic duty and roughly 20 percent will sacrifice nothing.

The sacrifice required of each person to do a civic duty often decreases with the number of people who do it. Figure 12.9 depicts the case where costs decrease

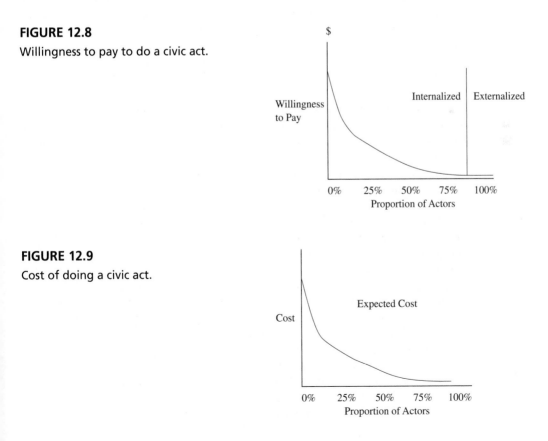

FIGURE 12.8

Willingness to pay to do a civic act.

FIGURE 12.9

Cost of doing a civic act.

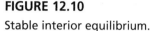

FIGURE 12.10

Stable interior equilibrium.

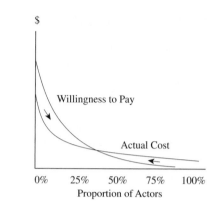

with the number of people who obey the norm. The decrease has a simple explanation: People are notoriously responsive to group pressures, variously described as conformity, herd effects, or social solidarity. With group pressures, an increase in an act's popularity lowers its cost. When most people help the police, a person who does so may feel that others will back him, so he runs less risk of retaliation from the criminal. When most employees in a company will report wrongdoing by their bosses, such as embezzling funds or disregarding environmental laws, each employee has less fear of retaliation and more hope of promotion from making such a report. As fewer people break the rules against smoking in airports, non-smokers feel less risk of confrontation when asking smokers to stop breaking the rules.

Figure 12.8 depicts a demand curve (willingness to pay) for civic acts, and Figure 12.9 depicts a supply curve (cost of supply). Figure 12.10 combines them. The demand and supply curves intersect roughly at 40 percent, which indicates the equilibrium level of civic acts. If the actual proportion equals 40 percent, people are willing to pay exactly what doing the civic duty costs, so no one changes his or her behavior. Furthermore, we can see that the equilibrium is stable. If the actual proportion is below 40 percent, people are willing to pay more than it costs to perform the civic act, so the proportion of actors increases towards 40 percent. If the actual proportion is above 40 percent, people are willing to pay less than its costs to perform the civic act, so the proportion of actors falls towards 40 percent.

In Figure 12.10, the willingness-to-pay curve has the usual downward slope of a demand curve. However, the cost curve in Figure 12.10, which is equivalent to the supply curve, also slopes down, which is not the usual shape of a supply curve. Even so, this account of civic acts closely tracks the usual analysis of demand and supply. Further increasing the supply curve's slope in Figure 12.10 dramatically changes the analysis. A startling effect occurs when the cost curve slopes down *more steeply* than the willingness-to-pay curve, as depicted in Figure 12.11. Instead of having a stable equilibrium at the intersection of the two curves, two stable equilibria exist as the corners of the graph. At one corner, the number of actors who do civic acts is zero, and at

FIGURE 12.11

Corner equilibria.

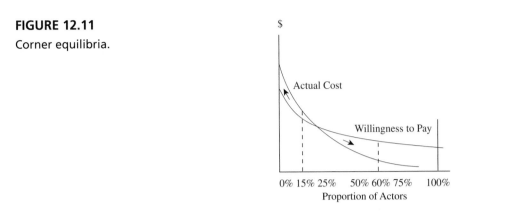

the other corner, the number is 100 percent. (A footnote explains why there are two equilibria.[15])

The society characterized by Figure 12.11 could end up in a situation where very few or very many citizens do civic acts. These two possibilities correspond to a world where many people help to suppress crime, or few people do so. Besides deterring criminals, law can help good citizens move to an equilibrium where many people perform civic acts and little crime occurs. In economic jargon, the criminal law "coordinates" good citizens so that society achieves a low-crime equilibrium.

This analysis illustrates a common feature of social norms: multiple equilibria. With multiple equilibria, state laws perform the important function of coordinating the behavior of good people, not just deterring wrongdoing by bad people. This brief discussion introduces students to an exciting new area of research in law and economics—the study of social norms.

Web Note 12.2

As we shall see in the following chapter, there are some clear and testable predictions of the economic theory that we have just outlined, and there is a considerable body of empirical work that we shall summarize there. You are no doubt aware that there are alternative theories of the decision to commit a crime. One of the most famous and widely held is what might be called the "socioeconomic" theory. On our website we summarize that theory and give some references to literature regarding it.

---

[15] Consider what happens when the number of actors doing civic acts is, say, 15 percent in Figure 12.11. At that point, the actual cost of civic acts exceeds what actors are willing to pay, so the number of actors performing civic acts will fall. The process continues until zero actors are performing civic acts. Alternatively, consider what happens when the number of actors doing civic acts is, say, 60 percent in Figure 12.11. At that point, the actual cost of civic acts is less than what actors are willing to pay, so the number of actors performing civic acts will rise. The process continues until 100 percent of actors are performing civic acts. The cause of this dynamic is greater downward slope of the supply curve relative to the demand curve, which can occur in an industry with rapidly increasing economies of scale.

Conclusion

We began this chapter by discussing the characteristics of a crime as distinguished in law. We then reinterpreted these facts by using an economic theory of criminal behavior. That theory holds that rational criminals compare the benefits of crime and the expected punishment. We used this behavioral theory to develop an economic theory of optimal punishment, based upon the goal of minimizing the sum of the social harm caused by crime and the cost of deterring it. We showed how to determine the optimal level of deterrence and how to allocate society's resources optimally among alternative ways to deter crime. Our task in the next chapter is to show how to use these models in formulating policy in the area of criminal law.

Suggested Readings

Becker, Gary S., *Crime and Punishment: An Economic Approach,* 76 J. Pol. Econ. 169 (1968).

Hart, H. L. A., Punishment and Responsibility (1968).

Katz, Leo, Bad Acts and Guilty Minds: Conundrums of the Criminal Law (1987).

Katz, Leo, Michael S. Moore, & Stephen F. Morse, eds., Foundations of Criminal Law (1999).

Moore, Michael S., Act and Crime: The Philosophy of Action and its Implications for Criminal Law (2010).

Posner, Richard A., *An Economic Theory of the Criminal Law,* 85 Colum. L. Rev. 1193 (1985).

13 Topics in the Economics of Crime and Punishment

We have strict statutes and most biting laws,
The needful bits and curbs to headstrong weeds,
Which for this fourteen years we have let slip; . . .
Now, as fond fathers,
Having bound up the threat'ning twigs of birch, . . .
Not to use, in time the rod more mocked becomes than feared:
so our decrees, . . . to themselves are dead;
And, liberty plucks justice by the nose,
The baby beats the nurse, and quite athwart
Goes all decorum.

SHAKESPEARE,
Measure for Measure, ACT I, SCENE 3

LIKE SHAKESPEARE in the preceding quote, American voters from 1980 to 2000 apparently thought that state authorities were too soft on crime—they "let slip" the "needful bits and curbs to headstrong weeds." Legislators responded to the cry of voters for harsher treatment of criminals by enacting "strict statutes and most biting laws." What was the result? In this chapter we review the statistical evidence on crime and punishment, and we try to determine whether people responded to harsher punishments as predicted by the economic theory of crime developed in the preceding chapter. We also summarize the economic literature on the death penalty, examine the connection between crime and drug addiction, and discuss the economics of handgun control.

I.   Crime and Punishment in the United States

A. Crime Rates

Trends in the rate of crime (the amount of crime divided by population) in recent decades in the United States can be summarized as follows:

1. From a peak in the mid-1930s, the rate of most crimes (both violent and nonviolent) decreased to a low point in the early 1960s.
2. Between the early 1960s and the mid- to late 1970s, a rapid and unprecedented increase in the rate of all crimes occurred.

3. Between the early 1980s and the early 1990s, the rate of most nonviolent crime among adults decreased markedly; the rate of violent crime decreased slightly among adults and increased among youth.

4. From the early 1990s to at least 2008, both violent and nonviolent crime continued to decline, but at a much slower rate than the declines of the 1990s.[1]

How do these rates compare with those of other countries? With respect to nonviolent crimes, the recent rates in the United States are roughly the same as those in other developed nations. More accurately, the recent trends in nonviolent-crime rates in other countries have been upward, while those in the United States have been declining, with the result that nonviolent-crime rates in the United States are now roughly equivalent to or even below those in other developed countries. Consider, for example, that in the early 1980s the burglary rate in Great Britain was significantly lower than the U.S. rate, but that by the early 2000s the Great Britain burglary rate was higher than the U.S. rate. Similarly, the automobile-theft rate in France in the early 1980s was lower than that in the United States; by the early 2000s the rate in France was greater than that in the United States. Finally, as early as 1984 the burglary rate in the Netherlands was almost twice that in the United States and has remained so.

Although the United States resembles Europe in rates of nonviolent crime, it differs significantly in rates of violent crimes. The United States has been the leader of the industrialized world in homicide rates (homicides divided by population) as long as records have been kept. For well over 100 years, large U.S. cities have had significantly higher homicide rates than similarly sized European cities. Nonetheless, the surge in U.S. homicides and other violent crimes beginning in the 1960s was unlike anything that has ever occurred in Europe. Even though homicide rates have always been higher in the United States than in Europe, homicide and other violent-crime rates in the United States have generally been falling recently. In fact, in 1991 there were approximately 24,700 homicides in the United States and about 16,600 in 2004, a drop of more than one-third.[2] The FBI estimated that there were 16,272 homicides in 2008. The already-low homicide rates in Europe have fallen in the last 10 years (with the curious exception of England, where they have risen), but they have not fallen as rapidly as have U.S. rates.

B. Imprisonment Rates

Legislators responded to the increase in crime by increasing the severity of punishment, especially imprisonment. The total number of prisoners in all jails and prison has risen sharply in the United States in recent years. In 1970, the incarceration rate in the United States was below one person in 400. Subsequently it quadrupled. In 2008,

---

[1] The principal sources for statistical information on crime are the U.S. Federal Bureau of Investigation's *Uniform Crime Reports* (annual) and the U.S. Department of Justice, Bureau of Justice Statistics, *Sourcebook of Criminal Justice Statistics* (annual).

[2] Violent crimes (murder, rape, robbery, and aggravated assault) increased by a small amount (2.5 percent) in 2005 after small declines in 2002–2004. Murder declined 2.4 percent in 2004 but was up 4.8 percent in 2005; the murder rate has been roughly constant from 2005 through 2008.

roughly one in every 100 adults was incarcerated, and roughly two in every 100 were on probation or parole.[3] As a proportion of the total population, the U.S. incarceration rate is five times the rate in Britain, nine times that in Germany, and 12 times that in Japan. Politicians responded to the public's perception of a crime epidemic with this unprecedented increase in the use of imprisonment in the United States of America.[4]

C. Causes of Crimes

The changes in crime rates prompt a search for possible causes. Here are some statistical facts that stand out.

First, most large cities in the United States have violent-crime rates that are two to seven times higher than those in their suburbs. While this fact suggests that urbanization contributes to crime, changes in urbanization do not align with changes in crime rates; so, the former cannot explain the latter.

Second, a disproportionate amount of criminals are young males. Arrest statistics suggest that two-thirds of all street crime in the United States is committed by persons under age 25, almost all of whom are male. Approximately 93 percent of all U.S. prisoners are male. Changes in crime rates often follow changes in the distribution of people by age. An increase in the proportion of adolescents will increase the rate of crime, all other things held equal. The discernible jump in all crimes in the early 1960s coincided with the maturing into adolescence (roughly ages 14 to 24) of the "baby boom" generation that had been born just after World War II, and the decline in crime in the 1980s coincided with the aging of the population.[5] The increase in the amount of crime between the 1960s and the 1980s, however, was so large that the increase in the number of 14- to 24-year-olds explains only a fraction of it. For example, one study found that the rise in the murder rate during the 1960s was more than 10 times greater than what one could have predicted from the changing age distribution of the population.[6]

---

[3] By the end of 2008, there were a total of 2,424,279 people confined: 1,518,559 in federal and state prisons; 785,556 in local jails; and 92,845 in juvenile detention facilities. An additional 4.8 million are on probation or parole. For a summary, see Adam Liptak, "1 in 100 U.S. Adults Behind Bars, New Study Says," *New York Times*, February 28, 2008, http://www.nytimes.com/2008/02/28/us/28cnd-prison.html?_r=2.

[4] Joke: A conservative is a liberal who has been mugged, and a liberal is a conservative who has been arrested.
Remark: In the 1980s, more liberals were being mugged than conservatives were being arrested.

[5] In 1950 there were 24 million people ages 14 to 24, and by 1960 that figure had increased only marginally to 27 million. However, within the next decade the number increased by 13 million, or by 1.3 million per year. In 1990 there were 1.5 million fewer boys ages 15 to 19 than there had been in 1980. This group accounted for 9.3 percent of the U.S. population in 1980 but for only 7.2 percent of the population in 1990. See Section IID for a theory about the reasons for these changes and a possible connection to the amount of crime.

[6] A detailed discussion of these figures and of alternative explanations for the crime wave of the 1960s may be found in JAMES Q. WILSON, THINKING ABOUT CRIME (rev. ed. 1983), pp. 13–25 (Ch. 1, "Crime Amidst Plenty: The Paradox of the Sixties") and pp. 223–249 (Ch. 12, "Crime and American Culture"). It is also important to note that this secular increase in the amount of crime was observed in *all* of the developed economies, not just in the United States.

Third, violent criminals and their victims in the United States are disproportionately African Americans. To illustrate, homicides are committed against the U.S. non-black population at about the same rate as against the nonminority populations in European countries and, in fact, at *lower* rates than in some European countries. Black victims of homicide elevate U.S. murder rates to the highest among developed countries. One of the most vitriolic policy debates in the United States concerns the connection between violence and race. One side blames discrimination as the cause, and the other side locates the problem in black society. (See the box, "African Americans and Crime.")

Fourth, a small number of people commit a large proportion of violent crimes. Approximately 6 percent of the young males of a given age commit 50 percent or more of all the serious crimes committed by all young males of that age. This remarkable fact is true in most countries, not just in the United States. The characteristics of this 6 percent of young males are remarkably consistent across different cultures. They tend to come from dysfunctional families, have close relatives (including parents) who are criminals, have low verbal-intelligence quotients, do poorly in school, are alcohol- and drug-abusers, live in poor and chaotic neighborhoods, and begin their misbehavior at a very young age.[7]

This sociological sketch suggests a connection between crime and poverty, which suggests a connection between crime and the economy. For example, an increase in unemployment rates might cause an increase in crime rates. In fact, this connection is weak. During the prosperous 1960s, the U.S. economy grew and the distribution of income became more equal; yet, the United States experienced a rapid increase in the amount of crime. During the economically prosperous 1990s, crime declined dramatically, even though the income distribution became less equal. (We will investigate the causes of this decline shortly.) And in the Great Recession of 2008–2010, the rise in unemployment rates from about 5 percent in 2007 to almost 10 percent in late 2010 has not been associated with higher crime rates. (See our further discussion of these relationships in Section IIB below.)

We have been discussing the social statistics of crime, which we relate to deterrence of crime. The economic theory of the previous chapter suggests that criminals are deterred partly by the severity of the punishment and partly by its certainty. Has this been prediction been borne out by events of the recent past? Perhaps so. The United States responded to increased crimes in the late 1960s and 1970s by longer prison sentences, not by increasing the certainty of punishment. To be concrete, the United States built more jails and hired more guards to punish criminals, rather than by hiring more police to catch them.[8] By definition, the *expected punishment* equals the severity of punishment times its probability. A possible explanation for the increased crime rates, at least through the early 1990s, one that is in keeping with the economic theory of the previous chapter, is that the expected punishment for committing a *serious* crime (violent or not) fell over the last four decades of the 20th century in the United States. In the 1950s it was 22 days in jail.

---

[7] For a discussion of the policy implications of these connections, see James Q. Wilson, *What to Do About Crime?*, COMMENTARY (September, 1994).

[8] There are definitional problems in counting police officers. (Should one, for example, include private security guards or only sworn, public police officers?) Setting these issues aside, in 2006 there were almost 700,000 police officers working for states, counties, municipalities, universities, transit systems, and other nonfederal governmental organizations. There were an additional 120,000 federal police officers, for a national total of about 820,000 police. Those figures have not increased much since 2006.

By the early 1980s it was just 11 days. For juveniles the expected punishment during this period was particularly low.[9] However, these figures began to change in the mid-1980s so that average expected punishment for a wide range of crimes rose. As we have seen, crimes began to fall in the early 1990s and have continued to fall throughout the first decade of the 21st century. These broad patterns seem to be explained by the economic theory of crime and punishment. But the connection between crime and expected punishment requires careful analysis using statistics, as we discuss later.

Web Note 13.1

On our website we provide up-to-date statistics on crime in the United States and other countries, links to websites with further information, and some comparative explanations of differences in the amount of crime in various countries.

B. Social Cost of Crime

Now we turn from the quantity of crime to its costs. We may divide the social cost of crime into the losses to victims (property and personal losses) and the cost of preventing crime (public and private). We can make a rough estimate of each of these elements in order to compute the social costs of crime in the United States in a recent year.

The easiest costs to document are state expenditures on preventing crime and punishing criminals. Spending on the criminal-justice system in 1992 constituted 7.5 percent of all governmental spending at the local, state, and federal levels. By 2002 the figure had fallen significantly, largely because the Gross Domestic Product (GDP) had risen so dramatically during the 1990s. The total amount spent annually by all levels of government in the United States on the criminal-justice system is well over $100 billion. Of that total, approximately one-third is spent on police protection. Federal and state prison systems cost about one-third of the total, and prosecutors, public defenders, probation officers, courts, recordkeeping, and so on account for the remaining one-third. More recent statistics are roughly the same, although somewhat distorted by the increase in anti-terrorist efforts.

Expenditures by individuals and private organizations to prevent crime are more difficult to estimate than state expenditures. This money is spent on alarms, private guards, security systems, placing identifying marks on valuable goods, and the like. In 1993, private expenditures to prevent crime in the United States amounted to approximately $65 billion. By 2003 the figure had risen to close to $90 billion. By 2008 the figure had risen to more than $100 billion. (We note from our discussion in the previous chapter that not all private expenditures reduce crime; some simply displaces crime.)

The value of lost property and the losses to individual victims of crime are the most difficult elements of the social costs of crime to estimate. The value of all stolen goods in 1992 was estimated to be $45 billion. We have only rough estimates of personal losses to victims: For example, the medical costs of attending to those injured in crimes was $5 billion in 1992, ignoring the many indirect costs of crime to the victims such as trauma, anxiety, and shattered lives. There are reasons to believe that these figures have not increased

---

[9] See Wilson, supra n. 7.

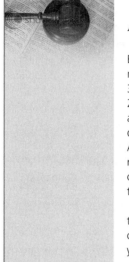

African Americans and Crime[10]

Blacks and whites had, in 1992, identical victimization rates for personal theft. However, for more serious theft (burglary, larceny, and automobile theft) the rate of black victimization was 33 percent higher than the rate for whites. More dramatically, in 1988 blacks accounted for 20 percent of the population in the 75 most populous urban counties in the United States but accounted for 54 percent of all murder victims in those counties.[11] Why are black Americans disproportionately victims of violent crime? Professor DiIulio concludes that affluent Americans move to safer communities, choose safer jobs, and enjoy relatively safe forms of recreation, whereas poverty prevents many black Americans from distancing themselves from criminals. (Note that most violent crime in the United States is *intra*racial: Black criminals tend to have black victims, and white criminals tend to have white victims.)[12]

A similar racial disparity exists among criminals. In the 75 most populous counties in the country, blacks account for 20 percent of the population but for 62 percent of all defendants in murder cases. In 1991 the arrest rate for violent crime for young black males was five times higher than for young white males (1,456 per 100,000 for black youth and 283 per 100,000 for white youth).

Disproportionate arrest rates resulted in a disproportionately African American prison population. In 1990, 48.9 percent of all state prisoners and 31.4 percent of all federal prisoners were black. (The proportions were almost the same in 2008.)[13] Why are black Americans disproportionately perpetrators of violent crime? Professor DiIulio points to the tragic fact that a disproportionate share of African American youth grow up in dysfunctional families and in neighborhoods in which delinquent and deviant behavior is common. Conversely, low crime rates among Chinese immigrants to the United States are often attributed to family and cultural characteristics.[14]

---

[10] The material in this box comes from John J. DiIulio Jr., *The Question of Black Crime*, THE PUBLIC INTEREST (Fall, 1994). See also the commentaries on that article by Glenn C. Loury, James Q. Wilson, Paul H. Robinson, Patrick A. Langan, and Richard T. Gill.

[11] For violent crimes of all types, the victimization rate in 1992 was 113 per 1,000 for teenage black males, 94 per 1,000 for teenage black females, 90 for teenage white males, and 55 for teenage white females. For slightly older black males (ages 20–34) the rate was 80; for white males of the same age the rate was 52. Finally, for adult black males between the ages of 35 and 64 the rate was 35; for adult white males, it was 18.

[12] Approximately 84 percent of the single-offender violent crimes committed by blacks are committed against other blacks, and about 73 percent of violent crimes committed by whites are committed against other whites.

[13] Some contend that the arrest, conviction, and imprisonment records reflect a racist criminal justice system. There is much evidence against this view. A recent National Academy of Sciences study said, "[F]ew criminologists would argue that the current gap between black and white levels of imprisonment is mainly due to discrimination in sentencing or in any of the other decision-making processes in the criminal justice system." Similarly, a 1991 RAND Corporation study of adult robbery and burglary defendants in 14 large urban areas found no evidence of racial or ethnic discrimination in conviction rates, disposition times, or other important indicators of outcomes.

[14] "During the 1960s, one neighborhood in San Francisco had the lowest income, the highest unemployment rate, the highest proportion of families with incomes under $4000 per year, the least educational attainment, the highest tuberculosis rate, and the highest proportion of substandard housing. . . . That neighborhood was called Chinatown. Yet in 1965, there were only five persons of Chinese ancestry committed to prison in the entire state of California." JAMES Q. WILSON & RICHARD J. HERRNSTEIN, CRIME AND HUMAN NATURE (1985).

significantly since the early 1990s. One reason is that the total amount of crime has declined in the last 20 years to levels not seen in the United States since the 1930s. Another reason is that the speed and skill with which medical personnel are now able to respond to traumatic injury lowers the medical costs of personal injuries, such as those from gunshot wounds.

If we add these elements, the total cost equals $500 billion, or approximately 4 percent of the U.S. gross domestic product. This number excludes some immeasurable costs. For example, imprisonment infects a significant group of criminals with AIDS.[15] This number also excludes the cost of reintegrating former prisoners into normal economic and social life after the surge in imprisonment. In 2007 approximately 700,000 prisoners were released from prison—a group equal in size to the population of a large city. Congress passed the Second Chance Act in 2007 to give the states a total of $100 million over the following two years to help the states design model programs for reintegration of these prisoners. There is no question that such programs are necessary: The best estimate is that two-thirds of those released prisoners will recidivate within three years.

QUESTION 13.1:   Do statistics support the perception that the United States has been swept by a wave of crime?

QUESTION 13.2:   If expenditures on preventing crime equal $200 billion and the costs of crime to victims equal at least $300 billion, could the United States save $500 billion by abandoning all efforts to prevent crime?

QUESTION 13.3:   How would economics try to answer the question, "Does crime increase or decrease as a society becomes more wealthy?"

QUESTION 13.4:   When statutes prescribe the exact punishment for each crime, the judge's discretionary power decreases and the prosecutor's increases. Predict how this change might affect the charges made against arrested persons.

II. Does Punishment Deter Crime?

In the previous chapter we outlined an economic theory of the decision to commit a crime. According to that theory, an increase in expected punishment causes a decrease in crime, holding other variables constant. The *deterrence hypothesis* holds that crime decreases significantly—in technical terms, the supply of crime is *elastic* with respect to punishment. If so, then increasing the resources that society devotes to the arrest, conviction, and punishment of criminals should reduce the harm caused by crime.

An alternative hypothesis holds that variations in the certainty and severity of punishment do *not* significantly deter criminals. Rather, crime is the result of a complex set

---

[15] Rucker C. Johnson & Steven Raphael, *Incarceration Trends and Racial Disparities in AIDS Infections*, Goldman School of Public Policy, University of California, Berkeley, Working paper (Fall 2008).

of economic and sociological factors (or possibly biological factors). The appropriate way to minimize the social costs of crime is to attack these root causes of crime—for example, to devote resources to job creation, income maintenance, family counseling, mental health, and drug and alcohol counseling.

Although public debate frames these two hypotheses as mutually exclusive, they might both be correct to some extent. If many variables cause crime, the optimal public policy for reducing it mixes criminal justice and socioeconomic programs.

Which hypothesis is true? We examine the relevant literature and then, at the end of this section, draw a tentative conclusion on the merits of alternative hypotheses. Much of the literature relies on econometrics, which is indispensible in the search for the causes of crime, but also susceptible to misuse and mistake.[16]

A. Deterrence

The usual statistical study of deterrence seeks to explain a certain kind of crime as a function of deterrence, economic, and sociological variables. These explanatory variables include, first, proxies for the probability of punishment (for example, the probabilities of being detected, arrested, and convicted) and the severity of punishment (for example, average prison sentence); second, labor market variables such as the unemployment rate and the income level of the jurisdiction; and third, socioeconomic variables such as the average age, race, and urbanization of the jurisdiction's population. The statistics may be from a single jurisdiction over time, or from different jurisdictions at the same point in time, or both.

Numerous empirical studies have this form. Here we discuss three especially noteworthy examples. First, a famous study by Isaac Ehrlich used data on robbery for the entire United States in 1940, 1950, and 1960 to estimate the deterrence hypothesis and concluded that, holding all other variables constant, the higher the probability of conviction for robbery, the lower the robbery rate.[17] Second, Alfred Blumstein and Daniel Nagin studied the relationship between draft evasion and penalties for that crime in the 1960s and 1970s. They concluded that a higher probability of conviction and a higher level of penalty caused a lower rate of draft evasion.[18] Third, a study by Kenneth

---

[16] We mention two general problems with all statistical studies of deterrence. First, the accuracy of the data on the number of crimes differs significantly among jurisdictions at any point in time, and within a jurisdiction at different points in time. For example, some crimes are almost always reported to the authorities; some are rarely reported; and these reporting discrepancies differ over time and among jurisdictions. These inaccuracies may create spurious statistical relationships. (See Web Note 13.1 for more on this topic.) Second, estimated models omit some important but difficult-to-measure variables, such as whether adults were abused as children. If omitted variables correlate with included variables, the estimated relationship will be biased. Over time, improvements in measuring variables and better statistical techniques tend to overcome these two weaknesses in deterrence studies.

[17] Isaac Ehrlich, *Participation in Illegitimate Activities: A Theoretical and Empirical Investigation*, 81 J. POL. ECON. 521 (1973). Ehrlich also found that there was no deterrent effect attributable to the severity of punishment, as measured by the average length of a prison sentence for robbery in the years 1940 and 1960, but that there was such a deterrent effect in 1950.

[18] Alfred Blumstein & Daniel Nagin, *The Deterrent Effect of Legal Sanctions on Draft Evasion*, 28 STAN. L. REV. 241 (1977).

Wolpin used time-series data from England and Wales over the lengthy period 1894–1967 to test for a deterrent effect in those countries. Wolpin found that crime rates in the United Kingdom were an inverse function of the probability and severity of punishment.[19]

These (and other) studies found a significant deterrence effect. The National Research Council of the U.S. National Academy of Sciences established the Panel on Research on Deterrent and Incapacitative Effects in 1978 to evaluate the many academic studies of deterrence. The panel concluded that "the evidence certainly favors a proposition supporting deterrence more than it favors one asserting that deterrence is absent."[20]

These studies seek to explain the "crime rate," which is a highly aggregated statistic. Rather than studying crime rates, another approach to measuring deterrence studies the behavior of small groups of people. We know that a relatively small proportion of the population commits a large proportion of the crime. Economists have had some success in predicting who will become violent criminals. (See box titled "Guilty of Future Crimes.") We describe two studies on deterring offenses by such people.

Guilty of Future Crimes

Social scientists have modestly increasing abilities to predict crime. For example, Peter Greenwood's study for RAND titled Selective Incapacitation (1982) found that high-rate criminal offenders could be predicted as having seven characteristics: (1) conviction of a crime while a juvenile; (2) use of illegal drugs as a juvenile; (3) use of illegal drugs during the last two years; (4) employment less than 50 percent of the time in the previous two years; (5) incarceration in a juvenile facility; (6) imprisonment during more than 50 percent of the last two years; and (7) a previous conviction for the current offense.

A controversial conclusion that some people reach is that criminals with these characteristics should be incapacitated in prison for a longer period than other criminals. For example, M. Moore, S. Estrich, D. McGillis, and W. Sperlman give "qualified endorsement" to a policy of "selective incapacitation" in Dangerous Offenders: the Elusive Target of Justice (1985). Of course, decisions about whether to grant bail, about the severity of punishment, and about parole are all currently made on the basis of predictions about the criminal disposition of the offender. In *Barefoot v. Estelle,* 463 U.S. 880 (1983), *reh. den.* 464 U.S. 874 (1983), the U.S. Supreme Court allowed psychiatric testimony on an individual's likely future dangerousness to be put before a jury that was deciding whether the defendant should be given the death penalty.

QUESTION 13.5: Does efficiency require the adjustment of punishment according to predictions about future crime? Is doing so unfair?

---

[19] Kenneth Wolpin, *An Economic Analysis of Crime and Punishment in England and Wales 1894–1967*, 86 J. Pol. Econ. 815 (1978). The data were better than any comparable data from the United States and, because of the length of the time period covered, allowed for considerable flexibility in the hypotheses tested.

[20] Blumstein, Cohen, & Nagin, eds., Deterrence and Incapacitation: Estimating the Effects of Criminal Sanctions on Crime Rates (1978). A critique of that report may be found in Ehrlich & Mark, *Fear of Deterrence*, 6 J. Legal Stud. 293 (1977).

First, Professor Ann Witte followed the post-release behavior of 641 convicted criminals for three years. She gathered information on whether the men were arrested again during that period (about 80 percent were), on their previous convictions and imprisonments, on their labor-market experience after release, and on whether they were addicted to alcohol or drugs. Professor Witte tested the hypothesis that conviction and imprisonment induced these high-risk offenders to engage in fewer crimes in the future. She concluded that the higher the probability of conviction and imprisonment, the lower the number of subsequent arrests per month out of prison.[21]

Second, Charles Murray and Louis Cox, Jr., tracked the records of 317 Chicago males, with an average age of 16, who had been imprisoned for the first time by the Illinois Department of Corrections. Notwithstanding their youth, this was a hardened group of young men: Before receiving their first prison sentences, they averaged 13 prior arrests per person; as a group, they had been charged with 14 homicides, 23 rapes, more than 300 assaults, more than 300 auto thefts, almost 200 armed robberies, and more than 700 burglaries. The average sentence for their offenses was 10 months. Murray and Cox followed these young offenders for about 18 months after their release and found that during that period, the group's arrest record fell by two-thirds. The authors concluded that imprisonment served as a deterrent to future crime for this high-risk group.[22]

Governments seldom conduct experiments for social scientists by changing criminal laws in order to test for deterrence effects. Sometimes, however, governments change such laws for political reasons, and the change presents social scientists with a "natural experiment" to test for deterrence. In July 2006, the Italian Parliament passed the Collective Clemency Bill, which provided for an immediate three-year reduction in the prison sentences of all inmates who had committed a crime before May 2, 2006, and been sentenced to imprisonment for a term of greater than three years. Approximately 22,00 inmates—about 40 percent of the Italian prison population—were released under the bill's terms on August 1, 2006. The bill further said that if a former inmate who had been released under the bill committed a crime within five years of his release, he would be required to serve the remaining sentence suspended by the pardon (which varied between one month and 36 months) and the sentence given for the newly committed crime.

Francesco Drago, Roberto Galbiati, and Pietro Vertova recognized that these terms created an interesting experiment in deterrence. The possible variations in the sentences that might be imposed on former inmates for the same crime in the future (consisting of the mandated sentence for the new crime plus the add-on from the time not served from the previous conviction) created a natural experiment that might be used to measure the effects

---

[21] Ann Witte, *Estimating the Economic Model of Crime with Individual Data,* 94 Q. J. Econ. 57 (1980). Additionally, she discovered that the strength of the deterrent effect varied between different classes of potential offenders. For those who engaged in serious, including violent, crimes, severity of punishment had a stronger deterrent effect than certainty of punishment. For those who engaged in property crimes, certainty of arrest and conviction had a stronger deterrent effect than severity of punishment. The deterrent effect was weakest for drug addicts. Lastly and somewhat surprisingly, the ease of subsequent employment had no significant effect on future criminal offenses.

[22] C. A. Murray & L. A. Cox, Jr., Beyond Probation: Juvenile Corrections and the Chronic Delinquent (1979). Note that Murray and Cox found that rearrest rates were higher for comparable juveniles who had *not* been imprisoned but instead were put on probation.

of increased prison sentences on the decision to commit a crime. Their statistical analysis concluded that "a marginal [one month] increase in the remaining sentence reduce[d] the probability of recidivism by 0.16 percent points." The authors went on to estimate an elasticity of crime with respect to prison sentences and found that figure to be approximately −0.74—that is, a 10 percent increase in prison sentence for committing a particular crime could be expected to lead to a 7.4 percent decrease in the amount of that crime committed.[23]

Economics has assimilated findings in cognitive psychology that are changing the analysis of deterrence. Perhaps the most important finding is that people are too short-sighted to be deterred by long criminal sentences. If the punishment increases from, say, two years in prison to three years, the additional years has little affect on deterring criminals, especially the young men who commit most violent crimes. Lee and McCrary demonstrated this fact in a remarkable study. The length of the sentence faced by a person who commits a crime increases sharply on the criminal's eighteenth birthday. Consequently, the deterrence hypothesis predicts a sharp decrease in crime when juvenile delinquents turn eighteen. A careful statistical analysis of Florida arrest data shows no discontinuity in the probability of committing a crime at the age of majority. So, the longer punishments when the criminal turns eighteen apparently are not deterring them from committing crime. This fact has a simple, powerful implication for criminal justice policy: Shortening sentences and redirecting expenditures away from prisons and towards police, which would decrease the severity of the punishment and increase its certainty, would deter more crimes at no more expense to taxpayers.[24]

In the same spirit as the Lee and McCrary finding, Paul Robinson of the University of Pennsylvania School of Law and John Darley of the Department of Psychology at Princeton University have argued that criminal law does not deter.[25] Let us be very careful about what the authors claim: They believe that the criminal justice system probably does deter crime, but they are very doubtful that criminal *laws* deter crime. They want to draw a distinction between such actions as the legislative manipulation of sentence length, which they believe does *not* have a deterrent effect, and such actions as increasing police patrols or the harshness of prison conditions, which they believe might deter crime.

The authors base their contention on findings in the behavioral sciences. They write that for criminal law to have a deterrent effect on a potential criminal's conduct choices, the "following three questions must all be answered in the affirmative:

1. Does the potential offender know, directly or indirectly, and understand the implications for him, of the law that is meant to influence him? That is, does the potential offender know which actions are criminalized by criminal

---

[23] Drago, Galbiati, & Vertova, *The Deterrent Effects of Prison: Evidence from a Natural Experiment*, 119 J. POL. ECON. 257 (2009).

[24] David Lee and Justin McCrary, "Crime, Punishment, and Myopia," NBER Working Paper No. W11491 (2005). An earlier study found some effect of harsher punishments at the age of majority. See Steven Levitt, *Juvenile Crime and Punishment*, 106 J. POL. ECON. 1156 (1998).

[25] Robinson & Darley, *Does Criminal Law Deter?: A Behavioral Science Investigation*, 24 OXFORD J. LEGAL STUD. 173 (2004).

codes, which actions are required, and which conditions will excuse actions which are otherwise criminal?

2. If he does know, will he bring such understanding to bear on his conduct choices at the moment of making his choices?

3. If he does know the rule and is able to be influenced in his choices, is his perception of his choices such that he is likely to choose compliance with the law rather than commission of the criminal offense? That is, do the perceived costs of noncompliance outweigh the perceived benefits of the criminal action so as to bring about a choice to forgo the criminal action?"[26]

Robinson and Darley argue that there is evidence that none of these premises is true. First, they report on surveys that they and others have conducted in different states about a limited number of legal rules to ascertain how well a random sample of citizens know prevailing criminal laws. One survey found that a survey of a "target population" (not the general population) of potential offenders found that 18 percent of them had no idea what the sanctions for several crimes would be; 35 percent said that they did not pay attention to what the sanction would be; and only 22 percent thought they knew exactly what the punishment would be. So, the authors conclude that "people rarely know the criminal law rules."[27]

Robinson and Darley also point out that the overall rate of conviction for crimes is extremely low—approximately 1.3 percent of all crimes result in a conviction, and the chances of a convicted criminal's receiving a prison sentence is about 100-to-1 for most offenses; "even the most serious offenses, other than homicide, have conviction rates of single digits." Many in the general population may not know these facts. Rather, they may believe that the chances of being detected, arrested, and convicted are much higher and are, therefore, deterred from committing crime. But career criminals and their friends and relatives are likely to know how low the conviction and punishment rates really are.

One of the most intriguing points that Robinson and Darley make is that the duration of prison sentences may not have a deterrent effect. They note that people adapt fairly quickly to changed circumstances; for instance, there is evidence that within six months of incarceration prisoners have returned to their pre-incarceration level of subjective well-being. And there is compelling evidence that in remembering experiences, we all suffer from "duration neglect"—that is, we do not accurately remember the duration of good or bad experiences. So, thoughts of imprisonment may deter those of us who have not been "inside," but perhaps those who have been imprisoned recall the experience as not as bad as they had anticipated.

Robinson and Darley summarize unpublished work by Anup Malani of the University of Chicago Law School on the deterrent effect of the felony-murder rule. That rule penalizes *any* death that occurs during the commission of a crime as if it were an intentional killing. Clearly, legislators passed the felony-murder rule in the hope that criminals would take greater care during the commission of a crime by, for example, not carrying a gun and might be deterred from committing serious crimes altogether. So, the hope was that the

---

[26] Id. at 175.

[27] They recognize that this is an overgeneralization. Many people know about important inflection points in the criminal sanctions, that, for example, the penalties for a given crime jump considerably when a juvenile becomes an adult. So, it should not be surprising to learn that when juveniles pass the age to become an adult, they commit fewer crimes. See Levitt, *supra* n. 24.

rule might not only lower the rate of serious injury in the commission of crimes but also lower the rate of serious crimes, such as robbery. Malani gathered data to see if he could establish the effects of the felony-murder rule on serious crime. Surprisingly, he found that the rule has had the perverse effect of "increase[ing] the rate of deaths during a robbery." Similarly with regard to rape, the overall effect of the rule was to increase the total deaths during rape by 0.15–0.16 percent. Why these perverse results obtain is still unclear.[28]

 Web Note 13.2

> We provide some additional information on the behavioral analysis of crime and punishment on our website.

B. Economic Conditions and Crime Rates

Committing a crime takes time and effort that could go elsewhere, such as earning money legally. A rational, amoral criminal responds to the opportunity cost of crime; so, an increase in the opportunities for earning income legally should cause a decrease in criminality. If opportunity cost has a powerful effect, then among the best policies for reducing the amount of crime are those that ameliorate economic and social conditions. For example, from 1991 to 2001 the United States had the longest period of peace-time prosperity without a recession in its history, and, as we know, this corresponded with a dramatic downturn in all sorts of crime, both violent and nonviolent. Was the economic prosperity a cause of the downturn in crime? We review briefly some empirical studies of the extent to which employment and income-enhancing policies reduce the amount of crime. (We do not discuss the statistical studies of the influence of early family life, heredity, and other noneconomic factors on crime rates.[29])

Perhaps unemployed workers commit crimes to gain income or to deal with their idle time and frustration, so that worsening employment conditions lead to an increase in the amount of property crimes. Is there a discernible relationship between cyclical fluctuations in economic conditions and crime rates? There is mixed evidence on this point. In a 1981 survey of the literature up to that date, Thomas Orsagh and Ann Witte found little evidence of a significant relationship.[30] Cook and Zarkin found a small increase in the number of burglaries and robberies during recent recessions, no correlation between the business cycle and homicides, and a countercyclical relationship between economic conditions and auto theft. They also found that long-term trends in crime rates were independent of the

---

[28] Randi Hjalmarsson, *Crime and Expected Punishment: Changes in Perceptions at the Age of Criminal Majority*, Am. L. & Econ. Rev. (forthcoming 2010).

[29] See, for example, Wilson & Herrnstein, *supra* n. 14.

[30] Orsagh & Witte, *Economic Status and Crime: Implications for Offender Rehabilitation*, 72 J. Crim. L. & Criminol. 1055 (1981). This study follows up a literature survey by Robert Gillespie. Gillespie found three studies that discovered a significant relationship between unemployment and crime and seven that did not. Robert W Gillespie, *Economic Factors in Crime and Delinquency: A Critical Review of the Empirical Evidence*, pp. 601–626 in Unemployment and Crime: Hearings Before the Subcommittee on Crime of the Committee on the Judiciary (House of Representatives; Washington, D.C.: U.S. Government Printing Office, 1978).

business cycle.[31] And as already noted, the continuing decline in crime through the Great Recession of 2008–2010 seems to indicate that there is a very weak connection between aggregate economic conditions and crime rates.

These negative results do not necessarily contradict the economic theory of deterrence. In that theory, the business cycle influences the opportunity cost of crime and also the opportunities for crime. These two influences work in opposite directions. As the economy worsens, criminals have fewer opportunities for legitimate earnings, and also fewer opportunities for crime. For example, unemployment creates a motive to sell cocaine and also reduces the number of potential customers.[32] It follows that as the economy improves, the opportunity cost of crime increases, but so, too, does the take to be had from successful crime. Which of these forces dominates is still somewhat in doubt. (We return to that connection in Section VII.)

C. Does Crime Pay?

Most people never commit crime, but some people make a career of it. These career criminals apparently believe that the benefits of crime exceed the expected punishments. Why do career criminals reach a different conclusion from the rest of us? Is crime very profitable for them, or is legitimate work unprofitable for them, or do they have special attitudes toward risk and special valuations of time?

To address these questions, James Q. Wilson and Allan Abrahamse (in *Does Crime Pay?* 9 JUSTICE QUARTERLY 359 (1992)) compared the gains from crime and from legitimate work for a group of career criminals in state prisons in three states. Wilson and Abrahamse divided prisoners into two groups: mid-rate offenders and high-rate offenders. Using data from the National Crime Survey's report of the average losses by victims in different sorts of crimes, the authors estimated the annual income for criminals.[33] They then compared these estimates of the income from crime with the prisoners' estimates of their income from legitimate sources. Two-thirds of the prisoners had reasonably stable jobs when they were not in prison and, on average, the prisoners believed that they made $5.78 per hour at those legitimate jobs.

---

[31] Philip J. Cook & Gary A. Zarkin, *Crime and the Business Cycle,* 14 J. LEGAL STUD. 115 (1985). This is, perhaps, surprising given the correlation between the business cycle and less serious property crimes and the usual belief that there is a correlation between those property crimes and homicides. See also Richard Freeman, *Crime and Unemployment,* in JAMES Q. WILSON, ED., CRIME AND PUBLIC POLICY (1983), and James Q. Wilson & Philip J. Cook, *Unemployment and Crime—What Is the Connection?,* 79 PUBLIC INTEREST 3 (1985).

[32] An excellent discussion of the literature on deterring crime through increasing the benefits of legal alternatives may be found in WILSON, THINKING ABOUT CRIME (rev. ed. 1983), pp. 137–142.

[33] For example, they estimated that the value of a stolen car was 20 percent of its market value. And following a study of drug dealing in Washington, D.C., they estimated that the net income of the average drug dealer was $2,000 per month. More recent survey evidence by Levitt and Venkatesh suggests that the annual incomes of most drug dealers is much less than that of minimum-wage employees (see *Freakonomics* Ch. 3 ("Why Do Drug Dealers Still Live with Their Moms?") (2006)). Levitt and Venkatesh have also written on the economics of street prostitution, showing that it is not at all financially rewarding (see "An Empirical Analysis of Street-Level Prostitution" (September, 2007) and *Superfreakonomics* Ch. 1 ("How Is a Street Prostitute Like a Department-Store Santa?") (2009)).

TABLE 13.1

Criminal and Legitimate Earnings per Year (1988 Dollars)

Crime type	High-Rate		Mid-Rate	
	Crime	Work	Crime	Work
Burglary/theft	$5,711	$5,540	$2,368	$7,931
Robbery	6,541	3,766	2,814	5,816
Swindling	14,801	6,245	6,816	8,113
Auto theft	26,043	2,308	15,008	5,457
Mixed	6,915	5,086	5,626	6,956

Source: Wilson & Abrahamse, *Does Crime Pay?*, 9 JUSTICE Q. 359, 367 (1992).

As Table 13.1 indicates, for mid-rate criminals, working pays more than crime for every type of crime except auto theft. For high-rate offenders, however, crime paid more than legitimate work for *all* crimes except burglary. These figures concern the income from crime, but not the major cost of crime to these criminals: time in prison. When the authors included those costs, the net income from crime fell below the income from legitimate work for both mid-rate and high-rate offenders.

Why, then, do career criminals commit crime? Wilson and Abrahamse consider and reject two explanations. First, the prisoners may have felt they had to commit crime because they had no meaningful opportunity for legitimate work. The authors doubt this view: Two-thirds of the prisoners were employed for some length of time during the period examined. Second, the prisoners may have had such serious problems with alcohol and drugs that they could not hold legitimate jobs. The authors argue that although two-thirds of the offenders had drinking or drug problems, the evidence from other studies indicates that these problems do not normally preclude legitimate employment. Wilson and Abrahamse conclude that career criminals are "temperamentally disposed to overvalue the benefits of crime and to undervalue its costs" because they are "inordinately impulsive or present-oriented." In economic terms, these people discount punishments for uncertainty and futurity more highly than other people do.

QUESTION 13.6: How could the collection of uniform crime statistics contribute to studies of deterrence?

QUESTION 13.7: Describe how statisticians might ideally separate the effect of the business cycle on the opportunity cost of crime and its profitability.

QUESTION 13.8: Assume that criminals discount risk and futurity more than other people. What policies might reduce crime by changing this fact?

D. Abortion and Crime

The economic analysis of crime hypothesizes that the level of punishment and its certainty, the level of legitimate economic opportunity, the age structure of the population, and other socioeconomic factors provide a relatively complete explanation for the level of crime in a particular time and place. The four-point pattern of recent crime in the United States that we outlined at the beginning of this chapter has been investigated using the independent variables that we just noted. However, a controversial article by John Donohue and Steve Levitt offers a very different explanation for the recent decline in the amount of crime—the legalization of abortion in 1973.[34]

The heart of their contention is that when the U.S. Supreme Court legalized abortion in *Roe v. Wade* in January 1973, there was a significant increase in the number of abortions—from under 750,000 in 1973 (when live births totaled 3.1 million) to 1.6 million legal abortions per year in 1980 (when live births totaled 3.6 million). Donohue and Levitt hypothesize that the increase in abortions can account for one-half of the observed decline in the amount of crime after 1991. All other factors taken together account for the remaining half. (We examine the other factors in Section VII.)

Donohue and Levitt divide legalized abortion's effect on the decline in crime into two effects—the "cohort size" effect and the "cohort quality" effect. The cohort size effect points to the reduction in the number of 18-year-old males beginning in 1991 as an important explanation of the decline in crime. But they also contend, controversially, that the "quality" of the young men who were not born because of abortion after 1973 was such that they would have been even more likely to commit crime and other antisocial acts than average 18-year-olds. The reasons are that "women who have abortions [teenage mothers, unmarried women, and the economically disadvantaged] are most likely to be those most at risk to give birth to children who would engage in criminal activity." Women tend to use abortion as a method of altering the timing of childbearing; they may wait until later when their economic or personal situation improves. Children are then born into better environments.

The authors point to five statistical factors in support of their hypothesis. First, there was a smaller number and proportion of the population in the high-crime ages in the early 1990s, in large part because of the increase in abortions beginning in 1973. Second, five states legalized abortion in 1970, before the Supreme Court legalized abortion in *Roe v. Wade,* and the decline in crime rates occurred earlier in those five states than it did in the rest of the country. Third, there is a statistically significant correlation between "higher rates of abortion in the late 1970s and early 1980s [and] lower crime rates [in those states] for the period 1985 to 1997." Fourth, there is no correlation between higher abortion rates in the mid- or late 1970s in a state and crime rates in that state between 1972 and 1985. And fifth, almost all of the decline in crime in the 1990s can be "attributed to reduction in crime among the cohorts born after abortion legalization[;] [t]here is little change in crime among older cohorts [over the last 30 years]."

Donohue and Levitt attribute about half of the entire decline in all crime in the 1990s to the effects of legalized abortion. Of that half, they attribute 50 percent to the "cohort size" effect and 50 percent to the "cohort quality" effect. However, their statistical research has not fared well under intense scrutiny. Abortion rates seem to lose their

---

[34] John J. Donohue III & Steven D. Levitt, *The Impact of Legalized Abortion on Crime,* 116 Q. J. ECON. 379 (2001). Interestingly the article first appeared on the SSRN Legal Scholarship network in 2000, from which there were a large number of downloads. *The New York Times* and other national publications reported on the study's findings well before the final version appeared in the *Quarterly Journal of Economics.*

significance when the regressions are redone by using more accurate crime rates of the age-relevant cohorts.[35] The only correction for inadequate econometric analysis is better econometric analysis, which the future will bring to the study of crime and abortion.

> ### Web Note 13.3
>
> For more on the Donohue and Levitt hypothesis, critiques of that hypothesis, an extension of the hypothesis that looks at the behavior of teenage girls, and links to other literature on the causes of the decline of crime in the 1990s, see our website.

III. Efficient Punishment

What forms of punishment do we actually use in the United States and how efficient are they? In this section we first examine the social benefits and costs of imprisonment and then look at the benefits and costs of monetary fines as a deterrent to crime. We argue that the U.S. criminal justice system relies too much on incarceration and too little on fines.

A. Imprisonment

1. The Social Benefits of Imprisonment

In principle, incarceration has at least four social benefits: (1) deterrence, (2) retribution, (3) rehabilitation, and (4) incapacitation. We have already discussed empirical evidence on deterrence. We consider the three remaining benefits in turn.

First, "retributivism" holds that justice requires punishing criminals in proportion to the seriousness of their crimes. In principle, varying the length of the sentence allows the state to adjust the shame and personal cost of imprisonment until it is proportional to the seriousness of the crime. You may think that economics concerns efficiency and has nothing to say about this problem of justice. In reality, economics has something to say about any explicit policy goal, including fairness. (See the box titled "Retribution and Economics.")

The next benefit allegedly derived from imprisonment is "rehabilitation," which means that prison changes criminals so that, after their release, they do not commit future crimes. For example, prison might teach the criminal a marketable job skill or provide religious instruction that induces them to eschew crime. The ideal of rehabilitation, which once enjoyed favor in the United States, has fallen out of favor, partly because rehabilitative programs show poor results.[36] Expenditures in U.S. prisons on counseling, job training, and general education have declined in recent years.

---

[35] Ted Joyce, *A Simple Test of Abortion and Crime*, 91 Rev. Econ. & Stat. 112 (2009). Our thanks go to Justin McCrary for advice on this difficult topic. See also Ted Joyce, "Abortion and Crime: A Review," NBER Working Paper, June, 2009. These and other criticisms of Donohue and Levitt's study are summarized in Web Note 13.3.

[36] See Francis Allen, The Decline of the Rehabilitative Ideal (1981).

Retribution and Economics

According to the principle of retribution, justice requires absolving the innocent and punishing the guilty in proportion to their crimes. Conversely, injustice results from punishing the innocent, absolving the guilty, or punishing the guilty out of proportion to the seriousness of their crimes. To avoid these injustices, officials who arrest and prosecute people must have good information about who did what. Given the cost of information, officials make mistakes. Punishing the innocent is called a "false positive" by statisticians, or a "Type I error." Not punishing the guilty is called a "false negative" or a "Type II error."

As officials increase the efficiency of the criminal-justice system, a point is reached where one type of error cannot be reduced without increasing errors of the other type. To illustrate, assume that the prosecutor ranks cases from weak to strong according to the probability of obtaining a conviction. A cutoff point is selected, above which all cases are prosecuted and below which cases are not prosecuted. Raising the cutoff, so that cases are only prosecuted with a high probability of obtaining a conviction, decreases false positives (punishing the innocent) and increases false negatives (not punishing the guilty). Lowering the cutoff has the opposite effect.

One way to choose the cutoff is by finding the point where the expected social cost of false positives equals the expected social cost of false negatives. If punishing an innocent person has more social cost than not punishing a guilty person, then the cutoff will be chosen at a point favoring the accused. Justice, as represented by the principle of retribution, and efficiency, as represented by minimizing the social costs of crime, come together when balancing false positives and false negatives. The two come together because the social cost of false imprisonment or mistaken release from prison depends upon beliefs about justice.

The final social benefit, "incapacitation," refers to the fact that, while confined, an offender cannot commit crimes against people outside prison. Even if prison fails to deter or rehabilitate, imprisonment may reduce crime by incapacitating criminals. Most recent studies indicate that about two-thirds of all inmates had criminal records before their current stay in prison. Additionally, between 25 percent and 50 percent of all offenders are arrested within a very short time of their release from prison—usually within six months to one year. And two-thirds will recidivate within three years. According to a Brookings Institution study, violent criminals who pass in and out of prison commit 12 serious crimes per year on average while out of prison (excluding drug crimes).[37]

From facts such as these, people conclude that incapacitation significantly lowers crime rates. These facts, however, require scrutiny. Two conditions must be met in order for incarceration to reduce crime rates. First, criminals incapacitated by imprisonment must not be replaced immediately by new criminals. For example, if imprisoning one drug dealer immediately results in his replacement by someone else, then incapacitation does not reduce total sales of drugs. In technical terms, *incapacitation is most effective at reducing crime when the supply of criminals is inelastic.* In general, inelastic supply results from a fixed factor of production. For example, an important drug dealer may have superior knowledge of illegal markets, so that after his arrest, no one else can quickly take his place.

---

[37] John J. DiIulio, *The Costs of Crime*, Brookings Review (Fall, 1994).

Second, in order for incarceration to reduce crime, imprisonment must reduce the total number of crimes committed by repeat offenders over their criminal careers. For some criminals, incarceration affects the timing, but not the number, of their crimes. To see why, consider that punishment typically grows more severe with each criminal conviction of a repeat offender. Suppose that after, say, the second conviction, the prospect of a very severe punishment for a third conviction causes this person to stop committing crimes. In this example, the fact that the person could not commit crimes while in jail after each of the first two convictions might not influence the total number of crimes the person committed. Rather, the time spent in jail just delayed the arrival of the day the criminal received the second conviction. The punishment for a third conviction could be so severe as to deter any further crime. In general, if a person commits crimes until the expected punishment exceeds the benefit, the deterrent effect of imprisonment determines how many crimes the person commits, and incapacitation has no independent effect. (See the box on "Three Strikes.")

Now consider the opposite kind of criminal. For this person, the urge to commit crime is irresistible in youth and fades with age. If the state keeps such a person in prison during her youth and releases her later in life, she will commit fewer crimes over her criminal career. Thus, incapacitation reduces the rate of crimes caused by youthfulness.

The fact that repeat offenders commit fewer crimes as they get older could be due to biological and sociological factors associated with aging, or it could be due to the higher expected penalties faced as their criminal records lengthen.

Distinguishing incapacitation effects and deterrence effects from incarceration is a complicated empirical issue. On the one hand, as we have seen, putting someone in jail or prison may reduce the amount of crime simply because the incarcerated cannot commit crimes. (The literature refers to this as "specific deterrence.") On the other hand, putting someone in jail or prison may reduce crime because other people observe the punishment meted out to a convicted criminal and decide not to commit a crime so as to avoid suffering the same punishment. (The literature refers to this as "general deterrence.") Either or both effects (or neither) are possible and disentangling them has proven to be a very taxing empirical task.

In the late 1990s, Dan Kessler and Steve Levitt published a paper in which they reported finding a method of distinguishing incapacitation and deterrence effects from incarceration and criminal sanctions generally.[38] In June 1982, voters in California passed a proposition (Proposition 8) that provided for immediate sentence enhancements for certain eligible crimes (murder, rape, robbery, burglary of a residence, and firearm assault): Upon conviction of any of the specified offenses, the defendant would receive a five-year increment to his or her incarceration for each prior conviction of a serious felony. The passage and implementation of the proposition provided what economists call a "natural experiment" to distinguish incapacitation from general deterrence. Kessler and Levitt recognized that any immediate decline in the amount of the crimes eligible for the sentence enhancements could not be attributed to incapacitative effects but rather to marginal deterrence effects. Kessler and Levitt found that there was an

---

[38] Daniel Kessler & Steven D. Levitt, *Using Sentence Enhancements to Distinguish Between Incapacitation and Deterrence,* 42 J. LAW & ECON. 343 (1998).

almost immediate decline of 4 percent in crimes eligible for sentence enhancements in California in the year after voters passed the proposition and that the declines in those crimes continued for years to come.[39] This is one of the most dramatic and careful studies finding a deterrence effect from criminal sanctions that can be distinguished from incapacitating effects of imprisonment.

2. The Social Costs of Imprisonment   The social costs of imprisonment include the direct costs of building, maintaining, and staffing prisons, and the opportunity cost of losing the productivity of imprisoned people. As to direct costs, recent

"Three Strikes" Law

California passed the nation's first "three strikes" legislation through a citizens' initiative in 1994. The measure passed with 72 percent of the votes, largely in reaction to the murder of 12-year-old Polly Klaas, who was kidnapped from a slumber party and murdered by a violent criminal who had recently been paroled. Three strikes laws, which have been passed in 26 states, call for significant sentence enhancement when an offender is convicted of his or her third felony. Usually, the first two offenses must be either violent or serious, but the third felony, which triggers the law, does not have to be either violent or serious. The sense of the laws is that someone who commits a third felony is a "habitual offender" and demonstrably not deterred by normal criminal sanctions. So, in California the sentence for the third felony is typically life in prison.

There are currently approximately 8,500 prisoners in California serving life sentences for a third felony. Of those, approximately 40 percent or 3,700 prisoners are serving that life sentence for a third felony that was neither violent nor serious. An initiative put to the voters in 2004 sought to remove nonviolent property and drug offenses from the list of three strikes felonies. But the measure was defeated, receiving slightly less than half of the votes.[40]

There is evidence that the three strikes law in California has been effective. Eric Helland and Alex Tabarrok did a sophisticated econometric study of the deterrent effect of the three strikes law and found that it "significantly reduces felony arrest rates among the class of criminals with two strikes by 17–20 percent."[41]

---

[39] The Kessler-Levitt study is criticized in Cheryl Marie Webster, Anthony N. Doob, & Franklin E. Zimring, *Proposition 8 and Crime Rates in California: The Case of the Disappearing Deterrent*, 5 CRIMINOLOGY & PUB. POL'Y 417 (2006). But see Levitt, *The Case of the Critics Who Missed the Point: A Reply to Webster et al.*, 5 CRIMINOLOGY & PUB. POL'Y 449 (2006).

[40] It is probably the case that the law on the books and the law in action are different with regard to third strike sentencing. Prosecutors rarely invoke the three strikes law if the third felony was not violent or serious. Also, California judges have decided that they can define a "felony" differently from how they are defined in statutes so that they can treat a nonviolent felony as if it were a misdemeanor that does not count as a third strike.

[41] Helland & Tabarrok, *Does Three Strikes Deter?: A Nonparametric Estimation*, 22 J. HUMAN RESOURCES 309 (2007). See also Emily Bazelon, *Arguing Three Strikes*, NEW YORK TIMES SUNDAY MAGAZINE, May 17, 2010; and FRANKLIN ZIMRING, GORDON HAWKINS & SAM KAMIN, PUNISHMENT AND DEMOCRACY: THREE STRIKES AND YOU'RE OUT IN CALIFORNIA (2001), who find that the three strikes laws have no discernible deterrent effect, are administratively awkward, and may cause significant injustices.

estimates are that it costs up to $40,000 per year to keep one prisoner in a maximum-security prison in the United States.

Turning to opportunity costs, inmates in U.S. prisons devote the bulk of their time to making highway signs, doing one another's laundry, preparing meals, and the like. More productive uses of their time surely could be found. One proposal, which former Chief Justice Warren Burger called "factories with fences," is to invite private industry to hire prisoners to produce marketable goods. At Attica State Prison in New York, a metal shop that manufactures file cabinets showed a profit of approximately $1.3 million in 1984. In Minnesota, Stillwater Data Processing, Inc.—a private, nonprofit corporation—employs inmates of a maximum-security prison as computer programmers. In Illinois, medium-security prisons often produce and market such valuable commodities as high school and college marching band uniforms. In North Carolina, female prison inmates serve as the staff that answers the state's tourism telephone hotline. Inmates highly prize those jobs and compete for them in terms of good behavior. However, there are legal obstacles that limit these developments, such as a federal law that makes transport of prison-made goods in interstate commerce illegal, and the "state-use" statutes that forbid the sale of prison-made goods to the governments of most states. Several states, eager to take advantage of the "factories with fences" idea, have repealed their state-use statutes.

Is there a cheaper method of deterring criminals than incarceration? One candidate that we shall look at shortly is the use of fines. Another is the use of high-technology monitoring equipment to enforce restrictions on criminals who are not in prison. For example, the terms of probation may prohibit a criminal from leaving a certain city, and the criminal may be required to report to his probation officer each week. In 1994, 40,000 criminals in the United States were wearing ankle bracelets that cannot be removed by them and that emit a signal enabling the police to locate them. The daily cost to the authorities of the ankle bracelet is $10, a fraction of the daily cost of imprisonment. Today those bracelets are equipped with GPS systems so that the exact location of the bracelet can be found at all times.

3. Sentencing Reform Two reforms in the sentencing of prisoners may have caused the sharp increase in the number of prisoners in the United States that we mentioned earlier. In 1980, most states followed a system called "indeterminate sentencing." Under indeterminate sentencing, the criminal statute prescribed an indefinite term for committing a particular offense, such as imprisonment "for not less than five years, nor more than ten years." The judge had discretion in determining the sentence within these broad boundaries. After the judge pronounced the sentence, the actual time served would be determined by the prison authorities and the parole board, depending on the prisoner's behavior and rehabilitative progress.[42]

In the mid- and late 1980s state and federal authorities replaced this system of judicial discretion with a system of determinate or mandatory sentencing. Under this system, the criminal statute prescribes a specific sentence for a particular crime—say, 15 years in prison for committing crime X. The offender becomes eligible for parole only after having served some fixed amount of time prescribed in the statute. Sometimes the judge

---

[42] The average violent offender in a state prison today spends only 40 percent of the sentence in prison.

reads the mandatory sentence from a grid. The vertical side of the grid lists crimes by their seriousness, ranging from a lesser felony to first-degree murder. Along the top of the grid, the history of the offender is scaled from 0 (a first-time offender) to 9 (a violent career criminal). Entries in the table increase in severity as one reads down or across. Judges have very little discretion to alter the sentence.[43]

We mentioned that the total number of prisoners in the United States rose to about 2.4 million in 2008. The principal reason for this increase is the mandatory sentencing of drug offenders. Today, 60 percent of all inmates in federal prisons and 20 percent of all those in state prisons are there on drug charges. (Later we analyze drug crimes.)

In complying with the requirements of mandatory sentencing, states are running out of prison space and money. For example, Texas today has about 240,000 offenders in prison, at an annual cost of $3 billion. In the early 1980s there were 188,000 prisoners, at an annual cost of $600 million. Federal law prevents the states from packing more prisoners into the same prisons.[44] Congress has tried to help the states by providing them with prison space under certain conditions.[45]

We have already considered (in the text box above) the workings and effects of three strikes laws. The economic wisdom of those laws is dubious. Imprisoning a 25-year-old for life would cost a phenomenally large sum of money, probably in excess of $1,000,000. In addition, keeping older inmates in prison is very costly and does not provide much social benefit. A California study found that the annual medical costs for prison inmates 55 and older may be $100,000. Moreover, only 2 percent of inmates over 55 who are released are ever rearrested.

In many states correctional spending has replaced health care spending as the fastest-growing component of the state budget. To reduce that correctional spending, many states are implementing criminal sentencing reforms. Michigan, for example, has recently abolished all of its mandatory minimum-sentencing drug laws. Louisiana eliminated some mandatory sentencing in favor of discretionary sentencing and amended its "three strikes" statute so as to count only violent felonies as the first two "strikes." Mississippi abolished discretionary parole in 1995 and brought it back for nonviolent first-time offenders in 2005. Eighteen other states have passed similar reforms of their sentencing laws.

---

[43] For a critique of mandatory sentencing and an argument by a former state court trial judge in Pennsylvania that the prior system of judicial discretion worked well, see LOIS G. FORER, A RAGE TO PUNISH: THE UNINTENDED CONSEQUENCES OF MANDATORY SENTENCING (1994).

[44] In North Carolina, inmates sued the state, contending that crowded state prisons violate the Eighth Amendment of the U.S. Constitution, which forbids cruel and unusual punishment. The 1988 agreement settling the suit stipulated that North Carolina would provide 50 square feet of space for each prisoner. With its current facilities, North Carolina can only house 21,400 prisoners and still satisfy this agreement. To keep the total state prison population at 21,400, the average time served by prisoners in North Carolina over the past seven years has fallen from 40 percent of the original sentence to 18.5 percent.

[45] In its 1994 anticrime act, Congress appropriated money for the federal government to build ten "regional prisons," designed to add 50,000 to 100,000 new prison spaces within the next five years. Congress invited the states to place their prisoners in these new facilities (thus, saving the states the politically painful cost of building their own new prisons), but only if the states would reform their criminal codes in several ways—most importantly by assuring the federal government that violent offenders would spend 85 percent of their sentence in prison.

Prisons for Profit and Factories with Fences

The U.S. government buys fighter planes, banking services, and hospital care from private companies. Why not pay private companies to confine prisoners? The profit motive spurs cost-cutting, quality control, and technological innovation, which make private businesses more efficient than the state. To illustrate, the Corrections Corporation of America, Inc., constructed the detention center of the U.S. Immigration and Naturalization Service in Houston for one-half the cost and in one-third the time required for the construction by the government of a comparable facility. CCA contends that its costs are generally about 6 percent below those of similar facilities operated by governmental bodies. CCA now owns 40 correctional facilities and manages some portion of the prisons in almost all the states and more than a dozen municipalities.

Another private company, Behavioral Systems Southwest, incarcerates 600 to 700 prisoners per day in leased hotels and large houses for a state prison system. The company deals only with low-risk prisoners and manages to detain them in its leased facilities for about $25 per day, compared with the $75 to $100 per-day cost of detention in a conventional facility.

Only a handful of privately operated prisons exist today in the United States, but penologists believe that the trend will broaden. The John Howard Association, a private, nonprofit group that lobbies for prisoners' rights, has not decided whether to support or oppose private prisons. The American Correctional Association is also adopting a wait-and-see attitude. However, the National Sheriffs Association and the American Federation of State, County and Municipal Employees, which represents 40,000 corrections employees, oppose privatization vigorously. (Can you see why?)

Prisons versus Social Programs

The prison population in the United States increased by almost a factor of five between 1980 and 2008—from 500,000 to almost 2.5 million people. As imprisonment became a much more likely punishment for conviction of a crime, the amount of many serious crimes fell dramatically. Prisons are expensive to build and expensive to operate. The best estimate we have is that the variable costs of incarceration are approximately $50,000 per year per prisoner. Because this society has so rapidly increased the number of prisoners, it may well be the case that we have reached the area of diminishing marginal social returns to further imprisonment. That is, the marginal social cost of imprisoning a further 100 prisoners—roughly $5 million—may be greater than its social benefits (in terms of crime deterred).

In an important recent study, John Donohue and Peter Siegelman calculated the marginal social return to further imprisonment and compared that return to that of spending an equal amount on social intervention programs designed to deter crime. Their conclusion was

(Continued)

that the social return on incarceration has fallen so that the elasticity of crime with respect to incarceration is approximately –0.15.[46]

That figure means that, for example, a 10 percent increase in spending on incarceration will cause a 1.5 percent drop in the amount of crime.

An economically informed policy that seeks to minimize the social costs of crime should take this elasticity and others into full consideration. For example, if we had evidence on the elasticity of crime with respect to spending on social programs and on policing and on other crime-deterring policies, we should allocate resources across these crime-deterring policies so as to get the greatest possible reduction in crime per dollar spent. There are estimates that suggest that the elasticity of crime with respect to expenditures on policing is 20 percent greater than that on incarceration, indicating that society should spend less on prisons and more on police. There are also estimates that the elasticity of crime with respect to expenditures on preschool programs is significantly higher than –0.15, suggesting that society should also transfer resources from prisons to preschools.

B. Fines

Imprisoning more people for longer periods may not be the most efficient way to reduce crime. A leading alternative to imprisonment is fines. In the previous chapter we examined the theory of fines, so our focus here is on the benefits and problems of implementing a system of fines for deterring crime.

Table 13.2 compares the use of fines and incarceration in several Western nations. Note the much greater reliance in Western Europe on fines as a punishment for

TABLE 13.2

Comparative Punishment for Selected Traditional Crimes, 1977

Country/ Jurisdiction	Total of Selected Defendants	Percent of All Defendants (in percent)	Incarceration (in Percent)	Fine Only (in Percent)	All Other (in Percent)
England, Wales	293,580	69	14	56	30
Germany	191,329	77	10	77	13
Sweden	29,121	67	13	43	44
U.S. Federal District Courts	16,057	56	39	5	56
Washington, D.C., Superior Court, 1974	1,847	38	32	4	64

The table and accompanying textual information are from Robert Gillespie, *Sanctioning Traditional Crimes with Fines: A Comparative Analysis,* 5 Int. J. Comp. Appl. Crim. Just. 197 (1981).

---

[46] See John J. Donohue III & Peter Siegelman, *Allocating Resources Among Prisons and Social Programs in the Battle Against Crime,* 27 J. Legal Stud. 1 (1998).

crimes, and the greater reliance in the United States on incarceration. What explains this difference? One possible explanation is that the United States' criminal population differs in significant ways from the European criminal population. For instance, Americans may use a gun or other dangerous weapon more frequently, thus deserving a stronger punishment. A second possibility is that a higher percentage of the U.S. criminal population consists of repeat offenders, for whom imprisonment may be the preferred sanction, and European criminals may tend to be first-time offenders, for whom fines may be the preferred sanction. A third possibility is that European criminals are more responsive to the threat of punishment than are criminals in the United States. Thus, authorities in this country must use more severe penalties to achieve the same level of deterrence that less severe sanctions generate in Europe. Finally, the difference may be due to different philosophical and cultural traditions. Europeans exhibit a distrust of imprisonment[47] as a deterrent, and Americans exhibit a distrust of fines.[48]

The typical fine in the United States is a fixed fine per offense, independent of the offender's wealth, with statutorily defined absolute maximums. By contrast, many European countries combine the use of the fixed-fine-per-offense system with an additional fine (called the "day fine" system) scaled according to the offender's income. Under this scheme, the prosecutor determines the defendant's recent daily income and recommends that the defendant be punished, if guilty, by being responsible for paying that daily income times a certain number of days. For a trivial crime, such as a traffic offense, the figure may be one day. For a serious crime, the number of days may rise to a maximum of 120.[49] Instead of paying the day fine all at once, the convicted person is allowed to spread the payments over a period of time. Spreading the payment overcomes the problem that fines can be large relative to income or wealth.

QUESTION 13.9: Competition among sellers improves the quality of goods for consumers. Could this mechanism work for the private supply of prisons?

QUESTION 13.10: How do full employment and high wages contribute to the power of fines as a deterrent?

---

[47] G. Mansell, *Comparative Correctional Systems: United States and Sweden,* 8 CRIM. L. BULL. 748 (1972).

[48] American Bar Association Project on Standards for Criminal Justice, STANDARDS RELATING TO SENTENCING ALTERNATIVES AND PROCEDURES (1971), and National Advisory Commission on Criminal Justice Standards and Goals, PROCEEDINGS OF THE NATIONAL CONFERENCE ON CRIMINAL JUSTICE (1973).

[49] For details on how the system works, see H. Thornstedt, *The Day-Fine System in Sweden,* 1975 CRIM. L. REV. 307. The reason that we may perceive criminal fines to be independent of the criminal's income and wealth is that we ignore the implicit economic effect of conviction on subsequent employment opportunities. John Lott, Jr., (in *Do We Punish High Income Criminals Too Heavily?* 30 ECON. INQ. 583 (1992)) shows that high-income criminals suffer a much larger loss in subsequent earnings due to a criminal conviction than do low- and medium-income criminals. Lott calculates that adding in this element of loss makes the total monetary penalty for crime (criminal fine plus the loss in subsequent earnings) steeply progressive.

IV. The Death Penalty

The ultimate punishment is death. In recent years, many countries have abandoned this sanction, and executions virtually ceased in the United States during the 1960s and have been very rare in the first decade of the twenty-first century. In 1972, the Supreme Court found the death penalty to be unconstitutional when applied "capriciously and discriminatorily."[50] This court decision provoked hostility among voters in some states, and many legislators responded by introducing legislation to revive capital punishment. After 1972, state legislatures amended their death statutes to comply with the Supreme Court's decision and to allow executions for the most serious crimes. In 1976 the Supreme Court upheld three revised state capital-punishment statutes as constitutional.[51] Currently, 37 states and the federal government have capital punishment statutes; 12 states and the District of Columbia do not.[52] Between 1976 and 2008, there were 1,224 executions of criminals in the United States, an average of approximately 37 people per year. There were 53 people executed in 2006, all of them men. The executions took place in 14 states—24 in Texas, 5 in Ohio, 4 in Florida, Oklahoma, North Carolina, and Virginia, and 1 each in Indiana, Alabama, Mississippi, South Carolina, Tennessee, California, Montana, and Nevada. All but one died by lethal injection. The number of prisoners on death row at the end of 2005 was 3,254. That is the fifth consecutive year that the number has fallen.[53] In 2008 there were 3,275 prisoners on death row. In 2009 there were 51 executions of prisoners; those occurred in 12 states. All but one of the executions in 2009 were by lethal injection; one was by electrocution. One prisoner died by firing squad in 2010, in Utah.

There have been, however, some interesting developments in the application of capital punishment in the United States. The peak year for executions since the reinstatement of the death penalty in 1976 was 1999, when there were 98 executions. Interestingly, only four states—Texas, California, Florida, and North Carolina—account for half of the additions to death row in recent years. And only two states—Oklahoma and Texas—account for half of the executions in recent years. Since 1999 the number of additions to death row in all the states has been decreasing. Indeed, in 2002 for the first time in a generation the number of prison inmates on death row dropped. These figures may indicate an important trend in American opinion. Although

---

[50] *Furman v. Georgia,* 408 U.S. 238 (1972). Justices Thurgood Marshall and William Brennan felt that the death penalty was cruel and unusual punishment (and, therefore, violated the Eighth Amendment to the Constitution) under any circumstances and, thus, would always be unconstitutional. (Justice Harry Blackmun announced in 1994, shortly before his retirement, that he, too, had come to believe that capital punishment was unconstitutional under any circumstances.) The other three justices of the majority were not prepared to go so far, holding instead that capital punishment was unconstitutional only when the state applied it capriciously and discriminatorily.

[51] *Profitt v. Florida,* 428 U.S. 242 (1976); *Jurek v. Texas,* 428 U.S. 252 (1976); and *Gregg v. Georgia,* 428 U.S. 153 (1976).

[52] Nebraska used to have the death penalty, but in 2008 the State Supreme Court declared the only method of execution (electrocution) to be unconstitutional. The state legislature has not written a new death statute.

[53] Forty-three percent of those on death row are African American. Approximately 1.5 percent are women. About 2 percent were 17 years old or younger.

public support for the death penalty is still strong (at 65 percent of those surveyed in 2006, down from 75 percent in the mid-1980s), it has been steadily declining for 20 years. And more than 50 percent of Americans believe that the death penalty is not administered fairly. Only 30 percent of Americans today believe that the death penalty deters homicide, down from 60 percent in 1985.

One reason for this declining support is the dramatic revelations in the mid- and late 1990s of the men on death row who were actually innocent. Since 1976 there have been a total of 304 condemned inmates who have been exonerated, mostly based on new evidence using new DNA techniques. In the late 1990s alone the State of Illinois released 13 people who had been wrongfully convicted of murders they did not commit and sentenced to death.[54] In early January 2003, outgoing Illinois Governor George Ryan pardoned an additional four Illinois inmates on death row whom he found to have been wrongfully convicted. On the last day of his administration Governor Ryan converted the death sentences of all 163 men and 4 women on Illinois' death row into life sentences.[55]

The literature on the economics of capital punishment focuses on the empirical question of whether executions deter murders. The debate has centered on statistical issues, such as the specification of the model to be estimated or the adequacy of the data. In this section we review this literature and draw some tentative conclusions about the deterrent effect of capital punishment.

Web Note 13.4

The dramatic findings of the conviction of innocent people have caused several states, including Illinois, to rethink the procedures by which courts impose the death penalty. To learn more about the new procedures and find additional information and links to articles about wrongful convictions, see our website. See also SCOTT TUROW, THE ULTIMATE PUNISHMENT: A LAWYER'S REFLECTIONS ON DEALING WITH THE DEATH PENALTY (2003).

A. The Deterrent Effect of Capital Punishment

The sociologist Thorsten Sellin made the first major study of the deterrent effect of the death penalty.[56] Sellin used four tests to detect a deterrent effect. First, he compared the homicide rates for adjacent states that did and did not have the death penalty. He discerned no difference in homicide rates among these adjacent states and, therefore,

---

[54] These exonerations were the result of heroic work by journalism students at Northwestern University and the work of Larry Marshall and his coworkers at the Center on Wrongful Convictions at the Northwestern University School of Law.

[55] See Samuel R. Gross, Kristen Jacoby, Daniel J. Matheson, Nicholas Montgomery, & Sujata Patil, *Exonerations in the United States, 1989 Through 2003,* 95 J. CRIM. L. & CRIMINOLOGY. 523 (2005) and Andrew Gelman, James S. Liebman, Valerie West, & Alexander Kiss, *A Broken System: The Persistent Pattern of Reversals of Death Sentences in the United States,* 1 J. EMP. LEGAL STUD. 209 (2004).

[56] THORSTEN SELLIN, CAPITAL PUNISHMENT (1967), pp. 135–160. See also T. SELLIN, THE PENALTY OF DEATH (1980).

inferred that the death penalty had no deterrent effect. Second, Sellin compared homicide rates within the same state before and after the abolition or restoration of the death penalty. He found no significant difference in those rates depending on the legal status of the death penalty. Third, Sellin looked at homicide rates within cities where executions had taken place and had been well publicized. There was no difference in homicide rates just before and just after executions. Lastly, he examined death rates for police officers in states that did and did not have the death penalty for murdering a police officer. The rate at which officers were killed was the same, regardless of whether that state executed the murderers of police officers.[57] Sellin's overall conclusion from these four tests was that the death penalty does not deter homicides.

Probabilistic Punishments: Good Economics, Bad Law

Most people dislike taking chances with very large stakes, such as their lives. The classical Chinese legal system took advantage of this fact to deter criminals cheaply and effectively.[58] A large number of crimes were punishable by death in imperial China, in principle. In reality, few criminals from noble families were executed, but many were threatened with execution. Criminals convicted of capital offenses had to pass through a series of rituals that resulted in random executions. In the last ritual, the names of everyone convicted of a capital offense were written on a scroll that was presented to the Emperor annually. The Emperor took a red brush and stroked it across the scroll. Anyone whose name was touched by red ink, which was a fraction of the names on the scroll, was executed. Anyone passing safely through this ritual several times was set free. The main advantage of this system was that many people could be deterred from committing serious crimes without actually executing very many people, and without significant cost to the state. Risk is cheap, effective punishment.

Public opinion, however, has turned decisively against random punishments, as dramatically illustrated by an infamous New York case. After a criminal was convicted of a felony, the judge explained that he would flip a coin to determine whether the young man would be set free or sentenced to prison. These facts found their way into the newspapers, producing an uproar, and the judge was eventually removed from the bench for misconduct and barred from serving as a New York judge again.[59]

QUESTION 13.11: What are the main sources of randomness in the contemporary criminal justice system?

QUESTION 13.12: Do you think that this randomness discourages or encourages crime?

[57] Some people assert that in the absence of the death penalty, hardened criminals have nothing to lose from killing prison guards or other inmates, and, therefore, will commit more of those murders.

[58] MARTIN SHAPIRO, COURTS: A COMPARATIVE AND POLITICAL ANALYSIS, pp. 157–193 (1981). See also NEIL DUXBURY, RANDOM JUSTICE: ON LOTTERIES AND LEGAL DECISION-MAKING (2002).

[59] W. G. Blair, "Flip of Coin Decides Jail Term in a Manhattan Criminal Case," *The New York Times* (Feb. 2, 1982); K. R. Shipp, "Ex-Jurist Who Made Coin-Toss Decision Is Barred from Being New York Judge Again," *The New York Times* (April 7, 1983).

The most famous study of the deterrent effect of capital punishment was by Isaac Ehrlich, an economist.[60] Ehrlich, following the Becker model that we explored in the previous chapter, assumed that the potential murderer balances the expected punishment against the expected benefit. Ehrlich allowed certain economic and social variables to measure the benefit of homicide to the killer. He included data on the unemployment rate, the labor-force participation rate, the level of wealth, the age composition of the population, and the racial composition of the population.[61]

Ehrlich took the criminal's expected costs of homicide to depend on three variables: the probability of being arrested for the crime (measured by the total number of arrests for homicide divided by the total number of reported homicides); the probability of being convicted of homicide (measured by the total number of convictions for homicide divided by the total number of arrests for homicide); and the probability of execution if convicted (measured by the total number of executions divided by the total number of convictions for homicide). Ehrlich predicted an inverse relationship between each of these three probabilities and homicide rates.

Using time-series data for the United States for the period 1933–1969, Ehrlich concluded that the homicide rate was negatively and significantly correlated with each of the three deterrence measures. Ehrlich's model also predicted that the strongest deterrent effect on homicides would arise from an increase in the probability of arrest; the next strongest, from an increase in the probability of conviction; and the next strongest, from an increase in the probability of execution. The data confirmed his predictions about the relative strength of each of these variables. The most dramatic of his conclusions was that one additional execution per year resulted in between seven and eight fewer homicides per year.[62]

Critics found two statistical shortcomings in the Ehrlich study. First, in Ehrlich's model of behavior, homicide rates could be a linear function of the independent variables, a multiplicative function, a logarithmic function, or some other form. Ehrlich offered no persuasive reason for the particular functional form in which he estimated his regression; yet, changing the functional form changed his results.[63]

Second, Ehrlich's results are much too sensitive to the time period over which the estimations were made. Recall that Ehrlich's original study covered the period

---

[60] Isaac Ehrlich, *The Deterrent Effect of Capital Punishment: A Question of Life and Death,* 65 AM. ECON. REV. 397 (1975). See also Ehrlich, *Capital Punishment and Deterrence: Some Further Thoughts and Additional Evidence,* 85 J. POL. ECON. 741 (1977).

[61] He justified inclusion of the race variable on the ground that legitimate employment opportunities for blacks, especially for young male blacks, are limited. Thus, there may be a greater tendency for blacks to commit property crimes and, because of the correlation between those crimes and homicide, to commit murder.

[62] The Department of Justice cited this particular result in its argument before the Supreme Court in *Gregg v. Georgia* in favor of the death penalty. Kenneth Wolpin did a study similar to Ehrlich's for England and Wales for the period 1929–1968 and concluded that an additional execution would have led to four fewer homicides. Wolpin, *Capital Punishment and Homicide: The English Experience,* 68 AM. ECON. REV. 422 (1978). An additional finding of the Ehrlich study—a finding frequently overlooked in the debate on the deterrent effect of capital punishment—is that the deterrent effect of an improvement in labor-market conditions is stronger than that of any of the criminal-justice-system variables.

[63] John Taylor, *Econometric Models of Criminal Behavior,* in ECONOMIC MODELS OF CRIMINAL BEHAVIOR (J. M. Heineke, ed. 1978).

1933–1969. In the last seven years of that period, the number of executions dropped precipitously, from 47 in 1962 to two in 1967 and to zero in 1968 and 1969. During those same seven years, crime rates escalated sharply. These facts commend excluding the period 1962–1969 from the data used in the regression. John Taylor and Peter Passell redid Ehrlich's study, excluding the period 1962–1969, and found that the statistical significance of the deterrent relationship between the number of executions and the number of homicides disappeared.[64]

In addition to these statistical problems, the critics identified a subtle theoretical problem. Ehrlich found that the number of homicides was an inverse function of the probability of being convicted for murder, which implies that the greater the conviction rate for homicide, the lower the number of murders. Suppose that juries know that if they convict a defendant of homicide, the chances of execution are extremely high. They may be reluctant to convict for first-degree murder. If so, then the following paradoxical behavior may result: Greater use of execution as the punishment for certain homicides might lead to *fewer* convictions for murder. This would reduce the deterrent effect of both capital punishment and of convictions on subsequent murderers.

There is evidence that precisely this sort of relationship occurred in Great Britain. Before the abolition of the death penalty in 1965, British judges had less discretion to avoid sentencing defendants guilty of first-degree homicide to execution than did juries and judges in the United States. Offenders who were found insane could not be executed. Before 1965 the percentage of murderers in Great Britain who were found to be insane was much larger than it was in the United States. Not surprisingly, the number of murderers in Great Britain found to be insane fell dramatically after 1965 when the death penalty was abolished. There was no sudden and dramatic improvement in the mental health of the British criminal class. Rather, British judges before 1965 were reluctant to sentence convicted murderers to death.

Professor Richard Lempert, using this insight into the connection between conviction and the reluctance to execute, reestimated Ehrlich's model and found that an increase in the use of the death penalty would have lowered the probability of a murderer's being convicted by 17 percent.[65]

After a lull in studies of the deterrent effect of capital punishment in the mid- and late 1980s and much of the 1990s, there has been a spate of new studies in the early part of this century. Why? Partly because there has been a wealth of additional experience and, therefore, data with which to perform econometric tests. Partly, too, because of the

---

[64] Passell & Taylor, *The Deterrent Effect of Capital Punishment: Another View,* 57 AM. ECON. REV. 445 (1977). In response to these criticisms, Ehrlich did a cross-sectional study of the deterrent effect of capital punishment on homicide for various states between 1940 and 1960. Ehrlich, *Capital Punishment and Deterrence: Some Further Thoughts and Additional Evidence,* 85 J. POL. ECON. 741 (1977). Again Ehrlich found a deterrent effect on homicide from increases in the probability of execution. This later study is not subject to the same criticisms that were made of the earlier work, but other objections have been raised to Ehrlich's use of cross-sectional data.

[65] Richard Lempert, *Desert and Deterrence: An Assessment of the Moral Bases of the Case for Capital Punishment,* 79 MICH. L. REV. 1177 (1981). Wolpin's work, mentioned above, also noted that, in order for his conclusions about the deterrent effect of the death penalty in England to hold, a change in the probability of execution of convicted murderers must not cause a change in the probability of conviction for murder.

very different experiences of the various states with the death penalty over the last 20 or so years—differences noted earlier in this chapter. For example, some of the states, such as Illinois, have had moratoria on executions, which could, in theory, lead to an increase in homicides if there is, in fact, a deterrent effect of capital punishment. Yet another reason for the new studies is the development of new, more powerful empirical techniques.

Some of the new studies have found a significant effect while others have found no significant deterrent effect of capital punishment. For instance, Lawrence Katz, Steven D. Levitt, and Ellen Shustorovich found no evidence of a deterrence effect of capital punishment. Indeed, they expect that none is likely to be found for the simple reason that there is very little fluctuation in the annual number of executions while the annual number of homicides varies widely.[66] By contrast, Dezhbakhsh and Shepherd, in an analysis of time-series data from 1960 to 2000, found a statistically significant negative causal relationship between capital punishment and the homicide rate. Indeed, the deterrent effect they found was very large—150 fewer homicides as a result of each execution.[67] Earlier, using a different data set, Dezhbakhsh, Rubin, and Shepherd also discovered a deterrent effect, with each execution deterring 18 subsequent homicides.[68] Finally, Mocan and Gittings, using monthly, county-level panel data spanning the period 1977–1997, found that taking commutations, executions, and crime rates into account, each execution deterred five subsequent homicides and each commutation caused five subsequent homicides.[69]

These new studies prompted John Donohue and Justin Wolfers to do a comprehensive survey of the new literature on the deterrent effect of the death penalty.[70] They draw attention to two pieces of anecdotal but telling evidence suggesting that there is no causal relationship between executions and the homicide rate. The first has to do with a comparison of the Canadian and United States homicide rates. The Canadian rate is about one-third that of the United States but it has fluctuated up and down over the last 50 years in uncanny imitation of the fluctuations in the U.S. homicide rate. And yet Canada has had no executions since 1962.

The second has to do with a comparison of homicide rates in those states that have the death penalty and those that do not. "There are six states that have not had the death penalty on the books at any point in our 1960 to 2000 sample. . . . Again the most striking finding is that the close co-movement of homicide rates in these two groups of states."[71]

---

[66] Lawrence Katz, Steven Levitt, & Ellen Shustorovich, *Prison Conditions, Deterrence, and Capital Punishment,* 5 AM. LAW & ECON. REV. 213 (2003).

[67] Hashem Dezhbakhsh & Joanna M. Shepherd, *The Deterrent Effect of Capital Punishment: Evidence from a Judicial Experiment,* 44 ECON. INQ. 512 (2006).

[68] Hashem Dezhbakhsh, Paul H. Rubin, & Joanna M. Shepherd, *Does Capital Punishment Have a Deterrent Effect?: New Evidence from Postmoratorium Panel Data,* 5 AM. LAW & ECON. REV. 344 (2003).

[69] H. Naci Mocan & R. Kaj Gittings, *Getting Off Death Row: Commuted Sentences and the Deterrent Effect of Capital Punishment,* 46 J. LAW & ECON. 453 (2003).

[70] John J. Donohue III & Justin Wolfers, *Uses and Abuses of Empirical Evidence in the Death Penalty Debate,* 58 STAN. L. REV. 791 (2005).

[71] Id. at 800-01. Donohue and Wolfers refer to these events as "Supreme Court-mandated natural experiments."

Donohue and Wolfers conclude that the new studies do not make a compelling case for the deterrent effect of the death penalty.

B. The Social Costs of Capital Punishment

Although the deterrent effect of capital punishment—the social benefit of the death penalty—remains an open question, the high administrative *costs* of capital punishment are not in doubt. Jury selection is more painstaking, because state statutes usually allow both the prosecution and the defense to challenge more jurors. A recent study of California capital cases found that jury selection in capital cases averaged 13 days, while jury selection in noncapital cases averaged three days.

Once the jury is selected, the trial itself is much more expensive in a capital case than in a noncapital case. Both the prosecution and the defense put on more complicated and thorough cases. One recent estimate suggests that a capital case costs the prosecution an average of $2 million. Moreover, the capital trial is typically divided into two trials: one to determine guilt, the other to assess the penalty. The safeguards that have been put in place in the penalty phase of the trial are so elaborate that it is not unusual for that phase to be nearly as long as the trial on the determination of guilt.

Finally, the post-conviction legal proceedings in death cases have become elaborate and expensive. Most states require automatic review of all capital cases by the state's highest court. Not only is this review directly expensive to the prosecution and the defense, it also diverts the scarce judicial resources of the state court of last resort from other pressing business. And, of course, the recent discoveries of wrongful convictions in capital cases have made both trials and post-conviction appeals more expensive (no doubt, correctly so) than ever.

Even excluding the appeals process, the costs of the death penalty to the state are high. Imprisonment on death row is twice as expensive as imprisonment among the normal prison population. Death-row inmates require more elaborate security and supervision. They cannot be employed in the usual prison enterprises, and consequently, they make little contribution to the revenues of the prison. Because of extreme stress, the inmates' medical and psychiatric costs are high on death row.

C. Conclusion on Deterrence and Capital Punishment

The statistical evidence does not support the firm conviction that executions deter homicides. Perhaps we will not ever obtain compelling statistical conclusions.[72] Separating the effect of executions from other variables requires good data on a large number of cases, data that may be very difficult to collect. Moreover, states restrict executions to such a small group of killers that statisticians have little data to analyze. And finally, the recent discovery of the large number of cases

---

[72] See Edward Leamer, *Let's Take the "Con" Out of Econometrics,* 73 AM. ECON. REV. 31 (1983). Professor Leamer uses an econometric study of the deterrent effect of capital punishment to demonstrate the impact of the investigator's prior beliefs on his conclusions. Id. pp. 40–43.

in which the death penalty was wrongfully imposed on innocent men has been extremely disturbing.

QUESTION 13.13:   Opponents and proponents of capital punishment deny that their beliefs depend on the presence or absence of deterrence effects,[73] yet Ehrlich's study provoked intense debate and outrage. What do these facts say about the contribution of econometrics to criminal law?

QUESTION 13.14:   In the eighteenth century, prisoners were not only executed, they were also whipped, branded, and mutilated. Can you think of any economic reasons why many modern states have eliminated these punishments, retaining only fines, imprisonment, and probation?

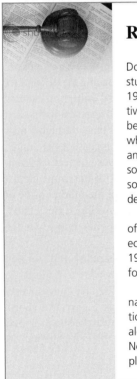

Racial Discrimination and the Death Penalty

Does the defendant's race significantly influence the probability of capital punishment? A study by Wolfgang and Amsterdam of 3000 rape convictions in 11 southern states between 1945 and 1965 showed that the execution of African Americans convicted of rape was relatively rare (13 percent). However, the study found that blacks were seven times more likely to be executed than whites convicted of the same crime, and a black man who had raped a white woman was 18 times more likely to be executed than when the victim and injurer were any other combination of race. These facts are consistent with the traditional hostility of some southern whites to sexual relations between black men and white women. A similar comparison of black and white executions for the same crimes in the North yielded much less evidence of race differences.

A different conclusion was reached for murder. For the period 1930–1967, the murder of a black person by another black person was slightly less likely to result in the murderer's execution than the murder of a white person by another white person. For the period 1967–1978, the statistics showed clearly that blacks were less likely to be sentenced to death for murder than were whites.

Behind such statistics lies a simple fact: The overrepresentation of blacks among criminals who commit capital crimes guarantees that capital punishment will result in the execution of blacks in greater proportion than their numbers in the general population. This fact alone will open capital punishment to the charge of racism in future political debates.[74] Nonetheless, the proportion of blacks sentenced to death raises worrisome concerns of implicit or explicit racial bias.

---

[73] For example, 90 percent of those in favor say that they are in favor of that sanction even if it could be shown to them conclusively that there is no deterrent effect. Vidmar & Ellsworth, *Public Opinion and the Death Penalty*, 26 STAN. L. REV. 1245 (1974).

[74] See Stanley Rothman & Stephen Powers, *Execution by Quota?*, 116 PUB. INTEREST 3 (1994). See also JOHN BLUME, THEODORE EISENBERG, & MARTIN T. WELLS, *Explaining Death Row's Population and Racial Composition*, 1 J. EMP LEGAL STUD. 165 (2004).

V. The Economics of Addictive Drugs and Crime

One of the popular explanations for increased crime is increased drug abuse. The use of such addictive drugs as heroin, crack cocaine, and PCP contributes to crime in three ways. First, some drug addicts need to commit crimes to generate incomes. Their habit is so debilitating that they cannot work at legitimate jobs, or they cannot earn enough working at legitimate jobs to pay for drugs. Second, drugs, like alcohol, may cause people to commit crimes by undermining their inhibitions and increasing the volatility of their moods. About 70 percent of those arrested in all large U.S. cities for robbery, weapons offenses, and larceny test positive for heroin, cocaine, or PCP. Third, drug dealing can be a lucrative business, and, therefore, a business worth protecting against competition. Drug dealers commit violent crimes against their competitors. Drug use contributes significantly to crime, so reducing the social costs of crime involves reducing the use of addictive drugs. We have already seen that a very high percentage of the almost 2.5 million persons in U.S. jails and prisons are there for drug offenses.

A. Punishing Drug Sales

Current policy in the United States seeks to break the connection between the use of addictive drugs and crime by curtailing the supply of drugs and by reducing the demand for them. One means of reducing the supply and lessening the use of illegal drugs is to increase the expected punishment for selling or using them. Some suppliers will leave the business of supplying drugs in favor of legitimate, less risky activities. At the same time, the higher market price caused by the restriction in supply may cause consumers to purchase fewer drugs.

Some economists have argued that this policy is incorrect because its factual premises are incorrect. Critics argue that addiction makes the demand for the drugs inelastic. Therefore, a restriction in supply and the resulting increase in the market price of the illegal drug will not cause the addict to reduce his consumption significantly. Instead, it will cause him to increase the amount of crime he commits to produce the greater revenue required to support his habit.

Figure 13.1 depicts this argument. The figure is divided into two panels representing two kinds of drug users. The left panel indicates demand for drugs by addicts, denoted D. The right panel indicates demand for drugs by nonaddicts, denoted D'. By "nonaddicts" we mean occasional users who are not physically dependent on drugs. Figure 13.1 shows the consequences of a successful campaign to interdict drugs and punish the suppliers and

FIGURE 13.1

Drug markets and price.

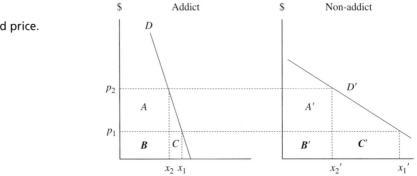

users. Before the campaign, the price of drugs is p_1, which results in drug use by addicts and nonaddicts denoted x_1 and x_1', respectively. After the campaign against drugs, the price rises to p_2. The price includes the purchase price and also the monetary equivalent of the risk of punishment caused by purchasing illegal drugs. At price p_2, addicts use drugs in the amount x_2. The fact that x_2 is *not* much less than x_1 indicates that demand by addicts is inelastic. At price p_2, nonaddicts use drugs in the amount x_2'. The fact that x_2' is *much* less than x_1' indicates that demand by addicts is elastic. Raising the price of drugs from p_1 to p_2 has little effect on drug use by addicts and a large effect on nonaddicts.

Now consider the effects of the increase in price on expenditures on drugs. Addicts purchase x_1 drugs at the low price p_1, which results in total expenditures of $p_1 \times x_1$, as indicated by areas $B + C$ in Figure 13.1. After the campaign against drugs, addicts purchase x_2 drugs at the higher price p_2, which results in total expenditures of $p_2 \times x_2$ as indicated by the areas $A + B$ in Figure 13.1. The campaign thus causes a large increase in expenditures on drugs by addicts, specifically an increase of $A - C$. Total expenditures go up because addicts continue buying almost the same quantity of drugs and paying a much higher price. Consequently, addicts will need a lot more money to buy drugs, and much of that money may come from property crimes. Thus, public policies that raise the cost of drugs to addicts may cause more crime rather than less. (The campaign against drugs, which raises prices, also causes total expenditures by nonaddicts to go *down* by $A' - C'$.)

This analysis exposes a dilemma: Public policies that raise the price of drugs have the good effect of reducing their use by nonaddicts. Less use by nonaddicts presumably implies fewer crimes committed by them, and also fewer nonaddicts becoming addicts. However, public policies that raise the price of drugs have the bad effect of substantially increasing expenditures on drugs by addicts. More expenditure on drugs by addicts implies more crimes committed by them in order to get more money for drugs.

The obvious response to these facts is to try to get the best of both worlds by raising the price to nonaddicts and not raising the price to addicts. In other words, the obvious response is a drug policy that discriminates in drug prices between addicts and nonaddicts. Successful price discrimination causes the addicts in Figure 13.1 to face the low price p_1 and the nonaddicts to face the high price p_2. As implemented in the United Kingdom and elsewhere, addicts can submit to medical examination and register their addictions. After registration, they can buy cheap drugs legally by prescription, much as people obtain medicinal drugs by prescription from a doctor. Consequently, addicts obtain a safe supply of drugs sufficient to maintain their habits. However, nonaddicts (or unregistered addicts) cannot obtain drugs legally from pharmacies; instead they must purchase drugs illegally at much higher prices.

We have discussed a system of prescription sales for addictive drugs that creates price discrimination between addicts and nonaddicts. Note that price discrimination in this system goes in the opposite direction from price discrimination practiced by profit-maximizing companies. The prescriptions system aims to lower the price of addictive drugs to consumers with inelastic demand (addicts), whereas profit-maximizing companies aim to raise the price of their products to consumers with inelastic demand.

The preceding analysis simplifies reality by sharply distinguishing between addicts and nonaddicts. Reality is more continuous than the sharp distinction in language suggests. The important point of the analysis is to lower the price for drug users with inelastic demand in order to reduce the harm that they cause. Thus, a recent Swiss experiment supplied free heroin to addicts who massively increased their daily doses;

yet, they significantly increased their participation in legitimate work and significantly reduced their income-generating criminal behaviors.[75]

B. Suppressing and Interdicting

In the preceding section, we criticized policies attempting to increase the expected punishment of the sellers of illegal drugs. Now we consider the failure of policies aimed at suppressing drug production and interdicting the importation of drugs.

First, consider attempts to limit the production of illegal drugs abroad. In the 1970s the U.S. government tried to eradicate opium production in Turkey, then the source of most of the raw opium that ultimately became heroin for the U.S. market. The program was moderately successful in Turkey, but Mexico began to grow opium and quickly became the supplier of 80 percent of the U.S. market. The U.S. government next began an eradication program in Mexico, but production simply moved elsewhere. The odds against the success of these programs are overwhelming. U.S. citizens demand approximately six tons of heroin per year. To make that much heroin requires about sixty tons of opium, which equals 2 to 3 percent of the total illicit production of opium in the world each year. The world market for opium and heroin is too large, and production is too flexible, for the United States to suppress.

Similarly, the attempt to restrict the import of illegal drugs has failed.[76] Small amounts of illegal drugs are so valuable that tens of thousands of dollars worth can be easily concealed in personal luggage on commercial airlines. The authorities cannot effectively monitor the millions of individuals who arrive in this country on commercial airlines. When one route is blocked, suppliers easily shift to alternative routes. Also, drug suppliers smuggle by boat into remote harbors or by airplane onto private rural airstrips. A recent survey article concludes, "It is difficult to imagine a more aggressive supply reduction effort than the one we've experienced, and yet student surveys show that drugs remain readily available at schools, and cocaine and heroin prices have fallen to about a third of their 1981 levels after controlling for inflation."[77]

C. Legalization

These dubious policies against drugs are very expensive. During the 1980s federal expenditures on drug enforcement tripled, from about $1 billion per year to more than $3 billion per year and then rose in the early 1990s to $6.7 billion per year. Although this figure is difficult to define precisely, the best available evidence (that of Jeffrey A. Miron and Katherine Waldock, *The Budgetary Impact of Ending Drug Prohibition* (2010)) is that by 2010 all levels of government in the United States were spending more than $41 billion per year to eradicate illegal drugs Miron and Waldock further estimate that legalizing currently

---

[75] For references, see Robert MacCoun, *Is the Addiction Concept Useful for Drug Policy?*, in NICK HEATHER & RUDY E. VUCHINICH, EDS., CHOICE, BEHAVIORAL ECONOMICS, AND ADDICTION (2003), 355–373, at page 368. Here's a relevant joke: When Keith Richards, a member of the rock band "The Rolling Stones," was arrested on another drug charge, he allegedly said, "Let's get things straight. I don't have a drug problem. I have a police problem."

[76] See Peter Reuter, *Can the Borders Be Sealed?*, 82 PUB. INTEREST 36 (1988). See also Jonathan P. Caulkins, Peter Reuter, Martin Y. Iguchi, & James Chiesa, *How Goes the 'War on Drugs'?*, RAND, DRUG POLICY RESEARCH CENTER, 2005.

[77] See generally MacCoun, *supra* n. 75.

illegal drugs would increase tax revenues for all levels of U.S. government by almost $47 billion per year. So, the total costs to U.S. society of our current regime of recreational drug suppression is approximately $88 billion per year—in direct expenditures of $41 billion in suppression and enforcement and an opportunity cost of forgone tax revenues of $47 billion.

While there is a strong economic case for decriminalizing drugs, there is a wide spectrum of legalization policies from which to choose. At one end is legalization with almost no governmental control. At the other end is total government control over the production and sale of drugs. In between is regulation with many possibilities—such as licensing of production and consumption; prohibition of sale to minors; regulations on the time, manner, and place of consumption and sale; more extensive programs to help addicts; and increasing education on the dangers of drug abuse.[78]

A comparison of drugs and alcohol suggests an alternative to the current failed policies. In the United States, alcohol is the direct cause of 80,000 to 100,000 deaths per year and a contributing factor in another 100,000 deaths. More than one-third of all serious crimes resulting in state prison sentences involve the abuse of alcohol. There are in the United States an estimated 20 million alcoholics or alcohol abusers. The annual social cost of alcohol abuse to the United States is estimated to be over $100 billion per year. Tobacco has similar social costs. Approximately 320,000 people die each year from consuming tobacco. By comparison, in 1985 only 3562 people died from the use of all illegal drugs. All of the social costs of illegal drugs are only a fraction of the social costs imposed by alcohol and tobacco.

In spite of the harm caused by alcohol, the American experiment with criminalizing its use in the 1920s failed. To illustrate, during the era of "prohibition" the murder rate soared to levels similar to those among drug dealers in the late 1980s. Then the murder rated plummeted when alcohol was decriminalized and regulated by the state, largely because the "alcohol wars" ceased. While alcohol causes crime, it seems that its prohibition caused even more crime.

Perhaps the same is true of drugs today. The murder rate might be even lower today if drugs were decriminalized and regulated by the state, bringing an end to the "drug wars." Repealing many of the current laws might lead to a moderate increase in drug abuse, but moderately more abuse in an environment of drug regulation is probably preferable to the current level of abuse in a criminal environment.[79]

In a recent study, Gary Becker, Kevin Murphy, and Michael Grossman explored some of the economic consequence of legalizing drugs.[80] They conclude that "a monetary tax

---

[78] For an illuminating discussion of the many varieties of legalization, see Mark Kleiman & Aaron Sager, *Drug Legalization: The Importance of Asking the Right Question,* 18 HOFSTRA L. REV. 527 (1990).

[79] For an argument that decriminalization would not lead to increased drug addiction, see Ethan Nadelman, *The Case for Legalization,* 82 PUB. INTEREST 3 (1988). For a more recent argument in favor of decriminalization, see ANDREW D. LEIPOLD, *The War on Drugs and the Puzzle of Deterrence,* 6 J. GENDER, RACE, JUST. 111 (2002).

[80] Becker, Murphy, & Grossman, *The Economic Theory of Illegal Goods: The Case of Drugs,* 114 J. POL. ECON. 38 (2006). Their investigation includes a broader consideration of *all* illegal goods, those for which "the social value [] is less than its private value." Their general conclusion is that in instances of goods with that characteristic, "it would be most effective to allow the good to be legal, and impose the right monetary tax to account for the discrepancy between private and social values." If that is the optimal policy, why has it been the case throughout history that societies have dealt with such illegal goods as prostitution, drugs, and gambling through suboptimal policies, such as bans? The authors suggest that "one answer to this discrepancy between actual and optimal policies depends on their different impacts on the consumption of middle class and poorer persons. Higher- and middle-level income families often prefer certain goods to be illegal rather than to endure higher taxes, while poor persons prefer the opposite. If the poor have much *less* political power, these goods would end up being illegal."

on a legal good could cause a greater reduction in output and increase in price than would optimal enforcement, even recognizing that producers may want to go underground to try to avoid a monetary tax."

In 1971 President Richard Nixon declared war on drugs. Judging from statistics on drug use and violence, we mostly lost this war. We cannot admit defeat, change tactics, and disengage because that would appear as if we are approving of drugs, rather like admitting defeat, disengaging, and withdrawing from Vietnam appeared as if we were approving of communism. Symbols can impede rationality. A rational approach to drugs would be to minimize the waste from addiction, crime, and imprisonment. Incarcerating vast numbers of young men (disproportionately African Americans) maximizes the waste. Instead, we should decriminalize, regulate, and tax, using tax revenues to finance advertising against drug use among youth.

QUESTION 13.15: During the "war on drugs" in the United States, the street price of most illegal drugs has remained stable or has fallen. What does this fact indicate about who is winning the "war"?

QUESTION 13.16: Use economics to compare three ways to reduce the *demand* for heroin: (i) the substitution of another, less dangerous, and less debilitating drug, such as methadone for heroin, to registered addicts; (ii) the free availability of the illegal substance to registered addicts; and (iii) a legal proscription on use, which is the current policy.

QUESTION 13.17: If violent criminals were tested immediately after arrest, do you think that more of them would test positive for the recent consumption of drugs or a hamburger? What, then, is the significance of the high rate of drug use among criminals?

VI. The Economics of Handgun Control

The United States has long had higher rates of violent crime than Western European nations. The United States also has higher rates of gun ownership, especially handguns, than most (but not all) European nations. In this section we explore whether widespread gun ownership causes crime, or whether crime causes widespread gun ownership. Criminals obtain guns to make crime easier and apprehension more difficult; so, guns tend to create crime. The potential victims of crime obtain guns to make their victimization harder and more risky for criminals; so, guns tend to reduce crime. We consider evidence on the relative strength of these two effects.

A. U.S. Gun Data

The correlation between the number of guns and the amount of crime is high. There are an estimated 200 million firearms in private possession in the United States, of which approximately 67 million are handguns. Approximately one-half of U.S.

households contain guns; the average number of guns per household is 4.5. There is an estimate that 100,000 schoolchildren take handguns to school each day.[81] Recall the horrifying episode in April, 1999, at Columbine High School near Denver, Colorado, in which two heavily armed young men shot and killed a number of their fellow students and their teachers before committing suicide.

Gun ownership and crime in the United States have changed in an interesting pattern for the past 50 years, which may or may not be causally related. During the 1960s and the 1970s the robbery rate in the United States increased sixfold, and the homicide rate doubled. The rate of handgun ownership almost doubled, too. There are approximately 640,000 crimes committed with handguns every year in the United States, but that figure has varied considerably since the mid-1980s. Generally, the trend in the number of handgun-related crimes has been down. There were about 11,000 homicides committed in the United States in 1992 with handguns. (For the sake of comparison, in the same year there were 87 murders by handgun in Japan, 22 in Great Britain, and 10 in Australia.) Since 1989, there has been a slow but unsteady increase in the number of handguns in private hands in the U.S., including a significant surge in sales in late 2008 and early 2009. Since 1989, there has been a relatively steady or even declining number of homicides committed by handguns, so that by 2008 approximately 10,000 of the 16,000 homicides were committed by handguns. On a per capita basis, the homicide rate has been falling since the early 1990s. Are these correlations causal or coincidental? Does the increased number of firearms cause more crime or less crime?

B. Gun Control

The effort to break the connection between handguns and crime has focused on two general methods of regulation: first, restrictions on the production and possession of handguns; and second, more severe punishment for those who use handguns in the commission of crimes.[82]

Since late in the nineteenth century, when governments passed the first laws regulating guns (specifically, concealed weapons), the first method of regulation has been the one most used by federal, state, and local governments. For example, in the 1930s Congress prohibited the use of the U.S. mail system for the sale of handguns across state lines; required the registration of machine guns, sawed-off shotguns, and silencers (weapons and equipment favored, at that time, by criminals), and the photographing and fingerprinting of registered owners of these weapons; and instituted a $200 tax to be paid whenever the ownership of these registered weapons was transferred.

The latest federal attempt at limiting the possession of handguns is the Brady Act (passed by Congress in late 1993 and named after James Brady, President Reagan's press secretary, who was shot in 1981 during an assassination attempt on the president).

---

[81] See Wilson, supra n. 7.

[82] About 80 percent of U.S. citizens (including about 60 percent of the membership of the National Rifle Association, typically thought to be the principal lobby against handgun regulations) favor more restrictions on the possession of firearms, especially handguns. Only 30 percent support a complete ban.

The act requires gun buyers to wait five business days and undergo a background check before taking possession of the guns they have purchased. Because good recordkeeping is vital to this act's success and because most states do not have good records, the act authorizes the federal government to spend up to $200 million per year to help states improve their recordkeeping. The goal is to replace the five-day waiting period with instant background checks within five years.[83]

Regulations like the Brady Act may prevent those people most likely to commit a crime from obtaining handguns legally. More than 20 states, containing half the population of the United States, already have similar waiting periods. The experience in those states is that 1 to 2 percent of prospective gun buyers are disqualified by the background check. For instance, California's background-check law has prevented about 12,000 people with a criminal record or a history of mental illness or drug abuse from buying handguns in a recent two-year period. A similar law in Illinois has prevented 2,000 people from buying handguns there. We have no evidence on how many of these people subsequently purchased handguns illegally.

At the local level, regulations have taken a different tack. It has been illegal to sell handguns in Chicago since April, 1982.[84] Recently, some local governments have offered to purchase guns from their residents, no questions asked. In 1992, St. Louis offered to pay $25 for each handgun turned in. The city collected 7,465 guns in the course of one month and melted them. Many public schools in large cities have metal detectors; the Clinton administration proposed random sweeps of housing projects to search for guns; and some localities have instituted random roadblocks to check cars for guns.

Besides these restrictions on production and possession, the punishment for violating handgun-possession regulations or for committing a crime with a handgun has increased. Several states have passed legislation that requires more severe and more certain punishment for those who carry a handgun without a permit. For example, the Massachusetts Bartley-Fox law in 1974 imposed a mandatory penalty of one year in prison without the possibility of probation, parole, or other diminution of sentence for failure to license a private handgun. Several studies have been conducted to measure the impact of Bartley-Fox, and the reported evidence suggests that the result of the law was, first, a reduction in the casual carrying of handguns, and, second, a decline in the proportion of assaults, robberies, and homicides committed with handguns.[85]

---

[83] The purpose of these checks is to keep handguns out of the hands of convicted felons, fugitives, minors, current and former drug addicts, and those who have been involuntarily committed for mental illness. The Act has, arguably, been effective. From 1994 to 2008 there were nearly two million firearms' purchases that were prevented by Brady background checks. Prosecutions of illegal sales or purchases. however. have been very rare.

[84] Rifles, shotguns, and ammunition are available to those who have an Illinois Firearm Owner's Identification card. This FOID takes up to 1 month to get, and even if a potential gun buyer has one, he or she must go through a waiting period before receiving the gun. Notwithstanding these efforts, there are hundreds of thousands of illegal handguns in Chicago. The reason is that it is extremely difficult for Chicago to seal its borders. Handguns come from the suburbs, where they are not as tightly regulated, or from the neighboring states of Indiana or Wisconsin. This experience suggests that local regulation is likely to be ineffective.

[85] See WILSON, THINKING ABOUT CRIME, pp. 135–136 (rev. ed. 1983). This reduction in homicides associated with other felonies occurred even though the total number of these offenses was going up in Boston and in other large cities.

Notwithstanding this evidence, the two types of regulation noted do not appear to have had a large effect on crime rates. There are reasons for doubting the major premise of those regulations—namely, that more handguns inevitably lead to more violent crime. If criminals know that honest citizens are less likely to have guns, they may perceive smaller risk from committing crime and may, therefore, commit more crime. But if criminals know that many private citizens have guns, they might be increasingly wary of committing crime. This observation muddies the direction of causation between handguns and crime. The standard argument is that more handguns cause more crime. But perhaps more handguns lead to less crime. If so, then reducing the number of handguns may lead to an increase in the amount of crime.[86]

Both casual and some detailed evidence[87] suggest that increases in handgun ownership have no simple causal connection to violent crime. The casual evidence notes that during the 1980s, the stock of privately owned handguns in the United States increased by more than a million units each year and that many crime rates fell. We have already seen a heightening of this pattern—increased private gun ownership and falling crime rates, including violent crime rates—during the 1990s. Additionally, a few countries, such as Switzerland and Israel, have a very high number of firearms per civilian household but do not have as much crime. Conversely, Mexico and South Africa have very strict handgun control laws, and these countries have murder rates more than twice as high as those in the United States. Florida's murder rate has been falling since the state made it easier for citizens to carry concealed weapons. (See Web Note 13.5 at the end of this section.)

Yet another fascinating piece of evidence on this matter is the correlation between private handgun ownership and "hot" burglaries. (A "hot" burglary is one in which there are people at home when the burglary occurs.) If homeowners can legally own handguns, then potential burglars will be less likely, all other things being equal, to invade houses in which someone is at home. However, if homeowners cannot legally own handguns, then burglars will not be as reluctant to invade when someone is at home. Thus, one ought to observe fewer "hot" burglaries in jurisdictions that allow homeowners to keep handguns. And, indeed, that is what one finds. The United States, Canada, and Great Britain have roughly equal burglary rates. However, the "hot" burglary rate in the United States (where private handgun ownership is generally allowed) is about 10 percent, and that in Canada and Great Britain (where private handgun ownership generally is not allowed) is about 50 percent.[88]

This issue, like many of the other issues we have studied in the economics of crime and punishment, is complex. Better empirical work is needed before we can reach firm conclusions on the relationship between handguns and crime that could point to definite policy recommendations. The issue is not so much a free market in guns versus banning their possession. Rather, the problem is to find specific regulations that actually succeed in reducing violent crime. For example, small-caliber guns fire bullets that usually wound without killing, whereas large-caliber guns fire bullets that kill. Banning

---

[86] Daniel Polsby, *The False Promise of Gun Control*, THE ATLANTIC MONTHLY (March, 1994), p. 57.

[87] Arthur Kellerman et al., N ENGL. J. MED. October 7, 1993.

[88] Our thanks to John Lott, Jr., for this evidence. See LOTT, MORE GUNS, LESS CRIME (1999), for an extension of this argument.

large-caliber pistols in the United States might cause a shift in demand to small-caliber pistols and many fewer deaths.

QUESTION 13.18: Use economics to predict the ranking by crime rates of the following situations:
a. no private person has a gun (effective prohibition).
b. only criminals have guns (ineffective prohibition on criminals).
c. everyone has easy access to guns.
d. only honest citizens have access to guns.

QUESTION 13.19: Is it possible to design and enforce a law so that only honest citizens have access to guns?

QUESTION 13.20: Gun control is politically unpopular in neighborhoods with the highest crime rates in the United States. Use economics to explain why.

QUESTION 13.21: About 38,000 Americans die of gunshot wounds each year. Fewer than half these deaths are homicides. Accidents and suicides account for 54 percent of firearms deaths. Assume that guns in honest households deter crimes and cause accidental deaths. How would you compare the costs of each?

Web Note 13.5

In *More Guns, Less Crime,* John R. Lott, Jr., has attempted to show that when a state passes a "concealed carry" law—a law allowing registered gun owners to carry concealed weapons—there is a discernible subsequent decline in crime in that state. Lott argues that criminals are rational and that if they know that either their victims or those nearby the scene of a crime may have concealed handguns and that, therefore, the possibility of serious injury or death to the criminal is high, they are less likely to commit crime. On our website we review Lott's arguments and survey the critique of his work.

VII. Explaining the Decline in Crime in the United States

In the almost two decades since 1991 serious crime in the United States has declined by almost 40 percent. What caused the decline? Steven Levitt, an economist, has identified four factors that caused the decline and six factors that some commentators falsely believe to have caused it.[89] This section describes the decline and its causes as identified by Levitt.

---

[89] Steven D. Levitt, *Understanding Why Crime Fell in the 1990s: Four Factors that Explain the Decline and Six that Do Not,* 18 J. ECON. PERSP. 163 (2004). We are going to suppress references to particular parts of this article in the remainder of the section. See also Steven D. Levitt & Thomas J. Miles, *Empirical Study of Criminal Punishment,* in A. MITCHELL POLINSKY & STEVEN SHAVELL, EDS., HANDBOOK OF LAW AND ECONOMICS, V. 1 (2007).

Recall that the decline in crime that began in the early 1990s affected both violent and nonviolent crime. Homicide rates fell by 43 percent from 1991 to 2001, reaching their lowest levels since the 1930s. The Federal Bureau of Investigation's (FBI's) indexes of violent and property crimes declined by 34 and 29 percent over the same period. Using data from the *Uniform Crime Reports* and the *National Crime Victimization Surveys*, Levitt summarizes these changes in the accompanying table, which we label Table 13.3.

He further shows that the declines in crime in the 1990s "affected all geographic areas and demographic groups. . . . The greatest percentage improvements in crime occurred within metropolitan statistical areas (MSAs) and especially among large cities with populations over 250,000."

The six factors that Levitt finds to have had little or no effect on the decline in U.S. crime in the 1990s are these: (1) the strong economy; (2) changing demographics; (3) better policing strategies; (4) gun control laws; (5) laws allowing the carrying of concealed weapons; and (6) the increased use of capital punishment.

TABLE 13.3
National Trends in Specific Categories of Crime

Crime Category and Data Source	Percentage Change in Crime Category, 1973–1991	Percentage Change in Crime Category, 1991–2001
Crimes reported to the police from UCR		
Violent crime	+82.9	−33.6
Homicide	+5.4	−42.9
Rape	+73.4	−24.8
Robbery	+50.0	−45.8
Aggravated assault	+118.1	−26.7
Property crime	+38.2	−28.8
Burglary	+3.0	−40.9
Larceny	+56.7	−23.2
Motor vehicle theft	+49.8	−34.6
Criminal victimization from the NCVS		
Violent crime	+1.6	−50.1
Rape	−20.0	−45.0
Robbery	−15.5	−53.3
Aggravated assault	−3.9	−56.9
Simple assault	+10.7	−47.0
Property crime	−32.0	−52.8
Burglary	−41.3	−55.6
Theft	−46.5	−51.6
Motor vehicle theft	+16.2	−58.6

Levitt, Table 2, p. 167.

1. The Strong Economy   The period from 1991 to 2001 was the longest period of continuous growth in U.S. history, with real GDP per capita increasing by almost 30 percent and the annual unemployment rate falling to around 4 percent. One might reasonably have predicted that this strong economy contributed to the decline in crime by giving potential criminals better opportunities to earn income legally. However, as we have already seen earlier in this chapter, there is no good empirical evidence to suggest a correlation or causal connection between the ups and downs of the economy and the rate of crime. Levitt suggests that at best a 1 percentage point improvement in the unemployment rate leads to a 1 percentage point decrease in property crime (and no change in violent crime). So, the 2 percentage point decline in the average unemployment rate between 1991 and 2001 could have contributed only to a 2 percentage point decrease in the property crime rate. But in fact the property crime rate fell by 30 percent. Moreover, one should doubt the importance of economy-wide factors in explaining crime because crime increased significantly during the 1960s at the same time that there was vigorous economic growth and has not apparently increased since the onset of the Great Recession in 2008.

2. Changing Demographics   We have already seen a strong causal connection between demography and crime: All other things being equal, the greater the proportion of young males in society, the greater the amount of crime. Conversely, the greater the proportion of older people, the lower the crime rate.[90] During the period under consideration, the percentage of 15- to 24-year-olds in the population increased from 13.7 percent to 14.6 percent, not enough to make much of a difference in the amount of crime. There were no other notable demographic changes during the period of declining crime—certainly nothing that could account for the dramatic decreases that occurred.

3. Better Policing Strategies   Early in the 1991–2001 period, New York City tried some innovative policing strategies, such as "community policing," and appointed a new, vigorous police commissioner. Because New York City had the greatest crime decline of any large city, commentators have often pointed to the change in policing strategies and the new commissioner as leading causes of the City's great success in fighting crime.[91]

Levitt doubts that either of these changes had much to do with the pattern of New York City's crime rate. First, the decline began before these changes were made. Moreover, there was no discernible acceleration in the trend—indeed, no change at

---

[90] "In 2001, people over the age of 65 had per capita arrest rates approximately one-fiftieth the level of 15- to 19-year-olds." The victimization rates of the elderly are about one-tenth those of teenagers.

[91] An influential theory underlying this change in policing strategies was the "broken windows" hypothesis attributable to James Q. Wilson & George L. Kelling, *Broken Windows: The Police and Neighborhood Safety*, THE ATLANTIC MONTHLY (March 1992), available at http://www.theatlantic.com/politics/crime/windows.htm. Professor Bernard E. Harcourt of the University of Chicago Law School criticizes the Wilson-Kelling hypothesis in *Illusion of Order: The False Promise of Broken Windows Policing* (2001).

all—at the point at which policing strategies changed or the new police commissioner assumed office. Second, the size of the New York City Police Department increased by 45 percent during the 1990s, a rate three times greater than the national average. As we will see, the increase in the number of police was far more important than the change in policing strategy. And third, most other cities did not institute the policing strategy changes that New York did, and yet they, too, had dramatic reductions in crime.[92]

4. Gun Control Laws   We have seen that there are more than 200 million firearms in private hands in the United States and that approximately 11,000 of the roughly 16,000 annual murders are by firearm. So, it might be the case that stricter gun control laws reduced crime—particularly homicide. However, Jens Ludwig and Philip Cook reported that those laws—notably the Brady Handgun Violence Prevention Act of 1993—had no statistically discernible effect on homicide trends.[93] Nor is there any other evidence proving that more strict gun control laws, or municipal policies to buy back guns, has had any effect on firearms violence.

5. Laws Allowing the Carrying of Concealed Weapons   Instead of making gun control laws more strict, some states have loosened restriction on carrying concealed weapons. An empirical paper claims that laws allowing registrants to carry concealed weapons has had dramatic downward effects on crime rates, but Levitt and others believe that this claim is unproved.[94] (See Web Note 13.5.)

6. Increased Use of Capital Punishment   There were four times as many people executed during the 1990s (478) as had been put to death in the 1980s (117). Levitt is almost certain that there was no effect on serious crime. First, few people on death row have actually been executed (53 executions in 2006 among 3,200 death-row inmates—less than 2 percent), and the delays in execution are so long that a "rational criminal should not be deterred by the threat of execution." In fact, "the likelihood of being executed conditional on committing murder is still less than 1 in 200." Many of those on death row would have a higher probability of dying violently in their home neighborhoods than dying on death row. Second, suppose that we take a figure from the deterrence literature that suggests that each execution deters six subsequent homicides. Then, "the observed increase in the death penalty from 14 executions in 1991 to 66 in 2001 would eliminate between 300 and 400 homicides, for a reduction of 1.5 percent in the homicide rate, or less than 125th of the observed decline in the homicide rate over this time period."

---

[92] An important (and controversial) fourth factor in New York, a factor that we have already explored, was the fact that New York City had abortion rates in the 1970s that were among the highest in the country. And New York State legalized abortion in 1970, three years before the Supreme Court's decision in *Roe v. Wade*, 410 U.S. 113 (1973). Be sure to see Web Note 13.3 for a critique of the hypothesis that there is a connection between abortion rates and later crime rates.

[93] Jens Ludwig & Philip J. Cook, *Homicide and Suicide Rates Associated with Implementation of the Brady Handgun Violence Prevention Act,* 284 J. Am. Med. Assoc. 585 (2000).

[94] See John R. Lott, Jr. & David B. Mustard, *Crime, Deterrence, and the Right to Carry Concealed Handguns,* 26 J. Legal Stud. 1 (1997). The hypothesis is extended in John R. Lott, Jr., More Guns, Less Crime: Understand Crime and Gun-Control Laws (1998).

C. Four Factors That Explain the Decline in U.S. Crime in the 1990s

The four factors to which Levitt gives credit for the decline in crime are these: (1) increases in the number of police; (2) the rising prison population; (3) the receding crack epidemic; and (4) the legalization of abortion in the early 1970s. We have already devoted an entire section to the argument and evidence regarding abortion's role in the decline in crime. Here we will summarize the other factors.

1. Increases in the Number of Police   The number of police can have an important deterring effect on crime. Thomas Marvell and Carlisle Moody estimated in the mid-1990s that the elasticity of crime with respect to the number of police is −0.30.[95] That is, a 10 percent increase in the number of police would cause a 3 percent decrease in crime. Levitt somewhat later found elasticities of crime with respect to the number of police to be in the range of −0.43 to −0.50.[96] (Note how much larger both of these estimates are than the elasticity of crime with respect to incarceration.) The total number of police officers in the United States increased by 50,000 to 60,000 during the 1990s, an increase of 14 percent. If we use an elasticity measure of −0.40, then we can attribute 5 to 6 percent of the decline in crime during our period to the increase in the number of police. That is, this factor alone explains between one-fifth and one-tenth of the overall decline.

2. The Rising Prison Population   We have already seen that the U.S. prison population quadrupled between 1980 and 2002. Slightly more than half that increase occurred during the 1990s. There is good evidence that the elasticity of crime with respect to expected punishment ranges between −0.10 and −0.40. (The evidence suggests a figure in the higher end of the range for violent crime and something toward the lower end of the range for property crime.) Assume an elasticity of −0.30 for violent crime with respect to expected punishment and −0.20 for property crime. Then, increases in expected punishment "can account for a reduction in crime of approximately 12 percent for the first two categories and 8 percent for property crime, or about one-third of the observed decline in crime."

3. The Receding Crack Epidemic   Crack cocaine, which is produced by heating a mixture of powder cocaine and baking soda into airy nuggets, appeared in the mid-1980s and found a lucrative and rapidly expanding market. The new form of cocaine was relatively inexpensive and produced an intense and short high. The competition to sell this illegal product was intense, so much so that gang violence associated with this competition became a significant problem in the United States beginning in 1985. As a result, homicide rates for young black males under the age of 25 rose very rapidly through the end of the 1980s.

---

[95] Thomas Marvell & Carlisle Moody, *Specification Problems, Police Levels, and Crime Rates,* 34 CRIMINOLOGY 609 (1996).

[96] Levitt, *Using Electoral Cycles in Police Hiring to Estimate the Effect of Police on Crime: A Reply,* 92 AM. ECON. REV. 1244 (2002). Levitt used changes in the number of firefighters as an instrument for changes in the number of police.

But then in the early 1990s the crack epidemic began to wane, and with it so did the very high homicide rate for young black males. That rate fell by almost 50 percent during the period 1991–2001, compared with a decline of 30 percent in the homicide rate for adult white males. Levitt estimates that the decline of crack cocaine might account for about 15 percent of the fall of all homicides during the decade. He estimates that the impact of less crack on other crimes is significantly smaller, perhaps 3 percent.

D. A Summary

The crime rate dropped 30 to 40 percent from 1991 to 2001 in almost all categories of crime and all regions. Levitt summarizes his explanation in Table 13.4. His heroic efforts provide a useful basis for discussion, but many puzzles remain, such as why Canada's experience with changing crime rates closely resembles that of the United States, even though Canada's policies were different.[97]

TABLE 13.4
Summarizing the Estimated Contribution of Various Factors to the Decline in Crime in the 1990s

Factor	Percentage Change in Crime that this Factor Accounts for Over the Period 1991–2001			
	Homicide	Violent Crime	Property Crime	Certainty Level of Estimated Impact
Strong economy	0	0	−2	High
Changing demographics	0	−2	−5	High
Better policing strategies	−1	−1	−1	Low
Gun control laws	0	0	0	Medium
Concealed weapons laws	0	0	0	High
Increased usage of capital punishment	−1.5	0	0	Medium
Increases in the number of police	−5.5	−5.5	−5.5	Medium
Increases in the prison population	−12	−12	−8	High
The decline of crack	−6	−3	0	Low
Legalized abortion	−10	−10	−10	Medium
Total of all factors considered	−36	−33.5	−31.5	
Actual change in UCR reported crime	−43	−34	−29	
Actual change in NCVS victimization	—	−50	−53	

Levitt, Table 5, p. 184.

---

[97] See Franklin E. Zimring, The Great American Crime Decline (2008).

Conclusion

In this chapter we have used the economic theory of crime and punishment to examine some pressing policy issues in criminal justice. Economic theory is valuable in framing the problems and the possible solutions, and empirical research is necessary to weigh the policy options designed to minimize the social costs of crime.

Suggested Readings and Viewings

Bar-Gill, Oren, & Alon Harel, *Crime Rates and Expected Sanctions: The Economics of Deterrence Revisited,* 30 J. LEGAL STUD. 485 (2001).

Harcourt, Bernard, & Jens Ludwig, *Broken Windows: New Evidence from New York City and a Five-City Social Experiment,* 73 U. CHI. L. REV. 271 (2006).

Krueger, Alan B., & Jitka Maleckova, *Education, Poverty, and Terrorism: Is There a Connection?,* 17 J. ECON. PERSP. 119 (2003).

Levitt, Steven D., *Using Electoral Cycles in Police Hiring to Estimate the Effect of Police on Crime,* 87 AM. ECON. REV. 270 (1997). See also Levitt, *Reply,* 92 AM. ECON. REV. 1244 (2002).

Milhaupt, Curtis, & Mark D. West, *The Dark Side of Private Ordering: An Institutional and Empirical Analysis of Organized Crime,* 67 U. CHI. L. REV. 41 (2000).

Simon, David, *The Wire,* Seasons 1 – 5 (HBO Productions, 2002–2008).

Stuntz, William, *Local Policing After the Terror,* 111 YALE L. J. 2137 (2002).

VENKATESH, SUDHIR, GANG LEADER FOR A DAY (2008).

Case Index

Name Index

535

Subject Index